QUANTITY	SYMBOL*	UNITS	QUANTITY	SYMBOL*	UNITS
Acceleration	$\mathbf{a}$	m/s^2	Entropy	S	J/K
Angle	θ, ϕ	rad	Force	$\mathbf{F}$	N
Angular acceleration	$\boldsymbol{\alpha}$	rad/s^2, s^{-2}	Frequency	f, ν	Hz
Angular frequency, angular speed, angular velocity	$\omega, \boldsymbol{\omega}$	rad/s, s^{-1}	Heat	Q	J
			Heat flow	H	J/s
Angular momentum	$\mathbf{L}$	$kg \cdot m^2/s$	Inductance	L	H
Atomic number	Z		Intensity	$I, S, \mathbf{S}$	W/m^2
Capacitance	C	F	Magnetic field	$\mathbf{B}$	T
Charge	q, Q, e	C	Magnetic flux	ϕ_B	$T \cdot m^2$
Charge density			Mass	m, M	kg
Line	λ	C/m	Mass number	A	
Surface	σ	C/m^2	Molar specific heat	C_V, C_P	$J/mol \cdot K$
Volume	ρ	C/m^3	Momentum	$\mathbf{p}$	$kg \cdot m/s$
Conductivity	σ	$\Omega^{-1} \cdot m^{-1}$	Period	T	s
Current	I	A	Power	P	W
Current density	$\mathbf{J}$	A/m^2	Pressure	P	Pa
Density	ρ	kg/m^3	Resistance	R	Ω
Dielectric constant	κ		Resistivity	ρ	$\Omega \cdot m$
Dipole moment, electric	$\mathbf{p}$	$C \cdot m$	Rotational inertia	I	$kg \cdot m^2$
Dipole moment, magnetic	$\boldsymbol{\mu}$	$A \cdot m^2$	Temperature	T	K
Distance, displacement, length, position	$x, y, z, s, d,$ $\ell, w, h, \mathbf{r}$	m	Time	t	s
			Torque	$\boldsymbol{\tau}$	$N \cdot m$
Electric field	$\mathbf{E}$	N/C, V/m	Specific heat	c	$J/kg \cdot k$
Electric flux	ϕ, ϕ_E	$N \cdot m^2/C$	Speed, velocity	$v, \mathbf{v}$	m/s
Electric potential	V	V	Volume	V	m^3
Electromotive force	$\mathcal{E}$	V	Wavelength	λ	m
Energy	E, U, K	J	Wavenumber	k	m^{-1}
			Work	W	J

*Boldface indicates vector quantities.

TRIGONOMETRY

Definition of angle (in radians): $\theta = \dfrac{s}{r}$

2π radians in complete circle
1 radian $\simeq 57.3° = 2.06$ arc sec

TRIGONOMETRIC FUNCTIONS

$\sin \theta = \dfrac{y}{r}$

$\cos \theta = \dfrac{x}{r}$

$\tan \theta = \dfrac{\sin \theta}{\cos \theta} = \dfrac{y}{x}$

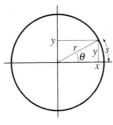

THE GREEK ALPHABET

	UPPERCASE	LOWERCASE
Alpha	A	α
Beta	B	β
Gamma	Γ	γ
Delta	Δ	δ
Epsilon	E	ε
Zeta	Z	ζ
Eta	H	η
Theta	Θ	θ
Iota	I	ι
Kappa	K	κ
Lambda	Λ	λ
Mu	M	μ
Nu	N	ν
Xi	Ξ	ξ
Omicron	O	o
Pi	Π	π
Rho	P	ρ
Sigma	Σ	σ
Tau	T	τ
Upsilon	Υ	υ
Phi	Φ	ϕ
Chi	X	χ
Psi	Ψ	ψ
Omega	Ω	ω

PHYSICS FOR SCIENTISTS AND ENGINEERS

RICHARD WOLFSON | JAY M. PASACHOFF

Taken from:

Physics for Scientists and Engineers, Third Edition
by Richard Wolfson and Jay M. Pasachoff

Cover Art *Electr1* by Barry Cronin

Taken from:

Physics, For Scientists and Engineers, Third Edition
by Richard Wolfson, Jay M. Pasachoff
Copyright 1999 by Addison Wesley Longman, Inc.
A Pearson Education Company
Boston, Massachusetts 02116

This special edition published in cooperation with Pearson Custom Publishing.

Printed in the United States of America

10 9 8 7 6 5 4 3 2 1

ISBN 0536-17026-6

2005460098

MT

Please visit our web site at *www.pearsoncustom.com*

PEARSON CUSTOM PUBLISHING
75 Arlington Street, Suite 300, Boston, MA 02116
A Pearson Education Company

Brief Contents

Contents

Preface

PHYSICS: CHALLENGE AND SIMPLICITY

Physics is fundamental. To understand physics is to understand how the world works, both at the everyday level and on scales of time and space so small and large that they defy intuition.

To the student, physics can be at once fascinating, challenging, subtle, and yet simple. Physics fascinates with its applications throughout science and engineering and in its revelation of unexpected phenomena like superconductivity, black holes, and chaos. It challenges with the need for precise thinking and skillful application of mathematics. Physics can be subtle, especially in describing phenomena at odds with everyday intuition. Most importantly, physics is simple. Its few fundamental laws are succinct, yet they encompass a universe of natural phenomena and technological devices.

GOALS OF THIS BOOK

This text is for science and engineering students. Its main goals are:

- to help students develop an understanding of the physical universe at its most fundamental level
- to explore a wide range of physics applications in science, technology, and everyday life
- to develop students' analytical and quantitative skills as applied to problems in science and engineering

The standard version of this text covers the full sequence of calculus-based university physics, and the extended version adds seven chapters on modern physics.

ORGANIZATION

The book is organized into six parts. Part 1 (Chapters 2 through 14) develops the basics of mechanics. Part 2 (Chapters 15 through 18) applies mechanics to the study of oscillations, waves, and fluids. Part 3 (Chapters 19 through 22) covers thermodynamics. Part 4 (Chapters 23–34) deals with electricity and magnetism. Part 5 (Chapters 35 through 37) treats optics. Part 6 (Chapters 38 and 39) briefly introduces relativity and quantum physics. Part 6 of the extended version (Chapters 38 through 45) expands the coverage of modern physics and its applications to atoms, molecules, and the solid state; nuclear physics and its applications; and particle physics and cosmology. Each part ends with a set of Cumulative Problems that synthesize concepts from the chapters in that part.

Distinguishing Features of the Third Edition

This third edition continues to hone the text and illustrations for clarity and precision, and to ensure that physics is tied closely with the latest in applications that are scientifically exciting and relevant to the student's everyday experience or future professional activities. Below we detail the many changes we've made, as well as describing new and continuing features designed to help students learn.

Improvements in Content This revision includes many substantial changes and improvements, most of which were suggested by instructors who have used the text or reviewed the manuscript. We've also added new pedagogical features to help develop both conceptual and quantitative understanding, and to test students' understanding of subtle concepts. Here are some of the more significant changes we've implemented in this edition.

- We extensively rewrote Chapters 5 (Force and Motion) and 6 (Using Newton's Laws) to account for the results of new research in physics education, especially the Force Concept Inventory.
- We substantially reorganized a number of other chapters to enhance the clarity and logical structure. For example, readers will find the presentations of magnetism and of physical optics much clearer due to chapter reorganization in this new edition. In all chapters, significant rewriting and art revisions improve clarity and provide tie-ins with preceding material.
- We revised the problem sets to include more "real-world" problems and a better balance of easy, multi-step, and challenging problems. In each chapter, up to 20 percent of the problems are new.
- A new category of "annotated figures" links text and art, using captions within the figure to guide students through complex concepts.
- A new feature, **Got It!** boxes, provide conceptual and largely non-quantitative reinforcement of students' understanding.
- The new **Math Toolbox** feature presents important mathematical tools separately from the main text.
- We have integrated *ActivPhysics*—the comprehensive simulation and visualization software—throughout the book, to provide a valuable option for both instructors and students. *ActivPhysics* helps students explore the major concepts from all parts of physics. Students can make predictions and test assumptions by changing variables and running the simulations. *ActivPhysics* references in the text, and icons in the margin, are strategically placed at common student trouble spots. Used in the classroom, lab, or for self-study, *ActivPhysics* will help the student develop imagery and intuition, and will reinforce the student's understanding of basic physics.
- We've updated for new scientific discoveries and technological developments, including the finding that neutrinos have mass, advances in superconductivity, and fiber optic technology, and many others.

Other features carry over from the second edition with significant revisions and improvements. These include

Applications and Examples A rich array of practical and up-to-date applications illustrates the use of physics principles in both technology and in natural phenomena. Applications range from the life sciences through the frontiers of technology, and include biomedical technology, antilock brakes, global warming, microelectronics, lasers, and much more. Some new applications and examples in this third edition include hybrid cars with flywheel energy storage; the digital video disc; kayaking; electrical models for the cell membrane; gel electrophoresis for protein separation; capacitive transducers; medical defibrillators, and many others. As in previous editions, we integrate many applications with the text and problem sets, rather than presenting just a few applications as guest essays.

Questions These follow the chapter synopsis and can be used for class discussion, in peer-based learning strategies, or to get students thinking about concepts before they begin work on quantitative problems.

Problems Science and engineering students learn physics best by working physics problems. This third edition contains nearly 3,000 end-of-chapter problems, with significant revision of the problem sets, especially in the early chapters. Problems range from simple confidence builders, to more complex and realistic multi-problems, to difficult **Supplementary Problems** that will challenge the best students. A section of unique **Paired Problems** for each chapter lets students practice problem-solving techniques on a pair of problems whose solutions involve closely related physical concepts or mathematical approaches. **Cumulative Problems** integrate material from the chapters of each major part of the text. Frequent text references to specific problems link text and problems in the common purpose of enhancing the student's understanding of physics.

Worked Examples These reinforce basic concepts, illustrate problem-solving strategies, and often serve to introduce "real-world" applications of physics. Most examples are followed by an exercise that further reinforces concepts and strategies. A **Similar Problems** line after each example points out related end-of-chapter problems.

Tip Boxes Tip boxes appear throughout the text and warn against common pitfalls or give helpful problem-solving hints.

Pedagogical Use of Color The book's design is an essential pedagogical feature. The carefully planned use of color in figures and in highlighting important equations and definitions, as well as the selection of photographs, all reinforce the text and enhance communication of concepts to the student. Specific colors are used consistently for different physical elements in the figures; for example, velocity vectors and graphs of velocity use the same color, while force vectors and graphs consistently use a different color. A list of elements and their colors follows this preface.

Chapter Synopses Chapter summaries emphasize key concepts and remind students of new terms and mathematical symbols. Each summary ends with a reminder of limitations and approximations used in the theories, models, and equations developed in the chapter.

Appendices and Endpapers The book's appendices and endpapers contain a mathematical review and a wealth of up-to-date physical data, conversion factors, and information on measurements systems.

PHYSICS AND MATHEMATICS

For many students, the university physics course is their first contact with practical applications of calculus. We recognize that students have a range of mathematical abilities, from those taking their first calculus course concurrently with physics to those fluent in both differential and integral calculus. The former will find our new Math Toolboxes, along with many of the Tip boxes and figures, helpful in building confidence in their mathematical skills; the latter will find a selection of challenging calculus-based problems.

In this book mathematics is a tool, not an end in itself. Therefore we always relate mathematical solutions and derivations back to the underlying physics. After deriving an equation or solving a sample problem, we frequently ask: "Does this result make sense?" We show that it does by examining easily understood special cases, thus building physical intuition along with mathematical confidence. We explore the meaning of equations verbally and through figures, ensuring that concepts are clear before students begin to use the material quantitatively.

SUPPLEMENTS

Professors and students alike find it useful to have supplements designed to complement their text. For the third edition, we offer a new expanded supplements package.

For the Instructor

Instructor's Solutions Manual (0-321-03578-X), prepared by Edw. S. Ginsberg, University of Massachusetts-Boston, includes worked solutions to all problems in the text. The solutions manual is now available on CD-ROM in TEX, techexplorer, and Microsoft Word, for easy editing and posting of homework solutions in documents or on the web (0-321-05149-1).

TestGen-EQ Computerized Test Bank is an expanded testbank that allows instructors to edit and change the order of questions, add entirely new questions in six different formats and print different versions of a test. The testbank is available for Windows (0-321-03579-8) and Macintosh (0-321-03580-1). A print version is also available (0-321-03590-9).

Transparency Acetates (0-321-03577-1) contain over 150 color acetates of figures from the text, useful in lectures and classroom discussions.

For the Student

Student Solutions Manual (0-321-03575-5), by Edw. S. Ginsberg, University of Massachusetts-Boston, includes detailed solutions to all the odd-numbered problems in the text.

Study Guide with ActivPhysics, is a book and CD package. The study guide, by Jeffrey J. Braun, University of Evansville, provides an overview of each chapter of *Physics for Scientists and Engineers* and summarizes definitions and key equations. The *ActivPhysics* worksheets and CD-ROM by Alan Van Heuvelen, The Ohio State University, and Paul D'Alessandris help students develop imagery and intuition by changing variables and running the simulations. *ActivPhysics* prompts students with questions that help develop a more thorough understanding, step by step. The *ActivPhysics* CD-ROM is dual platform, for both Macintosh and Windows. *Study Guide with ActivPhysics* is available in two volumes.

- *Volume 1 (covering Wolfson/Pasachoff—Physics for Scientists and Engineers Chapters 1–22)* 0-321-05148-3
- *Volume 2 (covering Wolfson/Pasachoff—Physics for Scientists and Engineers Chapters 23–45)* 0-321-05147-5.

Preparing for General Physics: Math Skill Drills and Other Useful Help, by Arnold D. Pickar of Portland State University, is a self-study workbook that reviews algebra and trigonometry topics for university physics (0-201-53802-4).

ACKNOWLEDGMENTS

A project of this magnitude is not the work of its author alone. Here we acknowledge the many people whose contributions made the book possible. Colleagues using the second edition at universities and colleges throughout the world have volunteered suggestions, and will find most of those incorporated here. Students in Middlebury's Physics 109–110 courses have made significant contributions to the book's accuracy and readability. RW's Middlebury colleagues Ann Broughton, Cris Butler, Jeff Dunham, Bob Prigo, Steve Ratcliff, Susan Watson, and Frank Winkler all provided substantial suggestions or help on this project. We are especially grateful to a group of "on call" reviewers who provided instant feedback to questions from author and editors during the revision: Jerry Hosken, *City College of San Francisco;* Andy Odel, *Northern Arizona University;* James Rohlf, *Boston University;* Gurbax Singh, *University of Maryland;* Robert Weidman, *Michigan Technological University.*

It is frustrating to find numerical errors in a textbook, especially in answers to problems. We have gone to great lengths to make this book as free from error as possible, and we credit the people who helped achieved this goal. Edw. S. Ginsberg, *University of Massachusetts-Boston,* meticulously checked all numerical results in examples, exercises, and end-of-chapter problems. Mark Coffey of the *University of Colorado at Boulder,* and John Bartelt of the *Stanford Linear Accelerator Center* provided valuable accuracy checks.

Prior to this revision, every chapter of the book was thoroughly reviewed by users of both this and competing texts. Reviewers made general as well as more detailed suggestions, nearly all of which we have been able to incorporate in the third edition. We are grateful to these reviewers, and to reviewers of the second edition:

Edward Adelson, *Ohio State University*
Vijendra Agarwal, *Moorhead State University*
William Anderson, *Phoenix College*
Gordon J. Aubrecht, *Ohio State University—Marion*
Paul Avery, *University of Florida*
Douglas Bennett, *University of California, Los Angeles*
Marvin Blecher, *Virginia Polytechnic Institute and State University*
Gary Bowman, *Northern Arizona University*
John Brient, *University of Texas at El Paso*
James H. Burgess, *Washington University*
Bernard Chasan, *Boston University*
Roger Clapp, *University of South Florida*
Claire D. Dewberry, *Florida Community College at Jacksonville*
Jeffrey Dunne, *Purdue University*
Robert J. Endorf, *University of Cincinnati*
Heidi Fearn, *California State University—Fullerton*
Shechao Feng, *University of California, Los Angeles*
Albert L. Ford, *Texas A & M University*
Ian Gatland, *Georgia Institute of Technology*
Edw. S. Ginsberg, *University of Massachusetts—Boston*
James Goff, *Pima Community College*
Alan I. Goldman, *Iowa State University*
Philip Goode, *New Jersey Institute of Technology*
Denise S. Graves, *Clark Atlanta University*
Donald Greenberg, *University of Alaska*
Phillip Gutierrez, *University of Oklahoma*
Stephen Hanzely, *Youngstown State University*
Kenneth Hardy, *Florida International University*
Gerald Harmon, *University of Maine at Orono*
Randy Harris, *University of California, Davis*
Warren Hein, *American Association of Physics Teachers*
Roger Herman, *The Pennsylvania State University*
P. G. Hjorth, *Technical University of Denmark*
Francis L. Howell, *University of North Dakota*
J. N. Huffaker, *University of Oklahoma*
Quinton Hurst, *Arizona State University*
Javed Iqbal, *University of British Columbia*
Wayne James, *University of South Dakota*
Karen Johnston, *North Carolina State University*
Evan Jones, *Sierra College*
Randy Knight, *California Polytechnic State University*
Dean Langely, *St. John's University*
Chew-Lean Lee, *Florida Community College*
Brian Logan, *University of Ottawa*

Peter Loly, *University of Manitoba*
Hilliard K. Macomber, *University of Northern Iowa*
David Markowitz, *University of Connecticut*
Daniel Marlow, *Princeton University*
Nolan Massey, *University of Texas at Arlington*
Ralph McGrew, *Broome Community College*
Victor Michalk, *Southwest Texas State University*
Allen Mincer, *New York University*
P. James Moser, *Bloomsburg University*
Vinod Nangia, *University of Minnesota*
Andrew Odell, *Northern Arizona University*
Robert Osborne, *Yakima Valley Community College*
Michael O'Shea, *Kansas State University*
George Parker, *North Carolina State University*
Graham Pearson, *Novia Scotia Agricultural College*
R. J. Peterson, *University of Colorado*
Slawomir Piatek, *New Jersey Institute of Technology*
Gerald Pogatshnik, *Southern Illinois University*
Joseph F. Polen, *Shasta College*
Talat Rahman, *Kansas State University*
Dennis Roark, *The King's College*
James Rohlf, *Boston University*
Alfons Schulte, *University of Central Florida*
Neil Shafer-Ray, *University of Oklahoma*
Gurbax Singh, *University of Maryland*
Roger F. Sipson, *Moorhead State University*
John Sperry, *Sierra College*
Lon D. Spight, *University of Nevada at Las Vegas*

Robert Sprague, *Foothill College*
Julien. C. Sprott, *University of Wisconsin-Madison*
Konrad M. Stein, *Golden West College*
Bryan H. Suits, *Michigan Technological University*
Leo Takahashi, *The Pennsylvania State University—Beaver Campus*
Frank Tanherlini, *College of the Holy Cross*
Karl Trappe, *University of Texas*
Michael Trinkala, *Hudson Valley Community College*
Loren Vian, *Centralia College*
Clarence Wagener, *Creighton University*
Robert Weidman, *Michigan Technological University*
George Williams, *University of Utah*
Robert J. Wilson, *Colorado State University*
Arthur Winston, *Gordon Institute*
David Yee, *City College of San Francisco*
John Yelton, *University of Florida*
Dale Yoder-Short, *Michigan Technological University*

We also thank editors Catherine Flack, Sami Iwata, Joan Marsh, and publisher Robin Heyden at Addison Wesley for their vigorous support of and collaboration on this project, and Ingrid Mount of Elm Street Publishing Services for her skillful efforts in bringing it to fruition. Finally, RW thanks his family, colleagues, and students for their patience during the intense process of revising this book.

Richard Wolfson
Jay M. Pasachoff

A Visual Guide to the Book

Tip
How Does the Battery Know? How does the battery in Fig. 28-5 "know" how much current to supply? How does it even "know" there are two resistors, and what their values are? For the brief instant when the circuit is first connected, the battery doesn't "know," and some rather complicated action occurs as charge moves from the battery, encounters resistance, and accumulates to establish the potential differences across the resistors. During that brief time the current is not the same everywhere. But very soon the circuit reaches a steady state, with the same current throughout. Later in this chapter, when we consider circuits with capacitors, we'll look in more detail at the approach to the steady state; for now, our analyses assume that circuits have already reached that state.

Tip boxes appear throughout the text to help a student with difficult concepts, warn against common pitfalls, and give problem-solving hints.

EXAMPLE 28-1	*Designing a Voltage Divider*

A light bulb with a resistance (when on) of $5.0\ \Omega$ is designed to operate at a current of 600 mA. To operate this lamp from a 12-V battery, what resistance should you place in series with it?

Solution
Let R_2 be the lamp and R_1 the unknown series resistor. Since resistors in series add, the current through both resistors is $I = \mathcal{E}/(R_1 + R_2)$, which is supposed to be 600 mA or 0.60 A. Solving for R_1 gives

$$R_1 = \frac{\mathcal{E} - IR_2}{I} = \frac{12\ \text{V} - (0.60\ \text{A})(5.0\ \Omega)}{0.60\ \text{A}} = 15\ \Omega.$$

You can also get this result by noting that the light bulb's proper operating voltage is $V = IR_2 = (0.60\ \text{A})(5.0\ \Omega) = 3.0\ \text{V}$. This is one-fourth of the battery voltage, so the light bulb's $5\text{-}\Omega$ resistance should be one-fourth of the total. That makes the total $20\ \Omega$, leaving $15\ \Omega$ for R_1.

EXERCISE Suppose that in Fig. 28-5 $R_1 = 470\ \Omega$. If the voltage across R_2 is 59% of the battery voltage, find R_2.

Answer: $676\ \Omega$

Some problems similar to Example 28-1: 23–25

Got It!
What is the voltage across the resistor R at the top of each circuit shown Fig. 28-7? In (*a*) the second resistor has the same resistance R, and in (*b*) the g is an open circuit (infinite resistance). Think about it first, then verify y answers using Equations 28-2.

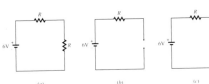

FIGURE 28-7 What's the voltage across the upper resistor in each circuit?

Got It! boxes provide conceptual reinforcement of a student's understanding.
Here the student is asked to stop and think about three simple circuits, to probe their understanding before moving on to the next topic. They are asked to apply what they have learned in a qualitative way, and then asked to verify using the equations.

If I is the current in the circuit of Fig. 28-5, then there must be a voltage $V_1 = IR_1$ across R_1 to drive the current through this resistor. Similarly, the voltage across R_2 is $V_2 = IR_2$. Thus, the voltage across the two resistors together is $V_1 + V_2 = IR_1 + IR_2$. But the battery is connected directly across this series combination, so we have

$$IR_1 + IR_2 = \mathcal{E}.$$

or

$$I = \frac{\mathcal{E}}{R_1 + R_2}.$$

Comparison with Ohm's law in the form $I = V/R$ shows that the two resistors in series behave like an equivalent resistance equal to the sum of their resistances. In an obvious generalization to more resistors in series, we have

$$R_{\text{series}} = R_1 + R_2 + R_3 + \cdots \qquad (28\text{-}1)$$

In other words, resistors in series add.
Given the current, we can use Ohm's law in the form $V = IR$ to solve for the voltage across each resistor:

$$V_1 = \frac{R_1}{R_1 + R_2}\mathcal{E} \qquad (28\text{-}2a)$$

and

$$V_2 = \frac{R_2}{R_1 + R_2}\mathcal{E}. \qquad (28\text{-}2b)$$

These expressions show that the battery voltage divides between the two resistors in proportion to their resistance. For this reason a series combination of resistors is called a **voltage divider**. Figure 28-6 depicts the voltages throughout the circuit of Fig. 28-5, and shows explicitly that the resistors divide the battery voltage.

Annotated figures guide a student through complex concepts.
Here we see potential difference in a simple circuit explained step-by-step. Leading the student through the graphical representation of this important, but tricky, concept can lead to a more thorough understanding of the phenomena of voltage.

FIGURE 28-6 Voltages in the circuit of Fig. 28-5, with $V = 0$ at the negative battery terminal. Note that there is no potential difference across the wires, since they have negligible resistance, and that potential increases across the battery and decreases across the resistors. Can you tell from the graph which resistance is greater? (Here we've "unrolled" the circuit so we can clearly show the voltage as a function of position around the circuit. But remember that the circuit is a closed loop, so the left and right ends of the graph represent the same physical point, namely the negative battery terminal.)

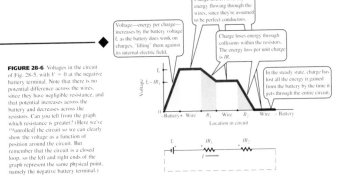

A rich array of **applications** reinforces understanding of underlying physics in both technology and natural phenomena. Applications range from the life sciences through the latest technology. They bring the subject alive by providing relevance of the theory to a student's everyday world.

Here DVDs are compared to CDs to give the student knowledge of this topical development.

Throughout the book, icons in the margins and references in the text link to the powerful simulation package *ActivPhysics*. The simulations in *ActivPhysics* provide an opportunity for students to make predictions and test those predictions. The student becomes an active participant through manipulation and visualization of hard-to-grasp concepts.

---

998 Chapter 37 Interference and Diffraction

| **EXAMPLE 37-8** | *Asteroid Alert!* |

An asteroid appears on a collision course with Earth, at a distance of 20×10^6 km. What is the minimum size asteroid that the 2.4-m-diameter diffraction-limited Hubble Space Telescope could resolve at this distance, using 550-nm reflected sunlight?

Solution

Resolving the asteroid means being able to distinguish its opposite edges in the telescope image and therefore to assess its size. Suppose the asteroid's long dimension (it might not be spherical) is ℓ. Then at a distance $L \gg \ell$ it subtends an angle given very nearly by $\theta = \ell/L$. Using this result in Equation 37-13b with the mirror diameter and wavelength given, we have

$$\frac{\ell}{L} = \frac{1.22\lambda}{D},$$

or

$$\ell = \frac{1.22\lambda L}{D} = \frac{(1.22)(550 \times 10^{-9}\text{ m})(20 \times 10^6\text{ m})}{2.4\text{ m}} = 5.6\text{ km}.$$

This is a potentially dangerous object, comparable in size to the asteroid that scientists believe caused the extinction of the dinosaurs, and somewhat larger than the comet fragments that slammed into Jupiter in 1994, causing Earth-sized disturbances on the giant planet.

EXERCISE Two ants stand 1 cm apart. Assuming diffraction-limited vision, at what distance could a human eye, with an iris aperture of 4 mm, tell that two are indeed separate creatures? Assume a wavelength of 550 nm, near the middle of the visible spectrum. (Other limitations of the human eye prevent its realizing this diffraction limit.)

Answer: 60 m

Some problems similar to Example 37-8: 55–59

| **APPLICATION** | *Movies on Disc: From CD to DVD* |

Standard audio CDs have a maximum playing time of 74 minutes—a value that's set by the optical diffraction limit. In the Application "CD Music, Continued" earlier in this chapter, we showed how a CD encodes information in "pits" $1.6\ \mu m$ apart and as short as $0.83\ \mu m$ in length. Standard CDs are read with 780-nm infrared laser light and the pit size and separation are chosen to ensure that diffraction effects at this wavelength don't cause the CD player's optical system to confuse adjacent pits. Ultimately, therefore, the 74-minute playing time is limited by the laser wavelength.

When CDs were first developed, inexpensive semiconductor lasers were available only in the infrared. But today's semiconductor lasers produce light well into the visible—with significantly shorter wavelengths than the infrared light used in CD players and CD-ROM drives. The new DVDs introduced in the late 1990s (read either "digital video disc" or "digital versatile disc") exploit these shorter-wavelength lasers.

Using laser wavelengths of 635 and 650 nm, DVDs can function with significantly lower pit sizes and spacings because of the lower diffraction limit at these shorter wavelengths (Fig. 37-39). Coupled with a two-layer structure (as opposed to the standard CD's single information layer) and more sophisticated data-compression schemes, the smaller pits and pit spacing give DVDs more than 12 times the information-storage capacity of standard CDs. That translates into more than two hours of high quality video and audio, as opposed to the CD's 74 minutes of audio alone. In computer use, it means a DVD can hold some 8.5 gigabytes of information as opposed to a CD's 680 megabytes (by comparison, a 3.5″ floppy disc holds only 1.44 MB). And DVDs can be made in two-sided versions, providing another doubling in capacity. Despite their high capacity, DVDs are physically the same size as CDs, and DVD players are compatible with standard CDs as well.

FIGURE 37-39 A comparison of a standard CD and a DVD. The smaller pit size and closer pit spacing of the DVD result in a much higher information storage capacity, and are made possible by the lower diffraction limit associated with the DVD player's shorter wavelength laser light. Both images are microphotographs of the same size region, about 8 μm on a side. The pits lie on a single spiral track that covers most of the disc.

(a) (b)

---

946 Chapter 36 Image Formation and Optical Instruments

last step in this equality follows from Equation for ℓ' and using the result in the equation

$$f = \frac{R}{2}$$

Thus the focal length of a spherical mirror We emphasize that the results derived based on the assumption that the spherical parabola. Equivalent ways of describing curvature radius is large compared with Fig. 36-12c and (2) that all rays reflecti nearly parallel to the mirror axis (the paraxings can't accurately reflect these conditiclearly the ray paths.

15.7 *ActivPhysics*
Spherical Mirror Problems

| **EXAMPLE 36-2** | *Sizing Up Hubble: A Concave Mirror* |

During assembly of the Hubble Space Telescope, a technician stood 3.85 m in front of the telescope's concave mirror and viewed his image (Fig. 36-13). Given the telescope's focal length of 5.52 m, find (a) the location and (b) the magnification of the technician's image. (c) Repeat for the case when the technician stands 15.0 m from the mirror.

Solution

Since the mirror is *concave*, the focal length f is *positive*.
(a) We can solve the mirror equation (Equation 36-2) to get

$$\frac{1}{\ell'} = \frac{1}{f} - \frac{1}{\ell} = \frac{\ell - f}{f\ell},$$

or

$$\ell' = \frac{f\ell}{\ell - f} = \frac{(5.52\text{ m})(3.85\text{ m})}{3.85\text{ m} - 5.52\text{ m}} = -12.7\text{ m}.$$

Why the *negative* answer? Because the technician is closer to the mirror than the focal point, so this is a *virtual* image located *behind* the mirror.
(b) Equation 36-1 gives the magnification:

$$M = -\frac{\ell'}{\ell} = -\frac{(-12.7\text{ m})}{3.85\text{ m}} = 3.30.$$

This *positive* answer indicates an *upright* image, enlarged about three times as shown in Fig. 36-13.
(c) If the technician stands 15.0 m from the mirror, similar calculations give

$$\ell' = \frac{f\ell}{\ell - f} = \frac{(5.52\text{ m})(15.0\text{ m})}{15.0\text{ m} - 5.52\text{ m}} = 8.73\text{ m}$$

and

$$M = -\frac{\ell'}{\ell} = -\frac{8.73\text{ m}}{15.0\text{ m}} = -0.582.$$

Some problems similar to Example 36-2: 3–9, 11–14

FIGURE 36-13 A technician standing in front of the Hubble Space Telescope mirror. Where and how big is the technician's image?

Now ℓ' is *positive*, so the image is *real* and in *front* of the mirror; the *negative* magnification shows that it's *inverted*, and it's reduced in size.

EXERCISE You're scrutinizing your nose using a handheld concave mirror with curvature radius 2.2 m. How far from your face should you hold the mirror to see your nose doubled in size?

Answer: 55 cm

Worked examples are an integral part of the text and reinforce basic concepts. Real world applications are interwoven to give relevance to a student's experience. Many worked examples are followed by **Exercises. Similar Problems** from the end-of-chapter problems are indicated for students who want to work more problems on the topic.

In principle, we could imagine making the interval Δt as close to zero as we like, and getting ever better approximations to the instantaneous velocity. In practice, given a graph of position versus time, an easy approach is to "eyeball" the tangent line to the graph at the point we're interested in: the slope of the tangent line is the slope of the graph at that point, and is therefore the instantaneous velocity. Figure 2-5 shows this approach. Note that the slope of the tangent line, and therefore the velocity, varies from place to place on the graph. That's the whole point of the instantaneous velocity–it's a quantity that can vary continually.

Got It!

Figure 2-6 shows position-versus-time graphs for several objects. Which object is moving with constant speed? Which reverses direction? Which starts slowly and then speeds up?

Often, we're given the position as a mathematical function of time. We could draw a graph and measure the slopes of tangent lines to find the velocity at different points. But calculus provides a quicker way. In calculus, the result of the limiting process described in Equation 2-2a is called the **derivative** of x with respect to t, and is given the special symbol dx/dt:

$$\frac{dx}{dt} = \lim_{\Delta t \to 0} \frac{\Delta x}{\Delta t}.$$

The quantities dx and dt are called **infinitesimals**; they represent vanishingly small quantities that result from the limiting process. We can then write Equation 2-2a as

$$v = \frac{dx}{dt}. \qquad (2\text{-}2b)$$

When we're given the position x as a function of time t, calculus provi[des a] simple way to calculate the velocity $v = dx/dt$. Consult the Math Toolbox i[f you] haven't yet seen derivatives in your calculus class, or if you need a refres[...]

Math Toolbox

Derivatives Do we need to go through an elaborate limiting process every [time] we want an instantaneous velocity? No! In calculus you either have or will d[erive] formulas for the derivatives of common functions. For example, any functi[on of] the form

$$x = bt^n,$$

where b and n are constants, has the derivative

$$\frac{dx}{dt} = bnt^{n-1}.$$

Derivatives of other common functions, including trig functions, exponen[tials] and logarithms, are listed in Appendix A. If a function is made up of a su[m of] terms, its derivative is just the sum of the derivatives of the individual te[rms.]

FIGURE 2-5 The instantaneous velocity at a given time is the slope of the tangent line at the point on the position-versus-time graph corresponding to that time. If the position-versus-time graph is not a straight line, then the instantaneous velocity varies with time.

Chapter Synopses emphasize key concepts and remind students of new terms and mathematical symbols. **Limitations to Keep in Mind** remind students of approximations, idealizations, and limited applications of physical concepts and equations. The **Problems You Should Be Able To Solve** section allows a student to evaluate their comprehension of the material in the chapter.

Math Toolboxes help a student through the math necessary for a full understanding of the physics. They emphasize math as a tool, in context with the physics.

CHAPTER SYNOPSIS ◆

Summary

1. Newton's **first law of motion** states that a body continues in uniform motion unless acted on by a nonzero net force. Uniform motion is a natural state; the study of motion then emphasizes not the cause of motion itself, but the cause of *changes* in motion.

2. Newton's **second law of motion** quantifies the change in motion brought about by a force. The law states that the rate of change of a body's momentum (product of mass and velocity; symbol **p**) is equal to the net force on the body:

$$\mathbf{F}_{net} = \frac{d\mathbf{p}}{dt}.$$

As long as the mass of the body does not change, Newton's second law can also be written in the form

$$\mathbf{F}_{net} = m\mathbf{a}.$$

Here $\mathbf{F}_{net}$ is the **net force** on a body—that is, the vector sum of all the individual interaction forces acting on the body. The SI unit of force is the **newton**, defined as the force that gives a 1-kg mass an acceleration of 1 m/s².

3. **Weight** is the force of gravity on an object: $\mathbf{W} = m\mathbf{g}$. In an accelerated frame of reference, the **apparent weight** differs from the gravitational force; in particular, the apparent weight of an object in free fall is zero.

4. Newton's **third law of motion** states that forces always come in pairs. When one object exerts a force on another, the second object exerts an oppositely directed force of equal magnitude back on the first. Newton's second and third laws together permit a consistent description of the motions of interacting objects.

5. Elastic objects such as springs provide a practical way of measuring forces. When the force exerted by a spring is directly proportional to the amount of stretch or compression, the spring is said to obey **Hooke's law**: the force is then given by

$$F = -kx. \quad \text{(Hooke's law)}$$

where k is the **spring constant**, with SI units of N/m.

Terms You Should Understand

(Pairs are closely related terms whose distinction is important; number in parentheses is chapter section where term first appears.)

dynamics (introduction)
Aristotle, Galileo, Newton (5-1)
force, net force, interaction force (5-2)
momentum (5-2)
Newton's laws of motion (5-2, 5-7)
inertia (5-2)
gravitational, electroweak, color forces (5-3)
mass, weight (5-5)
apparent weight (5-5, 5-8), weightlessness (5-5)
third-law pair (5-7)
normal force (5-7)
tension force, compression force (5-8)
Hooke's law (5-8)
spring constant (5-8)

Symbols You Should Recognize

F (5-2)
p (5-2)
N (5-4)
g (5-5)
W (5-5)
k (5-8)

Problems You Should Be Able to Solve

calculating force, mass, or acceleration from the other two quantities (5-4)
calculating weight or mass given the other (5-5)
solving for forces or accelerations in one-dimensional situations (5-6)
applying Newton's second and third laws together in one-dimensional situations (5-7)
determining spring force, extension/compression, or spring constant given the other two quantities (5-8)
determining apparent weight (5-8)

Limitations to Keep in Mind

Newton's laws apply only when relative velocities are much less than the speed of light; aside from that restriction, the basic material of this chapter is universally applicable.
Newton's laws are valid in inertial reference frames.
Newton's second law in the form $\mathbf{F} = m\mathbf{a}$ is valid only when mass remains constant; the form $\mathbf{F} = d\mathbf{p}/dt$ is more general.
Real springs deviate from ideal Hooke's law behavior when stretched or compressed substantially.

Questions will prompt a student to think about concepts in a chapter before they start on the problems.

652 Chapter 25 Electric Potential

QUESTIONS

1. Why can a bird perch on a high-voltage power line without getting electrocuted?
2. One proton is accelerated from rest by a uniform electric field, the other by a nonuniform electric field. If they move through the same potential difference, how do their final speeds compare?
3. Would a free electron move toward higher or lower potential?
4. The potential difference from A to B in Fig. 25-33 is zero since the two points are equidistant from the charge Q. How can this be, when a charge moving along the path shown clearly experiences an electric force not perpendicular to the path?

DANGER
ELECTROCUTION HAZARD
KEEP CLEAR
DEATH OR SERIOUS INJURY CAN RESULT FROM
CONTACT WITH LOAD, MACHINE OR VEHICLE
IF THEY BECOME ELECTRICALLY CHARGED

FIGURE 25-34 Question 12.

Paired Problems let a student practice problem-solving on a pair of problems whose solutions involve closely related physical concepts or mathematical approaches.

Almost 3000 **end-of-chapter problems,** ranging from confidence builders to realistic multi-problems, will help a student understand concepts and develop problem-solving skills. The problems are thought provoking and encourage critical thinking, and are relevant to a student's everyday life.

how this hazard ...
to someone on th...

Section 25-5 Potentials of Charged Conductors

52. (a) What is the maximum potential (measured from infinity) for the sphere of Example 25-3 before dielectric breakdown of air occurs at the sphere's surface? (Breakdown of air occurs at a field strength of 3 MV/m.) (b) What is the charge on the sphere when it's at this potential?
53. The spark plug in an automobile engine has a center electrode made from wire 2.0 mm in diameter. The electrode is worn to a hemispherical shape, so it behaves approximately like a charged sphere. What is the minimum potential on this electrode that will ensure the plug sparks in air? Neglect the presence of the second electrode.
54. A large metal sphere has three times the diameter of a smaller sphere and carries three times as much charge. Both spheres are isolated, so their surface charge densities ...form. Com...

...d (b) the electric
...re far apart. One
...other -10 nC.
... the spheres are
...potential on each
...uch charge must
...eve equilibrium?
... for the isolated.

...in diameter and
...part. Determine
...d strength at the
...midway between
...ce between the

Paired Problems

(Both problems in a pair involve the same principles and techniques. If you can get the first problem, you should be able to solve the second one.)

59. Three 50-pC charges sit at the vertices of an equilateral triangle 1.5 mm on a side. How much work would it take to bring a proton from very far away to the midpoint of one of the triangle's sides?
60. Repeat the preceding problem for the case when one of the charges is -50 pC and the proton is brought to the midpoint of the side between the two positive charges.
61. A pair of equal charges q lies on the x axis at $x = \pm a$. (a) Find expressions for the potential at points on the x axis for which $x > a$ and (b) show that your result reduces to a point-charge potential for $x \gg a$.
62. (a) For the charge distribution of the preceding problem, find an expression for the potential at *all* points on the y axis. (b) Show that your result reduces to a point-charge potential for $y \gg a$.
63. A 2.0-cm-radius metal sphere carries 75 nC and is surrounded by a concentric spherical conducting shell of radius 10 cm carrying -75 nC. (a) Find the potential difference between the shell and the sphere. (b) How would your answer change if the shell charge were changed to $+150$ nC?
64. A coaxial cable consists of a 2.0-mm-radius central wire carrying 75 nC/m, and a concentric outer conductor of radius 10 mm carrying -75 nC/m. (a) Find the

PROBLEMS

ActivPhysics can help with these problems:
Activities 11.9, 11.10.

Section 25-2 Potential Difference

1. How much work does it take to move a 50-μC charge against a 12-V potential difference?
2. The potential difference between the two sides of an ordinary electrical outlet is 120 V. How much energy does an electron gain when it moves from one side to the other?
3. It takes 45 J to move a 15-mC charge from point A to point B. What is the potential difference ΔV_{AB}?
4. Show that 1 V/m is the same as 1 N/C.
5. Find the magnitude of the potential difference between two points located 1.4 m apart in a uniform 650 N/C electric field, if a line between the points is parallel to the field.
6. A charge of 3.1 C moves from the positive to the negative terminal of a 9.0-V battery. How much energy does the battery impart to the charge?
7. Two points A and B lie 15 cm apart in a uniform electric field, with the path AB parallel to the field. If the potential difference ΔV_{AB} is 840 V, what is the field strength?
8. Figure 25-37 shows a uniform electric field of magnitude E. Find expressions for (a) the potential difference ΔV_{AB} and (b) ΔV_{BC}. (c) Use your result to determine ΔV_{AC}.

9. A proton, an alpha particle (a bare helium nucleus), and a singly ionized helium atom are accelerated through a potential difference of 100 V. Find the energy each gains.
10. The electric field within the membrane separating the inside and outside of a biological cell is approximately 8.0 MV/m, and is essentially uniform. If the membrane is 10 nm thick, what is the potential difference across the membrane?
11. What is the potential difference between the terminals of a battery that can impart 7.2×10^{-19} J to each electron that moves between the terminals?
12. Electrons in a TV tube are accelerated from rest through a 25-kV potential difference. With what speed do they hit the TV screen?
13. A 12-V car battery stores 2.8 MJ of energy. How much charge can move between the battery terminals before it is totally discharged? Assume the potential difference remains at 12 V, an assumption that is not realistic.
14. What is the charge on an ion that gains 1.6×10^{-15} J when it moves through a potential difference of 2500 V?
15. Two large, flat metal plates are a distance d apart, where d is small compared with the plate size. If the plates carry surface charge densities $\pm\sigma$, show that the magnitude of the potential difference between them is $V = \sigma d/\varepsilon_0$.
16. An electron passes point A moving at 6.5 Mm/s. At point B the electron has come to a complete stop. Find the potential difference ΔV_{AB}.
17. A 5.0-g obj... carri... ...arge of 3.8... ... It ... ...es a speed v w... ...difference ... ...the same ci...

C

d

E

$45°$

A — d — B

FIGURE 25-37 Problem 8.

Most of the problems are **referenced by section** to allow a student to refer easily to the relevant text.

Supplementary Problems drawn from throughout the chapter are more difficult problems that will challenge the best students.

Supplementary Problems

69. A conducting sphere 5.0 cm in radius carries 60 nC. It is surrounded by a concentric spherical conducting shell of radius 15 cm carrying -60 nC. (a) Find the potential at the sphere's surface, taking the zero of potential at infinity. (b) Repeat for the case when the shell also carries $+60$ nC.
70. Show that the result of Example 25-9 approaches the field of a point charge for $x \gg a$. *Hint:* You will need to apply the binomial theorem to the quantity $1/\sqrt{x^2 + a^2}$.
71. The potential on the axis of a uniformly charged disk at ... the potential 10 cm ... he disk radius and its

76. Repeat the preceding problem for the case $\lambda = \lambda_0(x/\ell)$. Why is your answer for $x \gg \ell$ different? *Hint:* What does this charge distribution resemble at large distances?
77. For the situation of Example 25-10, find an equation for the equipotential with $V = 0$ in the x-y plane. Plot the equipotential, and show that it passes through the points described in Example 25-10 and its exercise.
78. A disk of radius a carries a nonuniform surface charge density given by $\sigma = \sigma_0(r/a)$, where σ_0 is a constant. (a) Find the potential at an arbitrary point on the disk axis, a distance x from the disk center. (b) Use the result of (a) to find the electric field on the disk axis, and (c) show that the field reduces to an expected form for $x \gg a$.
79. An open-ended cylinder of radius a and length $2a$ carries charge q spread uniformly over its surface. Find the potential on the cylinder axis at its center. *Hint:* Treat the cylinder as a stack of charged rings, and integrate.

914 Part 4 Cumulative Problems

PART 4 Cumulative Problems

These problems combine material from chapters throughout the entire part or, in addition, from chapters in earlier parts, or they present special challenges.

1. An air-insulated parallel-plate capacitor has plate area 100 cm² and spacing 0.50 cm. The capacitor is charged and then disconnected from the charging battery. A thin-walled, nonconducting box of the same dimensions as the capacitor is filled with water at 20.00°C. The box is released at the edge of the capacitor and moves without friction into the capacitor (Fig. 1). When it reaches equilibrium the water temperature is 21.50°. What was the original voltage on the capacitor?

50 T/s while that in the right-hand solenoid is decreasing at 30 T/s. Find the current in the resistance wire shared by both triangles. Which way does the current flow?

B_{out} B_{out}

FIGURE 3 Cumulative Problem 3.

4. A long solenoid of length ℓ and radius R has a total of N ...

The student is asked to integrate knowledge from previous chapters to solve the **Cumulative Problems.** They test a student's understanding of a range of topics, and accumulation of knowledge.

The Authors

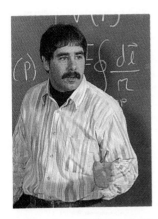

Richard Wolfson is Professor of Physics and George Adams Ellis Professor of the Liberal Arts at Middlebury College, where he has taught since 1976. He did undergraduate work at the Massachusetts Institute of Technology and Swarthmore College and holds the M.S. degree from the University of Michigan and Ph.D. from Dartmouth. He has published widely in scientific journals, including works ranging from medical physics research to experimental plasma physics, electronic circuit design, solar energy engineering, and theoretical astrophysics. He is also an interpreter of science for the nonspecialist, as a contributor to *Scientific American* and author of the book *Nuclear Choices: A Citizen's Guide to Nuclear Technology*. His videotaped course "Einstein's Relativity and the Quantum Revolution," produced by The Teaching Company, brings the key ideas of modern physics to nonscientists. Professor Wolfson has spent sabbatical years as Visiting Scientist at the National Center for Atmospheric Research in Boulder, Colorado, at St. Andrews University in Scotland, and at Stanford University.

Jay M. Pasachoff is Field Memorial Professor of Astronomy and Director of the Hopkins Observatory at Williams College. He was born and brought up in New York City. After attending the Bronx High School of Science, he received his A.B. degree from Harvard College and his A.M. and Ph.D. from Harvard University. He then held postdoctoral fellowships at Harvard and at the California Institute of Technology before going to Williams in 1972. His research has dealt mainly with solar physics, most recently the solar corona as studied at total eclipses, and with nuclear astrophysics, namely, the abundances of the light elements and their formation in the first minutes of the universe. Professor Pasachoff has spent sabbatical leaves at the University of Hawaii, at l'Institut d'Astrophysique in Paris, at the Institute for Advanced Study in Princeton, and at the Harvard-Smithsonian Center for Astrophysics. He is also author or co-author of major texts in physics, calculus, physical science, and astronomy.

Color Key for Figures

The artwork for this third edition is carefully designed to make effective use of color printing as a learning aid. In particular, we have assigned colors to the vector quantities that are so important in physics, and we have used those colors consistently throughout the book. The table below lists some important physical quantities, along with their text and graphic symbols and color assignments. We also include electric circuit symbols, which, to be consistent with usage in engineering, are printed in black.

Vector	Text Symbol	Graphic Symbol
Displacement	$\mathbf{r}, \boldsymbol{\ell}$	
Velocity	$\mathbf{v}$	
Acceleration	$\mathbf{a}$	
Force	$\mathbf{F}$	
Linear momentum	$\mathbf{p}$	
Angular velocity	$\boldsymbol{\omega}$	
Torque	$\boldsymbol{\tau}$	
Angular momentum	$\mathbf{L}$	
Electric field	$\mathbf{E}$	
Magnetic field	$\mathbf{B}$	
Electric dipole moment	$\mathbf{p}$	
Magnetic dipole moment	$\boldsymbol{\mu}$	
Electric charge		
Positive charge	q, Q	⊕
Negative charge	q, Q	⊖
Circuit symbols		
Battery, emf	$\mathcal{E}$	
Resistor	R	
Capacitor	C	
Inductor	L	
Switch	S	

Credits

Page abbreviations are as follows: (T) top, (C) center, (B) bottom, (L) left, (R) right.

429BR Courtesy of T.D. Rossing/Northern Illinois University

430 Courtesy of Fox Products, South Whitley, IN

431 From PSSC Physcis, 2nd ed., 1965 D.C. Heath and Co. with Education Development Center

432 ©Camerique/H. Armstrong Roberts

435L Courtesy of Dr. Gary Settles

435C ©The Harold E. Edgerton 1992 Trust/Palm Press

435R ©H. Armstrong Roberts

437 ©David R. Frazier Photolibrary

439L ©Greg Cranna/Stock Boston

439R ©Philippe Plailly/SPL/Photo Researchers, Inc.

441 ©Peter Rauter/Tony Stone Images

447 ©Bill Gallery/Stock Boston

448CL ©J.Cochin//Explorer/Photo Researchers, Inc.

448CR ©Fred McConnaughey/Photo Researchers, Inc.

448B Courtesy of Lawrence Livermore National Laboratory

449L ©Fredrik D. Bodin/Stock Boston

449R ©W.Eastep/The Stock Market

450 ©Wolfgang Kaehler

452TR Courtesy of Mercedes Benz

452TL ©Diane Schiumo/Fundamental Photographs

452C Courtesy of NASA

454 ©Dan McCoy/Rainbow

458T ©Tod Planck/Tony Stone Images

458B ©Larry Mulvehill/Photo Researchers, Inc.

459T ©J. Toers/George Hall Photos

459B ©Globus Brothers

460 ©Peter Menzel/Stock Boston

461 ONERA photo, H. Werle 1974, from Milton van Dyke, An Atlas of Fluid Motion

464B ©Bruce Thomas/The Stock Market

471 ©Ray Ellis/Photo Researchers, Inc.

472 ©NASA/SS/Photo Researchers, Inc.

474C ©Jay M. Pasachoff

474B ©1998 PhotoDisc, Inc.

477 ©G.R. Roberts

478 ©Robert Fried/Stock Boston

483 ©John Wilson White/Addison Wesley Longman

484 ©Manuel G. Velarde

485T ©Keith Wood/Tony Stone Images

485B ©Camerique/H. Armstrong Roberts

496 ©Paolo Koch/Photo Researchers, Inc.

505 ©Alexander Tsiaras/Photo Researchers, Inc.

507C ©Paul Silverman/Fundamental Photographs

507B ©Richard Megna/Fundamental Photographs

511T Courtesy of the Hartford Steam Boiler and Insurance Company

511C ©AP/Wide World

516 ©Bruce M. Wellman/Stock Boston

517 ©Jim Richardson/H. Armstrong Roberts

519 ©Jan Halaska/Photo Researchers, Inc.

523 ©David R. Austen/Stock Boston

527 Courtesy of Price Weber

529T ©Geoff Juckes/The Stock Market

529B ©Thomas Ives/The Stock Market

543 ©Sinclair Stammers/SPL/Photo Researchers, Inc.

546L ©David R. Frazier Photolibrary/Photo Researchers, Inc.

546R Courtesy of the Environmental Protection Agency

550 ©Rick Browne/Stock Boston

551 ©Martin Bond/SPL/Photo Researchers, Inc.

552T Courtesy of Lockheed

552B ©Hank Morgan/Photo Researchers, Inc.

569 ©Astrid and Hans Frieder Michler/SPL/Photo Researchers, Inc.

570 ©Gary Ladd

571L ©Richard Megna/Fundamental Photographs

571R Courtesy of Intel

573T ©Lawrence Berkeley Laboratory/SPL/Photo Researchers, Inc.

573C ©Richard Megna/Fundamental Photographs

1053L Courtesy of AT&T Bell Laboratories

1054 Courtesy of the Meggers Gallery, AIP

1057T Courtesy of the Institute of Theoretical Physics, Lund, Sweden

1057B Courtesy of Carl D. Anderson/California Institute of Technology

1058 ©AP/Wide World

1060T ©U.S. Navy/SPL/Photo Researchers, Inc.

1060B Courtesy of Ullstein Bilderdienst

1061 Courtesy of Ullstein Bilderdienst

1062 Courtesy of the Stein Collection, AIP

1064L Courtesy of Fermilab Visual Media Services

1064R Courtesy of CERN

1065T Courtesy of Ralph Crane

1065B ©Patrice Loiez/CERN/SPL/Photo Researchers, Inc.

1067 ©Joe Stancampiano and Karl Luttrell/National Geographic Society

1071 ©Dan McCoy/Rainbow

1072R ©Mark Marten/Los Alamos National Laboratory/Photo Researchers, Inc.

Extended

1044 ©Wexler/Burgess/SPL/Photo Researchers, Inc.

1046 Courtesy of The Exploratorium

1057T Courtesy of R. Giovanelli and H.R. Gillett/ CSIRO National Measurement Laboratory, Australia

1057B Courtesy of Alfred Leitner/Rensselaer Polytechnic Institute

1058 Courtesy of the AIP Niels Bohr Library, photo by Paul Ehrenfest

1063L ©Prof. P.M. Motta/SPL/Photo Researchers, Inc.

1063R ©CNRI/SPL/Photo Researchers, Inc.

1064 Courtesy of AT&T Bell Laboratories

1068 Courtesy of the AIP Niels Bohr Library

1074 Courtesy of the Lawrence Livermore National Laboratory

1076 Courtesy of Elisha Huggins, Dartmouth

1077T From C. Jonsson, Zeitscrift fer Physik, Springer-Verlag, Berlin, Heidelberg, New York

1077B Courtesy of the AIP, Meggers Gallery

1079 Courtesy of Paul Ehrenfest

1088 Courtesy of Don Eigler, IBM Almaden

1089L Courtesy of IBM

1089R Courtesy of IBM

1090L Courtesy of Don Eigler, IBM Almaden

1090R Courtesy of R.M. Penner, University of California, Irvine

1094 Courtesy of Fermilab Visual Media Services

1100 ©Ken Eward/Photo Researchers, Inc.

1113 Courtesy of the National Radio Astronomy Observatory

1115T Courtesy of Mike Matthews/JILA

1115B ©Richard Megna/Fundamental Photographs

1121T Courtesy of the Astronomical Data Center (ADC) catalog A6016, by Reader J., Corliss Ch.H.:1981, 'Line Spectra of the Elements', CRC Handbook of Chemistry and Physics; NSRDS-NBS 68

1121B Courtesy of Osram/Sylvania, Inc.

1124 ©SPL/Photo Researchers, Inc.

1126 Courtesy of D.A. Calvert/Royal Greenwich Observatory

1127TL ©Skelton Photography

1127TC ©Dan McCoy/Rainbow

1127TR ©Paul Shambroom/Photo Researchers, Inc.

1127C ©Dagmar Schilling/Peter Arnold, Inc.

1127B ©Dan McCoy/Rainbow

1133 ©Science Source/Photo Researchers, Inc.

1136 ©Geoff Tomplinson/SPL/Photo Researchers, Inc.

1150T ©1998 PhotoDisc, Inc.

1150B ©John Mead/SPL/Photo Researchers, Inc.

1152L ©IBM Research/Peter Arnold, Inc.

1152C Courtesy of Brookhaven National Laboratory and NYU Medi-Cal Center

1153T Courtesy of Conductus

1153B Courtesy of the American Superconductor Corp.

Wave Motion

Ocean waves carry energy thousands of kilometers before breaking on shore. These waves are produced by wind disturbing the ocean surface. Numerous smaller waves are superposed on the two large wave crests prominent in this photo.

It's a beautiful day at the beach, but the surf is a bit rough as ocean waves bring to shore energy imparted by a distant storm. Astronomers direct the Hubble Space Telescope to capture images of galaxies so distant that the light waves reaching Hubble have been traveling for 12 billion years. Your car breaks down and you use a cellular phone to summon help; your voice is carried on radio waves to the telephone network. A rock band energizes the air with its playing, and that energy is carried as sound waves to the audience's ears. An earthquake sends waves to the far corners of the planet, allowing geologists to pinpoint the quake and to study Earth's interior. Spectators in one section of a football stadium stand up, and soon a wave of standing fans sweeps around the stadium. Physicians probe the human body with ultrasound waves, whose reflections form images of inner structures (Fig. 16-1).

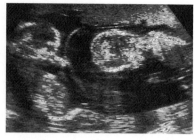

(a)

(b)

(c)

FIGURE 16-1 (a) Twin fetuses are evident in this image, produced by ultrasound waves reflecting in the human body. (b) This building in Kobe, Japan, was destroyed in the 1995 earthquake. Energy released in a quake propagates as a wave, shaking the ground as it passes. (c) Invisible electromagnetic waves carry cellular phone messages.

All of these examples involve **wave motion**. They have in common the motion—or **propagation**—of energy from one place to another. Matter, however, does not travel anywhere: those waves crashing on the beach don't carry water from the distant open ocean where the storm raged. Air does not travel from the rock band's loudspeakers to your ears. Spectators don't run around the football stadium. And though geologists across the planet know about the earthquake, no earth actually moves from the quake zone to distant seismographs. Our definition of a **wave** emphasizes this point:

A wave is a traveling disturbance that transports energy but not matter.

16-1 KINDS OF WAVES

You're familiar with many kinds of waves. Sound waves carry energy and information through the air; sound also propagates in solids and liquids. Water waves are obvious on the surface of lakes and seas; earthquake waves propagate invisibly through Earth's solid and liquid interior. The vibrating strings of violins and pianos involve waves propagating back and forth along the strings. All these are examples of **mechanical waves**, so called because each involves disturbances of a mechanical medium such as air, water, solid Earth, or a stretched string.

Other common waves include the light waves by which you see, radio waves that carry radio and TV signals, microwaves that cook your food, X rays that image your body's innards, and ultraviolet waves that can burn your skin. All these are examples of **electromagnetic waves**. These waves have many properties in common with mechanical waves, including the same basic mathematical description. However, electromagnetic waves don't involve a mechanical medium. Less familiar are waves used in the quantum mechanical description of the physical world at the atomic scale. These so-called matter waves govern the behavior of particles such as electrons and protons.

We explore wave motion in this chapter and the next, concentrating primarily on mechanical waves. Many of the phenomena and mathematical techniques we develop here will apply also to electromagnetic waves, which we study in Chapters 34–38, and to matter waves, introduced in Chapter 39 and explored further in the extended version of this text.

Mechanical Waves

What does wave motion have to do with what we've studied in earlier chapters? For mechanical waves, the answer is quite a lot. Because such waves involve disturbance of a mechanical system, they're ultimately governed by the interplay between force and mass described by Newton's laws.

Both the physics and the mathematics of wave motion have much in common with oscillatory motion that we studied in the preceding chapter. The interactions among particles that make up bulk matter can often be modeled by considering the particles to be masses coupled by springs that represent the forces acting between them. A disturbance from equilibrium in one region of the material sets up an oscillation that is then coupled to other regions. The result

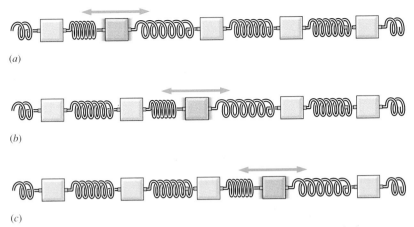

(a)

(b)

(c)

FIGURE 16-2 A long, narrow structure such as a stretched string or a rod can be modeled as a line of blocks connected by springs. (a) A disturbance from equilibrium sets the highlighted block at left oscillating, compressing and stretching the adjacent springs. (b–c) Because the blocks are coupled, the disturbance propagates to other regions of the medium, moving ever farther from its starting point as time advances. The propagating disturbance is a wave pulse.

is a propagating wave, carrying the disturbance throughout the material. Figure 16-2 illustrates this process.

The mass-spring model of Fig. 16-2 will help you understand wave motion by building on your knowledge of oscillatory motion. Those who go on to more advanced work in physics, engineering, or materials science will find many other examples—from semiconductor crystals to skyscrapers—where structures are effectively modeled as coupled mass-spring systems.

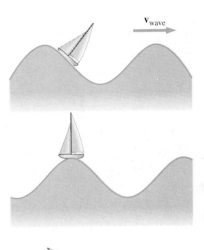

FIGURE 16-3 Waves on the open ocean disturb the boat, but it doesn't participate in their shoreward motion. Neither does the water itself, although water does move about locally as the wave passes (see Fig. 16-5).

Tip

What Do You Mean, A Wave Doesn't Transport Matter? Our definition of a wave emphasizes the transport of energy but not matter. But in Fig. 16-2 it sure looks like the individual blocks move. They *do* move, temporarily, executing small oscillations about their equilibrium positions, as the wave goes by. But they aren't transported from place to place. That's the important distinction. A mechanical wave is a disturbance of a medium, and while the wave is passing the particles making up the medium do move. But they only oscillate; they don't undergo a bulk displacement from one place to another. In contrast, the wave energy—manifested in the oscillations of the individual blocks shown in Fig. 16-2—does move from place to place (see Fig. 16-3).

16-2 WAVE PROPERTIES

Here we describe the physical properties that characterize different waves. You can visualize these properties and gain much more insight into wave motion through the wave animations provided in ActivPhysics Activity 10.1.

10.1
Properties of Mechanical Waves

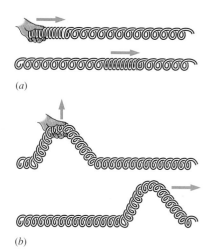

(a)

(b)

FIGURE 16-4 Waves on a stretched spring, like a Slinky. (a) Compressing a section of the spring produces a longitudinal wave pulse. (b) Displacing the spring perpendicular to its length produces a transverse wave pulse.

Amplitude

A wave disturbs a medium from its equilibrium state. The maximum value of the disturbance is the wave **amplitude**; this is the same as the definition of amplitude we gave in Chapter 15 for oscillatory motion. Amplitude measures whatever physical property is affected by the wave—the height of a water wave from the undisturbed water surface, the excess pressure of a sound wave, the extra tension or compression forces in the springs of Figs. 16-2 and 16-4, or the maximum displacement of a violin string from equilibrium.

Longitudinal and Transverse Waves

Figure 16-4 shows a section of a stretched spring (a Slinky is a good example). Imagine compressing part of the spring and then releasing it. The compression moves along the spring, constituting a traveling wave pulse (Fig. 16-4a). As the pulse passes along the spring, coils of the spring move slightly back and forth to bunch up and then relax again to their equilibrium positions. A wave such as this one, in which the medium moves back and forth along the same line on which the wave is propagating, is called a **longitudinal wave**. Another example of a longitudinal wave is sound, in which air molecules oscillate back and forth in the direction of the sound's propagation. We'll study sound waves in the next chapter.

Figure 16-4b shows another way to set up a wave on the stretched spring. Disturbing the spring at right angles to its long dimension and then releasing it sends a pulse down the spring. As the pulse passes, a section of the spring moves back and forth at right angles to the spring's long dimension, taking on the pulse shape and then relaxing back to equilibrium. A wave such as this, where the medium moves back and forth at right angles to the wave motion, is called a **transverse wave**. Examples of transverse mechanical waves include some types of earthquake waves and waves on musical instrument strings. Electromagnetic waves in vacuum are also transverse, but since there's no medium involved it won't be fully clear until Chapter 34 just what that means.

Unlike solids, liquids and gases (collectively called fluids) do not develop restoring forces in response to so-called shearing motions that displace one layer of fluid sideways relative to another. As a result, liquids and gases cannot support fully transverse waves confined entirely within the bulk material of the fluid. In contrast, fluids can support longitudinal waves because they develop restoring forces in response to compression.

Things get more complicated at the interface between two fluids, for example, water and air, or even the warm and cool layers in lakes. At such interfaces waves can exist with both longitudinal and transverse components. The familiar waves on the surface of water provide an example (Fig. 16-5).

FIGURE 16-5 A water wave has both longitudinal and transverse components, as parcels of water describe nearly circular paths around their equilibrium positions.

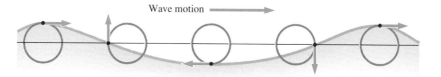

Waveforms

Wave disturbances come in many shapes, called **waveforms** (Fig. 16-6). An isolated disturbance, traveling through an otherwise undisturbed medium, is a **pulse**. A pulse occurs when a medium is disturbed only briefly, as in Fig. 16-4. At the opposite extreme is a **continuous wave**, produced when a medium is disturbed in a regular, periodic way. A **wave train** results from the more realistic case when a periodic disturbance lasts for a finite time.

Wavelength and Period

A continuous wave repeats itself in both space and time. The **wavelength** λ is the *distance* over which the wave pattern repeats, as measured at a *fixed time* (Fig. 16-7). The wave **period** T is the *time* for one complete wave cycle to pass a *fixed position*. The **frequency** f, or number of wave cycles passing a given point per unit time, is the inverse of the period.

Wave Speed

A wave travels at a characteristic speed through its medium. Under typical conditions, the speed of sound in air is 340 m/s. Small ripples on the surface of a pond move at about 20 cm/s, while earthquake waves move through Earth's outer crust at about 6 km/s. The physical properties of the medium, in connection with Newton's laws, ultimately determine wave speed. In Section 16-4 we'll see how this works for one simple yet important case.

Wave speed, wavelength, and period are related. In one wave period, a fixed observer sees one complete wavelength go by (Fig. 16-8). Thus, the wave moves one wavelength in one period, so its speed is

$$v = \frac{\lambda}{T} = \lambda f, \qquad (16\text{-}1)$$

where the second equality follows because the period and frequency are inverses.

16-3 MATHEMATICAL DESCRIPTION OF WAVE MOTION

Figure 16-9 shows a "snapshot" of a wave pulse at time $t = 0$. The pulse is moving to the right with speed v, and at $t = 0$ its peak coincides with $x = 0$. We can describe the pulse by giving the displacement y as a function of position x: $y = f(x)$, where the peak of the function f occurs where its argument is zero.

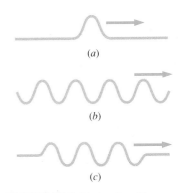

FIGURE 16-6 (*a*) A pulse, (*b*) a continuous wave, and (*c*) a wave train.

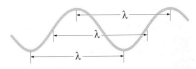

FIGURE 16-7 The wavelength λ is the distance over which the wave pattern repeats.

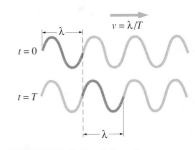

FIGURE 16-8 One full cycle— occupying a distance of one wavelength— passes a given point in one wave period. The wave speed is therefore $v = \lambda/T$.

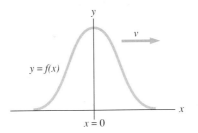

FIGURE 16-9 A "snapshot" of a wave pulse at time $t = 0$. The pulse is moving to the right with speed v.

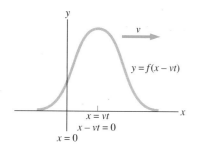

FIGURE 16-10 At a later time t the wave pulse has moved to the right a distance vt. It is described by the same function f, but now with argument $x - vt$.

Figure 16-10 shows the pulse some time t later. Moving at speed v, its peak is now located at $x = vt$. We can describe this displaced pulse by adjusting the function $y = f(x)$ so it peaks at $x = vt$ instead of at $x = 0$. The function f itself peaks where its argument is zero, so if we change the argument to $x - vt$ we will have just what we want: a function whose peak occurs when $x - vt = 0$, or $x = vt$. As time increases, so does vt and, therefore, the value of x that gives the location of the peak. Thus, the function $f(x - vt)$ correctly describes the moving pulse.

Although we considered a single pulse, the same argument applies to *any* function $f(x)$, including continuous waves. Quite generally, a wave moving in the positive x direction is described by some function of the form $f(x - vt)$, with v the wave speed. You can convince yourself that a wave moving in the negative x direction is described similarly by $f(x + vt)$.

A particularly important case is the **simple harmonic wave**, so called because the wave medium executes simple harmonic motion about equilibrium. We want a mathematical description of such a wave, starting first at a fixed time, say $t = 0$. Given such a description—which amounts to an expression for the wave displacement as a function of position x—we'll be able to generalize to all times by replacing x with $x - vt$, as we argued using Figs. 16-9 and 16-10.

A simple harmonic wave must be sinusoidal in shape, so a sine or cosine function will do. We'll choose cosine, an arbitrary choice that assumes the wave has its maximum displacement at $x = 0$. But what, exactly, should be the argument of that cosine function? Our wave has wavelength λ, so the interval from $x = 0$ to $x = \lambda$ should span one wavelength. The cosine function itself goes through a full cycle as its argument goes from 0 to 2π, so we want the argument of our cosine function to be zero at $x = 0$ and 2π when $x = \lambda$. Taking $2\pi x/\lambda$ for the argument of the cosine does this: substitute $x = 0$ and the result is zero; substitute $x = \lambda$ and the result is 2π. So our expression for the wave displacement at time $t = 0$ is

$$y(x, 0) = A\cos\left(\frac{2\pi x}{\lambda}\right),$$

where y is the displacement from equilibrium and A the amplitude (Fig. 16-11a). This expression holds at $t = 0$; to get an expression valid for all times, we replace x by $x \pm vt$:

$$y(x, t) = A\cos\left[\frac{2\pi(x \pm vt)}{\lambda}\right] = A\cos\left(\frac{2\pi x}{\lambda} \pm 2\pi ft\right), \qquad (16\text{-}2)$$

where the last step follows using $v/\lambda = f$ from Equation 16-1. Equation 16-2 shows that if we sit at a fixed position—say, $x = 0$—then the displacement varies in time as $y(0, t) = A\cos(2\pi ft)$, which we recognize as simple harmonic motion with **angular frequency** given by

$$\omega = 2\pi f = \frac{2\pi}{T}, \qquad (16\text{-}3)$$

as shown in Fig. 16-11b. Similarly, it is convenient to define the **wave number**, k:

$$k = \frac{2\pi}{\lambda}. \qquad (16\text{-}4)$$

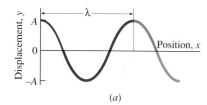

(a)

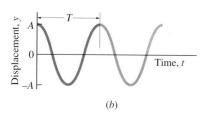

(b)

FIGURE 16-11 (a) "Snapshot," at time $t = 0$, of the simple harmonic wave described by Equation 16-2. The graph is the wave displacement as a function of position x. (b) The wave displacement at a fixed position, plotted as a function of *time*. The medium oscillates with angular frequency $\omega = 2\pi f = 2\pi/T$. Note the difference between (a) and (b); (a) shows the *spatial* variation at a *fixed time*, while (b) shows the *temporal* variation at a *fixed position*.

The wave number is the spatial analog of frequency; the latter describes the number of radians of wave cycle per unit *time,* the former the number of radians per unit *distance.* The definition of k shows that its units are m^{-1}. Using ω and k, we can rewrite Equation 16-2:

$$y(x, t) = A\cos(kx \pm \omega t). \tag{16-5}$$

The simple way in which k and ω enter this description of the wave is the reason these quantities are so often used. We can use Equation 16-1 with Equations 16-3 and 16-4 to write the wave speed in terms of ω and k:

$$v = \frac{\lambda}{T} = \frac{2\pi/k}{2\pi/\omega} = \frac{\omega}{k}. \tag{16-6}$$

Sometimes, especially when we're dealing with multiple waves, we may add a phase constant in the argument of the cosine in Equation 16-5, as we described in the Math Toolbox "Phase, Phase Constant, Phase Difference" in Chapter 15.

EXAMPLE 16-1	Surf's Up!

A surfing physicist paddles out beyond the breaking surf to a deep-water region where the ocean waves are sinusoidal in shape, with crests 14 m apart. The surfer rises a vertical distance 3.6 m from wave trough to crest, a process that takes 1.5 s. Find the wave speed, and describe it with an equation of the same form as Equation 16-5. Take a wave crest to be at $x = 0$ at time $t = 0$, with the positive x direction toward the open ocean.

Solution

Figure 16-11*b* shows that the time from trough to crest is half a period, so $T = 3.0$ s. Then Equation 16-1 gives

$$v = \frac{\lambda}{T} = \frac{14 \text{ m}}{3.0 \text{ s}} = 4.67 \text{ m/s}.$$

To use the form of Equation 16-5 we need the amplitude A, wave number k, and angular frequency ω. Figure 16-11 shows that the amplitude is half the trough-to-crest displacement, or 1.8 m, while Equations 16-3 and 16-4 give ω and k:

$$\omega = \frac{2\pi}{T} = \frac{2\pi}{3.0 \text{ s}} = 2.09 \text{ s}^{-1}, \, k = \frac{2\pi}{\lambda} = \frac{2\pi}{14 \text{ m}} = 0.449 \text{ m}^{-1}.$$

With the wave propagating in the $-x$ direction—toward shore—we take the plus sign in Equation 16-5, so the wave description is

$$y(x, t) = 1.8\cos(0.449x + 2.09t) \text{ m}.$$

EXERCISE The temporal and spatial variation of the waves in a microwave oven are described by $\cos(50.3x - 15.1t)$, with t in nanoseconds and x in meters. Find (a) the wave frequency in hertz, (b) the wavelength, and (c) the wave speed.

Answers: (a) 2.4 GHz; (b) 12.5 cm; (c) 3.00×10^8 m/s

Some problems similar to Example 16-1: 10, 13, 14

16-4 WAVES ON A STRING

A Stretched String

What determines how fast waves propagate in a mechanical medium? The answer lies in Newton's laws and the physical properties of the medium. Calculating the speed and other characteristics of waves in different materials is a significant job for professional physicists and materials scientists. Only in the simplest cases can mathematical analysis at our level yield the wave speed. One

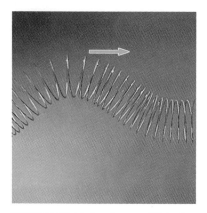

FIGURE 16-12 A pulse on a Slinky is an example of a transverse wave on an elongated structure. The pulse was produced by pulling the Slinky vertically at one point, then releasing.

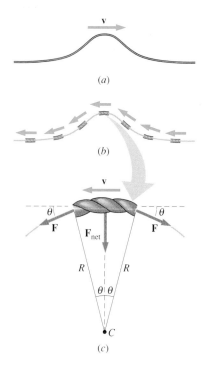

such case is that of transverse waves on a stretched string, which we're now going to look at in detail. Our results are directly applicable to musical instrument strings, suspension bridge cables, and many other elongated structures (Fig. 16-12).

Our string has mass per unit length μ in kilograms per meter, and is stretched to a tension force F in newtons. In equilibrium, the string lies along the x axis. Suppose we distort a section of it slightly by displacing it in the y direction. We want to show that wave motion results when the string is released and to determine the wave speed.

To find the speed, we need to apply Newton's law to the motion of the string. Figure 16-13a shows the wave pulse moving to the right with some speed v. It's easiest to apply Newton's law in a frame of reference moving with the uniform velocity of the pulse; in that frame the entire string is moving to the *left* at speed v. As a section of the string encounters the pulse, which is stationary in this frame of reference, its motion deviates from a straight line as it rides up over the pulse (Fig. 16-13b).

Whatever the pulse shape, we can describe a small enough section at the top as a circular arc of some radius R, as shown in Fig. 16-13c. Then a small section of string right at the top of the pulse undergoes circular motion with speed v and radius R; if its mass is m, Newton's law requires that a force of magnitude mv^2/R act toward the center of curvature in order to keep the string section on its circular path. This force is provided by the difference in string tension between the two ends of the section; as Fig. 16-13c shows, the section's curvature means the tension vectors at the two ends point in different directions. The tension at each end contributes a component $F \sin\theta$ toward the center of curvature, where θ is shown in Fig. 16-13c. Then the net force on the segment has magnitude $2F \sin\theta$ and points toward the center of curvature.

Now we make an additional assumption: that the disturbance of the string is small, in the sense that the string remains almost horizontal even at the pulse. Then the angle θ is small, and we can apply the approximation $\sin\theta \simeq \theta$. Therefore the net force on the string section becomes approximately $2F\theta$. Furthermore, the small-disturbance approximation means that the tension doesn't vary significantly from its undisturbed value, so the F in this expression is essentially the same F we're using to characterize the tension throughout the string. Finally, our curved string section forms a circular arc whose length, from Fig. 16-13c, is $2\theta R$. Multiplying by the mass per unit length μ gives its mass:

FIGURE 16-13 (a) A pulse moving to the right with speed v on a stretched string. (b) In the reference frame of the moving pulse, the string moves to the left. Individual segments of the string follow curved paths as they move through the pulse. (c) A blow-up of a small string segment at the top of the pulse. The net force on the segment is the vector sum of the tension forces $\mathbf{F}$ at the two ends; this force keeps the string segment in its path through the curved pulse. The angle θ is exaggerated; it is actually so small that $\sin\theta \simeq \theta$, making $F_{net} \simeq 2F\theta$. The quantity R is the curvature radius at the top of the pulse.

Remember that the analysis of (c) is done in a reference frame with the pulse at rest; in that frame, the string really does undergo circular motion at the top of the pulse. But in a reference frame in which the undisturbed string is at rest, the only motion is the back-and-forth motion of the string in the y direction (perpendicular to the string) as the pulse goes by.

$m = 2\theta R\mu$. Now we can apply Newton's law, equating the net force $2F\theta$ to the mass times acceleration:

$$2F\theta = \frac{mv^2}{R} = \frac{2\theta R\mu v^2}{R} = 2\theta\mu v^2.$$

Solving for the wave speed v then gives

$$v = \sqrt{\frac{F}{\mu}}. \qquad (16\text{-}7)$$

10.2
Speed of Waves on a String

Does this result make sense? The string tension provides the restoring force that drives the disturbed part of the string toward equilibrium. The greater the tension F, the greater the acceleration of the disturbed string, and thus the more rapidly the wave should propagate. The string's inertia, on the other hand, limits the acceleration with which the string responds to the force, and therefore a greater mass per unit length should slow the wave propagation. Equation 16-7, with F in the numerator and μ in the denominator, reflects both these trends.

We have made no assumption about wave shape other than to assume that the disturbance is small; therefore Equation 16-7 applies to small-amplitude pulses, continuous waves, and wave trains of any shape. In Section 16-6 we will derive Equation 16-7 using a more advanced analysis that gives a general equation shared by many systems that support propagating waves and will show explicitly that simple harmonic waves are among its solutions.

EXAMPLE 16-2	*Rock Climbing*

Two climbers are joined by a 43-m-long rope of total mass 5.0 kg. One climber strikes the rope with a fist, and 1.4 s later the second climber feels the effect. What is the rope tension?

Solution
Solving Equation 16-7 for the tension gives $F = \mu v^2$. Here $\mu = m/L$ and $v = L/t$, with L and m the rope length and mass and t the time interval. So we have

$$F = \mu v^2 = \left(\frac{m}{L}\right)\left(\frac{L}{t}\right)^2 = \frac{mL}{t^2} = \frac{(5.0 \text{ kg})(43 \text{ m})}{(1.4 \text{ s})^2} = 110 \text{ N}.$$

Is this number reasonable? A typical adult weighs between 500 and 1000 N, so the rope is supporting only a small fraction of the lower climber's weight—a reasonable situation.

EXERCISE A 4.5-g piano wire is under 680 N tension. If waves propagate along it at 320 m/s, what is its length?

Answer: 68 cm

Some problems similar to Example 16-2: 21, 24, 27, 29

16-5 WAVE POWER AND INTENSITY

A wave propagates because part of a medium communicates its motion to adjacent parts. In the process, energy passes through the medium. As always in mechanics, that energy is transferred by forces that do work.

In the case of a stretched string, it is the tension force that does work on the string, and this work results in energy transfer along the string in the direction of the wave propagation. As we showed in Section 7-7, power—the rate of

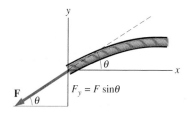

FIGURE 16-14 The force acting on the left end of the string is the tension force **F**. But since the string is moving downward, only the vertical component $F_y = F\sin\theta$ does any work. For small angles, $\sin\theta \simeq \theta \simeq \tan\theta$, and $\tan\theta$ is the slope—that is, the derivative dy/dx—of the string evaluated at the end of the segment.

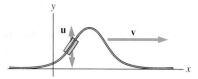

FIGURE 16-15 The speed u of the disturbed string is not the same as the wave speed v! The pulse moves in the x direction, from left to right along the string, while a section of the string moves back and forth in the y direction, perpendicular to the wave propagation, as the pulse passes by. Both the directions and the magnitudes of the two velocities **u** and **v** are different.

doing work—is the dot product of the force with the velocity. Figure 16-14 shows the section of string we considered earlier, now in the reference frame of the string. In that frame the left end of the displaced segment is moving downward as the pulse passes to the right, and, as we found earlier, the vertical component of the tension force on the left end alone is very nearly $-F\theta$, with the minus sign indicating the downward direction. Then the rate at which work is done by this force is

$$P = F_y u = -F\theta u,$$

where u is the vertical speed of the string segment.

Tip

The Medium Is Not the Wave The speed u is the speed at which the disturbed medium moves and is *not* the same as the wave speed v. For this transverse wave, the string motion is in fact at right angles to the wave propagation. Figure 16-15 emphasizes this distinction.

This expression for power holds for any wave shape; we now specialize to the case of a simple harmonic wave, described by Equation 16-5. The velocity u at which the string moves vertically is simply the derivative of the string displacement $y(x, t) = A\cos(kx - \omega t)$ with respect to time:

$$u = \frac{\partial y}{\partial t} = \omega A \sin(kx - \omega t),$$

where we used the chain rule for differentiation, differentiating cosine to get $-$sine, then multiplying by the derivative, $-\omega$, of the cosine's argument $kx - \omega t$. As Fig. 16-14 shows, the tangent of the angle θ is the slope, $\partial y/\partial x$, at the left end of the segment. In the small angle approximation, $\theta \simeq \tan\theta$. Then we have

$$\theta \simeq \frac{\partial y}{\partial x} = -kA \sin(kx - \omega t).$$

The minus sign shows that θ is *positive*—as in Fig. 16-14—when $\sin(kx - \omega t)$ is *negative*. Thus, the force is downward when the velocity **u** is downward, indicating that the tension force does work on the string segment.

Math Toolbox

Partial Derivatives Equation 16-5 gives the displacement in a simple harmonic wave as a function of *both position and time*. Figure 16-14 is a "snapshot" of the string *at an instant in time*. Therefore, the derivative is to be taken *with time fixed*. This qualification is important because the string displacement is a function of both x and t and changes if *either* of these variables changes. With functions of more than one variable, we use the symbol ∂ instead of the usual d to indicate a rate of change with respect to one variable while other variables are held fixed. Such derivatives, like $\partial y/\partial t$ and $\partial y/\partial x$, are called **partial derivatives**.

The rules for partial derivatives are exactly the same as for ordinary derivatives; you just treat as constants all variables other than the one with respect to which you're taking the derivative. Thus, in computing the string's velocity $u = \partial y/\partial t$, we treat x as a constant.

Using our expressions for u and θ, we can then write the power transmitted along the wave as

$$P = -F\theta u = F\omega k A^2 \sin^2(kx - \omega t).$$

The term $\sin^2(kx - \omega t)$ shows that the power fluctuates throughout the wave cycle. We're usually more interested in the *average* power, which we get by noting that the average value of $\sin^2$ is $\frac{1}{2}$ (see Fig. 16-16). Then the average power is simply

$$\bar{P} = \tfrac{1}{2}F\omega k A^2.$$

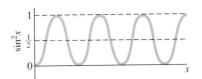

FIGURE 16-16 The function $\sin^2 x$ swings symmetrically between 0 and 1, so its average value is $\frac{1}{2}$.

We can give this expression more physical meaning if we use Equations 16-6 and 16-7 to write $k = \omega/v$ and $F = \mu v^2$, where v is the wave speed. Then we have

$$\bar{P} = \tfrac{1}{2}\mu\omega^2 A^2 v. \tag{16-8}$$

This equation makes sense since it shows that the power—the rate at which energy moves along the wave—is directly proportional to the wave speed v.

Although we derived Equation 16-8 for waves on a string, some aspects of the equation are common to all waves. In particular, wave power is always proportional to the wave speed and to the *square* of the wave amplitude.

EXAMPLE 16-3	*Wave Power*

A garden hose with 440 g of mass per meter of length is lying on the ground. You pull on the hose, producing 12 N of tension, then shake it from side to side to make waves (Fig. 16-17). At what average rate must you do work if you displace the hose 25 cm either side of its equilibrium position, completing two full back-and-forth cycles every second? What will be the distance between wave crests?

Solution
The work you do is transmitted along the hose as the energy of the wave, so you do work at the rate given by Equation 16-8. To use this equation we need the wave speed v and angular frequency ω. The former is given by Equation 16-7:

$$v = \sqrt{\frac{F}{\mu}} = \sqrt{\frac{12\text{ N}}{0.44\text{ kg/m}}} = 5.22\text{ m/s},$$

while the angular frequency is $\omega = 2\pi f = (2\pi)(2.0\text{ Hz}) = 12.6\text{ s}^{-1}$. Then the average power is

$$\bar{P} = \tfrac{1}{2}\mu\omega^2 A^2 v$$
$$= \tfrac{1}{2}(0.44\text{ kg/m})(12.6\text{ s}^{-1})^2(0.25\text{ m})^2(5.22\text{ m/s})$$
$$= 11\text{ W}.$$

This answer neglects any work done against friction between hose and ground.

Finally, Equation 16-1 gives the wavelength—the distance between wave crests:

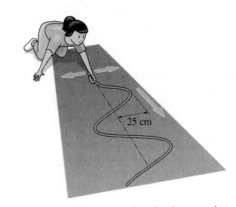

FIGURE 16-17 How much power does it take to send waves along the hose?

$$\lambda = \frac{v}{f} = \frac{5.22\text{ m/s}}{2.0\text{ Hz}} = 2.6\text{ m}.$$

EXERCISE A suspension bridge cable has 3800 kg/m and is under 230 MN tension. What power is required to send a 15-Hz wave with amplitude 5.0 mm along this cable?

Answer: 100 kW

Some problems similar to Example 16-3: 33–35, 38

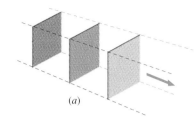

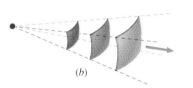

FIGURE 16-18 (a) A plane wave does not spread, so its intensity remains constant. (b) As a spherical wave spreads from a point source, its intensity decreases as the inverse square of the distance from the source.

Wave Intensity

The total power is useful in describing a wave confined to a narrow structure like a string for mechanical waves or a cable or optical fiber for electromagnetic waves. But when waves travel throughout a three-dimensional medium, like sound waves spreading out in air, it makes more sense to talk about the rate at which the wave carries energy across a unit area. This quantity defines the wave **intensity**:

> *The intensity of a wave is the average rate at which the wave carries energy per unit area across a surface perpendicular to the wave propagation.*

Since the rate of energy flow is power, the intensity is just the power per unit area carried by the wave; its units are W/m^2.

A **wavefront** is a surface over which the wave has constant phase. (Recall from Chapter 15 that *phase* means the argument of the function describing oscillatory motion; here we generalize to the argument of the function describing a wave. In the simple cases we've been dealing with, the wave phase is the quantity $x \pm vt$.) An example of a wavefront is a contiguous surface containing all points where the wave displacement is at its peak value. A **plane wave** is one whose wavefronts are planes. Since the wave energy doesn't spread out as the wave propagates, the intensity remains constant (Fig. 16-18a). But with waves from a localized source, the wave energy spreads over ever greater areas, and therefore the intensity decreases. **Spherical waves** originate from pointlike sources and their spherical wavefronts spread in all directions; since the area increases as the square of the distance from the source, the intensity decreases as the inverse square of the distance (Fig. 16-18b). If P is the total power emitted by the source, then the intensity at a distance r is given by

$$I = \frac{P}{A} = \frac{P}{4\pi r^2}, \quad \text{(spherical wave)} \tag{16-9}$$

since the area of a sphere is $4\pi r^2$. It isn't that wave energy is being lost; rather, the same energy is spread over ever greater areas as the waves propagate outward. Examples of spherical waves include light spreading out from a single light bulb, radio waves spreading from a small antenna, or sound from a localized source such as a single loudspeaker. In general, waves spreading out from a source are to a good approximation spherical at distances large compared to the source size.

Table 16-1 lists the intensities of various waves. For those entries whose sources are small compared with the distance listed, you can find the intensities at other distances using the inverse-square relation (see Problems 39–45).

TABLE 16-1 *Wave Intensities*

WAVE	INTENSITY, W/m^2
Sound, 4 m from loud rock band	1
Sound, jet aircraft at 50 m	10
Sound, whisper at 1 m	10^{-10}
Light, sunlight at Earth's orbit	1368
Light, sunlight at Jupiter's orbit	50
Light, 1 m from typical camera flash	4000
Light, at target of laser fusion experiment	10^{18}
TV signal, 5 km from 50 kW transmitter	1.6×10^{-4}
Microwaves, inside microwave oven	6000
Earthquake wave, 5 km from Richter 7.0 quake	4×10^4

EXAMPLE 16-4	*Reading Light*

The page of your book is 1.9 m from a 75-W light bulb, and the light is just barely adequate for reading. How far from a 40-W bulb would the page have to be to get the same light intensity? Treat the bulbs as sources of spherical light waves.

Solution

Equation 16-9 gives the intensity of a spherical wave in terms of the source power and distance. We want the same intensity from both bulbs; equating the intensities as given by Equation 16-9, we have

$$\frac{P_{75}}{4\pi r_{75}^2} = \frac{P_{40}}{4\pi r_{40}^2}$$

Solving for the unknown distance r_{40} then gives

$$r_{40} = r_{75}\sqrt{\frac{P_{40}}{P_{75}}} = (1.9 \text{ m})\sqrt{\frac{40 \text{ W}}{75 \text{ W}}} = 1.4 \text{ m}.$$

Although the 40-W bulb has only about half the power output, the decrease in distance is not as great because the intensity depends on the inverse *square* of the distance.

EXERCISE Use the entry in Table 16-1 for sunlight at Earth's orbit, along with Earth's distance from the Sun, to calculate the total power emitted by the Sun.

Answer: 3.9×10^{26} W

Some problems similar to Example 16-4: 39–41, 59

16-6 THE SUPERPOSITION PRINCIPLE AND WAVE INTERFERENCE

What happens if we launch two wave trains from opposite ends of a stretched string? Where they meet, experiment shows that the displacement of the string is just the sum of the displacements of the two wave trains (Fig. 16-19). It's also possible to prove this mathematically, under the small-amplitude approximation that led to Equation 16-7; we'll see this in the next section. The combining of two waves to form a composite wave is called **interference**. The interference is **constructive** if the waves reinforce each other (Fig. 16-19b) and **destructive** if they tend to cancel (Fig. 16-19c).

In most cases the displacement of a composite wave is the algebraic sum of the displacements of two or more interfering waves. This is generally true for waves whose amplitude is not too large, including most sound waves, and it's always true for light waves, at least in vacuum. Waves whose displacements simply add are said to obey the **superposition principle**.

Suppose we have two such waves, each described by Equation 16-5. Each could have a different frequency ω, wave number k, amplitude A, and propagation direction. Their relative phases might be different, so each might need a phase constant in Equation 16-5. If the two waves are given by

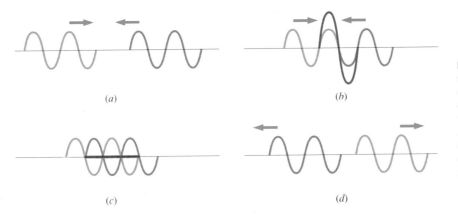

(a)

(b)

(c)

(d)

FIGURE 16-19 (*a*) Sinusoidal wave trains propagating in opposite directions. (*b*) As their crests overlap, they interfere constructively, producing the darker waveform; at this instant the two waves are said to be in phase. (*c*) A quarter cycle later, they are 180° or π radians out of phase and interfere destructively; the result is zero displacement (dark line). (*d*) The wave trains continue on their way, unaffected by their encounter.

$y_1(x, t) = A_1 \cos(k_1 x \pm \omega_1 t + \phi_1)$ and $y_2(x, t) = A_2 \cos(k_2 x \pm \omega_2 t + \phi_2)$, then their superposition is just

$$y(x, t) = A_1 \cos(k_1 x \pm \omega_1 t + \phi_1) + A_2 \cos(k_2 x \pm \omega_2 t + \phi_2). \quad (16\text{-}10)$$

That is, Equation 16-10 gives the displacement y at any position x and time t in the presence of the two waves whose displacements are $y_1(x, t)$ and $y_2(x, t)$.

Waves that do not obey the superposition principle include large-amplitude waves such as the sound waves from a thunderclap or explosion, the tidal bores that race up rivers in regions of high tides, and waves in complicated media. Mathematical analysis of these so-called nonlinear waves is quite difficult.

Wave interference and superposition occur throughout physics, from mechanical waves to light and sound, and even in the quantum-mechanical waves that govern behavior in the atomic and subatomic realms. Here and in the next chapter we present some interference phenomena, and we will consider the interference of light waves in much greater detail in Chapter 37.

Analysis of Complex Waves: Fourier Analysis

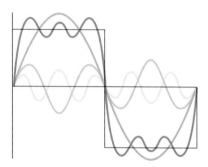

FIGURE 16-20 A square wave built up as a sum of simple harmonic waves, with frequencies in the ratio $1 : 3 : 5 : \ldots$ and amplitudes in the ratio $1 : \frac{1}{3} : \frac{1}{5} : \ldots$ Shown are the square wave (black), its first three harmonic components (green), and their sum (purple).

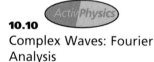

10.10

Complex Waves: Fourier Analysis

The superposition principle allows us to build complex wave shapes by superposing simpler ones—in particular, simple harmonic waves. Analysis of a complex wave in terms of its so-called harmonic components is termed **Fourier analysis**, after the French mathematician Jean Baptiste Joseph Fourier (1768–1830). Fourier showed that *any* periodic wave can be decomposed into a sum of simple harmonic terms. Figure 16-20 shows how a square wave—important, for example, as the waveform of the "clock" signal that determines the speed of your computer—can be represented as a superposition of individual sine waves. For this waveform the component sine waves have frequencies that are odd integer multiples of a fundamental frequency (e.g., the clock rate in your computer, for example: 350 MHz), and the higher frequencies decrease in amplitude as the inverse of the frequency. Mathematically, the time dependence of the square wave (e.g., its displacement at a fixed position, say $x = 0$) is given by

$$y(t) = A \sin(\omega t) + \tfrac{1}{3} A \sin(3\omega t) + \tfrac{1}{5} A \sin(5\omega t) + \ldots.$$

You can explore Fourier analysis for this and other examples with ActivPhysics Activity 10.10. Fourier analysis has many applications, ranging from music to structural engineering and communications because it helps us understand how a complex wave behaves if we know how its simple harmonic components behave. For example, the Fourier components of a complex sound waveform from a musical instrument determine the exact sound we hear (Fig. 16-21). Two different instruments playing the same note produce two different sets of Fourier components, so they sound different.

Dispersion

When wave speed is independent of wavelength, then the simple harmonic components making up a complex waveform travel at the same speed. As a

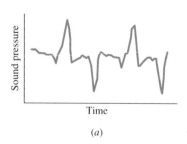

(a)

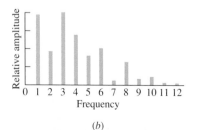

(b)

FIGURE 16-21 An electric guitar plays the note E, producing a complex waveform of which two cycles are shown in (a) as a plot of sound wave pressure variation versus time. (b) Fourier analysis shows the relative strengths of individual sine waves whose sum forms the complex waveform. Numbers on the horizontal axis are multiples of the fundamental frequency, and the height of each bar measures the amplitude of that frequency component. To reproduce the waveform faithfully, an audio system must be capable of reproducing not only the fundamental frequency but also the higher frequencies of the harmonic components.

result, the waveform maintains its shape. But for some media, wave speed depends on wavelength. Then, individual harmonic waves travel at different speeds, and a complex waveform changes shape as it moves. This phenomenon is called **dispersion**, and is illustrated in Fig. 16-22. Waves on the surface of deep water, for example, have speed given by

$$v = \sqrt{\frac{\lambda g}{2\pi}},\qquad(16\text{-}11)$$

where λ is the wavelength and g the acceleration of gravity. Because v depends on λ, the waves are dispersive. Long-wavelength waves from a storm at sea have the highest speeds and therefore reach shore well in advance of both the storm and the shorter wavelength waves. Dispersion is also important in communications systems; for example, dispersion of the square wave pulses carrying digital data sets the maximum lengths for wires and optical fibers used in computer networks.

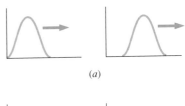

(a)

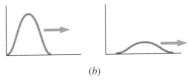

(b)

FIGURE 16-22 (a) A wave pulse in a nondispersive medium holds its shape as it propagates. (b) In a dispersive medium, the pulse changes shape as it propagates.

Beats

In Fig. 16-19 we saw the superposition of two waves of the same frequency and amplitude. When they were in phase, they interfered everywhere constructively; when they were 180° out of phase, the interference was everywhere destructive. But what if two waves with slightly different frequencies interfere? Then their interference is constructive at some points and destructive at others, resulting in a waveform whose amplitude itself varies (Fig. 16-23). We can analyze this phenomenon by writing the composite waveform as the sum of two equal-amplitude waves of slightly different frequencies, according to Equation 16-10. If we consider just the time variation at the fixed position $x = 0$, then this sum is

$$y(t) = A\cos\omega_1 t + A\cos\omega_2 t.$$

We can express this in a more enlightening form using the trigonometric identity $\cos\alpha + \cos\beta = 2\cos\left(\dfrac{\alpha-\beta}{2}\right)\cos\left(\dfrac{\alpha+\beta}{2}\right)$ given in Appendix A. Then we have

$$y(t) = 2A\cos(\tfrac{1}{2}(\omega_1 - \omega_2)t)\cos(\tfrac{1}{2}(\omega_1 + \omega_2)t).$$

The second cosine factor in this equation represents a sinusoidal oscillation at the average of the two individual frequencies. The first term oscillates at a lower frequency—half the difference of the individual frequencies. If we think of the entire term $2A\cos(\tfrac{1}{2}(\omega_1 - \omega_2)t)$ as the "amplitude" of the higher frequency

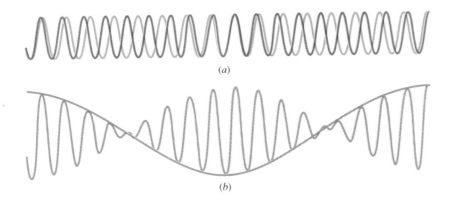

(a)

(b)

FIGURE 16-23 (a) Two waves with slightly different frequencies. Where the two are in phase, they interfere constructively. Where they are out of phase, the interference is destructive. The amplitude of the resulting waveform (b) varies with a frequency equal to the difference of the frequencies of the two interfering waves. The gray curve represents the term $2A\cos[\tfrac{1}{2}(\omega_1 - \omega_2)t]$ that describes this amplitude variation.

oscillation, then this amplitude itself varies with time, as Fig. 16-23 shows. Note that there are *two* amplitude peaks for each cycle of the slow oscillation, so the frequency with which the amplitude varies is simply $\omega_1 - \omega_2$.

For sound waves, interference of two nearly equal frequencies results in variations in sound intensity called **beats**; the closer the two frequencies, the longer the period between beats. In twin-engine aircraft, for example, pilots synchronize engine speeds by reducing the beat frequency toward zero. Beating of electromagnetic waves forms the basis for some very sensitive measurements; modern optical techniques, for example, allow us to detect beat frequencies in the millihertz range arising from the interference of light waves whose frequencies are around 10^{14} Hz.

ActivPhysics Activity 10.7 lets you experiment with beating waves of different frequencies; with ActivPhysics you can also hear actual beats from the interference of sound waves.

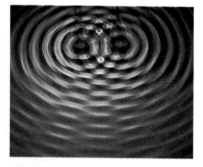

10.7
Beats and Beat Frequency

Interference in Two Dimensions

Waves propagating in two and three dimensions exhibit a rich variety of interference patterns. Figure 16-24 shows one of the simplest and most important examples—the interference of waves from two point sources oscillating at the same frequency. Points on a line passing perpendicular midway between the sources are equidistant from both sources, and therefore waves arrive at this line in phase. Thus, they interfere constructively, producing a high amplitude on this center line. Some distance away, though, is a set of points on which waves arrive exactly half a period out of phase. They therefore interfere destructively, giving rise to a **nodal line** on which the wave amplitude is very small. Since waves travel half a wavelength in half a period, the nodal line occurs where the distances to the two sources differ by half a wavelength. Additional nodal lines occur where those distances differ by $1\frac{1}{2}$ wavelengths, $2\frac{1}{2}$ wavelengths, and so forth.

Two-source interference also arises when plane waves pass through two small apertures which act as sources of circular or spherical wavefronts (Fig. 16-25a). Such two-slit interference experiments are of considerable importance in optics and in modern physics and are of historical interest because they were first used to demonstrate the wave nature of light (Fig. 16-25b). We will explore optical interference further in Chapter 37.

FIGURE 16-24 Interference of circular water waves from two point sources (at rear) shows clearly the pattern of nodal lines, or regions of low wave amplitude resulting from destructive interference.

FIGURE 16-25 (a) Interference pattern produced by passing plane waves through two apertures. Dark curves (purple) are nodal lines, with low wave amplitude; light curves (pink) mark constructive interference giving rise to high amplitude. The situation shown here is just like that of Fig. 16-24 except that now instead of two sources we use a barrier with two slits that turn plane waves into circular waves. (b) Interference pattern produced by shining laser light through two narrow slits. Photographic film was placed at the right end of an optical setup analogous to (a), thus capturing a pattern of alternating light and dark regions.

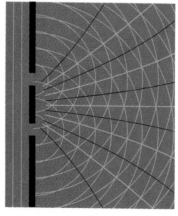

(a)

(b)

| EXAMPLE 16-5 | *Calm Water* |

Ocean waves pass through two small openings in a breakwater. The openings are $d = 20$ m apart, as shown in Fig. 16-26. You're in a small boat on a perpendicular line midway between the two openings, 75 m from the breakwater. You row 33 m parallel to the breakwater and, for the first time, find yourself in relatively calm water. What is the wavelength of the waves?

Solution

Finding calm water means finding a point P where the waves interfere destructively. That means waves from openings A and B arrive at P out of phase by half a cycle—that is, waves from A arrive half a period later than those from B. The first time that happens is when AP is longer than BP by the distance the waves go in half a period—that is, by half a wavelength. Mathematically, $AP - BP = \frac{1}{2}\lambda$. In Fig. 16-26 we've lightly shaded two right triangles whose hypotenuses are the lengths AP and BP. Applying the Pythagorean theorem gives

$$AP = \sqrt{(75 \text{ m})^2 + (43 \text{ m})^2} = 86.5 \text{ m}$$

$$BP = \sqrt{(75 \text{ m})^2 + (23 \text{ m})^2} = 78.4 \text{ m} .$$

Then

$$\lambda = 2(AP - BP) = 2(86.5 \text{ m} - 78.4 \text{ m}) = 16 \text{ m} .$$

EXERCISE On another day waves of a different wavelength impinge on the breakwater in Fig. 16-26. Still 75 m from the breakwater, you now row 38 m from the center line and find yourself in the first region of *maximum* wave amplitude. What is the wavelength on this day?

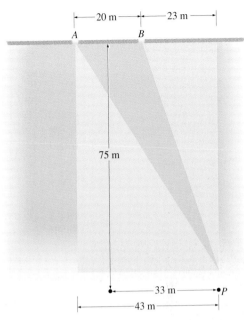

FIGURE 16-26 Calm water at P implies that paths AP and BP differ by half a wavelength.

Answer: 9.0 m

Some problems similar to Example 16-5: 51, 52, 69, 70

16-7 THE WAVE EQUATION

Our only quantitative analysis of wave propagation in this chapter involved waves on a stretched string, and in that analysis we found only the speed of the waves. We did not explicitly show that wave functions of the form $f(x \pm vt)$ are compatible with Newton's law applied to the string. Here we derive the so-called linear **wave equation** that is satisfied not only by waves on a stretched string but by any other waves that satisfy the superposition principle. The wave equation gives a complete description of the wave motion. We will see the wave equation again in Chapter 34 when we consider electromagnetic waves.

Figure 16-27 again shows our stretched string and the forces at opposite ends of a small segment of the string with mass dm and extending from x to $x + dx$. Under the small-angle approximation, the net force is nearly vertical and Fig. 16-27 shows that its magnitude is

$$dF_y \simeq F \sin \theta_2 - F \sin \theta_1 \simeq F(\tan \theta_1 - \tan \theta_2) ,$$

where the last step follows because for small angles $\sin \theta \simeq \theta \simeq \tan \theta$. But the tangents are the slopes dy/dx at opposite ends of the string segment, so

$$dF_y = F(\tan \theta_1 - \tan \theta_2) = F\left(\left.\frac{\partial y}{\partial x}\right|_{x+dx} - \left.\frac{\partial y}{\partial x}\right|_x\right) .$$

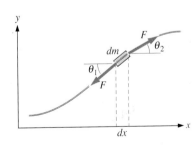

FIGURE 16-27 A portion of the stretched string, showing the forces on a short segment of mass dm. The forces at opposite ends point in slightly different directions, producing a net downward force. The vertical distortion is exaggerated for clarity; actually, the string remains very nearly horizontal.

(See the Math Toolbox on page 400 for the meaning of the symbol ∂.) The term in parentheses is the change in the first derivative over the interval dx; dividing through by dx would give the rate of change of the first derivative—that is, the second derivative $\partial^2 y/\partial x^2$. So we can write

$$dF_y = F\frac{\partial^2 y}{\partial x^2}dx$$

for the net force on the segment. Since the string has mass per unit length μ and is nearly horizontal, the segment's length is essentially dx and therefore its mass is $dm = \mu dx$. Knowing the force, we can then apply Newton's law $F_{net} = ma$ to get

$$F\frac{\partial^2 y}{\partial x^2}dx = \mu\, dx\frac{\partial^2 y}{\partial t^2},$$

where we have written the acceleration as the second time derivative of the displacement. Canceling dx, we can write

$$\frac{\partial^2 y}{\partial x^2} = \frac{\mu}{F}\frac{\partial^2 y}{\partial t^2}.$$

But Equation 16-7 shows that $\mu/F = 1/v^2$, with v the wave speed. So we have

$$\frac{\partial^2 y}{\partial x^2} = \frac{1}{v^2}\frac{\partial^2 y}{\partial t^2}. \tag{16-12}$$

This is the linear **wave equation**. Any time the analysis of a physical system leads to an equation of this form, then that system supports waves propagating with speed v—that is, with speed given by the inverse of the square root of whatever quantity multiplies $\partial^2 y/\partial t^2$. For our string wave that quantity was μ/F, but for another type of wave it would be some other combination of physical quantities (see Problem 53 for one example).

It's a simple matter to show that any harmonic wave of the form $y = A\cos(kx - \omega t)$ satisfies the wave equation. To do so, we twice differentiate this function with respect to x and t:

$$\frac{\partial^2}{\partial x^2}[A\cos(kx - \omega t)] = \frac{\partial}{\partial x}[-kA\sin(kx - \omega t)] = -k^2 A\cos(kx - \omega t)$$

$$\frac{\partial^2}{\partial t^2}[A\cos(kx - \omega t)] = \frac{\partial}{\partial t}[\omega A\sin(kx - \omega t)] = -\omega^2 A\cos(kx - \omega t).$$

Substituting these results in Equation 16-12 gives

$$-k^2 A\cos(kx - \omega t) = \frac{1}{v^2}[-\omega^2 A\cos(kx - \omega t)]$$

or, canceling the cosine term and the minus sign,

$$v^2 = \frac{\omega^2}{k^2}.$$

But we found earlier that $v = \omega/k$ for a harmonic wave, so this equation is an identity. Thus, we've shown by direct substitution that the harmonic wave $A\cos(kx - \omega t)$ satisfies the wave equation 16-12. In Problem 54 you can show that *any* function of the form $f(x \pm vt)$ also satisfies the wave equation. You can also show that the sum of two different solutions to the wave equation is also a solution, thus verifying that waves that satisfy this equation obey the superposition principle.

CHAPTER SYNOPSIS

Summary

1. A **wave** is a propagating disturbance that carries energy but not matter. A wave is **longitudinal** if the disturbance displaces the medium in the direction of propagation, and **transverse** if the displacement is perpendicular to the wave propagation. A wave may have any shape, from a single **pulse** to a **continuous wave**. The peak value of the wave disturbance is the wave **amplitude**.

2. A continuous wave is a periodic disturbance characterized by its **wavelength** λ—the distance between wave crests— and its **period** T—the time between crests measured at a fixed point. A wave travels one wavelength in one period, so its speed is

$$v = \frac{\lambda}{T} = f\lambda,$$

where $f = 1/T$ is the wave **frequency**.

3. A wave propagating in the x direction is described by a function of the quantity $x \pm vt$. In the special case of a **simple harmonic wave**, that function is sinusoidal and may be written

$$y(x, t) = A\cos(kx \pm \omega t),$$

where y is the displacement of the medium, A the amplitude, $k = 2\pi/\lambda$ the **wave number**, and $\omega = 2\pi f = 2\pi/T$ the **angular frequency**. The wave speed v is then $v = \lambda/T = \omega/k$.

4. Applying Newton's law for small-amplitude displacements of a stretched string shows that the waves propagate with speed $v = \sqrt{F/\mu}$, where F is the string tension and μ the mass per unit length.

5. Waves carry energy at a rate proportional to the wave speed and to the square of the wave amplitude. For waves propagating in three dimensions, the rate of energy flow is characterized by the **intensity**, or power per unit area through an area at right angles to the wave propagation. For **plane waves** the intensity remains constant as the wave propagates without spreading, but for the more realistic case of spherical waves from a localized source, the waves spread and their intensity drops as the inverse square of the distance from the source.

6. Many waves obey the **superposition principle**, meaning that their wave displacements simply add when the waves overlap or **interfere**. Wave interference is **constructive** if the overall amplitude is enhanced and **destructive** when it is diminished. In two dimensions, wave interference results in patterns including **nodal lines** where the combined wave amplitude is a minimum.

7. Complex waves may be analyzed as sums of simple harmonic waves of different wavelengths. When wave speed is independent of wavelength, a complex wave retains its shape. But if wave speed varies with wavelength, a complex waveform exhibits **dispersion**, changing shape as it propagates.

8. Many waves of sufficiently small amplitude satisfy the linear **wave equation**,

$$\frac{\partial^2 y}{\partial x^2} = \frac{1}{v^2}\frac{\partial^2 y}{\partial t^2},$$

and those that do then obey the superposition principle.

Terms You Should Understand

(Pairs are closely related terms whose distinction is important; number in parentheses is chapter section where term first appears.)

wave, mechanical wave (16-1)
amplitude (16-2)
longitudinal wave, transverse wave (16-2)
pulse, continuous wave, wave train (16-2)
wavelength, period, frequency (16-2)
simple harmonic wave (16-3)
wave number, angular frequency (16-3)
partial derivative (16-4)
intensity (16-5)
plane wave, spherical wave (16-5)
superposition principle (16-6)
Fourier analysis (16-6)
dispersion (16-6)
interference, constructive and destructive (16-6)
beats (16-6)
nodal line (16-6)
wave equation (16-7)

Symbols You Should Recognize

k, ω (16-3)
$kx \pm \omega t$ (16-3)
μ (16-4)
∂ (16-4)

Problems You Should Be Able to Solve

solving for wavelength, period, or speed from the other two quantities (16-2)

solving for frequency, wavelength, or speed from the other two quantities (16-2)

converting among period, frequency, and angular frequency (16-3)

converting between wavelength and wave number (16-3)

solving for angular frequency, wave number, or speed from the other two quantities (16-3)

writing mathematical expressions for simple harmonic waves (16-3)

solving for speed, tension, or mass per unit length involved with waves on a stretched string, given two of those quantities (16-4)

calculating the wave power propagating on a stretched string (16-5)

calculating the intensity of spherical waves (16-5)

describing quantitatively simple interference situations, including beats and nodal lines in two dimensions (16-6)

Limitations to Keep in Mind

Many of the results developed in this chapter—including the wave speed on stretched strings and the superposition principle—apply only for small-amplitude waves.

QUESTIONS

1. What distinguishes a wave from an oscillation?
2. Red light has a longer wavelength than blue light. Compare their frequencies.
3. Consider a light wave and a sound wave with the same wavelength. Which has the higher frequency?
4. In what sense is "the wave" passing through the crowd at a football game really a wave?
5. A car stops suddenly. The subsequent stopping of cars behind it can be described as a "wave" that propagates back into the traffic. In what sense is this a wave? What are some factors that determine its speed?
6. Must a wave be either transverse or longitudinal? Explain.
7. Does a wave pulse have a period? A frequency? A speed? An amplitude? Explain.
8. Explain in words why the speed of a wave is given by λ/T.
9. As a wave propagates on a stretched string, the string moves back and forth sideways. Is the string speed related to the wave speed? Explain.
10. If you doubled the tension in a string, what would happen to the speed of waves on the string?
11. The wave number k is sometimes called the *spatial frequency*. Why is this name appropriate?
12. A heavy cable is hanging vertically, its bottom end free. How will the speed of transverse waves near the top and bottom of the cable compare? Why?
13. Why won't waves propagate on a string that's not under tension?
14. If you halve the amplitude of your side-to-side shaking of the garden hose in Example 16-3, what would happen to the power you need to supply?
15. As a wave propagates down an ideal, uniform string, does the rate at which it carries energy change?
16. The intensity of waves from a spherical source decreases as the inverse square of the distance from the source. How does the wave amplitude depend on distance?
17. The intensity of light from a localized source decreases as the inverse square of the distance from the source. Does this mean that the light loses energy as it propagates?
18. The speed of small-amplitude waves on a stretched string is independent of wavelength. Do you expect that the speed of large-amplitude waves should increase or decrease with increasing wavelength? Give a physical reason for your answer.
19. An upward and a downward pulse, otherwise identical in shape, are propagating in opposite directions along a stretched string. At the instant they overlap completely, the displacement of the string is exactly zero everywhere. How does this situation differ from true equilibrium? *Hint:* Where is the wave energy?
20. A lightning flash in Earth's southern hemisphere produces radio waves that give a burst of static in nearby radios. But a radio receiver appropriately located in the northern hemisphere detects a long whistle whose pitch decreases with time. What does this say about the speed of these radio waves as a function of frequency? (Electrical properties of the upper atmosphere cause this phenomenon; in vacuum all radio and other electromagnetic waves travel at the same speed.)
21. Do the nodal lines in Fig. 16-24 move as the waves propagate?
22. Is the wave amplitude on a nodal line exactly zero? Why?
23. The maximum frequency the human ear can detect is about 20 kHz. If you walk into a room in which two sources are emitting sound waves at 100 kHz and 102 kHz, will you hear anything? Explain.

PROBLEMS

ActivPhysics can help with these problems:
Activities 10.1, 10.2, 10.7, 10.10.

Section 16-2 Wave Properties

1. Ocean waves with 18-m wavelength travel at 5.3 m/s. What is the time interval between wave crests passing under a boat moored at a fixed location?

2. Ripples in a shallow puddle are propagating at 34 cm/s. If the wave frequency is 5.2 Hz, what are (a) the period and (b) the wavelength?

3. An 88.7-MHz FM radio wave propagates at the speed of light. What is its wavelength?

4. One end of rope is tied to a wall. You shake the other end with a frequency of 2.2 Hz, producing waves whose wavelength is 1.6 m. What is their propagation speed?

5. A 145-MHz radio signal propagates along a cable. Measurement shows that the wave crests are spaced 1.25 m apart. What is the speed of the waves on the cable? Compare with the speed of light in vacuum.

6. Calculate the wavelengths of (a) a 1.0-MHz AM radio wave, (b) a channel 9 TV signal (190 MHz), (c) a police radar (10 GHz), (d) infrared radiation from a hot stove (4.0×10^{13} Hz), (e) green light (6.0×10^{14} Hz), and (f) 1.0×10^{18} Hz X rays. All are electromagnetic waves that propagate at 3.0×10^8 m/s.

7. Detecting objects by reflecting waves off them is effective only for objects larger than about one wavelength. (a) What is the smallest object that can be seen with visible light (maximum frequency 7.5×10^{14} Hz)? (b) What is the smallest object that can be detected with a medical ultrasound unit operating at 5 MHz? The speed of ultrasound waves in body tissue is about 1500 m/s.

8. A seismograph located 1200 km from an earthquake detects waves from the quake 5.0 min after the quake occurs. The seismograph oscillates in step with the waves, at a frequency of 3.1 Hz. Find the wavelength of the waves.

9. In Fig. 16-28 two boats are anchored offshore and are bobbing up and down on the waves at the rate of six complete cycles each minute. When one boat is up the other is down. If the waves propagate at 2.2 m/s, what is the minimum distance between the boats?

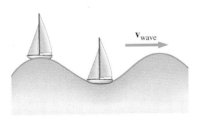

FIGURE 16-28 Problem 9.

Section 16-3 Mathematical Description of Wave Motion

10. Ultrasound used in a particular medical imager has frequency 4.8 MHz and wavelength 0.31 mm. Find (a) the angular frequency, (b) the wave number, and (c) the wave speed.

11. An ocean wave has period 4.1 s and wavelength 10.8 m. Find (a) its wave number and (b) its angular frequency.

12. Find (a) the amplitude, (b) the wavelength, (c) the period, and (d) the speed of a wave whose displacement is given by $y = 1.3 \cos(0.69x + 31t)$, where x and y are in cm and t is in seconds. (e) In which direction is the wave propagating?

13. A simple harmonic wave of wavelength 16 cm and amplitude 2.5 cm is propagating along a string in the negative x direction at 35 cm/s. Find (a) the angular frequency and (b) the wave number. (c) Write a mathematical expression describing the displacement y of this wave (in centimeters) as a function of position and time. Assume the displacement at $x = 0$ is a maximum when $t = 0$.

14. Figure 16-29 shows a simple harmonic wave at time $t = 0$ and later at $t = 2.6$ s. Write a mathematical description of this wave.

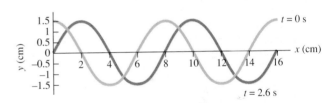

FIGURE 16-29 Problem 14.

15. What are (a) the amplitude, (b) the frequency in hertz, (c) the wavelength, and (d) the speed of a water wave whose displacement is $y = 0.25 \sin(0.52x - 2.3t)$, where x and y are in meters and t in seconds?

16. A sound wave with frequency 256 Hz (the musical note middle C) is propagating in air at 343 m/s. How far apart are two points on the wave that differ in phase by $\frac{\pi}{2}$ or $90°$?

17. At time $t = 0$, the displacement in a transverse wave pulse is described by $y = \dfrac{2}{x^4 + 1}$, with both x and y in cm. Write an expression for the pulse as a function of position x and time t if it is propagating in the positive x direction at 3 cm/s.

18. Plot the answer to the previous problem as a function of position x for the two cases $t = 0$ and $t = 4$ s, and verify that your plots are consistent with the pulse speed of 3 cm/s.

19. Figure 16-30*a* shows a wave plotted as a function of position at time $t = 0$, while Fig. 16-30*b* shows the same wave plotted as a function of time at position $x = 0$. Find (a) the wavelength, (b) the period, (c) the wave speed, and (d) the direction of propagation.

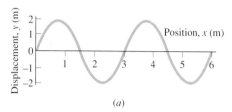

(a)

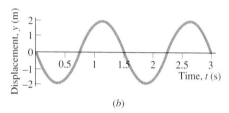

(b)

FIGURE 16-30 Problems 19, 20.

20. Write a mathematical description of the wave in the preceding problem.

Section 16-4 Waves on a String

21. The main cables supporting New York's George Washington Bridge have a mass per unit length of 4100 kg/m and are under tension of 250 MN. At what speed would a transverse wave propagate on these cables?

22. A transverse wave 1.2 cm in amplitude is propagating on a string; the wave frequency is 44 Hz. The string is under 21 N tension and has mass per unit length of 15 g/m. Determine (a) the wave speed and (b) the maximum speed of a point on the string.

23. A transverse wave with 3.0-cm amplitude and 75-cm wavelength is propagating on a stretched spring whose mass per unit length is 170 g/m. If the wave speed is 6.7 m/s, find (a) the spring tension and (b) the maximum speed of any point on the spring.

24. A rope is stretched between supports 12 m apart; its tension is 35 N. If one end of the rope is tweaked, the resulting disturbance reaches the other end 0.45 s later. What is the total mass of the rope?

25. A 3.1-kg mass hangs from a 2.7-m-long string whose total mass is 0.62 g. What is the speed of transverse waves on the string? *Hint:* You can ignore the string mass in calculating the tension but not in calculating the wave speed. Why?

26. Transverse waves propagate at 18 m/s on a string whose tension is 14 N. What will be the wave speed if the tension is increased to 40 N?

27. The density of copper is 8.29 g/cm³. What is the tension in a 1.0-mm-diameter copper wire that propagates transverse waves at 120 m/s?

28. A 100-m-long wire has a mass of 130 g. A sample of the wire is tested and found to break at a tension of 150 N. What is the maximum propagation speed for transverse waves on this wire?

29. A 25-m-long piece of 1.0-mm-diameter wire is put under 85 N tension. If a transverse wave takes 0.21 s to travel the length of the wire, what is the density of the material comprising the wire?

30. A mass m_1 is attached to a wire of linear density 5.6 g/m, and the other end of the wire run over a pulley and tied to a wall as shown in Fig. 16-31. The speed of transverse waves on the horizontal section of wire is observed to be 20 m/s. If a second mass m_2 is added to the first, the wave speed increases to 45 m/s. Find the second mass. Assume the string does not stretch appreciably.

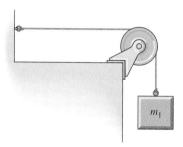

FIGURE 16-31 Problem 30.

31. A steel wire can tolerate a maximum tension per unit cross-sectional area of 2.7 GN/m² before it undergoes permanent distortion. What is the maximum possible speed for transverse waves in a steel wire if it is to remain undistorted? Steel has a density of 7.9 g/cm³.

32. A uniform cable hangs vertically under its own weight. Show that the speed of waves on the cable is given by $v = \sqrt{yg}$, where y is the distance from the bottom of the cable.

Section 16-5 Wave Power and Intensity

33. A rope with 280 g of mass per meter is under 550 N tension. A wave with frequency 3.3 Hz and amplitude 6.1 cm is propagating on the rope. What is the average power carried by the wave?

34. A motor drives a mechanism that produces simple harmonic motion at one end of a stretched cable. The frequency of the motion is 30 Hz, and the motor can supply energy at an average rate of 350 W. If the cable has linear density 450 g/m and is under 1.7 kN tension, (a) what is the maximum wave amplitude that can be driven down the cable? (b) If the motor were replaced by a larger one capable of supplying 700 W, how would the maximum amplitude change?

35. A 600-g Slinky is stretched to a length of 10 m. You shake one end at the frequency of 1.8 Hz, applying a time-average power of 1.1 W. The resulting waves propagate along the Slinky at 2.3 m/s. What is the wave amplitude?

36. A simple harmonic wave of amplitude 5.0 cm, wavelength 70 cm, and frequency 14 Hz is propagating on a wire with linear density 40 g/m. Find the wave energy per unit length of the wire.

37. Figure 16-32 shows a wave train consisting of two cycles of a sine wave propagating along a string. Obtain an expression for the total energy in this wave train, in terms of the string tension F, the wave amplitude A, and the wavelength λ.

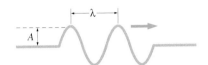

FIGURE 16-32 Problem 37.

38. A steel wire with linear density 5.0 g/m is under 450 N tension. What is the maximum power that can be carried by transverse waves on this wire if the wave amplitude is not to exceed 10% of the wavelength?

39. A loudspeaker emits energy at the rate of 50 W, spread in all directions. What is the intensity of sound 18 m from the speaker?

40. The light intensity 3.3 m from a light bulb is 0.73 W/m². What is the power output of the bulb, assuming it radiates equally in all directions?

41. Use data from Appendix E to determine the intensity of sunlight at (a) Mercury and (b) Pluto.

42. A 9-W laser produces a beam 2 mm in diameter. Compare its light intensity with that of sunlight at noon, about 1 kW/m².

43. Light emerges from a 5.0-mW laser in a beam 1.0 mm in diameter. The beam shines on a wall, producing a spot 3.6 cm in diameter. What are the beam intensities (a) at the laser and (b) at the wall?

44. A large boulder drops from a cliff into the ocean, producing circular waves. A small boat 18 m from the impact point measures the wave amplitude at 130 cm. At what distance will the amplitude be 50 cm?

45. Use Table 16-1 to determine how close to a rock band you should stand for it to sound as loud as a jet plane at 200 m. Treat the band and the plane as point sources. Is this assumption reasonable?

Section 16-6 The Superposition Principle and Wave Interference

46. Consider two functions $f(x \pm vt)$ and $g(x \pm vt)$ that both satisfy the wave equation (Equation 16-12). Show that their sum also satisfies the wave equation.

47. Two wave pulses are described by $y_1(x, t) = \dfrac{2}{(x - t)^2 + 1}$,

$y_2(x, t) = \dfrac{-2}{(x - 5 + t)^2 + 1}$, where x and y are in cm

and t in seconds. (a) What is the amplitude of each pulse? (b) At $t = 0$, where is the peak of each pulse, and in what direction is it moving? (c) At what time will the two pulses exactly cancel?

48. The triangular wave of Fig. 16-33 can be described by the following sum of simple harmonic terms:

$$y(x) = \frac{8}{\pi^2}\left(\frac{\sin x}{1^2} - \frac{\sin 3x}{3^2} + \frac{\sin 5x}{5^2} - \cdots\right).$$

Plot the sum of the first three terms in this series for x ranging from 0 to 2π, and compare with the first cycle shown in Fig. 16-33. (See also ActivPhysics Activity 10.7.)

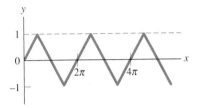

FIGURE 16-33 A triangular wave (Problem 48).

49. You're in an airplane whose two engines are running at 560 rpm and 570 rpm. How often do you hear the sound intensity increase as a result of wave interference?

50. Two waves have the same angular frequency ω, wave number k, and amplitude A, but they differ in phase: $y_1 = A\cos(kx - \omega t)$ and $y_2 = A\cos(kx - \omega t + \phi)$. Show that their superposition is also a simple harmonic wave, and determine its amplitude A_s as a function of the phase difference ϕ.

51. What is the wavelength of the ocean waves in Example 16-5 if the calm water you encounter at 33 m is the *second* calm region on your voyage from the center line?

52. The two loudspeakers shown in Fig. 16-34 emit identical 500-Hz sound waves. Point P is on the first nodal line of the interference pattern. Use the numbers shown to calculate the speed of the sound waves.

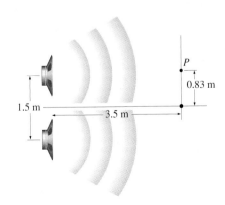

FIGURE 16-34 Problem 52.

Section 16-7 The Wave Equation

53. The following equation arises in analyzing the behavior of shallow water:

$$\frac{\partial^2 y}{\partial x^2} - \frac{1}{gh}\frac{\partial^2 y}{\partial t^2} = 0,$$

where h is the equilibrium depth and y the displacement from equilibrium. Give an expression for the speed of waves in shallow water. (Here *shallow* means the water depth is much less than the wavelength.)

54. Use the chain rule for differentiation to show explicitly that any function of the form $f(x \pm vt)$ satisfies the wave equation (Equation 16-12).

Paired Problems

(Both problems in a pair involve the same principles and techniques. If you can get the first problem, you should be able to solve the second one.)

55. A wave on a taut wire is described by the equation $y = 1.5\sin(0.10x - 560t)$, where x and y are in cm and t is in seconds. If the wire tension is 28 N, what are (a) the amplitude, (b) the wavelength, (c) the period, (d) the wave speed, and (e) the power carried by the wave?

56. A wave given by $y = 23\cos(0.025x - 350t)$, with x and y in mm and t in seconds, is propagating on a cable with mass per unit length 410 g/m. Find (a) the amplitude, (b) the wavelength, (c) the frequency in Hz, (d) the wave speed, and (e) the power carried by the wave.

57. A spring of mass m and spring constant k has an unstretched length ℓ_0. Find an expression for the speed of transverse waves on this spring when it has been stretched to a length ℓ.

58. When a 340-g spring is stretched to a total length of 40 cm, it supports transverse waves propagating at 4.5 m/s. When it's stretched to 60 cm, the waves propagate at 12 m/s. Find (a) the unstretched length of the spring and (b) its spring constant.

59. At a point 15 m from a source of spherical sound waves, you measure a sound intensity of 750 mW/m². How far do you need to walk, directly away from the source, until the intensity is 270 mW/m²?

60. Figure 16-35 shows two observers 20 m apart, on a line that connects them and a spherical light source. If the observer nearest the source measures a light intensity 50%

greater than the other observer, how far is the nearest observer from the source?

61. Two motors in a factory produce sound waves with the same frequency as their rotation rates. If one motor is running at 3600 rpm and the other at 3602 rpm, how often will workers hear a peak in the sound intensity?

62. Two radio waves with frequencies of approximately 50 MHz interfere. The composite wave is detected and fed to a loudspeaker, which emits audible sound at 500 Hz. What is the percentage difference between the frequencies of the two radio waves?

Supplementary Problems

63. For a transverse wave on a stretched string, the requirement that the string be nearly horizontal is met if the amplitude is much less than the wavelength. (a) Show this by drawing an appropriate sketch. (b) Show that, under this approximation that $A \ll \lambda$, the maximum speed u of the string must be considerably less than the wave speed v. (c) If the amplitude is not to exceed 1% of the wavelength, how large can the string speed u be in relation to the wave speed v?

64. A 64-g spring has unstretched length 25 cm. With a 940-g mass attached, the spring undergoes simple harmonic motion with angular frequency 6.1 s⁻¹. What will be the speed of transverse waves on this spring when it's stretched to a total length of 40 cm?

65. An ideal spring is compressed until its total length is ℓ_1, and the speed of transverse waves on the spring is measured. When it's compressed further to a total length ℓ_2, waves propagate at the *same* speed. Show that the uncompressed spring length is just $\ell_1 + \ell_2$.

66. An ideal spring is stretched to a total length ℓ_1. When that length is doubled, the speed of transverse waves on the spring triples. Find an expression for the unstretched length of the spring.

67. A 1-megaton nuclear explosion produces a shock wave whose amplitude, measured as excess air pressure above normal atmospheric pressure, is 1.4×10^5 Pa (1 Pa = 1 N/m²) at a distance of 1.3 km from the explosion. An excess pressure of 3.5×10^4 Pa will destroy a typical wood-frame house. At what distance from the explosion will such houses be destroyed? Assume the wavefront is spherical.

68. Show that the time it takes a wave to propagate up the cable in Problem 32 is $t = 2\sqrt{\ell/g}$, where ℓ is the cable length.

69. In Example 16-5, how much farther would you have to row to reach a region of maximum wave amplitude?

70. Suppose the wavelength of the ocean waves in Example 16-5 were 8.4 m. How far would you have to row from the center line, staying 75 m from the breakwater, in order to find (a) the first and (b) the second region of relative calm?

|←——— 20 m ———→|←——— $x = ?$ ———→|

FIGURE 16-35 Problem 60.

Sound and Other Wave Phenomena

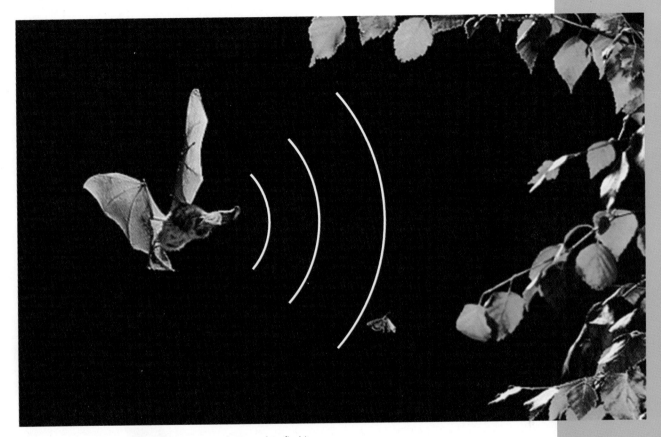

A bat uses high-frequency sound waves to navigate and to find its prey.

Sound waves are longitudinal mechanical waves that propagate through gases, liquids, and solids. We think of sound waves primarily in connection with the sounds we hear, but **audible** sound comprises only a small part of the range of sound waves important both in the natural world and in technology. The human ear is sensitive to sounds in the range from approximately 20 Hz to 20 kHz; below this range is **infrasound** arising, for example, from the vibration of massive structures like buildings. Above the audible range lies **ultrasound**, used in medical diagnostics and treatment, location of underwater objects, analysis of materials, and even microscopy. Many animals can detect sounds above the range audible to humans; bats, in particular, use ultrasound for navigation.

The generation and propagation of sound waves involves a number of wave phenomena beyond those introduced in Chapter 16. Here we describe the properties of sound waves, then explore these additional wave phenomena.

17-1 SOUND WAVES IN GASES

All materials are, to some degree, compressible. That means a force applied to the material results in a change in volume. According to Newton's third law, the material in turn exerts a force. In gases it's simplest to characterize that force in terms of **pressure**, or force per unit area.

Applying a force to one part of a gas immediately compresses only that part. But the increased pressure is communicated to adjacent regions, and the result is a propagating longitudinal wave—a sound wave. Figure 17-1 shows a hollow

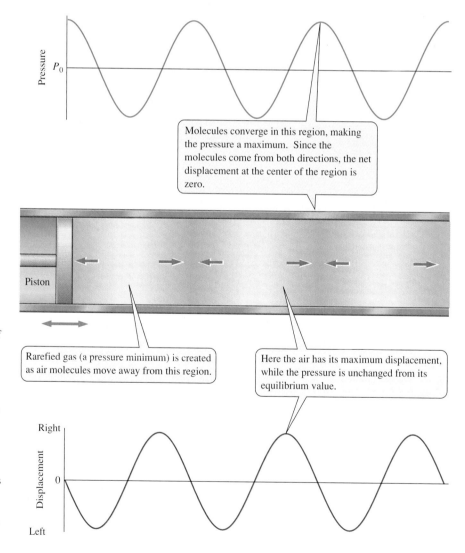

Molecules converge in this region, making the pressure a maximum. Since the molecules come from both directions, the net displacement at the center of the region is zero.

Rarefied gas (a pressure minimum) is created as air molecules move away from this region.

Here the air has its maximum displacement, while the pressure is unchanged from its equilibrium value.

FIGURE 17-1 A sound wave in a hollow pipe consists of alternating regions of compression and rarefaction propagating through the air. Arrows show the instantaneous displacements of the air from equilibrium as it undergoes oscillatory motion. Note that regions where the pressure is a maximum or minimum correspond to zero displacement. The displacement is highly exaggerated; normally, displacements of air in a sound wave are less than 1% of the wavelength. The pressure and displacement are $\pi/2$ or 90° out of phase. We assume that the pipe continues forever to the right; otherwise, the waves would spread out at the open end to make audible sound. However, they might also reflect back into the pipe and complicate the picture.

pipe closed at one end by a movable piston. Moving this piston back and forth alternately rarefies and compresses the air, with the pressure varying slightly about its equilibrium value. That equilibrium pressure itself arises from random motion of the air molecules, which we'll examine in detail in Chapter 20. Collisions among the rapidly moving molecules communicate changes in pressure to adjacent volumes of air, with the result that the compression and rarefaction induced by the piston propagate down the pipe as a sound wave.

The piston's movement communicates not only pressure changes but also motion to the air. As Fig. 17-1 shows, adjacent volumes of air have displacements in opposite directions; the region where those air volumes meet is either a pressure maximum or minimum, depending on whether air has moved into or out of the region. Since the displacement must be zero where oppositely displaced air masses meet, the displacement and pressure variation are therefore out of phase. So the sound wave consists of alternating regions of compression and rarefaction, and correspondingly of back-and-forth air motion, propagating down the pipe.

You might wonder whether you could hear the sound depicted in Fig. 17-1. We've assumed the pipe continues indefinitely, but if instead it's open at the right end, then the waves will spread through the surrounding air. If the piston is moving at a frequency in the audible range, then you'll hear the sound as a pure tone. An organ pipe is an obvious example of a system similar to our pipe; so are instruments such as trumpets and clarinets, with their flaring open ends designed to transfer the most sound energy to the surrounding air.

Tip

The Air Motion Is Not the Wave Motion Is Not the Molecular Motion As always, a wave transports energy but not matter. The back-and-forth motion of the air is a manifestation of the wave's passage, just as is the sideways motion of a string as a transverse wave passes. Although the air moves back and forth, it undergoes no overall change in position. And its speed is *not* the wave speed.

There's another important distinction to be made. The back-and-forth air motion refers to the *average* motion of a group of air molecules. Individually, those molecules are whizzing around with random motion at much higher speeds. In fact, for reasons we'll see in Chapter 20, the typical speed of that random motion is roughly the same as the wave speed. The back-and-forth motion of the air as the wave passes is just a small effect superposed on the individual random molecular motions.

The variations suggested in Fig. 17-1 are highly exaggerated. The pressure changes even in the loudest audible sound are about one ten-thousandth of the equilibrium air pressure, and the maximum displacement is a tiny fraction of a wavelength.

17-2 THE SPEED OF SOUND IN GASES

In the preceding chapter we found the speed of transverse waves on a stretched string to be given by $v = \sqrt{F/\mu}$. Here the string tension F is the force that tends to restore the string to equilibrium, while μ—the mass per unit length—measures the inertia associated with the string's mass. We might expect the speed of sound to depend on analogous factors—a restoring force and inertia. In a gas that restoring force is provided by the gas pressure P, while the density ρ—mass per unit volume—measures the inertia. So is the sound speed given by $v = \sqrt{P/\rho}$? Almost: dimensional analysis (see Problem 1) shows that this quantity does indeed have the units of velocity, but dimensional analysis cannot tell whether we have exactly the right constant factors. In fact, for reasons we'll see in Chapter 21, the exact expression is

$$v = \sqrt{\frac{\gamma P}{\rho}} \quad \text{(sound speed in a gas)}, \qquad (17\text{-}1)$$

where γ is a constant that depends on the nature of the gas. For a gas consisting of simple particles—helium atoms, for example, or the electron-proton mixtures that characterize matter at very high temperatures—γ has the value $\frac{5}{3}$. For diatomic molecules like N_2 and O_2 that comprise air, γ takes the lower value $\frac{7}{5}$. And for more complicated molecules γ is lower still; in triatomic CO_2, for example, γ is close to $\frac{4}{3}$.

EXAMPLE 17-1	*"Donald Duck" Talk*

Under normal atmospheric conditions, air pressure is 1.01×10^5 N/m^2, and there are 2.51×10^{25} air molecules per cubic meter. Air is essentially 21% oxygen (O_2) and 79% nitrogen (N_2). (a) Find the speed of sound in air and in helium (He) with the same pressure and number of molecules per unit volume. (b) For each gas, find the frequency of a sound wave whose wavelength is 64 cm.

Solution

The masses of oxygen and nitrogen molecules are 32 u and 28 u respectively, so the density of air is

$$\rho = [(0.21)(32 \text{ u}) + (0.79)(28 \text{ u})]$$
$$\times (1.66 \times 10^{-27} \text{ kg/u})(2.51 \times 10^{25} \text{ m}^{-3}) = 1.20 \text{ kg/m}^3,$$

where we've weighted the masses of the individual molecules according to their abundances. Then we have

$$v = \sqrt{\frac{\gamma P}{\rho}} = \sqrt{\frac{(7/5)(1.01 \times 10^5 \text{ N/m}^2)}{1.20 \text{ kg/m}^3}} = 343 \text{ m/s}.$$

The atomic weight of helium is 4 u, giving $\rho = (4 \text{ u})(1.66 \times 10^{-27} \text{ kg/u})(2.51 \times 10^{25} \text{ m}^{-3}) = 0.167$ kg/m^3. Then, using $\gamma = \frac{5}{3}$ for a monatomic gas, we have

$$v = \sqrt{\frac{\gamma P}{\rho}} = \sqrt{\frac{(5/3)(1.01 \times 10^5 \text{ N/m}^2)}{0.167 \text{ kg/m}^3}} = 1000 \text{ m/s}.$$

Both these speeds are, incidentally, close to the mean speeds of the random molecular motion in the two gases—not surprising, since it's ultimately collisions between gas molecules that transmit the wave energy.

Writing Equation 16-1 in terms of the frequency $f = 1/T$ then gives

$$f_{\text{air}} = \frac{v}{\lambda} = \frac{343 \text{ m/s}}{0.64 \text{ m}} = 536 \text{ Hz}$$

$$f_{\text{He}} = \frac{v}{\lambda} = \frac{1000 \text{ m/s}}{0.64 \text{ m}} = 1560 \text{ Hz}.$$

If you've ever heard someone speak after inhaling helium, you've experienced directly the effect of the different sound speeds calculated in this example. Wavelengths in human speech are set by the geometry of the vocal cords and throat, so a rise in sound speed increases the frequency—resulting in the high-pitched, "Donald Duck" speech of the helium inhaler.

EXERCISE Find the sound speed in hydrogen (H_2) under standard conditions. The number of particles per cubic meter in this case is the same as for air. Take $\gamma = \frac{7}{5}$ since hydrogen is diatomic.

Answer: 1.3 km/s

Some problems similar to Example 17-1: 6–8, 12, 14

17-3 SOUND INTENSITY

In Section 16-5 we calculated the power carried in a wave on a stretched string by finding the rate at which one section of string did work on the next section. That rate was $F_y u$, with F_y the y component of the string tension and u the speed *of the string*. Here we do the analogous calculation for sound waves.

Let s be the air's displacement from equilibrium, so $u = \partial s / \partial t$ is its speed. The air motion in a sound wave is driven by the force associated with the pressure *change* ΔP from the equilibrium value. Since pressure is force per unit area, the force exerted *by* one region of the air *on* an adjacent region of area A is ΔPA, and the power is therefore $\Delta PAu = \Delta PA(\partial s / \partial t)$. Dividing by A gives the power per unit area, or intensity:

$$I = \Delta P \frac{\partial s}{\partial t}.$$

In a simple harmonic wave both pressure and displacement vary sinusoidally in space and time with amplitudes ΔP_0 and s_0:

$$\Delta P = \Delta P_0 \cos(kx - \omega t) \qquad (17\text{-}2a)$$

$$s = -s_0 \sin(kx - \omega t), \qquad (17\text{-}2b)$$

where we've chosen cosine and sine, and the minus sign on s, for consistency with Fig. 17-1. Using these expressions in our equation for intensity gives

$$I = \Delta P \frac{\partial s}{\partial t} = \Delta P_0 \cos(kx - \omega t) \frac{\partial}{\partial t} [-s_0 \sin(kx - \omega t)]$$

$$= s_0 \omega \Delta P_0 \cos^2(kx - \omega t).$$

As in Chapter 16, we're more interested in the intensity averaged over one cycle; since the average of $\cos^2$ is $\frac{1}{2}$, we have

$$\bar{I} = \tfrac{1}{2} s_0 \omega \Delta P_0. \qquad (17\text{-}3a)$$

Finally, we can relate the pressure amplitude ΔP_0 and displacement amplitude s_0. Figure 17-2 shows a thin slab of air in a sound wave. On one side of the slab, whose thickness is dx, the pressure is P; on the other side, it is $P + dP$. The slab has area A, so the net force on it is $dF = [P - (P + dP)]A = -A\,dP$, where the minus sign indicates a leftward force in Fig. 17-2 when dP is positive. The volume of the slab is $A\,dx$, so its mass is $dm = A\rho\,dx$, with ρ the density. Solving Newton's law for acceleration gives $a = F/m$; here the force is dF and the mass is dm, so

$$a = \frac{dF}{dm} = \frac{-A\,dP}{A\rho\,dx} = -\frac{1}{\rho} \frac{\partial P}{\partial x}$$

is the acceleration of the slab. We've used the partial derivative because the pressure is a function of both position and time, and here we want its

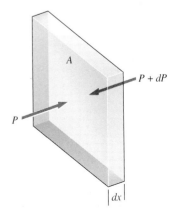

FIGURE 17-2 A thin slab of air in a sound wave has area A and thickness dx. The pressure on one side is P and on the other side $P + dP$, giving a net force of magnitude $A\,dP$ on the slab.

TABLE 17-1 *Sound Intensity*

SOURCE	INTENSITY, W/m²	INTENSITY LEVEL, dB	
Space shuttle, at 50 m	10^5	170	
Eardrum ruptures	10^4	160	
Jet aircraft, at 50 m	10	130	
Rock band, at 4 m	1	120	← Threshold of pain
Subway	10^{-2}	100	
City traffic	10^{-4}	80	
Normal conversation, at 1 m	10^{-6}	60	
Mosquito	10^{-8}	40	
Whisper, at 1 m	10^{-10}	20	
Normal breathing	10^{-11}	10	
Threshold of hearing	10^{-12}	0	

variation with position only. Using Equations 17-2, we can write $a = \dfrac{\partial^2 s}{\partial t^2} = -s_0 \omega^2 \cos(kx - \omega t)$ and $\dfrac{\partial P}{\partial x} = -k\Delta P_0 \sin(kx - \omega t)$. So the acceleration amplitude is $s_0\omega^2$ and the amplitude of $\partial P/\partial x$ is $k\Delta P_0$. Using our Newton's law equation to relate these amplitudes gives

$$s_0\omega^2 = \frac{k\Delta P_0}{\rho}.$$

Solving this equation first for s_0 and then for ΔP_0 and using the results in Equation (17-3a) gives two alternative forms for the sound wave intensity:

$$\bar{I} = \tfrac{1}{2}s_0\omega\Delta P_0 = \frac{\Delta P_0^2}{2\rho v} \qquad (17\text{-}3b)$$

$$\bar{I} = \tfrac{1}{2}s_0\omega\Delta P_0 = \tfrac{1}{2}\rho\omega^2 s_0^2 v, \qquad (17\text{-}3c)$$

where we've used Equation 16-6 to write the wave speed $v = \omega/k$. Note that both these expressions depend on the *square* of the disturbed quantity, as advertised in Section 16-5. Table 17-1 lists intensities for some common sounds.

You might wonder whether "intensity" when applied to sound waves means the same thing as "loudness." Intensity does ultimately determine loudness, but the physiology of hearing is such that your perception of loudness is nowhere near directly proportional to sound intensity. In the next section we look specifically at the human ear and quantify the relation between intensity and loudness.

Sound and the Human Ear

The intensity of normal sound waves ranges widely from small to truly minuscule values, and the ear is a remarkable instrument both in its ability to respond to these weak waves and in the wide range of amplitudes it can handle. Figure 17-3 shows the minimum intensity and the threshold of pain for the human ear, as functions of frequency.

| APPLICATION | *Stereo Controls* |

Your stereo system probably has a "loudness" switch that you're supposed to turn on at low volumes. The shape of the curves in Fig. 17-3 is the reason for this switch. At high volumes (i.e., high intensities), the curves are not far from being flat, meaning that sounds of the same power but different frequencies are perceived at essentially the same volume. But at low volumes the curves turn upward at both ends of the frequency scale, showing that it takes greater intensity at high and low frequencies to give the same perceived volume. The "loudness" control switches in a circuit that boosts the high and low frequencies to compensate for this effect.

FIGURE 17-3 Minimum and maximum sound intensities for a typical human ear, as functions of frequency. The ear responds to sounds in the entire shaded region. Note the logarithmic scales. Intensities are shown in both watts per square meter and in decibels. Sounds above the threshold of pain are also heard, but prolonged exposure can damage the ears. Ranges for three common sounds are marked on the diagram.

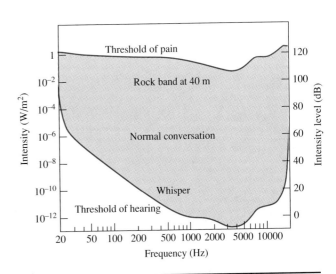

| EXAMPLE 17-2 | *Response of the Human Ear* |

(a) Find the displacement and pressure amplitudes of the weakest sound to which the typical human ear can respond. (b) Over a wide frequency range, the threshold of pain is about 1 W/m². Find the displacement and pressure amplitudes for this sound.

Solution

(a) Figure 17-3 shows that the weakest sound for human perception is in the frequency range from 3 kHz to 4 kHz, where the minimum intensity is about 10^{-13} W/m². Equation 17-3b shows that the pressure amplitude is independent of frequency; solving for ΔP_0 then gives

$$\Delta P_0 = \sqrt{2\rho v \bar{I}} = \sqrt{(2)(1.2 \text{ kg/m}^3)(343 \text{ m/s})(10^{-13} \text{ W/m}^2)}$$

$$= 10^{-5} \text{ N/m}^2,$$

where we used the density and sound speed from Example 17-1. Since normal air pressure is 10^5 N/m², this amplitude represents a variation of only one part in ten billion! The corresponding displacement is also impressively small. Taking $f = 3.5$ kHz as typical of the frequency range for minimum intensity and solving Equation 17-3c for s_0 gives

$$s_0 = \sqrt{\frac{2\bar{I}}{\rho\omega^2 v}} = \sqrt{\frac{(2)(10^{-13} \text{ W/m}^2)}{(1.2 \text{ kg/m}^3)[2\pi(3500 \text{ Hz})]^2(343 \text{ m/s})}}$$

$$= 10^{-12} \text{ m},$$

where we used $\omega = 2\pi f$. This number is one hundredth of an atomic diameter! That your eardrum can detect and transmit to your brain information about such small amplitude motions is truly astounding. (b) With 1-kHz waves at the 1 W/m² threshold of pain, similar calculations give $\Delta P_0 = 29$ N/m² and $s_0 = 1 \times 10^{-5}$ m, or one hundredth of a millimeter.

EXERCISE In a whispered conversation, the sound intensity 1 m from the source is about 100 pW/m². Under these conditions, what are (a) the total power falling on a typical adult eardrum of area 60 mm² and (b) the displacement amplitude, assuming a frequency of 850 Hz?

Answers: (a) 6×10^{-15} W; (b) 0.13 nm

Some problems similar to Example 17-2: 15, 16, 18, 20

Decibels

The human ear responds to sound intensities and frequencies covering many orders of magnitude; that's why Fig. 17-3 is plotted with logarithmic scales. Because of this wide range, it makes sense to quantify sound levels with a unit proportional to the logarithm of the actual intensity. Such a unit is the **decibel** (dB), defined by

$$\beta = 10 \log\left(\frac{I}{I_0}\right), \tag{17-4}$$

where β is the sound **intensity level** in decibels and where $I_0 = 10^{-12}$ W/m^2 is a reference level chosen as the threshold of hearing at 1 kHz. The decibel is one-tenth of a bel, a less frequently used unit named for telephone inventor Alexander Graham Bell. Since the logarithm of 10 is 1, each factor-of-10 increase in sound intensity over the reference level of 10^{-12} W/m^2 represents an increase of 10 dB. Your actual perception of loudness is somewhat subjective, depending not only on the intensity level but also on frequency and duration; in general, for intensity levels above about 40 dB, the perceived loudness approximately doubles for every 10 dB increase in intensity level. One consequence of this relation is the enormous power increase needed to produce really loud sounds.

Sound levels over 120 dB are generally painful, while continuous exposure to levels in excess of 90 dB can lead to hearing loss. Table 17-1 includes common sound intensity levels in dB; we've also included a decibel scale on Fig. 17-3.

Got It!

Remember that the intensity of waves from a pointlike source falls off in proportion to the inverse square of the distance (see Equation 16-9). So a 10-fold increase in distance corresponds to a 100-fold drop in intensity. Does that mean the decibel level also drops by a factor of 100? If not, by how much does it drop?

EXAMPLE 17-3	*Turn Down the TV!*

Your little sister is watching TV, and the sound is blasting your ears at 75 dB. You yell to her to turn it down, and she drops the intensity level to 60 dB. By what factor has the power dropped?

Solution

The intensity level has dropped by 15 dB, corresponding to 1.5 orders of magnitude in actual intensity. So the intensity—and therefore the power emitted by the speakers—drops by a factor $10^{-1.5}$, or to about one thirtieth of its original value. We can get this result more formally by writing Equation 17-4 for each value and subtracting. Designating the initial and final values by the subscripts 1 and 2, we have:

$$\beta_2 - \beta_1 = 10 \log\left(\frac{I_2}{I_0}\right) - 10 \log\left(\frac{I_1}{I_0}\right) = 10 \log\left(\frac{I_2}{I_1}\right).$$

Solving for the logarithm gives $\log(I_2/I_1) = (\beta_2 - \beta_1)/10$; exponentiating in base 10 then gives

$$10^{\log(I_2/I_1)} = \frac{I_2}{I_1} = 10^{(\beta_2 - \beta_1)/10} = 10^{(60\,\text{dB} - 75\,\text{dB})/10}$$

$$= 10^{-1.5} = 0.032.$$

This substantial power reduction results in only a modest reduction in perceived loudness; since the loudness changes by roughly a factor of 2 for each 10 dB change in intensity level, the reduced volume will sound between one-fourth and one-half as loud as before.

Tip

Working with Decibels Decibels are designed for ease in calculating sound intensity levels. That's why we could do this example in a few sentences and get the same result as a paragraph of equations. Note also that decibels are dimensionless because the decibel measure always involves intensity ratios.

EXERCISE At the softest passage in a piece of music, your loudspeakers put out a sound level of 48 dB; the actual power delivered by the speakers at this time is 7.8 mW. If you perceive the loudest music to be eight times as loud as the softest, what will be the greatest power the speakers must deliver during this piece?

Answer: 7.8 W

Some problems similar to Example 17-3: 22, 24, 25, 28

17-4 SOUND WAVES IN LIQUIDS AND SOLIDS

Although less compressible than gases, liquids and solids also support longitudinal sound waves. In general, a material's compressibility is described by its **bulk modulus of elasticity**, or the ratio of the change in pressure to the fractional change in volume:

$$B = -\frac{\Delta P}{\Delta V / V},\qquad(17\text{-}5)$$

where the minus sign arises because a positive pressure increase corresponds to a decrease in volume. Because the denominator in this expression is dimensionless, B has the units of pressure. The bulk modulus is essentially a measure of a material's elasticity, with a large value of B describing a "stiff" material, one that is hard to compress. The stiffer the material, the stronger the restoring forces that develop in response to compression; at the same time, response to compressional forces depends on inertia as measured by the material density. Therefore, it's not surprising that the speed of sound in a material is given by

$$v = \sqrt{\frac{B}{\rho}}.\qquad(17\text{-}6)$$

This is the analog of Equation 17-1 for solids and liquids. Table 17-2 lists sound speeds in some common materials. The stiffness of solids and liquids results in greater sound speeds than in gases, although greater density makes the increase less dramatic than it would otherwise be.

Wave propagation in solids is a complex subject. A simple model for a solid consists of individual atoms linked by springs representing the interatomic electrical forces (Fig. 17-4)—a three-dimensional version of the model system we used to introduce wave motion in Chapter 16 (see Fig. 16-2). Such a structure supports not only longitudinal but also transverse waves. Furthermore, unless the structure is perfectly symmetric, wave properties differ depending on propagation direction. The analysis of possible wave modes is the focus of much contemporary work by solid-state physicists.

TABLE 17-2 *Sound Speeds in Selected Materials**

MATERIAL	SOUND SPEED (m/s)
Gases	
Air (0°C)	331
Air (20°C)	343
Carbon dioxide	259
Hydrogen	1284
Liquids (at 25°)	
Benzene	1295
Mercury	1450
Water	1497
Solids	
Aluminum	6420
Copper	5010
Glass (Pyrex)	5640
Lead	1960
Neoprene	1600
Steel	5940

*At normal atmospheric pressure. Sound speed generally increases with temperature because, as we show in Chapter 20, sound speed is related to the random thermal speeds of molecules.

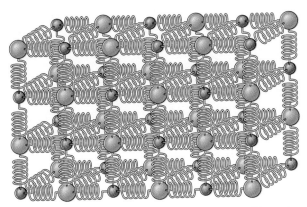

FIGURE 17-4 A simple model for a solid, showing atoms connected by springs. This structure supports both longitudinal and transverse waves.

17-5 WAVE REFLECTION AND REFRACTION

You shout in a mountain valley and hear echoes reverberating off the valley walls. You look in a mirror and see light from your face reflected off the silvered surface. A metal screen in your microwave oven's door turns back potentially harmful waves and keeps them where they'll heat your food. A doctor's ultrasound probes your body, bouncing back to reveal internal structures. A bat navigates flawlessly in response to echoes from a cave wall. All these are examples of wave **reflection**.

You can see that wave reflection *must* occur when a wave hits a medium in which it can't propagate; otherwise, where would the wave energy go? Figure 17-5 details the reflection process for waves on a stretched string, in the two cases where the string end is (*a*) clamped at a rigid wall and (*b*) free to move up and down. In the first case the wave amplitude must remain zero at the end, so

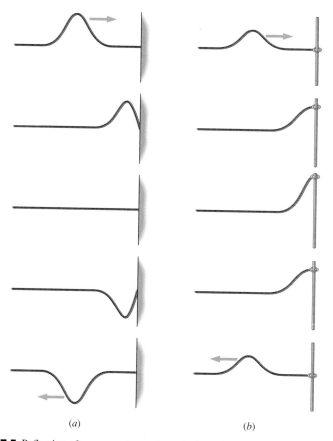

(*a*)   (*b*)

FIGURE 17-5 Reflection of a wave pulse at the end of a string. Conditions at the end determine the details of the reflection. In (*a*) the string is rigidly clamped, so the wave amplitude must be zero at the end and therefore the incident and reflected pulses interfere destructively. That means the reflected pulse must be inverted. In (*b*) the string is free to move up and down on a frictionless rod, and the wave displacement at the end is a maximum; therefore the pulse reflects without inverting.

FIGURE 17-6 Partial reflection at a junction between two different strings. Here the right-hand string is heavier, so the reflected pulse is inverted.

the incident and reflected pulses interfere destructively and the reflected wave is therefore inverted. In the second case the displacement is a maximum at the free end, and the reflected wave is not inverted.

Between the extremes of a rigid wall and a perfectly free end lies the case of one string connected to another with a different mass per unit length. In this case some wave energy is transmitted to the second string and some reflected back along the first (Fig. 17-6).

The phenomenon of partial reflection and transmission at a junction of strings has its analog in the behavior of all sorts of waves at interfaces between different media. For example, shallow water waves are partially reflected if the water depth changes abruptly. Light incident on even the clearest glass undergoes partial reflection because of the difference in light-transmitting capabilities of air and glass (Fig. 17-7). Partial reflection of ultrasound waves at interfaces of body tissues with different densities makes ultrasound a valuable medical diagnostic.

When waves strike an interface between two media at an oblique angle, and are capable of propagating in the second medium, then the phenomenon of **refraction** occurs. In refraction, the direction of wave propagation changes because of a difference in wave speed between the two media. Fig. 17-8 shows the refraction of water waves at an interface between two different water depths. It's often convenient to describe the direction of wave propagation, especially in cases of reflection and refraction where the direction changes, by drawing lines called **rays** that are perpendicular to the wavefronts. We've superposed some rays on Fig. 17-8; note in addition to the refracted ray, there's a weak reflected ray, as well. When the wave speed in a medium changes continuously with position, then the propagation direction also changes continuously and the rays become curves. We discuss the mathematics of refraction in Chapter 35.

FIGURE 17-7 Even though glass is transparent, partial reflection of light occurs at the interface between air and glass. Here the Dallas skyline is reflected in a glass-walled building.

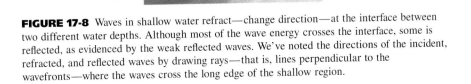

FIGURE 17-8 Waves in shallow water refract—change direction—at the interface between two different water depths. Although most of the wave energy crosses the interface, some is reflected, as evidenced by the weak reflected waves. We've noted the directions of the incident, refracted, and reflected waves by drawing rays—that is, lines perpendicular to the wavefronts—where the waves cross the long edge of the shallow region.

APPLICATION	*Probing the Earth*

Waves propagating and reflecting inside the Earth allow geologists to deduce the structure of the planet's interior, from its largest features to the locations of oil and gas deposits. The waves used include those generated naturally by earthquakes, as well as waves produced intentionally with explosives.

The interior of Earth supports two types of earthquake-generated waves. These are longitudinal waves, which geologists call P waves, and transverse waves called S waves (Fig. 17-9). (Additional wave types propagate near the surface, but not through the interior.) Recall that solids support both longitudinal and transverse waves, while only longitudinal waves can propagate in liquids. This fact provides our most direct evidence that Earth has a liquid core. Since the transverse S waves do not propagate in liquid, they leave a "shadow zone" as shown in Fig. 17-10. Measuring the extent of the shadow zone with a network of seismic stations lets geologists infer the size of the liquid core.

Longitudinal waves—or P-waves—do propagate through the liquid core. Detection of P-waves partially reflected from within the core led geologists to propose an inner core structure. Propagation times for waves passing through this inner core proved shorter than for those passing through the outer core alone, giving evidence that the inner core is solid, with a higher sound speed. Detailed analysis of P-waves from nuclear weapons tests led to geologists' best measurements of the core sizes; the solid inner core is about 1200 km in radius and is surrounded by the 2300-km-thick liquid outer core (Fig. 17-11).

Probing with seismic waves on a smaller scale helps in the search for oil and gas. Using small explosive charges or special machinery that vigorously "thumps" the ground, geologists generate seismic waves that reflect from rock layers a few hundred meters to a few kilometers down. They detect the reflected waves a short distance from their source. Increasingly, this technique is being used on even smaller scales by environmental scientists to map water supplies and the spread of pollutants in groundwater.

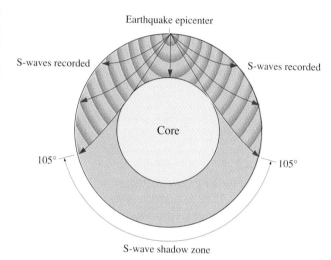

FIGURE 17-10 Transverse waves (S-waves) cannot propagate in liquids, so the presence of a shadow zone for earthquake-generated S-waves is evidence for Earth's liquid core. Bending of the rays occurs because of changes in wave speed with depth.

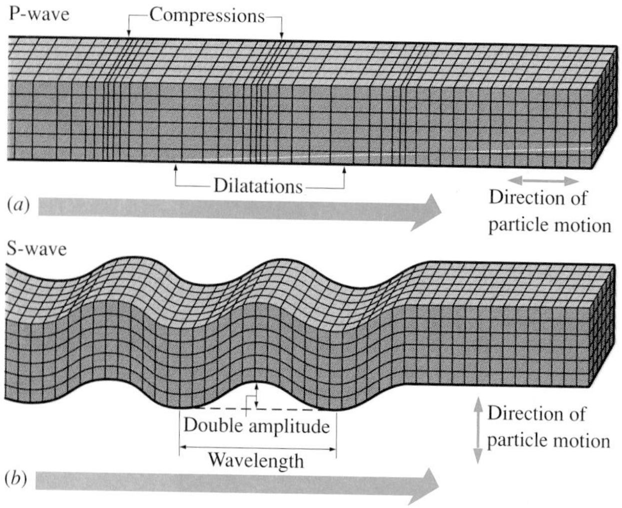

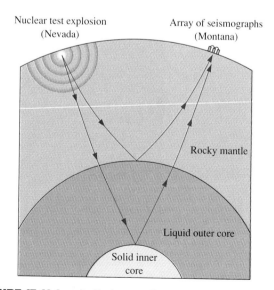

FIGURE 17-11 Longitudinal waves (P-waves) do propagate in the liquid core. The P-waves from nuclear explosions are partially reflected at the boundaries of the inner and outer cores; precise timing of these "echoes" gives the sizes of the cores.

FIGURE 17-9 The structure of compressional P waves and transverse S waves in Earth's interior. Only the P waves can propagate in both liquid and solid regions.

17-6 STANDING WAVES

Imagine a string clamped tightly at both ends. Waves can propagate back and forth on this string by reflecting at its ends. But because the ends are clamped, the wave displacement at the ends must always be zero. Only certain waves can satisfy this requirement; as Fig. 17-12 suggests, they're those for which an integer number of half wavelengths just fits on the length L of the string.

The wave structures shown in Fig. 17-12 are called **standing waves**, so named because they essentially stand still, confined to the length of the string, and they don't propagate anywhere. Instead, the string at each point executes simple harmonic motion perpendicular to the direction of the undisturbed string. We can understand and describe standing waves mathematically by considering that they arise from the superposition of two waves propagating in opposite directions and reflecting at the ends of the string. If we take the x axis to coincide with the string, then we can write the string displacements in two such waves as $y_1(x, t) = A\cos(kx - \omega t)$ for the wave propagating in the $+x$ direction (recall Equation 16-5), and $y_2(x, t) = -A\cos(kx + \omega t)$ for the wave propagating in the $-x$ direction. (The minus sign in y_2 accounts for the phase change that occurs on reflection.) Their superposition is then

$$y(x, t) = y_1 + y_2 = A[\cos(kx - \omega t) - \cos(kx + \omega t)].$$

Appendix A lists a trig identity for the difference of two cosines:

$$\cos\alpha - \cos\beta = -2\sin[\tfrac{1}{2}(\alpha + \beta)]\,\sin[\tfrac{1}{2}(\alpha - \beta)];$$

applying this identity with $\alpha = kx - \omega t$ and $\beta = kx + \omega t$ gives

$$y(x, t) = 2A\sin kx \sin \omega t. \tag{17-7}$$

Equation 17-7 is the mathematical description of a standing wave, and it affirms our qualitative description that each point on the string simply oscillates up and down. Pick any point—that is, any fixed value of x—and Equation 17-7 does indeed describe simple harmonic motion in the y direction, through the factor $\sin \omega t$. The amplitude of that motion depends on the point x you've chosen, and is given by the factor that multiplies $\sin \omega t$, namely $2A\sin kx$.

Because the string is clamped at both ends, the amplitude at the ends must be zero. Our amplitude factor $2A\sin kx$ does give $y = 0$ in Equation 17-7 at $x = 0$, but what about at $x = L$? Here we'll get zero only if $\sin kL = 0$—and that requires kL to be a multiple of π (recall that the sine function is zero when its argument is 0, π, 2π, . . .). So we must have $kL = m\pi$, where m is any integer. But the wave number, k, is related to the wavelength λ by $k = 2\pi/\lambda$. Our condition $kL = m\pi$ can then be written

$$L = \frac{m\lambda}{2}, \quad m = 1, 2, 3, \ldots \tag{17-8}$$

This is just the condition we already guessed at from Fig. 17-12, namely that the string length L be an integer number of half wavelengths.

Given a particular string length L, Equation 17-8 limits the allowed standing waves on the string to a discrete set whose wavelengths follow from the equation. Those allowed waves are called **modes**, and the integer m is the **mode number**. The $m = 1$ mode is the **fundamental**, and is the longest wavelength standing wave that can exist on the string. The higher modes are called **harmonics**. You can explore standing waves with ActivPhysics 10.4, 10.5, and 10.6.

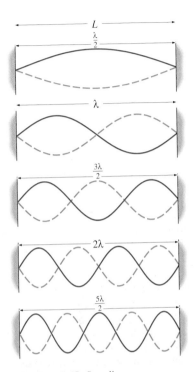

FIGURE 17-12 Standing waves on a string. Clamped rigidly at both ends, the string can accommodate only an integer number of half wavelengths. Shown are the fundamental and four harmonics. Solid line is the string at one instant, dashed line one-half cycle later. Nodes—points where the displacement is always zero—occur at the ends in all cases, and in between for the harmonics.

ActivPhysics

10.4, 10.5, 10.6
Standing Waves on a String

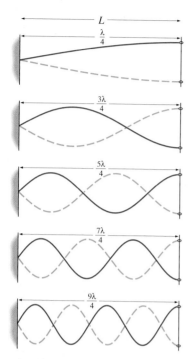

FIGURE 17-13 When one end of the string is fixed and the other free, the string can accommodate only an odd number of quarter wavelengths. (Here the string is clamped at the left end, but at the right end is attached to a ring that slides without friction along a vertical pole.)

Figure 17-12 shows that there are points where the string does not move at all. These include, obviously, the two clamped ends. For all but the fundamental, they also include one or more points in between. Points of zero displacement in a standing wave are called **nodes**. Points where the amplitude of the wave displacement is a maximum, in contrast, are **antinodes**.

When a string is clamped rigidly at one end but free at the other, its clamped end is a node but its free end is an antinode. Figure 17-13 shows that the string length must then be an odd multiple of a quarter wavelength—a result that you can also get from Equation 17-7 by requiring $\sin kL = 1$ to give maximum amplitude at $x = L$ (see Problem 41).

Standing Wave Resonance

We've discussed standing waves in terms of constraints on the wavelength λ rather than on the frequency f. But because waves on a string have a fixed speed v, and because $f\lambda = v$, Equation 17-8's discrete set of allowed wavelengths corresponds to a set of discrete frequencies, as well. The lowest allowed frequency, called the fundamental frequency, corresponds to the longest wavelength; the harmonics have higher frequencies. With ActivPhysics Activity 10.4 you can actually listen to the different harmonics of a vibrating string.

Because a stretched string can oscillate in any of its allowed frequencies, resonant behavior that we discussed in Chapter 15, Section 15-7, can occur close to any of those frequencies. Buildings and other structures, in analogy with our simple string, support a variety of standing wave modes. For example, a skyscraper is like the string of Fig. 17-13, its base clamped to Earth but its top free to swing. Engineers must be sure to identify all possible modes of structures they design, in order to avoid harmful resonances. The disastrous oscillations of the Tacoma Narrows Bridge shown in Fig. 15-32 are actually torsional standing waves.

ActivPhysics Activity 10.4 lets you try to get a string oscillating at *any* frequency you choose. You'll find that you can produce oscillations of significant amplitude only for frequencies very close to the allowed mode frequencies.

Other Standing Waves

Standing waves are common phenomena. Water waves in confined spaces exhibit standing waves, and entire lakes can develop very slow oscillations corresponding to low-mode-number standing waves. Standing electromagnetic waves occur inside closed metal cavities; in microwave ovens the nodes of the standing-wave pattern would result in "cold" spots were not either the food or the source of microwaves kept in motion. Standing waves are common in mechanical systems. And even atomic structure can be understood in terms of standing waves associated with electrons.

In a novel variant on musical wind instruments, engineers seeking to eliminate ozone-destroying chemicals now used in refrigerators have developed so-called thermoacoustic refrigerators, in which high-amplitude standing sound waves provide the compression and expansion necessary to extract heat (more on this in Chapter 22).

FIGURE 17-14 Complex standing wave patterns arise in two and three dimensions. Here, a computer model of standing-wave oscillations in the Sun provides insights into physical conditions deep in the solar interior. Red and blue areas represent oscillatory motion in opposite directions.

Standing-wave patterns in two- and three-dimensional systems can be quite complex, as Fig. 17-14 suggests.

Musical Instruments

Our analysis of standing waves on strings applies directly to stringed musical instruments such as violins, guitars, and pianos. Standing-wave vibrations in the instrument strings are communicated to the air as sound waves, usually through the intermediary of a sounding box or electronic amplifiers. For instruments in the violin family, the body of the instrument itself undergoes standing wave vibrations, excited by the vibration of the string, that establish each individual instrument's peculiar sound quality (Fig. 17-15a). Similarly, the stretched membranes of drums exhibit a variety of standing wave patterns representing the allowed modes on these two-dimensional surfaces (Fig. 17-15b).

Wind instruments, in contrast, generate standing sound waves in air columns, analogous to the pipe we considered in Fig. 17-1. These must be open at one end to allow sound to escape; in many instruments the column is effectively open at both ends. An open end has its pressure fixed at atmospheric pressure; it is therefore a pressure node and thus, from Fig. 17-1, a displacement antinode. As a result, an instrument open at one end supports odd integer multiples of a quarter wavelength (Fig. 17-16a), in analogy with Fig. 17-13. An instrument open at both ends, on the other hand, supports integer multiples of a half wavelength (Fig. 17-16b).

ActivPhysics

10.5
Tuning a Stringed Instrument

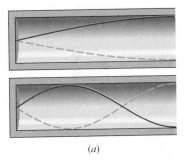

(a)

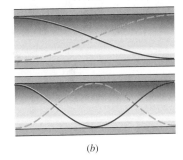

(b)

FIGURE 17-16 Graphs showing displacement of standing sound waves in wind instruments. Solid and dashed lines are one-half cycle apart. Shown are the fundamental and the lowest harmonic that the instrument can support. (a) An instrument with one end open must have a node at the closed end and an antinode at the open end, so it supports odd integer multiples of a quarter wavelength. (b) With both ends open antinodes occur at both ends, so the instrument supports integer multiples of a half wavelength.

(a)

(b)

FIGURE 17-15 (a) Standing waves on a violin, imaged using holographic interference of laser light waves. (b) Standing waves on a drum.

EXAMPLE 17-4	*The Double Bassoon*

The double bassoon (Fig. 17-17) is the lowest pitched instrument in a normal orchestra. The instrument is "folded" to achieve an effective air column 5.5 m long, and it acts like a pipe open at both ends. What is the frequency of the double bassoon's fundamental note?

Solution

Because the double bassoon acts like a pipe open at both ends, Fig. 17-16b shows that its fundamental mode has a wavelength twice that of the air column, or 11 m. Equation 16-1, $v = \lambda f$, then gives

$$f = \frac{v}{\lambda} = \frac{343 \text{ m/s}}{11 \text{ m}} = 31 \text{ Hz},$$

where we found the sound speed in Table 17-2. This frequency is the note B_0, and lies near the low-frequency limit of the human ear.

The actual length of the double bassoon's air column is 4.8 m, but the instrument's detailed shape alters the standing wave modes, giving a greater effective length. Like most wind

FIGURE 17-17 The double bassoon, whose air column is about 5 m long, is the lowest pitched instrument in a standard orchestra. The instrument is "folded" to achieve its long air column in a more compact space.

instruments, the bassoon has a number of holes that, when uncovered, alter the positions of the antinodes and therefore change the pitch.

EXERCISE The C clarinet has an effective length of 32.8 cm, and for its lowest notes it functions as a pipe closed at one end. What is the fundamental frequency of this instrument?

Answer: 261 Hz

Some problems similar to Example 17-4: 50, 52–55

A vibrating string or air column can support many modes, each corresponding to a different frequency and wavelength. In general, a mixture of modes exists simultaneously, a superposition of many simple harmonic waves. The method of Fourier analysis, introduced in Section 16-6, is useful in describing the distribution of individual modes. Different musical instruments favor different modes, which is what gives each its distinctive sound (Fig. 17-18).

FIGURE 17-18 Waveforms of a clarinet (above) and oboe (below) playing the same note. Although the fundamental frequencies are the same, the waveforms and the resulting sounds are quite different because of the different mixtures of standing wave modes in the two instruments.

EXAMPLE 17-5	*Measuring the Sound Speed*

Resonance in hollow pipes provides an accurate means of measuring the speed of sound. In a particular experiment, a pipe 1.300 m long is closed at one end with a diaphragm that can be made to oscillate at an arbitrary frequency, while the other end is open to the atmosphere. A microphone monitors the sound intensity at the open end. Experimentally, the lowest diaphragm frequency that causes the intensity to peak is found to be 66.29 Hz. (a) What is the sound speed in the pipe? (b) At what frequency will the next resonance occur?

Solution

Figure 17-16a shows that a pipe open at one end supports standing waves with the pipe length L an odd quarter multiple of a wavelength. Thus, for the 66.29-Hz fundamental, $L = \frac{1}{4}\lambda$, so $\lambda = 4L$, and the sound speed is

$$v = f\lambda = (66.29 \text{ Hz})(4)(1.300 \text{ m}) = 344.7 \text{ m/s}.$$

The next resonance occurs when $L = \frac{3}{4}\lambda$ or $\lambda = \frac{4}{3}L$; the corresponding frequency is

$$f = \frac{v}{\lambda} = \frac{344.7 \text{ m/s}}{(\frac{4}{3})(1.300)} = 198.9 \text{ Hz}.$$

EXERCISE In air at 20°C and 30% humidity, the speed of sound is 343.8 m/s. Under these conditions the fundamental resonant frequency in a hollow pipe is 1148 Hz. When the humidity increases to 80%, the resonant frequency rises to 1150 Hz. What is the sound speed at 80% humidity?

Answer: 344.4 m/s.

Some problems similar to Example 17-5: 43, 55

17-7 THE DOPPLER EFFECT

The speed v of a wave is its speed relative to the medium through which it propagates. A point source at rest in the medium radiates waves uniformly in all directions (Fig. 17-19). But when the source moves, wave crests bunch up in the direction toward which the source is moving, resulting in a decreased wavelength (Fig. 17-20). In the opposite direction, wave crests spread out and the wavelength increases. You can see this effect simulated with ActivPhysics Activity 10.8.

The wave speed is determined by the properties of the medium, so it doesn't change with source motion. Thus the relation $v = \lambda f$ still holds. This means that an observer in front of the moving source, where λ is smaller, experiences a higher wave frequency as more wave crests pass per unit time. Similarly, an observer behind the source experiences a lower frequency. This change in wavelength and frequency from a moving source is the **Doppler effect** or **Doppler shift**, after the Austrian physicist Christian Johann Doppler (1803–1853).

To analyze the Doppler effect, let λ be the wavelength measured when the source is stationary, and λ' the wavelength when the source is moving at speed u through a medium where the wave speed is v. At the source, the time between wave crests is the wave period T, and a wave crest moves one wavelength λ in this time. But during the same time T, the moving source covers a distance uT, after which it emits the next wave crest. So the distance between wave crests, as seen by an observer in front of the moving source, is

$$\lambda' = \lambda - uT.$$

Writing $T = \lambda/v$, this becomes

$$\lambda' = \lambda - u\frac{\lambda}{v} = \lambda\left(1 - \frac{u}{v}\right). \qquad \text{(source approaching)} \qquad \text{(17-9a)}$$

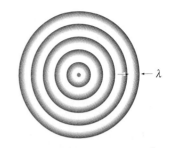

FIGURE 17-19 Circular waves from a source at rest with respect to the medium.

10.8, 10.9
Doppler Effect

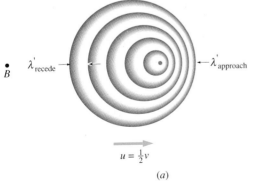

$u = \frac{1}{2}v$

(a)

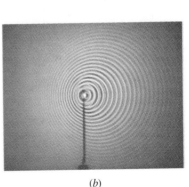

(b)

FIGURE 17-20 (a) When the source moves through the medium, the wavelength is shortened in the direction of motion and increased in the opposite direction. Observers at A and B therefore detect higher and lower frequencies, respectively. In the case shown, the source speed u is half the wave speed v. (b) Doppler effect in water waves produced by a moving source tapping the water surface at regular intervals. Which way is the source moving?

FIGURE 17-21 Speed trap! Police radar works by measuring the Doppler shift of radio waves reflected off moving cars.

The situation is similar in the direction opposite the source motion, except that now the wavelength *increases* by the amount $\lambda u/v$, giving

$$\lambda' = \lambda\left(1 + \frac{u}{v}\right). \qquad \text{(source receding)} \qquad (17\text{-}9b)$$

We can recast these expressions in terms of frequency using the relations $\lambda = v/f$ and $\lambda' = v/f'$, where f' is the frequency of waves from the moving source as measured by an observer at rest in the medium. Substituting these relations in our expressions for λ' and solving for f' gives

$$f' = \frac{f}{1 \pm u/v}, \qquad \text{(Doppler shift, moving source)} \qquad (17\text{-}10)$$

for the Doppler-shifted frequency, where the $+$ and $-$ signs correspond to receding and approaching sources, respectively.

You've probably experienced the Doppler effect for sound when standing near a highway. A loud truck approaches with a high-pitched sound "aaaaaaaaaaa." As it passes, the pitch drops abruptly: "aaaaaaaaaeiooooooooooo," and stays low as the truck recedes. Practical uses of the Doppler effect are numerous. Measuring the Doppler shift in reflected ultrasound allows measurement of blood flow and fetal heartbeat. Police radar works by measuring the Doppler shift of high-frequency radio waves reflected from moving cars (Fig. 17-21). The Doppler shift of starlight reveals stellar motions, while Doppler-shifted light from distant galaxies is evidence that our entire universe is expanding.

EXAMPLE 17-6	*The Wrong Note*

A car speeds down the highway with its stereo blasting. An observer with perfect pitch is standing by the roadside and, as the car approaches, notices that a musical note that should be G ($f = 392$ Hz) sounds like A (440 Hz). How fast is the car moving?

Solution

Solving Equation 17-10 for the source speed u, we have

$$u = v\left(1 - \frac{f}{f'}\right) = (343 \text{ m/s})\left(1 - \frac{392 \text{ Hz}}{440 \text{ Hz}}\right) = 37.4 \text{ m/s}$$

$$= 135 \text{ km/h}.$$

EXERCISE What is the shift in frequency of a 1.2-kHz m ambulance siren when the ambulance is approaching at 130 km/h?

Answer: $\Delta f = 140$ Hz

Some problems similar to Example 17-6: 56, 57, 59

Moving Observers

A Doppler shift in frequency, but not wavelength, also occurs when a moving observer approaches a stationary source—meaning a source at rest with respect

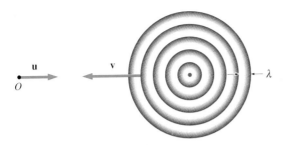

to the wave medium. Figure 17-22 shows how this comes about. An observer moving with speed u toward a stationary source of waves with wave speed v is moving at speed $v + u$ relative to the wave crests (recall Chapter 3, Section 3-5 on relative motion). Since the distance between wave crests is the wavelength λ, the moving observer will measure a time T' between wave crests given by

$$T' = \frac{\lambda}{v + u}.$$

As far as the moving observer is concerned, this time T' is the wave period—the time for the wave cycle to repeat itself fully. Since frequency and period are inverses, the moving observer measures a wave frequency f' given by $f' = 1/T' = (v + u)/\lambda$. We can recast this expression in terms of the frequency f measured by an observer at rest by noting that, in the rest frame of the source, $f\lambda = v$ or $\lambda = v/f$. Using this result in our expression for the shifted frequency gives

$$f' = \frac{v + u}{\lambda} = f\frac{v + u}{v} = f(1 + u/v).$$

Had the observer been moving away from the source, the relative speed would have been $v - u$, and we would have $f' = f(1 - u/v)$. Thus, in general, the shifted frequency measured by a moving observer is

$$f' = f(1 \pm u/v), \quad \text{(Doppler shift, moving observer)} \qquad (17\text{-}11)$$

with the positive sign for an observer approaching the source, negative for an observer receding. For observer velocities u very small compared with the wave speed v, Equations 17-10 and 17-11 give essentially the same results, as you can show in Problem 61. Problem 76 shows how to combine Equations 17-10 and 17-11 to get a general expression for the Doppler shift when both source and observer are in motion. ActivPhysics Activities 10.8 and 10.9 simulate the Doppler effect for moving sources, moving observers, and situations where both source and observer move.

Waves from a stationary source that reflect from a moving object undergo a Doppler shift *twice*. First, because the frequency as received at the reflecting object is shifted, according to Equation 17-11, due to the object's motion relative to the source. Then a stationary observer sees the reflected waves as coming from a moving source, so there's another shift, this time given by Equation 17-10. Police radar and other Doppler-based speed measurements make use of this double Doppler shift that occurs on reflection (see Problems 77–80).

The Doppler Effect for Light

Although light and other electromagnetic waves do not require a material medium, they, too, are subject to the Doppler shift. Both Doppler formulas we've derived here apply to electromagnetic waves, but only in the limit where the relative speed between source and observer is much less than the 3×10^8 m/s speed of light.

The Doppler shift for electromagnetic waves is the same whether it's the source that moves or the observer. This reflects a profound fact at the root of Einstein's relativity, a fact that we hinted at in Chapter 3 and will explore in Chapter 38: that "stationary" and "moving" are meaningful only as relative terms. Electromagnetic waves, unlike mechanical waves, do not require a medium—and therefore terms such as "stationary source" and "moving observer" are meaningless. All that matters is the relative motion between source and observer.

17-8 SHOCK WAVES

Equation 17-9a suggests that wavelength goes to zero if a source approaches at exactly the wave speed. This happens because wave crests can't get away from the source, so they pile up just ahead of it to form a large-amplitude wave called a **shock wave** (Fig. 17-23a). When the source moves faster than the wave speed, waves pile up on a cone whose half angle is given by $\sin \theta = v/u$, as shown in Fig. 17-23b. The ratio u/v is called the **Mach number**, and the cone angle is the **Mach angle**. The speeds of supersonic aircraft are often stated in terms of Mach number; for example, the Concorde, the world's only supersonic passenger plane, flies at Mach 2.

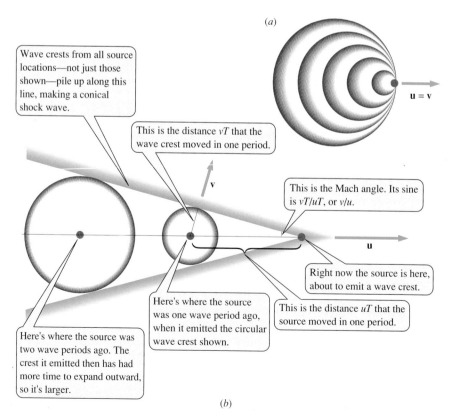

(a)

Wave crests from all source locations—not just those shown—pile up along this line, making a conical shock wave.

This is the distance vT that the wave crest moved in one period.

This is the Mach angle. Its sine is vT/uT, or v/u.

$u = v$

v

u

Right now the source is here, about to emit a wave crest.

Here's where the source was one wave period ago, when it emitted the circular wave crest shown.

This is the distance uT that the source moved in one period.

Here's where the source was two wave periods ago. The crest it emitted then has had more time to expand outward, so it's larger.

FIGURE 17-23 Formation of shock waves. (a) When the source (blue dot) moves at just the wave speed, wave crests emitted in the direction of the source motion remain right at the source. This pileup of wave crests at one place is the shock wave. (b) When the source moves faster than the wave speed, the source travels farther in a given time than do the expanding wave crests. The crests pile up along a cone whose half-angle is the Mach angle, $\sin^{-1}(v/u)$. Can you determine the Mach number from this diagram?

(b)

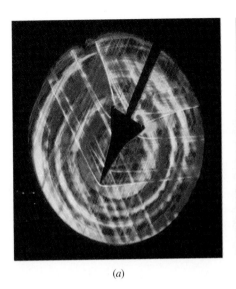

(a)

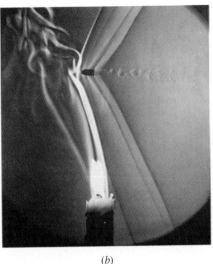

(b)

(c)

FIGURE 17-24 (a) Shock waves (red lines) trail from a model of a delta-winged orbiter in a wind tunnel. Shocks from real supersonic aircraft are the sonic booms that can damage buildings and marine life. (b) A bullet passes through a candle flame, trailing shock waves and disrupting the air flow above the flame. Photos (a) and (b) were both made with a technique that images regions of enhanced density, such as the air that "piles up" behind a shock wave. (c) A powerboat's wake is also a shock wave.

Shock waves occur in a wide variety of physical situations (Fig. 17-24). Sonic booms are shock waves from supersonic aircraft. The bow wave of a boat is a shock wave on the water surface. On a much larger scale, a huge shock wave forms in space as the solar wind—a high-speed flow of particles from the Sun—encounters Earth's magnetic field.

CHAPTER SYNOPSIS

Summary

1. **Sound waves** are longitudinal mechanical waves propagating in gases, liquids, or solids. The speed of sound in gases is given by

$$v = \sqrt{\frac{\gamma P}{\rho}},$$

with P the pressure, ρ the density, and γ a constant that depends on the nature of the gas molecules. More generally, the speed of sound is given by $v = \sqrt{B/\rho}$, where the **bulk modulus** B measures the elastic properties of the medium.

2. The intensity of sound, like that of any wave, depends on the square of the wave disturbance. In sound the medium undergoes both displacement and pressure changes, and the intensity can be written as

$$\overline{I} = \frac{\Delta P_0^2}{2\rho v} = \tfrac{1}{2}\rho\omega^2 s_0^2 v,$$

where ΔP_0 and s_0 are the pressure and displacement amplitudes, ω the angular frequency, and v the wave speed.

3. Audible sound covers many orders of magnitude in intensity, and the human ear responds logarithmically to sound intensity. A convenient measure of intensity is the **decibel** level, defined by

$$\beta = 10 \log\left(\frac{I}{I_0}\right),$$

where $I_0 = 10^{-12}$ W/m^2 is approximately the threshold of hearing at 1 kHz.

4. Wave **reflection** occurs whenever the medium changes abruptly. Complete reflection occurs if a wave cannot propagate in the new medium. More generally, a wave is partially reflected and partially transmitted at an interface between two media.

5. **Standing waves** arise when a vibrating medium is bounded. Each point in a standing wave undergoes simple harmonic motion. When the system is constrained so that there can be no displacement at either end, then its length must be an integer number of half wavelengths:

$$L = \frac{n\lambda}{2}.$$

If one end is fixed and the other free, then an odd integer number of quarter wavelengths must fit between the ends. The longest wavelength—and lowest frequency—standing wave is the **fundamental**; higher frequencies are the **harmonics**.

6. The **Doppler effect** is the change in frequency due to the motion of a wave source or observer. For mechanical waves, the Doppler-shifted frequency from a moving source is

$$f' = \frac{f}{1 \pm u/v},$$

where f is the frequency emitted when the source is at rest, v the wave speed, and u the source speed with respect to the medium. The positive sign applies to a source receding from the observer, the minus sign to an approaching source. For a stationary source and a moving observer, the Doppler shift is given by

$$f' = f(1 \pm u/v).$$

7. **Shock waves** are formed by sources moving through a medium at speeds greater than the wave speed. Shock waves are large-amplitude disturbances that form a cone of half angle $\theta = \sin^{-1}(v/u)$ with apex at the moving source.

Terms You Should Understand

(Pairs are closely related terms whose distinction is important; number in parentheses is chapter section where term first appears.)

audible sound, infrasound, ultrasound (introduction)
pressure (17-1)
decibel (17-3)
bulk modulus (17-4)
reflection, partial reflection (17-5)
refraction (17-5)
standing wave (17-6)
node, antinode (17-6)
mode (17-6)
Doppler effect (17-7)
shock wave (17-8)
Mach number, Mach angle (17-8)

Symbols You Should Recognize

γ (17-2)	s (17-3)
P (17-2)	β (17-3)
ρ (17-2)	f', λ' (17-7)

Problems You Should be Able to Solve

calculating sound speed from pressure, density, and constant γ (17-2)
relating frequency and wavelength of waves in different gases (17-2)
solving for sound intensity, displacement amplitude, or pressure amplitude (17-3)
working with intensity level in decibels (17-3)
solving for reflected and transmitted amplitude with waves on strings (17-5)
finding frequency and wavelength of allowed standing wave modes (17-6)
determining Doppler-shifted frequency and wavelength (17-7)
evaluating shock-wave angles (17-8)

Limitations to Keep in Mind

Expressions for sound speed apply only for small-amplitude waves.
When applied to light and other electromagnetic waves, the Doppler shift formulas developed in this chapter are approximations good when the source speed is small compared with the speed of light.

QUESTIONS

1. Consider a light wave and a sound wave with the same wavelength. Which has the higher frequency?
2. If you double the pressure of a gas while keeping its density the same, what happens to the sound speed?
3. Water is about 1000 times more dense than air, yet the speed of sound in water is greater than in air. How is this possible?
4. Why can't astronauts on the moon communicate with sound?
5. In a sound wave, do the displacement and pressure peak at the same point or at different points? Why?
6. Does an increase of 1 dB in sound level correspond to a definite change in the intensity as measured in W/m²? Explain.
7. If the decibel level drops by half, does the sound intensity in W/m² also drop by half? Explain.
8. What property of the human ear makes the decibel scale particularly useful?
9. A loudspeaker is blaring at only 10 dB below the threshold of pain. By what factor must its power be increased to reach that threshold?
10. Figure 17-3 is drawn for a typical human ear. How might the figure change as a person ages?
11. Is it meaningful to talk about sound with a negative decibel level? Explain.

12. Why do you see a reflection of yourself in a perfectly clear glass window?
13. Which string in Fig. 17-6 has the greater mass per unit length?
14. If you place a perfectly clear piece of glass in perfectly clear water, you can still see the glass. Why?
15. Standing waves don't propagate. In what sense, then, are they waves?
16. Do standing waves satisfy the wave equation? You can answer without doing any math; just think about the superposition principle.
17. Light from distant galaxies is red shifted relative to nearby galaxies. Assuming this red shift is due to the Doppler shift, what does it say about the distant galaxies' motion relative to Earth?
18. When a wave source moves relative to the medium, a stationary observer measures changes in both wavelength and frequency. But when the observer moves and the source is stationary, only the frequency changes. Why the difference?
19. Why does a boat easily produce a shock wave on the water surface, while it takes very high-speed aircraft to produce sonic booms?

PROBLEMS

ActivPhysics can help with these problems:
Activities 10.3, 10.4, 10.5, 10.6, 10.8, 10.9.

Sections 17-1 and 17-2 Sound Waves and the Speed of Sound in Gases

1. Show that the quantity $\sqrt{P/\rho}$ has the units of speed.
2. Dimensional analysis alone suggests that the sound speed in a gas should be given roughly by $\sqrt{P/\rho}$. By how much would an estimate based on this simple analysis be in error for a gas with $\gamma = \frac{7}{5}$?
3. Find the wavelength, period, angular frequency, and wave number of a 1.0-kHz sound wave in air under the conditions of Example 17-1.
4. (a) Determine an approximate value for the speed of sound in miles per second. (b) Suppose you see a lightning flash and, 10 s later, hear the thunder. How many miles away did the flash occur? Neglect the travel time for the light (why?)
5. Timers in sprint races start their watches when they see smoke from the starting gun, not when they hear the sound (Fig. 17-25). Why? How much error would be introduced by timing a 100-m race from the sound of the shot?

FIGURE 17-25 Problem 5.

6. The factor γ for nitrogen dioxide (NO_2) is 1.29. Find the sound speed in NO_2 at a pressure of 4.8×10^4 N/m² and density 0.35 kg/m³.
7. At standard atmospheric pressure (1.0×10^5 N/m²), what density of air would make the sound speed 1.0 km/s?
8. The Sun's outer atmosphere, or corona, has about 10^8 electrons and an equal number of protons per cubic centimeter. The pressure of this electron-proton gas is about 3×10^{-3} N/m², and it behaves like a monatomic gas with $\gamma = \frac{5}{3}$. To one significant figure, what is the sound speed in the corona?
9. A gas with density 1.0 kg/m³ and pressure 8.0×10^4 N/m² has sound speed 365 m/s. Are the gas molecules monatomic or diatomic?
10. By what percentage would the sound speed in pure oxygen (O_2) differ from that in air with the same pressure and number of particles per unit volume? Consult Example 17-1.
11. Saturn's moon Titan has one of the solar system's thickest atmospheres. Near Titan's surface, atmospheric pressure is 50% greater than standard atmospheric pressure on Earth, while the density in molecules per unit volume is one-third that of Earth's atmosphere. If Titan's atmosphere is essentially all nitrogen (N_2), what is the sound speed?
12. Divers in an underwater habitat breathe a special mixture of oxygen and neon, with pressure 6.2×10^5 N/m² and density 4.5 kg/m³. The effective γ value for the mixture is 1.61. Find the frequency in this mixture for a 50-cm-wavelength sound wave, and compare with its frequency in air under normal conditions.
13. You see an airplane straight overhead at an altitude of 5.2 km. Sound from the plane, however, seems to be coming from a point back along the plane's path at a 35° angle to the vertical (Fig. 17-26). What is the plane's speed, assuming an average 330 m/s sound speed?

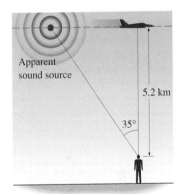

FIGURE 17-26 Problem 13.

14. A mixture of oxygen and nitrogen with the pressure and molecules per cubic meter given in Example 17-1 has sound speed 339 m/s. What fraction of the molecules are oxygen?

Section 17-3 Sound Intensity

15. Sound intensity in normal conversation is about 1 µW/m². What is the displacement amplitude of air in a 2.5-kHz sound wave with this intensity?
16. The eardrum ruptures at a sound intensity of 10 kW/m². What is the amplitude of the sound-wave pressure variation at this intensity, in air under normal conditions? Compare with standard atmospheric pressure, about 10^5 N/m².
17. A speaker produces 440-Hz sound with total power 1.2 W, radiating equally in all directions. At a distance of 5.0 m, what are (a) the average intensity, (b) the decibel level, (c) the pressure amplitude, and (d) the displacement amplitude?

18. A "tweeter" loudspeaker emitting 5.0 kHz sound has an oscillation amplitude of 1 μm. What must be the oscillation amplitude of a "woofer" speaker producing the same sound intensity at 30 Hz?

19. What is the approximate frequency range over which sound with intensity 10^{-12} W/m^2 can be heard? Consult Fig. 17-3.

20. The radius of the hydrogen atom is 0.0529 nm. (a) What is the intensity of a 100-Hz sound wave whose displacement amplitude is this size? (b) Repeat for a 2.0 kHz wave. Is either sound audible? Consult Fig. 17-3.

21. What are the intensity and pressure amplitudes in sound waves with intensity levels of (a) 65 dB and (b) −5 dB?

22. A 1-dB increase in sound level is about the minimum change the human ear can perceive. By what factor is the sound intensity increased if the level changes by 1 dB?

23. (a) What is the decibel level of a sound wave whose pressure amplitude is 2.9×10^{-4} N/m^2? (b) Consult Fig. 17-3 to determine the approximate lowest frequency at which this sound would be audible.

24. If the pressure amplitude of a sound wave doubles, what happens to (a) the intensity in W/m^2 and (b) the decibel level?

25. Show that a doubling of sound intensity corresponds to very nearly a 3 dB increase in the decibel level.

26. Sound intensity from a localized source decreases as the inverse square of the distance, according to Equation 16-9. If the distance from the source doubles, what happens to (a) the intensity and (b) the decibel level?

27. At a distance 2.0 m from a localized sound source you measure the intensity level as 75 dB. How far away must you be for the perceived loudness to drop in half (i.e., to an intensity level of 65 dB)?

28. An amplifier is supplying a loudspeaker with 50 mW of power, and the resulting sound level where you are sitting is 46 dB. How much power must the amplifier supply for you to perceive a fourfold increase in loudness?

29. Sound intensity from a certain extended source drops as $1/r^n$, where r is the distance from the source. If the intensity level drops by 3 dB every time the distance is doubled, what is n?

30. (a) Show that the decibel level may be written

$$\beta = 20 \log\left(\frac{\Delta P}{P_0}\right),$$

where ΔP is the sound-wave pressure amplitude and P_0 is a reference pressure. (b) Find the value of P_0.

Section 17-4 Sound Waves in Liquids and Solids

31. The bulk modulus for tungsten is 2.0×10^{11} N/m^2, and its density is 1.94×10^4 kg/m^3. Find the sound speed in tungsten.

32. The density of aluminum is 2700 kg/m^3. Use the sound speed in Table 17-2 to find aluminum's bulk modulus.

33. The speed of sound in body tissues is essentially the same as in water. Find the wavelength of 2.0 MHz ultrasound used in medical diagnostics.

34. A 1-m-long lead bar and a 1-m-long steel bar are side by side. If they are simultaneously struck a blow on one end, how much sooner will the resulting pressure pulse arrive at the far end of the steel bar?

35. Mechanical vibration induces a sound wave in a mechanism consisting of a 12-cm-long steel rod attached to a 3.0-cm-long neoprene block. How long does it take the wave to propagate through this structure?

36. An acoustic microscope is a device that uses high-frequency ultrasound for imaging; such microscopes are especially useful in the semiconductor industry. The smallest structures that can be imaged by the acoustic microscope (or any other microscope that uses waves of any kind to probe its specimens) have sizes on the order of a wavelength. What is the smallest structure that can be imaged by an acoustic microscope using 4.5-GHz ultrasound in liquid helium, where the sound speed is 240 m/s?

37. The bulk modulus of the steel whose sound speed is given in Table 17-2 is 1.6×10^{11} N/m^2. A 0.50-mm-diameter wire made from this steel can withstand a tension force of 50 N before it deforms permanently. Is it possible to put this wire under enough tension that the speed of transverse waves on the wire is the same as the sound speed in the wire? Answer by calculating the tension required.

Section 17-6 Standing Waves

38. A 2.0-m-long string is clamped at both ends. (a) What is the longest wavelength standing wave that can exist on this string? (b) If the wave speed is 56 m/s, what is the lowest standing-wave frequency?

39. When a stretched string is clamped at both ends, its fundamental standing-wave frequency is 140 Hz. (a) What is the next higher frequency? (b) If the same string, with the same tension, is now clamped at one end and free at the other, what is the fundamental frequency? (c) What is the next higher frequency in case (b)?

40. The A-string (440 Hz) on a piano is 38.9 cm long and is clamped tightly at both ends. If the string is under 667 N tension, what is its mass?

41. Show that only odd harmonics are allowed on a taut string with one end tight and the other free.

42. A string is clamped at both ends and tensioned until its fundamental vibration frequency is 85 Hz. If the string is then held rigidly at its midpoint, what is the lowest frequency at which it will vibrate?

43. Show that the standing-wave condition of Equation 17-8 is equivalent to the requirement that the time it takes a wave to make a round trip from one end of the medium to the other and back be an integer multiple of the wave period.

44. The wave speed on a taut wire is 320 m/s. If the wire is 80 cm long, and is vibrating at 800 Hz, how far apart are the nodes?

45. "Vibrato" in a violin is produced by sliding the finger back and forth along the vibrating string. The G-string on a particular violin measures 30 cm between the bridge and its far end and is clamped rigidly at both points. Its

fundamental frequency is 197 Hz. (a) How far from the end should the violinist place a finger so that the G-string plays the note A (440 Hz)? (b) If the violinist executes vibrato by moving the finger 0.50 cm to either side of the position in part (a), what range of frequencies results?

46. Estimate the fundamental frequency of the human vocal tract by assuming it to be a cylinder 15 cm long that is closed at one end.

47. A bathtub 1.7 m long contains 13 cm of water. By sloshing water back and forth with your hand, you can build up large-amplitude oscillations. Determine the lowest frequency possible for such a resonant oscillation, using the fact that the speed of waves in shallow water of depth h is $v = \sqrt{gh}$. *Hint:* At resonance in this case, the wave has a crest at one end and a trough at the other.

48. What length is necessary for an organ pipe (Fig. 17-27) to produce a 22-Hz tone (a) if the pipe is closed at one end and (b) if it's open at both ends?

FIGURE 17-27 What length pipe organ will produce a 22-Hz tone? (Problem 48)

49. What would be the fundamental frequency of the double bassoon of Example 17-4, if it were played in helium under conditions of Example 17-1?

50. An organ pipe is closed at one end and has a fundamental frequency of 50 Hz. What are the mode numbers and frequencies of the next two higher frequencies it can play?

51. An astronaut smuggles a double bassoon (Example 17-4) to Mars and plays the instrument's fundamental note. If it sounds at 23 Hz, what is the sound speed on Mars?

52. A guitar's G note that should be 392 Hz is playing a bit flat, at 381 Hz. By what percentage should the string tension be increased? Assume the string does not stretch significantly.

Section 17-7 The Doppler Effect

53. A car horn emits 380-Hz sound. If the car moves at 17 m/s with its horn blasting, what frequency will a person standing in front of the car hear?

54. The stationary siren on a firehouse is blaring at 85 Hz. What is the frequency perceived by a firefighter racing toward the station at 120 km/h?

55. A fire truck's siren at rest wails at 1400 Hz; standing by the roadside as the truck approaches, you hear it at 1600 Hz. How fast is the truck going?

56. Red light emitted by hydrogen atoms at rest in the laboratory has wavelength 656 nm. Light emitted in the same process on a distant galaxy is received at Earth with wavelength 708 nm. Describe the galaxy's motion relative to Earth.

57. The dominant frequency emitted by an airplane's engines is 1400 Hz. (a) What frequency will you measure if the plane approaches you at half the sound speed? (b) What frequency will you measure if the plane recedes at half the sound speed?

58. A wave source approaches you at constant speed, and you measure a wave frequency f_1. As the source passes and then recedes, you measure frequency f_2. Find expressions for (a) the source speed and (b) the frequency emitted if the source were stationary, both in terms of f_1, f_2, and the wave speed v.

59. You're standing by the roadside as a truck approaches, and you measure the dominant frequency in the truck noise at 1100 Hz. As the truck passes the frequency drops to 950 Hz. What is the truck's speed?

60. You're between two loudspeakers emitting 180-Hz tones. How fast would you have to walk or run to perceive a beat frequency of 1.5 Hz between the two?

61. Use the binomial approximation to show that Equations 17-10 and 17-11 give the same result in the limit $u \ll v$.

Section 17-8 Shock Waves

62. What will be the cone angle for a supersonic aircraft traveling at Mach 2.5 (2.5 times the sound speed)?

63. Figure 17-28 shows a projectile in supersonic flight, with shock waves clearly visible. By making appropriate

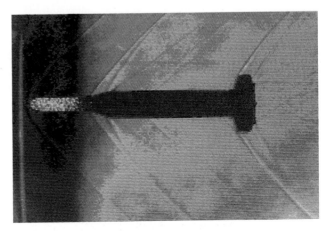

FIGURE 17-28 Problem 63.

measurements, determine the projectile's speed as compared with the sound speed.

64. A supersonic plane flies directly over you at 2.2 times the sound speed. You hear its sonic boom 19 s later. What is the plane's altitude, assuming a constant 340 m/s sound speed?

Paired Problems

(Both problems in a pair involve the same principles and techniques. If you can get the first problem, you should be able to solve the second one.)

65. A 1.0-W sound source emits uniformly in all directions. Find (a) the intensity and (b) the decibel level 12 m from the source.

66. At a distance 3.5 m from a localized sound source the intensity level is 84 dB. (a) What will it be 8.0 m from the source? (b) What is the total power emitted by the source?

67. A pipe 80 cm long is open at both ends. When the pipe is immersed in a gas mixture, the frequency of a certain harmonic is 280 Hz and the next higher harmonic is 350 Hz. Determine (a) the sound speed and (b) the mode numbers of the two harmonics.

68. A 1.5-m-long pipe has one end open. Among its possible standing-wave frequencies is 225 Hz; the next higher frequency is 375 Hz. Find (a) the fundamental frequency and (b) the sound speed.

69. Find the wave speed in a medium where a 28 m/s source speed causes a 3% increase in frequency measured by a stationary observer.

70. A wave source recedes from you at 8.2 m/s, and the wavelength you measure is 20% greater than what you would measure were the source at rest. What is the wave speed?

Supplementary Problems

71. The sound speed in air at 0°C is 331 m/s, and for temperatures within a few tens of degrees of 0°C it increases at the rate 0.590 m/s for every °C increase in temperature. How long would it take a sound wave to travel 150 m over a path where the temperature rises linearly from 5°C at one end to 15°C at the other end?

72. Rods of lead and steel are joined end-to-end; the total length is 6.0 m. If a sound wave takes 1.8 ms to traverse this structure, how long is the lead rod?

73. A rectangular trough is 2.5 m long and is much deeper than its length, so Equation 16-11 applies. Determine the wavelength and frequency of (a) the longest and (b) the next longest standing waves possible in this trough. Why isn't the higher frequency twice the lower?

74. Show by direct substitution (with appropriate differentiation) that Equation 17-7 satisfies the wave Equation 16-12.

75. A supersonic airplane flies directly over you at 6.5 km altitude. You hear its sonic boom 13 s later. What is the plane's Mach number?

76. A wave source moves at speed u_s through a medium where the wave speed is v. An observer moves with speed u_o. If the wave frequency as emitted by the source is f, show that the observer measures a frequency given by $f' = f(v \pm u_o)/(v \mp u_s)$, where the signs are interpreted as in Equations 17-10 and 17-11.

77. Consider an object moving at speed u through a medium, and reflecting sound waves from a stationary source back toward the source. The object receives the waves at the shifted frequency given by Equation 17-11, and when it re-emits them they are shifted once again, this time according to Equation 17-10. Find an expression for the overall frequency shift that results, and show that, for $u \ll v$, this shift is approximately $2fu/v$.

78. Obstetricians use ultrasound to monitor fetal heartbeat. If 5.0-MHz ultrasound reflects off the moving heart wall with a 100-Hz frequency shift, what is the speed of the heart wall? *Hint:* The heart *reflects* the waves, so consider the result of the preceding problem.

79. What is the frequency shift of a 70-GHz police radar signal when it reflects off a car moving at 120 km/h? (Radar waves travel at the speed of light.) *Hint:* See Problem 77.

80. In an extraordinarily sensitive experiment, physicists at Harvard University recently measured the growth rate of crystals by reflecting a laser beam off the crystal surface. The reflected and transmitted beams were combined, and the resulting beat frequency—arising from the very small Doppler shift—was measured. (a) For a laser frequency of 5×10^{14} Hz, what beat frequency results from a crystal growth rate of 0.2 nm/s? (b) What fraction is the frequency shift of the original laser frequency?

Fluid Motion

A tornado owes its destructive power to the swirling winds that develop as the fluid air responds to pressure and gravitational forces.

A tornado whirls across a darkened sky. A jetliner takes off, propelled by hot gases and supported by air pressure on its wings. A stream of gas leaves the surface of a giant star and forms a cosmic whirlpool before it plunges into a black hole. Your car brakes to a stop, the force of your foot on the brake pedal amplified by the effect of fluid in the brake cylinders. Your own body is sustained by air moving in and out of your lungs, and by the flow of blood throughout your tissues. All these examples involve fluid motion.

Fluid is matter that flows under the influence of external forces. The intermolecular forces are weaker in fluids than in solids, and as a result the molecules move around readily rather than being locked into the rigid structure that characterizes a solid. In a liquid, those forces are still significant enough to keep the molecules in close contact, while in a gas they are almost negligible and the molecules are usually widely spaced. In either case, mobility of the individual molecules means that fluids cannot resist so-called shear forces that tend to slide one layer of material past another. For example, you can't make a pile of water the way you can of, say, sand. This inability to resist shear forces means that a fluid spreads out to take the shape of its container.

18-1 DESCRIBING FLUIDS: DENSITY AND PRESSURE

If we could observe a fluid on the molecular scale, we would find large numbers of molecules in continuous motion, colliding frequently with each other and with the walls of their containers. This molecular behavior is governed by the laws of mechanics, and in principle we could study fluids by applying those laws to all the individual molecules. But even a drop of water contains about 10^{21} molecules; to calculate the motions of all those molecules would take the fastest computers many times the age of the universe!

Because the number of molecules is so large, we approximate a fluid by considering it to be continuous rather than composed of discrete particles. In this approximation, valid for fluid samples large compared with the distance between molecules, we describe the fluid by specifying macroscopic properties such as density and pressure.

Density

Density (symbol ρ, the Greek rho) measures the mass per unit volume; its SI units are kg/m^3. The density of water under normal conditions is about 1000 kg/m^3; that of air is about a factor of 1000 smaller. Because their molecules are essentially in contact, liquids are **incompressible**, meaning that their densities remain nearly constant. In contrast, gases, with relatively large distances between their molecules, are **compressible**; their densities change readily.

Pressure

Pressure measures the normal force per unit area exerted by a fluid (Fig. 18-1a). If the pressure is uniform over an area, then we have

$$P = \frac{F}{A};$$ (18-1a)

if pressure varies over an area, we consider the force dF on an infinitesimal area dA and write

$$P = \frac{dF}{dA}.$$ (18-1b)

The SI pressure unit is N/m^2, given the name **pascal** (Pa) after the French mathematician, scientist, and philosopher Blaise Pascal (1623–1662). Another commonly used pressure unit is the **atmosphere** (atm), defined as Earth's normal atmospheric pressure at sea level and equal to 1.013×10^5 Pa (14.7 pounds per square inch). Problems 6 and 7 introduce several other pressure units.

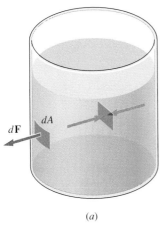

FIGURE 18-1 (*a*) Pressure is the force per unit area exerted by a fluid, either on its container walls or an adjacent volume of fluid. (*b*) At a given point, a fluid exerts the same pressure in all directions.

(*a*) (*b*)

Pressure is a scalar quantity; at a given point in a fluid, pressure is exerted equally in all directions (Fig. 18-1*b*), so it makes no sense to associate a direction with it. This property explains an aspect of pressure that you may find puzzling. Although the atmosphere bears down on your body with a pressure of 14.7 pounds on every square inch, you certainly don't feel that burden. Why not? Because the force associated with this pressure is everywhere perpendicular to your body, and your body fluids respond by compressing until they're at the same pressure. If you've had your ears "pop" in a fast elevator or airplane, or when diving underwater, you know the pain that can develop when pressure forces on your body are temporarily imbalanced.

18-2 FLUIDS AT REST: HYDROSTATIC EQUILIBRIUM

For a fluid to remain at rest, the net force everywhere in the fluid must be zero. When this condition is met, the fluid is in **hydrostatic equilibrium**. In the absence of any external forces, hydrostatic equilibrium requires that the pressure be constant throughout the fluid; otherwise pressure differences would result in forces acting on the fluid, and the fluid would move in response. As Fig. 18-2

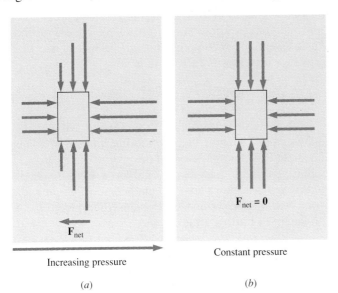

$F_{net} = 0$

F_{net}

Increasing pressure

Constant pressure

(*a*) (*b*)

FIGURE 18-2 (*a*) If pressure varies with position, then there is a net pressure force on a volume of fluid. In the absence of external forces, the fluid then cannot be in hydrostatic equilibrium. (*b*) When the pressure is constant, the net pressure force is zero. In the absence of external forces, the fluid is then in hydrostatic equilibrium.

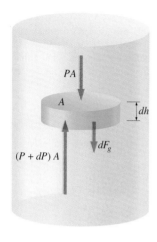

FIGURE 18-3 Forces on a fluid element in hydrostatic equilibrium include gravity and the pressure forces on top and bottom.

suggests, it is pressure *difference,* rather than pressure itself, that gives rise to net forces within fluids.

Hydrostatic Equilibrium with Gravity

For a fluid to be in hydrostatic equilibrium in the presence of gravity, there must be a pressure force to counteract the gravitational force. Since pressure forces arise only from pressure differences, the fluid pressure must therefore vary with depth.

Figure 18-3 shows the forces on a fluid element of area A, thickness dh, and mass dm. A gravitational force acts downward on this fluid element; for it to be in equilibrium there must therefore be an upward pressure force—and that requires a greater pressure on the lower side of the fluid element. Suppose the pressures at the top and bottom are P and $P + dP$, respectively. Since pressure is force per unit area, the net pressure force on the fluid element is therefore

$$dF_{\text{press}} = (P + dP)A - PA = A\,dP.$$

The gravitational force is $dF_{\text{grav}} = -g\,dm$, where the minus sign designates the downward direction. But the mass dm is the density times the volume, so

$$dF_{\text{grav}} = -g\,dm = -g\rho A\,dh.$$

Hydrostatic equilibrium requires that these forces sum to zero:

$$A\,dP - g\rho A\,dh = 0,$$

or

$$\frac{dP}{dh} = \rho g. \tag{18-2}$$

This equation shows that dP/dh—the variation in pressure with depth h—is positive, confirming our expectation that pressure increases with depth. For a liquid, which is essentially incompressible, ρ is constant and Equation 18-2 shows that pressure increases linearly with depth:

$$P = P_0 + \rho gh, \tag{18-3}$$

where P_0 is the pressure at the liquid surface.

Equation 18-2 applies to any fluid in a uniform gravitational field; Equation 18-3 follows from Equation 18-2 for the special case of a liquid. It's also possible to integrate Equation 18-2 to find the pressure in a gas, such as Earth's atmosphere, that's subject to the gravitational force. Because the gas density is not constant, this is a little more involved mathematically—but not beyond the reach of a first-year calculus student. Problem 70 explores the variation of pressure with height in Earth's atmosphere.

EXAMPLE 18-1	Ocean Depths

(a) At what water depth is the pressure twice atmospheric pressure? (b) What is the water pressure at the bottom of the 11.3-km-deep Marianas trench in the North Pacific, the deepest point in the ocean? Atmospheric pressure P_0 is 1.0×10^5 Pa, and the density of water is 1000 kg/m^3.

Solution

At twice atmospheric pressure, $P = 2P_0$ in Equation 18-2. Solving for the depth h then gives

$$h = \frac{P - P_0}{\rho g} = \frac{2.0 \times 10^5 \text{ Pa} - 1.0 \times 10^5 \text{ Pa}}{(1000 \text{ kg/m}^3)(9.8 \text{ m/s}^2)} = 10 \text{ m}.$$

Since pressure increases linearly with depth, the pressure continues to increase by 1.0×10^5 Pa for every 10 m of depth. In the Marianas trench, 11.3×10^3 m deep, the pressure increase is then

$$P - P_0 = (11.3 \times 10^3 \text{ m})(1.0 \times 10^5 \text{ Pa}/10 \text{ m}) = 1.1 \times 10^9 \text{ Pa}.$$

This is over 1000 times atmospheric pressure, or more than 8 tons per square inch! Creatures living at these depths are in pressure equilibrium with their surroundings; to bring them to the surface for study, scientists must maintain their natural pressure or they will explode (Fig. 18-4). A similar plight awaits scuba divers who hold their breath while ascending; air in the lungs expands, bursting the alveoli.

EXERCISE A submarine is designed for depths to 1500 m. How much pressure must it withstand if its interior is maintained at normal atmospheric pressure?

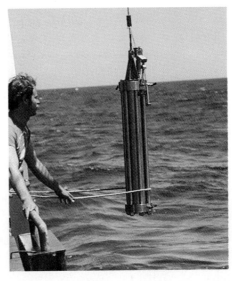

FIGURE 18-4 Oceanographers bring deep ocean water to the surface in a container that maintains deep-sea creatures at their natural pressure.

Answer: 1.5×10^7 Pa

Some problems similar to Example 18-1: 17–19

EXAMPLE 18-2	A Swimming Pool

A swimming pool is 15 m wide and, at the deep end, 3.0 m deep. Find the force of the water on the pool wall at the deep end.

Solution

The pressure in the pool varies from surface to bottom, so we can't simply multiply the pressure by the area to find the force. Instead, we consider the force on a small strip of height dh and pool width W, as shown in Fig. 18-5. This strip has area $dA = W dh$, so the force on it is $dF = P dA = PW dh$. Using Equation 18-3 for the pressure, and integrating to get the total force, we have

$$F = \int dF = \int_{h=0}^{h=H} (P_0 + \rho g h) W dh = W(P_0 h + \tfrac{1}{2}\rho g h^2)\big|_0^H$$

$$= P_0 W H + \tfrac{1}{2}\rho g W H^2,$$

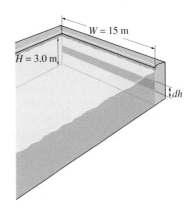

FIGURE 18-5 Since pressure varies with depth, calculating the force on the pool wall involves integrating over the vertical position. A suitable area element is a strip of width W and height dh.

where H is the pool depth. Using $P_0 = 1.0 \times 10^5$ Pa for atmospheric pressure, $\rho = 1000$ kg/m³ for water, and the pool dimensions gives $F = 5.2$ MN.

EXERCISE The spent fuel storage pool at a nuclear reactor measures 20 m long by 10 m wide by 6.5 m deep and is filled with water. What force must its longer sides be capable of withstanding?

Answer: 17 MN

Some problems similar to Example 18-2: 23, 24

Measuring Pressure

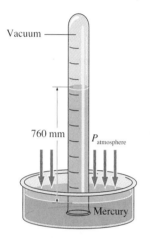

FIGURE 18-6 A mercury barometer. Normal air pressure supports a mercury column 760 mm high.

The variation in liquid pressure with depth is the basis of several common pressure-measuring instruments. Figure 18-6 shows a simple **barometer**. Atmospheric pressure acts on the open pool of liquid mercury, pushing the liquid into the evacuated tube. Since $P_0 = 0$ in the vacuum at the top of the tube, Equation 18-3 becomes simply $P = \rho g h$, showing that the height h of the mercury column is directly proportional to the atmospheric pressure P at the bottom of the column. In mercury, standard atmospheric pressure of 1.013×10^5 Pa supports a mercury column 760 mm or 29.92 inches high (see Problem 6). The actual value of atmospheric pressure usually varies slightly from one place to another, and is of interest to meteorologists because pressure variations drive the air motions we call wind and indirectly cause other weather phenomena. Weather forecasters often report atmospheric pressure in mm or inches of mercury.

Barometers use mercury because its high density makes for a relatively short instrument; Example 18-1 shows that a water-filled barometer would need to be 10 m long to measure atmospheric pressure. The same underlying fact—that atmospheric pressure can support a water column 10 m high—puts a limitation on water pumps that operate by suction. No matter how good a vacuum a suction pump can produce, atmospheric pressure can't push water up more than 10 m. Pumping from greater depths requires a submerged pump or one that somehow increases the pressure at the pumping depth.

Measurement of pressure differences is accomplished with a **manometer**, a U-shaped tube containing liquid and open at both ends (Fig. 18-7). A pressure difference between the ends of the tube results in a difference in height of the two liquid surfaces; Equation 18-3 shows that this height difference is directly proportional to the pressure difference.

Mercury barometers and manometers are the classic pressure measuring instruments, and understanding their simple operation helps elucidate the meaning of pressure. But pressure-measuring devices in use today are often electronic, using the pressure force on a solid material to alter electrical properties in a way that produces an electrical signal proportional to the pressure.

When one end of a manometer, or other pressure-difference instrument, senses atmospheric pressure, the pressure it reads is called **gauge pressure**, meaning the pressure in excess of atmospheric pressure. Inflation pressures for tires and sports equipment are given in gauge pressure; a tire inflated to 200 kPa (about 30 pounds/in²) actually has an absolute pressure of about 300 kPa because the 100-kPa atmospheric pressure is not included in the specification. Tire gauges read gauge, not absolute, pressure.

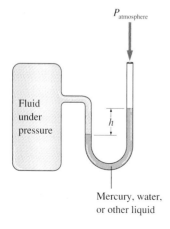

FIGURE 18-7 A manometer used to measure pressure difference between a closed container and the ambient atmosphere. Height difference h is proportional to the pressure difference.

Pascal's Law

Equation 18-3 shows that an increase in surface pressure P_0 results in the same pressure increase throughout the fluid. More generally, a pressure increase anywhere in a fluid is felt throughout the fluid—a fact first recognized by Pascal and now known as **Pascal's law**. Pascal applied this principle in his invention of the hydraulic press; today hydraulic systems, based on Pascal's law, are used to control machinery ranging from automobile brake systems, to aircraft wings, to bulldozers, cranes, and robots (Fig. 18-8).

FIGURE 18-8 Arrows indicate the hydraulic cylinders that actuate this power shovel.

EXAMPLE 18-3	*A Hydraulic Lift*

In the hydraulic lift shown in Fig. 18-9, a 120-cm-diameter piston supports a car. If the total mass of the piston and car is 3200 kg, what should be the diameter of the smaller piston if an applied force of 450 N is to maintain the system in equilibrium? Neglect the mass of the smaller piston and any pressure variation with height.

Solution

The small piston exerts a pressure $P = F_1/A_1 = F/\pi r_1^2$, with r_1 its radius and F_1 the 450-N applied force. Pascal's law says that this pressure is transmitted equally throughout the system; at the large piston it produces a force $F_2 = PA_2$. This force supports the weight mg of piston and car; therefore we have

$$mg = PA_2 = P\pi r_2^2 = \frac{F_1}{\pi r_1^2}\,\pi r_2^2 = F_1\frac{r_2^2}{r_1^2}.$$

Solving for r_1 gives

$$r_1 = r_2\sqrt{\frac{F_1}{mg}} = (60 \text{ cm})\sqrt{\frac{450 \text{ N}}{(3200 \text{ kg})(9.8 \text{ N/kg})}} = 7.2 \text{ cm},$$

or a diameter of 14.4 cm. Note that the 450-N force is effectively multiplied by the ratio of the piston areas, ultimately supporting a weight of nearly 32,000 N.

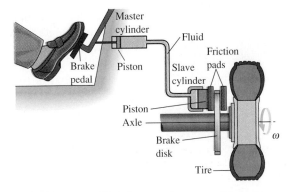

FIGURE 18-10 Simplified diagram of an automobile braking system, showing master cylinder and one of the slave cylinders. The slave cylinder pushes the brake pads against the rotating brake disk, stopping it and the attached wheel.

Are we getting something for nothing here? No. Work done in moving the small piston—the product of force with distance moved—is equal to the work done on the large piston. Since the force on the large piston is much greater, the distance moved is much smaller, and energy is conserved.

EXERCISE Figure 18-10 shows an automobile braking system. The brake pedal applies a force to a piston in the "master cylinder," and the resulting pressure increase is transmitted to "slave cylinders" that operate the brakes. The master cylinder has an interior diameter of 8.0 mm, and it operates two slave cylinders each with diameter 3.2 cm. (Two separate systems each operating two wheels are provided on modern cars for safety in the event of a hydraulic fluid leak.) If a 750-N force is applied to the master cylinder, what force does each of the two slave cylinders exert on its brake pads?

Answer: 12 kN

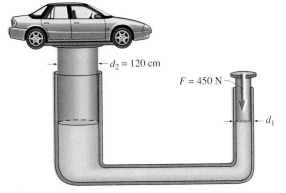

FIGURE 18-9 A hydraulic lift (Example 18-3).

Some problems similar to Example 18-3: 28–30

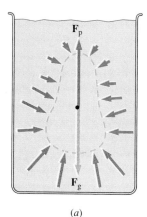

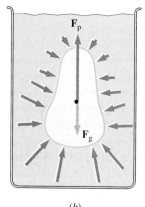

(a)

(b)

FIGURE 18-11 (a) In hydrostatic equilibrium, the upward pressure force $\mathbf{F}_p$ is equal to the weight $\mathbf{F}_g$ of any fluid volume. (b) If the fluid is replaced by a solid object, the pressure force remains the same but the gravitational force generally changes. The direction of the net force on the object depends on whether it is more or less dense than the fluid.

18-3 ARCHIMEDES' PRINCIPLE AND BUOYANCY

Drop a rock into water and it sinks. Drop a cork and it floats. Why the difference?

Figure 18-11a shows the upward pressure force on an arbitrary fluid volume balancing the downward gravitational force. Now imagine replacing the fluid volume by a solid object of identical shape (Fig. 18-11b). The remaining fluid hasn't changed, so it continues to exert an upward force on the object—a force whose magnitude equals the weight of the *original fluid volume*. This force is called the **buoyancy force**, and in giving its magnitude we've stated **Archimedes' principle**:

> **Archimedes' principle: The buoyant force on an object is equal to the weight of the fluid displaced by the object.**

If the submerged object weighs more than the displaced fluid, then the gravitational force exceeds the buoyancy force and it sinks. If the object weighs less than the displaced fluid, the buoyancy force is greater and it rises. Therefore, an object floats or sinks depending on whether its average density is greater or less than that of the fluid. In between is the case of **neutral buoyancy**, when an object's average density is the same as that of the fluid. Fish, submarines, and balloons are often in neutral buoyancy (Fig. 18-12).

(a) (b)

FIGURE 18-12 (a) A hot-air balloon at constant altitude is in neutral buoyancy. (b) So is a fish, whose gas-filled swim bladder compresses or expands to maintain the same average density as water. In both cases the net buoyancy force is equal in magnitude to the gravitational force.

EXAMPLE 18-4	*Aerogels, Archimedes, and the King's Crown*

Physicists have developed new materials called *aerogels* that are at once amazingly light (Fig. 18-13a) and surprisingly strong (Fig. 18-13b). A particular piece of aerogel is made

FIGURE 18-13 (a) Aerogels, made from silicon dioxide, are so tenuous that the buoyant force of air significantly reduces the apparent weight. Here a ghostly blue slab of aerogel rests on freshly beaten egg whites. (b) Aerogels are surprisingly strong. Here an aerogel slab with mass under 1 g supports a 100-g mass.

(a) (b)

from 1.00 g of silicon dioxide. Yet its apparent weight on a scale is 7.35 mN. How does the aerogel's density compare with that of air?

Solution

The aerogel's apparent weight is less than its actual weight $m_{gel}g = 9.8$ mN because of the upward buoyant force of the air. That force is equal to the weight of displaced air, or $F_b = m_{air}g$. The *volume* of displaced air is that of the aerogel, so $m_{air} = \rho_{air}V_{gel}$. But the aerogel's volume is $V_{gel} = m_{gel}/\rho_{gel}$. Putting this all together gives the buoyant force:

$$F_b = m_{air}g = \rho_{air}V_{gel}g = \rho_{air}\frac{m_{gel}}{\rho_{gel}}g = W_{gel}\frac{\rho_{air}}{\rho_{gel}},$$

where $W_{gel} = m_{gel}g$ is the gel's actual weight. Its apparent weight is then $W_{apparent} = W_{gel} - F_b$. Using our expression for F_b and solving for the density ratio ρ_{gel}/ρ_{air} then gives

$$\frac{\rho_{gel}}{\rho_{air}} = \frac{W_{gel}}{W_{gel} - W_{apparent}} = \frac{9.8 \text{ mN}}{9.8 \text{ mN} - 7.35 \text{ mN}} = 4.0 .$$

The density of air is about 1.2 kg/m³, so the aerogel's density is only 4.8 kg/m³—compared with 1000 kg/m³ for water.

The buoyant force of air significantly reduces the aerogel's apparent weight because its density is only a few times that of air. Buoyancy actually lowers the apparent weights of all objects when weighed in air, but usually the effect is negligible because typical densities are on the order of 1000 times that of air.

Archimedes (c. 287–212 B.C.), one of the greatest scientists of ancient Greece, purportedly used his principle to determine

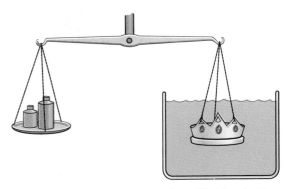

FIGURE 18-14 Archimedes purportedly verified that the king's crown was pure gold by finding its apparent weight when submerged in water.

the density of the king's crown, and thus verify that it was indeed made of gold. Archimedes achieved a nonnegligible buoyancy force by suspending the crown in water (see Fig. 18-14 and Problem 34).

EXERCISE Salvage experts recover a shipment of steel beams from a sunken ship. What will be the tension in a cable lifting a 750-kg beam through water with density 1.0 g/cm³? The density of the steel is 7.9 g/cm³ and the lifting is at constant speed.

Answer: 6.4 kN

Some problems similar to Example 18-4: 31–34

Floating Objects

Archimedes' principle still holds for a floating object. But now the buoyant force must balance the object's weight—and this can happen only if the fluid displaced by the submerged part of the object has a weight equal to that of the object. This condition determines how high in the water the object floats, as Fig. 18-15 and the following examples illustrate.

(a)   (b)

FIGURE 18-15 Supertankers, (a) empty and (b) fully loaded. In both cases the buoyant force supports the full weight of the ship and cargo. The buoyant force is equal to the weight of the displaced water, so the fully loaded ship must displace more water and therefore floats lower in the water.

Got It!

A glass of water, with an ice cube floating in it, is full to the brim. Will it overflow as the ice cube melts?

EXAMPLE 18-5	The Tip of the Iceberg

The average density of a typical arctic iceberg is 0.86 that of sea water. What fraction of an iceberg's volume is submerged?

Solution

The buoyant force supports the entire weight of the iceberg, so the weight of the displaced water is equal to the iceberg weight. If V_{sub} is the volume of ice that's submerged, then the weight of an equal volume of water—and therefore the magnitude of the buoyant force—is

$$F_b = W_{water} = m_{water}g = \rho_{water}V_{sub}g .$$

The weight of the iceberg is

$$W_{ice} = m_{ice}g = \rho_{ice}V_{ice}g ,$$

where V_{ice} is the volume of the entire iceberg. Equating the iceberg weight to the magnitude of the buoyant force, we have

$$\rho_{ice}V_{ice}g = \rho_{water}V_{sub}g ,$$

so

$$\frac{V_{sub}}{V_{ice}} = \frac{\rho_{ice}}{\rho_{water}} = 0.86 .$$

Roughly six-sevenths of an arctic iceberg is therefore submerged (Fig. 18-16).

FIGURE 18-16 Most of an iceberg's volume is submerged because its density is only slightly less than that of water.

EXAMPLE 18-6	An Overloaded Boat

A flat-bottomed rowboat has length $\ell = 3.2$ m, width $w = 1.1$ m, and is 28 cm deep. Empty, it has a mass of 130 kg. (a) How much of the boat is submerged when it is empty? (b) What is the total mass it could carry without taking on water?

Solution

In equilibrium, the total weight of the boat and its load must be supported by the buoyant force of the water. By Archimedes' principle, this force is equal to the weight of water displaced by the boat. Letting y be the depth to which the boat is submerged, we have

$$\ell wy\rho_{water}g = Mg .$$

Here ρ_{water} is the density of water, and ℓwy the submerged volume, so the term on the left is the weight of displaced water and is therefore equal to the magnitude of the buoyant force. The quantity M is the total mass of the boat plus its load, so the term on the right is the weight supported by the buoyant force. Solving for y, we have

$$y = \frac{M}{\ell w\rho_{water}} = \frac{(130 \text{ kg})}{(3.2 \text{ m})(1.1 \text{ m})(1000 \text{ kg/m}^3)} = 3.7 \text{ cm}$$

for the empty boat.

To find the absolute maximum load, we set y equal to the boat's 28-cm depth, and solve for M:

$$M = \ell wy\rho_{water} = (3.2 \text{ m})(1.1 \text{ m})(0.28 \text{ m})(1000 \text{ kg/m}^3)$$

$$= 986 \text{ kg} .$$

This is the total mass; subtracting the 130-kg boat mass gives 856 kg for the maximum load.

EXERCISE A rectangular bar of soap floats with 3.5 cm extending below the water surface and 1.5 cm above. What is its density?

Answer: 700 kg/m^3

Some problems similar to Examples 18-5 and 18-6: 35–37, 40

The Center of Buoyancy

A boat will float if its average density is less than that of water. But will it float upright? That depends. We found in Chapter 14 that the force of gravity acts as though it were all concentrated at a point called the center of gravity. Does the buoyancy force also act at the center of gravity? No: The buoyancy force on an object is precisely the force that would act on a volume of water identical in size and shape to the submerged part of the object. Since the buoyancy force and gravitational force would keep that water volume in equilibrium, the two forces must act at the same point—otherwise there could be torques that would set the water into rotation. So the buoyancy force acts at the center of gravity not of the object but of the water that would be there if the object weren't. Normally, therefore, the center of gravity and **center of buoyancy**, as it's called, are not the same point.

For a floating object to be in stable equilibrium, the forces of gravity and buoyancy must not only sum to zero, but they must also produce no net torque. Consider the boat shown in Fig. 18-17a, whose center of buoyancy lies above its center of gravity. If it tips a bit to the side, a torque develops that tends to restore it to equilibrium. But if the boat were so ill designed, or so overloaded, that its center of gravity was above its center of buoyancy, then any deviation from a perfectly upright position would produce a torque that would tip the boat over (Fig. 18-17b). So the first priority of a marine engineer is to ensure that any watercraft design puts the center of gravity below the center of buoyancy, and the first priority of any boat operator is to keep it that way!

Got It!

Explain, in terms of center of gravity and center of buoyancy, why you're not supposed to stand up in a canoe.

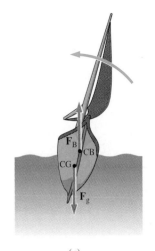

(a)

(b)

FIGURE 18-17 (a) When the center of buoyancy (CB) is above the center of gravity (CG), the torque that develops if the boat tips tends to restore it to its upright position. (b) If the center of gravity is above the center of buoyancy, a torque develops that tips the boat over.

18-4 FLUID DYNAMICS

We now turn our attention to moving fluids, which are described by the flow velocity at each point in the fluid and at each instant of time. Figure 18-18 shows some flow velocity vectors in a river. We can describe flow velocity either with individual vectors, as in Fig. 18-18a, or by drawing continuous lines called **streamlines** that are everywhere tangent to the local flow direction (Fig. 18-18b). Their spacing is a measure of flow speed, with closely spaced streamlines indicating high speed. Small particles, such as smoke or dyes, are

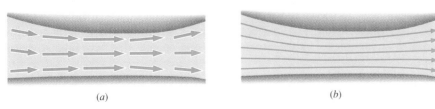

(a)   (b)

FIGURE 18-18 (a) Flow vectors in a river. Note the higher speed where the river narrows. (b) Streamlines are an alternative way of representing the flow. Note that lines are closer where the flow speed is higher.

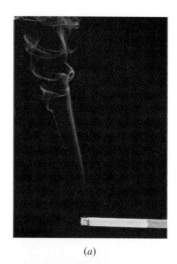

FIGURE 18-19 In this aerodynamic test, smoke particles trace streamlines in the airflow over a car. Can you tell where the flow is fastest?

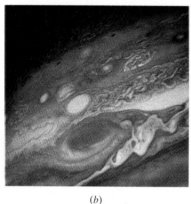

(a)

(b)

FIGURE 18-20 (a) Smoke from a burning cigarette first rises in a steady flow, but soon the flow becomes unsteady. (b) Unsteady flows in Jupiter's atmosphere, photographed by a Voyager spacecraft.

often introduced into moving fluids because they follow streamlines and therefore give a visual indication of the flow velocity pattern (Fig. 18-19).

We distinguish two types of fluid motion. In **steady flow**, the pattern of fluid motion remains the same at each point, even though individual fluid elements are in continual motion. When you look at a river in steady flow, for example, it always looks the same, even though you're not seeing the same water each time you look. At a given point in the river, the water velocity, density, and pressure are always the same. **Unsteady flow**, in contrast, involves fluid motion that changes with time even at a fixed point. The blood in your arteries is in unsteady flow; with each contraction of the heart ventricles, the pressure rises, and the flow velocity increases. Figure 18-20 shows other examples of steady and unsteady flow. We will restrict our quantitative description of fluid motion to steady flow.

Like all other motion in classical physics, fluid motion is governed by Newton's laws. Indeed, it is possible to write Newton's second law in a form that involves explicitly the fluid velocity as a function of position and time. But the resulting equation is difficult to solve in any but the simplest cases. Instead of applying Newton's law directly, we will approach fluid dynamics from the point of view of energy conservation. As in mechanics, energy conservation provides a shortcut to problem solving; the price of that shortcut is the lack of some details.

Conservation of Mass: The Continuity Equation

In mechanics we had no trouble keeping track of the individual objects. But a fluid is continuous and deformable, so it's not easy to follow an individual fluid element as it moves. Yet fluid is conserved; as it moves and deforms, new fluid is neither created nor destroyed. The **continuity equation** is a mathematical statement of this fact.

To develop the continuity equation, consider a steady fluid flow represented by streamlines, as shown in Fig. 18-21a. We have shaded a **flow tube**—a small tubelike region bounded on its sides by a set of streamlines and on its ends by areas at right angles to the streamlines. We choose the flow tube to have

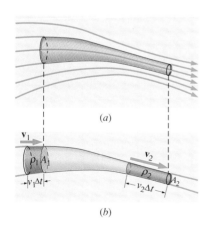

(a)

(b)

FIGURE 18-21 (a) A flow tube. In steady flow, the rate at which fluid enters the tube equals the rate at which it leaves the tube. (b) Fluid elements of equal mass entering and leaving the tube.

sufficiently small cross-sectional area that fluid velocity and other fluid properties do not vary significantly over any cross section; however, fluid properties may vary along the flow tube. Although our flow tube has no physical boundaries, it nevertheless acts like a pipe of the same shape because fluid flows *along,* not across the streamlines. In steady flow, the rate at which fluid enters the tube at its left end equals the rate at which it exits at the right; otherwise, the amount of fluid in the pipe would change and the fluid properties would not be independent of time.

Figure 18-21*b* shows a small fluid element just about to enter the flow tube, a process that will take some time Δt. Suppose the fluid is moving at speed v_1; since it takes time Δt to cross the tube end, its length is $v_1 \Delta t$. With cross-sectional area A_1, length $v_1 \Delta t$, and density ρ_1, the mass of the entering fluid element is

$$m = \rho_1 A_1 v_1 \Delta t .$$

Another fluid element is shown just about to leave the tube. Suppose it has the *same* mass m as the entering fluid element. Then it must exit the tube in the *same* time Δt, in order to keep the total mass in the tube constant. But its mass can be written

$$m = \rho_2 A_2 v_2 \Delta t .$$

Equating our two expressions for m shows that

$$\rho_1 v_1 A_1 = \rho_2 v_2 A_2 . \tag{18-4a}$$

Since the endpoints of the tube are arbitrary, we conclude that the quantity $\rho v A$ must have the same value anywhere along the flow tube:

$$\rho v A = \text{constant along a flow tube} . \quad \text{(any fluid)} \tag{18-4b}$$

What is this quantity $\rho v A$ that is constant along a flow tube? Its SI units are $(\text{kg/m}^3)(\text{m/s})(\text{m}^2)$, or simply kg/s. The quantity $\rho v A$ is therefore the **mass flow rate** or mass of fluid per unit time passing through the flow tube. Equations 18-4a and 18-4b are equivalent expressions of the continuity equation, both stating that the mass flow rate is constant along a flow tube in steady flow.

For a liquid, the density ρ is essentially constant, and the continuity equation 18-5 becomes simply

$$v A = \text{constant along a flow tube} . \quad \text{(liquid)} \tag{18-5}$$

Now the constant quantity is just $v A$, with units of $(\text{m/s})(\text{m}^2)$, or m^3/s. The quantity $v A$ is the **volume flow rate**; in a fluid of constant density, constancy of mass flow rate also implies constancy of volume flow rate because a given mass of fluid does not change volume. In the form 18-5, the continuity equation makes obvious physical sense. Where the liquid has a large cross-sectional area, it can flow relatively slowly to transport a given volume of fluid per unit time. But where the area is more constricted, the flow must be faster to carry the same volume per unit time. With a gas, obeying Equation 18-4 but not necessarily 18-5, the situation is slightly more ambiguous, as density variations also play a rôle in the continuity equation. For flow speeds below the speed of sound in a gas, it turns out that lower area implies a higher flow speed just as for a liquid. But when gas flow speed exceeds the sound speed, density changes become so great that flow speed actually decreases with lower area.

EXAMPLE 18-7	*Ausable Chasm*

In the lower part of its valley, the Ausable River in upstate New York is about 40 m wide. Under typical early summer conditions, it is 2.2 m deep and flows at 4.5 m/s. Just before it reaches Lake Champlain, the river enters Ausable Chasm, a deep gorge cut through rock (Fig. 18-22). At its narrowest, the gorge is only 3.7 m wide at the river surface. If the flow rate in the gorge is 6.0 m/s, how deep is the river at this point? Assume that the river has a rectangular cross section, with uniform flow speed over a cross section.

Solution

Writing the cross-sectional area as the product of width w and depth d, Equation 18-5 becomes

$$v_1 w_1 d_1 = v_2 w_2 d_2 .$$

Solving for the gorge depth d_2 gives

$$d_2 = \frac{v_1 w_1 d_1}{v_2 w_2} = \frac{(4.5 \text{ m/s})(40 \text{ m})(2.2 \text{ m})}{(6.0 \text{ m/s})(3.7 \text{ m})} = 18 \text{ m} ,$$

or about 60 feet!

FIGURE 18-22 The Ausable River in upstate New York cuts through a narrow chasm. To accommodate the flow, water depth in the chasm is much greater than elsewhere.

EXERCISE A 2.5-cm-diameter pipe is full of water flowing at 1.8 m/s. If the pipe narrows to 2.0-cm diameter, what is the flow speed in the narrow section?

Answer: 2.8 m/s

Some problems similar to Example 18-7: 43–45

Conservation of Energy: Bernoulli's Equation

We now turn to conservation of fluid energy. Figure 18-23 shows the same fluid element of mass m as it enters and again as it leaves a flow tube. If it enters with

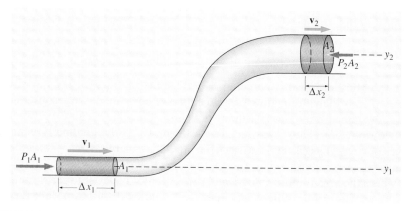

FIGURE 18-23 A flow tube showing the same fluid element entering and leaving. The work done by pressure and gravitational forces equals the change in kinetic energy of the fluid element.

speed v_1 and leaves with speed v_2, the change in its kinetic energy is

$$\Delta K = \tfrac{1}{2}m(v_2^2 - v_1^2).$$

The work-energy theorem (Equation 7-16) equates this change to the net work done on the fluid element. As the element enters the tube, it's subject to a pressure force P_1A_1 from the fluid to its left. This external force acts over the length Δx_1 of the fluid element as it enters, so it does work $W_1 = P_1A_1\Delta x_1$. Similarly, as it leaves the tube the fluid element experiences a force P_2A_2 from the fluid to its right. Because this force is opposite to the flow direction, it does negative work $W_2 = -P_2A_2\Delta x_2$. There are also pressure forces that adjacent volumes of fluid within the flow tube exert on each other, but by Newton's third law these internal forces cancel in pairs and therefore do no net work. Forces from adjacent flow tubes act at right angles to the flow, so they, too, do no net work. Finally, the fluid element rises a distance $y_2 - y_1$ as it traverses the tube; therefore gravity does negative work $W_3 = -mg(y_2 - y_1)$. (Here we assume the flow tube is narrow enough that height variations across either end of the tube are insignificant.) Summing the three contributions to the work and applying the work-energy theorem, we have

$$W_1 + W_2 + W_3 = \Delta K,$$

or

$$P_1A_1\Delta x_1 - P_2A_2\Delta x_2 - mg(y_2 - y_1) = \tfrac{1}{2}m(v_2^2 - v_1^2).$$

The quantities $A_1\Delta x_1$ and $A_2\Delta x_2$ are the volumes of the fluid element as it enters and leaves the flow, respectively. If we restrict ourselves to incompressible fluids, then those two volumes are equal. Dividing through by this common volume $V = A\Delta x$ and noting that $m/V = \rho$, our equation becomes

$$P_1 + \tfrac{1}{2}\rho v_1^2 + \rho g y_1 = P_2 + \tfrac{1}{2}\rho v_2^2 + \rho g y_2, \tag{18-6a}$$

or

$$P + \tfrac{1}{2}\rho v^2 + \rho g y = \text{constant along a flow tube}. \tag{18-6b}$$

This is called **Bernoulli's equation**, after the Swiss mathematician Daniel Bernoulli (1700–1782).

What do the terms in Bernoulli's equation mean? The quantity $\tfrac{1}{2}\rho v^2$ looks like the kinetic energy $\tfrac{1}{2}mv^2$, except it has mass per unit volume ρ instead of mass m. It's therefore the kinetic energy per unit volume, or kinetic energy density. Similarly, $\rho g y$ is the gravitational potential energy per unit volume. What about the pressure P? It, too, has the units of energy density, and represents the internal energy of the fluid. Bernoulli's equation therefore says that the total energy per unit volume of fluid is conserved as the fluid moves.

Bernoulli's equation in the form 18-6 applies to incompressible fluids. It neglects fluid friction, also called *viscosity*, that may dissipate fluid kinetic energy. It also neglects energy transfers associated with machinery such as turbines or pumps that may extract or add to the fluid's energy. Engineers often include those effects in deriving Bernoulli's equation.

18-5 APPLICATIONS OF FLUID DYNAMICS

The laws of mass and energy conservation we have just written for fluids can be used to analyze a wide variety of natural and technological phenomena involving fluid motion. As we give examples of their applications, remember that those laws are based in the same physical principles—particularly Newton's laws—that we used to describe mechanical systems.

EXAMPLE 18-8	Draining a Tank

A large, open tank is filled to a height h with liquid of density ρ. What is the speed of the liquid emerging from a small hole at the base of the tank (Fig. 18-24)?

Solution

We apply Bernoulli's equation to the emerging fluid, calculating the quantity $P + \frac{1}{2}\rho v^2 + \rho g y$ at the hole ($y = 0$) and at the tank top ($y = h$). At both these points the fluid is open to the atmosphere, so the pressure at both points is atmospheric pressure, P_a. If the tank area is large compared with the hole area, fluid at the tank top will be moving very slowly and we can make the approximation $v_{top} \simeq 0$. Then Bernoulli's equation

becomes

$$P_a + \tfrac{1}{2}\rho v_{hole}^2 = P_a + \rho g h.$$

Solving for the outflow speed at the hole gives

$$v_{hole} = \sqrt{2gh}.$$

This is the same result we would get by dropping an object through the distance h—and for the same reason: conservation of energy. Draining a gram of water from the hole is energetically equivalent to removing a gram of water from the top and dropping it through the distance h. Just as the speed of a falling object is independent of its mass, so is the speed of the liquid independent of its density.

As the liquid drains the height h decreases, and so does the flow rate. Problem 67 explores this situation further.

EXERCISE Suppose the top of the tank in Example 18-8 is sealed and pressurized to twice atmospheric pressure. What now is the outflow speed at the hole?

Answer: $\sqrt{2(P_a/\rho + gh)}$

Some problems similar to Example 18-8: 48, 49, 59, 67

FIGURE 18-24 Example 18-8. How fast does the liquid emerge from the tank?

Venturi Flows

A constriction in a pipe carrying incompressible fluid—a liquid or a gas moving at well below its sound speed—requires that flow speed increase in order to maintain constant mass flow. Such a constriction is called a **venturi**. Bernoulli's equation requires that the pressure be lower in the venturi. Example 18-9 shows how this effect is used to measure fluid flow.

| EXAMPLE 18-9 | A Venturi Flowmeter |

Figure 18-25 shows a pipe of cross sectional area A_1 with a venturi constriction of area A_2. A pressure gauge senses pressure differences between the venturi and the unconstricted pipe. The pipe carries an incompressible fluid of density ρ. Find an expression for the flow speed in the unconstricted pipe as a function of the pressure difference ΔP.

Solution

The gravitational term in Bernoulli's equation is the same in the pipe and venturi, so the equation becomes simply

$$P_1 + \tfrac{1}{2}\rho v_1^2 = P_2 + \tfrac{1}{2}\rho v_2^2,$$

where the subscripts 1 and 2 refer to the unconstricted pipe and venturi, respectively. We can relate the two speeds using the continuity equation for an incompressible fluid, Equation 18-5:

$$v_1 A_1 = v_2 A_2.$$

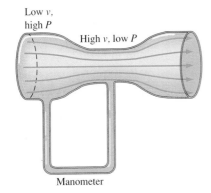

Low v, high P

High v, low P

Manometer

FIGURE 18-25 A venturi flowmeter, with a manometer used to measure the pressure difference between unconstricted pipe and venturi. Bernoulli's equation shows that the pressure difference depends on flow speed.

Solving for v_2 and using the result in Bernoulli's equation gives

$$P_1 - P_2 = \tfrac{1}{2}\rho v_2^2 - \tfrac{1}{2}\rho v_1^2 = \frac{1}{2}\rho\left(\frac{v_1 A_1}{A_2}\right)^2 - \tfrac{1}{2}\rho v_1^2$$

$$= \frac{1}{2}\rho v_1^2\left[\left(\frac{A_1}{A_2}\right)^2 - 1\right].$$

Solving for v_1 in terms of the pressure difference $\Delta P = P_1 - P_2$ then gives

$$v_1 = \sqrt{\frac{2\Delta P}{\rho[(A_1/A_2)^2 - 1]}}.$$

This is the flow speed; multiplying by the area A_1 would give the volume flow rate.

Tip

Combine Information Bernoulli's equation alone could not solve this example; instead we needed both Bernoulli's equation (conservation of energy) and the continuity equation (conservation of mass). You've frequently encountered problems like this where you need to invoke several distinct physical laws. As you attempt new problems, be sure to consider all the laws that might be applicable.

EXERCISE A 1.0-cm-diameter venturi flowmeter is inserted in a 2.0-cm-diameter pipe carrying water (density 1000 kg/m^3). What are (a) the flow speed in the pipe and (b) the volume flow rate if the pressure difference between venturi and unconstricted pipe is 17 kPa?

Answers: (a) 1.5 m/s; (b) 0.473 L/s

Some problems similar to Example 18-9: 46, 47, 51, 57, 58

The venturi phenomenon is put to good use in the carburetor, a device that mixes fuel with air to provide a combustible mixture to a gasoline engine. Liquid fuel is introduced at a venturi in the air stream heading to the engine. Lower pressure at the venturi causes fuel to be forced through a small nozzle, where it mixes thoroughly with the air (Fig. 18-26; see also Problem 65). Small gasoline engines and older cars use carburetors, but fuel injection systems have largely supplanted carburetors in modern cars.

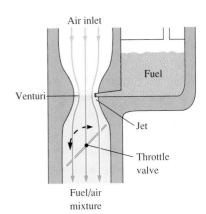

Air inlet

Fuel

Venturi

Jet

Throttle valve

Fuel/air mixture to engine

FIGURE 18-26 Simplified view of a carburetor. Pressure difference between the top of the fuel, at atmospheric pressure, and lower pressure in the venturi forces fuel into the air stream. Throttle plate controls the rate of air flow and therefore the engine speed; it's what's connected to the gas pedal in automobile engines using carburetors.

The occurrence of lower pressure with higher flow speeds, and vice versa—often called the **Bernoulli effect**—has numerous manifestations. The dirt around a prairie dog's hole is mounded up in a way that forces wind to accelerate over the hole, resulting in lower pressure above the hole (Fig. 18-27). Biologists speculate that prairie dogs have evolved this design to provide natural ventilation. Sometimes the Bernoulli effect can be strikingly counterintuitive. Figure 18-28 shows a ping-pong ball suspended by a *downward* blowing airflow in an inverted funnel. Rapid divergence of the flow results in lower speed and therefore higher pressure below the ball.

Got It!

Cholesterol buildup reduces the diameter of a small section of a major artery. Will the blood pressure in this section be higher or lower than elsewhere? (Consider the flow as being steady, even though blood flow is decidedly not.)

FIGURE 18-27 Do prairie dogs shape the entrances to their holes to provide ventilation by lowering air pressure above the hole?

FIGURE 18-28 A ping-pong ball supported by a downward-flowing air stream.

Flight and Lift

Airplanes, helicopters, and birds are supported in flight by aerodynamic forces resulting from their dynamic interaction with the air. Hydrofoil boats, water skis, and high-performance sailboards have analogous interactions with water. Projectiles such as baseballs and missiles, although not supported by the air, have their trajectories substantially modified by aerodynamic forces.

One of the simplest examples of aerodynamic **lift** is the helicopter. Its whirling blades are tilted so they force air downward as they move, just like a giant fan (Fig. 18-29). By Newton's third law, the air exerts an upward force on the blades, ultimately supporting the helicopter. An airplane wing works in the same way, except that it moves forward in a straight line instead of describing a circle. Wings are shaped to maximize the downward deflection of the air even with the wing horizontal, but in principle even a flat board would function as a

FIGURE 18-29 Helicopter blades are tilted to deflect air downward. By Newton's third law, the deflected air exerts an upward force on the blade, ultimately supporting the copter. Airflow is depicted in the frame of reference of the moving blade.

FIGURE 18-31 Vertical component (lift) of the aerodynamic force $\mathbf{F}_a$ supports the entire weight $\mathbf{F}_g$ (140 MN or 150 tons) of this A300 Airbus. Engine force $\mathbf{F}_e$ balances the horizontal component (drag) to keep the plane moving at constant speed.

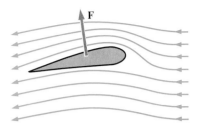

FIGURE 18-30 Flow past a wing. The wing deflects the initially horizontal flow downward; in reaction, the air exerts an upward lift force on the wing. Curved shape enhances lift, but is not essential. Note closer-spaced streamlines above the wing, indicating higher speed and therefore lower pressure.

wing if it were tilted to the oncoming air. Figure 18-30 shows the airflow around a wing. Note how the flow, initially horizontal, leaves the wing moving downward—a clear indication that the wing has exerted a downward force on the air. In a third-law pair with this downward force is the upward force that supports the airplane (Fig. 18-31).

A spinning ball provides another example of aerodynamic lift. Figure 18-32a shows the airflow around a baseball that's not spinning; the flow is symmetric on top and bottom of the ball. But if the pitcher sets the ball spinning in the direction shown in Fig. 18-32b, air dragged around the top is deflected downward. This does not happen symmetrically on the bottom because of differences in the flow pattern between the forward and backward directions. The result is a net downward air deflection and, therefore, an upward force on the ball. If the spin is reversed, the "lift" force will be downward; if the spin axis is turned vertical, the ball will veer left or right (Fig. 18-33).

Bernoulli's equation is frequently invoked to explain lift forces. It is true, as Figs. 18-30 and 18-31b suggest, that flow speeds are higher, and therefore—according to Bernoulli's equation—pressures are lower on top of a wing or a spinning ball. Forces associated with that pressure difference provide the lift, so Bernoulli's equation does help explain what's going on. But those pressure differences and the flow speeds associated with them are manifestations of a simpler underlying phenomenon—the force pairs of Newton's third law.

(a)   (b)

FIGURE 18-32 (a) Flow is symmetric around a non-spinning ball, so air passes the ball with no net deflection. Therefore there is no lift force on the ball. (b) When the ball spins it drags air with it, causing a downward air deflection and therefore giving rise to a lift force. Note also the higher flow speed and therefore lower pressure above the ball. Small curves represent turbulent eddies that form behind the ball.

FIGURE 18-33 Aerodynamic forces ($\mathbf{F}_a$) give the spinning curve ball its curved trajectory.

APPLICATION	*Wind Energy*

Bernoulli's equation states that fluid energy is conserved. If, however, we put moving machinery in a fluid flow, that machinery may add energy, as do pumps, or it may extract energy, as do windmills and other turbines (Fig. 18-34).

Where the wind is blowing with speed v, Bernoulli's equation shows that kinetic energy of fluid motion is present with density $\frac{1}{2}\rho v^2$. A wind turbine can extract fluid kinetic energy from the flow, converting it to the mechanical energy of moving machinery and ultimately to electricity.

What is the rate at which a turbine can extract energy from the wind? If the air approaching the turbine in Fig. 18-34 has speed v, then in time Δt a column of air with length $v\,\Delta t$ flows past the turbine. If the turbine sweeps out an area A, then the volume passing in time Δt is $vA\,\Delta t$. Since the kinetic energy density is $\frac{1}{2}\rho v^2$, the kinetic energy ΔK passing the turbine is

$$\Delta K = (\tfrac{1}{2}\rho v^2)(vA\,\Delta t) = \tfrac{1}{2}\rho v^3 A\,\Delta t.$$

Dividing through by $A\,\Delta t$ gives the energy per time per unit area—that is, the power per unit area available from the wind:

$$\text{Wind power per unit area} = \tfrac{1}{2}\rho v^3.$$

Unfortunately the wind turbine can't extract *all* the kinetic energy, for if it did the air would come to a complete stop behind the turbine and the pressure would build up, halting the flow. A thorough analysis shows that the maximum rate for wind energy extraction is $\frac{8}{27}\rho v^3$, amounting to about 59% of the total kinetic energy. For air (density 1.2 kg/m^3) with a wind speed of 10 m/s, this gives 356 watts for every square meter swept out by the turbine. Under ideal conditions, the best practical wind turbines can achieve 80 percent of the theoretical maximum energy extraction.

Because wind power scales as the cube of the wind speed, regions where winds are strong and steady have considerable potential for producing wind energy. In the United States those regions are concentrated near the coasts and in the Great Plains; estimates suggest that large-scale wind development could supply 20% or more of the nation's electrical energy. Thanks to intensive wind development over the past two decades, California already gets 1% of its electricity from the wind, at costs competitive with conventional sources (Fig. 18-35).

Wind is rarely constant, so wind-generated energy must either be stored somehow or used to supplant other energy sources at those times when wind is available. The effect of

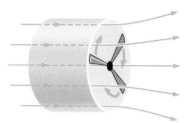

FIGURE 18-34 A set of rotating blades—a turbine—in a fluid flow. If external forces turn the turbine, then the turbine acts as a pump, doing work on the fluid and increasing fluid energy. If the fluid turns the turbine, then the turbine extracts energy from the fluid. Can you tell from the streamlines which this turbine is doing?

wind fluctuations can be minimized by connecting generators at diverse locations to a common electrical grid.

Wind generators have fewer adverse environmental effects than most other means of generating electricity. They may present aesthetic problems, especially on mountain ridges, and their mounting towers do take land area. On the other hand, activities such as farming and livestock grazing can continue even in dense "wind farms" like the one shown in Fig. 18-35.

FIGURE 18-35 "Wind farm" at Altamont Pass, California, has more than 6,000 wind turbines and produces an average power of more than 100 MW. California's total wind capacity of nearly 2 GW is the equivalent of two large nuclear or coal-fired power plants.

18-6 VISCOSITY AND TURBULENCE

Our discussion of the spinning baseball suggests that air is "dragged" by objects moving through it. This indeed happens, not only when a fluid is in motion relative to a solid object but even when it moves with different speeds on different streamlines. This phenomenon—called fluid friction or **viscosity**—ultimately arises from momentum transfers among individual molecules with components of motion perpendicular to the flow.

Viscosity is often negligible, especially when fluid is far from a solid boundary. But near such boundaries viscosity is always important because forces between fluid and boundary bring the fluid to a complete stop right at the boundary surface. It's this boundary effect that produces drag forces on objects moving through fluids—and it's the same viscous drag at the surfaces of airplane and ship propellers that exerts a force on the fluid. Without viscosity propellers would just spin uselessly and planes and ships would go nowhere.

Fluid flowing in narrow channels or pipes is always close to a solid boundary, so here viscosity is always important. The result is a nonuniform flow profile, as shown in Fig. 18-36. Viscosity is the dominant force in fluids confined to very small spaces, such as the lubricating oils separating metal surfaces in machinery. Similarly, viscosity plays a more important role in blood flow through capillaries than it does in major arteries and veins.

The importance of viscosity depends not only on the dimensions of the flow channel but also on the fluid itself. Water, for example, is relatively inviscid while molasses is extremely viscous. But again, it's a question of scale: viscosity plays only a small role in the flow of a river, but to a bacterium wiggling its flagella for propulsion, water is far more viscous than molasses dripping off a spoon.

Viscosity also plays an important role in stabilizing fluid flows that would otherwise become **turbulent**, or chaotically unsteady (Fig. 18-37). Turbulence ultimately results from the growth of waves that gain energy at the expense of the flow. When many wave modes are present at once the flow becomes completely chaotic, changing continuously in unpredictable ways. There is not yet a fully satisfactory theory of turbulence, so this area of fluid dynamics is the focus of much contemporary research. Researchers continue to find remarkable connections between the behavior of turbulent fluids and of seemingly unrelated phenomena such as the growth of crystals, the shapes of mountain ranges, and population fluctuations in ecological systems.

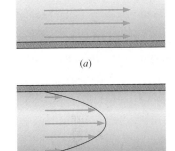

(a)

(b)

FIGURE 18-36 (a) Inviscid flow in a pipe would be uniform. (b) Viscosity reduces the flow velocity, especially near the walls, resulting in a nonuniform flow profile.

(a)   (b)

FIGURE 18-37 (a) An initially uniform flow of liquid (red area) soon becomes turbulent. (b) This turbulent flow shows a striking pattern of whirlpool-like eddies.

CHAPTER SYNOPSIS

Summary

1. **Fluid** is matter that readily deforms and flows under the influence of forces. Fluids are characterized by **density**, or mass per unit volume, and **pressure**, or force per unit area. Liquids are nearly **incompressible**, meaning liquid density hardly changes. Gases are **compressible**, capable of large density changes, but such changes generally occur only when flow speeds approach or exceed the sound speed.

2. In **hydrostatic equilibrium** there is no net force on any element of a fluid. In the absence of external forces, hydrostatic equilibrium implies uniform pressure throughout the fluid. In the presence of gravity, fluid pressure increases with depth so pressure forces balance the gravitational force; in a liquid, that increase is described by

$$P = P_0 + \rho gh,$$

   where P_0 is the surface pressure and h the depth.

3. In hydrostatic equilibrium, a pressure increase at any point is transmitted throughout the fluid, a fact known as **Pascal's law**.

4. **Buoyancy** is the upward pressure force on an object wholly or partly immersed in a fluid. The buoyancy force is equal to the weight of fluid displaced by the object—a fact known as **Archimedes' principle**. If an object is less dense than the fluid, the buoyancy force exceeds the gravitational force, and the object rises.

5. A moving fluid is characterized by its flow velocity at each point in space and time. In **steady flow** the velocity is always the same at a given point; such flow is represented by **streamlines** that mark the paths of the fluid elements. In **unsteady flow** the flow velocity varies with time as well as position.

6. The laws of conservation of mass and conservation of energy provide a simplified description of a fluid in steady flow. Both laws are applied to a narrow **flow tube**—a volume bounded by nearby streamlines. Conservation of mass results in the **continuity equation**:

$$\rho vA = \text{constant along a flow tube},$$

   where A is the tube area and ρvA the **mass flow rate**. In a liquid, or a gas with flow speed well below the sound speed, the density ρ is constant and therefore the **volume flow rate** vA remains constant along a flow tube.

   In steady, incompressible flow in the absence of viscosity or other forms of energy loss or addition, conservation of energy yields **Bernoulli's equation**:

$$P + \tfrac{1}{2}\rho v^2 + \rho gh = \text{constant along a flow tube}.$$

   The continuity equation and Bernoulli's equation together help explain a great many fluid phenomena; other phenomena, such as airplane flight, are more simply explained through the paired forces of Newton's third law.

7. Fluid friction, or **viscosity**, is especially important near fluid boundaries, particularly in narrowly confined flows. Viscosity exerts a stabilizing influence on flows that would otherwise become **turbulent**, or chaotically unstable.

Terms You Should Understand

(Pairs are closely related terms whose distinction is important; number in parentheses is chapter section where term first appears.)

fluid (introduction)
density (18-1)
compressible, incompressible (18-1)
pressure (18-1)
pascal (18-1)
hydrostatic equilibrium (18-2)
barometer, manometer (18-2)
gauge pressure (18-2)
Pascal's law (18-2)
buoyancy force (18-3)
Archimedes' principle (18-3)
streamlines (18-4)
steady flow, unsteady flow (18-4)
flow tube (18-4)
continuity equation (18-4)
mass flow rate, volume flow rate (18-4)
Bernoulli's equation (18-4)
Bernoulli effect (18-5)
lift (18-5)
viscosity (18-6)
turbulence (18-6)

Symbols You Should Recognize

P (18-1)
ρ (18-1)
Pa (18-1)

Problems You Should Be Able to Solve

calculating pressure from force and vice versa (18-1)
calculating pressure as a function of depth in liquids (18-2)
analyzing simple hydraulic systems (18-2)
determining density given apparent weight of submerged objects (18-3)
determining floating position of buoyant objects (18-3)
using the continuity equation to determine flow speeds (18-4)
using the continuity equation and Bernoulli's equation together to solve fluid dynamics problems (18-5)

Limitations to Keep in Mind

Treating matter as a continuous fluid is an approximation valid only when the spacing between molecules is much smaller than any length of interest—including the wavelength of any significant wave motion.

Bernoulli's equation applies only to incompressible flows—that is, to liquids or to gases moving at much less than the sound speed.

QUESTIONS

1. Explain the difference between hydrostatic equilibrium, steady flow, and unsteady flow.
2. Why do your ears "pop" when you drive up a mountain?
3. The cabins of commercial jet aircraft are usually pressurized to the pressure of the atmosphere at about 2 km above sea level. Why don't you feel the lower pressure on your entire body?
4. Water pressure at the bottom of the ocean arises from the weight of the overlying water. Does this mean that the water exerts pressure only in the downward direction? Explain.
5. The three containers in Fig. 18-38 are filled to the same level and are open to the atmosphere. How do the pressures at the bottoms of the three containers compare?

FIGURE 18-38 Question 5.

6. Municipal water systems often include tanks or reservoirs mounted on hills or towers. Besides water storage, what function might these reservoirs have?
7. Why is it easier to float in the ocean than in fresh water?
8. Figure 18-39 shows a cork suspended from the bottom of a sealed container of water. The container is on a turntable rotating about a vertical axis, as shown. Explain the position of the cork.

FIGURE 18-39 Question 8.

9. An ice cube is floating in a cup of water. Will the water level rise, fall, or remain the same when the cube melts?

10. Meteorologists in the United States usually report barometer readings in "inches." What are they talking about?
11. A mountain stream, frothy with entrained air bubbles, presents a serious hazard to hikers who fall into it, for they may sink in the stream where they would float in calm water. Why?
12. Why are dams thicker at the bottom than at the top?
13. It's not possible to breathe through a snorkel from a depth greater than a meter or so (Fig. 18-40). Why not?

FIGURE 18-40 Why don't snorkels work at more than a meter or so of depth (Question 13)?

14. Most humans float naturally in fresh water. Yet the body of a drowning victim generally sinks, often rising several days later after bodily decomposition has set in. What might explain this sequence of floating, sinking, and floating again?
15. A helium-filled balloon stops rising long before it reaches the "top" of the atmosphere, while a cork released from the bottom of a lake rises all the way to the surface of the water. Explain the difference between these two behaviors.
16. A barge filled with steel beams overturns in a lake, spilling its cargo. Does the water level in the lake rise, fall, or remain the same?
17. Imagine a vertical cylinder filled with water and set rotating about its axis. If pieces of wood and stone are introduced into the cylinder, where will each end up?
18. When gas in steady, subsonic flow through a tube encounters a constriction, its flow speed increases. When it flows supersonically in the same situation, flow speed decreases in the constriction. What must be happening to the gas density at the constriction in the supersonic case?
19. Under what conditions can a gas be treated as incompressible?
20. As you drive along a highway and are passed by a large truck, your car may experience a force toward the truck. Explain the origin of this force in terms of the Bernoulli effect.

FIGURE 18-41 A ball supported by air from a hair dryer. Why is it in stable equilibrium? (Question 21)

21. A ball supported by an upward-flowing air column (Fig. 18-41) is essentially in stable equilibrium; if the ball is displaced slightly in any direction, it returns to its original position. Explain. *Hint:* How do you expect the flow speed to vary with horizontal position from the center of the air column?

22. A pump is submerged at the bottom of a 200-ft-deep well. Does it take more power to pump water to the surface when the well is full of water or nearly empty? Or doesn't it matter?

23. Why do airplanes take off into the wind?

24. Is the turbine in Fig. 18-34 adding or removing energy from the flow? How can you tell?

25. Is the flow speed behind a wind turbine greater or less than the flow speed in front? Is the pressure behind the turbine greater or less than in front? Is there a violation of Bernoulli's equation here? Explain.

PROBLEMS

Section 18-1 Describing Fluids: Density and Pressure

1. The density of molasses is $1600 \ \text{kg/m}^3$. Find the mass of the molasses in a 0.75-liter jar.

2. Salad dressing is made from one part (by volume) of vinegar (density $1.0 \ \text{g/cm}^3$) to three parts olive oil (density $0.92 \ \text{g/cm}^3$). What is the average density of the dressing?

3. The density of atomic nuclei is about $10^{17} \ \text{kg/m}^3$, while the density of water is $10^3 \ \text{kg/m}^3$. Roughly what fraction of the volume of water is *not* empty space?

4. Compressed air with mass 8.8 kg is stored in a gas cylinder with a volume of $0.050 \ \text{m}^3$. (a) What is the density of the compressed air? (b) How large a volume would the same gas occupy at typical atmospheric density of $1.2 \ \text{kg/m}^3$?

5. A plant hangs from a 3.2-cm-diameter suction cup affixed to a smooth horizontal surface (Fig. 18-42). What is the maximum weight that can be suspended (a) at sea level and (b) in Denver, where atmospheric pressure is about 0.80 atm?

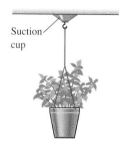

Suction cup

FIGURE 18-42 Problem 5.

6. The pressure unit **torr** is defined as the pressure that will support a column of mercury 1 mm high. Meteorologists often give barometric pressure in **inches of mercury**, defined analogously. Express each of these units in SI. The density of mercury is $1.36 \times 10^4 \ \text{kg/m}^3$.

7. Measurement of small pressure differences, for example, between the interior of a chimney and the ambient atmosphere, is often given in **inches of water**, where one inch of water is the pressure that will support a 1-in.-high water column. Express this unit in SI.

8. (a) What is the weight of a column of air with cross-sectional area $1 \ \text{m}^2$ extending from Earth's surface to the top of the atmosphere? (b) What is the weight of the entire atmosphere?

9. The fuselage of a 747 jumbo jet is roughly a cylinder 60 m long and 6 m in diameter. If the interior of the plane is pressurized to 0.75 atm, what is the net pressure force tending to separate half the cylinder from the other half when the plane is flying at 10 km, where air pressure is about 0.25 atm? (The earliest commercial jets suffered structural failure from just such forces; modern planes are better engineered.)

10. A 4300-kg circus elephant balances on one foot (Fig. 18-43). If the foot is a circle 30 cm in diameter, what pressure does it exert on the ground?

FIGURE 18-43 Problem 10.

11. A paper clip is made from wire 1.5 mm in diameter. You unbend a paper clip and push the end against the wall. What force must you exert to give a pressure of 120 atm?

12. Continuously running exhaust hoods in a university chemistry building keep the inside air pressure slightly lower than outside. A student notices that a 150-N force is necessary to start opening a 1.2 m by 2.3 m door. The door is hinged on one of its 2.3-m vertical sides, and the handle is mounted on the other side. What is the pressure difference between inside and outside? Give in pascals and as a fraction of atmospheric pressure. *Hint:* Think about torque.

13. When a couple with a total mass of 120 kg lies on a water bed, the pressure in the bed increases by 4700 Pa. What surface area of the two bodies is in contact with the bed?

14. A fully loaded Volvo station wagon has a mass of 1950 kg. If each of its four tires is inflated to a gauge pressure of 230 kPa, what is the total tire area in contact with the road?

15. The emergency escape window of a DC-9 jetliner measures 50 cm by 90 cm. The interior pressure is 0.75 atm, and the plane is at an altitude where atmospheric pressure is 0.25 atm. Is there any danger that a passenger could open the window? Answer by calculating the force needed to pull the window straight inward.

Section 18-2 Fluids at Rest: Hydrostatic Equilibrium

16. Calculate the height of a mercury column that can be supported by air at 1.0 atm pressure. Mercury's density is 1.36×10^4 kg/m^3.

17. What is the density of a fluid whose pressure increases at the rate of 100 kPa for every 6.0 m of depth?

18. A research submarine can withstand external pressures of 50 MPa when its internal pressure is 100 kPa. How deep can it dive?

19. Scuba equipment provides the diver with air at the same pressure as the surrounding water. But at pressures greater than about 1 MPa, the nitrogen in air becomes dangerously narcotic. At what depth does nitrogen narcosis become a hazard?

20. Hot gases rising in a chimney produce a slightly lower air pressure in the chimney, which in turn ensures that these gases can't escape into the surrounding building. The pressure difference, called draft, is often measured with a manometer as shown in Fig. 18-44. If the difference in water levels in the manometer tube is 0.04 in. (typical of an oil furnace), by how much does the chimney pressure differ from atmospheric pressure?

21. A vertical tube open at the top contains 5.0 cm of oil (density 0.82 g/cm^3) floating on 5.0 cm of water. Find the *gauge* pressure at the bottom of the tube.

22. A vertical tube 1.0 cm in diameter and open at the top contains 5.0 g of oil (density 0.82 g/cm^3) floating on 5.0 g of water. Find the *gauge* pressure (a) at the oil-water interface and (b) at the bottom.

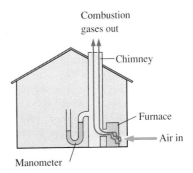

FIGURE 18-44 Water manometer used on a chimney (Problem 20).

23. A 1500-m-wide dam holds back a lake 95 m deep. What force does the water exert on the dam?

24. Show that the force on the wall in Example 18-2 can be found by multiplying the wall area by the average of the pressures at top and bottom of the wall. Why does this work?

25. A U-shaped tube open at both ends contains water and a quantity of oil occupying a 2.0-cm length of the tube, as shown in Fig. 18-45. If the oil's density is 0.82 times that of water, what is the height difference h?

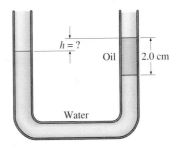

FIGURE 18-45 Problem 25.

26. A child attempts to drink water through a 100-cm-long straw, but finds that the water rises only 75 cm. By how much has the child reduced the pressure in her mouth below atmospheric pressure?

27. Barometric pressure in the eye of a hurricane is 0.91 atm (27.2 inches of mercury). How does the level of the ocean surface under the eye compare with that under a distant fair-weather region where the pressure is 1.0 atm?

28. A hydraulic cylinder moving a robotic arm has a diameter of 5.0 cm and can exert a maximum force of 5.6 kN. (a) What pressure must the hydraulic lines be capable of withstanding? (b) The cylinder at the other end of the hydraulic system has a 1.0-cm diameter. What force must be applied to it to get the maximum force out of the cylinder driving the arm?

29. A garage lift has a 45-cm-diameter piston supporting the load. Compressed air with a maximum pressure of

500 kPa is applied to a small piston at the other end of the hydraulic system. What is the maximum mass the lift can support?

30. Figure 18-46 shows a hydraulic lift operated by pumping fluid into the hydraulic system. The large cylinder is 40 cm in diameter, while the small tube leaving the pump is 1.7 cm in diameter. A total load of 2800 kg is raised 2.3 m at a constant rate. (a) What volume of fluid passes through the pump? (b) What is the pressure at the pump outlet? (c) How much work does the pump do? (d) If the lifting takes 40 s, what is the pump power? Neglect pressure variations with height, and neglect also the weight of the fluid raised.

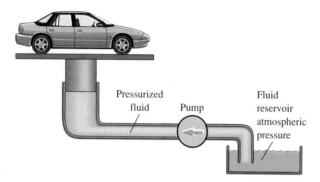

FIGURE 18-46 Problem 30 (diameters are not to scale).

Section 18-3 Archimedes' Principle and Buoyancy

31. On land, the most massive concrete block you can carry is 25 kg. How massive a block could you carry underwater, if the density of concrete is 2300 kg/m³?
32. A 5.4-g jewel has an apparent weight of 32 mN when submerged in water. Could the jewel be diamond (density 3.51 g/cm³)?
33. The density of styrofoam is 160 kg/m³. What per cent error is introduced by weighing a styrofoam block in air, which exerts an upward buoyancy force, rather than in vacuum? The density of air is 1.2 kg/m³.
34. Archimedes purportedly used his principle to verify that the king's crown was pure gold, by weighing the crown while it was submerged in water (see Fig. 18-14). Suppose the crown's actual weight was 25.0 N. What would be its apparent weight if it were made of (a) pure gold and (b) 75% gold and 25% silver, by volume? The densities of gold, silver, and water are 19.3 g/cm³, 10.5 g/cm³, and 1.00 g/cm³, respectively.
35. A partially full beer bottle with interior diameter 52 mm is floating upright in water, as shown in Fig. 18-47. A drinker takes a swig and replaces the bottle in the water, where it now floats 28 mm higher than before. How much beer did the drinker drink?

FIGURE 18-47 Problem 35.

36. A glass beaker measures 10 cm high by 4.0 cm in diameter. Empty, it floats in water with one-third of its height submerged. How many 15-g rocks can be placed in the beaker before it sinks?
37. A typical supertanker has mass 2.0×10^6 kg and carries twice that much oil. If 9.0 m of the ship is submerged when it's empty, what is the minimum water depth needed for it to navigate when full? Assume the sides of the ship are vertical.
38. A balloon contains gas of density ρ_g and is to lift a mass M, including the balloon but not the gas. Show that the minimum mass of gas required is

$$m = \frac{M\rho_g}{\rho_a - \rho_g},$$

where ρ_a is the atmospheric density.
39. (a) How much helium (density 0.18 kg/m³) is needed to lift a balloon carrying two people in a basket, if the total mass of people, basket, and balloon (but not gas) is 280 kg? (b) Repeat for a hot air balloon, whose air density is 10% less than that of the surrounding atmosphere.
40. A 55-kg swimmer climbs onto a styrofoam block whose density is 160 kg/m³. If the water level comes right to the top of the styrofoam, what is the block's volume?

Sections 18-4 and 18-5 Fluid Dynamics and Applications

41. A fluid is flowing steadily, roughly from left to right. At left it is flowing rapidly; it then slows down, and finally speeds up again. Its final speed at right is not as great as its initial speed at left. Sketch a streamline pattern that could represent this flow.
42. Show that pressure has the units of energy density.
43. A typical mass flow rate for the Mississippi River is 1.8×10^7 kg/s. Find (a) the volume flow rate and (b) the flow speed in a region where the river is 2.0 km wide and an average of 6.1 m deep.
44. A fire hose 10 cm in diameter delivers water at the rate of 15 kg/s. The hose terminates in a nozzle 2.5 cm in diameter. What are the flow speeds (a) in the hose and (b) in the nozzle?

45. A typical human aorta, or main artery from the heart, is 1.8 cm in diameter and carries blood at a speed of 35 cm/s. What will be the flow speed around a clot that reduces the flow area by 80%?

46. If the blood pressure in the unobstructed artery of the previous problem is 16 kPa gauge (about 120 mm of mercury, in the unit commonly reported by doctors), what will it be at the clot? The density of blood is 1060 kg/m³. (Too low a pressure can actually collapse the artery, momentarily cutting off blood flow.)

47. In Fig. 18-48 a horizontal pipe of cross-sectional area A is joined to a lower pipe of cross-sectional area $\frac{1}{2}A$. The entire pipe is full of liquid with density ρ, and the left end is at atmospheric pressure P_a. A small open tube extends upward from the lower pipe. Find the height h_2 of liquid in the small tube (a) when the right end of the lower pipe is closed, so the liquid is in hydrostatic equilibrium, and (b) when the liquid flows with speed v in the upper pipe.

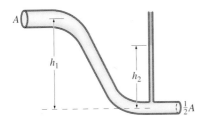

FIGURE 18-48 Problem 47.

48. A can of height h is full of water. At what height y should a small hole be cut so the water initially goes as far horizontally as it does vertically, as shown in Fig. 18-49?

FIGURE 18-49 Problem 48.

49. The water in a garden hose is at a gauge pressure of 140 kPa and is moving at negligible speed. The hose terminates in a sprinkler consisting of many small holes. What is the maximum height reached by the water emerging from the holes?

50. Water emerges from a faucet of diameter d_0 in steady, near vertical flow with speed v_0. Show that the diameter of the falling water column is given by $d = d_0[v_0^2/(v_0^2 + 2gh)]^{1/4}$, where h is the distance below the faucet (Fig. 18-50).

FIGURE 18-50 The diameter of the water column varies as the fourth root of the distance from the faucet (Problem 50).

51. The venturi flowmeter shown in Fig. 18-51 is used to measure the flow rate of water in a solar collector system. The flowmeter is inserted in a pipe with diameter 1.9 cm; at the venturi of the flowmeter the diameter is reduced to 0.64 cm. The manometer tube contains oil with density 0.82 times that of water. If the difference in oil levels on the two sides of the manometer tube is 1.4 cm, what is the volume flow rate?

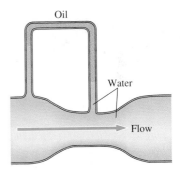

FIGURE 18-51 Problem 51.

52. A drinking straw 20 cm long and 3.0 mm in diameter stands vertically in a cup of juice 8.0 cm in diameter. A section of straw 6.5 cm long extends above the juice. A child sucks on the straw, and the level of juice in the glass begins dropping at 0.20 cm/s. (a) By how much does the pressure in the child's mouth differ from atmospheric pressure? (b) What is the greatest height from which the child could drink, assuming this same mouth pressure?

Paired Problems

(Both problems in a pair involve the same principles and techniques. If you can get the first problem, you should be able to solve the second one.)

53. A steel drum has volume 0.23 m³ and mass 16 kg. Will it float in water when filled with (a) water or (b) gasoline (density 860 kg/m³)? Neglect the thickness of the steel.

54. A 260-g circular pan 20 cm in diameter has straight sides 6.0 cm high and is made from metal of negligible thickness. To what maximum depth can the pan be filled with water and still float on water?

55. A spherical rubber balloon with mass 0.85 g and diameter 30 cm is filled with helium (density 0.18 kg/m³). How many 1.0-g paper clips can you hang from the balloon before it loses its buoyancy?

56. A string of negligible diameter has mass per unit length 1.4 g/m. You tie a 3-m-long piece of the string to a spherical helium balloon 23 cm in diameter and find that the balloon floats with 1.8 m of string off the floor. Find the combined mass of the balloon and helium.

57. Water at a pressure of 230 kPa is flowing at 1.5 m/s through a pipe, when it encounters an obstruction where the pressure drops by 5%. What fraction of the pipe's area is obstructed?

58. A venturi flowmeter in an oil pipeline has a radius half that of the pipe. The flow speed in the unconstricted flow is 1.9 m/s. If the pressure difference between the unconstricted flow and the venturi is 16 kPa, what is the density of the oil?

59. Find an expression for the volume flow rate from the siphon shown in Fig. 18-52, assuming the siphon area A is much less than the tank area.

FIGURE 18-52 Problems 59, 60.

60. (a) Find the initial siphon flow speed in Fig. 18-52 if the tank is sealed, with its top at only one-fourth of atmospheric pressure. Answer in terms of atmospheric pressure P_a, liquid density ρ, height h, and g. (b) What is the maximum distance between the bend at the top of the siphon

and the liquid level in the tank for which the siphon will work under these conditions, assuming the liquid is water? (Give a numerical value here.)

Supplementary Problems

61. A 1.0-m-diameter tank is filled with water to a depth of 2.0 m and is open to the atmosphere at the top. The water drains through a 1.0-cm-diameter pipe at the bottom; that pipe then joins a 1.5-cm-diameter pipe open to the atmosphere, as shown in Fig. 18-53. Find (a) the flow speed in the narrow section and (b) the water height in the *sealed* vertical tube shown.

FIGURE 18-53 Problem 61.

62. How massive an object can be supported by a 5.0-cm-diameter suction cup mounted on a vertical wall, if the coefficient of friction between cup and wall is 0.72? Assume normal atmospheric pressure.

63. Figure 18-54 shows a simplified diagram of a Pitot tube, used for measuring aircraft speeds. The tube is mounted on the underside of the aircraft wing with opening A at right angles to the flow and opening B pointing into the flow. The gauge prevents airflow through the tube. Use Bernoulli's equation to show that the air speed relative to the wing is given by $v = \sqrt{2\Delta P/\rho}$, where ΔP is the pressure difference between the tubes and ρ is the density of air. *Hint:* The flow must be stopped at B, but continues past A with its normal speed.

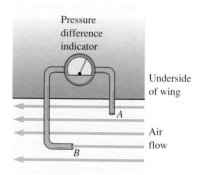

FIGURE 18-54 Problem 63.

64. A ship's hull has a V-shaped cross section, as shown in Fig. 18-55. The ship has vertical height h_0 from keel to deck and a total length ℓ perpendicular to the plane of Fig. 18-54. Empty, the hull extends underwater to a depth h_1, as shown. Find an expression for the maximum load the ship can carry, in terms of the water density ρ and the quantities h_0, h_1, ℓ, and θ shown in the figure.

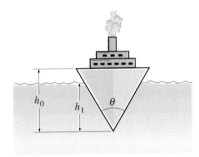

FIGURE 18-55 Problems 64, 72.

65. With its throttle valve wide open, an automobile carburetor has a throat diameter of 2.4 cm. With each revolution, the engine draws 0.50 L of air through the carburetor. At an engine speed of 3000 rpm, what are (a) the volume flow rate, (b) the airflow speed, and (c) the difference between atmospheric pressure and air pressure in the carburetor throat? The density of air is 1.2 kg/m³.

66. A wind turbine has a blade diameter of 65 m. What is the theoretical maximum power output of this turbine in winds of (a) 10 m/s and (b) 15 m/s? (c) If the machine actually achieves 50% of its theoretical maximum output, how many such turbines would be needed to displace a 1-GW nuclear power plant, assuming an average wind speed of 12 m/s?

67. A can of height h and cross-sectional area A_0 is initially full of water. A small hole of area $A_1 \ll A_0$ is cut in the bottom of the can. Find an expression for the time it takes all the water to drain from the can. *Hint:* Call the water depth y, use the continuity equation to relate dy/dt to the outflow speed at the hole, then integrate.

68. A pencil is weighted so it floats vertically with length ℓ submerged. It's pushed vertically downward without being totally submerged, then released. Show that it undergoes simple harmonic motion with period $T = 2\pi\sqrt{\ell/g}$.

69. A circular pan of liquid (density ρ) is centered on a horizontal turntable rotating with angular speed ω. Its axis coincides with the rotation axis, as shown in Fig. 18-56. Atmospheric pressure is P_a. Find expressions for (a) the pressure at the bottom of the pan and (b) the height of the liquid surface as functions of the distance r from the axis, given that the height at the center is h_0.

FIGURE 18-56 Problem 69.

70. Density and pressure in Earth's atmosphere are proportional: $\rho = P/h_0 g$, where h_0 is a constant with the approximate value 8200 m and g is the acceleration of gravity. (a) Integrate Equation 18-2 for this case to show that atmospheric pressure as a function of height h above the surface is given by $P = P_0 e^{-h/h_0}$, where P_0 is the surface pressure. (b) At what height will the pressure have dropped to half its surface value?

71. (a) Use the result of the preceding problem to express Earth's atmospheric density as a function of height (this is simple). (b) Use the result of (a) to find the height below which half of Earth's atmospheric mass lies (this will require integration).

72. Find the center of buoyancy of the ship shown in Fig. 18-55.

PART 2 Cumulative Problems

1. A cylindrical log of total mass M and uniform diameter d has an uneven mass distribution that causes it to float in a vertical position, as shown in Fig. 1. (a) Find an expression for the length ℓ of the submerged portion of the log when it is floating in equilibrium, in terms of M, d, and the water density ρ. (b) If the log is displaced vertically from its equilibrium position and released, it will undergo simple harmonic motion. Find an expression for the period of this motion, neglecting viscosity and other frictional effects.

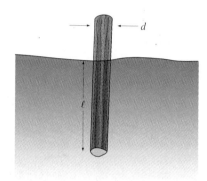

FIGURE 1 Cumulative Problem 1.

2. A cable of total mass m and length ℓ hangs vertically, with a mass M attached to its bottom end, as shown in Fig. 2. The mass is given a sudden sideways blow that starts a low-amplitude transverse pulse propagating up the cable. Show that the time it takes the pulse to reach the top of the cable is

$$t = 2\left(\sqrt{\frac{(m + M)\ell}{mg}} - \sqrt{\frac{M\ell}{mg}}\right).$$

FIGURE 2 Cumulative Problem 2.

3. Let P_0 and ρ_0 be the atmospheric pressure and density at Earth's surface. Assume that the ratio P/ρ is the same throughout the atmosphere (this implies that the temperature is uniform). Show that the pressure a vertical height z above the surface is given by $P(z) = P_0 e^{-\rho_0 gz/P_0}$, for z much less than Earth's radius (this amounts to neglecting Earth's curvature, and thus taking g to be constant).

4. A piece of rope of length ℓ and mass m has its two ends spliced together to form a continuous loop. The loop is set spinning at so high a rate that it forms a circle with essentially uniform tension. It is then placed in contact with the ground, where it rolls, without slipping, like a rigid hoop. The loop is rolling on level ground when it rolls over a stick that produces a small distortion (see Fig. 3). As a result, two pulses, initially coinciding, propagate along the loop in opposite directions. (a) Where will they again coincide? (b) Through what angle will the loop have rotated while the pulses are separated?

FIGURE 3 Cumulative Problem 4.

5. A U-shaped tube containing liquid is mounted on a table that tilts back and forth through a slight angle, as shown in Fig. 4. The diameter of the tube is much less than either the height of its arms or their separation. When the table is rocked very slowly or very rapidly, nothing particularly dramatic happens. But when the rocking takes place at a few times per second, the liquid level in the tube oscillates violently, with maximum amplitude at a rocking frequency of 1.7 Hz. Explain what is going on, and find the total length of the liquid including both vertical and horizontal portions.

FIGURE 4 Cumulative Problem 5.

Part Three

Thermodynamics

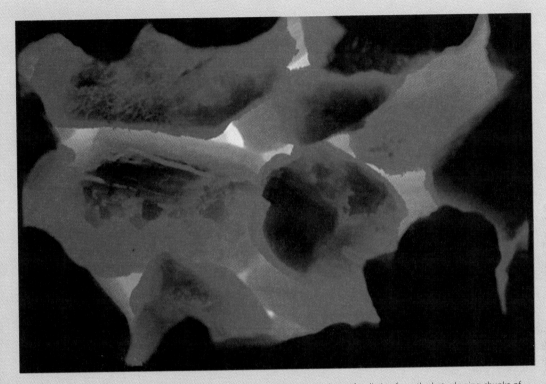

Coal burns, releasing its stored chemical energy as heat—here largely in the form of radiation from the hot, glowing chunks of coal. Burning coal supplies much of the world's electrical energy, as electric power plants convert a fraction of the heat released into useful work. Carbon dioxide from combustion of coal affects heat transfer in Earth's atmosphere, causing the global warming that scientists now believe is attributable to human activities. All these processes—heat transfer, conversion of thermal energy to useful work, and climate change—are governed by the laws of thermodynamics.

Without the Sun's heat, the Earth would be a lifeless, frozen rock. Without the heat from burning fuels, we humans would be confined to the tropics. Nearly all our transportation systems use engines driven by the heat released in combustion. Even our bodies could not function without mechanisms to regulate the flow of heat. The study of heat and temperature, and their connection with the all important concept of energy, comprises the branch of physics called thermodynamics. The next four chapters probe the fundamental physics and many practical applications of thermodynamics.

19 Temperature and Heat

Thermogram of a house, taken with an infrared scanning device, shows regions of greatest heat loss in red and yellow, lowest in blue and black. Understanding heat flow allows engineers to design systems that keep buildings comfortable and helps scientists predict the effect of human activities on Earth's climate.

The next four chapters deal with the physics of heat, temperature, and related phenomena. Our own bodies provide a qualitative sense of what it means for things to be "hot" or "cold." Here we'll quantify this sense and explore the behavior of matter under different thermal conditions. And we will learn something our sense of temperature could never tell us—namely, how thermal phenomena reflect the laws of mechanics operating on a microscopic scale.

19-1 MACROSCOPIC AND MICROSCOPIC DESCRIPTIONS

Some physical properties—for example, mass—apply equally to microscopic objects such as atoms and molecules and to macroscopic objects such as cars, gas cylinders, and planets. But others—for example, temperature and pressure—have no meaning on a microscopic scale. We speak of the temperature and pressure of air, but it makes no sense to ask about the temperature or pressure of an individual air molecule. The study of temperature, heat, and related macroscopic properties comprises the branch of physics called **thermodynamics**.

The thermodynamic behavior of matter is determined by the behavior of its constituent atoms and molecules in response to the laws of mechanics. **Statistical mechanics** is the branch of physics that relates the macroscopic description of matter to the underlying microscopic processes. Historically, thermodynamics was developed before the atomic theory of matter was well established. The subsequent explanation of thermodynamics in terms of statistical mechanics—the mechanics of atoms and molecules—was a triumph for classical physics. At the same time, the few thermodynamic phenomena that could not be explained successfully with classical physics helped point the way to the development of the quantum theory. In our study of thermal phenomena, we will interweave the macroscopic and microscopic descriptions to provide the fullest understanding of both viewpoints.

19-2 TEMPERATURE AND THERMODYNAMIC EQUILIBRIUM

Take a bottle of soda from the refrigerator and leave it on the kitchen counter. Eventually it reaches room temperature and then stays there. You don't need a scientific definition of temperature to recognize this; your sense of touch suffices to tell you that the soda's temperature eventually stops changing.

The key point here is that the soda and the room have reached a kind of equilibrium—not the static equilibrium of force balance that we explored in Chapter 14, but a **thermodynamic equilibrium**. We define this new type of equilibrium by saying that when two systems—in this case the soda bottle and the surrounding air—are placed together until no further change occurs in any macroscopic property, then the two have reached thermodynamic equilibrium with each other. When we use the term "equilibrium" in the next four chapters, we'll always mean thermodynamic equilibrium.

The concept of thermodynamic equilibrium does not require a prior notion of temperature. To determine whether two systems are in equilibrium, we can consider *any* macroscopic properties. Typical properties include length, volume, pressure, and electrical resistance, as well as temperature. If any macroscopic property changes when two systems are placed together, then the systems were not originally in thermodynamic equilibrium. Once changes cease, then the systems have reached equilibrium.

We've used the phrase "placed together" to describe arranging two systems so they can come to thermodynamic equilibrium. A more precise phrase would be "placed in *thermal contact*." Two systems are in **thermal contact** if heating one

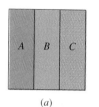

(a)   (b)

FIGURE 19-1 (a) Systems A and C are each in thermal contact with B, but not with each other, and both A and C have reached thermodynamic equilibrium with B. (b) If A and C are put in thermal contact, their macroscopic properties don't change—showing that A and C were already in thermodynamic equilibrium.

FIGURE 19-2 The coil at the center of this thermostat is a bimetallic strip that bends with increasing temperature, actuating a switch that controls a furnace.

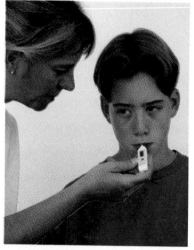

of them results in macroscopic changes in the other. For example, put two metal cups of water in contact, and place a heater in one of them; the water in both cups gets hotter. In that case the cups are in thermal contact. Do the same with styrofoam cups, or separate the metal cups with a layer of styrofoam, and heating one cup has little effect on the other. In that case the two systems are **thermally insulated**. Thermal contact need not imply direct physical contact and—as the styrofoam cups show—physical contact alone may not ensure thermal contact.

Using the concept of thermodynamic equilibrium, we can now define quantitatively what we mean by temperature. We first state what it means for two systems to have the same temperature:

> Two systems have the same temperature if they are in thermodynamic equilibrium.

Conversely, two systems that are not in thermodynamic equilibrium do not have the same temperature.

A simple experimental fact makes it possible to compare systems that aren't in thermal contact. Consider two systems A and C in thermal contact with a third system B, but not with each other (Fig. 19-1a). If we wait until A and C are both in thermodynamic equilibrium with B, then bring A and C into contact (Fig. 19-1b), we find that no further changes occur—indicating that A and C are already in equilibrium. This fact is so fundamental to the rest of thermodynamics that it is called the **zeroth law of thermodynamics**:

> *Zeroth law of thermodynamics: If two systems A and C each are in thermodynamic equilibrium with system B, then A and C are in thermodynamic equilibrium with each other.*

19-3 MEASURING TEMPERATURE

Rephrased in terms of temperature, the zeroth law says that if system A has the same temperature as system B, and system B has the same temperature as system C, then A and C have the same temperature. This property allows us to make quantitative measurements of temperature.

A **thermometer** is a system with some conveniently observed macroscopic property that changes with temperature. The length of the mercury column indicates temperature in a mercury thermometer. A strip made of two different metals bends when heated, turning the indicating needle on a dial-type thermometer or closing a switch that starts a furnace (Fig. 19-2). Electrical resistance has long been used in science and engineering to measure temperature and is rapidly replacing mercury in medical and other applications (Fig. 19-3).

To use a thermometer, we simply put it in contact with the system whose temperature we're trying to measure and let the two come to thermodynamic equilibrium. The value of whatever macroscopic property has changed then gives a quantitative indication of temperature. The zeroth law assures us that this process is consistent, in that two systems for which the thermometer gives the same reading must have the same temperature.

FIGURE 19-3 An electronic digital fever thermometer. For this thermometer, electrical resistance is the macroscopic property that changes with temperature.

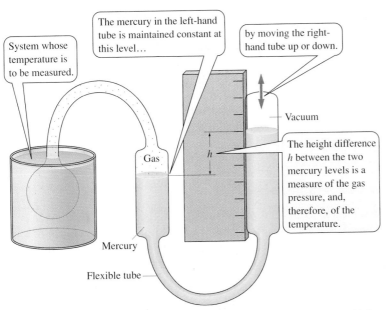

FIGURE 19-4 A constant-volume gas thermometer. The gas pressure increases with increasing temperature and decreases with decreasing temperature. The closed tube at right is raised or lowered to keep the mercury level in the left-hand tube constant, thus maintaining constant gas volume. The height difference h between the mercury levels is then a measure of gas pressure and, therefore, of temperature.

Gas Thermometers and the Kelvin Scale

We need a standard against which to calibrate different types of thermometers. Gas thermometers—using either the pressure or the volume of a gas to indicate temperature—operate over an extremely wide temperature range and are therefore used to define the temperature scale.

Figure 19-4 shows a **constant-volume gas thermometer**, whose temperature indication is the pressure of gas held at constant volume. Temperature is taken to be a linear function of the gas pressure. Two points are needed to define a linear function. One point corresponds to zero gas pressure in the thermometer, and we define the temperature at that point to be zero (see Fig. 19-5). The second point is established by the **triple point** of water—the unique temperature at which solid, liquid, and gas phases of water can coexist in equilibrium (more on the triple point in Chapter 20). The SI temperature unit, the **kelvin** (symbol K; *not* "degrees kelvin" or °K), is defined by setting the triple point at exactly 273.16 K. The temperature of a constant-volume gas thermometer is then

$$T = 273.16 \frac{P}{P_3}, \tag{19-1}$$

where P is the thermometer pressure at an arbitrary temperature T and P_3 its pressure at the triple point (see Fig. 19-5).

Since a gas cannot have negative pressure, the zero of the kelvin scale represents an absolute lower limit on temperature, and is called **absolute zero**. We'll explore the meaning of absolute zero further in Chapter 22. Figure 19-6 shows some important physical situations on the kelvin scale.

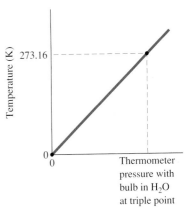

FIGURE 19-5 Kelvin temperature scale defined using a constant-volume gas thermometer.

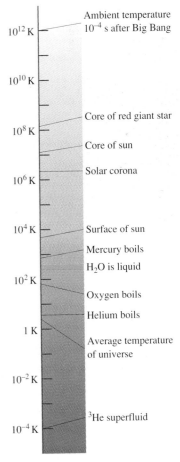

FIGURE 19-6 Some physical processes on the kelvin scale. Chart is logarithmic to display a wide temperature range. Because of the logarithmic scale, it's not possible to show absolute zero on the diagram.

What kind of gas should we use in our thermometer? It doesn't matter. That's the beauty of gas thermometry, and the reason it's used to set the temperature scale. What is important is the amount of gas: experimentally, we find that *all* gases behave exactly the same way as the quantity of gas in the thermometer becomes arbitrarily small (we'll see why in the next chapter). Thus Equation 19-1 is precisely valid only in the limit as the amount of gas shrinks to zero. But we don't really need to reach that limit; it suffices to take several measurements, using decreasing amounts of gas in each, and then extrapolate the ratio P/P_3 in Equation 19-1 to the value it would have as the amount of gas becomes arbitrarily small.

Other Temperature Scales

Other scales in common use include the Celsius (°C), Fahrenheit (°F), and Rankine (°R) scales (Fig. 19-7), although the latter two are largely limited to the United States. One Celsius degree represents the same temperature difference as one kelvin, but the zero of the Celsius scale occurs at 273.15 K, so

$$T_C = T - 273.15 , \tag{19-2}$$

where T_C is the Celsius temperature and T the temperature in kelvins. The Celsius scale was chosen so the melting point of ice at standard atmospheric pressure—the ice point—is at exactly 0°C, while the boiling point of water at standard atmospheric pressure—the steam point—is at 100°C. The triple point of water occurs at 0.01°C, which accounts for the 273.15 difference between the kelvin and Celsius scales as well as for the difference of 0.01 in the constants of Equations 19-1 and 19-2. Equation 19-2 shows that absolute zero occurs at -273.15°C.

The Fahrenheit scale, which is part of the British system of units, is defined with the ice point at 32°F and the steam point at 212°F (Fig. 19-7). As a result, the relation between the Fahrenheit and Celsius scales is

$$T_F = \tfrac{9}{5}T_C + 32 . \tag{19-3}$$

FIGURE 19-7 Relations among the four temperature scales.

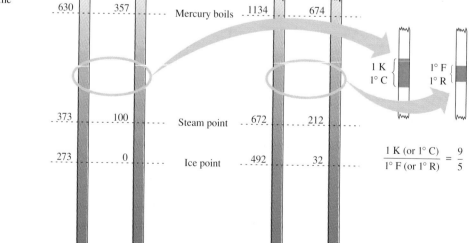

The Rankine scale is often used in engineering work in the United States. A Rankine degree is the same size as a Fahrenheit degree, but the zero of the Rankine scale coincides with the zero of the kelvin scale, so 0°R is absolute zero.

EXAMPLE 19-1	*Temperature Scales*

What is normal body temperature (98.6°F) on the Celsius and kelvin scales? If you have a fever of 101.6°F, by how much has your temperature risen on each of these scales?

Solution
Solving Equation 19-3 for T_C gives

$$T_C = \tfrac{5}{9}(T_F - 32) = \tfrac{5}{9}(98.6 - 32.0) = 37.0°C.$$

Then Equation 19-2 gives the kelvin temperature:

$$T = T_C + 273.2 = 310.2 \text{ K}.$$

A kelvin and a degree Celsius are the same size, and are both larger than a degree Fahrenheit by the factor $\tfrac{9}{5}$, so a rise of 3.0°F is equivalent to a rise of

$$\frac{3.0}{9/5} = 1.7°C = 1.7 \text{ K}.$$

EXERCISE A meteorologist on a Canadian radio station reports a high temperature of 24°C. What is the corresponding Fahrenheit temperature?

Answer: 75°F

Some problems similar to Example 19-1: 2–8

19-4 TEMPERATURE AND HEAT

A lighted match will burn your finger, yet it wouldn't provide much heat in a cold room. A large vat of water, although much cooler than the match, would do a better job heating the room. This example shows our intuitive sense of the difference between temperature and heat: Heat measures an *amount* of "something," while temperature measures the *strength* of that "something."

What is that "something"? Before the early 1800s, heat was considered a material fluid, called **caloric**, that flowed from hot bodies to colder ones. But observations made by the American-born scientist Benjamin Thompson in the late 1700s began to shed doubt on the caloric theory. Thompson was appointed director of the Bavarian arsenal, where he supervised the boring of cannon. Thompson recognized that essentially limitless amounts of heat could be produced in the boring process, and he concluded that heat could not be a conserved fluid. Instead, he suggested, heating was associated with mechanical work done by the boring tool.

In the half-century following Thompson's observations, the caloric theory gradually faded in popularity as a series of experiments confirmed the association between heating and mechanical energy. These experiments culminated in the work of the British physicist and brewer James Joule (1818–1889), who explored the relation between heat and mechanical, electrical, and chemical energy. In 1843, Joule quantified the relation between heat and energy, bringing thermal phenomena under the powerful conservation-of-energy law. In recognition of this major synthesis in physics, the SI unit of energy is named after Joule (Fig. 19-8). In Chapter 21 we will explore in detail the relation between heat and energy, and will show Joule's experiment in Fig. 21-2.

Our everyday experience of heat is nearly always associated with the movement of energy from one body to another. We rarely make statements about the actual amount of "heat" in an object—we're concerned instead that the temperature be appropriate. We want the furnace to transfer energy to our house in the winter and are satisfied when the house reaches a certain temperature, not when

FIGURE 19-8 In SI-based Australia, energy content of foods is given in joules rather than calories.

it contains a certain amount of "heat." The scientific definition of heat reflects this natural inclination to think of heat as energy in transit:

> Heat is energy being transferred from one object to another because of a temperature difference alone.

Strictly speaking, the word **heat** refers only to energy in transit. Once heat has been transferred to an object, we say that the **internal energy** of the object has increased, but not that it contains more heat. This distinction reflects the fact that processes other than heating—such as the transfer of mechanical or electrical energy—can also change an object's temperature. The next chapter explores this relation between heat and internal energy.

19-5 HEAT CAPACITY AND SPECIFIC HEAT

Experimentally, we find the heat ΔQ transferred to an object and the resulting change ΔT in the object's temperature are directly proportional. We write

$$\Delta Q = C\Delta T, \qquad (19\text{-}4)$$

where C is called the **heat capacity** of the object. Since heat is a measure of energy transfer, its unit is the joule, and therefore the units of heat capacity are J/K. The heat capacity C applies to a specific object and depends on its mass and on the substance from which it's made. We characterize different substances in terms of **specific heat** c, or heat capacity per unit mass. The heat capacity of an object is then the product of its mass and specific heat, so we can write

$$\Delta Q = mc\Delta T. \qquad (19\text{-}5)$$

The SI units of specific heat are J/kg·K. Figure 19-9 illustrates the difference between heat capacity and specific heat, while Table 19-1 lists specific heats of common materials.

Historically, thermodynamic phenomena were first studied before scientists knew the relation between heat and energy. Consequently other units were

Heat capacity
The heat capacity C of the iguana is the energy ΔQ per unit temperature change that must be transferred to the *whole iguana* to raise its temperature:

$C = \dfrac{\Delta Q}{\Delta T}$ (SI units: J/K)

Specific Heat
The specific heat c is the energy ΔQ per unit temperature change that must be transferred to the iguana *per unit mass* to raise its temperature:

$c = \dfrac{\Delta Q}{m\Delta T}$ (SI units: J/kg·K)

c is a property not of this particular iguana but of the material–mostly water–from which it's made.

FIGURE 19-9 The difference between heat capacity and specific heat, as exemplified by a Galapagos marine iguana. These cold-blooded organisms forage in cold shore waters, and to warm up they emerge periodically and bask on the hot black rocks of the shore.

TABLE 19-1 *Specific Heats of Some Common Materials**

	Specific Heat, c	
Substance	**SI Units: J/kg·K**	**cal/g·°C, kcal/kg·°C, or Btu/lb·°F**
Aluminum	900	0.215
Copper	386	0.0923
Iron	447	0.107
Glass	753	0.18
Mercury	140	0.033
Steel	502	0.12
Stone (granite)	840	0.20
Water:		
Liquid	4184	1.00
Ice, −10°C	2050	0.49
Wood	1400	0.33

* Temperature range 0°C to 100°C except as noted.

defined for heat. The **calorie** (cal) was defined as the heat needed to raise the temperature of one gram of water from 14.5°C to 15.5°; consequently, the specific heat of water in this temperature range is 1 cal/g·°C. Several different definitions of the calorie exist today, based on different methods for establishing the heat-energy equivalence. In this book we use the so-called thermochemical calorie, defined as exactly 4.184 J. The "calorie" used in describing the energy content of foods is actually a kilocalorie. In the English system, still widely used in engineering in the United States, the unit of heat is the **British thermal unit** (Btu). One Btu is the amount of heat needed to raise the temperature of one pound of water from 63°F to 64°F, and is equal to 1055 J.

EXAMPLE 19-2	*Waiting to Shower*

Your whole family has taken showers before you, dropping the temperature in the water heater to 18°C. If the heater holds 150 kg of water, how much energy will it take to bring it to 50°C? If the energy is supplied by a 5.0-kW electric heating element, how long will that take?

Tip

Is That C or K? It doesn't matter when we're talking about temperature *differences*. That's why we could mix units, multiplying the specific heat in J/kg·K by the difference of Celsius temperatures.

Solution

The heat required is given by Equation 19-5:

$$\Delta Q = mc\,\Delta T = (150 \text{ kg})(4184 \text{ J/kg·K})(50°C - 18°C)$$
$$= 2.0 \times 10^7 \text{ J},$$

where we found the specific heat of water in Table 19-1. The heating element supplies energy at the rate of 5.0 kW, or 5.0×10^3 J/s; at that rate the time needed to supply 2.0×10^7 J is

$$\Delta t = \frac{2.0 \times 10^7 \text{ J}}{5.0 \times 10^3 \text{ J/s}} = 4000 \text{ s}, \quad \text{or a little over an hour}.$$

EXERCISE (a) How much heat does it take to bring a 3.4-kg iron skillet from 20°C to 130°C? (b) If the heat is supplied by a stove burner at the rate of 2.0 kW, how long will it take to heat the pan?

Answers: (a) 166 kJ; (b) 84 s

Some problems similar to Example 19-2: 19, 23–25, 28

For many substances, the specific heat is nearly independent of temperature over wide temperature ranges. When the specific heat does vary significantly with temperature, we write Equation 19-5 in the limit of very small temperature change dT and heat dQ, and integrate to find the heat required for larger changes. Problem 73 explores this situation.

Strictly speaking, values of heat capacity and specific heat depend on whether an object's pressure or its volume changes as it's heated. For solids and liquids, which don't expand much, the distinction is not very important. But it makes a big difference whether a gas is confined to a fixed volume or allowed to expand when heated. Consequently, for gases we need to define two different specific heats, depending on which of volume or pressure is held constant. We'll deal with that issue in Chapter 21, where we explore the behavior of gases in the context of fundamental laws of thermodynamics.

The Equilibrium Temperature

When two objects at different temperatures are in thermal contact, heat flows from the hotter object to the cooler one until they reach thermodynamic equilibrium. If the two objects are thermally insulated from their surroundings, then all the energy leaving the hotter object ends up in the cooler one. Mathematically, this statement may be written

$$m_1 c_1 \, \Delta T_1 + m_2 c_2 \, \Delta T_2 = 0 \,, \qquad (19\text{-}6)$$

where mc is the heat capacity of an object of mass m and specific heat c, and ΔT is the temperature change of that object. For the hotter object, ΔT is negative, so the two terms in Equation 19-6 have opposite signs. One term represents the outflow of heat from the hotter object, the other inflow into the cooler object.

Got It!

A hot rock with mass 250 g is dropped into an equal mass of cool water. Which temperature changes more, that of the rock or the water? Explain.

EXAMPLE 19-3	*Cooling Down*

An aluminum frying pan with mass 1.5 kg is heated on a stove to 180°C, then plunged into a sink containing 8.0 kg of water at room temperature (20°C). Assuming that none of the water boils, and that no heat is lost to the surroundings, what is the equilibrium temperature of the water and pan?

Solution

We write Equation 19-6 in the form

$$m_p c_p (T - T_p) + m_w c_w (T - T_w) = 0 \,,$$

where the subscripts p and w refer to the pan and the water, and where the equilibrium temperature T is the same for both. Solving for T then gives

$$T = \frac{m_p c_p T_p + m_w c_w T_w}{m_p c_p + m_w c_w} \,.$$

Using the given values of m_p, T_p, m_w, and T_w, and taking c_p and c_w from Table 19-1, we find that $T = 26°C$.

EXERCISE You take a 1.0-L bottle of soda from a 4.0°C refrigerator and put it in an insulated cooler chest whose heat capacity is negligible. Also in the chest is a wooden cutting board of mass 2.1 kg and temperature 24°C. When you open the chest much later, what will be the temperature of the soda? Soda has essentially the same density (1.0 kg/L) and specific heat as water. Neglect the heat capacity of the soda bottle itself.

Answer: 12°C

Some problems similar to Example 19-3: 34–36, 59, 60

19-6 HEAT TRANSFER

How is heat transferred between two objects? Engineers need to know so they can design systems to control heat transfer, as in heating or cooling a building. Scientists need to know so they can anticipate temperature changes, as in the global warming that seems to be resulting from combustion of fossil fuels and other human activities.

Three heat-transfer mechanisms commonly occur. These are conduction, a process involving direct physical contact; convection, involving energy transfer by the bulk flow of a fluid; and radiation, or energy transfer by electromagnetic waves. In a given situation, one of the three may dominate, or we may have to take all three into account.

Conduction

Conduction is the transfer of heat through direct physical contact. Microscopically, conduction occurs because molecules in a hotter region transfer energy to those of an adjacent cooler region through collisions. The effect of these collisions in a given material is quantified by the material's **thermal conductivity**, k, whose SI units are W/m·K. Common materials exhibit a broad range of thermal conductivities, from about 400 W/m·K for copper—a good conductor of heat—to 0.029 W/m·K for styrofoam, a good thermal insulator.

Figure 19-10 shows a slab of material with thickness Δx and cross-sectional area A. Suppose one face of the material is held at temperature T and the other at $T + \Delta T$. Intuitively, we might expect the rate of heat flow through the slab to increase with increasing area A and to decrease with increasing thickness Δx. Of course, the heat-flow rate must also depend on the thermal conductivity of the material. We expect further that heat will flow from the hotter to the cooler face of the slab, with the heat-flow rate dependent also on the temperature difference between the two faces. Our intuition is borne out experimentally: for a slab of uniform thickness, the heat-flow rate H is given by

$$H = -kA \frac{\Delta T}{\Delta x}. \qquad (19\text{-}7)$$

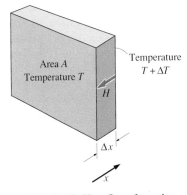

FIGURE 19-10 Heat flows from the hotter to the cooler face of the slab, at a rate H that depends on the slab area A, thickness Δx, temperature difference ΔT, and thermal conductivity k.

Since H is a rate of energy flow, its units are joules/second, or watts. The minus sign in Equation 19-7 shows that heat transfer is opposite to the direction of increasing temperature, that is, from hotter to cooler.

Table 19-2 lists thermal conductivities for some common materials. Both SI and British units are listed since the latter are commonly used in calculations involving heat loss in buildings. Note the wide range of thermal conductivities in Table 19-2. Metals are exceptionally good conductors because they contain free electrons that move quickly, transferring energy with them. Gases, on the other hand, are poor conductors because the wide spacing of their molecules makes for infrequent energy transfers. Good heat insulators, such as fiberglass and styrofoam, owe their insulating properties to a physical structure that traps small volumes of air or other gas.

TABLE 19-2 *Thermal Conductivities**

	Thermal Conductivity, k	
Material	**SI Units: W/m·K**	**British Units: Btu·in./h·ft²·°F**
Air	0.026	0.18
Aluminum	237	1644
Concrete (varies with mix)	1	7
Copper	401	2780
Fiberglass	0.042	0.29
Glass	0.7–0.9	5–6
Goose down	0.043	0.30
Helium	0.14	0.97
Iron	80.4	558
Steel	46	319
Styrofoam	0.029	0.20
Water	0.61	4.2
Wood (pine)	0.11	0.78

* Temperature range 0°C to 100°C.

EXAMPLE 19-4	*Warming a Lake*

A lake with a flat bottom and steep sides has surface area 1.5 km^2 and is 8.0 m deep. On a summer day, the surface water is at a temperature of 30°C, while the bottom water is at 4.0°C. What is the rate of heat conduction through the lake? Assume that the temperature declines uniformly from surface to bottom.

Solution

The lake resembles the slab of Fig. 19-10. Taking the thermal conductivity of water from Table 19-2, Equation 19-7 gives

$$H = -kA \frac{\Delta T}{\Delta x}$$

$$= -(0.61 \text{ W/m·K})(1.5 \times 10^6 \text{ m}^2) \frac{30°C - 4.0°C}{8.0 \text{ m}}$$

$$= -3.0 \times 10^6 \text{ W}.$$

The minus sign indicates that heat flows in the direction of decreasing temperature, or downward into the lake. Were the surface and bottom temperatures not maintained, heat flow would eventually bring the entire lake to a uniform temperature.

EXERCISE A concrete wall 20 cm thick measures 2.2 m high by 11 m wide. On the inside, the temperature is 20°C; outside, it's −10°C. What is the heat-flow rate through the wall?

Answer: 3.6 kW

Some problems similar to Example 19-4: 38, 39, 42, 46

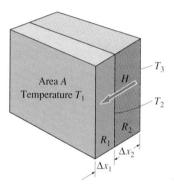

FIGURE 19-11 A composite slab. The heat-flow rate H is the same through both sections.

Equation 19-7 is strictly correct only when the temperature varies uniformly from one surface to the other. This is the case in practical problems where two surfaces at different temperatures have the same area. With other geometries— as in evaluating heat loss through the insulation surrounding a cylindrical pipe— we need to write $\Delta T/\Delta x$ as the derivative dT/dx and integrate to relate the heat loss and the temperature difference. Problems 74 and 75 explore this situation.

Often heat flows through several different materials. A building wall, for example, may contain wood, plaster, fiberglass insulation, and other materials. Figure 19-11 shows such a composite structure, with temperature T_1 on one side and T_3 on the other. The heat-flow rate H must be the same through both slabs since energy doesn't accumulate or disappear at the interface between the two. Then Equation 19-7 gives

$$H = -k_1 A \frac{T_2 - T_1}{\Delta x_1} = -k_2 A \frac{T_3 - T_2}{\Delta x_2}, \qquad (19\text{-}8)$$

where k_1 and k_2 are the thermal conductivities of the two materials, and T_2 is the temperature at the interface. We would like to express the heat-flow rate in terms of the surface temperatures T_1 and T_3 alone, without having to worry about the intermediate temperature T_2. To do so, it's convenient to define the **thermal resistance**, R, of each slab:

$$R = \frac{\Delta x}{kA}. \qquad (19\text{-}9)$$

The SI units of R are K/W. Unlike the thermal conductivity, k, which is a property of a *material*, R is a property of a *particular piece* of material, reflecting both its conductivity and its geometry. In terms of thermal resistance, Equation 19-8 becomes

$$H = -\frac{T_2 - T_1}{R_1} = -\frac{T_3 - T_2}{R_2},$$

so

$$R_1 H = T_1 - T_2$$

and

$$R_2 H = T_2 - T_3.$$

Adding these two equations gives

$$(R_1 + R_2)H = T_1 - T_2 + T_2 - T_3 = T_1 - T_3,$$

or
$$H = \frac{T_1 - T_3}{R_1 + R_2}. \qquad (19\text{-}10)$$

Equation 19-10 shows that the composite slab acts like a single slab whose thermal resistance is the sum of the resistances of the two slabs that compose it. We could easily extend this treatment to show that the thermal resistances of three or more slabs add when the slabs are arranged so the same heat flows through all of them.

In the United States, the insulating properties of building materials are usually described in terms of the **R-factor**, $\mathcal{R}$, which is the thermal resistance for a slab of unit area:

$$\mathcal{R} = RA = \frac{\Delta x}{k}. \qquad (19\text{-}11)$$

The units of $\mathcal{R}$, although rarely stated, are ft²·°F·h/Btu. This means that $\mathcal{R}$-19 fiberglass insulation, now in common use as a wall insulation in the northern part of the United States, has a heat loss of $\frac{1}{19}$ Btu per hour for each square foot of insulation for each degree Fahrenheit temperature difference across the insulation (see Fig. 19-12).

FIGURE 19-12 This $\mathcal{R}$-19 fiberglass insulation loses 1/19 Btu per hour per square foot for every °F temperature difference.

EXAMPLE 19-5	*Insulation, Heat Loss, and the Price of Oil*

Figure 19-13 shows a house whose walls consist of plaster ($\mathcal{R} = 0.17$), $\mathcal{R}$-11 fiberglass insulation, plywood ($\mathcal{R} = 0.65$), and cedar shingles ($\mathcal{R} = 0.55$). The roof is the same construction except it uses $\mathcal{R}$-30 fiberglass insulation. The average outdoor temperature in winter is 20°F, and the house is maintained at 70°F. The house's oil furnace produces 100,000 Btu for every gallon of oil, and oil costs 94¢ per gallon. How much does it cost to heat the house for a month?

Solution

The R-factors for the walls and roof are

$$\mathcal{R}_{\text{wall}} = \mathcal{R}_{\text{plaster}} + \mathcal{R}_{\text{fiberglass}} + \mathcal{R}_{\text{plywood}} + \mathcal{R}_{\text{shingles}}$$
$$= 0.17 + 11 + 0.65 + 0.55 = 12.4,$$

and

$$\mathcal{R}_{\text{roof}} = 0.17 + 30 + 0.65 + 0.55 = 31.4.$$

The total wall area is

$$A_{\text{wall}} = (28 \text{ ft} + 36 \text{ ft} + 28 \text{ ft} + 36 \text{ ft})(10 \text{ ft})$$
$$+ (28 \text{ ft})(8.08 \text{ ft}) = 1506 \text{ ft}^2,$$

where the second term in the sum is the area of the two triangular portions of the side walls, whose height is (14 ft) (tan30°), or 8.08 ft. These $\mathcal{R}$-12.4 walls lose 1/12.4 Btu/h·ft²·°F, and the temperature difference across them is 50°F, so the total heat-loss rate through the walls is

$$H_{\text{walls}} = (\tfrac{1}{12.4} \text{ Btu/h·ft}^2\text{·°F})(1506 \text{ ft}^2)(50\text{°F}) = 6073 \text{ Btu/h}.$$

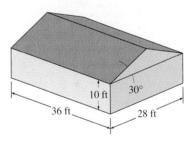

FIGURE 19-13 House for Example 19-5.

The area of the pitched roof is increased over that of a flat roof by the factor 1/cos30°, so the heat-loss rate through the roof is

$$H_{\text{roof}} = (\tfrac{1}{31.4} \text{ Btu/h·ft}^2\text{·°F}) \frac{(36 \text{ ft})(28 \text{ ft})}{\cos 30°} (50\text{°F})$$
$$= 1853 \text{ Btu/h}.$$

The total heat-loss rate is then

$$H = 6073 \text{ Btu/h} + 1853 \text{ Btu/h} = 7926 \text{ Btu/h}.$$

In a month, this results in a total heat loss of

$$Q = (7926 \text{ Btu/h})(30 \text{ days/month})(24 \text{ h/day})$$
$$= 5.71 \times 10^6 \text{ Btu}.$$

With 10^5 Btu per gallon of oil burned, this requires 57.1 gallons of oil, at a cost of (57.1 gal) ($0.94/gal) = $53.58.

This estimate is low; losses through windows and doors are substantial, and cold air infiltration results in additional heat loss. A more accurate analysis would also consider heat lost to the ground and solar energy gained through the windows. Problem 67 provides a more realistic look at heat loss in this house.

EXERCISE In the house of Example 19-5, how much money would be saved each month if the wall insulation were increased to the same $\mathcal{R} = 30$ as in the roof?

Answer: $24.80

Some problems similar to Example 19-5: 43, 45, 47, 48, 67

Convection

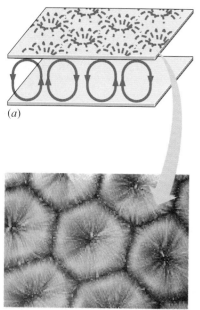

Convection is heat transfer by the bulk motion of a fluid. Convection occurs because a fluid becomes less dense when heated and therefore rises. Figure 19-14a shows two plates held at different temperatures, with fluid between them. Fluid heated by the lower plate rises and transfers heat to the upper plate. The cooled fluid then sinks, and the process repeats. The pattern of rising and sinking fluid often acquires a striking regularity, as shown in Fig. 19-14b.

Convection is important in many technological and natural environments. When you heat water on a stove, convection carries heat from the bottom of the pan to the top. Houses usually rely on convection from heat sources near floor level to circulate warm air throughout a room. Insulating materials such as fiberglass and goose down trap air and thereby inhibit convection that would otherwise cause excessive heat loss from our houses and our bodies. Convection associated with solar heating of Earth's surface drives the vast air movements that establish our overall climate. Violent convective movements, such as those in thunderstorms, are associated with localized temperature differences. On a much longer time scale, convection in Earth's mantle is involved in continental drift (Fig. 19-15). Convection plays a crucial role in many astrophysical processes, including the generation of magnetic fields in stars and planets.

As with conduction, the convective heat-loss rate often is approximately proportional to the temperature difference. But the calculation of convective heat loss is complicated because of the need to understand the details of the associated fluid motion. The study of convection processes is an important research area in many fields of contemporary science and engineering.

FIGURE 19-14 (a) Schematic diagram showing convection between two plates at different temperatures. (b) Top view of convection cells in a laboratory experiment.

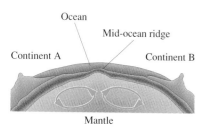

FIGURE 19-15 Slow convection in Earth's mantle brings up material at the mid-ocean ridges. Here continents A and B are drifting apart as the ocean widens.

Radiation

Turn an electric stove burner to "high," and it glows a brilliant red-orange. Set it on "low," and it does not appear hot, yet you can still tell it is by holding your hand near it. In both cases the burner is losing energy by emitting **radiation**. In later chapters, we will investigate the nature of radiation in terms of electromagnetic phenomena and atomic theory. Our stove-burner example suggests that radiation increases rapidly with temperature. Experiment confirms this: the rate of energy loss by radiation is given by the **Stefan-Boltzmann law**:

$$P = e\sigma AT^4, \tag{19-12}$$

where the energy loss rate P is in watts, A is the surface area of the emitting surface, T the temperature in kelvins, and σ a constant called the **Stefan-**

Boltzmann constant, approximately 5.67×10^{-8} W/m²·K⁴. The quantity e is called the **emissivity** of the material. It is a dimensionless number ranging from 0 to 1 that measures the material's effectiveness in emitting radiation.

The rate of energy loss by radiation depends on the fourth power of the temperature. Therefore radiation is generally less important at low temperatures but dominates at high temperatures. A house loses only modest heat through radiation, while very hot things such as the Sun, light bulb filaments, or molten metal lose most of their energy by radiation (Fig. 19-16)—although any object above absolute zero radiates some energy. In vacuum, where conduction and convection cannot occur, all heat transfer occurs by radiation. That's why Thermos bottles and Dewar flasks—whose insulation is the vacuum between layers of glass—are coated with shiny material that reflects radiation.

FIGURE 19-16 Foundry worker pouring molten gold concentrate. Radiation is the dominant mode of heat loss from the hot liquid metal, as evidenced by its bright glow.

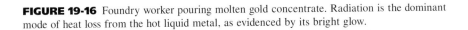

| EXAMPLE 19-6 | *The Sun's Temperature* |

The Sun radiates energy at the rate $P = 3.9 \times 10^{26}$ W, and its radius is 7.0×10^8 m (Fig. 19-17). Assuming the Sun to be a blackbody (emissivity = 1), what is its surface temperature?

Solution

The radiated power is given by the Stefan-Boltzmann law, Equation 19-12. Solving this equation for T and using $4\pi R^2$ for the surface area of the Sun gives

$$T = \left(\frac{P}{4\pi R^2 \sigma} \right)^{1/4}$$

$$= \left[\frac{3.9 \times 10^{26} \text{ W}}{4\pi (7.0 \times 10^8 \text{ m})^2 (5.7 \times 10^{-8} \text{ W/m}^2 \cdot \text{K}^4)} \right]^{1/4}$$

$$= 5.8 \times 10^3 \text{ K},$$

in agreement with observational measurements.

EXERCISE What is the surface area of a 100-W light bulb filament at a temperature of 3100 K? Assume the filament has emissivity $e = 1$.

Answer: 1.9×10^{-5} m²

FIGURE 19-17 What is the Sun's surface temperature?

Some problems similar to Example 19-6: 52–54, 63, 64

When an object is in thermodynamic equilibrium with its surroundings, it must emit and absorb radiation at the same rate; otherwise it would gain or lose energy and its temperature change from that of its surroundings. Then, since Equation 19-12 gives the rate of energy emission, it must also give the rate of absorption. Furthermore, for emission and absorption to be equal at a given temperature, the quantity e appearing in Equation 19-12 must be the same in both processes. A perfect emitter has $e = 1$ and must therefore also be a perfect absorber. Since it absorbs all radiation incident on it, such an object would appear black at room temperature and is therefore called a **blackbody**. (A blackbody would, however, glow brightly at high temperature.) A shiny object, in contrast, reflects radiation incident on it. So it has $e \simeq 0$, and is therefore also a poor emitter of radiation. That's why wood stoves and stovepipes are painted black; if they were shiny less heat would be radiated into the room to warm its occupants (and more would go up the chimney, by convection).

When an object is not in thermodynamic equilibrium, its temperature T differs from the surrounding temperature T_0. The object still emits energy at the rate $P_e = e\sigma A T^4$ set by its own temperature, but now it absorbs at the rate $P_a = e\sigma A T_0{}^4$ set by its surroundings. The net rate at which the object loses energy through radiation is the difference between these two quantities, or:

$$P_{\text{net}} = e\sigma A(T^4 - T_0{}^4). \qquad (19\text{-}13)$$

When $T = T_0$ we recover the result $P_{\text{net}} = 0$, as we argued must be the case for an object in equilibrium with its surroundings; when $T < T_0$ Equation 19-13 gives a negative energy loss rate, indicating that the object gains energy from its surroundings.

Examples of objects decidedly not in thermodynamic equilibrium with their surroundings include the Sun and the filament in Example 19-6. In that example, we were justified in neglecting the absorbed power because the surrounding temperature T_0 is in both cases so much less than the object's temperature that, when raised to the fourth power, it makes the absorbed power totally negligible.

Got It!

You set an electric stove burner on "high" but forget to put a pan on it; soon the burner glows red hot. What's the dominant mode of heat loss from the burner in this case? Now you put a pan of water on the burner and bring the water to a vigorous boil. What's the dominant mode of heat transfer (a) from burner to pan and (b) from the bottom of the pan to the top of the water surface?

19-7 THERMAL ENERGY BALANCE

When an object is in thermodynamic equilibrium with its surroundings, its temperature remains constant. But it could also maintain a constant temperature, different from its surroundings, by balancing energy gain and loss. A house in winter provides a good example of this **thermal energy balance**. Unheated, the house would come to equilibrium at the outdoor temperature. Heated, it loses energy because of the temperature difference between itself and its environment, but this loss is balanced by energy input from a furnace, solar collector, electricity, or other source (Fig. 19-18).

The principle of thermal energy balance is used throughout science and engineering to predict temperatures under different conditions. It's also used to determine the sizes of heat sources needed to achieve desired temperatures. When heat is supplied to an object, its temperature initially rises. But so does the heat-loss rate, which increases with the temperature difference between the object and its surroundings. Eventually the loss rate equals the rate of energy input. The object is then in thermal energy balance at a constant temperature. The following examples and application explore thermal energy balance.

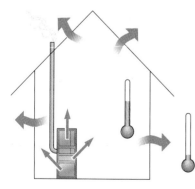

FIGURE 19-18 A house in thermal energy balance. Energy from the furnace balances heat loss, maintaining the house at a constant temperature higher than that of its surroundings.

EXAMPLE 19-7	*A Water Heater*

A poorly insulated electric water heater loses heat at the rate of 40 W for each Celsius degree difference between the water and its surroundings. The tank is heated by a 2.5-kW electric heating element. If the heater is located in a 15°C basement, what will be its temperature if the heating element operates continuously?

Solution

The heating element supplies energy at the rate $H_{in} = 2.5$ kW, while the heater loses energy at the rate $H_{out} = (40 \text{ W}/°\text{C})(\Delta T)$, where ΔT is the temperature difference between the water and its surroundings. In thermal energy balance the heat input equals the heat loss, so we have

$$(40 \text{ W}/°\text{C})(\Delta T) = 2.5 \text{ kW} ,$$

or

$$\Delta T = \frac{2.5 \text{ kW}}{40 \text{ W}/°\text{C}} = 63°\text{C} .$$

With the basement at 15°C, the water temperature is then 78°C.

EXERCISE A home heating system supplies heat at the maximum rate of 40 kW. If the house loses 1.1 kW for each °C between inside and outside, what is the minimum outdoor temperature for which the heating system can maintain 20°C inside?

Answer: −16°C

Some problems similar to Example 19-7: 51, 54, 58, 65, 66

EXAMPLE 19-8	*A Solar Greenhouse*

Figure 19-19 shows a solar-heated greenhouse. The south-facing diagonal wall is made of double-pane glass ($\mathcal{R} = 1.8$), while the other walls are opaque and have R-factors of 30. Heat loss through the floor is negligible. The intensity of sunlight on the glass, averaged over a typical day, is 120 W/m². If the outdoor temperature is 15°F, what will be the temperature in the greenhouse?

Solution

We first calculate the heat-loss rate for the greenhouse. The total area of insulated wall is

$$A_w = (10 \text{ ft})(20 \text{ ft}) + 2[\tfrac{1}{2}(10 \text{ ft})^2] = 300 \text{ ft}^2 ,$$

so the heat-loss rate through these $\mathcal{R}$-30 walls is

$$H_w = \frac{A_w \Delta T}{\mathcal{R}_w} = \frac{300 \Delta T}{30} = 10\Delta T \text{ Btu}/\text{h}\cdot°\text{F} .$$

Similarly, the glass area is

$$A_g = (20 \text{ ft})(10\sqrt{2} \text{ ft}) = 283 \text{ ft}^2 ,$$

so the heat-loss rate through the glass is

$$H_g = \frac{A_g \Delta T}{\mathcal{R}_g} = \frac{283 \Delta T}{1.8} = 157\Delta T \text{ Btu}/\text{h}\cdot°\text{F} .$$

If the greenhouse is to be in thermal energy balance, the total heat-loss rate of $167\Delta T$ Btu/h·°F must be balanced by the energy gained from the Sun. The average solar input, which we denote S, is 120 W/m², or

$$S = (120 \text{ W}/\text{m}^2)[3.413(\text{Btu}/\text{h})/\text{W}](0.0929 \text{ m}^2/\text{ft}^2)$$
$$= 38.0 \text{ Btu}/\text{h}\cdot\text{ft}^2 ,$$

where we obtained the conversion factors from Appendix C. Then the total solar gain on the 283-ft² glass is

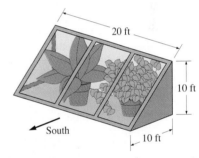

FIGURE 19-19 Solar greenhouse for Example 19-8.

$$(283 \text{ ft}^2)(38.0 \text{ Btu}/\text{h}\cdot\text{ft}^2) = 1.075 \times 10^4 \text{ Btu}/\text{h} .$$

Equating the heat loss to the solar gain gives

$$167\Delta T \text{ Btu}/\text{h}\cdot°\text{F} = 1.075 \times 10^4 \text{ Btu}/\text{h} ,$$

so

$$\Delta T = \frac{1.075 \times 10^4 \text{ Btu}/\text{h}}{167 \text{ Btu}/\text{h}\cdot°\text{F}} = 64°\text{F} .$$

With the outdoors at 15°F, the greenhouse temperature is then 79°F.

EXERCISE A cubical doghouse measures 4.0 ft on a side, and its four walls and roof have $\mathcal{R} = 8.5$, including an insulated door. Heat loss to the ground is negligible. If the dog's metabolism produces energy at the average rate of 45 W, what will be the doghouse temperature when the outside temperature is −5°F?

Answer: 11°F

Some problems similar to Example 19-8: 55, 67

APPLICATION	*The Greenhouse Effect and Global Warming*

Among the most serious environmental challenges of the twenty-first century is global warming, brought on as human activity alters the composition of Earth's atmosphere (Fig. 19-20). Among the likely consequences are a rise in sea level and shifts in rainfall patterns that could jeopardize our ability to feed the burgeoning human population. With warming rates well in excess of naturally occurring climate change, many plant and animal species might perish from inability to adapt or migrate fast enough to escape inhospitable conditions. Less probable but potentially disastrous consequences include sudden, radical shifts in ocean circulation patterns that could leave Europe—now warmed by the Gulf Stream—with a climate like that of northern Labrador.

Scientific analysis of global warming is complex and not without controversy. By the mid-1990s, however, a substantial majority of climate scientists had concluded that signs of global warming were already evident, and that warming was likely to become much more obvious over the next few decades. In 1996, the authoritative Intergovernmental Panel on Climate Change (IPCC) published a carefully worded statement that "the balance of evidence suggests a discernible human influence on global climate."* IPCC scientists based their conclusion in part on direct evidence, including a rise in global temperature and the occurrence of record hottest years and even decades at the twentieth century's end. But equally compelling was indirect evidence from patterns of climatic change—for example, the occurrence of more intense precipitation—that corroborate computer model predictions for the effects of human-induced global warming. By now there is near-universal agreement in the scientific community that human activities will bring a still warmer climate in the coming decades. However, the details of how much warming, how fast, where, and with what consequences remain less certain.

But though the details are complex, the basic physics is straightforward. Earth itself is essentially in thermal energy balance. Sunlight heats the planet, which in turn radiates energy as infrared radiation. Earth's temperature is established by the balance between solar input and infrared radiation into space. Figure 19-21 shows that our planet presents an effective area πR_E^2 to the incident sunlight. The rate of solar energy input at the top of the atmosphere is then $\pi R_E^2 S$, where S is the power per unit area in sunlight. Above the atmosphere, $S = 1.37$ kW/m², but about 30% of the sunlight is reflected back into space, giving an effective solar intensity $S = 960$ W/m². Figure 19-21 also shows that Earth radiates from its entire surface area $4\pi R_E^2$. If Earth were a blackbody ($e = 1$), Equation 19-12 would give a total energy loss rate $P = \sigma 4\pi R_E^2 T^4$.

* *Climate Change 1995: The Science of Climate Change* (Contribution of Working Group I to the Second Assessment Report of the Intergovernmental Panel on Climate Change), J. T. Houghton et al., eds. (Cambridge University Press, 1996).

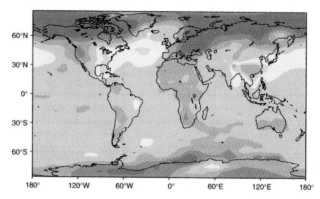

FIGURE 19-20 Global temperature changes according to a computer model simulating the period from 1880 to 2049, based on projected increases in carbon dioxide and atmospheric aerosols (particulate matter). Darkest red areas represent a 5°C temperature increase; darkest blue areas indicate a 2°C decrease. Simulation is for conditions during the northern hemisphere winter.

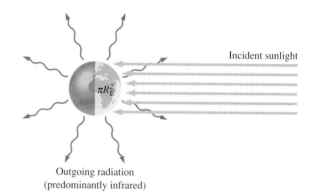

FIGURE 19-21 Earth's temperature is determined by the balance of incoming sunlight and outgoing infrared radiation. The planet presents an effective area πR_E^2 to sunlight, but radiates from its entire surface.

Equating energy gain and loss rates would give

$$\pi R_E^2 S = \sigma 4\pi R_E^2 T^4,$$

or

$$T = \left(\frac{S}{4\sigma}\right)^{1/4} = \left(\frac{960 \text{ W/m}^2}{(4)(5.67\times10^{-8} \text{ W/m}^2\cdot\text{K})}\right)^{1/4}$$

$$= 255 \text{ K} = -18°C.$$

This number is certainly the right order of magnitude, but is considerably lower than the measured global average temperature of about 14°C.

What's missing in our simple calculation that would account for the 32°C discrepancy? The answer lies in the composition of Earth's atmosphere. A number of atmospheric gas molecules absorb infrared radiation, reradiating some to space but some back to Earth. As a result, Earth's surface temperature must be higher than it would be in the absence of those gases in order to achieve the same rate of infrared radiation escaping to outer space. This phenomenon is called the **greenhouse effect** because the infrared-absorbing gases play the same role as greenhouse glass: they let incident sunlight through but impede escaping infrared, helping to keep the greenhouse temperature higher than it otherwise would be.

The 32°C temperature increase we've just described is due to the **natural greenhouse effect**, caused primarily by atmospheric water vapor and carbon dioxide. It's good thing we have the natural greenhouse effect; otherwise Earth would be intolerably cold, as our calculation suggests. The planet Mars has insignificant quantities of greenhouse gases, and it's much colder relative to Earth than its greater distance from the Sun would imply. On the other hand the greenhouse effect can get out of control; Venus' surface temperature is hotter than an oven, thanks to an overabundance of greenhouse gases. Earth's temperature is in a delicate balance between too little and too much greenhouse effect.

Unfortunately that balance is changing. The single most significant human contribution to atmospheric greenhouse gases is carbon dioxide, which results primarily from burning fossil fuels and accounts for nearly two-thirds of the human-induced enhancement of the greenhouse effect. The CO_2 content of Earth's atmosphere has risen steadily throughout the industrial age (Fig. 19-22), and now produces roughly the same excess heating as would a 1.6-kW/m^2 increase in the intensity of sunlight.

CO_2 emissions continue to rise, driven by such factors as rapid industrialization in the developing world and decreases in average automobile fuel efficiency in the U.S. (recall Fig. 7-21). It's definitely too late to prevent global warming altogether. With a concerted effort, though, the average temperature increase might be held to about 2 C°—a rise that, although small, still implies significant climatic change. In 1997, a global conference on greenhouse warming produced the first international treaty with binding requirements on some nations to reduce their greenhouse gas emissions. The treaty reductions will help, but in themselves will not be enough to prevent continued increases in atmospheric CO_2 and with them a rise in global temperature.

Current projections, based on computer models that couple the physics and chemistry of the atmosphere and oceans with responses of the biosphere and assumptions about the development of human society, suggest a global average temperature increase of some 1–3.5°C over the next century, with 2°C a best estimate. These values may seem modest, but they represent a rate of change far in excess of what humankind has previously experienced (Fig. 19-23). Furthermore, the projected warming is not spread evenly over the planet, but tends to be greatest in the polar regions. Significant climatic change will almost certainly accompany even a global average temperature rise of 1–2°C.

There remain uncertainties in predicting both the extent of global warming and its effects. Physical, chemical, and biological mechanisms, many poorly understood, may help stabilize global warming, or they may exacerbate it. New technologies may help alleviate the problem or they may contribute to it. Global warming presents an enormous challenge to scientists and engineers—and to all the world's citizens.

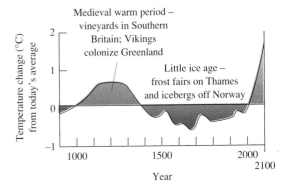

FIGURE 19-23 Global average temperature change over 1200 years, including the best estimate by the Intergovernmental Panel on Climate Change for the next century. The IPCC's 2°C projection is considerably larger than natural variations over the past thousand years; even the latter had obvious effects on climate. Furthermore, the projected increase due to global warming will occur far more rapidly than any recent natural changes, giving ecosystems little time to adapt. Although a 2°C rise may seem small, changes only a few times larger—but in the opposite direction—are associated with the difference between Earth's present climate and the last ice age.

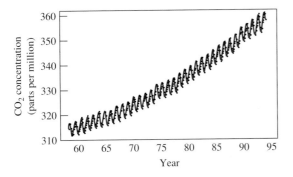

FIGURE 19-22 Atmospheric CO_2 concentration as measured at Mauna Loa, Hawaii, over the past four decades. Annual variations reflect seasonal changes in vegetation. The overall trend shows an increase that has been occurring since the beginning of the industrial age.

CHAPTER SYNOPSIS

Summary

1. Heat and related phenomena may be viewed from either the macroscopic viewpoint of **thermodynamics** or the microscopic viewpoint of **statistical mechanics**.

2. Two systems are in **thermodynamic equilibrium** if none of their macroscopic properties change when they are brought into thermal contact. Systems in thermodynamic equilibrium have the same **temperature**.

3. The **zeroth law of thermodynamics** states that two systems in thermodynamic equilibrium with a third system are in thermodynamic equilibrium with each other. This law allows the establishment of temperature scales.

4. A **thermometer** is a system with a convenient macroscopic property that serves to indicate temperature. **Gas thermometers** are used to establish the **kelvin** temperature scale of the SI system.

5. **Heat** is energy being transferred between objects as a result of a temperature difference.

6. **Specific heat** measures the ratio of heat to temperature change for a unit mass of a given material:

$$c = \frac{1}{m}\frac{\Delta Q}{\Delta T}.$$

Heat capacity is the ratio of heat to temperature change for a given object:

$$C = mc = \frac{\Delta Q}{\Delta T}.$$

7. Heat transfer occurs mainly by three distinct mechanisms:
   a. **Conduction** is direct transfer of heat through physical contact, and involves energy exchange through molecular collisions. The conduction rate H through a slab of material depends on the **thermal conductivity** k of the material, the slab thickness Δx and slab area A, and on the temperature difference across the slab:

   $$H = -kA\frac{\Delta T}{\Delta x}.$$

   Thermal resistance, $R = \Delta x/kA$ and **R-factor**, $\mathcal{R} = \Delta \bar{x}/k$, also characterize heat conduction through materials.

   b. **Convection** is heat transfer through bulk motion of a fluid, as when heated air rises. Convection is difficult to describe quantitatively but is an important process in many natural and technological systems.

   c. **Radiation** is energy in the form of electromagnetic waves that can travel through empty space. The rate at which a hot surface of temperature T and area A loses energy by radiation is

   $$P = e\sigma AT^4,$$

   where e is a number between 0 and 1 that describes the effectiveness of the surface as a radiation emitter

and σ is the universal **Stefan-Boltzmann constant**, $\sigma = 5.67 \times 10^{-8}$ W/m²·K.

8. **Thermal energy balance** exists when an object gains and loses energy at the same rate, thereby maintaining a constant temperature. If either energy gain or loss changes, the temperature rises or falls until heat loss again balances gain.

Terms You Should Understand

(Pairs are closely related terms whose distinction is important; number in parentheses is chapter section where term first appears.)

thermodynamics, statistical mechanics (19-1)
thermodynamic equilibrium (19-2)
thermal contact, thermal insulation (19-2)
thermometer, gas thermometer (19-3)
kelvin (19-3)
calorie, British thermal unit (19-4)
specific heat, heat capacity (19-5)
conduction, convection, radiation (19-6)
thermal conductivity (19-6)
thermal resistance, R-factor (19-6)
Stefan-Boltzmann law (19-6)
emissivity (19-6)
blackbody (19-6)
thermal energy balance (19-7)
greenhouse effect (19-7)

Symbols You Should Recognize

T (19-3)	k (19-6)
K, °C, °F (19-3)	$R, \mathcal{R}$ (19-6)
cal, Btu (19-4)	e (19-6)
c, C (19-5)	σ (19-6)
H (19-6)	

Problems You Should Be Able to Solve

converting among different temperature scales (19-3)
converting among different energy units (19-4)
calculating the equilibrium temperature of a mixture (19-5)
evaluating heat loss given thermal conductivity, resistance, or R-factor (19-6)
evaluating radiant heat loss (19-6)
determining temperature in thermal energy balance (19-7)

Limitations to Keep in Mind

When specific heat varies significantly over a temperature range, Equation 19-4 must be written in terms of the derivative dQ/dT and then integrated to find the heat.

Equation 19-7 applies exactly only when the thermal conductivity is independent of temperature and the geometry is that of a rectangular slab. Otherwise it must be written in terms of the derivative dT/dx and integrated to relate heat loss and temperature difference.

QUESTIONS

1. Two identical-looking physical systems are in the same macroscopic state. Must they be in the same microscopic state? Explain.
2. Two identical-looking physical systems are in the same microscopic state. Must they be in the same macroscopic state? Explain.
3. If system *A* is not in thermodynamic equilibrium with system *B*, and *B* is not in equilibrium with *C*, can you draw any conclusions about the temperatures of the three systems?
4. Given that there are three main mechanisms of heat transfer, how would you construct a good insulator?
5. Does a thermometer measure its own temperature, or the temperature of its surroundings? Explain.
6. To get an accurate body temperature measurement, you must hold a glass-and-mercury fever thermometer under your tongue for about 3 minutes. Some electronic fever thermometers require less than a minute. What might account for the difference?
7. Why is it better to define temperature scales in terms of a physical state, such as the triple point of water, rather than by having an official, standard thermometer stored at the International Bureau of Weights and Measures?
8. Compare the relative sizes of the kelvin, the degree Celsius, the degree Fahrenheit, and the degree Rankine.
9. Does a vacuum have temperature? Explain.
10. If you put a thermometer in direct sunlight, what do you measure? The air temperature? The temperature of the Sun? Some other temperature?
11. Why does the temperature in a stone building usually vary less than in a wooden building?
12. Why do large bodies of water exert a temperature-moderating effect on their surroundings?
13. A Thermos bottle consists of an evacuated, double-wall glass liner. The glass is coated with a thin layer of aluminum. How does a Thermos bottle work?
14. Stainless-steel cookware often has a layer of aluminum or copper embedded in the bottom. Why?
15. What method of energy transfer dominates in baking? In broiling?
16. After a calm, cold night the temperature a few feet above ground often drops just as the Sun comes up. Explain in terms of convection.
17. Solar collectors often have a copper absorber surface coated with a black paint, whose emissivity is nearly 1 for visible and infrared radiation. Better results can be achieved, though, with a "selective surface," whose emissivity is high for visible light but low for the infrared radiation associated with lower temperatures than the Sun's. Why is this?
18. Glass and fiberglass are made from the same material, yet have dramatically different thermal conductivities. Why?
19. A thin layer of glass does not offer much resistance to heat conduction. Yet double-glazed windows provide substantial energy savings. Why?
20. The insulating value of a double-glazed window actually decreases if the spacing is made too great. Why might this be?
21. To keep your hands warm while skiing, you should wear mittens instead of gloves. Why?
22. Since Earth is exposed to solar radiation, why doesn't Earth have the same temperature as the Sun?
23. On a clear night, a solar collector will often cool well below the ambient air temperature. Why? Why doesn't this happen on a cloudy night?
24. Is Earth in perfect energy balance? If not, why not?

PROBLEMS

Section 19-1 Macroscopic and Microscopic Descriptions

1. The macroscopic state of a carton capable of holding a half-dozen eggs is specified by giving the number of eggs in the carton. The microscopic state is specified by telling where each egg is in the carton. How many microscopic states correspond to the macroscopic state of a full carton?

Section 19-3 Measuring Temperature

2. A Canadian meteorologist predicts an overnight low of $-15°C$. How would a U.S. meteorologist express that same prediction?
3. Normal room temperature is 68°F. What is this in Celsius?
4. The outdoor temperature rises by 10°C. What is the rise in Fahrenheit?
5. At what temperature do the Fahrenheit and Celsius scales coincide?
6. Give equations for Rankine temperature in terms of (a) kelvins and (b) °F.
7. The normal boiling point of nitrogen is 77.3 K. Express this in Celsius and Fahrenheit.
8. A sick child's temperature reads 39.1 on a Celsius thermometer. What's the child's temperature on the Fahrenheit scale?
9. A constant-volume gas thermometer is filled with air whose pressure is 101 kPa at the normal melting point of ice. What would its pressure be at (a) the normal boiling point of water, (b) the normal boiling point of oxygen

(90.2 K), and (c) the normal boiling point of mercury (630 K)?

10. A constant-volume gas thermometer is at 55 kPa pressure at the triple point of water. By how much does its pressure change for each kelvin temperature change?

11. The temperature of a constant-pressure gas thermometer is directly proportional to the gas volume. If the volume is 1.00 L at the triple point of water, what is it at water's normal boiling point?

12. In the gas thermometer of Fig. 19-24, the height h is 60.0 mm at the triple point of water. When the thermometer is immersed in boiling sulfur dioxide the height drops to 57.8 mm. What is the boiling point of SO_2 in kelvins and in degrees Celsius?

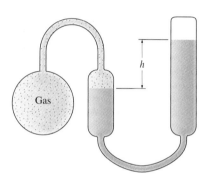

FIGURE 19-24 Problem 12.

13. A constant-volume gas thermometer supports a 72.5-mm-high mercury column when it's immersed in liquid nitrogen at $-196°C$. What will be the column height when the thermometer is in molten lead at $350°C$?

Sections 19-4 and 19-5 Temperature and Heat, Heat Capacity and Specific Heat

14. The average human diet contains about 2000 kcal per day. If all this food energy is released rather than being stored as fat, what is the approximate average power output of the human body?

15. If your mass is 60 kg, what is the minimum number of calories you would "burn off" climbing a 1700-m-high mountain? (The actual metabolic energy used would be much greater.)

16. Walking at 3 km/h requires an energy expenditure rate of about 200 W. How far would you have to walk to "burn off" a 300-kcal hamburger?

17. Typical fats contain about 9 kcal per gram. If the energy in body fat could be utilized with 100% efficiency, how much mass could a 78-kg person lose running a 26.2-mile marathon? The energy expenditure rate for that mass is 125 kcal/mile.

18. You expend 150 kcal while exercising for 5 minutes. If your mass is 60 kg and you're essentially water, by how much would your temperature increase if you had no heat loss?

19. A circular lake 1.0 km in diameter is 10 m deep (Fig. 19-25). Solar energy is incident on the lake at an average rate of 200 W/m^2. If the lake absorbs all this energy and does not exchange heat with its surroundings, how long will it take to warm from 10°C to 20°C?

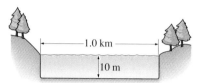

FIGURE 19-25 Problem 19.

20. You bring a 350-g wrench into the house from your car. The house is 15°C warmer than the car, and it takes 2.52 kJ of energy to warm the wrench by this amount. Find (a) the heat capacity of the wrench and (b) the specific heat of the metal it's made from.

21. How much heat is required to raise an 800-g copper pan from 15°C to 90°C if (a) the pan is empty; (b) the pan contains 1.0 kg of water; (c) the pan contains 4.0 kg of mercury?

22. Initially, 100 g of water and 100 g of another substance listed in Table 19-1 are at 20°C. Heat is then transferred to each substance at the same rate for 1.0 min. At the end of that time the water is at 32°C and the other substance at 76°C. (a) What is the other substance? (b) What is the heating rate?

23. How much power does it take to raise the temperature of a 1.3-kg copper pipe by 15°C/s?

24. How long will it take a 625-W microwave oven to bring 250 mL of water from 10°C to the boiling point?

25. You insert your microwave oven's temperature probe in a roast and start it cooking. You notice that the temperature goes up 1°C every 20 s. If the roast has the same specific heat as water, and if the oven power is 500 W, what is the mass of the roast? Neglect heat loss.

26. Two neighbors return from Florida to find their houses at a frigid 15°F. Each house has a furnace with heat output of 100,000 Btu/h. One house is made of stone and weighs 75 tons. The other is made of wood and weighs 15 tons. How long does it take each house to reach 65°F? Neglect heat loss, and assume the entire house mass reaches the same 65°F temperature.

27. A stove burner supplies heat at the rate of 1.0 kW, a microwave oven at 625 W. You can heat water in the microwave in a paper cup of negligible heat capacity, but the stove requires a pan whose heat capacity is 1.4 kJ/K. (a) How much water do you need before it becomes quicker to heat on the stovetop? (b) What will be the rate at which the temperature of this much water rises?

28. When a nuclear power plant's reactor is shut down, radioactive decay continues to produce heat at about 10% of the reactor's normal power level of 3.0 GW. In a major accident, a pipe breaks and all the reactor cooling water is

lost. The reactor is immediately shut down, the break sealed, and 420 m³ of 20°C water injected into the reactor. If the water were not actively cooled, how long would it take to reach its normal boiling point?

29. A 1.2-kg iron tea kettle sits on a 2.0-kW stove burner. If it takes 5.4 min to bring the kettle and the water in it from 20°C to the boiling point, how much water is in the kettle?

30. An alpine rescue team finds a 73-kg hypothermia victim whose body temperature has dropped to 34°C. They wrap the victim in blankets, reducing his heat loss to near zero. Shivering violently, the victim's own metabolism releases energy at the rate of 190 W. (a) How long will it take to warm his body to the normal 37°C? Assume the body is essentially water. (b) How many 230-kcal chocolate bars would it take to supply the energy needed to heat the victim's body?

31. Two cars collide head-on at 90 km/h. If all their kinetic energy ended up as heat, what would be the temperature increase of the wrecks? The specific heat of the cars is essentially that of iron.

32. A 1500-kg car moving at 40 km/h is brought to a sudden stop. If all the car's energy is dissipated in heating its four 5.0-kg steel brake disks, by how much do the disk temperatures increase?

33. A leaf absorbs sunlight with intensity 600 W/m². The leaf has a mass per unit area of 100 g/m², and its specific heat is 3800 J/kg·K. In the absence of any heat loss, at what rate would the leaf's temperature rise?

34. A child complains that her cocoa is too hot. The cocoa is at 90°C. Her father pours 2 oz of milk at 3°C into the 6 oz of cocoa. Assuming milk and cocoa have the same specific heat as water, what is the new temperature of the cocoa?

35. A piece of copper at 300°C is dropped into 1.0 kg of water at 20°C. If the equilibrium temperature is 25°C, what is the mass of the copper?

36. Vegetables with mass 2.2 kg, specific heat 0.92 cal/g·°C, and temperature 4.0°C are added to 4.5 kg of soup stock (essentially water) at 80°C. What is the equilibrium temperature?

37. A thermometer of mass 83.0 g is used to measure the temperature of a 150-g water sample. The thermometer's specific heat is 0.190 cal/g·°C, and it reads 20.0°C before immersion in the water. The water temperature is initially 60.0°C. What does the thermometer read after it comes to equilibrium with the water?

Sections 19-6 and 19-7 Heat Transfer and Thermal Energy Balance

38. Find the heat-loss rate through a 1.0-m² slab of (a) wood and (b) styrofoam, each 2.0 cm thick, if one surface is at 20°C and the other at 0°C.

39. The top of a steel wood stove measures 90 cm × 40 cm, and is 0.45 cm thick. The fire maintains the inside surface of the stove top at 310°C, while the outside surface is at 295°C. Find the rate of heat conduction through the stove top.

40. How thick a concrete wall would be needed to give the same insulating value as $3\frac{1}{2}$ inches of fiberglass?

41. Building heat loss in the United States is usually expressed in Btu/h. What is 1 Btu/h in SI?

42. An 8.0 m × 12 m house is built on a concrete slab 23 cm thick. What is the heat-loss rate through the floor if the interior is at 20°C while the ground is at 10°C?

43. What is the R-factor of a wall that loses 0.040 Btu each hour through each square foot for each °F temperature difference?

44. Compute the R-factors for 1-inch thicknesses of air, concrete, fiberglass, glass, styrofoam, and wood.

45. A biology lab's walk-in cooler measures 3.0 m × 2.0 m × 2.3 m and is insulated with 8.0-cm-thick styrofoam. If the surrounding building is at 20°C, at what average rate must the cooler's refrigeration unit remove heat in order to maintain 4.0°C in the cooler?

46. One end of an iron rod 40 cm long and 3.0 cm in diameter is in ice water, the other in boiling water. (See Fig. 19-26.) The rod is well insulated so there's no heat lost out the sides. What is the heat-flow rate along the rod?

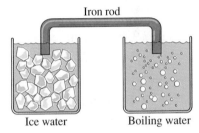

FIGURE 19-26 Problem 46.

47. (a) What is the R-factor for a wall consisting of $\frac{1}{4}$-in. pine paneling, $\mathcal{R}$-11 fiberglass insulation, $\frac{3}{4}$-in. pine sheathing, and 2.0-mm aluminum siding? (b) What is the heat-loss rate through a 20 ft × 8 ft section of wall when the temperature difference across the wall is 55°F?

48. You're considering installing a 5 ft × 8 ft picture window in a north-facing wall that now has $\mathcal{R}$-19 insulation. The window has $\mathcal{R}$ = 2.1 ft²·°F·h/Btu. If you install the window, how much more oil, at 100,000 Btu per gallon, will you have to burn in a winter month when the outdoor temperature averages 15°F and the indoor temperature is 68°F?

49. Repeat the preceding problem for a south-facing window where the average sunlight intensity is 180 W/m².

50. A flat-roofed house measures 28 ft × 28 ft × 9 ft high and has $\mathcal{R}$ = 30 for its roof and $\mathcal{R}$ = 20 for its walls. The house next door has the same height, the same wall and roof construction, the same square shape, but twice the floor area. If the houses are kept at the same temperature, compare their heating bills. Neglect losses through the floors.

51. A house is insulated so its total heat loss is 370 W/°C. On a night when the outdoor temperature is 12°C the owner throws a party, and 40 people come. The average power output of the human body is 100 W. If there are no other

heat sources in the house, what will be the house temperature during the party?

52. A 1000-W electric clothes iron has surface area 300 cm² and emissivity $e = 0.97$. If the surface temperature of the iron is 500 K and its surroundings are at 300 K, (a) what is the *net* rate of energy transfer by radiation from the iron? (b) What must be the rate of energy transfer by conduction and convection?

53. An electric stove burner has surface area 325 cm² and emissivity $e = 1.0$. The burner is at 900 K and the electric power input to the burner is 1500 W. If room temperature is 300 K, what fraction of the burner's heat loss is by radiation?

54. An electric current passes through a metal strip 0.50 cm × 5.0 cm × 0.10 mm, heating it at the rate of 50 W. The strip has emissivity $e = 1.0$ and its surroundings are at 300 K. What will be the temperature of the strip if it's enclosed in (a) a vacuum bottle transparent to all radiation and (b) an insulating box with thermal resistance $R = 8.0$ K/W that blocks all radiation?

55. The average human body produces heat at the rate of 100 W and has total surface area of about 1.5 m². What is the coldest outdoor temperature in which a down sleeping bag with 4.0-cm loft (thickness) can be used without the body temperature dropping below 37°C? Consider only conductive heat loss.

56. The Intergovernmental Panel on Climate Change estimates that human-produced greenhouse gases currently have a climatic effect roughly equivalent to an increase in the intensity of sunlight of 2.5 W/m². What increase in global temperature should be attributable to these gases? (Your answer is only an estimate because your calculation ignores feedbacks and other important effects.)

57. Scientists worry that a nuclear war could inject enough dust into the upper atmosphere to reduce significantly the amount of solar energy reaching Earth's surface. If an 8% reduction in solar input occurred, what would happen to Earth's 287-K average temperature?

58. Sunlight intensity varies with the inverse square of the distance from the Sun; at Earth's orbit the intensity is 1.37 kW/m². Use data from Appendix E to calculate the average temperatures of Mars and Venus if those planets' atmospheres contained no greenhouse gases, and treating each as a blackbody ($e = 1$). Compare with the measured surface temperatures of about 220 K and 730 K, respectively. Does either planet have a significant greenhouse effect?

Paired Problems

(Both problems in a pair involve the same principles and techniques. If you can get the first problem, you should be able to solve the second one.)

59. A blacksmith heats a 1.1-kg iron horseshoe to 550°C, then plunges it into a bucket containing 15 kg of water at 20°C. What is the final temperature?

60. A 2.3-kg cast-iron frying pan is plunged into 7.5 kg of water at 22°C. If the equilibrium temperature is 30°C, what was the pan's initial temperature?

61. What is the power output of a microwave oven that can heat 430 g of water from 20°C to the boiling point in 5.0 minutes? Neglect the heat capacity of the container.

62. A nuclear power plant is being started up after refueling. If it takes 1.5 hours to bring the reactor's 5.4×10^6 kg of cooling water from 10°C to its 350°C operating temperature, what is the reactor's thermal power output? Neglect the heat capacity of the reactor vessel and plumbing.

63. A cylindrical log 15 cm in diameter and 65 cm long is glowing red hot in a fireplace. If it's emitting radiation at the rate of 34 kW, what is its temperature? The log's emissivity is essentially 1.

64. A star whose surface temperature is 50 kK radiates 4.0×10^{27} W. If the star behaves as a blackbody, what is its radius?

65. An enclosed rabbit hutch has a thermal resistance of 0.25 K/W. If you put a 50-W heat lamp in the hutch on a day when the outside temperature is −15°C, what will be the hutch temperature? Neglect the rabbit's metabolism.

66. The walls of a home refrigerator have a thermal resistance of 0.090 K/W. What is the average rate at which the refrigerator must transfer heat in order to maintain the interior at 4°C in a room where the temperature is 21°C?

Supplementary Problems

67. Rework Example 19-5, now assuming that the house has 10 single-glazed windows, each measuring 2.5 ft × 5.0 ft. Four of the windows are on the south, and admit solar energy at the average rate of 30 Btu/h·ft². *All* the windows lose heat; their R-factor is 0.90. (a) What is the total heating cost for the month? (b) How much is the solar gain worth?

68. What are the SI units of R-factor? Express the R-factor for 6-in fiberglass insulation ($\mathcal{R} = 19$ ft²·°F·h/Btu) in SI.

69. My house currently burns 160 gallons of oil in a typical winter month when the outdoor temperature averages 15°F and the indoor temperature averages 66°F. Roof insulation consists of $\mathcal{R} = 19$ fiberglass, and the roof area is 770 ft². If I double the thickness of the roof insulation, by what percentage will my heating bills drop? A gallon of oil yields about 100,000 Btu of heat.

70. A black woodstove with surface area 4.6 m² is made from cast iron 4.0 mm thick. The interior wall of the stove is at 650°C while the exterior is at 647°C. (a) What is the rate of heat conduction through the stove wall? (b) What is the rate of heat loss by radiation from the stove? (c) Use the results of (a) and (b) to find how much heat the stove loses by a combination of conduction and convection in the surrounding air.

71. A copper pan 1.5 mm thick and a cast iron pan 4.0 mm thick are sitting on electric stove burners; the bottom area of each pan is 300 cm². Each contains 2.0 kg of water

whose temperature is rising at the rate of 0.15 K/s. Find the temperature difference between the inside and outside bottom of each pan.

72. What should be the average temperature on Pluto, at its 5.9×10^{12}-m distance from the Sun? Treat Pluto as a blackbody.

73. At low temperatures the specific heat of a solid is approximately proportional to the cube of the temperature; for copper the specific heat is given by $c = 31(T/343 \text{ K})^3$ J/g·K. When heat capacity is not constant, Equations 19-4 and 19-5 must be written in terms of the derivative dQ/dT and integrated to get the total heat involved in a temperature change. Find the heat required to bring a 40-g sample of copper from 10 K to 25 K.

74. When area or heat conductivity are not constant, Equation 19-7 must be written in terms of the derivative dT/dx:

$$H = -kA\frac{dT}{dx} \qquad (19\text{-}14)$$

and must be integrated to get the relation between the temperature difference and heat loss. Consider a truncated cone with faces of radii R_1 and R_2 and length ℓ, as shown in Fig. 19-27. If the temperatures on the faces are T_1 and T_2, respectively, and if insulation prevents heat loss out the sides, show that the heat flow rate is given by $H = \pi k R_1 R_2 (T_1 - T_2)/\ell$. *Hint:* Divide the cone into thin slabs and write the area of each in terms of its distance x from the left face. Use this expression for the area in Equation 19-14, multiply through by dx/A, and integrate, noting that H must be the same throughout the cone.

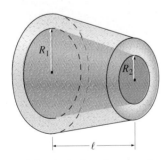

FIGURE 19-27 What is the heat flow rate through the cone? The insulation prevents heat loss out the sides (Problem 74).

75. A pipe of length ℓ and radius R_1 is surrounded by insulation of outer radius R_2 and thermal conductivity k. Use the methods of the preceding problem to show that the heat loss rate through the insulation is

$$H = \frac{2\pi k \ell (T_1 - T_2)}{\ln(R_2/R_1)}.$$

Hint: Consider the heat flow through a thin layer of thickness dr and temperature difference dT as shown in Fig. 19-28.

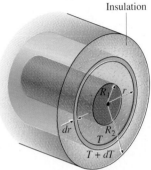

FIGURE 19-28 An insulated pipe. Blue cylinder is a layer of thickness dr for use in calculating the heat loss (Problem 75).

76. An object of heat capacity C J/K is surrounded by insulation with thermal resistance R K/W. The object is initially at temperature T_1 and its surroundings are at the constant temperature T_0. (a) If there is no source of heat in the object, show that its temperature T as a function of time t is described by the equation

$$C\frac{dT}{dt} = -\frac{1}{R}(T - T_0).$$

(b) Show by substitution that the solution to this equation is

$$T = T_0 + (T_1 - T_0)e^{-t/RC}.$$

Show that this solution gives reasonable results for $t = 0$ and as $t \to \infty$.

77. A house is at 20°C on a winter day when the outdoor temperature is -15°C. Suddenly the furnace fails. Use the result of the previous problem to determine how long it will take the house temperature to reach the freezing point. The heat capacity of the house is 6.5 MJ/K, and its thermal resistance is 6.67 mK/W.

20 The Thermal Behavior of Matter

Melting is one of the changes matter undergoes when its temperature increases. Here molten steel pours from a red-hot crucible.

Matter responds to heating in a variety of ways. It may get hotter or it may melt. It may experience changes in size or shape, or in pressure. In this chapter, we seek to understand the thermal behavior of matter. We start with a particularly simple state—the gaseous state—whose behavior can largely be explained by applying Newtonian mechanics at the molecular level. We then move to the more complicated cases of liquids and solids, whose behavior is still grounded in the molecular properties of matter, but whose description at the level of this text is necessarily more empirical.

20-1 GASES

Gas is matter in a rarefied state. Molecules of a gas are so far apart that they spend most of their time moving freely, and only rarely interact with one another. That makes gas behavior and its physical explanation particularly simple. In studying gas behavior, we will develop a clear understanding of the relation between macroscopic properties—such as temperature and pressure—and the underlying microscopic properties of gas molecules.

The Ideal Gas Law

The macroscopic state of a gas in thermodynamic equilibrium is determined completely by its temperature, pressure, and volume. Moreover, it turns out that all gases exhibit, to a very good approximation, the same relation among these three quantities.

A simple system for studying gas behavior consists of a gas-filled cylinder sealed by a movable piston (Fig. 20-1). As we explore this system here and in the next chapter, keep in mind that it's not just a pedagogical abstraction. Practical devices including engines, pumps, and air compressors contain piston-cylinder systems, while human lungs, balloons, the blood-borne gas bubbles that cause the "bends" in scuba divers, and many other natural systems involving confined gases are analogous to our piston-cylinder system. ActivPhysics Activity 8.4 provides a simulation of a gas in a piston-cylinder system.

If we maintain the system of Fig. 20-1 at constant temperature (for example, by immersing it in a bath of water) and move the piston to vary the gas volume, we find that the pressure varies inversely with volume. If we increase the temperature while holding volume fixed, the pressure rises in direct proportion to the temperature. If we double the amount of gas while holding temperature and volume constant, we find that the pressure doubles. Putting all these experimental results together, we can write

$$PV = NkT, \tag{20-1}$$

with P, V, and T the pressure, volume, and temperature, respectively, and N the number of molecules in the gas. The constant k is **Boltzmann's constant**, after the Austrian physicist Ludwig Boltzmann (1844–1906), who was instrumental in developing the microscopic description of thermal phenomena. Its value is $k = 1.38 \times 10^{-23}$ J/K.

Equation 20-1 is the **ideal gas law**. Most real gases obey this law to a very good approximation. Later we'll see just why and how real gas behavior deviates, usually just slightly, from the ideal expressed in Equation 20-1.

Because the number of molecules, N, in a typical gas sample is astronomically large, we often express the ideal gas law in terms of the number of **moles** (mol) of gas molecules. The mole is an SI unit useful for measuring the amount of anything that comes in large numbers; one mole of anything consists of Avogadro's number of that thing, where Avogadro's number is approximately $N_A = 6.022 \times 10^{23}$. (Formally, Avogadro's number is defined as the number of carbon-12 atoms in 1 gram of carbon-12. It's named after the Italian chemist Amadeo Avogadro, 1776–1856.)

FIGURE 20-1 A piston-cylinder system.

8.4
Ideal Gas Law

If we have n moles of a gas, then $N = nN_A$ is the number of molecules, so the ideal gas law becomes

$$PV = nN_A kT = nRT, \qquad (20\text{-}2)$$

where the constant $R = N_A k = 8.314$ J/K·mol is called the **universal gas constant**.

EXAMPLE 20-1	STP

What is the volume occupied by 1.00 mol of an ideal gas at standard temperature and pressure (STP), where $T = 0°C$ and $P = 101.3$ kPa?

Solution

Solving the ideal gas law for the volume V, and expressing temperature in kelvins, we have

$$V = \frac{nRT}{P} = \frac{(1.00 \text{ mol})(8.314 \text{ J/K·mol})(273 \text{ K})}{1.013 \times 10^5 \text{ Pa}}$$
$$= 22.4 \times 10^{-3} \text{ m}^3 = 22.4 \text{ L}.$$

EXERCISE If the gas of Example 20-1 is cooled to $-120°C$ and compressed into a 2.0-L container, what will be its pressure?

Answer: 636 kPa

Some problems similar to Example 20-1: 3, 6, 8, 11

The ideal gas law is remarkably simple. Neither the form of the law nor the constants k and R depend on the substance making up the gas or on the mass of the individual gas molecules. Yet most real gases follow the ideal gas law very closely over a wide range of pressures. This nearly ideal behavior is what gives gas thermometers their high precision over a wide temperature range.

Kinetic Theory of the Ideal Gas

Why do gases obey such a simple relation among temperature, pressure, and volume? Here we answer that question with a microscopic analysis of the ideal gas that is based ultimately in the laws of Newtonian mechanics.

To understand how matter in the gaseous state should behave, we make a number of simplifying assumptions:

1. The gas consists of a very large number of identical molecules, each with mass m but with negligible size and no internal structure. This assumption is approximately true for real gases when the distance between molecules is large compared with their size. The molecules' negligible size means that intermolecular collisions are so rare we can neglect them. (We'll see later that neglecting collisions is not essential, but it will simplify our analysis. ActivPhysics Activity 8.1 explores the role of molecular collisions.)

2. The molecules do not exert any action-at-a-distance forces on each other. This means there are no potential energy changes to be considered, so each molecule's kinetic energy remains unchanged. Thus the only form of molecular energy that's important is kinetic energy. This assumption is fundamental to the nature of an ideal gas.

3. The molecules are moving in random directions with a distribution of speeds that is independent of direction.

4. Collisions with the container walls are elastic, conserving the molecules' energy and momentum. This is where we'll tie our gas model to the laws of Newtonian mechanics.

8.1
Characteristics of a Gas

Consider N molecules of gas confined inside a rectangular container extending a length ℓ in the x direction (Fig. 20-2). Each time a gas molecule collides with a container wall, it exerts a force on the wall. There are so many molecules (assumption 1) that individual collisions aren't evident; instead the wall experiences an essentially constant average force. The gas pressure P is a measure of this force pushing on a unit area. We're going to find an expression for this pressure and show that it can be put in the same form as the ideal gas law.

To find the pressure, consider one molecule colliding with the right-hand wall in Fig. 20-2. Since the collision is elastic (assumption 4), the y component of the molecule's velocity remains unchanged, while the x component reverses sign (Fig. 20-3). Thus the molecule undergoes a momentum change of magnitude $2mv_{xi}$, where i labels this particular molecule. After colliding with the right-hand wall, nothing will change the molecule's x velocity (assumption 2) until it hits the left-hand wall and its x velocity again reverses. So it will be back at the right-hand wall in the time $\Delta t_i = 2\ell/v_{xi}$ that it takes to go back and forth along the container.

Now each time our molecule collides with the right-hand wall, it delivers momentum $2mv_{xi}$ to the wall. Newton's second law says that force is the rate of change of momentum; since we've just found the time interval between collisions, we can calculate the average force $\overline{F}_i$ due to the one molecule we're considering:

$$\overline{F}_i = \frac{\Delta p}{\Delta t} = \frac{2mv_{xi}}{(2\ell/v_{xi})} = \frac{mv_{xi}^2}{\ell}.$$

To get the total force on the wall, we sum over all N molecules with their different x velocities; dividing by the wall area A then gives the force per unit area, or pressure:

$$P = \frac{\overline{F}}{A} = \frac{\sum \overline{F}_i}{A} = \frac{\sum mv_{xi}^2/\ell}{A} = \frac{m \sum v_{xi}^2}{A\ell}.$$

The last step follows because both the box length ℓ and molecular mass m are the same for all molecules, so they factor out of the sum. We can simplify our expression for pressure by noting that the denominator $A\ell$ is just the volume, V, of the rectangular container. Let's also multiply by 1 in the form N/N, with N the number of molecules. Then we have

$$P = \frac{m \sum v_{xi}^2}{A\ell} = \frac{mN}{V} \frac{\sum v_{xi}^2}{N}.$$

In the final expression here, the term $\sum v_{xi}^2/N$ is just the average of the squares of all the x velocity components of all the molecules; we designate this quantity $\overline{v_x^2}$. So the pressure becomes

$$P = \frac{mN}{V} \overline{v_x^2}.$$

We still haven't used our assumption 3, that the molecules move in random directions with speed distribution independent of direction. If we grab a molecule at random, that means we're just as likely to find it moving in the x direction, the y direction, the z direction, or any direction in between—and its speed, on average, won't depend on its direction of motion. So the average quantities $\overline{v_x^2}$, $\overline{v_y^2}$, and $\overline{v_z^2}$ must be equal; otherwise one of the directions would be favored with molecules moving faster. Since the three directions x, y, and z are perpendicular, the average of the molecular speeds squared is given by

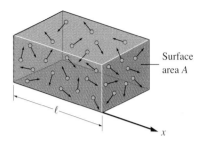

FIGURE 20-2 Gas molecules confined to a rectangular box.

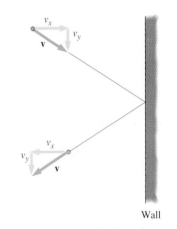

FIGURE 20-3 A molecule undergoes an elastic collision with the container wall, reversing its x component of velocity and transferring momentum $2mv_x$ to the wall.

$\overline{v^2} = \overline{v_x^2} + \overline{v_y^2} + \overline{v_z^2}$. Since we've just argued that all three terms on the right must be equal, we can then write $\overline{v^2} = 3\overline{v_x^2}$, or $\overline{v_x^2} = \frac{1}{3}\overline{v^2}$. Then our expression for pressure becomes

$$P = \frac{mN}{3V}\overline{v^2}.$$

Multiplying through by V, and by 1 in the form 2/2, we have

$$PV = \tfrac{2}{3}N(\tfrac{1}{2}m\overline{v^2}). \tag{20-3}$$

This looks a lot like the ideal gas law (Equation 20-1)! On the left is product PV, showing that pressure and volume are indeed inversely proportional if other quantities are held fixed. On the right is N, showing that pressure is indeed proportional to the amount of gas. But instead of kT we have $\frac{2}{3}(\frac{1}{2}m\overline{v^2})$. Take a good look at the quantity in parentheses: you'll see that it's just the average kinetic energy of a gas molecule.

Think about what we've done here. We applied the fundamental laws of mechanics to an ideal gas and came up with an equation (20-3) that looks like the experimentally verified ideal gas law, except that it's expressed in terms of a microscopic quantity—molecular kinetic energy—rather than the macroscopic quantity temperature. Since Equation 20-3 describes the behavior of an ideal gas, it *must be* the ideal gas law. Comparing our equation with the ideal gas law in the form 20-1, we see that for the equations to be equivalent, we must have

$$\tfrac{1}{2}m\overline{v^2} = \tfrac{3}{2}kT. \tag{20-4}$$

Our derivation leading to Equation 20-3 shows why, in terms of Newtonian mechanics, a gas obeying our four assumptions should obey the ideal gas law. In Equation 20-4 we get an added bonus—a microscopic understanding of the meaning of temperature:

> **Temperature measures the average kinetic energy associated with random translational motion of the molecules.**

EXAMPLE 20-2	*Molecular Energy*

What is the average kinetic energy of a molecule in air at room temperature? What would be the speed of a nitrogen molecule with this energy?

Solution

The average kinetic energy is given by Equation 20-4, where room temperature is about 20°C (293 K):

$$\tfrac{1}{2}m\overline{v^2} = \tfrac{3}{2}kT = \tfrac{3}{2}(1.38\times10^{-23}\text{ J/K})(293\text{ K})$$

$$= 6.07\times10^{-21}\text{ J}.$$

A nitrogen molecule consists of two nitrogen atoms (atomic mass 14 u; see Appendix D), so its mass is

$$m = 2(14\text{ u})(1.66\times10^{-27}\text{ kg/u}) = 4.65\times10^{-26}\text{ kg}.$$

The kinetic energy is $K = \frac{1}{2}mv^2$, so

$$v = \sqrt{\frac{2K}{m}} = \sqrt{\frac{2(6.07\times10^{-21}\text{ J})}{4.65\times10^{-26}\text{ kg}}} = 511\text{ m/s}.$$

Not surprisingly, this is of the same order of magnitude as the sound speed ($\approx$340 m/s) in air at room temperature. At the microscopic level, the speed of the individual molecules sets an approximate upper limit on the maximum rate at which information can be transmitted by disturbances—that is, sound waves—propagating through the gas.

EXERCISE Find the speed of a hydrogen molecule (H_2) with average kinetic energy at 300 K.

Answer: 1.9 km/s

Some problems similar to Example 20-2: 14–16

We'll call the speed calculated in Example 20-2 the **thermal speed**; in terms of temperature, Equation 20-4 shows that it's given by

$$v_{th} = \sqrt{\frac{3kT}{m}}. \qquad (20\text{-}5)$$

v_{th} is also called the **root mean square** (rms) speed, because it comes from taking the square root of a quantity—the temperature T or average molecular kinetic energy K—that contains the average of the speeds squared.

The Distribution of Molecular Speeds

The quantity $\frac{3}{2}KT$ in Equation 20-4 gives the average kinetic energy of all the molecules in a gas, but it doesn't tell us about any one molecule. Similarly, the thermal speed of Equation 20-5 is a typical molecular speed, but again it doesn't tell us much about what to expect for the speed of any individual molecule.

Sometimes we want to know more than just these average quantities. For example, is the range of molecular speeds limited to a narrow band about the thermal speed? Or are there many molecules moving much faster? Such fast molecules would be important in determining, for example, the chemical reaction rates in a gas mixture, or the tendency of an atmosphere to escape the gravitational field of its planet.

In the 1860s, the Scottish physicist James Clerk Maxwell considered the sharing of energy that must result from collisions among the molecules of a gas. Although we've neglected such collisions, their presence changes none of our earlier conclusions as long as the collisions are elastic; in fact, collisions are responsible for bringing a gas into thermodynamic equilibrium. Maxwell showed that molecular collisions result in a speed distribution where the number of molecules in a small speed range Δv about some speed v is given by

8.2, 8.3
Maxwell-Boltzmann Distribution

$$N(v)\,\Delta v = 4\pi N\left(\frac{m}{2\pi kT}\right)^{3/2} v^2 e^{-mv^2/2kT}\,\Delta v, \qquad (20\text{-}6)$$

where N is the total number of molecules in the gas, m the molecular mass, k Boltzmann's constant, and T the temperature. The quantity $N(v)$ is the number of molecules per unit speed range; multiplying by a small speed range Δv gives $N(v)\Delta v$, the actual number of molecules in that range. Equation 20-6 is known as the **Maxwell-Boltzmann distribution**. Figure 20-4 shows plots of this distribution for the same gas sample at two different temperatures. Each curve exhibits a single peak; this is the most probable value for a molecule's speed. Because the curve is not symmetric about the peak, the most probable speed lies below the thermal speed (see Problem 72). Figure 20-4 shows what Equation 20-4 already told us: that an increase in temperature corresponds to an increase in mean thermal speed. But it also shows something averages alone could not reveal: that an increase in temperature results in a broader speed distribution, with relatively fewer molecules near the most probable speed. ActivPhysics Activity 8.2 lets you explore the Maxwell-Boltzmann distribution for a simulated gas; you can pick a speed range on a graph of the distribution and you'll see highlighted just which molecules in the gas have speeds in that range.

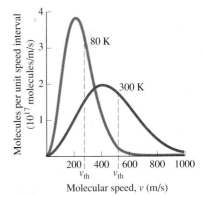

FIGURE 20-4 Maxwell-Boltzmann distribution of molecular speeds for 10^{20} nitrogen molecules (N_2) at temperatures of 80 K and 300 K. Also marked is the thermal speed $v_{th} = \sqrt{3kT/m}$; note that it isn't quite the same as the most probable speed, which is the speed value where the curve has its peak. Areas under both curves correspond to the total number of molecules and are therefore the same.

Our world would be very different if molecules in a gas all shared a single speed, or even if the distribution of molecular speeds were more symmetric than the Maxwell-Boltzmann distribution. Because the "tail" of the distribution extends to high speeds, there are always a significant number of high-energy molecules even in a relatively cool gas. It's easier for these high-energy molecules to break the bonds holding them in the liquid, so they're the ones that go first when the liquid evaporates. Without the high-energy tail of the Maxwell-Boltzmann distribution, Earth's atmosphere would be much drier and rain far less frequent. Loss of the highest-energy molecules during evaporation also leaves the average energy—and therefore the temperature—of the remaining molecules lower. That explains the process of evaporative cooling—a process our own bodies use to help regulate temperature.

The high-energy tail of the Maxwell-Boltzmann distribution also determines chemical reaction rates, and explains even such mundane phenomena as the spoiling of unrefrigerated food. Higher-energy molecules are more likely to collide vigorously enough to combine or break apart to form new chemical species. The exponential term in Equation 20-6 shows that increasing the temperature even slightly disproportionately increases the number of high-energy molecules (see Problem 22). For that reason, chemical reaction rates increase dramatically with increasing temperature. Biochemical reactions are no exception, and that's why even the roughly 20°C difference between refrigerator temperature and room temperature makes such a big difference in how long you can keep food before it spoils.

Real Gases

Though the ideal gas law is a good approximation to the behavior of real gases, the assumptions leading to its derivation are not entirely realistic. Real gases therefore exhibit deviations from ideal behavior.

Our derivation of the ideal gas law assumed gas molecules are noninteracting point particles. But real molecules take up space, and they do collide. Figure 20-5 shows that each molecule prevents others from approaching closer than one molecular radius, thereby reducing the total volume available to the molecules. When molecules are close, furthermore, electrical effects result in a weak attractive force called the **van der Waals force**. In Chapter 23 we'll see how the van der Waals force arises from fundamental principles of electricity (see Fig. 23-30). As molecules move apart they do work to overcome the van der Waals force, and as a result the molecular kinetic energy drops. Correcting for both the nonzero molecular size and the effect of the van der Waals force gives the **van der Waals equation**, which we state without further derivation:

$$\left(P + \frac{n^2 a}{V^2}\right)(V - nb) = nRT, \tag{20-7}$$

where a and b are constants that depend on the particular gas. For low particle densities n/V, both correction terms in the van der Waals equation become negligible, showing that a rarefied gas closely follows the ideal gas law.

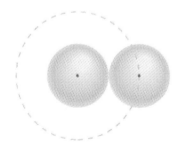

FIGURE 20-5 Two spherical gas molecules cannot get closer than a center-to-center separation of twice their radius. This effect reduces the total volume available to the molecules.

EXAMPLE 20-3	Van der Waals Effects

The constants a and b in the van der Waals equation for nitrogen have the values $a = 0.14$ Pa·m^6/mol^2, $b = 3.91 \times 10^{-5}$ m^3/mol. If 1.000 mol of nitrogen is confined to a volume of 2.000 L, and is at pressure of 10.00 atm, by how much does its temperature as predicted by the van der Waals equation differ from the ideal gas prediction?

Solution

Converting to SI units, we have $P = 1.013 \times 10^6$ Pa and $V = 2.000 \times 10^{-3}$ m^3. Then the ideal gas law predicts a temperature

$$T_{ideal} = \frac{PV}{nR} = \frac{(1.013 \times 10^6 \text{ Pa})(2.000 \times 10^{-3} \text{ m}^3)}{(1.000 \text{ mol})(8.314 \text{ J/K·mol})} = 244 \text{ K}.$$

The van der Waals equation predicts a temperature

$$T_{van} = \frac{(P + n^2 a/V^2)(V - nb)}{nR} = 247 \text{ K},$$

using the given values of a, b, n, P, and V. Under these conditions, nitrogen deviates from ideal gas behavior by only about 1%.

EXERCISE If the gas volume in Example 20-3 is halved while the pressure is held constant, by what percentage will the ideal and van der Waals temperature calculations differ?

Answer: 9.4%

Some problems similar to Example 20-3: 17–19

20-2 PHASE CHANGES

Step out of a steamy shower and you'll find the bathroom mirror all fogged up. Why? Because a gas of H$_2$O molecules has condensed on the cool mirror to make a film of liquid water. Climb a mountain on a winter day and you may be treated to the lovely spectacle of every rock, every branch, even every pine needle covered with a delicate coating of frost. Why? Because gaseous water from the air has solidified directly onto these surfaces. Spray a carbon-dioxide fire extinguisher and you'll see flakes of dry ice—solid CO$_2$ that formed directly from the rapidly cooling CO$_2$ gas expelled from the extinguisher.

What's happening here is a **phase change** that turns a gas into a liquid or even a solid. Intermolecular forces, negligible in the ideal gas approximation and weak in the van der Waals model, become dominant and bind the molecules into close proximity, sliding past each other in a liquid or locked into the rigid structure of a solid. You're familiar with other phase changes, too. You've observed ice melting and water freezing. You may have seen liquid nitrogen boiling at a mere 77 K (-196°C), or watched a welding torch melt its way through steel.

In this section we consider first such individual phase changes, then put phase changes in the broader context of the behavior of matter in response to general changes in temperature and pressure.

Heat and Phase Changes

Drop some ice cubes into a drink, stir, and wait a few minutes. What's the temperature of the drink? The answer is remarkably simple: it's 0°C, and it stays there as long as there's any ice left. The melting of a pure solid such as ice takes place at a fixed temperature (although, as we'll soon see, that temperature may depend on pressure). During the melting process, energy goes into breaking the molecular bonds that hold the material in its solid form. This increases the potential energy associated with separation of the molecules, but not their kinetic energy. We've just seen in Section 20-1 that temperature is related to molecular *kinetic* energy. Since molecular kinetic energy doesn't change during melting, neither does temperature.

FIGURE 20-6 Temperature versus time for what's initially a block of ice at −20°C, supplied with energy at a constant rate. The temperature doesn't change as the ice melts, nor when it boils; during these times the energy being absorbed goes into breaking molecular bonds. We've indicated a gap in the boiling time; otherwise this part of the graph would be inordinately long. Can you see from Table 20-1 why that would be? Can you tell from the graph whether ice or water has the greater specific heat?

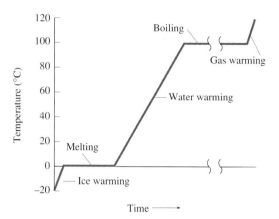

Figure 20-6 shows what happens if we take a block of ice from the freezer at, say, −20°C and supply energy at a constant rate, perhaps with a flame or by putting the ice in a microwave oven. At first the ice warms up, but soon it reaches its 0°C melting point. It continues to absorb energy, but with no temperature increase until it's all melted. Then its temperature once again increases. If we continue heating, the water eventually reaches its 100°C boiling point and then the temperature again remains constant as liquid water turns to gas. Finally, with continued heating, the gas temperature rises.

The amount of energy required to change the phase of a unit mass of material is called a **heat of transformation**; for the solid-to-liquid change it's the **heat of fusion**, L_f, and for the liquid-to-gas change it's the **heat of vaporization**, L_v. Less familiar is the **heat of sublimation** characterizing a change from solid directly to gas. Since the heat of transformation is the energy required per unit mass, the energy required to change the phase of a mass m is

$$Q = Lm. \tag{20-8}$$

To reverse the phase change—for example, to freeze water—requires removing the energy given by Equation 20-8. Table 20-1 lists heats of transformation for some common materials at atmospheric pressure.

Got It!

You bring a pot of water to boil, then forget about it. Ten minutes later you come back to the kitchen to find the water still boiling. What's its temperature?

TABLE 20-1 *Heats of Transformation (At Atmospheric Pressure)*

SUBSTANCE	MELTING POINT, K	L_f, kJ/kg	BOILING POINT, K	L_v, kJ/kg
Alcohol, ethyl	159	109	351	879
Copper	1357	205	2840	4726
Lead	601	24.7	2013	858
Mercury	234	11.3	630	296
Oxygen	54.8	13.8	90.2	213
Sulfur	388	38.5	718	287
Water	273	334	373	2257
Uranium	1406	82.8	4091	1875

Heat transfers associated with phase changes are typically quite large. The heat of fusion of water, for example, is 334 kJ/kg or 80 cal/g—meaning that it takes as much energy to melt one gram of ice as it does to raise the resulting water from 0°C to 80°C.

EXAMPLE 20-4	*Meltdown!*

In a serious accident, a nuclear power plant's reactor vessel cracks, and all the cooling water drains out (Fig. 20-7). Although nuclear fission stops, radioactive decay continues to heat the reactor's 2.5×10^5-kg uranium core at the rate of 120 MW. Once the core reaches its melting point, how much energy will it take to melt the core? How long will the melting take?

Solution

Using the heat of fusion from Table 20-1 in Equation 20-8 gives

$$Q = mL_f = (2.5 \times 10^5 \text{ kg})(82.8 \text{ kJ/kg}) = 2.07 \times 10^{10} \text{ J}.$$

At a heating rate of 120 MW ($= 1.2 \times 10^8$ J/s), the melting will take

$$\frac{2.07 \times 10^{10} \text{ J}}{1.2 \times 10^8 \text{ J/s}} = 172 \text{ s},$$

or less than 3 minutes! Failsafe emergency cooling systems are essential in preventing nuclear meltdowns.

EXERCISE (a) Find the energy needed to melt a 500-g block of lead at its melting point. (b) If the energy is supplied with a 1.1-kW torch, how long will the melting take?

Answers: (a) 12.4 kJ; (b) 11 s

Some problems similar to Example 20-4: 30, 32, 34–37

FIGURE 20-7 Workers practice picking up radioactive debris in a full-scale model of the damaged Three Mile Island nuclear reactor. The TMI reactor experienced a partial meltdown, although its pressure vessel did not crack.

The heats of transformation measure only the energy associated with phase changes, during which temperature doesn't change. To calculate the heat needed to change first the temperature and then the phase, we need to consider both the specific heat and the heat of transformation:

EXAMPLE 20-5	*Meltdown in the Kitchen?*

You put 650 g of water at 20°C in a pan on a 1.5-kW stove burner and forget about it. How long will it take to boil the pan dry, assuming all the burner's energy goes into the water?

Solution

First we calculate the energy needed to raise the water to its boiling point. Using the appropriate specific heat from Table 19-1 in Equation 19-4 gives

$$Q_1 = mc\Delta T = (0.65 \text{ kg})(4.184 \text{ kJ/kg·K})(80 \text{ K}) = 218 \text{ kJ}.$$

Equation 20-8, with data from Table 20-1, then gives the energy needed to transform all the water to the gaseous state:

$$Q_2 = mL_v = (0.65 \text{ kg})(2257 \text{ kJ/kg}) = 1467 \text{ kJ}.$$

So total energy needed is 218 kJ + 1467 kJ = 1685 kJ; at a heating rate of 1.5 kW, this takes 1685 kJ/1.5 kJ/s = 1123 s, or about 19 minutes.

Tip

Break a Problem into Separate Parts To work this example required solving two separate problems, one about temperature change and one about boiling. You'll often need to break a complex problem into several simpler ones, as this example suggests.

EXERCISE You put 100 g of ice at 0°C in a 625-W microwave oven. How long will it take until you have water at 90°C?

Answer: 114 s

Some problems similar to Example 20-5: 37–42

EXAMPLE 20-6	*Enough Ice?*

200 g of ice at $-10°C$ is added to 1.0 kg of water at 15°C in an insulated container. Is there enough ice to cool the water to 0°C? If so, how much ice and water are present once equilibrium is reached?

Solution

First we determine whether there is enough ice. To bring the ice to its melting point and melt all of it requires

$$Q_1 = mc\,\Delta T + mL_f$$
$$= (0.20 \text{ kg})(2.05 \text{ kJ/kg·K})(10 \text{ K}) + (0.20 \text{ kg})(334 \text{ kJ/kg})$$
$$= 4.1 \text{ kJ} + 66.8 \text{ kJ} = 70.9 \text{ kJ},$$

where we used data from Tables 19-1 and 20-1, and where the temperature change in °C is equal to its value in kelvins. (Here we've algebraically combined the two subproblems mentioned in the tip in Example 20-5.)

Cooling the water to 0°C extracts an amount of heat given by

$$Q_2 = mc\,\Delta T = (1.0 \text{ kg})(4.184 \text{ kJ/kg·K})(15 \text{ K}) = 62.8 \text{ kJ}.$$

This is far more than the 4.1 kJ needed to bring the ice to 0°C, but not quite the 70.9 kJ needed to leave it all melted. So there's enough ice to cool the water to 0°C, with some left over. How much? Our calculation of Q_1 shows that 4.1 kJ go into raising the ice temperature. Of the 62.8 kJ extracted from the water, the remaining 58.7 kJ go to melting ice. From Equation 20-6, the amount of ice melted is then

$$m = \frac{Q}{L_f} = \frac{58.7 \text{ kJ}}{334 \text{ kJ/kg}} = 0.176 \text{ kg} = 176 \text{ g}.$$

Thus we're left with 24 g of ice in 1176 g of water, all at 0°C.

EXERCISE Determine the final mix and temperature in Example 20-6 if the initial amount of ice is 100 g.

Answer: all water at 5.9°C

Some problems similar to Example 20-6: 43–47, 49

Phase Diagrams

Mountaineers in the Himalayas can't get their coffee as hot as you can at a lower altitude. Why not? Because the boiling point of water drops with the decreasing pressure at higher altitudes. This makes good physical sense, since it's easier for molecules to escape the liquid when there's less pressure from the surrounding air. Remember that the temperature doesn't change while the water is boiling, so it won't do the mountaineers any good to turn up the flame or heat their coffee longer—eventually it will just boil away!

In general, the temperatures at which phase changes occur—the melting and boiling points—depend on pressure. We can explore these effects with a **phase diagram** that shows where the solid, liquid, and gas phases lie on a plot of pressure versus temperature. Each substance has a different phase diagram, although most are qualitatively similar. Figure 20-8 shows a phase diagram for a typical substance such as carbon dioxide. (Water, with whose phase changes you're most familiar, has a slightly unusual phase diagram that we discuss in the next section. However, most of our general discussion here applies to water as well.)

The phase diagram of Fig. 20-8 divides *T-P* space into three regions corresponding to the solid, liquid, and gas phases. The lines separating these regions mark the phase transitions. Our everyday experience suggests that heating brings a solid to its melting point, turns it to liquid, raises the liquid temperature to the boiling point, and then turns it to a gas—just as we showed for water in Fig. 20-6. But Fig. 20-8 shows that this sequence doesn't always occur. At low enough pressure (line AB in Fig. 20-8), heating brings the substance right across the solid-gas transition. For carbon dioxide, normal atmospheric pressure lies in this lower region of the curve; that's why dry ice (solid CO_2) turns directly into

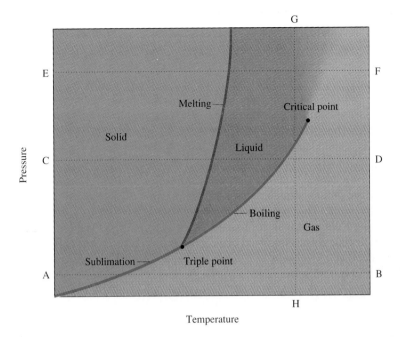

Temperature

FIGURE 20-9 Carbon dioxide subliming from solid to gas. The gray mist is actually a cloud of water droplets that condensed on contact with the cool CO_2 gas.

gas, a process called **sublimation** (Fig. 20-9). At higher pressures (line CD in Fig. 20-8), heating a substance gives the normal solid-liquid-gas sequence. (At room temperature, for example, a carbon-dioxide fire extinguisher is at a high enough pressure that the CO_2 is liquid.) But at still higher pressures (line EF), above the so-called **critical pressure** marked by the **critical point** in the phase diagram, heating turns the solid into a thick fluid whose properties gradually change from liquidlike to gaslike with continued heating; at these supercritical pressures, there's no sharp phase transition between liquid and gas.

We generally think of changing solid or liquid, or liquid to gas, by applying heat. But our phase diagram (Fig. 20-8) shows that we can also accomplish phase changes by varying the pressure. Lowering the pressure on a liquid at fixed temperature, for example (line GH in the phase diagram), will cause the liquid to boil and become a gas. You may have seen a demonstration in which water at room temperature is placed in an enclosed chamber and the air pumped out; when the pressure gets low enough, the water boils vigorously (Fig. 20-10).

Don't let Figure 20-8 fool you into thinking that phase transitions occur instantaneously as a substance jumps from, say, the solid to the liquid region of its phase diagram. If you started a substance at point C and supplied heat at a constant rate, keeping the pressure constant, the substance would move gradually across line CD in its phase diagram. Its temperature would increase at a rate determined by the power of the heat source and the specific heat of the solid; then it would pause on the solid-liquid transition for the time it took the entire sample to melt—a time determined by the heat of fusion. It would then move across the liquid region of the diagram, and then pause again on the liquid-gas transition until it had all turned to gas. This process is in fact just what we described for water in Fig. 20-6.

The dividing curves on Fig. 20-8 are regions where two phases can coexist in equilibrium. Ice floating in water at atmospheric pressure is one example; as long

FIGURE 20-10 Water boiling at room temperature in an evacuated flask.

as any ice remains, the system sits at a fixed point on the solid-liquid dividing line in the phase diagram. It's because melting, boiling, and sublimation occur along curves rather than at specific points in the phase diagram that terms such as "melting point" and "boiling point" are meaningless unless a pressure is specified. Water freezes at 0°C and boils at 100°C—but only at normal atmospheric pressure. So melting and boiling points do not make for good temperature standards. But there's one unique point in the phase diagram where the curves for melting, boiling, and sublimation all meet. That's the **triple point**, where solid, liquid, and gas can all coexist in equilibrium. Temperature and pressure at the triple point have unique, unambiguous values. If you put a substance in a sealed container and manipulate the temperature and pressure until all three phases remain indefinitely in the container, then you know you're at the triple point. That's why the triple point of water—at 273.16 K—is used to define the Kelvin temperature scale, as we discussed in Chapter 19. But you won't reach that point at normal atmospheric pressure; for the water the triple point occurs at a pressure of 0.006 atmospheres (that's the pressure at an altitude of about 35 km).

Phase diagrams display a lot of information in compact form. But even they can't do justice to the rich variety of thermal behavior exhibited by different substances. For example, a phase diagram doesn't show directly how volume changes with temperature and pressure. Furthermore, many substances have more complicated phase diagrams with different subphases, associated with changes in crystalline structure or molecular bonding. Full description of the thermal behavior of a given substance requires a three-dimensional diagram with axes representing temperature, pressure, and volume. We leave that for more advanced works on thermodynamics.

20-3 THERMAL EXPANSION

We've explored changes of temperature and phase that occur when matter is heated. But heating can also result in pressure or volume changes. For a gas held at constant pressure, for example, the ideal gas law shows that volume increases in direct proportion to the temperature rise.

The volume and pressure relations in the liquid and solid phases are not quite so simple. Liquids and solids are far less compressible than gases, so thermal expansion is less pronounced. On the microscopic level, the molecules in a liquid or solid are closely spaced; to move them requires that we do work against large (electrical) forces.

We can characterize the change in the volume of a substance with temperature in terms of its **coefficient of volume expansion**, β, defined as the fractional change in volume when the substance undergoes a small temperature change ΔT:

$$\beta = \frac{\Delta V/V}{\Delta T}. \tag{20-9}$$

This equation assumes that β is independent of temperature; if it varies significantly then we would need to define β in terms of the derivative dV/dT (see Problem 76). Our definition of β also assumes constant pressure; we could entirely inhibit thermal expansion with appropriate pressure increases.

Often we want to know how one linear dimension of a solid changes with temperature. This is especially true with long, rodlike structures where the absolute change is greatest along the long dimension (Fig. 20-11). We then

(a)

(b)

FIGURE 20-11 A power line sags as its length increases on a hot summer day.

TABLE 20-2 *Expansion Coefficients**

SOLIDS	$\alpha(\mathrm{K}^{-1})$	LIQUIDS AND GASES	$\beta(\mathrm{K}^{-1})$
Aluminum	24×10^{-6}	Air	3.7×10^{-3}
Brass	19×10^{-6}	Alcohol, ethyl	75×10^{-5}
Copper	17×10^{-6}	Gasoline	95×10^{-5}
Glass (Pyrex)	3.2×10^{-6}	Mercury	18×10^{-5}
Ice	51×10^{-6}	Water, 1°C	-4.8×10^{-5}
Invar†	0.9×10^{-6}	Water, 20°C	20×10^{-5}
Steel	12×10^{-6}	Water, 50°C	50×10^{-5}

*At approximately room temperature unless noted.
† Invar, consisting of 64% iron and 36% nickel, is an alloy designed to minimize thermal expansion.

speak of the **coefficient of linear expansion**, α, defined by

$$\alpha = \frac{\Delta L/L}{\Delta T}. \tag{20-10}$$

The volume expansion coefficient and linear expansion coefficient α are related in a simple way: $\beta = 3\alpha$, as you can show in Problem 79. This relation means that either of these coefficients fully characterizes the thermal expansion of a material. However, the linear expansion coefficient α is really only meaningful with solids, because liquids and gases deform readily and therefore do not generally expand proportionately in all directions. Table 20-2 lists expansion coefficients for some common substances.

EXAMPLE 20-7	*Thermal Expansion*

A steel girder is 15 m long at $-20°C$. It is used in the construction of a building where temperature extremes of $-20°C$ to $40°C$ are expected. By how much does the girder length change between these extremes?

Solution

Table 20-2 gives the coefficient of linear expansion for steel: $\alpha = 12\times10^{-6}\ \mathrm{K}^{-1}$. Equation 20-10 then gives

$\Delta L = \alpha L \Delta T = (12\times10^{-6}\ \mathrm{K}^{-1})(15\ \mathrm{m})(60\ \mathrm{K}) = 1.1\ \mathrm{cm}$.

EXERCISE A telescope assembly includes an aluminum rod 1.3 m long at 10°C. What is the maximum allowable temperature if the rod length is not to increase by more than 0.50 mm?

Answer: 26°C

Some problems similar to Example 20-7: 51–54

What happens when a hollow object expands? In Fig. 20-12, you might expect that the hole would shrink as material expands into it. Actually, as Fig. 20-13 shows, *every* linear dimension expands in the same proportion, causing the interior space to expand, too.

FIGURE 20-12 How will the size of the hole change when the object expands?

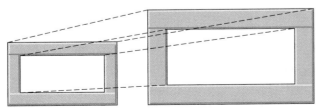

FIGURE 20-13 A hollow solid made of rectangular slabs. As the slabs expand, so does the interior space.

EXAMPLE 20-8	*Spilled Gasoline*

A car's gasoline tank is made of steel and has internal dimensions 60 cm × 60 cm × 20 cm at 10°C. It is filled with gasoline at 10°C. If the temperature now increases to 30°C, by how much does the volume of the tank increase? How much gasoline spills out of the tank?

Solution

The initial volume of the tank is

$$V = (0.60 \text{ m})(0.60 \text{ m})(0.20 \text{ m}) = 0.072 \text{ m}^3.$$

Equation 20-9 then gives the volume increases:

$$\Delta V = \beta V \Delta T,$$

so $\quad \Delta V_{\text{tank}} = (3)(12 \times 10^{-6} \text{ K}^{-1})(0.072 \text{ m}^3)(20 \text{ K})$

$$= 5.18 \times 10^{-5} \text{ m}^3,$$

and

$$\Delta V_{\text{gas}} = (95 \times 10^{-5} \text{ K}^{-1})(0.072 \text{ m}^3)(20 \text{ K}) = 1.37 \times 10^{-3} \text{ m}^3.$$

Since Table 20-2 gives the coefficient of linear expansion, α, for solids, we used $\beta = 3\alpha$ in calculating the volume change of the tank.

The expansion of the steel tank is negligible compared with that of the gasoline, so we lose 1.32×10^{-3} m³, or 1.32 L of gasoline. Don't fill your gas tank to the very top!

EXERCISE A farmer milks a cow into a 20-L steel milk pail; the milk comes from the cow at approximately 37°C. If the pail is initially full and also at 37°C, how much empty space will there be when it's been cooled to 3°C? The average thermal expansion coefficient for milk in this temperature range is 2.0×10^{-4} K⁻¹.

Answer: 112 mL

Some problems similar to Example 20-8: 60, 62, 76

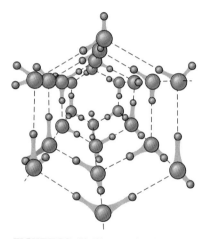

FIGURE 20-15 Water molecules in an ice crystal form an open structure, giving solid water a lower density than the liquid state.

Thermal Expansion of Water

The entry for water at 1°C in Table 20-2 is remarkable, for the negative expansion coefficient shows that water at this temperature actually *contracts* on heating (Fig. 20-14). This unusual behavior occurs because ice has a relatively open crystal structure (Fig. 20-15), and therefore is less dense than liquid water. That's why ice floats. Immediately above the melting point, the intermolecular forces (so-called hydrogen bonds) that hold H₂O molecules together in ice still exert an influence, giving cold liquid water a lower density than at slightly higher temperatures. At 4°C water reaches its maximum density, and above this temperature the effect of molecular kinetic energy in keeping molecules apart wins out over intermolecular forces. From there on water exhibits the more normal behavior of expansion with increasing temperature.

This unusual property of water near its melting point is reflected in its phase diagram, shown in Fig. 20-16. Notice that the solid-liquid boundary extends leftward from the triple point, in contrast to the more typical behavior we showed in Fig. 20-8. That means that ice at a fixed temperature will melt if the pressure is *increased*—an unusual property known as pressure melting (see Question 26 for more on this).

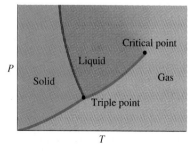

FIGURE 20-16 Phase diagram for water. Compare the solid-liquid boundary here with that of Fig. 20-8.

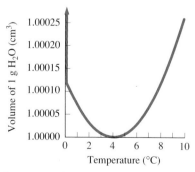

FIGURE 20-14 Volume of one gram of water near its melting point. Below 4°C, water actually expands when cooled. Graph rises vertically at 0°C, showing that solid ice would be way off scale at about 1.1 cm³. This is because ice's density is only about 90% of water.

The anomalous behavior of water has important consequences for life. If ice did not float, then ponds, lakes, and even oceans would freeze solid from the bottom up, making aquatic life impossible. What actually happens, instead, is that a thin layer of ice forms on the surface, insulating the water below and keeping it liquid; as a result, ice cover in temperate climates rarely exceeds a meter or so. Because water has the greatest density at 4°C, water at this temperature sinks to the bottom. At lake depths greater than a few meters, sunlight is inadequate to raise the temperature, which therefore remains year-round at 4°C.

Thermal Stresses

By enclosing a liquid or gas in a rigid container, or by tightly clamping the ends of a solid in place, we can inhibit thermal expansion. When heated, the material must then experience a pressure increase. If a container is unable to withstand this increase, it will burst (Fig. 20-17). If a solid is restrained along only one dimension, it will deform and perhaps crack (Fig. 20-18). Similarly, when a solid is clamped at both ends and cooled, tension forces develop that may cause it to break. Finally, if a solid is heated or cooled unevenly, part of the material expands or contracts at a different rate from the surrounding material. Again, the resulting forces may damage the material.

FIGURE 20-17 Industrial disaster! This boiler burst from overpressure caused by thermal expansion.

FIGURE 20-18 Thermal expansion distorted these railroad tracks, causing a derailment.

CHAPTER SYNOPSIS

Summary

1. An **ideal gas** is described by the **ideal gas law**, a relation among pressure, temperature, volume, and amount of gas.

$$PV = NkT.$$

Here N is the number of gas molecules and $k = 1.38 \times 10^{-23}$ J/K is **Boltzmann's constant**. The ideal gas law may also be written

$$PV = nRT,$$

where n is the number of moles and $R = 8.314$ J/K·mol is the **universal gas constant**.

2. **Kinetic theory** provides a description of the ideal gas in terms of the microscopic physics of large numbers of molecules. Kinetic theory relates temperature to the average translational kinetic energy of the gas molecules:

$$\tfrac{1}{2}m\overline{v^2} = \tfrac{3}{2}kT.$$

3. **Real gases** deviate from ideal behavior at high densities and low temperatures, where molecular size and intermolecular forces become significant. Real gases are described approximately by the **van der Waals equation**:

$$\left(P + \frac{n^2 a}{V^2}\right)(V - nb) = nRT,$$

where a and b are constants describing a particular gas.

4. Most substances can exist in several **phases**, including solid, liquid, and gas. During a **phase change**, energy is transferred to or from a substance without any temperature change. The energy per unit mass associated with phase changes from solid to liquid and liquid to gas are, respectively, the **heat of fusion** and the **heat of vaporization**. The **heat of sublimation** characterizes the solid-gas transition.

5. A **phase diagram** shows solid, liquid, and gaseous phases as regions on a plot of pressure versus temperature. Important points in the diagram are the **triple point**, defining the

unique temperature and pressure where all three phases can coexist in equilibrium, and the **critical point**, where the boundary between liquid and gas phases ceases to be distinct.

6. Most substances expand when heated at constant pressure. The change in volume is given by

$$\Delta V = \beta V \Delta T,$$

where β is the **coefficient of volume expansion**. The change in length of a solid is given by a similar expression:

$$\Delta L = \alpha L \Delta T,$$

where $\alpha = \beta/3$ is the **coefficient of linear expansion**. Water provides an important exception to the general rule that substances expand when heated: In the range from 0°C to 4°C, water contracts on heating.

7. If a substance is held rigidly, so that thermal expansion or contraction cannot occur, then **thermal stresses** develop that may cause damage.

Terms You Should Understand

(Pairs are closely related terms whose distinction is important; number in parentheses is chapter section where term first appears.)

ideal gas (20-1)
ideal gas law (20-1)
Boltzmann's constant (20-1)
universal gas constant (20-1)
Maxwell-Boltzmann distribution (20-1)
van der Waals equation (20-1)
phase, phase change (20-2)
phase diagram (20-2)

heat of transformation; heats of fusion and vaporization (20-2)
critical point (20-2)
triple point (20-2)
coefficients of volume and linear expansion (20-3)

Symbols You Should Recognize

N (20-1) $\overline{v^2}$ (20-1)
k (20-1) L, L_f, L_v (20-2)
N_A (20-1) α, β (20-3)
R (20-1)

Problems You Should Be Able to Solve

evaluating ideal gas properties (20-1)
relating temperature and molecular kinetic energy (20-1)
evaluating gas properties in the van der Waals approximation (20-1)
determining energy involved in phase changes (20-2)
calculating thermal expansion (20-3)

Limitations to Keep in Mind

The ideal gas law is an approximation valid for rarefied gases where molecular size and intermolecular forces are not important. For most gases under normal conditions the law provides an excellent approximation.

Despite our everyday experience, the distinction between liquid and gas is not always clear-cut. Similarly, the temperature regimes in which the different phases can exist depend on pressure and may sometimes run counter to common experience.

Equations 20-7 and 20-8 are strictly valid only for temperature changes small enough that the expansion coefficients β and α remain essentially constant.

QUESTIONS

1. If the volume of an ideal gas is increased, must the pressure drop proportionately? Explain.
2. According to the ideal gas law, what should the volume of a gas be at absolute zero? Why is this result absurd?
3. Why are you supposed to check the pressure in a tire when the tire is cold?
4. The average *speed* of the molecules in a gas increases with increasing temperature. What about the average *velocity?*
5. Suppose you start running while holding a jar of air. Do you change the average speed of the air molecules? The average velocity? The temperature?
6. Do all molecules in a gas have the same speed? If so, how does this come about? If not, how can the notion of temperature be meaningful?
7. The speed of sound in a gas is closely related to the thermal speed of the molecules. Why?

8. Two different gases are at the same temperature, and both are at low enough densities that they behave like ideal gases. Do their molecules have the same thermal speeds? Explain.
9. The atmosphere of a small planet such as Earth contains very little of the lighter gases such as hydrogen and helium. The massive planet Jupiter has an atmosphere rich in light gases. Explain, using the concepts of thermal speed and escape speed (see Chapter 9, Section 9-4).
10. Is the van der Waals force attractive or repulsive? Justify your answer in terms of the sign of the term $n^2 a/V^2$ appearing in the van der Waals equation, assuming that the parameter a is positive.
11. Some people think that ice and snow must be at 0°C. Is this always true? Under what circumstances must it be true? Could you paraphrase the same arguments for another substance? Try steel, for example.

12. What is the temperature of water just under the ice layer of a frozen lake? At the bottom of the lake?

13. Deep lakes usually "turn over" twice each year. During the overturn, water from the lake bottom gets mixed with surface water, while at other times deep water and surface water do not mix. Under what conditions should such an overturn occur?

14. What's the temperature at the bottom of Lake Michigan?

15. How is it possible to have liquid water at 0°C?

16. Some ice and water have been together in a glass for a long time. Is the water hotter than the ice?

17. Does it take more heat to melt a gram of ice at 0°C than to bring the resulting water to the boiling point? Once at the boiling point, does it take more heat to boil all the water than it did to bring it from the melting point to the boiling point?

18. Why does removing the plastic wrap from a package of frozen hamburger help it to thaw faster?

19. Why do we use the triple point of water for thermometer calibration? Why not just use the melting point or boiling point?

20. When the average temperature drops below freezing in winter, regions near large lakes remain warmer for some time. Why?

21. Must all substances exhibit solid, liquid, and gas phases? What might happen before a substance reaches the gas phase? Consider sugar, for example.

22. How is it possible to have boiling water at a temperature other than 100°C?

23. Why does the water in a car radiator boil explosively when you remove the radiator cap?

24. How does a pressure cooker work?

25. Why does a double boiler prevent food from burning?

26. Figure 20-19 shows a thin, flexible wire draped over an ice cube, with weights tied on either end of the wire. If the weights are heavy enough, the wire will gradually melt its

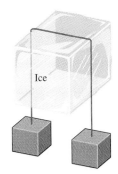

FIGURE 20-19 Questions 26–27.

way through the ice cube, nevertheless leaving the cube in one piece. Explain this phenomenon in terms of the phase diagram for water (Fig. 20-16).

27. Could you perform the experiment in Fig. 20-19 on a dry ice cube? Explain by comparing Figs. 20-8 and 20-16.

28. Earth's inner core is solid and is surrounded by a liquid outer core made of the same material but cooler. How is this possible?

29. Suppose mercury and glass had the same coefficient of volume expansion. Could you build a mercury thermometer?

30. Why are the coefficients of volume expansion generally greater for liquids than for solids?

31. A bimetallic strip consists of thin pieces of brass and steel bonded together (Fig. 20-20). Such strips are often used in thermostats. What will happen when the strip is heated? *Hint:* Consult Table 20-2.

Brass
Steel

FIGURE 20-20 Question 31.

32. Why are power lines more likely to break in winter?

PROBLEMS

ActivPhysics can help with these problems:
Activities 8.1–8.4.

Section 20-1 Gases

1. At Mars's surface, the planet's atmosphere has a pressure only 0.0070 times that of Earth, and an average temperature of 218 K. What is the volume of 1 mole of the Martian atmosphere?

2. How many molecules are in an ideal gas sample at 350 K that occupies 8.5 L when the pressure is 180 kPa?

3. What is the pressure of an ideal gas if 3.5 moles occupy 2.0 L at a temperature of −150°C?

4. An ideal gas occupies a volume V at 100°C. If the gas pressure is held constant, by what factor does the volume change (a) if the Celsius temperature is doubled and (b) if the kelvin temperature is doubled?

5. If 2.0 mol of an ideal gas are at an initial temperature of 250 K and pressure of 1.5 atm, (a) what is the gas volume? (b) The pressure is now increased to 4.0 atm, and the gas volume drops to half its initial value. What is the new temperature?

6. The solar corona is an extended atmosphere of hot (2×10^6 K) gas surrounding the cooler visible surface of the Sun. The gas pressure in the solar corona is about 0.03 Pa. What is the coronal density in particles per cubic meter? Compare with Earth's atmosphere.

7. A pressure of 1.0×10^{-10} Pa is readily achievable with laboratory vacuum apparatus. If the residual air in this

"vacuum" is at 0°C, how many air molecules are in one liter?

8. A cubical metal box with thin walls measures 10 cm on each side. It is filled with 0.50 mol of an ideal gas at 180 K, and is surrounded by air at atmospheric pressure. What is the net pressure force on each side of the box?

9. A helium balloon occupies 8.0 L at 20°C and 1.0 atm pressure. The balloon rises to an altitude where air pressure is 0.65 atm and the temperature is −10°C. What is its volume when it reaches equilibrium at the new altitude? (Neglect tension forces in the material of the balloon.)

10. A compressed air cylinder stands 100 cm tall and has an internal diameter of 20.0 cm. At room temperature, the pressure is 180 atm. (a) How many moles of air are in the cylinder? (b) What volume would this air occupy at 1.0 atm and room temperature?

11. An aerosol can of whipped cream is pressurized at 440 kPa when it's refrigerated at 3°C. The can warns against temperatures in excess of 50°C. What is the maximum safe pressure for the can?

12. A student's dormitory room measures 3.0 m × 3.5 × 2.6 m. (a) How many air molecules does it contain? (b) What is the total translational kinetic energy of these molecules? (c) How does this energy compare with the kinetic energy of the student's 1200-kg car going 90 km/h?

13. A 3000-ml flask is initially open while in a room containing air at 1.00 atm and 20°C. The flask is then closed and immersed in a bath of boiling water. When the air in the flask has reached thermodynamic equilibrium, the flask is opened and air allowed to escape. The flask is then closed and cooled back to 20°C. (a) What is the maximum pressure reached in the flask? (b) How many moles escape when air is released from the flask? (c) What is the final pressure in the flask?

14. What is the thermal speed of hydrogen (H_2) molecules at 800 K?

15. In which gas are the molecules moving faster: hydrogen (H_2) at 75 K or sulfur dioxide (SO_2) at 350 K?

16. The principal gases in Earth's atmosphere are N_2, O_2, and Ar, with smaller amounts of CO_2 and H_2O. In air at 300 K, what are the thermal speeds of these gases?

17. The van der Waals constants for helium gas (He) are $a = 0.0341$ L²·atm/mol² and $b = 0.0237$ L/mol. What is the temperature of 3.00 mol of helium at 90.0 atm pressure if the gas volume is 0.800 L? How does this result differ from the ideal gas prediction?

18. At what pressure does the van der Waals calculation of temperature for the gas of Example 20-3 differ by 10% from the ideal gas calculation?

19. Because the correction terms (n^2a/V^2 and $−nb$) in the van der Waals equation have opposite signs, there is a point at which the van der Waals and ideal gas equations predict the same temperature. For the gas of Example 20-3, at what pressure does that occur?

20. Plot the Maxwell-Boltzmann distribution of molecular speeds for samples of monatomic helium gas (He) containing 10^{18} atoms at temperatures of 50 K and 250 K.

21. In a sample of 10^{24} hydrogen (H_2) molecules, how many molecules have speeds between 900 and 901 m/s (a) at a temperature of 100 K and (b) at 450 K?

22. Room temperature (about 293 K) is only about 6.5% higher than a typical refrigerator temperature (about 275 K). To show how important the high-energy tail of the Boltzmann distribution is in determining food spoilage rates, find the percent increase in the number of oxygen molecules in air with speeds in the range 1350 m/s to 1351 m/s as the temperature goes from 275 K to 293 K. You should find it to be much greater than the corresponding 6.5% increase in temperature.

Section 20-2 Phase Changes

23. How much energy does it take to melt a 65-g ice cube?

24. It takes 200 J to melt an 8.0-g sample of one of the substances in Table 20-1. What is the substance?

25. If it takes 840 kJ to vaporize a sample of liquid oxygen, how large is the sample?

26. Carbon dioxide sublimes (changes from solid to gas) at 195 K. The heat of sublimation is 573 kJ/kg. How much heat must be extracted from 250 g of CO_2 gas at 195 K in order to solidify it?

27. Find the energy needed to convert 28 kg of liquid oxygen at its boiling point into gas.

28. A stove burner supplies heat to a pan at the rate of 1500 W. How long will it take to boil away 1.1 kg of water, from the time the water is at its boiling point?

29. If a 1-megaton nuclear bomb were exploded deep in the Greenland ice cap, how much ice would it melt? Assume the ice is initially at about its freezing point, and consult Appendix C for the appropriate energy conversion.

30. How much ice can a 625-W microwave oven melt in 1.0 min, if the ice is initially at 0°C?

31. What is the power of a microwave oven that takes 20 min to boil dry a 300-g cup of water initially at its boiling point?

32. At winter's end, Lake Superior's 82,000-km² surface is frozen to a depth of 1.3 m. The density of ice is 917 kg/m³. (a) How much energy does it take to melt the ice? (b) If the ice disappears in 3 weeks, what is the average power supplied to melt it?

33. A refrigerator extracts energy from its contents at the rate of 95 W. How long will it take to freeze 750 g of water already at 0°C?

34. The size of industrial air conditioning and refrigeration equipment is often given in tons, meaning the number of tons of water at its melting point that the unit could freeze in one day. (This unit is a holdover from the days when ice was cut from lakes in winter.) What is the rate of heat extraction, in watts, of a 15-ton refrigeration unit?

35. At its "thaw" setting a microwave oven delivers 210 W. How long will it take to thaw a frozen 1.8-kg roast, assuming the roast is essentially water and is initially at 0°C?

36. An ice layer 50 cm thick covers a lake; soot from air pollution covers the ice and absorbs 75% of the incident sunlight, whose time-average intensity is 200 W/m². How long will it take to melt the ice, assuming an initial temperature of about 0°C? The density of ice is 917 kg/m³.

37. A 100-g block of ice, initially at −20°C, is placed in a 500-W microwave oven. (a) How long must the oven be on to produce water at 50°C? (b) Make a graph showing temperature versus time during this entire interval.

38. Repeat Example 20-6 if the initial mass of ice is 50 g.

39. How much energy does it take to melt 10 kg of ice initially at −10°C? Consult Table 19-1.

40. Water is brought to its boiling point and then allowed to boil away completely. If the energy needed to raise the water to the boiling point is one-tenth of that needed to boil it away, what was the initial temperature?

41. A 250-g piece of ice at 0°C is placed in a 500-W microwave oven and the oven run for 5.0 min. What is the temperature at the end of this time?

42. During a nuclear accident, 420 m³ of emergency cooling water at 20°C are injected into a reactor vessel where the reactor core is producing heat at the rate of 200 MW. If the water is allowed to boil at normal atmospheric pressure, how long will it take to boil the reactor dry?

43. What is the minimum amount of ice in Example 20-6 that will ensure a final temperature of 0°C?

44. What would have to be the initial ice temperature in Example 20-6 in order that the final mixture ends up with more than 200 g of ice?

45. A 500-g chunk of solid mercury at its 234 K melting point is added to 500 g of liquid mercury at room temperature (293 K). Determine the equilibrium mix and temperature.

46. Repeat the preceding problem if the initial amount of liquid is 1.0 kg.

47. A bowl contains 16 kg of punch (essentially water) at a warm 25°C. What is the minimum amount of ice at 0°C that will cool the punch to 0°C?

48. Water at 300 K is sprinkled onto 200 g of molten copper at its 1356-K melting point. The water boils away, leaving solid copper still at 1356 K. How much water does this take? Assume that the only heat loss from the copper is to the liquid water.

49. A 50-g ice cube at −10°C is placed in an equal mass of water. What must be the initial water temperature if the final mixture still contains equal amounts of ice and water?

50. A 40-kg block of aluminum is initially at 50°C. A jet of steam at 100°C hits the block and condenses, and the resulting water drops off before its temperature changes. How much steam must hit the block to raise its temperature to 100°C?

Section 20-3 Thermal Expansion

51. A Pyrex glass marble is 1.00000 cm in diameter at 20°C. What will be its diameter at 85°C?

52. At 0°C, the hole in a steel washer is 9.52 mm in diameter. To what temperature must it be heated in order to fit over a 9.55-mm-diameter bolt?

53. Suppose a single piece of welded steel railroad track stretched 5000 km across the continental United States. If the track were free to expand, by how much would its length change if the entire track went from a cold winter temperature of −25°C to a hot summer day at 40°C?

54. A glass marble 1.000 cm in diameter is to be dropped through a hole in a steel plate. At room temperature the hole diameter is 0.997 cm. By how much must the steel temperature be raised so that the marble will fit through the hole?

55. The tube in a mercury thermometer is 0.10 mm in diameter. What should be the volume of the thermometer bulb if a 1.0-mm rise is to correspond to a temperature change of 1.0°C? Neglect the expansion of the glass.

56. A 2000-mL graduated cylinder is filled with liquid at 350 K. When the liquid is cooled to 300 K, the cylinder is full only to the 1925-mL mark. Use Table 20-2 to identify the liquid.

57. A steel ball bearing is encased in a Pyrex glass cube 1.0 cm on a side. At 330 K, the ball bearing fits tightly in the cube. At what temperature will it have a clearance of 1.0 μm all around?

58. Gasoline comes from its underground tank at 10°C. On a summer day, how much gas can you put in your car's 60-L tank if the tank is not to overflow when the gas reaches the ambient temperature of 25°C?

59. A rod of length L_0 is clamped rigidly at both ends. Its temperature increases in the middle by an amount ΔT, and in the ensuing expansion it cracks to form two straight pieces, as shown in Fig. 20-21. Find an expression for the distance d shown in the figure, in terms of L_0, ΔT, and the coefficient of linear expansion, α.

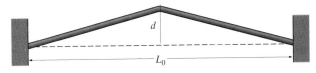

FIGURE 20-21 Problem 59.

60. A 250-ml Pyrex glass beaker is filled to the brim with ethyl alcohol; both beaker and alcohol are at 20°C. How much alcohol spills over the top when the temperature is increased to 30°C?

Paired Problems

(Both problems in a pair involve the same principles and techniques. If you can get the first problem, you should be able to solve the second one.)

61. What is the density, in moles per m³, of air in a tire whose absolute pressure is 300 kPa at 34°C?
62. Venus's atmospheric pressure is 90 times that of Earth, and its average temperature is 730 K. What is the volume of 1 mole of Venus's atmosphere?
63. What power is needed to melt 20 kg of ice in 6.0 min?
64. How long will it take a 140-W heat source to vaporize 250 g of ethyl alcohol already at its boiling point?
65. You put 300 g of water into a 500-W microwave oven and accidentally set the time for 20 min instead of 2.0 min. If the water is initially at 20°C, how much is left at the end of 20 min?
66. If 4.5×10^5 kg of emergency cooling water at 10°C are dumped into a malfunctioning nuclear reactor whose core is producing energy at the rate of 200 MW, and if no circulation or cooling of the water is provided, how long will it be before half the water has boiled away?
67. Describe the composition and temperature of the equilibrium mixture after 1.0 kg of ice at −40°C is added to 1.0 kg of water at 5.0°C.
68. Repeat the preceding problem if the ice is initially at −80°C and if there are initially only 200 g of liquid water.

Supplementary Problems

69. How long will it take a 500-W microwave oven to vaporize completely a 500-g block of ice initially at 0°C?
70. The thermal resistance of a refrigerator's walls is 0.12 K/W. During a power failure you put a 15-kg block of ice at 0°C in the refrigerator, bringing the interior temperature to 0°C. If room temperature is 20°C, how long will the ice last?
71. A solar-heated house (Fig. 20-22) stores energy in 5.0 tons of Glauber salt ($Na_2SO_4 \cdot 10H_2O$), a substance that melts at 90°F. The heat of fusion of Glauber salt is 104 Btu/lb, and

FIGURE 20-22 A solar-heated house (Problem 71).

the specific heats of the solid and liquid are, respectively, 0.46 Btu/lb·°F and 0.68 Btu/lb·°F. After a week of sunny weather, the storage medium is all liquid at 95°F. Then a cool, cloudy period sets in during which the house loses heat at an average rate of 20,000 Btu/h. (a) How long is it before the temperature of the storage medium drops below 60°F? (b) How much of this time is spent at 90°F?

72. By differentiating Equation 20-6, show that the most probable molecular speed in the Maxwell-Boltzmann distribution is lower than the thermal speed by a factor of $\sqrt{2/3}$.
73. Show that the coefficient of volume expansion of an ideal gas at constant pressure is just the reciprocal of its kelvin temperature.
74. A constant-volume gas thermometer is made from Pyrex glass. If the thermometer is calibrated at the triple point of water and then used to determine the boiling point of water, how much error will be introduced by ignoring the expansion of the glass?
75. Water's coefficient of volume expansion in the temperature range from 0°C to about 20°C is given approximately by $\beta = a + bT + cT^2$, where T is in Celsius and $a = -6.43 \times 10^{-5}$ °C^{-1}, $b = 1.70 \times 10^{-5}$ °C^{-2}, and $c = -2.02 \times 10^{-7}$ °C^{-3}. Show that water has its greatest density at approximately 4.0°C.
76. When the expansion coefficient varies with temperature, Equation 20-7 should be written $\beta = \dfrac{1}{V}\dfrac{dV}{dT}$. If a sample of water occupies 1.00000 L at 0°C, find its volume at 12°C. Use the information from the preceding problem, and integrate the equation above.
77. Ignoring air resistance, find the height from which you must drop an ice cube at 0°C so it melts completely on impact. Assume no heat exchange with the environment.
78. The timekeeping of an old clock is regulated by a brass pendulum 20.0 cm long. If the clock is accurate at 20°C but is in a room at 18°C, how long will it be before the clock is in error by 1 minute? Will it be too fast or too slow?
79. Prove the relation $\beta = 3\alpha$ (page 509) by considering a cube of side s and therefore volume $V = s^3$ that undergoes a small temperature change dT and corresponding length and volume changes ds and dV.
80. One of the dangers of global warming is a rise in sea level that could inundate some coastal areas. Most people assume such a rise would come from melting ice, but, in fact, the primary cause would be expansion of sea water. Estimate the rise due to expansion in the event of a 2°C rise in the average temperature of the entire ocean. Treat the ocean as a body of water of constant 3.8 km depth (the average depth of the oceans) at 20°C. Your answer is an overestimate; among other things, it doesn't include the effects of salinity changes, nor processes in the cold, deep ocean where, as Table 20-2 shows, water's expansion coefficient is very different than it is at 20°C.

Heat, Work, and the First Law of Thermodynamics

21

A jet aircraft engine, shown here being repaired, converts energy released in burning fuel to mechanical motion. Jet engines, gasoline and diesel engines, and electric power plants all rely on thermodynamics to effect energy conversion.

How do we change the temperature of a substance? One approach involves heat transfer between substances at different temperatures. Another approach—which you've experienced if you ever pulled a rope too quickly through your hands, or touched a drill bit just after drilling a hole, or smelled your car's brakes burning as you went down a steep hill—involves mechanical energy. Here we explore this second approach to temperature change and, in the process, come to a deeper understanding of the relation between heat and mechanical energy.

21-1 THE FIRST LAW OF THERMODYNAMICS

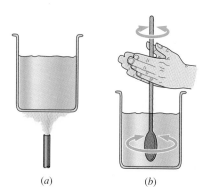

FIGURE 21-1 Either a flame or mechanical agitation will raise the water temperature.

8.6
Heat, Internal Energy, and First Law of Thermodynamics

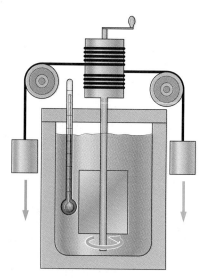

FIGURE 21-2 In Joule's apparatus, potential energy of the falling weights is converted to kinetic energy of the rotating paddle, which in turn becomes internal energy of the water.

Heat is energy being transferred from one object to another because of a temperature difference alone. As a result of heat transfer, a substance undergoes changes in its thermodynamic state—its temperature, pressure, and volume may change, and it may undergo a change of phase. But we can accomplish these same changes with mechanical energy. As Fig. 21-1 suggests, we can raise the temperature of water by heating with a flame or by stirring violently with a spoon. For the flame to heat the water, the flame temperature must exceed the water temperature. But the spoon can have the same temperature as the water, since it's the mechanical energy of the spoon's motion that raises the water temperature. We use the term **work** to describe energy transfer that does not require a temperature difference. This sense is consistent with our earlier use of the word *work* to describe mechanical energy transfer. Sometimes that energy ends up as stored potential energy, but often it results in a temperature change—as when we do work against frictional forces. That both heat and mechanical work can raise temperature is what made possible Joule's quantitative identification of heat as a form of energy (Fig. 21-2).

What happens to energy transferred to a system through either heat or mechanical work? It ends up changing the **internal energy** of the system—that is, the sum of the different kinds of energy associated with all the individual particles making up the system. For an ideal gas, internal energy is the total kinetic energy of the gas molecules. More complicated substances include potential energy as well; fuels such as gasoline or uranium, for example, have considerable internal potential energy. ActivPhysics Activity 8.6 explores the microscopic details of internal energy.

If we keep track of all energy entering and leaving a system—both heat and work—we find that the change in the system's internal energy depends only on the net amount of energy added to or removed from the system. In one sense this is hardly surprising; it's just an extension of the idea of energy conservation to include heat as well as mechanical work. But in another way it's remarkable: it doesn't matter at all *how* energy is transferred to or from the system—by heating, by mechanical work, or by some combination of the two. All that matters is the total energy transferred. This statement constitutes the **first law of thermodynamics**:

> *First law of thermodynamics: The change in the internal energy of a system depends only on the net heat transferred to the system and the net work done by the system, and is independent of the particular processes involved.*

Mathematically, the first law reads

$$\Delta U = Q - W, \tag{21-1}$$

where ΔU is the change in a system's internal energy, Q the heat transferred *to* the system, and W the work done *by* the system. Thus a positive Q represents an energy gain for the system, while a positive W represents an energy loss; that's why the minus sign appears in Equation 21-1. This convention on the signs of Q and W is used because the first law was developed in connection with engines, which take heat from a source and give out mechanical work. Keeping track of energy transfers in an engine is easier if both the heat input and the work output are considered positive quantities; their difference is then the change in internal energy.

The first law of thermodynamics says that the change in a system's internal energy doesn't depend on the details of the energy transfer—only on the total amount of energy transferred. We could transfer a given quantity of energy by heating, by mechanical work, or by some combination of the two, and the effect would be the same. For this reason internal energy is called a **thermodynamic state variable**, meaning a quantity whose value doesn't depend on how a system got into its particular state. Temperature and pressure are also thermodynamic state variables; heat and work are not.

We're frequently concerned with *rates* of energy flow. Differentiating the first law with respect to time gives a statement about these rates:

$$\frac{dU}{dt} = \frac{dQ}{dt} - \frac{dW}{dt}, \tag{21-2}$$

where dU/dt is the rate of change of a system's internal energy, dQ/dt the rate of heat transfer to the system, and dW/dt the rate at which the system does work on its surroundings.

EXAMPLE 21-1	*Nuclear Power, Thermal Pollution*

A nuclear power plant's reactor supplies energy at the rate of 3.0 GW (1 GW = 10^9 W), boiling water to produce steam that turns a turbine-generator (Fig. 21-3). The spent steam is then condensed through thermal contact with water taken from a river and sent back to the reactor. If the power plant produces electrical energy at the rate of 1.0 GW, at what rate is heat transferred to the river?

Solution

Here the system consists of the power plant and its reactor, so dU/dt in Equation 21-2 represents the rate of change of internal energy in the nuclear fuel. Since that internal energy is being converted to other forms, dU/dt is negative; its value is -3.0 GW. On the other hand, dW/dt is the rate at which the plant does work—i.e., the rate at which it supplies electrical energy to the external world. Thus $dW/dt = +1.0$ GW. Solving for the heat-transfer rate then gives

$$\frac{dQ}{dt} = \frac{dU}{dt} + \frac{dW}{dt} = -3.0 \text{ GW} + 1.0 \text{ GW} = -2.0 \text{ GW}.$$

Does this make sense? Since a positive Q represents heat transferred *to* the system, the minus sign in our answer shows that heat is transferred *from* the power plant to the river at the rate of 2.0 GW. The numbers in this example are typical for large nuclear and coal-burning power plants, and show that about two-thirds of the energy extracted from the fuel is wasted in heating the environment. We'll see in the next chapter just why this waste occurs.

Tip

Identify the System Thermodynamics problems often deal with energy flows into and out of a system. Before attacking a problem, be sure you're clear on just what constitutes the system. The first law holds no matter how you define the system, but the meanings of the various quantities change with that definition. In Example 21-1, for example, we could have excluded the nuclear fuel from the system. The net result— 2 GW dumped to the river—would have been the same, but now we would have had an additional heat input of 3 GW and no change in internal energy.

EXERCISE Gasoline burning in an automobile engine releases energy at the rate of 160 kW. Heat is exhausted through the car's radiator at the rate of 51 kW and out the exhaust at 50 kW. An additional 23 kW goes to frictional heating within the machinery of the car. What fraction of the fuel energy is available for propelling the car?

Answer: 22.5%

Some problems similar to Example 21-1: 4–6

FIGURE 21-3 A nuclear power plant, showing two reactor buildings and a large cooling tower. The plant takes in water from the river in the foreground. The water absorbs waste heat and then passes through the cooling tower before returning to the river. Example 21-1 shows that two-thirds of the energy produced in the reactor is discarded as waste heat.

21-2 THERMODYNAMIC PROCESSES

The first law relates two kinds of energy transfers—heat and work—that can change a system's thermodynamic state. Although the first law applies to *any* system, it is easiest to understand when applied to an ideal gas. The ideal gas law (Equation 20-2) relates the temperature, pressure, and volume of a given gas sample: $PV = nRT$. The thermodynamic state of the gas is completely determined by any two of the quantities P, V, or T. We'll find it convenient to work with pressure and volume, representing different states of a system as points on a coordinate system whose vertical and horizontal axes represent pressure and volume, respectively. This is called a **PV diagram**.

Reversible and Irreversible Processes

Imagine heating a gas sample by immersing it in a large reservoir of water whose temperature we can control (Fig. 21-4). If the gas and water temperatures are equal, the gas will stay in thermodynamic equilibrium. If we then raise the reservoir temperature very slowly, both water and gas temperatures will rise essentially in unison, and the gas will remain in equilibrium. Such a slow change is called a **quasi-static process**. Because a system undergoing a quasi-static process is always in thermodynamic equilibrium, its overall change from one state to another is then described by a continuous sequence of points—a curve—in its PV diagram (Fig. 21-5).

We could reverse this heating process by very slowly lowering the reservoir temperature; the gas would then cool while remaining essentially in thermodynamic equilibrium and would go back along the same path in its PV diagram. Because the system can be made to traverse the same path in the PV diagram going either way, a quasi-static process is also called a **reversible process**. A process like the sudden plunging of the gas sample into boiling water is, in contrast, **irreversible** (Fig. 21-6). During an irreversible process the system is not in equilibrium, and thermodynamic variables like temperature and pressure

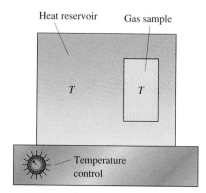

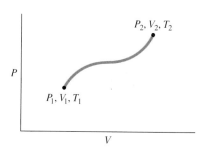

FIGURE 21-4 A quasi-static, or reversible, process. The gas sample is heated by immersion in a heat reservoir whose temperature is slowly increased. The entire gas sample is always at essentially the same temperature as the reservoir, so it is always in a well-defined thermodynamic state.

FIGURE 21-5 Because a system undergoing a quasi-static change is always in thermodynamic equilibrium, the change may be described by a succession of states—a continuous path—in its PV diagram.

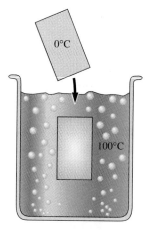

FIGURE 21-6 Plunging a gas sample at 0°C into boiling water is an irreversible process. It takes some time for the gas to reach equilibrium at the higher temperature, during which time the gas itself has no well-defined thermodynamic state.

do not have well-defined values. It therefore makes no sense to think of a path in the *PV* diagram. A process may be irreversible even though it returns a system to its original state. The distinction lies not in the end states but in the *process* that takes the system between states.

There are many ways to change the thermodynamic state of a system. Here we consider several important special cases as they apply to an ideal gas system. These special cases illustrate the physical principles behind a myriad of technological devices and natural phenomena, from the operation of a gasoline engine to the propagation of a sound wave to the oscillations of a star.

Our system consists of an ideal gas confined to a cylinder sealed with a movable piston (Fig. 21-7). The piston and cylinder walls are perfectly insulating—they block all heat transfer—while the bottom is a perfect conductor of heat. We can change the thermodynamic state of the gas mechanically, by moving the piston, or thermally, by transferring heat through the bottom. We will consider only reversible processes, which we can describe by paths in the *PV* diagram for the gas.

FIGURE 21-7 A gas-cylinder system. The cylinder walls are perfectly insulating, but the bottom is a perfect conductor of heat.

Work and Volume Changes

Before examining specific processes, we develop a relation between volume change and work that holds for all processes. If *A* is the cross-sectional area of our piston and cylinder and *P* the gas pressure, then $F = PA$ is the force the gas exerts on the piston (Fig. 21-8a). If the piston moves a small distance Δx, then the work done by the gas is

$$\Delta W = F \Delta x = PA \Delta x = P \Delta V,$$

where $\Delta V = A \Delta x$ is the change in gas volume. The work ΔW is positive when the volume increases, indicating that the gas does work on the piston, and negative if ΔV is negative, indicating work done on the gas. Pressure may vary with volume, in which case our result is strictly valid only in the limit of very small volume changes. To find the work associated with a larger volume change, we take the limit $\Delta V \to 0$, and integrate over the volume change:

$$W = \int dW = \int_{V_1}^{V_2} P\,dV, \qquad (21\text{-}3)$$

where V_1 and V_2 are the initial and final volumes. Figure 21-8b shows the geometrical interpretation of this equation: the work done by the gas is simply the area under the *PV* curve.

Now that we have a relation between pressure, volume, and work, we will explore several basic thermodynamic processes, in each of which we hold one of the thermodynamic variables constant. These processes approximate what goes on in a wide variety of real systems ranging from engines to sound waves to

8.5
Work Done by a Gas

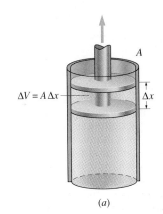

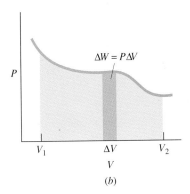

FIGURE 21-8 (*a*) The gas exerts a pressure force *PA* on the piston of area *A*, so the work done in moving the piston a small distance Δx is $PA \Delta x$, or $P\Delta V$. (*b*) On the *PV* diagram, this work corresponds to the area of the dark strip of width ΔV. The total work to take the system from volume V_1 to V_2 is the area under the *PV* curve between V_1 and V_2.

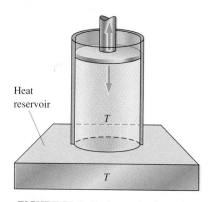

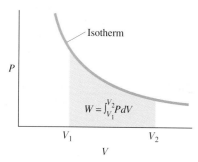

FIGURE 21-9 During an isothermal process, the piston moves slowly while the system is held in thermal contact with a heat reservoir at fixed temperature.

FIGURE 21-10 *PV* diagram for an isothermal process, showing a particular isotherm—a curve of constant temperature. Since $PV = nRT$ for an ideal gas, the pressure and volume are inversely related at constant temperature, so the isotherm is a hyperbola. The work done during an isothermal expansion from volume V_1 to V_2 is the area under the isotherm.

weather systems. We will restrict ourselves to quasi-static processes, so in each case the process in question is reversible and can be described by a path in the *PV* diagram.

Isothermal Processes

To perform a reversible **isothermal process**, we place the heat-conducting bottom of our gas cylinder in good thermal contact with a heat reservoir whose temperature is held constant (Fig. 21-9). We then move the piston to change the volume of the system, doing so slowly enough that the gas remains in equilibrium with the heat reservoir. The system then moves from its initial state to its final state along a curve of constant temperature—an **isotherm**—in the *PV* diagram (Fig. 21-10). The work done in the process is given by Equation 21-3 and is equal to the area under the isotherm.

For an ideal gas, we can relate pressure *P* and volume *V* through the ideal gas law:

$$P = \frac{nRT}{V}.$$

Then Equation 21-3 becomes

$$W = \int_{V_1}^{V_2} \frac{nRT}{V} \, dV.$$

For an isothermal process, the temperature *T* is constant, giving

$$W = nRT \int_{V_1}^{V_2} \frac{dV}{V} = nRT \ln V \Big|_{V_1}^{V_2} = nRT \ln\left(\frac{V_2}{V_1}\right).$$

The internal energy of an ideal gas consists only of the kinetic energy of its molecules which, in turn, depends only on the temperature. We showed this in the preceding chapter for a gas of structureless point particles and will extend it later in this chapter to gases consisting of more complicated molecules. Thus, there is no change in the internal energy of an ideal gas during an isothermal process. The first law of thermodynamics then gives

$$\Delta U = 0 = Q - W$$

so

$$Q = W = nRT \ln\left(\frac{V_2}{V_1}\right). \quad \text{(isothermal process)} \qquad (21\text{-}4)$$

Does this result $Q = W$ make sense? Recall that Q is the heat transferred to the gas, while W is the work done by the gas. Therefore, our result says that when an ideal gas does work W on the external world with no change in temperature, it must absorb an equal amount of heat from outside. Similarly, if work is done on the gas, then the gas must reject an equal amount of heat to the outside if its temperature is not to change. ActivPhysics Activity 8.10 lets you simulate the isothermal process described in our derivation of Equation 21-4.

8.10

Isothermal Process

| EXAMPLE 21-2 | *A Diver Exhales* |

A scuba diver (Fig. 21-11) is swimming at a depth of 25 m, where the pressure is 3.5 atm (recall Example 18-1). The air she exhales forms bubbles 8.0 mm in radius. How much work is done by each bubble as it expands on rising to the surface? Assume that the bubbles remain at the uniform 300 K temperature of the surrounding water.

Solution

Since the bubbles remain at constant temperature, the process is isothermal and Equation 21-4 applies. Just before they break the surface, the bubbles are at essentially 1 atm pressure, so their pressure has decreased by a factor of 3.5. The ideal gas law, $PV = nRT$, shows that when temperature is constant, pressure and volume are inversely related. Therefore, the bubble volume has increased by a factor of 3.5. To apply Equation 21-4, we also need the quantity nRT for a bubble. We can get this from the ideal gas law using the given radius of the bubbles at 3.5 atm pressure:

$$nRT = PV = P(\tfrac{4}{3}\pi r^3),$$

so Equation 21-4 becomes

$$W = nRT \ln\left(\frac{V_2}{V_1}\right) = \tfrac{4}{3}\pi r^3 P \ln\left(\frac{V_2}{V_1}\right)$$

$$= \tfrac{4}{3}\pi (8.0\times10^{-3}\ \text{m})^3 (3.5\ \text{atm})(1.01\times10^5\ \text{Pa/atm}) \ln(3.5)$$

$$= 0.95\ \text{J}.$$

FIGURE 21-11 How much work do the diver's exhaled air bubbles do as they rise? (Example 21-2)

Where does this energy go? As a bubble expands, it pushes water outward and, ultimately, upward. It therefore raises the gravitational potential energy of the ocean. When the bubble breaks the surface, this excess potential energy becomes kinetic energy, appearing in the form of small waves on the water surface.

EXERCISE Consider 3.2 mol of an ideal gas in contact with a heat reservoir at 320 K. Find the work done by the gas if its volume doubles.

Answer: 5.9 kJ

Some problems similar to Example 21-2: 11, 13–16

Constant-Volume Processes and Specific Heat

A **constant-volume process** (also called an isometric, isochoric, or isovolumic process) occurs in a rigid, closed container whose volume cannot change. In our piston-cylinder arrangement, we could tightly clamp the piston for a constant-volume process. Because the piston doesn't move, the gas does no work, and the first law becomes simply

$$Q = \Delta U. \qquad (21\text{-}5)$$

To express this result in terms of a temperature change ΔT, we introduce the **molar specific heat at constant volume**, C_V, defined by the equation

$$Q = nC_V\Delta T, \qquad (21\text{-}6)$$

where n is the number of moles. This molar specific heat is like the specific heat defined in Chapter 19, except that with a gas it's more convenient to consider the heat per mole rather than per unit mass. Introducing the definition of C_V into Equation 21-5 gives

$$nC_V\Delta T = \Delta U. \qquad (21\text{-}7)$$

8.8

Active Physics

Isochoric (Constant V) Process

Solving for C_V then gives

$$C_V = \frac{1}{n}\frac{\Delta U}{\Delta T}.$$ (21-8)

For an ideal gas, the internal energy is a function of temperature alone, so $\Delta U/\Delta T$ has the same value no matter what process the gas undergoes. Therefore Equation 21-7, relating the temperature change ΔT and internal energy change ΔU, applies not only to a constant-volume process, but also to *any* ideal gas process. Why, then, have we been so careful to label C_V the specific heat *at constant volume?* Although the relation $nC_V\Delta T = \Delta U$ holds for any process, it is only when no work is done that the first law allows us to write $Q = \Delta U$, and therefore only for a constant-volume process that Equation 21-6 holds.

Isobaric Processes and Specific Heat

Isobaric means constant pressure. Processes occurring in systems exposed to the nearly constant pressure of Earth's atmosphere, for example, are essentially isobaric. This includes most chemical and biochemical reactions. Even though these processes don't generally involve the gas phase, the fact of constant pressure nevertheless simplifies their thermodynamic analysis.

In a reversible isobaric process, a system moves along an isobar, or curve of constant pressure, in its PV diagram (Fig. 21-12). The work done as the volume changes from V_1 to V_2 is the area under the isobar, or

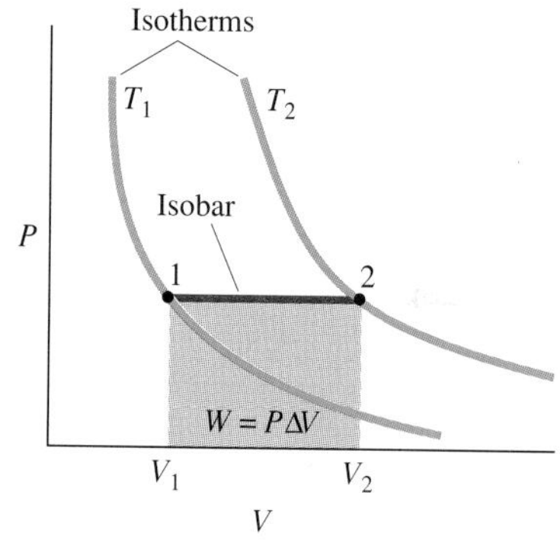

$$W = P(V_2 - V_1) = P\,\Delta V,$$ (21-9)

a result we could obtain formally by integrating Equation 21-3.

Solving the first law (Equation 21-1) for Q and using our expression for work gives

$$Q = \Delta U + W = \Delta U + P\,\Delta V.$$

For an ideal gas, we've just found that the change in internal energy is given by $\Delta U = nC_V\Delta T$ for *any* process. Therefore

$$Q = nC_V\Delta T + P\,\Delta V$$ (21-10)

for an ideal gas undergoing an isobaric process. We define the **molar specific heat at constant pressure**, C_P, as the heat required to raise one mole of gas through a unit temperature change at constant pressure, or

$$Q = nC_P\Delta T.$$

Equation 21-10 can then be written

$$nC_P\Delta T = nC_V\Delta T + P\,\Delta V. \quad \text{(isobaric process)}$$ (21-11)

This is a useful form for calculating temperature changes in an isobaric process, if we know both specific heats C_P and C_V. However, we really need only one of these specific heats, for a simple relation holds between the two. The ideal gas law, $PV = nRT$, allows us to write

$$P\,\Delta V = nR\,\Delta T$$

FIGURE 21-12 PV diagram for an isobaric process. The gas moves along the isobar from state 1 to state 2, doing work $P\Delta V$ in the process. Also shown are isotherms for the initial and final temperatures.

for an isobaric process. Using this expression in Equation 21-11 gives

$$nC_P\Delta T = nC_V\Delta T + nR\Delta T,$$

so
$$C_P = C_V + R. \qquad (21\text{-}12)$$

Does this result make sense? Specific heat measures the heat needed to cause a given temperature change. In a constant-volume process, no work is done and all the heat goes into raising the internal energy and thus the temperature of an ideal gas. In a constant-pressure process, work is done and some of the added heat ends up as mechanical energy, leaving less energy available for raising the temperature. Therefore, in a constant-pressure process, *more* heat is needed to achieve a given temperature change, so the specific heat at constant pressure is larger than at constant volume, as reflected in Equation 21-12.

Why didn't we distinguish specific heats at constant volume and constant pressure much earlier? Because we were concerned mostly with solids and liquids, whose coefficients of expansion are far lower than those of gases. As a result of its relatively small expansion, the work done by a solid or liquid is much less than that done by a gas. Since work is what gives rise to the difference between C_V and C_P, the distinction is less significant for solids and liquids. As a practical matter, measured specific heats are usually at constant pressure, because enormous forces would be needed to prevent volume changes in solids or liquids. The simulations in ActivPhysics Activity 8.7 will help you understand the difference between specific heats at constant volume and constant pressure.

8.7
Heat Capacity

8.9
Isobaric Process

Adiabatic Processes

In an **adiabatic process**, no heat transfer occurs between a system and its environment. The simplest way to achieve this is to surround the system with perfect thermal insulation. Even without insulation, processes that occur quickly are often approximately adiabatic because they're over before significant heat transfer has had time to occur. In a gasoline engine, for example, compression of the gasoline-air mixture and subsequent expansion of the combustion products are nearly adiabatic because they occur so rapidly that little heat flows through the cylinder walls during the process.

Since the heat Q is zero in an adiabatic process, the first law becomes simply

$$\Delta U = -W. \quad \text{(adiabatic process)} \qquad (21\text{-}13)$$

This says that if a system does work on its surroundings, then—in the absence of heat transfer—its internal energy must decrease by the same amount. Microscopically, this internal energy loss occurs in a gas-cylinder system when molecules collide with the moving piston, returning to the gas with less energy (Fig. 21-13).

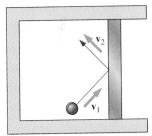

(a) Stationary piston

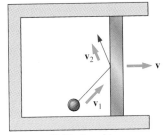

(b) Moving piston

FIGURE 21-13 *(a)* Molecules bouncing off a stationary piston rebound with no loss of speed. Here the gas is doing no work, and its internal energy remains constant. *(b)* Molecules bouncing off an outward-moving piston give some energy to the piston and rebound with lower speed. The internal energy of the gas decreases as its molecules do work on the piston. If the piston were moving inward the molecules would gain energy, and the piston would be doing work on the gas.

8.11
Adiabatic Process

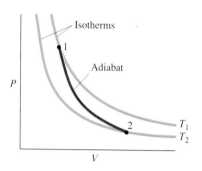

FIGURE 21-14 *PV* curve for an adiabatic process (red) shows that the pressure drops more than in an isothermal process going between the same two volumes. Two isotherms shown are for the initial and final temperatures of the adiabatic process. The adiabatic path is steeper because the gas loses internal energy as it does work.

As a gas expands adiabatically, its volume increases while its internal energy and temperature decrease. The ideal gas law, $PV = nRT$, then requires that the pressure decrease as well—and by more than it would in an isothermal process where T remains constant. In a *PV* diagram, the path of an adiabatic process—called an **adiabat**—therefore drops more steeply than the isotherms (Fig. 21-14).

The accompanying Math Toolbox details the mathematics involved in finding the shape of the adiabatic path; the result is

$$PV^{\gamma} = \text{constant} = P_0 V_0^{\gamma}, \quad \text{(adiabatic process)} \qquad (21\text{-}13a)$$

where $\gamma = C_P/C_V$ is the ratio of the specific heats and P_0 and V_0 are the values of P and V at some reference point, which could be any point in the process.

Because $C_P = C_V + R$, the ratio $\gamma = C_P/C_V$ is always greater than 1. Therefore an adiabatic process with a given volume change results in a greater pressure change than would a comparable isothermal process, as reflected in the steeper adiabatic path in Fig. 21-14. Physically, the adiabatic path is steeper because the gas loses internal energy as it does work, so its temperature drops.

Got It!

The ideal gas law says $PV = nRT$, but Equation 21-13a says $PV^{\gamma} = \text{constant}$. How can both equations be correct? Give an explanation that invokes the difference between adiabatic and isothermal processes.

We can find the temperature change in an adiabatic process by using the ideal gas law to eliminate pressure from Equation 21-13a. Writing that equation in the form $(PV)(V^{\gamma-1}) = (P_0 V_0)(V_0^{\gamma-1})$ and substituting for PV from the ideal gas law gives $nRTV^{\gamma-1} = nRT_0 V_0^{\gamma-1}$. Dividing both sides by nR gives

$$TV^{\gamma-1} = \text{constant} = T_0 V_0^{\gamma-1} \qquad (21\text{-}13b)$$

for the relation between temperature and volume in an adiabatic process. We could have written the adiabatic equation in yet a third way, eliminating V in favor of T and P (see Problem 28).

Math Toolbox

Deriving the Adiabatic Relation We derive the *PV* relation for an adiabatic process by integrating over a sequence of infinitesimal adiabatic changes. Equation 21-7, which holds for *any* process, shows that the internal energy change accompanying an infinitesimal temperature change is $dU = nC_V dT$. The work done in the process is $dW = P dV$ so, with $Q = 0$ for an adiabatic process, the first law becomes

$$nC_V dT = -P dV.$$

We now eliminate dT by differentiating the ideal gas law, allowing *both* P and V to change:

$$nR dT = d(PV) = P dV + V dP.$$

Solving for dT, substituting in our first-law statement, and multiplying through by R leads to

$$C_V V dP + (C_V + R)P dV = 0.$$

But $C_V + R = C_P$; substituting this and dividing through by $C_V PV$ gives

$$\frac{dP}{P} + \frac{C_P}{C_V}\frac{dV}{V} = 0\,.$$

Defining $\gamma \equiv C_P/C_V$ and integrating gives

$$\ln P + \gamma \ln V = \ln(\text{constant})\,,$$

where we've chosen to call the constant of integration $\ln(\text{constant})$. Since $\gamma \ln V = \ln V^\gamma$, it follows by exponentiation that

$$PV^\gamma = \text{constant}\,,$$

where the constant is the quantity $P_0 V_0^\gamma$ at a point where P and V have the known values P_0 and V_0.

EXAMPLE 21-3	*Diesel Power*

Ignition of the fuel in a diesel engine (Fig. 21-15) occurs on contact with air heated by compression as the piston moves to the top of its stroke. (In this way a diesel differs from a gasoline engine, in which a spark ignites the fuel.) The compression occurs fast enough that very little heat flows out of the gas, so the process is essentially adiabatic. If a temperature of 500°C is required for ignition, what must be the compression ratio (ratio of maximum to minimum cylinder volume) of the diesel engine? Air has a specific heat ratio γ of 1.4, and before compression its temperature is 20°C.

Solution

Equation 21-13b gives the relation between temperature and volume in an adiabatic process. Writing T_0 and V_0 for the temperature and volume at the bottom of the piston stroke, and T_1 and V_1 for the top of the stroke, Equation 21-13b becomes

$$T_1 V_1^{\gamma-1} = T_0 V_0^{\gamma-1}\,.$$

Solving for the compression ratio V_0/V_1 gives

$$\frac{V_0}{V_1} = \left(\frac{T_1}{T_0}\right)^{1/(\gamma-1)} = \left(\frac{773\ \text{K}}{293\ \text{K}}\right)^{1/0.4} = 11\,.$$

Practical diesel engines have considerably higher compression ratios to ensure reliable ignition. Conversely, compressional heating places an upper limit on the compression ratios of gasoline engines, where ignition by hot air would circumvent the carefully timed spark ignition system (see Problem 26).

FIGURE 21-15 (*a*) Cutaway diagram of a diesel engine. (b) One cylinder of the engine, shown with the piston at the bottom of its stroke (maximum volume), and (*c*) with the piston at the top of its stroke (minimum volume). The compression ratio is the ratio $V_{\text{max}}/V_{\text{min}}$. In a diesel, this ratio is high enough that adiabatic compression alone brings the fuel-air mixture to ignition temperature. Expansion of the burning fuel-air mixture then pushes the piston down, and this is what powers the engine. Not shown are intake and exhaust valves, nor fuel injectors.

(a)

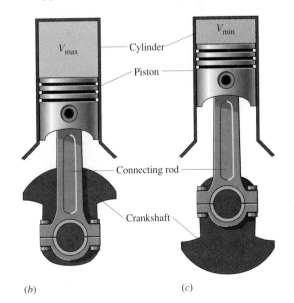

(b)　　　　(c)

EXAMPLE 21-4	*Adiabatic and Isothermal Expansion*

Two identical gas-cylinder systems each contain 0.060 mol of ideal gas at 300 K and 2.0 atm pressure. The specific heat ratio γ is 1.4. The gas samples are allowed to expand, one adiabatically and one isothermally, until both are at 1.0 atm pressure. What are the final temperatures and volumes of each?

Solution

The initial volume V_0 of both samples may be obtained from the ideal gas law, $PV = nRT$. Solving for V gives

$$V_0 = \frac{nRT_0}{P_0} = \frac{(0.060 \text{ mol})(8.314 \text{ J/K·mol})(300 \text{ K})}{(2.0 \text{ atm})(1.013 \times 10^5 \text{ Pa/atm})}$$
$$= 7.39 \times 10^{-4} \text{ m}^3 = 0.739 \text{ L} .$$

For the isothermal sample, T remains constant at 300 K. With constant temperature, $PV = $ constant, so as the pressure drops in half, the volume doubles, becoming 1.48 L.

For the adiabatic expansion, solving Equation 21-13a for the volume gives

$$V = \left(\frac{P_0}{P}\right)^{1/\gamma} V_0 = \left(\frac{2.0 \text{ atm}}{1.0 \text{ atm}}\right)^{1/1.4} (0.739 \text{ L}) = 1.21 \text{ L} .$$

The temperature follows from Equation 21-13b:

$$TV^{\gamma-1} = \text{constant} = T_0 V_0^{\gamma-1} ,$$

or

$$T = T_0 \left(\frac{V_0}{V}\right)^{\gamma-1} = (300 \text{ K}) \left(\frac{0.739 \text{ L}}{1.21 \text{ L}}\right)^{0.4} = 246 \text{ K} .$$

Since we knew both P and V, we could equally well have determined the temperature from the ideal gas law.

In this example, both gas samples do work against the outside world as they expand. In the isothermal process, energy leaving the system as work is replaced by energy entering as

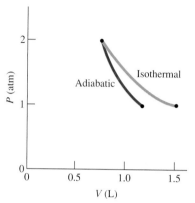

FIGURE 21-16 *PV* diagram showing isothermal and adiabatic processes of Example 21-4.

heat, so the temperature and internal energy remain constant. But heat cannot flow during the adiabatic process, so the work done is at the expense of the internal energy of the gas. As a result, the gas temperature drops, and the volume does not increase as much. Figure 21-16 shows both processes on a *PV* diagram.

EXERCISE A bicycle pump compresses 0.30 L of air, initially at 14°C and 1 atm pressure, to 4 times atmospheric pressure. The process occurs rapidly enough that it is essentially adiabatic. What are the volume and temperature of the compressed air? For air, $\gamma = 1.4$.

Answers: $V = 0.11$ L, $T = 153$°C

Some problems similar to Examples 21-3 and 21-4: 19, 22–26

How much work is done during an adiabatic process? Since there's no heat transfer, $W = -\Delta U$. But we've found that $\Delta U = nC_V \Delta T$ for *any* process. Therefore in an adiabatic process

$$W = -nC_V \Delta T = nC_V(T_1 - T_2) ,$$

where T_1 and T_2 are the initial and final temperatures. We can express this result in terms of pressure and volume changes by solving the ideal gas law, $PV = nRT$, for temperature and using the result in the equation above:

$$W = nC_V \frac{P_1 V_1 - P_2 V_2}{nR} .$$

But $R = C_P - C_V$, so

$$\frac{C_V}{R} = \frac{C_V}{C_P - C_V} = \frac{1}{(C_P/C_V) - 1} = \frac{1}{\gamma - 1} .$$

Then our expression for the adiabatic work becomes

$$W = \frac{P_1 V_1 - P_2 V_2}{\gamma - 1} . \tag{21-14}$$

We could also have obtained this result by direct integration of Equation 21-3 for an adiabatic process (see Problem 61).

The smog shown in Fig. 21-17*a* is an unfortunate manifestation of our high-energy industrial society. The presence of that smog is closely related to the adiabatic processes we've just considered.

Normally, atmospheric temperature decreases with altitude at a so-called **lapse rate** of about 6.5°C per kilometer. The main reason for the decrease is that sunlight first heats Earth's surface, which then transfers heat to the atmosphere. Now consider a parcel of air that for some reason starts moving upward. That initial rise could occur because the air is over a darker region, like pavement, that absorbs more solar energy. The heated air parcel, being less dense than the surrounding air, then rises under the influence of the buoyancy force we discussed in Chapter 18. Or the rise could occur as horizontally moving air is forced upward to clear an obstruction. Or it could be that hot air and other gases are belched out of a smokestack or automobile exhaust pipe. Whatever the reason, the air parcel starts upward. We want to know what happens next.

(*a*)

(*b*)

FIGURE 21-17 (*a*) Smog over Los Angeles. The smog is trapped because adiabatic expansion cools rising smog to the same temperature as the surrounding air. (*b*) In the violently unstable thunderstorm, adiabatic cooling is not sufficient to bring rising or falling parcels of air to thermal equilibrium.

As the air parcel rises, the pressure of the surrounding air drops, and the parcel therefore expands to maintain pressure equilibrium. Now, air is a good thermal insulator, so a parcel of reasonable size exchanges little heat with its surroundings. Its expansion is therefore adiabatic, and thus, its temperature drops as it expands. The decrease in pressure with altitude is such that dry air cools adiabatically at the rate of about 10°C per kilometer as it rises. If the surrounding air has the typical lapse rate of 6.5°C/km, then the rising parcel cools faster. Even if it started out hotter than its surroundings, it will soon reach an altitude where it is at the same temperature (Fig. 21-18*a*). Then it will no longer be buoyant, and its upward motion will

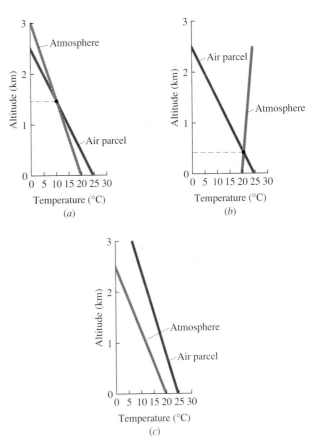

FIGURE 21-18 Conditions governing atmospheric stability. Blue lines show temperature versus altitude in the stationary atmosphere. Red lines are the rates at which rising air parcels cool adiabatically with increasing altitude. (*a*) Under normal stable conditions, adiabatic cooling occurs more rapidly and a parcel heated at ground level soon reaches equilibrium with the surrounding air, here at about 1.4 km. (*b*) A temperature inversion. Blue line shows air temperature increasing with altitude. Here equilibrium of a heated parcel occurs at low altitude, trapping pollutants near the ground. (*c*) When the lapse rate exceeds the adiabatic cooling rate, the air is unstable. A rising parcel continues to rise, without reaching equilibrium.

soon cease. Air under these conditions is therefore stable, in that a rising parcel soon reaches an equilibrium altitude. You can convince yourself that a falling parcel—falling because it's cooler than its surroundings—will also reach equilibrium.

Under stable conditions, smog-forming pollutants cannot escape to the upper atmosphere. Instead, they're trapped at an altitude where adiabatic cooling brings them to the same temperature as the surrounding air. The greater the difference between the actual lapse rate and the approximately 10°C/km adiabatic cooling rate, the stronger the "trapping" of the air and its pollutants. The most serious problems arise during a **temperature inversion**, in which the air temperature actually increases with height (Fig. 21-18b). A rising parcel still cools adiabatically, and now its temperature drops so quickly relative to its surroundings that the parcel is strongly trapped at low altitudes.

Sometimes the atmospheric lapse rate exceeds the rate of adiabatic cooling. This can occur on crisp, clear days when the ground is strongly heated, or it can occur with moist air for which the adiabatic cooling rate is only about 6°C/km. In this case a rising parcel cools more slowly than its surroundings, so its buoyancy increases and it accelerates upward (Fig. 21-18c). A falling parcel, similarly, accelerates downward. Under these conditions the air is unstable. The puffy cumulus clouds that form on an otherwise clear summer day are associated with plumes of warm air that rise through the unstable air until they're cool enough that moisture condenses to form clouds. A more dramatic example is the thunderstorm of Fig. 21-17b, in which unstable air undergoes violent up- and downdrafts driven by the heat of vaporization released as water vapor condenses. Problem 41 explores these issues of atmospheric stability.

Cyclic Processes

8.12, 8.13

Cyclic Process

Many natural and technological systems undergo **cyclic processes**, in which the system returns periodically to the same thermodynamic state. Engineering examples include engines, refrigerators, and air compressors, whose mechanical construction ensures cyclic behavior. Many natural oscillations, like those of a sound wave or a pulsating star, are essentially cyclic.

Cyclic processes often involve the four simple processes we've just outlined, which are summarized in Table 21-1. We've seen that the work done in any reversible process is just the area under the *PV* curve describing that process. A cyclic process returns to the same point in the *PV* diagram, so it generally involves both expansion and compression of the gas (Fig. 21-19). During expansion the gas does work on its surroundings; during compression work gets done on the gas. The net work is the difference between the two. Figure 21-19b shows that this work is the area—measured as pressure times volume—enclosed by the cyclic path in the *PV* diagram.

TABLE 21-1 *Ideal Gas Processes*

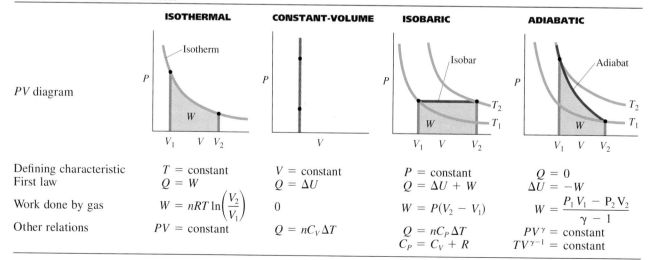

	ISOTHERMAL	CONSTANT-VOLUME	ISOBARIC	ADIABATIC
Defining characteristic	$T = $ constant	$V = $ constant	$P = $ constant	$Q = 0$
First law	$Q = W$	$Q = \Delta U$	$Q = \Delta U + W$	$\Delta U = -W$
Work done by gas	$W = nRT \ln\left(\dfrac{V_2}{V_1}\right)$	0	$W = P(V_2 - V_1)$	$W = \dfrac{P_1 V_1 - P_2 V_2}{\gamma - 1}$
Other relations	$PV = $ constant	$Q = nC_V \Delta T$	$Q = nC_P \Delta T$ $C_P = C_V + R$	$PV^\gamma = $ constant $TV^{\gamma-1} = $ constant

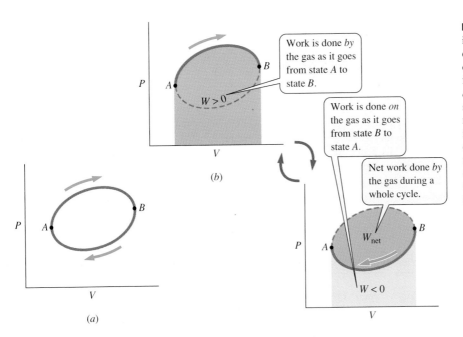

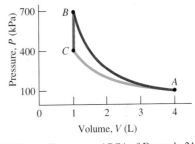

FIGURE 21-19 (*a*) A cyclic path for an ideal gas, traversed clockwise in the *PV* diagram. (*b*) The work done during a cycle. Work is done *by* the gas as it goes from state *A* to state *B*, and work is done *on* the gas as it returns from state *B* to state *A*. Since the area under each curve represents the associated work, the area inside the cycle represents the net work done by the gas. If the cycle were traversed counterclockwise rather than clockwise, the area inside the cycle would instead be the net work done *on* the gas.

EXAMPLE 21-5 | *A Cyclic Process*

An ideal gas with $\gamma = 1.4$ occupies 4.0 L at 300 K and 100 kPa pressure. It is compressed adiabatically to one-fourth of its original volume, then cooled at constant volume to 300 K, and finally allowed to expand isothermally to its original volume. How much work is done on the gas?

Solution

Figure 21-20 shows the cyclic path *ABCA* in the *PV* diagram. To calculate the work done on the gas, we consider the work involved in moving along each of the sections *AB*, *BC*, and *CA*. The adiabatic work W_{AB} is given by Equation 21-14:

$$W_{AB} = \frac{P_A V_A - P_B V_B}{\gamma - 1}.$$

We know P_A, V_A, and V_B. To get P_B, we solve the adiabatic relation $P_B V_B^\gamma = P_A V_A^\gamma$ to obtain

$$P_B = P_A \left(\frac{V_A}{V_B}\right)^\gamma.$$

Then the adiabatic work is

$$W_{AB} = \frac{P_A[V_A - (V_A/V_B)^\gamma V_B]}{\gamma - 1}$$

$$= \frac{(1.0 \times 10^5 \text{ Pa})[4.0 \times 10^{-3} \text{ m}^3 - (4^{1/4})(1.0 \times 10^{-3} \text{ m}^3)]}{0.4}$$

$$= -741 \text{ J}.$$

The minus sign indicates that work is done *on* the gas during this adiabatic compression.

FIGURE 21-20 The cyclic process *ABCA* of Example 21-5 includes adiabatic (*AB*), constant volume (*BC*), and isothermal (*CA*) sections.

No work is done during the constant-volume process *BC*, while the isothermal work W_{CA} is given by Equation 21-4:

$$W_{CA} = nRT \ln\left(\frac{V_A}{V_C}\right).$$

The quantity nRT is given by the ideal gas law, $nRT = PV$, where we can evaluate P and V at any point along the isotherm because it's a curve of constant temperature. We know these values at point *A*, so the isothermal work becomes

$$W_{CA} = P_A V_A \ln\left(\frac{V_A}{V_C}\right)$$

$$= (1.0 \times 10^5 \text{ Pa})(4.0 \times 10^{-3} \text{ m}^3)\ln\left(\frac{4.0 \text{ L}}{1.0 \text{ L}}\right) = 555 \text{ J}.$$

The net work is then

$$W_{ABC} = W_{AB} + W_{BC} + W_{CA}$$

$$= -741\,\text{J} + 0\,\text{J} + 555\,\text{J} = -187\,\text{J}.$$

The minus sign indicates that net work is done on the gas.

We could achieve the cyclic process described here with our simple gas-cylinder system by first insulating the bottom of the cylinder and moving the piston to compress the gas to one-fourth its original volume. We would then clamp the piston in place to maintain constant volume and cool the gas to 300 K by placing the cylinder in contact with a heat reservoir whose temperature was slowly decreased. Finally, we would maintain contact with the 300 K heat reservoir while allowing the gas to expand to its original volume.

Since the system returns to its original state, its internal energy undergoes no net change. That means any work done on

it must be rejected to its surroundings as heat. Since no heat flows during the adiabatic process *AB*, and since the gas *absorbs* heat during its isothermal expansion *CA*, the heat rejection takes place entirely during the constant-volume cooling period *BC*.

EXERCISE The gas of this example starts at state *A* in Fig. 21-20 and is compressed adiabatically until its temperature is 400 K. It's then cooled while maintaining constant volume until it reaches 300 K, then allowed to expand isothermally back to state *A*. Find (a) the net work done on the gas and (b) the minimum volume reached.

Answers: (a) 45.7 J; (b) 1.95 L

Some problems similar to Example 21-5: 20, 21, 27, 31–33, 55, 56, 63

21-3 SPECIFIC HEATS OF AN IDEAL GAS

We've found that the thermodynamic behavior of an ideal gas depends on the specific heats C_V and C_P. What are the values of those quantities?

Our ideal gas model of Chapter 20 assumed the gas molecules were structureless point particles. The only energy of such particles is their translational kinetic energy, and the internal energy U of the gas is the sum of all the molecular translational energies. But the average kinetic energy is directly proportional to the temperature:

$$\tfrac{1}{2}m\overline{v^2} = \tfrac{3}{2}kT.$$

If we have n moles of gas, the internal energy is then

$$U = nN_A\left(\tfrac{1}{2}m\overline{v^2}\right) = \tfrac{3}{2}nN_A kT,$$

where N_A is Avogadro's number. But $N_A k = R$, the gas constant, so

$$U = \tfrac{3}{2}nRT.$$

Using this result in Equation 21-8 for the molar specific heat gives

$$C_V = \frac{1}{n}\frac{\Delta U}{\Delta T} = \tfrac{3}{2}R. \qquad (21\text{-}15)$$

For this simple gas of structureless particles, the adiabatic exponent γ is then

$$\gamma = \frac{C_P}{C_V} = \frac{C_V + R}{C_V} = \frac{\tfrac{5}{2}R}{\tfrac{3}{2}R} = \frac{5}{3} = 1.67. \qquad (21\text{-}16)$$

Some gases, notably the inert gases helium (He), neon (Ne), argon (Ar), and others in the last column of the periodic table, have adiabatic exponents and specific heats given by these equations. But others do not. At room temperature, for example, hydrogen (H_2), oxygen (O_2), and nitrogen (N_2) obey adiabatic laws with γ very nearly $\frac{7}{5}$ (= 1.4). Solving Equation 21-16 for C_V shows that for these gases

$$C_V = \frac{R}{\gamma - 1} = \frac{R}{\frac{7}{5} - 1} = \frac{5}{2}R.$$

On the other hand, sulfur dioxide (SO_2) and nitrogen dioxide (NO_2) have specific heat ratios close to 1.3 and therefore volume specific heats of about $3.4R$.

What's going on here? A clue lies in the structure of individual gas molecules, reflected in their chemical formulas. The inert gas molecules are **monatomic**, consisting of single atoms. To the extent that these atoms behave like our model's structureless mass points, the only kind of energy they can have is kinetic energy associated with their translational motion. We can think of that kinetic energy as being a sum of *three* terms, each associated with motion in one of the three mutually perpendicular directions. We call each separate term in the expression for the energy of a system a **degree of freedom**, meaning a way that system can take on energy. So a monatomic molecule has three degrees of freedom.

In contrast, hydrogen, oxygen, and nitrogen molecules are **diatomic**, as shown in Fig. 21-21a. Although a gas of such molecules should still obey the ideal gas law $PV = nRT$, the molecules differ in one important respect from mass points: In addition to translational kinetic energy, they can have rotational energy as well. If we continue to model individual atoms as structureless mass points, then a diatomic molecule should be able to rotate about either of two axes, both mutually perpendicular and also perpendicular to the line joining the atoms, as suggested in Fig. 21-21b. Rotation about the axis joining the atoms is meaningless if the atoms are true mass points. Then the kinetic energy of a diatomic molecule consists of *five* terms, three for the three directions of translational motion and two for rotational motions about the two mutually perpendicular axes. So a diatomic molecule has five degrees of freedom. We'll now see how this difference between *three* degrees of freedom for monatomic molecules versus *five* for diatomic molecules accounts for the difference between their specific heats.

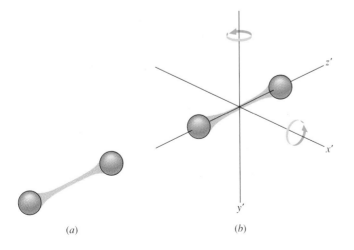

FIGURE 21-21 (*a*) "Dumbbell" model of a diatomic molecule, (*b*) showing that the diatomic molecule can rotate about two of three mutually perpendicular axes.

The Equipartition Theorem

We showed in Chapter 20 that the average translational kinetic energy associated with a gas molecule's motion in one direction is $\frac{1}{2}kT$. We then argued that all three directions of motion are equally probable, making the molecular kinetic energy, on average, $\frac{3}{2}kT$. The argument from one direction to three is statistical, based on the assumption that random collisions will "share" energy equally among the possible motions. When a molecule can rotate as well as translate, energy should be shared also among possible rotational motions.

Not only is energy shared, but it's shared equally. The nineteenth century Scottish physicist James Clerk Maxwell first proved this fact, which is now known as the **equipartition theorem**:

> Equipartition theorem: *When a system is in thermodynamic equilibrium, the average energy per molecule is* $\frac{1}{2}kT$ *for each degree of freedom*.

We can use the equipartition theorem to calculate the specific heat of a diatomic molecule. Each molecule has five degrees of freedom, three translational and two rotational. The average energy of a molecule is then $5(\frac{1}{2}kT) = \frac{5}{2}kT$, so the total internal energy in n moles of a diatomic gas is

$$U = nN_A(\tfrac{5}{2}kT) = \tfrac{5}{2}nRT.$$

Equation 21-8 then gives the specific heat at constant volume:

$$C_V = \frac{1}{n}\frac{\Delta U}{\Delta T} = \tfrac{5}{2}R. \qquad \text{(diatomic molecule)}$$

Our result $C_P = C_V + R$ still holds, since it was derived from the first law of thermodynamics without regard to molecular structure, so

$$C_P = \tfrac{7}{2}R$$

and

$$\gamma = \frac{C_P}{C_V} = \frac{7}{5} = 1.4.$$

These results describe the observed behavior of diatomic gases like hydrogen, oxygen, and nitrogen at room temperature.

EXAMPLE 21-6	*Mixing Gases*

A gas mixture consists of 2.0 mol of oxygen (O_2) and 1.0 mol of argon (Ar). What is the volume specific heat of the mixture?

Solution

Being diatomic, each oxygen molecule has five degrees of freedom. Then the equipartition theorem gives the total internal energy of all the oxygen molecules:

$$U_{O_2} = nN_A(\tfrac{5}{2}kT) = (2.0 \text{ mol})(\tfrac{5}{2}RT) = 5.0RT,$$

where we used $N_A k = R$. Similarly, the internal energy associated with all the monatomic argon molecules is

$$U_{Ar} = nN_A(\tfrac{3}{2}kT) = (1.0 \text{ mol})(\tfrac{3}{2}RT) = 1.5RT.$$

Then the total internal energy of the gas is

$$U = U_{O_2} + U_{Ar} = 6.5RT,$$

so

$$C_V = \frac{1}{n}\frac{\Delta U}{\Delta T} = \frac{6.5R}{3.0 \text{ mol}} = 2.2R.$$

EXERCISE Find the specific heat at constant volume and the adiabatic index γ for a mixture of equal numbers of nitrogen (N_2) and helium (He) molecules.

Answers: $C_V = 2R$, $\gamma = 1.5$

Some problems similar to Example 21-6: 42–45

A polyatomic molecule like NO_2 (Fig. 21-22) can rotate about any of three perpendicular axes and therefore has three rotational degrees of freedom. With a total of six degrees of freedom, the internal energy of n moles is then

$$U = (nN_A)(6)(\tfrac{1}{2}kT) = 3nRT,$$

so

$$C_V = \frac{1}{n}\frac{dU}{dT} = 3R,$$

$$C_P = C_V + R = 4R,$$

and

$$\gamma = \frac{C_P}{C_V} = \frac{4}{3} = 1.33.$$

These values are reasonably close to the experimental values $\gamma = 1.29$ and $C_V = 3.47R$, although the agreement is noticeably poorer than for monatomic and diatomic gases.

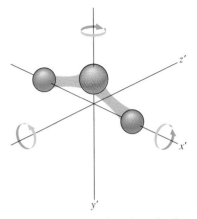

FIGURE 21-22 A triatomic molecule like NO_2 has significant rotational inertia about each of the three axes, and therefore has three rotational degrees of freedom.

Quantum Effects

Accounting for the effect of molecular structure on gas behavior seems a remarkable triumph for Newtonian physics. But hidden in our treatment of the specific heats of gases is an assumption that Newtonian physics alone can't justify, namely the treatment of atoms as structureless mass points. After all, real atoms have size and should be able to rotate. So why doesn't even a monatomic molecule have six degrees of freedom, three for rotation as well as three for translation? And if real atoms have size, a dumbbell-shaped diatomic molecule should be able to rotate about an axis through its atoms, giving it, too, three rotational degrees of freedom. Thus the fact that atoms have nonzero size suggests that both monatomic and diatomic molecules should have the same specific heat—whose value should be different from what's observed in either case. This difficulty greatly perplexed physicists at the end of the 19th century. What's wrong?

In trying to model individual atoms and molecules, we're pushing the limits of classical physics, approaching a realm where a quantum-mechanical description is necessary. In quantum mechanics, the energy associated with a periodic motion such as molecular rotation comes only in discrete multiples of some minimum amount. The minimum energy needed for rotation of monatomic molecules, or of diatomic molecules about the axis through the two atoms, is so large that at normal temperatures there isn't enough thermal energy to get these rotations going. So the atoms really do behave like structureless mass points— not because they are, but because they can't rotate. Our analysis of the specific heats of gases based on molecular structure is therefore correct—but only because of a hidden conclusion from quantum mechanics that lets us treat the individual atoms as nonrotating mass points.*

The fact of **quantization**—the restriction of energies to certain discrete values—is also evident in the behavior of specific heats as a function of temper-

*For more on this issue, see "Specific heats and the equipartition law," by Clayton A. Gearhart, *American Journal of Physics,* vol. 64, August 1996, p. 995.

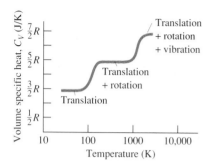

FIGURE 21-23 Volume specific heat of H_2 gas as a function of temperature. Below 20 K hydrogen is liquid and above 3200 K it dissociates into individual atoms.

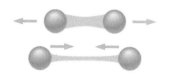

FIGURE 21-24 At high temperatures a diatomic molecule has enough energy to undergo vibrational motion.

ature, shown for hydrogen (H_2) in Fig. 21-23. In the region from about 250 K to 750 K, the specific heat has very nearly the value $\frac{5}{2}R$ that our dumbbell model predicts. But below about 100 K, hydrogen's specific heat is close to the $\frac{3}{2}R$ we expect for a monatomic molecule. There's a good reason for this: at these low temperatures, the thermal energy is well below the minimum needed for molecular rotation. So the molecules, although diatomic, can't rotate and therefore have only their three translational degrees of freedom. Thus at low temperatures, hydrogen's specific heat is that of a monatomic gas.

As the temperature rises, rotation becomes possible and the specific heat rises to the value $\frac{5}{2}R$ characteristic of diatomic molecules. At still higher temperatures, above about 3000 K, it rises to approximately $\frac{7}{2}R$. Here a new motion has become energetically possible, namely the vibration of molecules like miniature mass-spring systems (Fig. 21-24). Each molecule gains two more degrees of freedom, one for the kinetic energy and one for the potential energy associated with this vibrational motion, and so the specific heat goes up.

Are you bothered by the strange restrictions quantum mechanics imposes on the rotation and vibration of molecules? You should be! Nothing in the physics you've studied until now, and nothing in your everyday experience, suggests that a rotating object can't have any amount of energy you care to give it. But quantum mechanics deals with a realm of objects much smaller than those of our daily experience. The quantization of energy levels is only one of many unusual things that occur in the quantum realm. We will explore more quantum phenomena in Chapter 39.

CHAPTER SYNOPSIS

Summary

1. The **first law of thermodynamics** states that the change in a system's internal energy depends only on the net energy transfer to or from the system by any combination of heat or work. Thus the first law extends energy conservation to processes involving heat transfer. Mathematically, the change ΔU in a system's internal energy is the difference between the heat Q transferred *to* the system and the work W done *by* the system:

$$\Delta U = Q - W.$$

2. A **thermodynamic process** takes a system from one thermodynamic state to another. A **quasi-static process** occurs slowly enough that the system moves through a sequence of equilibrium states, so the process can be described by a path in the PV diagram. The work done by a system undergoing a quasi-static process that takes its volume from V_1 to V_2 is

$$W = \int_{V_1}^{V_2} P\,dV.$$

3. Four basic processes are **isothermal** (constant temperature), **constant volume**, **isobaric** (constant pressure), and **adiabatic** (no heat transfer). For an ideal gas, the work done and the relations among various thermodynamic variables are summarized in Table 21-1 in the text. A **cyclic process** takes a system around a closed path in its PV diagram, returning to its original state.

4. An ideal gas is characterized by its **molar specific heat at constant volume**, C_V, and its **molar specific heat at constant pressure**, C_P. The heat Q required to raise the temperature of n moles an amount ΔT is given by $Q = nC\Delta T$, where C is the specific heat appropriate to the condition—constant volume or pressure—under which the temperature change occurs. The specific heats are related by $C_P = C_V + R$, where R is the gas constant.

5. The **equipartition theorem** states that the average molecular energy per **degree of freedom** in thermodynamic equilibrium is $\frac{1}{2}kT$. Monatomic molecules have three degrees of freedom, associated with the three directions of translational motion; this leads to a volume specific heat $C_V = \frac{3}{2}R$. Diatomic molecules also undergo rotation, adding two more degrees of freedom and giving a volume specific heat of $\frac{5}{2}R$.

Terms You Should Understand

(Pairs are closely related terms whose distinction is important; number in parentheses is chapter section where term first appears.)

work (21-1)
internal energy (21-1)
first law of thermodynamics (21-1)
thermodynamic state, state variable (21-1)
quasi-static process (21-2)
reversible process, irreversible process (21-2)
isothermal process (21-2)
constant-volume process (21-2)
isobaric process (21-2)
molar specific heat at constant volume,
     . . . at constant pressure (21-2)
adiabatic process (21-2)
cyclic process (21-2)
degrees of freedom (21-3)
equipartition theorem (21-3)

Symbols You Should Recognize

ΔU (21-1) C_V, C_P (21-2) γ (21-2)

Problems You Should Be Able to Solve

calculating internal energy change, heat transfer, or work from the other two (21-1)
relating volume, pressure, and temperature changes for the basic ideal gas processes (21-2)
determining work done in basic ideal gas processes (21-2)
determining work involved in cyclic processes (21-2)
evaluating specific heats based on molecular structure (21-3)

Limitations to Keep in Mind

The ideal gas, with its internal energy a function of temperature alone, is an approximation. In real gases the weak forces among molecules make the internal energy depend slightly on volume as well.
Most relations developed in this chapter are valid only in the quasi-static limit; real processes may approach but not actually achieve this limit.

QUESTIONS

1. In Chapter 8 we wrote the conservation of energy principle in the form $K + U =$ constant. In what way is the first law of thermodynamics a broader statement than that?
2. The temperature of the water in a jar is raised by violently shaking the jar. Which of the terms Q and W in the first law of thermodynamics is involved in this case?
3. In Example 21-1, we considered the electric power leaving a power plant as part of the work done by the power plant. Why did we include the electric power with the work rather than with the heat?
4. What is the difference between heat and internal energy?
5. Some water is tightly sealed in a perfectly insulated container. Is it possible to change the water temperature? Explain.
6. Is the internal energy of a van der Waals gas a function of temperature alone? Why or why not?
7. Are the initial and final equilibrium states of an irreversible process describable by points in a PV diagram? Explain.
8. Why can an irreversible process not be described by a path in a PV diagram?
9. Does the first law of thermodynamics apply to an irreversible process?
10. Is it possible to have a process that is isothermal but irreversible? Explain.
11. A quasi-static process begins and ends at the same temperature. Is the process necessarily isothermal?

12. Figure 21-25 shows two processes, A and B, which connect the same initial and final states, 1 and 2. For which process is more heat added to the system?

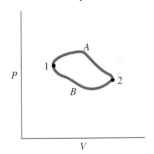

FIGURE 21-25 Question 12.

13. Two identical gas-cylinder systems are taken from the same initial state to the same final state, but by different processes. Is the work done in each case necessarily the same? The heat added? The change in internal energy?
14. When you let air out of a tire, the air seems cool. Why? What kind of process is occurring?
15. Blow on the back of your hand with your mouth wide open. Your breath will feel hot. Now tighten your lips into a small opening, and blow again. Now your breath feels cool. Why?
16. How is it possible to have $PV^\gamma =$ constant in an adiabatic process and yet have $PV = nRT$?

17. Water is boiled in an open pan. Of which of the four specific processes we considered is this an example?

18. Is it possible to involve an ideal gas in a process that is simultaneously isothermal and isobaric? Is there any real substance that could undergo such a process? Give an example.

19. Three identical gas-cylinder systems expand from the same initial state to final states that have the same volume. One system expands isothermally, one adiabatically, and one isobarically. Which does the most work? Which does the least work?

20. If the relation $\Delta U = nC_V\Delta T$ holds for any ideal gas process, why do we call C_V the molar specific heat at constant volume?

21. Why is the specific heat at constant pressure greater than at constant volume?

22. Imagine a gas of very complicated molecules, each with several hundred degrees of freedom. What, approximately, is the specific heat ratio γ of this gas? Is it easy or hard to change the gas temperature?

23. In what sense can a gas of diatomic molecules be considered an ideal gas, given that its molecules are not point particles?

PROBLEMS

ActivPhysics can help with these problems:
Activities 8.5–8.13.

Section 21-1 The First Law of Thermodynamics

1. In a perfectly insulated container, 1.0 kg of water is stirred vigorously until its temperature rises by 7.0°C. How much work was done on the water?

2. In a closed but uninsulated container, 500 g of water is shaken violently until its temperature rises by 3.0°C. The mechanical work required in the process is 9.0 kJ. (a) How much heat is transferred during the shaking? (b) How much mechanical energy would have been required had the container been perfectly insulated?

3. A 40-W heat source is applied to a gas sample for 25 s, during which time the gas expands and does 750 J of work on its surroundings. By how much does the internal energy of the gas change?

4. What is the rate of heat flow into a system whose internal energy is increasing at the rate of 45 W, given that the system is doing work at the rate of 165 W?

5. The most efficient large-scale electric power generating systems use high-temperature gas turbines and a so-called combined cycle system that maximizes the conversion of thermal energy into useful work. One such plant produces electrical energy at the rate of 360 MW, while extracting energy from its natural gas fuel at the rate of 670 MW. (a) At what rate does it reject waste heat to the environment? (b) Find its efficiency, defined as the percent of the total energy extracted from the fuel that ends up as electrical energy.

6. In a certain automobile engine, 17% of the total energy released in burning gasoline ends up as mechanical work. What is the engine's mechanical power output if its heat output is 68 kW?

7. Water flows over Niagara Falls (height 50 m) at the rate of about 10^6 kg/s. Suppose that all the water passes through a turbine connected to an electric generator producing 400 MW of electric power. If the water has negligible kinetic energy after leaving the turbine, by how much

has its temperature increased between the top of the falls and the outlet of the turbine?

Section 21-2 Thermodynamic Processes

8. An ideal gas expands from the state (P_1, V_1) to the state (P_2, V_2), where $P_2 = 2P_1$ and $V_2 = 2V_1$. The expansion proceeds along the straight diagonal path AB shown in Fig. 21-26. Find an expression for the work done by the gas during this process.

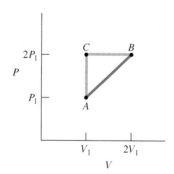

FIGURE 21-26 Poblems 8, 9.

9. Repeat the preceding problem for a process that follows the path ACB in Fig. 21-26.

10. Oceanographers lower an underwater habitat to the ocean floor. A hatch at the bottom of the habitat is open, so water can enter to compress the air and thus keep the air pressure inside equal to the pressure of the surrounding water. The habitat is lowered slowly enough that the inside air remains at the same temperature as the water. But the water temperature decreases with depth, in such a way that the air pressure and volume are related by $P = P_0\sqrt{V_0/V}$, where P_0 and V_0 are the surface values. The habitat's volume is 17 m³ and it's initially full of air at normal atmospheric pressure. It's then lowered to a depth where the pressure is 1.4 atmospheres. Find (a) the air volume at this depth and (b) the work done on the air as the habitat is lowered. *Hint:* You'll need to do an integral.

11. A balloon contains 0.30 mol of helium. It rises, while maintaining a constant 300 K temperature, to an altitude where its volume has expanded 5 times. How much work is done by the gas in the balloon during this isothermal expansion? Neglect tension forces in the balloon.

12. The balloon of the preceding problem starts at a pressure of 100 kPa and rises to an altitude where the pressure is 75 kPa, maintaining a constant 300 K temperature. (a) By what factor does its volume increase? (b) How much work does the gas in the balloon do?

13. How much work does it take to compress 2.5 mol of an ideal gas to half its original volume while maintaining a constant 300 K temperature?

14. An ideal gas expands to 10 times its original volume, maintaining a constant 440 K temperature. If the gas does 3.3 kJ of work on its surroundings, (a) how much heat does it absorb, and (b) how many moles of gas are there?

15. A 0.25 mol sample of an ideal gas initially occupies 3.5 L. If it takes 61 J of work to compress the gas isothermally to 3.0 L, what is the temperature?

16. As the heart beats, blood pressure in an artery varies from a high of 125 mm of mercury to a low of 80 mm of mercury. These values are gauge pressures—i.e., excesses over atmospheric pressure. An air bubble trapped in the artery has diameter 1.52 mm when the blood pressure is at its minimum. (a) What will be its diameter at maximum pressure? (b) How much work does the blood (and ultimately the heart) do in compressing this bubble, assuming the air remains at the same 37.0°C temperature as the blood?

17. It takes 600 J to compress a gas isothermally to half its original volume. How much work would it take to compress it by a factor of 10 starting from its original volume?

18. A gas undergoes an adiabatic compression during which its volume drops to half its original value. If the gas pressure increases by a factor of 2.55, what is its specific heat ratio γ?

19. A gas with $\gamma = 1.4$ is at 100 kPa pressure and occupies 5.00 L. (a) How much work does it take to compress the gas adiabatically to 2.50 L? (b) What is its final pressure?

20. A gas sample undergoes the cyclic process $ABCA$ shown in Fig. 21-27, where AB lies on an isotherm. The pressure at point A is 60 kPa. Find (a) the pressure at B and (b) the net work done on the gas.

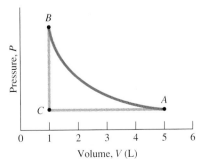

FIGURE 21-27 Problems 20, 21.

21. Repeat the preceding problem taking AB to be on an adiabat and using a specific heat ratio of $\gamma = 1.4$.

22. Warm winds called Chinooks (a Native American term meaning "snow eaters") sometimes sweep across the plains just east of the Rocky Mountains. These winds carry air from high in the mountains down to the plains rapidly enough that the air has no time to exchange significant heat with its surroundings (Fig. 21-28). On the day of a Chinook wind, pressure and temperature high in the Colorado Rockies are 62.0 kPa and −11.0°C, respectively. (a) What will be the air temperature when the Chinook has carried it to the plain where pressure is 86.5 kPa? (b) How much work is done on what was initially a cubic meter of air as it descends to the plain?

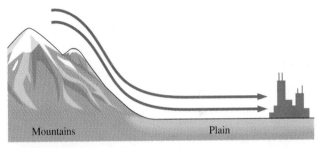

FIGURE 21-28 Chinook winds carry air from the low pressure and low temperature of the high Rocky Mountains to the higher pressure at the plains. How much does the air temperature increase? (Problem 22)

23. A gasoline engine has a compression ratio of 8.5. If the fuel-air mixture enters the engine at 30°C, what will be its temperature at maximum compression? Assume the compression is adiabatic and that the mixture has $\gamma = 1.4$.

24. By how much must the volume of a gas with $\gamma = 1.4$ be changed in an adiabatic process if the pressure is to double?

25. By how much must the volume of a gas with $\gamma = 1.4$ be changed in an adiabatic process if the kelvin temperature is to double?

26. Volvo's B5340 engine, used in the V70 series cars, has a compression ratio of 10.2 (see Example 21-3 for the meaning of this term). If air at 320 K and atmospheric pressure fills an engine cylinder at its maximum volume, (a) what will be the air temperature at the point of maximum compression? (b) What will be the pressure at this point? Assume the compression is adiabatic, with $\gamma = 1.4$.

27. A gas expands isothermally from state A to state B, in the process absorbing 35 J of heat. It is then compressed isobarically to state C, where its volume equals that of state A. During the compression, 22 J of work are done on the gas. The gas is then heated at constant volume until it returns to state A. (a) Draw a PV diagram for this process. (b) How much work is done on or by the gas during the complete cycle? (c) How much heat is transferred to or from the gas as it goes from B to C to A?

28. Derive an equation relating pressure and temperature in an adiabatic process.

29. A 2.0 mol sample of ideal gas with molar specific heat $C_V = \frac{5}{2}R$ is initially at 300 K and 100 kPa pressure. Determine the final temperature and the work done by the gas when 1.5 kJ of heat is added to the gas (a) isothermally, (b) at constant volume, and (c) isobarically.

30. Prove that the slope of an adiabat at a given point in a PV diagram is γ times the slope of the isotherm passing through the same point.

31. An ideal gas with $\gamma = 1.67$ starts at point A in Fig. 21-29, where its volume and pressure are 1.00 m^3 and 250 kPa, respectively. It then undergoes an adiabatic expansion that triples its volume, ending at point B. It's then heated at constant volume to point C, then compressed isothermally back to A. Find (a) the pressure at B, (b) the pressure at C, and (c) the net work done on the gas.

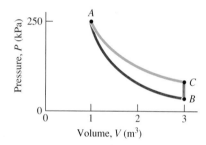

FIGURE 21-29 Problem 31.

32. The gas of Example 21-5 starts at state A in Fig. 21-20 and is compressed adiabatically until its volume is 2.0 L. It's then cooled while maintaining constant pressure until it reaches 300 K, then allowed to expand isothermally back to state A. Find (a) the net work done on the gas and (b) the minimum volume reached.

33. The gas of Example 21-5 starts at state A in Fig. 21-20 and is heated at constant volume until its pressure has doubled. It's then compressed adiabatically until its volume is one-fourth its original value, then cooled at constant volume to 300 K, and finally allowed to expand isothermally to its original state. Find the net work done on the gas.

34. A 25 L sample of an ideal gas with $\gamma = 1.67$ is at 250 K and 50 kPa. The gas is compressed isothermally to one-third of its original volume, then heated at constant volume until its state lies on the adiabatic curve that passes through its original state, and then allowed to expand adiabatically to that original state. Find the net work involved. Is work done on or by the gas?

35. A 25 L sample of an ideal gas with $\gamma = 1.67$ is at 250 K and 50 kPa. The gas is compressed adiabatically until its

pressure triples, then cooled at constant volume back to 250 K, and finally allowed to expand iothermally to its original state. (a) How much work is done on the gas? (b) What is the minimum volume reached? (c) Sketch this cyclic process in a PV diagram.

36. A 25 L sample of ideal gas is at 250 K and 50 kPa. The gas is heated at constant volume until its pressure triples, then cooled at constant pressure until its temperature is back to 250 K, and finally allowed to expand isothermally to its original state. (a) How much work is done on the gas? (b) What is the minimum volume reached? (c) Sketch this cyclic process in a PV diagram.

37. A bicycle pump consists of a cylinder 30 cm long when the pump handle is all the way out. The pump contains air ($\gamma = 1.4$) at 20°C. If the pump outlet is blocked and the handle pushed until the internal length of the pump cylinder is 17 cm, by how much does the air temperature rise? Assume that no heat is lost.

38. A tightly sealed flask contains 5.0 L of air at 0°C and 100 kPa pressure. How much heat is required to raise the air temperature to 20°C? The molar specific heat of air at constant volume is 2.5R.

39. A balloon contains 5.0 L of air at 0°C and 100 kPa pressure. How much heat is required to raise the air temperature to 20°C, assuming the gas stays in pressure equilibrium with its surroundings? Neglect tension forces in the balloon. The molar specific heat of air at constant volume is 2.5R.

40. A piston-cylinder system has initial volume 1.0 L and contains ideal gas at 300 K and 1.0 atm, with $C_V = 2.5R$. The piston is held fixed and the cylinder placed in contact with a heat reservoir at 600 K. Once equilibrium is reached, the gas is allowed to expand isothermally. When the pressure reaches 1.0 atm, the gas is cooled at constant pressure to 300 K. This cyclic process is repeated once a second. (a) Draw a PV diagram for the process. (b) What is the rate at which the gas does work?

41. Problem 70 in Chapter 18 shows that pressure as a function of height in Earth's atmosphere is given approximately by $P = P_0 e^{-h/h_0}$, where P_0 is the surface pressure and $h_0 = 8.2$ km. A parcel of air, initially at the surface and at a temperature of 10°C, rises as described in Application: Smog Alert on page 529. (a) What will be its temperature when it reaches 2.0 km altitude? (b) If the temperature of the surrounding air decreases at the normal lapse rate of 6.5°C/km, is the atmosphere stable or unstable under the conditions of this problem?

Section 21-3 Specific Heats of an Ideal Gas

42. A gas mixture contains 2.5 mol O_2 and 3.0 mol Ar. What are the molar specific heats at constant volume and pressure for this mixture?

43. A mixture of monatomic and diatomic gases has specific heat ratio $\gamma = 1.52$. What fraction of the molecules are monatomic?

44. What should be the approximate specific heat ratio of a gas consisting of 50% NO_2 ($\gamma = 1.29$), 30% O_2 ($\gamma = 1.4$), and 20% Ar ($\gamma = 1.67$)?

45. A gas mixture contains monatomic argon and diatomic oxygen. An adiabatic expansion that doubles its volume results in the pressure dropping to one-third of its original value. What fraction of the molecules are argon?

46. You have 2.0 mol of an ideal diatomic gas whose molecules can rotate but not vibrate. Suppose you arrange to give the gas 8.0 kJ of energy in such a way that it all goes initially into translational motion of the molecules. When equilibrium is reached, what will be the gas temperature?

47. How much of a triatomic gas with $C_V = 3R$ would you have to add to 10 mol of monatomic gas to get a mixture whose thermodynamic behavior was like that of a diatomic gas?

48. By how much does the temperature of (a) an ideal monatomic gas and (b) an ideal diatomic gas (with molecular rotation but no vibration) change in an adiabatic process in which 2.5 kJ of work are done on each mole of gas?

Paired Problems

(Both problems in a pair involve the same principles and techniques. If you can get the first problem, you should be able to solve the second one.)

49. A 5.0 mol sample of ideal gas with $C_V = \frac{5}{2}R$ undergoes an expansion during which the gas does 5.1 kJ of work. If it absorbs 2.7 kJ of heat during the process, by how much does its temperature change? *Hint:* Remember that Equation 21-7 holds for *any* ideal gas process.

50. External forces compress 21 mol of ideal monatomic gas; during the process the gas transfers 15 kJ of heat to its surroundings, yet its temperature rises by 160 K. How much work was done on the gas?

51. A gas with $\gamma = \frac{5}{3}$ is at 450 K at the start of an expansion that triples its volume. The expansion is isothermal until the volume has doubled, then adiabatic the rest of the way. What is the final gas temperature?

52. A gas with $\gamma = \frac{7}{5}$ is at 273 K when it's compressed isothermally to one-third of its original volume, then further compressed adiabatically to one-fifth of its original volume. What is its final temperature?

53. An ideal gas with $\gamma = 1.4$ is initially at 273 K and 100 kPa. The gas expands adiabatically until its temperature drops to 190 K. What is its final pressure?

54. An ideal gas with $\gamma = 1.3$ is initially at 273 K and 100 kPa. The gas is compressed adiabatically to 240 kPa pressure. What is its final temperature?

55. The curved path in Fig. 21-30 lies on the 350-K isotherm for an ideal gas with $\gamma = 1.4$. (a) Calculate the net work done on the gas as it goes around the cyclic path $ABCA$. (b) How much heat flows into or out of the gas on the segment AB?

56. Repeat part (a) of the preceding problem for the path $ACDA$ in Fig. 21-30. (b) How much heat flows into or out of the gas on the segment CD?

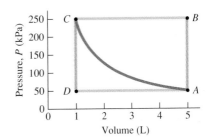

FIGURE 21-30 Problems 55, 56.

Supplementary Problems

57. An 8.5-kg rock at 0°C is dropped into a well-insulated vat containing a mixture of ice and water at 0°C. When equilibrium is reached there are 6.3 g less ice. From what height was the rock dropped?

58. A piston-cylinder arrangement containing 0.30 mol of nitrogen at high pressure is in thermal equilibrium with an ice-water bath containing 200 g of ice. The pressure of the ambient air is 1.0 atm. The gas is allowed to expand isothermally until it is in pressure balance with its surroundings. After the process is complete, the bath contains 210 g of ice. What was the original gas pressure?

59. Repeat Problem 8 for the case when the gas expands along a path given by $P = P_1 \left[1 + \left(\dfrac{V - V_1}{V_1} \right)^2 \right]$. Sketch the path in the PV diagram, and determine the work done.

60. A piston-cylinder arrangement contains 1.0 g of water at 50°C. The piston, which has negligible mass, is free to move and is exposed to atmospheric pressure (1.0 atm). The system is heated to 200°C. Assuming that liquid water is incompressible and that steam is an ideal gas with volume specific heat 4.3R, determine (a) the work done by the system and (b) the heat added to it.

61. Show that the application of Equation 21-3 to an adiabatic process results in Equation 21-14.

62. Find an expression for the molar specific heat at constant volume of an ideal gas in terms of its adiabatic exponent γ.

63. An ideal gas is taken clockwise around the circular path shown in Fig. 21-31. (a) How much work does the gas do? (b) If there are 1.3 moles of gas, what is the maximum temperature reached?

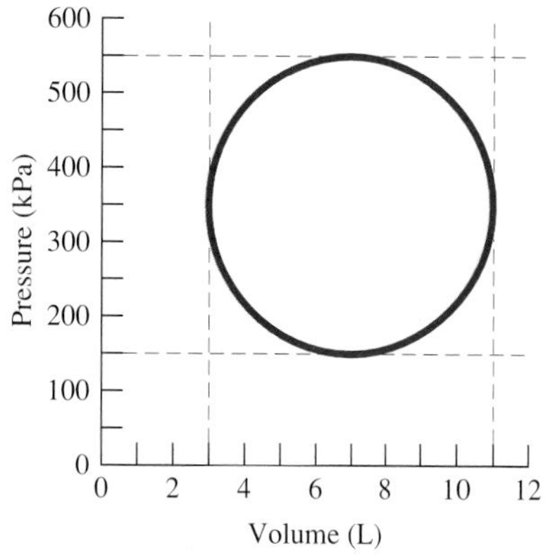

FIGURE 21-31 Problem 63.

64. A piston-cylinder system contains 0.50 mol of hydrogen (H_2) at 400 K and 300 kPa. An identical system contains 0.50 mol of helium (He) under identical conditions. Each gas undergoes an expansion that quadruples the system volume. Calculate the work done by each, if the expansion is (a) isothermal and (b) adiabatic.

65. Show that the work done by a van der Waals gas undergoing isothermal expansion from volume V_1 to V_2 is

$$W = nRT \ln\left(\frac{V_2 - nb}{V_1 - nb}\right) + an^2\left(\frac{1}{V_2} - \frac{1}{V_1}\right),$$

where a and b are the constants in Equation 20-5.

66. The compression and rarefaction in a sound wave occur fast enough that very little heat flow occurs, making the process essentially adiabatic. Show in this case that the bulk modulus (Equation 17-5) becomes $B = \gamma P$, and then show that Equation 17-6 leads to Equation 17-1 for the sound speed. *Hint:* Write Equation 17-5 in derivative form:

$$B = -V\frac{dP}{dV}.$$

67. A horizontal piston-cylinder system containing n mol of ideal gas is surrounded by air at temperature T_0 and pressure P_0. If the piston is displaced slightly from equilibrium, show that it executes simple harmonic motion with angular frequency $\omega = AP_0/\sqrt{MnRT_0}$, where A and M are the piston area and mass, respectively. Assume the gas temperature remains constant.

68. Repeat the preceding problem, now assuming that no heat flows into or out of the gas.

69. A cylinder of cross-sectional area A is closed by a massless piston. The cylinder contains n mol of ideal gas with specific heat ratio γ, and is initially in equilibrium with the surrounding air at temperature T_0 and pressure P_0. The piston is initially at height h_1 above the bottom of the cylinder. Sand is gradually sprinkled onto the piston until it has moved downward to a final height h_2. Find the total mass of the sand if the process is (a) isothermal and (b) adiabatic.

The Second Law of Thermodynamics

22

A power plant's cooling towers transfer waste heat to the environment. In a typical power plant, two-thirds of the energy released from the fuel ends up as waste heat—a consequence of the second law of thermodynamics.

The first law of thermodynamics relates heat and other forms of energy. Much of our world works because of this relation. Cars run on energy extracted from the heat of burning gasoline. Most of the electrical energy that powers lights and motors and computers originates in heat released in burning fuels or fissioning uranium. Our own bodies run on energy that was once released as heat deep in the Sun's core. But the first law doesn't tell the whole story. Heat and mechanical energy are not exactly the same thing, and the difference between them makes the conversion of heat to work a more subtle task than the first law alone would imply.

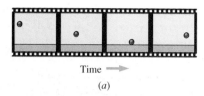

Time ⟶

(a)

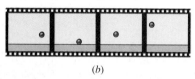

(b)

FIGURE 22-1 A movie of a bouncing ball makes sense whether it's shown forward or backward.

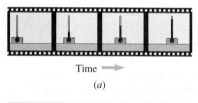

Time ⟶

(a)

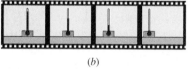

(b)

FIGURE 22-2 Movie of a block warming as friction dissipates its kinetic energy. The reverse sequence would never happen, even though it does not violate energy conservation.

22-1 REVERSIBILITY AND IRREVERSIBILITY

Figure 22-1 shows a movie of a bouncing ball. We can run it forward or backward and still have a plausible sequence of physical events. Figure 22-2 shows a movie of another simple physical process. A block slides along a table, eventually coming to a stop. Friction warms the block, so we see its temperature rise. Play this one in reverse, and it makes no sense. We never see a block at rest suddenly start to move, cooling in the process. Yet energy could be conserved if it did, so the first law of thermodynamics would be satisfied.

Beat an egg, and the yolk and white quickly blend. You would be surprised if, on reversing the beater, the scrambled yolk and white separated—yet nothing in the laws of mechanics would prevent it. Or put cups of cold and hot water in thermal contact. The hot water gets colder, and the cold water gets hotter. The reverse never occurs—even though energy would be conserved if it did.

Most events are **irreversible**, in the sense of the block, the egg, and the water. What is the origin of this irreversibility? In each case we start with matter in an organized state. In the sliding block all molecules share a common motion. The egg is organized so all the yolk molecules are in one place. The hot water has a greater number of energetic molecules. Of all the possible states into which matter might arrange itself, these *organized* states are relatively rare. There are many more *chaotic* states—for instance, all the possible arrangements of molecules in a scrambled egg—that have less organization. When a system evolves, chances are it will end up in a less organized state, simply because there are far more such states available to it. It's then very unlikely to assume spontaneously a more organized state.

A key word here is *spontaneous*. We could restore a system to a more organized state—for example, by putting one cup of lukewarm water on the stove and the other in the refrigerator—but then we have to carry out a rather deliberate and energy-consuming process.

Thermodynamic processes can also be irreversible, as we discussed in the preceding chapter. Plunging a cool gas sample into boiling water, for example, creates a temporarily more organized state in which the gas is separated into a hotter region—i.e., a region of higher mean molecular energy—right near the container walls and a cooler region in the interior (recall Fig. 21-6). But this is not a state of thermodynamic equilibrium, and molecular collisions soon equalize the mean molecular energy throughout the gas, restoring thermodynamic equilibrium. At the same time, the organization represented by separate hotter and cooler regions disappears. A spontaneous return to the organized state is highly improbable, and in this sense the process is irreversible.

Irreversibility is a probabilistic notion. Events that *could* occur without violating the principles of Newtonian physics nevertheless *don't* occur because they're too improbable. A practical consequence is that it's difficult to harness the considerable energy tied up as internal energy associated with random molecular motions because those motions won't spontaneously become organized. That makes much of the world's energy unavailable for doing useful work.

22-2 THE SECOND LAW OF THERMODYNAMICS

Heat Engines

It is impossible to convert *all* the internal energy of a system to useful work. But devices called **heat engines** can extract *some* of that internal energy. Examples of

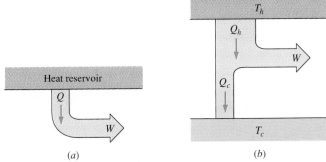

FIGURE 22-3 (*a*) Energy flow diagram for a perfect heat engine, which extracts heat Q from a reservoir and delivers an equal amount of work. (*b*) A real engine delivers as work only a fraction of the heat Q_h extracted from the high-temperature reservoir; the remainder is rejected to the low-temperature reservoir.

heat engines include gasoline and diesel engines, fossil-fueled and nuclear power plants, and jet aircraft engines.

Conceptually, we characterize a heat engine with a diagram showing heat flowing into the engine and work emerging. Figure 22-3*a* is such an energy-flow diagram for a "perfect" heat engine—one that extracts heat from a heat reservoir and converts it all to work. Such an engine would do exactly what we argued against in the preceding section—it would convert the random energy of thermal motion entirely into the ordered motion associated with mechanical work. In fact a perfect heat engine is impossible, for the same reason that we can't unscramble an egg or cause a block to accelerate spontaneously at the expense of its internal energy. This fact comprises one statement of the **second law of thermodynamics**:

> *Second law of thermodynamics (Kelvin-Planck statement): It is impossible to construct a heat engine operating in a cycle that extracts heat from a reservoir and delivers an equal amount of work.*

This version of the second law was formulated by Lord Kelvin and Max Planck. The phrase "in a cycle" means that a practical engine must go through a repeated sequence of steps, as in the back-and-forth motions of the pistons in a gasoline engine.

A simple heat engine consists of a gas-cylinder system and a heat reservoir, the latter kept hot, perhaps, by burning a fuel. With the gas initially at high pressure, we place the cylinder in contact with the heat reservoir. The gas expands and does work W on the piston. In this isothermal process, the gas extracts heat $Q = W$ from the reservoir. Eventually the gas reaches pressure equilibrium and stops expanding. The piston must then be returned to its original position if it's to do more work.

If we just push the piston back, we'll have to do as much work as was extracted during the expansion, and our engine will produce no net work. Instead we can cool the gas to reduce its volume, through thermal contact with a cool reservoir. But then some energy leaves the system as heat rather than work, as shown conceptually in Fig. 22-3*b*. Our engine extracts heat from a source and delivers mechanical work, but over a full cycle the amount of work is always less than the heat extracted. The remaining energy is rejected to the lower temperature reservoir, usually the environment. In practical terms, much of the energy

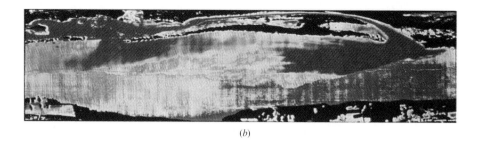

(b)

FIGURE 22-4 Real heat engines necessarily reject heat to the environment. (a) Water circulates through a car engine, absorbing waste heat, then on through the car's radiator. The radiator, a system of thin tubes exposed to the flow of air through the car's front grille, transfers waste heat to the air. Here a motorist adds antifreeze to the cooling water. (b) Power plants usually transfer waste heat to a nearby body of water. This infrared photo shows hot water (red) discharged from a power plant at the right end of the photo; black areas represent land, while yellow and gray regions are cooler parts of the river. Downstream is to the left.

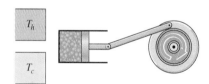

FIGURE 22-5 A simple heat engine. The gas absorbs heat from the hot reservoir, does work on the piston and wheel, and rejects heat to the cool reservoir. The two heat reservoirs can be moved to bring either one into thermal contact with the cylinder.

FIGURE 22-6 PV diagram for the engine of Fig. 22-5. AB and DC are isotherms at the temperatures of the hot and cool reservoirs, respectively; AD and BC are adiabatic curves.

released from fuels in car engines and power plants ends up as waste heat (Fig. 22-4).

The second law of thermodynamics states that we can't build a perfect heat engine. But how close can we come? Since we pay for the fuel that heats the high-temperature reservoir, it's clearly advantageous to minimize the rejected heat. We define the **efficiency** of an engine as the ratio of work W output by the engine in one cycle to the heat Q_h absorbed from the high-temperature reservoir,

$$e = \frac{W}{Q_h}.$$

Since the process is cyclic, there's no net change in internal energy over one cycle. Then the first law of thermodynamics, $\Delta U = Q - W$, ensures that the work done is the difference between the heat Q_h extracted from the high-temperature reservoir and the heat Q_c rejected to the cool reservoir. So the efficiency is

$$e = \frac{Q_h - Q_c}{Q_h} = 1 - \frac{Q_c}{Q_h}. \tag{22-1}$$

Figure 22-5 shows a simple heat engine whose efficiency we can readily calculate. The engine consists of a cylinder containing an ideal gas, sealed by a movable piston. The piston is connected to a rod that drives a wheel; as the piston goes back and forth, the wheel turns continually. The engine gets its energy from a heat reservoir maintained at a high temperature T_h, and it rejects heat to a cooler reservoir at temperature T_c.

Figure 22-6 shows how the engine works. It starts with the piston in its leftmost position, so the gas volume is at its minimum. This state is point A in the PV diagram of Fig. 22-6. At this point, we bring the high-temperature reservoir into thermal contact with the cylinder. The gas absorbs an amount of heat Q_h from the

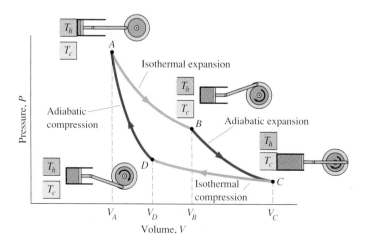

hot reservoir and expands isothermally along path AB in the PV diagram. Since the temperature remains constant during this process, so does the internal energy. The first law then shows that the engine does work $W = Q$ on the piston and wheel. At state B, we remove the hot reservoir. The expansion is now adiabatic, and follows path BC in the PV diagram. We design the engine so that, when the piston reaches its rightmost position, the gas temperature has cooled to T_c. This state is point C in the PV diagram, and is the state of maximum gas volume. We then bring the cool reservoir into thermal contact with the cylinder. The wheel's inertia keeps it turning, and the wheel does work on the gas, compressing it isothermally from state C to state D. This work ends up as heat rejected to the cool reservoir. Finally, at state D, we remove the cool reservoir from contact with the cylinder and allow the compression to continue adiabatically until the gas temperature has risen to T_h and the piston is once again in its leftmost position, with the gas compressed to its minimum volume. ActivPhysics Activity 8.14 provides a simulation of the entire cycle that shows this process more clearly than can a drawn picture.

ActivPhysics

8.14
Carnot Cycle

The engine we have just described undergoes a cyclic process consisting of four reversible steps, two isothermal and two adiabatic. This cycle is called a **Carnot cycle**, and the engine a **Carnot engine**, after the French engineer Sadi Carnot (1796–1832), who explored the properties of such an engine even before the first law of thermodynamics was formulated. The particular configuration of the engine is not important, nor is the choice of an ideal gas as the engine's **working fluid**. What distinguishes the Carnot cycle from others is the sequence of thermodynamic processes and the fact that these processes are reversible. The Carnot engine is an example of a **reversible engine**—one in which thermodynamic equilibrium is maintained so that all steps could, in principle, be reversed.

What is the efficiency of a Carnot engine? To find out, we need the heats Q_h and Q_c absorbed and rejected during the isothermal parts of the cycle shown in Fig. 22-6. We developed Equation 21-4 to deal with such isothermal processes. Applying that equation gives the heat Q_h absorbed during the isothermal expansion AB:

$$Q_h = nRT_h \ln\left(\frac{V_B}{V_A}\right),$$

and the heat Q_c rejected during the isothermal compression CD:

$$Q_c = -nRT_c \ln\left(\frac{V_D}{V_C}\right) = nRT_c \ln\left(\frac{V_C}{V_D}\right).$$

We put the minus sign here because our statement of the first law describes Q as the heat *absorbed*, while Equation 22-1 for the engine efficiency requires that Q_c be the heat *rejected*. To calculate engine efficiency according to Equation 22-1, we need the ratio Q_c/Q_h:

$$\frac{Q_c}{Q_h} = \frac{T_c \ln(V_C/V_D)}{T_h \ln(V_B/V_A)}. \tag{22-2}$$

This expression can be simplified by applying Equation 21-13b to the adiabatic processes BC and DA in the Carnot cycle:

$$T_h V_B^{\gamma-1} = T_c V_C^{\gamma-1} \quad \text{and} \quad T_h V_A^{\gamma-1} = T_c V_D^{\gamma-1}.$$

Dividing these two equations gives

$$\left(\frac{V_B}{V_A}\right)^{\gamma-1} = \left(\frac{V_C}{V_D}\right)^{\gamma-1} \quad \text{or} \quad \frac{V_B}{V_A} = \frac{V_C}{V_D},$$

so Equation 22-2 becomes simply

$$\frac{Q_c}{Q_h} = \frac{T_c}{T_h}.$$

Using this result in Equation 22-1 then gives the efficiency of the Carnot engine:

$$e_{\text{Carnot}} = 1 - \frac{T_c}{T_h}, \qquad (22\text{-}3)$$

where the temperatures are measured on an absolute scale (Kelvin or Rankine). Equation 22-3 tells us that the efficiency of a Carnot engine depends only on the highest and lowest temperatures of the working fluid. For a practical engine, the low temperature is usually the ambient temperature of the environment. Then to maximize the efficiency, we must make the high temperature as high as possible. Real engines represent a compromise between efficiency and the ability of materials to withstand high temperatures and pressures.

EXAMPLE 22-1	A Carnot Engine

A Carnot engine extracts 240 J of heat from a high-temperature reservoir during each cycle. It rejects 100 J of heat to a reservoir at 15°C. How much work does the engine do in one cycle? What is its efficiency? What is the temperature of the hot reservoir?

Solution

The first law of thermodynamics requires that energy not rejected as heat be delivered as work, so the engine does

$$W = 240 \text{ J} - 100 \text{ J} = 140 \text{ J}$$

of work. The efficiency is defined by Equation 22-1 as the ratio of work to heat extracted from the hot reservoir:

$$e = \frac{W}{Q_h} = \frac{140 \text{ J}}{240 \text{ J}} = 0.583 = 58.3\% .$$

Knowing the efficiency, we can solve Equation 22-3 for the high temperature to get

$$T_h = \frac{T_c}{1 - e} = \frac{288 \text{ K}}{1 - 0.583} = 691 \text{ K} = 418°\text{C} .$$

Note that in using Equation 22-3 we must work with absolute temperatures.

EXERCISE A Carnot engine operates between heat reservoirs at 520 K and 280 K. (a) What is its efficiency? (b) If it produces useful work at the rate of 400 W, at what rate does it reject waste heat?

Answers: (a) 46%; (b) 467 W

Some problems similar to Example 22-1: 5–8

Engines, Refrigerators, and the Second Law

Why are we putting so much emphasis on one particular device, namely the Carnot engine? Because our understanding of the Carnot engine will lead to insights into the broader question of how much useful work we can hope to extract from the internal thermal energy of *any* system. That, in turn, will help us to understand practical limitations on humankind's attempts to harness even more energy, and will ultimately bring us to a deeper and more universal understanding of the second law of thermodynamics.

So why is the Carnot engine so special? Couldn't we build a different kind of engine with greater efficiency? The answer is no. The special role of the Carnot cycle is embodied in **Carnot's theorem**:

> **Carnot's theorem: All reversible Carnot engines operating between temperatures T_h and T_c have the same efficiency (given by Equation 22-3), and no other engine operating between the same two temperatures can have a greater efficiency.**

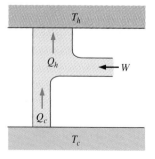

FIGURE 22-7 Energy flow diagram for a real refrigerator. The device takes in mechanical work and transfers heat from the cool to the hot reservoir.

To prove Carnot's theorem, we introduce the **refrigerator**. A refrigerator is the opposite of an engine: It extracts heat from a cool reservoir and rejects it to a hotter one, taking in work in the process (Fig. 22-7). A refrigerator forces heat

FIGURE 22-8 A perfect refrigerator would require no work to transfer heat from a cool object to a hotter one. The second law of thermodynamics rules out such a device.

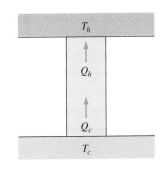

to flow the way it doesn't spontaneously go—from cold to hot—but to do so it requires work. A household refrigerator cools its contents and warms the house (you can feel the heat coming out the back), but in the process it uses electricity. That heat doesn't flow spontaneously from cold to hot constitutes another statement of the second law of thermodynamics, this one due to the German physicist Rudolph Clausius (1822–1888):

> **Second law of thermodynamics (Clausius statement): It is impossible to construct a refrigerator operating in a cycle whose sole effect is to transfer heat from a cooler object to a hotter one.**

The Clausius statement rules out a "perfect" refrigerator, like that shown in Fig. 22-8.

Suppose the Clausius statement were false. Then we could build the device of Fig. 22-9a, consisting of a reversible Carnot engine and a perfect refrigerator. In each cycle the engine would extract, say, 100 J from the hot reservoir, put out 60 J of useful work, and reject 40 J to the cool reservoir. The perfect refrigerator could transfer the 40 J back to the hot reservoir. The net effect would then be to extract 60 J from the hot reservoir and convert it entirely to work (Fig. 22-9b)—and we would have a perfect heat engine, in violation of the Kelvin-Planck statement of the second law. A similar argument shows that if a perfect heat engine is possible, so is a perfect refrigerator (see Problem 27). So the Clausius and Kelvin-Planck statements of the second law of thermodynamics are equivalent, in that if one is false then so is the other.

Because the Carnot engine is reversible, we could run it backward and reverse its path in the PV diagram of Fig. 22-6. Each process would run in reverse, and the engine would extract heat from the cool reservoir, take in work, and reject heat to the hot reservoir. It would be a refrigerator. Although real refrigerators are not designed exactly like engines, the two are, in principle, interchangeable.

We're now ready to prove Carnot's assertion that Equation 22-3 gives the maximum engine efficiency. Consider again the Carnot engine shown in Fig. 22-9a. It extracts 100 J of heat and delivers 60 J of work, so it's 60% efficient. Suppose we had another engine operating between the same two reservoirs, but with 70% efficiency. Since the Carnot engine is reversible, we can run it as a refrigerator. If we then put the two together, we get the device of Fig. 22-10a. Its

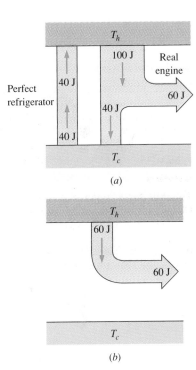

FIGURE 22-9 (a) A real heat engine combined with a perfect refrigerator. (b) The combination is equivalent to a perfect heat engine.

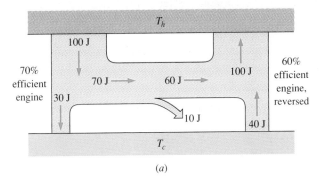

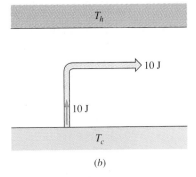

FIGURE 22-10 (a) A 60% efficient reversible engine run as a refrigerator, along with a hypothetical engine with 70% efficiency. (b) The combination is equivalent to a perfect heat engine delivering 10 J per cycle.

net effect is to extract 10 J of heat from the cool reservoir and deliver 10 J of work—so it's a perfect heat engine, in violation of the second law (Fig. 22-10b). We could make the same argument for any combination of a reversible Carnot engine and another, more efficient engine. It's therefore impossible to make an engine that's more efficient than a reversible Carnot engine, and thus, Equation 22-3 gives the maximum possible efficiency for *any* heat engine operating between the same two fixed temperatures.

Irreversible engines, because they involve processes that dissipate organized motion, are necessarily *less* efficient. So are many reversible engines, if their heat exchange does not take place solely at the highest and lowest temperatures available (see Problem 54). The ordinary gasoline engine is a case in point; even if it could be made perfectly reversible, its efficiency would be less than that of a comparable Carnot engine (see Problem 61).

22-3 APPLICATIONS OF THE SECOND LAW OF THERMODYNAMICS

The world abounds with thermal energy, but the second law of thermodynamics imposes a fundamental limitation on our ability to turn that energy to our own uses. Any device we construct that involves the interchange of heat and work is a heat engine or refrigerator, and is therefore subject to the second law.

Limitations on Heat Engines

Most of the electricity used in the United States is produced in large power plants that are basically heat engines powered by fossil fuels such as coal, oil, or natural gas, or by nuclear fission of uranium (Fig. 22-11). Figure 22-12 shows a schematic diagram of such a power plant. The working fluid is water, heated in a boiler and converted to steam at high pressure. The steam expands adiabatically against the blades of a turbine—a fanlike device that spins when struck by the steam. The turbine turns a generator that converts mechanical work into electrical energy (more on this in Chapter 31).

Steam leaving the turbine is still in the gaseous state, and is hotter than the water supplied to the boiler. Here's where the second law enters! Had the water

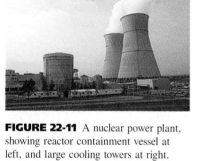

FIGURE 22-11 A nuclear power plant, showing reactor containment vessel at left, and large cooling towers at right. The cooling towers transfer some waste heat to the air, reducing but not eliminating thermal pollution of adjoining waters.

FIGURE 22-12 Schematic diagram of a typical electric power plant. Temperature of the working fluid (steam/water) is indicated at three points. $T_2 < T_1$ because the turbine has converted some of the steam's internal energy into mechanical work. $T_3 < T_2$ because the condenser has extracted additional internal energy and rejected it as waste heat. More significant is the energy extraction associated with the phase change from gas to liquid in the condenser; this energy, too, is sent to the environment as waste heat.

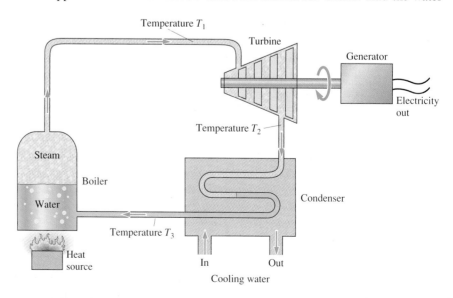

returned to its original state, we would have extracted as work all the energy acquired in the boiler, in violation of the second law. To use the steam again, we run it through a **condenser**—a device where pipes carrying the steam are in contact with large volumes of cool water, typically from a river, lake, or ocean. The condensed steam, now cool water, is fed back into the boiler to repeat the cycle.

The maximum steam temperature in a power plant is limited by the materials used in its construction. For a fossil-fueled plant, current technology permits high temperatures around 650 K. Potential damage to nuclear fuel rods limits the temperature in a nuclear plant to around 570 K. Cooling-water temperature averages about 40°C (310 K), so the maximum possible efficiencies for these power plants, given by Equation 22-3, are

$$e_{fossil} = 1 - \frac{310 \text{ K}}{650 \text{ K}} = 0.52 = 52\%$$

and

$$e_{nuclear} = 1 - \frac{310 \text{ K}}{570 \text{ K}} = 0.46 = 46\% \,.$$

Temperature differences between the exhausted steam and the cooling water, mechanical friction, and the need to divert energy for driving pumps and pollution control devices all reduce efficiency further, to about 40% for fossil-fueled plants and 34% for nuclear plants. This means that, when we make electricity, roughly two-thirds of the fuel energy released ends up as waste heat.

A typical large power plant produces 1000 MW of electricity, so another 2000 MW of waste heat is dumped into the cooling water. This rate of energy addition can cause a large temperature rise in even a major river, and can lead to serious ecological problems. The need for power plant cooling water—imposed on us by the second law of thermodynamics—is so great that a substantial fraction of all rainwater falling on the United States eventually finds its way through the condensers of power plants (see Problem 13).

To reduce this "thermal pollution," power plants employ cooling towers—expensive devices which release waste heat to the air rather than to water. Environmental effects of the heat released to the air are less serious than with heated water, although the increase in humidity can bring about unfortunate changes in local weather (Fig. 22-13).

FIGURE 22-13 Fog forms above the cooling towers of a large coal-fired electric power plant.

EXAMPLE 22-2	*Vermont Yankee*

The Vermont Yankee nuclear power plant at Vernon, Vermont, produces 540 MW of electric power, while energy from nuclear fission is released as heat at the rate of 1590 MW. Steam produced in the reactor enters the turbine at a temperature of 556 K and is discharged to the condenser at 313 K. Water from the Connecticut River is pumped through the condenser at the rate of 2.27×10^4 kg/s.

What is the maximum efficiency of the power plant, as limited by the second law of thermodynamics? What is the actual efficiency? How much does the temperature of the cooling water rise? How many houses like that of Example 19-5 could be heated with the waste heat from Vermont Yankee?

Solution

The second-law efficiency is given by Equation 22-3:

$$e = 1 - \frac{T_c}{T_h} = 1 - \frac{313 \text{ K}}{556 \text{ K}} = 0.437 = 43.7\% \,.$$

The actual efficiency is the ratio of electric power output to the rate of heat extraction from the nuclear fuel:

$$e = \frac{dW/dt}{dQ_h/dt} = \frac{540 \text{ MW}}{1590 \text{ MW}} = 0.340 = 34.0\% \,.$$

Waste heat is discharged to the river at a rate given by the difference between the thermal power output and the electric power output:

$$\frac{dQ_c}{dt} = \frac{dQ_h}{dt} - \frac{dW}{dt} = 1590 \text{ MW} - 540 \text{ MW} = 1050 \text{ MW} \,.$$

We can relate the waste power output to the temperature rise using Equation 19-5:

$$\Delta T = \frac{\Delta Q_c}{mc} = \frac{dQ_c/dt}{c\ dm/dt}$$

$$= \frac{1050 \times 10^6 \text{ W}}{(4184 \text{ J/kg·°C})(2.27 \times 10^4 \text{ kg/s})} = 11.1\text{°C},$$

where we used the given values of heat and mass per unit time for the ratio $\Delta Q/m$. The house of Example 19-5 uses 7926 Btu/h, or 2.3×10^{-3} MW. Then the waste heat from Vermont Yankee could heat $(1050 \text{ MW})/(2.4 \times 10^{-3} \text{ MW/house}) = 457{,}000$ houses. This number is unrealistic because most houses aren't as energy efficient as the one in Example 19-5; nevertheless, it shows that waste heat from power plants is a potentially valuable source for heating buildings.

EXERCISE A 40% efficient coal-fired power plant produces 1100 MW of electric power. (a) If spent steam leaves the turbine at 350 K, what is the lowest possible value for the steam temperature as it leaves the boiler? (b) If the plant is cooled with essentially the entire 4.4×10^4-kg/s flow of a river, by how much does the river temperature rise?

Answers: (a) 583 K; (b) 9.0°C

Some problems similar to Example 22-2: 10–12, 47, 48, 60

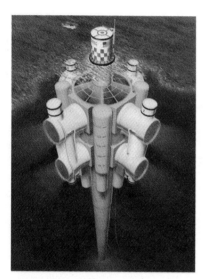

FIGURE 22-14 Artist's conception of an OTEC power plant.

Gasoline and diesel engines provide another pervasive example of heat engines. A typical automobile engine has a theoretical maximum efficiency of just over 50%, but irreversible thermodynamic processes make the actual efficiency much lower. Mechanical friction dissipates additional energy, and the end result is that less than 20% of the fuel energy is available at the driving wheels. Problems 61 and 62 explore the thermodynamics of the gasoline engine.

We wouldn't be so concerned with efficiency if we didn't have to pay for fuel. Even a very small temperature difference can drive a heat engine, although with low efficiency. Surface temperatures in the tropical oceans are around 25°C (298 K), while hundreds of meters down the water temperature is only about 5°C (278 K). A heat engine operating between these temperatures would have an efficiency of only $1 - 278 \text{ K}/298 \text{ K} = 0.07$ or 7%. Nevertheless, there are large amounts of warm ocean water, and its energy—solar in origin—is free. Substantial engineering problems remain before such **ocean thermal energy conversion** (OTEC) becomes practical, but pilot plants are already being tested (Fig. 22-14).

Another solar-powered heat engine uses mirrors to concentrate sunlight, heating a fluid and driving a turbine. Several hundred megawatts of such **solar-thermal power plants** have been built in California, and are generating power at rates just a few cents above those of conventional power plants (Fig. 22-15).

Refrigerators and Heat Pumps

FIGURE 22-15 This solar-thermal power plant in California's Mojave Desert generates 90 MW of electricity. Sun-tracking parabolic reflectors concentrate sunlight on pipes carrying synthetic oil, which then transfers the energy to boil water that drives a steam turbine.

Reversing a heat engine gives a refrigerator, which takes in mechanical work and transfers heat from cooler to hotter (Fig. 22-16). The heat coming out the back of your home refrigerator comprises both the energy removed from the refrigerator's contents as well as the energy that was supplied as electricity to run the refrigerator. A well-designed refrigerator should minimize the amount of work (or its equivalent, electrical energy) needed to extract a given amount of heat. But again, the second law of thermodynamics imposes limitations on even the best refrigerator.

The **coefficient of performance** (COP) is the ratio of heat extracted at the lower temperature to work input by a refrigerator:

$$\text{COP} = \frac{Q_c}{W} = \frac{Q_c}{Q_h - Q_c}. \tag{22-4}$$

For a reversible Carnot engine, we found in deriving Equation 22-3 that the heat ratio Q_c/Q_h is equal to the temperature ratio T_c/T_h. The best refrigerator we can build operates in a reversible Carnot cycle, so for this refrigerator the heat and temperature ratios are also equal. Then the COP becomes

$$\text{COP} = \frac{T_c}{T_h - T_c}. \qquad (22\text{-}5)$$

As the high and low temperatures become arbitrarily close, Equation 22-5 shows that the COP becomes large—meaning that the refrigerator requires relatively little work to do its job. But if we wish to effect heat transfer between two widely separated temperatures, then the COP drops and the work becomes considerable. In the limit of very large T_h, the COP approaches zero, indicating that we're simply converting mechanical work into a nearly equal amount of heat, and transferring very little additional heat from the cool reservoir. In operating a real refrigerator, we would like to minimize the work needed. But Equation 22-5—like Equation 22-3 for a heat engine—imposes a fundamental limitation on that minimum amount of work.

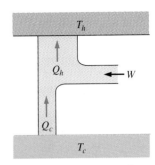

FIGURE 22-16 Energy flow diagram for a refrigerator.

EXAMPLE 22-3	*A Home Freezer*

A typical home freezer operates between a low of 0°F (-18°C) and a high of 86°F (30°C). What is the maximum possible COP of this freezer? With this COP, how much electrical energy would be required to freeze 500 g of water, initially at 0°C?

Solution
Equation 22-5 gives the COP:

$$\text{COP} = \frac{T_c}{T_h - T_c} = \frac{255 \text{ K}}{303 \text{ K} - 255 \text{ K}} = 5.3 \,.$$

To produce 500 g of ice takes

$$Q_c = mL_f = (0.50 \text{ kg})(334 \text{ kJ/kg}) = 170 \text{ kJ} \,,$$

where we obtained the heat of fusion from Table 20-1. This Q_c is the heat that must be removed from the low-temperature end

of the freezer. The COP is the ratio of the heat removed to the work done, so

$$W = \frac{Q_c}{\text{COP}} = \frac{170 \text{ kJ}}{5.3} = 32 \text{ kJ} \,.$$

In a real freezer, the COP would be lower, and the work correspondingly higher, because of irreversible processes in the refrigeration cycle.

EXERCISE (a) What is the COP of a refrigerator that maintains its interior at 4°C while exhausting heat at 40°C? (b) At what average rate does the refrigerator consume electricity if it extracts heat from its contents at the rate of 300 W?

Answers: (a) 7.7; (b) 39 W

Some problems similar to Example 22-3: 16–20

Refrigerators are not confined to kitchens. An air conditioner is a refrigerator designed to cool an entire room or building. A heat pump is a refrigerator that cools a building in the summer and heats it in the winter (Fig. 22-17). Heat pumps are widely used in the southern United States, where in winter they pump energy from the cool outside air to the warm house. A heat pump requires electricity, but it supplies more energy as heat than it uses in electricity. The excess energy comes from the outdoor environment. Heat pumps operating from the constant 10°C temperature found two meters below the ground have been used for years in Scandinavian countries and are becoming more popular in the northern United States and Canada.

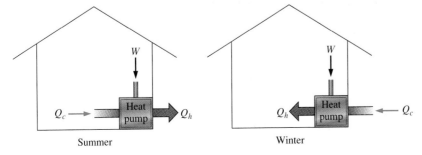

FIGURE 22-17 A heat pump. In summer the device acts as a refrigerator that cools the house interior by transferring heat to the outdoor environment. In winter its operation reverses, so it pumps heat from outdoors into the house. The work, W, is typically in the form of electricity.

EXAMPLE 22-4	*A Heat Pump*

A Carnot heat pump extracts energy from the ground at 10°C and transfers it to water at 70°C. The water is circulated to heat a building. (a) What is the COP of the heat pump? (b) What is its electrical power consumption if it supplies heat at the rate of 20 kW? (c) Compare the operating cost of the heat pump with that of an oil furnace if oil costs 93¢ per gallon and electricity costs 10¢ per kWh. (A gallon of oil releases about 30 kWh of heat when burned.)

Solution

Equation 22-5 gives the COP:

$$\text{COP} = \frac{T_c}{T_h - T_c} = \frac{283 \text{ K}}{343 \text{ K} - 283 \text{ K}} = 4.7 .$$

Equation 22-4 shows what this means: for every kWh of electricity used, the pump transfers an additional 4.7 kWh of heat from the ground, providing a total of 5.7 kWh. The pump supplies heat at the rate of 20 kW, so the electrical power needed is

$$P_{electric} = \frac{20 \text{ kW}}{5.7} = 3.5 \text{ kW} .$$

At 10¢/kWh, it costs 35¢ per hour to run the pump. Since oil supplies 30 kWh/gallon, we would need to burn two-thirds of a gallon per hour to get 20 kW, at a cost of $(\frac{2}{3}$ gal/h)(93¢/gal) $=$ 62¢ per hour.

Real heat pumps run at closer to half their theoretical maximum COP, and initial installation costs are much more expensive than for oil heat, so economics do not necessarily favor heat pumps.

If we're concerned about energy and not just cost, we should also consider the source of electricity. If this is a thermal power plant operating at an efficiency of, say, 33%, then the power plant uses three units of fuel energy for each unit it supplies to the heat pump. The overall efficiency of heat pump and power plant could actually be less than that of the oil furnace (see Problem 24).

EXERCISE A house requires 12 kW of heating power. If electricity costs 8.5¢/kWh, what is the minimum COP required if a heat pump is to operate for less than $5 per day?

Answer: 3.9

Some problems similar to Example 22-4: 22, 23, 63

22-4 THE THERMODYNAMIC TEMPERATURE SCALE

None of the practical thermometers we introduced in Chapter 19 works at all temperatures; even helium gas thermometers become useless below about 1 K.

The operation of a reversible Carnot engine between two fixed temperatures provides another way of measuring temperature that works at *any* temperature. Measuring the heats Q_c and Q_h, or one of these and the work output, allows us to calculate the temperature ratio. If one temperature is known, we can then determine the other. Although this may seem a rather obscure way to measure temperature, it is actually used in certain experiments at very low temperature. And it provides an absolute way of defining temperature that can, in principle, be used at any temperature. The temperature scale so defined is called the **thermodynamic temperature scale**.

The zero of the thermodynamic scale—**absolute zero**—is absolute in that it represents a state of maximum order. This is reflected in the fact that a heat engine rejecting heat at absolute zero would operate at 100% efficiency, as suggested by Equation 22-3 with $T_c = 0$. Unfortunately, there are no heat reservoirs at absolute zero, and it can be shown that it is impossible to cool anything to this temperature in a finite number of steps. The statement that it is impossible to reach absolute zero in a finite number of steps is called the **third law of thermodynamics**.

22-5 ENTROPY AND THE QUALITY OF ENERGY

If offered a joule of energy, would you rather have it delivered in the form of mechanical work, heat from an object at 1000 K, or heat from an object at 300 K? Your answer might depend on what you want to do. To lift or accelerate a mass, you would be smart to take your energy as work. But if you want to keep warm, then heat from the 300 K object would be perfectly acceptable.

If, on the other hand, you're not sure what you want to do with the energy, then which should you take? The second law of thermodynamics makes the answer clear: you should take the work. Why? Because you could use it directly as mechanical energy, or you could, through friction or other irreversible processes, use it to raise the temperature of something.

If you chose 300-K heat for your joule of energy, then you could supply a full joule only to objects cooler than 300 K. You couldn't do mechanical work unless you ran a heat engine. With its maximum temperature only a little above ambient, your engine would be very inefficient, and you could only extract a small fraction of a joule of mechanical energy. Nor could you heat anything hotter than 300 K, unless you ran a refrigerator—and that would take additional work. You would be better off with 1000-K heat since you could transfer it to anything cooler than 1000 K, or could run a heat engine to produce up to 0.70 joule of mechanical energy.

Taking your energy in the form of work gives you the most options. Anything you can do with a joule of energy, you can do with the work. Heat is less versatile, with 300-K heat the least useful of the three. We're not talking here about the quantity of energy—we have exactly one joule in each case—but about **energy quality**, indicated by its ability to do a variety of useful tasks. Schematically, we can describe energy quality on a diagram like Fig. 22-18. We can readily convert an entire amount of energy from higher to lower quality, but the second law of thermodynamics prevents us from going in the opposite direction with 100% efficiency.

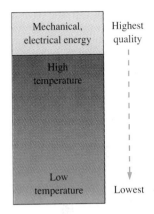

FIGURE 22-18 Energy quality measures the versatility of different energy forms. Electrical energy ranks with mechanical energy because it flows without the need for a temperature difference, thus qualifying as work.

APPLICATION	*Energy Quality, End Use, and Cogeneration*

Energy quality has important implications for our efficient use of energy, suggesting that we try to match the quality of available energy sources to our energy needs. Figure 22-19 shows a breakdown of United States energy use by quality; it makes clear that much of our energy demand is for relatively low-quality heat. Although we can do anything we want with a high-quality energy source like flowing water or electricity, it makes sense to put our high-quality energy to high-quality uses, and use lower-quality sources to meet other needs. For example, we often heat water with electricity—a great convenience to the homeowner, but a thermodynamic folly, for in so doing we convert the highest-quality form of energy into low-grade heat. If our electricity comes from a thermal power plant, we already threw away two-thirds of the energy from fuel as waste heat. It makes little sense to run an elaborate and inefficient heat engine only to have its high-quality output of electricity used for low-temperature heating. On the other hand, if we heat our water by burning a fuel directly at the water heater, then we can, in principle, transfer all the fuel's energy to the water. Another approach to matching energy quality with energy needs is to combine the production of steam for heating with the generation of electricity. Used in Europe for years, such **cogeneration** is gaining popularity in the United States.

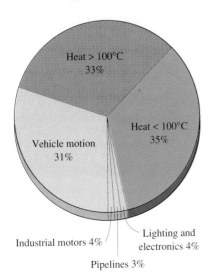

FIGURE 22-19 Energy use in the United States, organized by energy quality.

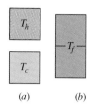

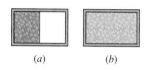

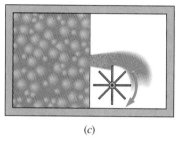

FIGURE 22-20 Two objects, initially at different temperatures, come to equilibrium at an intermediate temperature T_f. No energy is lost, but the system does lose its ability to do work.

FIGURE 22-21 (*a*, *b*) Adiabatic free expansion. Gas initially confined to one side of an insulated container expands to fill the entire container. The gas energy remains constant but its quality deteriorates. (*c*) A means of extracting useful work from the gas in the initial state of Fig. 22-21.

Entropy

How can we quantify the notion of energy quality? Imagine bringing two identical objects, initially at different temperatures, into thermal contact (Fig. 22-20). Heat flows from the hotter to the cooler object until they reach the same temperature. If they're thermally insulated from their environment there's no energy lost in the process. But something has changed: The system has lost the ability to do useful work. In the initial state we could have run a heat engine using the two objects as its hot and cool reservoirs. In the final state there's no temperature difference and therefore no way to run a heat engine. The quantity of energy has stayed the same, but its quality has decreased. Can we find some system property that reflects this change?

Figure 22-21 shows another system whose energy quality deteriorates without any loss of total energy. We start with a gas confined to one side of an insulated container; the other side is evacuated. Remove the partition, and the gas expands freely to fill the container. Since the container is insulated, the process is adiabatic, and no heat flows out. Since the gas expands into a vacuum, it does no work either. Therefore, its energy stays constant. But again we've lost the ability to do work. Starting with the initial state, we could have made the gas run a turbine between the high pressure region and the vacuum, extracting useful work (Fig. 22-21*c*). In the final state there's no pressure difference and therefore no way to run the turbine. Again, can we find a quantity that describes this decrease in energy quality?

To find the quantity we're after, consider an ideal gas undergoing a Carnot cycle—that is, a cycle of two isothermal and two adiabatic processes (recall Fig. 22-6). In deriving Equation 22-3 for the efficiency of this cycle we found that

$$\frac{Q_c}{Q_h} = \frac{T_c}{T_h},\qquad(22\text{-}6)$$

where Q_c was the heat *rejected* from the system to the low-temperature reservoir at T_c and Q_h the heat *added* from the reservoir at T_h.

We now change the definition of Q_c so it also means heat *added* to the system. This redefinition just changes the sign of Q_c, so now Equation 22-6 can be written

$$\frac{Q_c}{T_c} + \frac{Q_h}{T_h} = 0.$$

We can generalize this result to any reversible cycle by approximating the cycle as a sequence of adiabatic and isothermal steps (Fig. 22-22). Figure 22-22's caption shows how summing over the individual hot and cold isothermal segments then gives

$$\sum \frac{Q}{T} = 0.$$

We can approximate the closed cycle ever closer by more and more adiabatic and isothermal segments. In the limit the approximation becomes exact and the sum becomes an integral:

$$\oint \frac{dQ}{T} = 0,\qquad(22\text{-}7)$$

where the circle on the integral sign indicates that we integrate over all the heat transfers along a *closed* path.

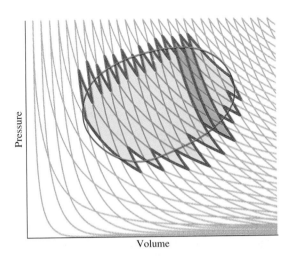

Volume

FIGURE 22-22 An arbitrary reversible cycle approximated by a sequence of adiabatic and isothermal steps. The region may be divided into elongated Carnot cycles like the two emphasized near the upper right. Heat is transferred to or from the gas only on the isothermal segments, all of which lie on the jagged approximation to the closed curve. The quantity $\dfrac{Q_c}{T_c} + \dfrac{Q_h}{T_h}$ for each individual cycle is determined from the isothermal segments only; therefore the sum of these quantities going around the entire cycle is equal to the sum of its values—namely zero—over the individual Carnot cycles.

Equation 22-7 tells us that there is some quantity S, a small amount of which is given by $dS = dQ/T$, that does not change when we take a system around a cyclic path. This quantity S is called **entropy**. If we take a system around a path that isn't closed, then its entropy will, in general, change. That change is given by integrating $dS = dQ/T$ over the path in question:

$$\Delta S = \int_1^2 \frac{dQ}{T}, \qquad (22\text{-}8)$$

where ΔS is the change in entropy between the two thermodynamic states 1 and 2. Note that entropy has the units J/K.

What good is this concept of entropy? Equation 22-8 shows that there's no entropy change when we take a system from some initial state and eventually return it to that state. Now suppose we take a system part way around a closed path, from state 1 to state 2 shown in Fig. 22-23. The entropy change from state 2 back to state 1 must be exactly opposite the change from 1 to 2, so that the change going around the closed path is zero. But this must be true no matter how we get from state 2 to state 1, as suggested by the two possible paths in Fig. 22-23. That is, the entropy change given by Equation 22-8 is independent of path; it is a property only of the initial and final states themselves. Like pressure, temperature, and volume, entropy is a thermodynamic state variable—a quantity that characterizes a given state independently of how a system got into that state.

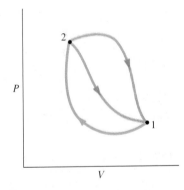

FIGURE 22-23 Entropy change is zero when the system returns to its original state. Therefore the entropy change from state 2 to state 1 is the same on both return paths shown. In fact, entropy change is always independent of path.

EXAMPLE 22-5	*Entropy*

An object of mass m and specific heat c is heated from temperature T_1 to temperature T_2. What is the change in its entropy?

Solution
Equation 22-8 gives the entropy change. To evaluate the integral in this equation we must relate dQ and T. Here we can do so because we know the specific heat: a small temperature change dT requires a heat dQ given by

$$dQ = mc\,dT.$$

Then Equation 22-8 becomes

$$\Delta S = \int_1^2 \frac{dQ}{T} = \int_{T_1}^{T_2} mc\,\frac{dT}{T} = mc\ln\left(\frac{T_2}{T_1}\right). \qquad (22\text{-}9)$$

EXERCISE What is the specific heat of a substance if 1.0 kg of it undergoes an entropy increase of 260 J/K when its temperature doubles?

Answer: 375 J/kg·K

Some problems similar to Example 22-5: 32, 33, 37, 38

Equation 22-8 is meaningful only for reversible processes since an irreversible process takes a system temporarily into thermodynamic disequilibrium, in which temperature is not well defined. But because entropy doesn't depend on how a system got into its thermodynamic state, we can calculate the entropy change during an *irreversible* process by finding a *reversible* process that takes the system between the same two states, then using Equation 22-8 to calculate the entropy change for the reversible process.

At the beginning of this section we considered two irreversible processes in which energy quality deteriorated even though total energy remained constant. We can come to understand the meaning of entropy by calculating entropy changes for these two processes.

Irreversible Heat Transfer

Figure 22-24 repeats Fig. 22-20, showing two objects, initially at temperatures T_h and T_c, placed in thermal contact until they reach a common temperature T_f. The total energy of the system remains unchanged, but energy quality deteriorates. We can calculate the entropy change by considering reversible processes that take the two objects to the final temperature T_f. We could, for example, place each in contact with a heat reservoir at its initial temperature and then gradually change the temperature until it reaches T_f. The entropy change for the cool object would then be

$$\Delta S_c = \int_{T_c}^{T_f} \frac{dQ}{T}.$$

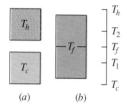

FIGURE 22-24 The two objects of Fig. 22-20, with a temperature scale showing the intermediate temperatures T_1 and T_2 used in evaluating the entropy change.

Although we might evaluate this integral (see Problem 42), note instead that there must be some intermediate temperature T_1 *that lies between* T_c and T_f, for which

$$\Delta S_c = \frac{Q_c}{T_1},$$

where Q_c is the heat absorbed by the cool object. We've marked T_1 on Fig. 22-24. Similarly, the entropy change for the hot object is

$$\Delta S_h = \int_{T_h}^{T_f} \frac{dQ}{T} = \frac{Q_h}{T_2},$$

where T_2 *lies between* T_h and T_f.

The entropy change of the system is then

$$\Delta S = \Delta S_c + \Delta S_h = \frac{Q_c}{T_1} + \frac{Q_h}{T_2}.$$

But the two objects are insulated, so any heat gained by the cool object in the actual irreversible process is equal to the heat lost by the hot object. Thus $Q_h = -Q_c$, and the entropy change becomes

$$\Delta S = \frac{Q_c}{T_1} - \frac{Q_c}{T_2} = Q_c \left(\frac{1}{T_1} - \frac{1}{T_2} \right).$$

Now T_1 lies *below* the equilibrium temperature T_f and T_2 lies *above* T_f. That makes ΔS a *positive* quantity—meaning that entropy has *increased* during the irreversible heat transfer.

Adiabatic Free Expansion

Figure 22-21 showed a gas undergoing an irreversible adiabatic free expansion. Neither the temperature nor the internal energy changes during the process, but energy quality deteriorates. We can calculate the entropy change by considering a reversible process that takes the gas between the same initial and final states. Since the final and initial temperatures are equal, one such process is an isothermal expansion. Equation 21-4 gives the heat added during such an expansion:

$$Q = nRT \ln\left(\frac{V_2}{V_1}\right).$$

Since the temperature is constant, the entropy change of Equation 22-9 becomes

$$\Delta S = \int \frac{dQ}{T} = \frac{1}{T}\int dQ = \frac{Q}{T} = nR \ln\left(\frac{V_2}{V_1}\right). \tag{22-10}$$

Since the final volume V_2 is larger than V_1, the entropy has *increased*.

In calculating this entropy change, we used the heat Q that would be required during a reversible isothermal process. Of course, no heat is transferred during the actual adiabatic free expansion. Nevertheless the entropy change is the same as for the reversible isothermal process that takes the system between the same initial and final states—and that process does involve heat transfer.

Entropy and the Availability of Work

Entropy increases during both the irreversible processes we just considered. Earlier, we argued that those processes result in a deterioration of energy quality, in that both systems lose the ability to do work. Suppose we had let the gas in Fig. 22-21 undergo a reversible isothermal expansion instead of the adiabatic free expansion. Then it would have done work given by Equation 21-4:

$$W = nRT \ln\left(\frac{V_2}{V_1}\right).$$

After the irreversible free expansion, the gas can no longer do this work, even though its energy is unchanged. Comparing with the entropy change of Equation 22-10, we see that the energy that becomes unavailable to do work is

$$E_{\text{unavailable}} = T\Delta S. \tag{22-11}$$

Equation 22-11 is an example of a more general relation between entropy and the quality of energy:

> **Entropy and the Quality of Energy: During an irreversible process in which the entropy of a system increases by ΔS, energy $E = T_{\text{min}}\Delta S$ becomes unavailable to do work, where T_{min} is coolest temperature available to the system.**

This statement shows that entropy provides our desired measure of energy quality. Given two systems with identical energy content, the one with the lower entropy contains the higher-quality energy. An entropy increase always corresponds to a degradation in energy quality, in that some energy becomes unavailable to do work.

EXAMPLE 22-6	*Entropy and Energy Quality*

A cylinder contains 5.0 mol of compressed gas at 300 K, confined to 2.0 L. If the cylinder is discharged into a 150-L vacuum chamber and its temperature remains at 300 K, how much energy becomes unavailable to do work?

Solution

This is essentially an adiabatic free expansion, so Equations 22-10 and 22-11 give

$$E_{unavailable} = T\Delta S = nRT \ln\left(\frac{V_2}{V_1}\right)$$

$$= (5.0 \text{ mol})(8.314 \text{ J/K·mol})(300 \text{ K}) \ln\left(\frac{152 \text{ L}}{2.0 \text{ L}}\right)$$

$$= 54 \text{ kJ}.$$

EXERCISE Astronauts pressurize an evacuated space station by discharging 670 mol of air from a 200-L cylinder into the station's 15-m³ volume. The gas temperature remains at 290 K. How much work becomes unavailable as a result of this process?

Answer: 7.0 MJ

Some problems similar to Example 22-6: 44, 45

Entropy and the Second Law of Thermodynamics

We started this chapter by arguing that natural processes are generally irreversible, going from ordered states to disordered states. It's this loss of order—as when a hot and a cold object eventually reach the same temperature—that makes energy unavailable to do work. Entropy is a measure of this disorder. Given the tendency of systems to evolve toward disordered states, we can make a statement about entropy that is, in fact, a general statement of the second law of thermodynamics:

> *Second law of thermodynamics: The entropy of a closed system can never decrease.*

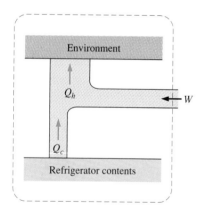

FIGURE 22-25 A refrigerator decreases the entropy of its contents, but only when work is done on the system from outside.

At best, the entropy of a closed system remains constant—and this happens only in an ideal, reversible process. If anything irreversible occurs—a slight amount of friction or a deviation from exact thermodynamic equilibrium—then entropy increases. There's no going back. As entropy increases, some energy becomes unavailable to do work, and nothing within the closed system can restore that energy to its original quality. This statement of the second law in terms of entropy is equivalent to our previous statements about the impossibility of perfect heat engines and refrigerators, for the operation of either device would require a decrease in entropy.

What about a system that isn't closed? Can't we decrease its entropy? Yes—but only by supplying high-quality energy from outside. Running a refrigerator decreases the entropy of its contents (Fig. 22-25). But we must do work on the refrigerator to effect this entropy decrease—to make heat flow in the direction it doesn't normally go. If we enlarge our closed system to include the power plant or whatever else supplies the refrigerator with work, we would find that the entropy of this new closed system does not decrease. The entropy decrease at the refrigerator is offset by entropy increases elsewhere in the system (Fig. 22-26). If irreversible processes occur anywhere in the system, then there is a net entropy increase.

Any system whose entropy seems to decrease—that gets more rather than less organized—cannot be a closed system. If we enlarge the system boundaries to encompass anything that might exchange energy with the original system, then the entropy of the larger system will not decrease. Ultimately, we can enlarge the system to include the entire universe. Then we have the ultimate statement of the second law:

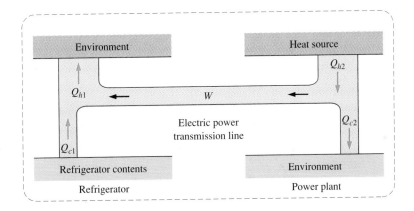

FIGURE 22-26 When the source of work for the refrigerator is included in the system, then the entropy of the entire system can at best remain constant.

> *Second law of thermodynamics: The entropy of the universe can never decrease.*

As examples of this broad statement, consider the growth of a living thing from the random mix of molecules in its environment, or the construction of a sky-scraper from materials that were originally dispersed about Earth, or the appearance of ordered symbols on a printed page from a bottle of ink. All these are processes in which matter goes from near chaos to a highly organized state—akin to separating yolk and white from a scrambled egg. They are certainly processes in which entropy decreases. But Earth is not a closed system. It gets high-quality energy from the Sun, energy that is ultimately responsible for life and all its actions. If we consider the Earth-Sun system, then the entropy decrease associated with life and civilization is more than balanced by the entropy increase associated with nuclear fusion inside the Sun. We living things represent a remarkable phenomenon—the organization of matter in a universe governed by a tendency toward disorder. But we do not escape the second law of thermodynamics. Our highly organized selves and society, and the entropy decreases they represent, come into being only at the expense of greater entropy increases elsewhere in the universe.

CHAPTER SYNOPSIS

Summary

1. **Irreversible processes** decrease a system's organization or order. Because there are many more ways to arrange matter in disorganized states, the probability that a disorganized state will become spontaneously organized is impossibly small. The many equivalent statements of the **second law of thermodynamics** embody this fact.

2. A **heat engine** extracts heat from a hot reservoir and converts some of it to useful work. Applied to heat engines, the second law says that it is impossible to build a perfect heat engine that converts all the heat to work. In particular, no engine operating between temperatures T_h and T_c can be more efficient than a reversible **Carnot engine**; thus

$$e = \frac{W}{Q_h} \le e_{\text{Carnot}} = 1 - \frac{T_c}{T_h}.$$

This second-law limitation on efficiency means that real engines like automobile engines and power plants reject a great deal of waste heat to their environments.

3. A **refrigerator** extracts heat Q_c from a cool reservoir and transfers it to a hotter one. The second law of thermodynamics implies that a perfect refrigerator is impossible; real refrigerators must take in work W. The **coefficient of performance** measures the efficiency of a refrigerator:

$$\text{COP} = \frac{Q_c}{W} \le \text{COP}_{\text{Carnot}} = \frac{T_c}{T_h - T_c},$$

where the inequality shows that no refrigerator can have a higher COP than a reversible refrigerator operating on a Carnot cycle.

4. The second-law limit on the efficiency of a heat engine defines the **thermodynamic temperature scale**. **Absolute zero** corresponds to a state of maximum order, but the **third**

law of thermodynamics states that it is impossible to reach absolute zero in a finite number of thermodynamic steps.

5. **Energy quality** describes the ability of a given quantity of energy to do work. The highest-quality energy is mechanical or electrical, followed by the energy associated with large temperature differences, followed by ever smaller temperature differences. Higher-quality energy can be converted to lower quality with 100% efficiency, but the second law prohibits the reverse process from occurring with 100% efficiency.

6. **Entropy** measures the relative disorder of a system, so increasing entropy corresponds to decreasing energy quality. Entropy is a thermodynamic state variable; its value depends only on the state of a system and not on how the system got into that state. The entropy difference between two states can be found by evaluating the expression

$$\Delta S = \int_1^2 \frac{dQ}{T}$$

for any reversible process connecting those states.

7. In terms of entropy, the second law of thermodynamics asserts that the entropy of the universe can never decrease. In this form, the second law is a universal statement about the tendency of systems to evolve toward states of greater disorder.

Terms You Should Understand

(Pairs are closely related terms whose distinction is important; number in parentheses is chapter section where term first appears.)

irreversible process (22-1)
second law of thermodynamics (22-2, 22-5)

heat engine, refrigerator (22-2)
efficiency (22-2), coefficient of performance (22-3)
thermodynamic temperature scale (22-4)
absolute zero (22-4)
third law of thermodynamics (22-4)
energy quality (22-5)
entropy (22-5)

Symbols You Should Recognize

T_c, T_h (22-2)   COP (22-3)
Q_c, Q_h (22-2) ΔS (22-5)
e (22-2)

Problems You Should Be Able to Solve

calculating efficiencies and waste heat of engines (22-2, 22-3)
calculating COP and related quantities for refrigerators and heat pumps (22-3)
calculating entropy changes for simple thermodynamic processes (22-5)
calculating loss of available work associated with entropy increase (22-5)

Limitations to Keep in Mind

The second law of thermodynamics, unlike physical laws you have encountered previously, is fundamentally *statistical*. It rules out events not because they violate basic laws of mechanics but because they're simply too improbable.

A completely reversible process is an idealization that cannot be realized in the macroscopic world where friction and other energy-dissipation mechanisms are present.

QUESTIONS

1. Which of the following processes is irreversible?
   a. Stirring sugar into coffee
   b. Building a house
   c. Demolishing a house with a wrecking crane
   d. Demolishing a house by taking it apart piece-by-piece
   e. Warming a bottle of milk by transferring it directly from a refrigerator to stove top
   f. Writing a sentence
   g. Harnessing the energy of falling water in order to drive machinery

2. Could you cool the kitchen by leaving the refrigerator door open? Explain.

3. Could you heat the kitchen by leaving the oven open? Explain.

4. Why don't we simply refrigerate the cooling water of a power plant before it goes to the plant, thereby increasing the plant's efficiency?

5. Should a car get better mileage in the summer or the winter? Explain.

6. Is there a limit to the maximum temperature that can be achieved by focusing sunlight with a lens? If so, what is it?

7. Name some irreversible processes that occur in a real engine.

8. A power company claims that electric heat is one hundred per cent efficient. Discuss this claim.

9. A hydroelectric power plant, using the energy of falling water, can operate with an efficiency arbitrarily close to one hundred per cent. Why?

10. To maximize the COP of a refrigerator, should you strive for a large or a small temperature difference? Explain.

11. The manufacturer of a heat pump claims that the device will heat your home using only energy already available in the ground. Is this true?

12. Why are heat pumps more widely used in warmer climates?

13. Proponents of ocean thermal energy conversion don't seem bothered by efficiencies so low as to be intolerable in fossil-fueled or nuclear power plants. Why the difference?

14. What might be done with the waste heat from power plants?

15. Does sunlight represent high- or low-quality energy? Explain; see also Question 6.

16. If new materials were developed that could withstand higher temperatures than those now encountered in power plants, how would that help us save energy?

17. The heat Q added during adiabatic free expansion is zero. Why can't we then argue from Equation 22-8 that the entropy change is zero?

18. Energy is conserved, so why can't we recycle it as we do materials?

19. A power plant provides electricity to run a heat pump. Can the heat output of the pump be greater than the heat extracted from the power plant's fuel?

20. Why does the evolution of human civilization not violate the second law of thermodynamics?

PROBLEMS

ActivPhysics can help with these problems:
Activity 8.14.

Section 22-1 Reversibility and Irreversibility

1. The egg carton shown in Fig. 22-27 has places for one dozen eggs. (a) How many distinct ways are there to arrange six eggs in the carton? (b) Of these, what fraction correspond to all six eggs being in the left half of the carton? Treat the eggs as distinguishable, so an interchange of two eggs gives rise to a new state.

FIGURE 22-27 An egg carton (Problem 1).

2. A gas consists of four distinguishable molecules, all moving with the same speed v either to the left or to the right. A microscopic state is specified by telling which molecules are moving in which direction. (a) How many possible microscopic states are there? (b) How many of these correspond to all four molecules moving in the same direction? (c) What is the probability of finding the gas with all its molecules moving in one direction? Repeat parts (a–c) for a gas of (d) 10 molecules and (e) a more typical value, 10^{23} molecules.

3. Estimate the energy that could be extracted by cooling the world's oceans by 1°C. How does your estimate compare with humanity's yearly energy consumption of about 2.5×10^{20} J?

4. Two grains of salt and two grains of pepper are mixed. (a) If the mixture is shaken randomly and then divided into two equal parts, what is the approximate probability that all the salt will be in one part and all the pepper in another? Repeat for the case when (b) 10 grains and (c) 1000 grains of each are mixed.

Sections 22-2 and 22-3 The Second Law and Its Applications

5. What are the efficiencies of reversible heat engines operating between (a) the normal freezing and boiling points of water, (b) the 25°C temperature at the surface of a tropical ocean and deep water at 4°C, and (c) a 1000°C candle flame and room temperature?

6. A cosmic heat engine might operate between the Sun's 5600-K surface and the 2.7-K temperature of intergalactic space. What would be its efficiency?

7. A reversible Carnot engine operating between helium's melting point and its 4.25-K boiling point has an efficiency of 77.7%. What is the melting point?

8. A Carnot engine extracts 890 J from a 550-K reservoir during each cycle and rejects 470 J to a cooler reservoir. (a) How much work does it do each cycle? (b) What is its efficiency? (c) What is the temperature of the cool reservoir? (d) If the engine undergoes 22 cycles per second, what is its mechanical power output?

9. The maximum temperature in a nuclear power plant is 570 K. The plant rejects heat to a river where the temperature is 0°C in the winter and 25°C in the summer. What are the maximum possible efficiencies for the plant in these seasons? Why might the plant not achieve these efficiencies?

10. The minimum flow in the Connecticut River is 3.40×10^4 kg/s. By how much will the Vermont Yankee nuclear power plant described in Example 22-2 heat the entire river?

11. A power plant's electrical output is 750 MW. Cooling water at 15°C flows through the plant at 2.8×10^4 kg/s, and its temperature rises by 8.5°C. Assuming the plant's only energy loss is to the cooling water and that the cooling water is effectively the low-temperature reservoir, find (a) the rate of energy extraction from the fuel, (b) the plant's efficiency, and (c) its highest temperature.

12. A power plant extracts energy from steam at 250°C and delivers 800 MW of electric power. It discharges waste heat to a river at 30°C. The overall efficiency of the plant is 28%. (a) How does this efficiency compare with the maximum possible at these temperatures? (b) What is the rate of waste heat discharge to the river? (c) How many houses, each requiring 18 kW of heating power, could be heated with the waste heat from this plant?

13. The electric power output of all the thermal electric power plants in the United States is about 2×10^{11} W, and these plants operate at an average efficiency around 33%. What is the rate at which all these plants use cooling water, assuming an average 5°C rise in cooling-water temperature? Compare

with the 1.8×10^7 kg/s average flow at the mouth of the Mississippi River.

14. Consider a Carnot engine operating between temperatures T_h and T_c, where T_c is still above the ambient temperature T_0 (Fig. 22-28). It should be possible to operate a second engine between T_c and T_0. Show that the maximum overall efficiency of such a two-stage engine is the same as that of a single engine operating between T_h and T_0.

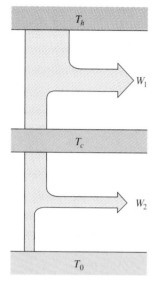

FIGURE 22-28 A two-stage engine (Problem 14).

15. A Carnot engine absorbs 900 J of heat each cycle and provides 350 J of work. (a) What is its efficiency? (b) How much heat is rejected each cycle? (c) If the engine rejects heat at 10°C, what is its maximum temperature?

16. What is the COP of a reversible refrigerator operating between 0°C and 30°C?

17. How much work does a refrigerator with a COP of 4.2 require to freeze 670 g of water already at its freezing point?

18. An industrial freezer operates between 0°C and 32°C, consuming electrical energy at the rate of 12 kW. Assuming the freezer is perfectly reversible, (a) what is its COP? (b) How much water at 0°C can it freeze in 1 hour?

19. A 4.0 L sample of water at 9.0°C is put into a refrigerator. The refrigerator's 130-W motor then runs for 4.0 min to cool the water to the refrigerator's low temperature of 1.0°C. (a) What is the COP of the refrigerator? (b) How does this compare with the maximum possible COP if the refrigerator exhausts heat at 25°C?

20. A refrigerator maintains an interior temperature of 4°C while the temperature near its heat exhaust is 30°C. The refrigerator's insulation is imperfect, and heat leaks into the refrigerator at the rate of 340 W. Assuming the refrigerator is reversible, at what rate must it consume electrical energy to maintain a constant 4°C interior?

21. A heat pump consumes electrical energy at the rate P_e. Show that it delivers heat at the rate $(COP + 1)P_e$.

22. A store is heated by an oil furnace that supplies 30 kWh of heat from each gallon. The store's owners are considering

switching to a heat pump system. Oil costs 87¢/gallon, and electricity costs 7.8¢/kWh. What is the minimum heat pump COP that will result in a savings in heating costs?

23. A heat pump transfers heat between the interior of a house and the outside air. In the summer the outside air averages 26°C, and the pump operates by chilling water to 5°C for circulation throughout the house. In winter the outside air averages 2°C, and the pump operates by heating water to 80°C for circulation throughout the house. (a) Find the coefficients of performance in summer and winter. How much work does the pump require (b) for each joule of heat removed from the house in summer and (c) for each joule supplied to the house in winter?

24. A house is heated by a heat pump with COP = 2.3. The heat pump is run by electricity generated in a power plant whose efficiency is 28%. (a) What is the overall efficiency of this process, defined as the ratio of heat delivered to the house to heat released from fuel at the power plant? (b) Could the efficiency so defined ever exceed 100%?

25. A 0.20-mol sample of an ideal gas goes through the Carnot cycle of Fig. 22-29. Calculate (a) the heat Q_h absorbed, (b) the heat Q_c rejected, and (c) the work done. (d) Use these quantities to determine the efficiency. (e) Find the maximum and minimum temperatures, and show explicitly that the efficiency as defined in Equation 22-1 is equal to the Carnot efficiency of Equation 22-3.

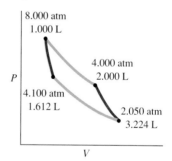

FIGURE 22-29 Problem 25 (diagram is not to scale).

26. Show that it is impossible for two adiabats to intersect. *Hint:* Suppose two adiabats do intersect. Connect them by a suitable isotherm to form a three-step cycle. Show that a heat engine operating in this cycle would have 100% efficiency, in violation of the second law.

27. Use appropriate energy flow diagrams to show that the existence of a perfect heat engine would permit the construction of a perfect refrigerator, thus violating the Clausius statement of the second law.

Section 22-4 The Thermodynamic Temperature Scale

28. A small sample of material is taken through a Carnot cycle between a reservoir of boiling helium at 1.76 K and an unknown lower temperature. During the process, 7.5 mJ of heat are absorbed from the helium, and 0.44 mJ rejected at the lower temperature. What is the unknown low temperature?

29. A Carnot engine operating between a vat of boiling sulfur and a bath of water at its triple point has an efficiency of 61.95%. What is the boiling point of sulfur?

30. A heat engine operating between a hotter reservoir of boiling hydrogen and a cooler one of boiling helium has 79.1% efficiency. What is the ratio of hydrogen to helium boiling temperatures?

Section 22-5 Entropy and the Quality of Energy

31. Calculate the entropy change associated with melting 1.0 kg of ice at 0°C.

32. You heat 250 g of water from 10°C to 95°C. By how much does the entropy of the water increase?

33. A 2.0-kg sample of water is heated to 35°C. If the entropy change is 740 J/K, what was the initial temperature?

34. Melting a block of lead already at its melting point results in an entropy increase of 900 J/K. What is the mass of the lead? *Hint:* Consult Table 20-1.

35. A shallow pond contains 94,000 kg of water. In winter it's entirely frozen. By how much does the entropy of the pond increase when the ice, already at 0°C, melts and then heats to its summer temperature of 15°C?

36. Figure 22-30 shows a 500-g copper block at 80°C dropped into 1.0 kg of water at 10°C. (a) What is the final temperature? (b) What is the entropy change of the system?

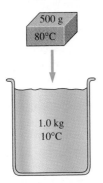

FIGURE 22-30 Problem 36.

37. The temperature of n moles of ideal gas is changed from T_1 to T_2 while the gas volume is held constant. Show that the corresponding entropy change is $\Delta S = nC_V \ln(T_2/T_1)$.

38. The temperature of n moles of ideal gas is changed from T_1 to T_2 while gas pressure is held constant. Show that the corresponding entropy change is $\Delta S = nC_P \ln(T_2/T_1)$.

39. A 5.0-mol sample of an ideal diatomic gas $(C_V = \frac{5}{2}R)$ is initially at 1.0 atm pressure and 300 K. What is the entropy change if the gas is heated to 500 K (a) at constant volume, (b) at constant pressure, and (c) adiabatically?

40. The interior of a house is maintained at 20°C while the outdoor temperature is -10°C. The house loses heat at the rate of 30 kW. At what rate does the entropy of the universe increase because of this irreversible heat flow?

41. A 250-g sample of water at 80°C is mixed with 250 g of water at 10°C. Find the entropy changes for (a) the hot water, (b) the cool water, and (c) the system.

42. Two identical objects of mass m and specific heat c at initial temperatures T_h and T_c are placed together in an insulated box and allowed to come to equilibrium. Show that the system's entropy increase is $\Delta S = mc \ln \dfrac{(T_h + T_c)^2}{4T_h T_c}$.

43. A 5.0-mol sample of ideal monatomic gas undergoes the cycle shown in Fig. 22-31, in which the process BC is isothermal. Calculate the entropy change associated with each of the three steps, and show explicitly that there is zero net entropy change over the full cycle.

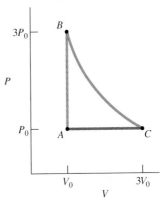

FIGURE 22-31 Problem 43.

44. In an adiabatic free expansion, 8.7 mol of ideal gas at 450 K expand 10-fold in volume. How much energy becomes unavailable to do work?

45. Ideal gas occupying 1.0 cm³ is placed in a 1.0-m³ vacuum chamber, where it expands adiabatically. If 6.5 J of energy become unavailable to do work, what was the initial gas pressure?

46. Make an argument based on Fig. 22-20 to show that a perfect refrigerator would decrease the entropy of the universe, in violation of the second law.

Paired Problems

(Both problems in a pair involve the same principles and techniques. If you can get the first problem, you should be able to solve the second one.)

47. Cooling water circulates through a reversible Carnot engine at 3.2 kg/s. The water enters at 23°C and leaves at 28°C; the average temperature is essentially that of the engine's cool reservoir. If the engine's mechanical power output is 150 kW, what are (a) its efficiency and (b) its highest temperature?

48. A reversible Carnot engine operates between 300 K and 640 K, running at 45 cycles per second. In each cycle the engine extracts 2.7 kJ from the high-temperature reservoir. Find (a) the efficiency and (b) the mechanical power output. (c) The low-temperature reservoir is provided by a flow of 300-K cooling water. If the water temperature increases 2.5°C, what is the flow rate?

49. Which would provide the greatest increase in efficiency of a Carnot engine, a 10 K increase in the maximum temperature or a 10 K decrease in the minimum temperature?

50. Which would provide the greatest increase in the COP of a reversible refrigerator, a decrease of 10 K in the maximum temperature or an increase of 10 K in the minimum temperature?

51. It costs $180 to heat a house with electricity in a typical winter month. (Electric heat simply converts all the incoming electrical energy to heat.) What would be the monthly heating bill following conversion to an electrically powered heat pump system with COP = 2.1?

52. It costs $140 each summer to operate a home air conditioner with a COP of 1.7. What will be the yearly savings in upgrading to a more efficient model with a COP of 2.4, assuming the same amount of heat is to be extracted from the house?

53. A reversible engine contains 0.20 mol of ideal monatomic gas, initially at 600 K and confined to 2.0 L. The gas undergoes the following cycle:

   - Isothermal expansion to 4.0 L.
   - Isovolumic cooling to 300 K.
   - Isothermal compression to 2.0 L.
   - Isovolumic heating to 600 K.

   (a) Calculate the net heat added during the cycle and the net work done. (b) Determine the engine's efficiency, defined as the ratio of the work done to only the heat *absorbed* during the cycle.

54. (a) Determine the efficiency for the cycle shown in Fig. 22-32, using the definition given in the preceding problem. (b) Compare with the efficiency of a Carnot engine operating between the same temperature extremes. Why are the two efficiencies different?

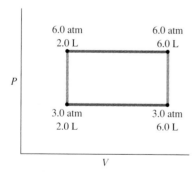

FIGURE 22-32 Problem 54.

55. You dump three 10-kg buckets of 10°C water into an empty tub, then add one 10-kg bucket of 70°C water. By how much does the entropy of the water increase?

56. Find the entropy change when a 2.4-kg aluminum pan at 155°C is plunged into 3.5 kg of water at 15°C.

Supplementary Problems

57. You're lying in a bathtub of water at 42°C. Suppose, in violation of the second law of thermodynamics, that the water spontaneously cooled to room temperature (20°C) and that the energy so released was transformed into your gravitational potential energy. Estimate the height to which you would rise above the bathtub.

58. An engine with mechanical power output 8.5 kW extracts heat from a source at 420 K and rejects it to a 1000-kg block of ice at its melting point. (a) What is its efficiency? (b) How long can it maintain this efficiency if the ice is not replenished?

59. A solar-thermal power plant is to be built in a desert location where the only source of cooling water is a small creek with average flow of 100 kg/s and an average temperature of 30°C. The plant is to cool itself by boiling away the entire creek. If the maximum temperature achieved in the plant is 500 K, what is the maximum electric power output it can sustain without running out of cooling water?

60. The McNeil generating station in Burlington, Vermont, is one of the world's largest wood-fired power plants. Here are some facts about the McNeil plant:

   - The electric power output is 59 MW.
   - Fuel consumption is 1.2×10^6 kg of wood per day. The wood's energy content is 1.4×10^7 J/kg, and 85% of this energy is released in burning.
   - Steam enters the plant's turbine at 1000°F and leaves at 200°F.
   - Cooling water circulates through the condenser at 1.8×10^5 kg/min, and its temperature increases by 18°F.

   Calculate the plant's efficiency in three ways: (a) Using only the third fact above to get the maximum possible efficiency; (b) using only the first and second facts; and (c) using only the first and fourth facts. What might account for the discrepancy between the second and third parts?

61. Gasoline engines operate approximately on the **Otto cycle**, consisting of two adiabatic and two constant-volume segments. The Otto cycle for a particular engine is shown in Fig. 22-33. (a) If the gas in the engine has specific heat ratio γ, find the engine's efficiency, assuming all processes are reversible. (b) Find the maximum temperature, in terms of the minimum temperature T_{min}. (c) How does the efficiency compare with that of a Carnot engine operating between the same two temperature extremes? *Note:* Fig. 22-33 neglects the intake of fuel-air and the exhaust of combustion products, which together involve essentially no net work.

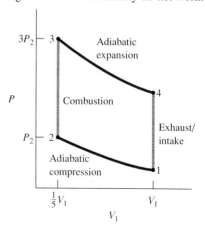

FIGURE 22-33 Otto cycle (Problems 61, 62).

62. The compression ratio r of an engine is the ratio of maximum to minimum gas volume. For the engine of the preceding problem, Fig. 22-33 shows that the compression ratio is 5. (a) Find an expression for the engine efficiency as a function of compression ratio. Assume that pressure continues to triple during the combustion phase, as shown in Fig. 22-33. (b) Make a graph of efficiency versus r, and on the same plot show also the efficiency of a Carnot engine operating between the same temperature extremes.

63. A heat pump designed for southern climates extracts heat from outside air and delivers air at 40°C to the inside of a house. (a) If the average outside temperature is 5°C, what is the average COP of the heat pump? (b) Suppose the pump is used in a northern climate where the average winter temperature is −10°C. Now what is the COP? (c) Two *identical* houses, one in the north and one in the south, are heated by this pump. Both houses maintain indoor temperatures of 19°C. What is the ratio of electric power consumption in the two houses? *Hint:* Think about heat loss as well as COP!

64. The specific heat of copper in the range from a few K to about 50 K is given by $c = aT^3$, where $a = 7.68 \times 10^{-4}$ J/kg·K⁴. Find the entropy change in a 200-g piece of copper as it's heated from 10 K to 25 K.

65. A Carnot engine extracts heat from a block of mass m and specific heat c that is initially at temperature T_{h0} but which has no heat source to maintain that temperature. The engine rejects heat to a reservoir at a constant temperature T_c. The engine is operated so its mechanical power output is proportional to the temperature difference $T_h - T_c$:

$$P = P_0 \frac{T_h - T_c}{T_{h0} - T_c},$$

where T_h is the instantaneous temperature of the hot block and P_0 is the initial power output. (a) Find an expression for T_h as a function of time, and (b) determine how long it takes for the engine's power output to reach zero.

66. You have 50 kg of steam at 100°C, but no heat source to maintain it in that condition. You also have a heat reservoir at 0°C. Suppose you operate a reversible heat engine with

this system, so the steam gradually condenses and cools until it reaches 0°C. (a) Calculate the total entropy change of the steam and subsequent water. (b) Calculate the total entropy change of the reservoir. (c) Find the total amount of work that the engine can do. *Hint:* Consider the entropy change of the entire system. This change occurs as the result of a reversible process that supplies useful work. But if it had occurred irreversibly, how much energy would have become unavailable to do work?

67. An ideal diatomic gas undergoes the cyclic process described in Fig. 22-34. Fill in the blank spaces in the table below:

	P	V	T	$U - U_A$	$S - S_A$
A	P_0	V_0	T_0	0	0
B	$3.4P_0$	V_0			
C					
D	P_0	$3.0V_0$			

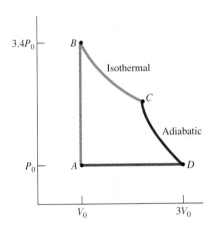

FIGURE 22-34 Cyclic process for Problem 67. Process BC is isothermal while CD is adiabatic. Diagram is not accurately scaled, and the location of point C is not quantitatively correct.

PART 3 *Cumulative Problems*

1. Figure 1 shows the thermodynamic cycle of a diesel engine. Note that this cycle differs from that of a gasoline engine (see Fig. 22-33) in that combustion takes place isobarically. As with the gasoline engine, the compression ratio r is the ratio of maximum to minimum volume; $r = V_1/V_2$. In addition, the so-called *cutoff ratio* is defined by $r_c = V_3/V_2$. Find an expression for the engine's efficiency, in terms of the ratios r and r_c and the specific heat ratio γ. Although your expression suggests that the diesel engine might be less efficient than the gasoline engine (see Problem 61 of Chapter 22), the diesel's higher compression ratio more than compensates, giving it a higher efficiency.

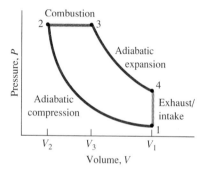

FIGURE 1 Cumulative Problem 1.

2. Deep in intergalactic space, an astronaut releases a thin-walled spherical container of radius R and negligible mass, containing a mass M of liquid water at temperature T_0 (Fig. 2). The container's surface is painted black to give it emissivity $e = 1$. The amount of radiation incident on the sphere from outside is negligible (since the temperature of intergalactic space is only 2.7 K). (a) Find an expression for the temperature of the liquid water as a function of time, assuming its heat conductivity is high enough that the water remains at essentially uniform temperature. (b) Taking $M = 100$ kg, $R = 29$ cm, and $T_0 = 300$ K, find the time from when the sphere is deployed until the water is completely frozen.

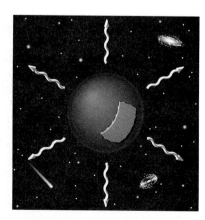

FIGURE 2 Cumulative Problem 2.

3. Equation 21-4 gives the work done by an ideal gas undergoing an isothermal expansion from volume V_1 to volume V_2. Find the analogous expression for a van der Waals gas described by Equation 20-7. Is the work done equal to the heat transferred to the gas in this case? Why or why not?

4. A solid sphere of mass m and radius R is made from a material with specific heat c, and is initially at a uniform temperature T_1. The sphere is surrounded by insulation of thermal conductivity k and thickness a (see Fig. 3). The temperature outside the insulation is fixed at T_0. (a) Assuming conduction is the only significant heat-loss mechanism, find an expression for the magnitude of the sphere's heat-loss rate as a function of its temperature T. (b) Assuming the temperature throughout the sphere remains uniform, find an expression for the temperature T as a function of time.

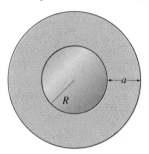

FIGURE 3 Cumulative Problem 4.

5. The ideal Carnot engine shown in Fig. 4 operates between a heat reservoir and a block of ice with mass M. An external energy source maintains the reservoir at a constant temperature T_h. At time $t = 0$ the ice is at its melting point T_0, but it is insulated from everything except the engine, so it is free to change state and temperature. The engine is operated in such a way that it extracts heat from the reservoir at a constant rate P_h. (a) Find an expression for the time t_1 at which the ice is all melted, in terms of the quantities given and any other appropriate thermodynamic parameters. (b) Find an expression for the mechanical power output of the engine as a function of time for times $t > t_1$. (c) Your expression in (b) holds only up to some maximum time t_2. Why? Find an expression for t_2.

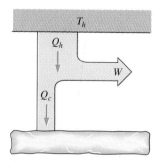

FIGURE 4 Cumulative Problem 5.

34 Maxwell's Equations and Electromagnetic Waves

Electromagnetic waves include light and the radio waves essential to modern communications. This antenna communicates with orbiting satellites.

At this point we have introduced the four fundamental laws of electromagnetism—Gauss's law for electricity, Gauss's law for magnetism, Ampère's law, and Faraday's law—that govern the behavior of electric and magnetic fields throughout the universe. We have seen how these laws describe the electric and magnetic interactions that make matter act as it does and have explored many practical devices that exploit the laws of electromagnetism. Here we extend the fundamental laws to their most general form and show how they predict the existence of electromagnetic waves. Those waves include the light, radio, TV, microwaves, X-rays, ultraviolet, and infrared with which we see, communicate, cook our food, diagnose our diseases, learn about the universe beyond Earth, and perform a myriad of other tasks from the mundane to the profound.

Electromagnetic waves are certainly among the most important manifestations of electromagnetism. After showing how electromagnetic waves arise from fundamental principles, we'll take a brief look at some of their properties. The next three chapters, on optics, then examine in detail the behavior of the electromagnetic waves we call visible light.

34-1 THE FOUR LAWS OF ELECTROMAGNETISM

Table 34-1 summarizes the four laws as we introduced them in earlier chapters. As you look at these four laws together, you can't help noticing some strong similarities. On the left-hand sides of the equations, the two laws of Gauss are identical but for the interchanging of $\mathbf{E}$ and $\mathbf{B}$. Similarly, the laws of Ampère and Faraday have left-hand sides that differ only in the interchange of $\mathbf{E}$ and $\mathbf{B}$.

On the right-hand sides, things are more different. Gauss's law for electricity involves the charge enclosed by the surface of integration, while Gauss's law for magnetism has zero on the right-hand side. Actually, though, these laws are similar. Since we have no experimental evidence for the existence of isolated magnetic charge, the enclosed magnetic charge on the right-hand side of Gauss's law for magnetism is zero. If and when magnetic monopoles are discovered, then the right-hand side of Gauss's law for magnetism would be nonzero for any surface enclosing net magnetic charge.

The right-hand sides of Ampère's and Faraday's laws are distinctly different. In Ampère's law we find the current—the flow of electric charge—as a source of magnetic field. We can understand the absence of a similar term in Faraday's law because we have never observed a flow of magnetic monopoles. If we had such a flow, then we would expect this magnetic current to produce an electric field.

Two of the differences among the laws of electromagnetism would be resolved if we knew for sure that magnetic monopoles exist. That current theories of elementary particles suggest the existence of monopoles is a tantalizing hint that there may be a fuller symmetry between electric and magnetic phenomena. The search for symmetry, based not on logic or experimental evidence but on an intuitive sense that nature should be simple, has motivated some of the most important discoveries in physics. We'll see next how symmetry considerations help lead us, finally, to the complete set of fundamental laws of electromagnetism.

TABLE 34-1 *Four Laws of Electromagnetism (still incomplete)*

LAW	MATHEMATICAL STATEMENT	WHAT IT SAYS
Gauss for $\mathbf{E}$	$\oint \mathbf{E} \cdot d\mathbf{A} = \dfrac{q}{\varepsilon_0}$	How charges produce electric field; field lines begin and end on charges
Gauss for $\mathbf{B}$	$\oint \mathbf{B} \cdot d\mathbf{A} = 0$	No magnetic charge; magnetic field lines do not begin or end
Faraday	$\oint \mathbf{E} \cdot d\boldsymbol{\ell} = -\dfrac{d\phi_B}{dt}$	Changing magnetic flux produces electric field
Ampère (steady currents only)	$\oint \mathbf{B} \cdot d\boldsymbol{\ell} = \mu_0 I$	Electric current produces magnetic field

34-2 AMBIGUITY IN AMPÈRE'S LAW

There remains one difference between the equations of electricity and magnetism that would not be resolved by the discovery of magnetic monopoles. On the right-hand side of Faraday's law we find the term $d\phi_B/dt$ that describes changing magnetic flux as a source of electric field. We find no comparable term in Ampère's law. Are we missing something? Is it possible that a changing electric flux produces a magnetic field? So far, we've given no experimental evidence for such a conjecture. It's suggested only by our sense that the near symmetry between electricity and magnetism is not a coincidence. If a changing electric flux did produce a magnetic field, just as a changing magnetic flux produces an electric field, then we would expect a term $d\phi_E/dt$ on the right-hand side of Ampère's law.

When we first stated Ampère's law in Chapter 30, we emphasized that it applied only to *steady* currents. Why that restriction? Figure 34-1 shows a situation in which current is *not* steady, namely the *RC* circuit we discussed in Chapter 28. Initially current flows in this circuit to carry charge onto the plates of the capacitor. But the current gradually decreases to zero as the capacitor becomes fully charged. While it's flowing, the current should produce a magnetic field. Let's try to use Ampère's law to calculate that field.

Ampère's law says that the line integral of the magnetic field around any closed loop is proportional to the encircled current:

$$\oint \mathbf{B} \cdot d\boldsymbol{\ell} = \mu_0 I.$$

By the encircled current, we mean the current through *any open surface* bounded by the loop. Figure 34-2 shows four such surfaces. The same current flows through surfaces 1, 2, and 4, because each of them is pierced by a current-carrying wire. But no current pierces surface 3, because the right end of that surface lies in the insulating gap between the capacitor plates. Charge flows onto the plates of the capacitor, but it doesn't flow through that gap. So for surfaces 1, 2, and 4, the right-hand side of Ampère's law is $\mu_0 I$, but for surface 3 it's zero. Thus Ampère's law is ambiguous in this case of a changing current.

This ambiguity does not arise with steady currents. In an *RC* circuit the steady-state current is everywhere zero, and thus the right-hand side of Ampère's law is zero for *any* surface. It's only when currents are changing with time that there may be situations like that of Fig. 34-2 where Ampère's law becomes ambiguous. That's why the form of Ampère's law we have used until now is strictly valid only for steady currents.

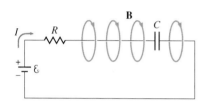

FIGURE 34-1 A charging *RC* circuit, showing some magnetic field lines surrounding the current-carrying wire.

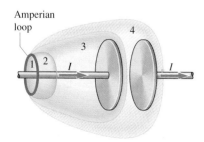

FIGURE 34-2 Ampère's law relates the line integral around an amperian loop to the current through *any open surface* bounded by that loop. Figure 34-2 shows four such surfaces, all bounded by the same circular loop. Surface 1 is the flat, circular disk bounded by the loop. The others are all like soap bubbles in the process of being blown after dipping the loop into a soap solution; they're open at the left end, so if current does pass through a surface, it does so at the right end only. Current in the wires passes through surfaces 1, 2, and 4, but not 3, so Ampère's law is ambiguous.

Can we salvage Ampère's law, extending it to cover unsteady currents without affecting its validity in the steady case? Symmetry between Ampère's and Faraday's laws has already suggested that a changing electric flux might produce a magnetic field. Between the plates of a charging capacitor there is an electric field whose magnitude is increasing (Fig. 34-3). That means there is a changing electric flux through surface 3 of Fig. 34-2.

It was the Scottish physicist James Clerk Maxwell who, about 1860, suggested that a changing electric flux should give rise to a magnetic field. Since that time many experiments, including direct measurement of the magnetic field inside a charging capacitor, have confirmed Maxwell's remarkable insight. Maxwell quantified his idea by introducing a new term into Ampère's law:

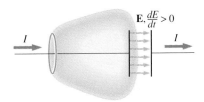

FIGURE 34-3 There is a changing electric field in the charging capacitor and, therefore, a changing electric flux through surface 3 of Fig. 34-2.

$$\oint \mathbf{B} \cdot d\boldsymbol{\ell} = \mu_0 I + \mu_0 \varepsilon_0 \frac{d\phi_E}{dt}. \tag{34-1}$$

Now there's no ambiguity. The integral is taken around any loop, I is the current through *any* surface bounded by the loop, and ϕ_E is the electric flux through that surface. With our charging capacitor, Equation 34-1 gives the same magnetic field no matter which surface we choose. For surfaces 1, 2, and 4 of Fig. 34-2, the current I makes all the contribution to the right-hand side of the equation. For surface 3, through which no current flows, the right-hand side of Equation 34-1 comes entirely from the changing electric flux. You can readily verify that the term $\varepsilon_0 d\phi_E/dt$ has the units of current, and that, for the charging capacitor, this term is numerically equal to the current I (see Problem 3).

Although changing electric flux is not the same thing as electric current, it has the same effect as a current in producing a magnetic field. For this reason Maxwell called the term $\varepsilon_0 d\phi_E/dt$ the **displacement current**. The word "displacement" has historical roots that don't provide much physical insight. But the word "current" is meaningful in that the effect of displacement current is indistinguishable from that of real current in producing magnetic fields. Although we developed the idea of displacement current using the specific example of a charging capacitor, we emphasize that Ampère's law in its now complete form (Equation 34-1) is truly universal: *any* changing electric flux results in a magnetic field. That fact will prove crucial in establishing the existence of electromagnetic waves.

EXAMPLE 34-1	*Displacement Current Produces Magnetic Field*

A parallel-plate capacitor with circular plates a distance d apart is charged through long, straight wires as shown in Fig. 34-4. The potential difference between the plates is increasing at the rate dV/dt. Find an expression for the magnetic field as a function of position between the plates.

Solution

With long, straight feed wires, the situation has cylindrical symmetry. The only magnetic field with this symmetry has

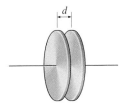

FIGURE 34-4 A circular capacitor (Example 34-1).

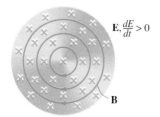

FIGURE 34-5 Electric and magnetic fields between the circular capacitor plates. The electric field strength is increasing, so the displacement current is in the same direction as the electric field. Pointing the right thumb in this direction then shows that the magnetic field circles clockwise.

circular field lines and a magnitude that depends only on the radial distance r from the symmetry axis, as shown in Fig. 34-5. A magnetic field line within the capacitor encircles no conduction current—no flow of charge—but it does encircle a changing electric field and therefore a displacement current. If the field line has radius r, the encircled electric flux is

$$\phi_E = \int \mathbf{E} \cdot d\mathbf{A} = \pi r^2 E = \pi r^2 \frac{V}{d},$$

where the uniformity of the field allows us to calculate the field as the ratio of potential difference to plate spacing and the flux as a simple product of field and area. Then the displacement current is

$$I_D = \varepsilon_0 \frac{d\phi_E}{dt} = \frac{\varepsilon_0 \pi r^2}{d} \frac{dV}{dt}.$$

With cylindrical symmetry, the line integral on the left-hand side of Ampère's law becomes

$$\oint \mathbf{B} \cdot d\boldsymbol{\ell} = 2\pi r B.$$

Equating this quantity to μ_0 times the encircled displacement current gives

$$2\pi r B = \frac{\mu_0 \varepsilon_0 \pi r^2}{d} \frac{dV}{dt},$$

so

$$B = \frac{\mu_0 \varepsilon_0 r}{2d} \frac{dV}{dt}.$$

This field, with its magnitude increasing linearly with r, should remind you of the magnetic field inside a cylindrical wire (see Example 30-4). Problem 4 extends this calculation to the field outside the capacitor.

We can find the direction of the induced magnetic field just as we did for the fields of ordinary conduction currents: Point your right thumb in the direction of the current and your right fingers curl in the direction of the magnetic field. But which way does the displacement current go? In this example the electric field strength is increasing, so $d\phi_E/dt$ is positive, and the displacement current is in the direction of the electric field (see Fig. 34-5). If the electric field strength were decreasing, the displacement current would be opposite the field.

The induced magnetic field in a practical capacitor is minuscule, as the following exercise illustrates. We'll soon see, however, that the significance of displacement-current-induced magnetic fields is vastly greater than in this simple example.

EXERCISE In 1984 D. F. Bartlett and T. R. Corle of the University of Colorado first measured the magnetic field inside a charging capacitor using a sensitive magnetometer called a superconducting quantum interference detector (SQUID). They used a capacitor with circular plates spaced 1.22 cm, connected across a 340-V peak sine-wave generator operating at 1.25 kHz. What was the peak magnetic field strength 3.0 cm from the capacitor axis?

Answer: 3.65×10^{-11} T, less than one millionth of Earth's magnetic field

Some problems similar to Example 34-1: 4–6

34-3 MAXWELL'S EQUATIONS

It was Maxwell's genius to recognize that Ampère's law should be modified to reflect the symmetry suggested by Faraday's law. The consequences of Maxwell's discovery go far beyond anything he could have imagined. To honor Maxwell, the four complete laws of electromagnetism are given the collective name **Maxwell's equations**. This full and complete set of equations, first published in 1864, governs the behavior of electric and magnetic fields everywhere. Table 34-2 summarizes Maxwell's equations.

These four simple, compact statements are all it takes to describe classical electromagnetic phenomena. Everything electric or magnetic that we have considered and will consider—from polar molecules to electric current; resistors, capacitors, inductors, and transistors; solar flares and cell membranes; electric generators and thunderstorms; computers and TV sets; the northern lights and fusion reactors—all these can be described using Maxwell's

TABLE 34-2 *Maxwell's Equations*

LAW	MATHEMATICAL STATEMENT	WHAT IT SAYS	EQUATION NUMBER
Gauss for $\mathbf{E}$	$\oint \mathbf{E} \cdot d\mathbf{A} = \dfrac{q}{\varepsilon_0}$	How charges produce electric field; field lines begin and end on charges	(34-2)
Gauss for $\mathbf{B}$	$\oint \mathbf{B} \cdot d\mathbf{A} = 0$	No magnetic charge; magnetic field lines do not begin or end	(34-3)
Faraday	$\oint \mathbf{E} \cdot d\boldsymbol{\ell} = -\dfrac{d\phi_B}{dt}$	Changing magnetic flux produces electric field	(34-4)
Ampère	$\oint \mathbf{B} \cdot d\boldsymbol{\ell} = \mu_0 I + \mu_0 \varepsilon_0 \dfrac{d\phi_E}{dt}$	Electric current and changing electric flux produce magnetic field	(34-5)

equations. And despite this wealth of phenomena, we have yet to discuss a most important manifestation of electromagnetism, namely electromagnetic waves. We've put off waves until now because they, unlike electromagnetic phenomena we've already introduced, depend crucially on Maxwell's extension of Ampère's law. It's easiest to understand electromagnetic waves when they propagate through empty space, so before beginning our study of waves we'll first simplify Maxwell's equations for the case of a vacuum.

Maxwell's Equations in Vacuum

Consider Maxwell's equations in a region free of any matter—in vacuum. We've learned enough about electromagnetism to anticipate that the fields themselves will still be able to interact, change, and carry energy even in the absence of matter. To express Maxwell's equations in vacuum, we simply remove all reference to matter—that is, to electric charge:

$$\oint \mathbf{E} \cdot d\mathbf{A} = 0 \qquad \text{(Gauss, } \mathbf{E}\text{)} \qquad\qquad (34\text{-}6)$$

$$\oint \mathbf{B} \cdot d\mathbf{A} = 0 \qquad \text{(Gauss, } \mathbf{B}\text{)} \qquad\qquad (34\text{-}7)$$

$$\oint \mathbf{E} \cdot d\boldsymbol{\ell} = -\frac{d\phi_B}{dt} \qquad \text{(Faraday)} \qquad\qquad (34\text{-}8)$$

$$\oint \mathbf{B} \cdot d\boldsymbol{\ell} = \mu_0 \varepsilon_0 \frac{d\phi_E}{dt}. \qquad \text{(Ampère)} \qquad\qquad (34\text{-}9)$$

In vacuum the symmetry is complete, with electric and magnetic fields appearing in the equations on an equal footing. With charge and current absent in a vacuum, the only source of either field is a change in the other field—as shown by the time derivatives on the right-hand sides of Faraday's and Ampère's laws.

34-4 ELECTROMAGNETIC WAVES

Faraday's law shows that a changing magnetic field induces an electric field. Ampère's law shows that a changing electric field induces a magnetic field. Together, the two laws suggest the possibility of **electromagnetic waves**, in which each type of field continually induces the other, resulting in an electromagnetic disturbance that propagates through space as a wave. We'll now confirm this qualitative suggestion with a rigorous demonstration, directly from Maxwell's equations, that electromagnetic waves are indeed possible. In the process we'll discover the properties of electromagnetic waves and will come to a deep understanding of the nature of light.

A Plane Electromagnetic Wave

Here we describe the simplest type of electromagnetic wave—a plane wave in vacuum. Recall from Chapter 16 that a plane wave is one whose properties don't vary in directions perpendicular to the wave propagation, so its wavefronts are planes (see Fig. 16-18). A plane wave is an approximation to the more realistic case of a spherical wave expanding from a localized source, but it's a good approximation at distances from the wave source that are large compared with the wavelength. Light waves reaching Earth from the Sun, for example, or radio waves miles from the transmitter, are essentially plane waves.

In vacuum, it turns out that the electric and magnetic fields of an electromagnetic wave are perpendicular to each other. They're both also perpendicular to the direction of wave propagation—making the electromagnetic wave a transverse wave, as defined in Chapter 16. To be concrete, we'll take the x direction to be the direction of propagation, the y direction that of the electric field, and the z direction that of the magnetic field (Fig. 34-6). We won't prove that this configuration of three mutually perpendicular directions is the only

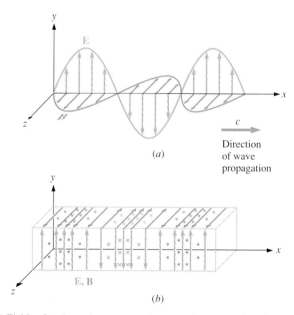

FIGURE 34-6 Fields of a plane electromagnetic wave, shown at a fixed instant of time. (a) Field vectors for points on the x axis show the sinusoidal variation in the fields. The electric and magnetic fields are perpendicular but in phase; they're also perpendicular to the propagation direction. (b) A partial representation of the field lines, which actually extend forever in both directions. Here the lines are pictured only in a finite rectangular slab. Lines on the facing surfaces of the slab are shown as arrows; lines going through the slab appear as dots or crosses depending on whether they're emerging from or going into the slab. Spacing of the field lines reflects the sinusoidal variation shown in (a).

one possible for an electromagnetic wave (although in vacuum it is; see Problem 11). What we will do, though, is prove that this configuration satisfies Maxwell's equations—thus showing that such electromagnetic waves are indeed possible. Before we can do that, we need a mathematical description of our plane electromagnetic wave.

In Chapter 16 we found that a sinusoidal wave propagating in the x direction is represented by a function of the form $A \sin(kx - \omega t)$, where A is the wave amplitude, k the wave number, and ω the angular frequency. For the mechanical waves of Chapters 16 and 17, the function $A \sin(kx - \omega t)$ described some physical quantity such as the height of a water wave or pressure variation in a sound wave. In an electromagnetic wave, the corresponding physical quantities are the electric and magnetic fields—which are vector quantities. It turns out that these two wave fields, although perpendicular, are in phase—meaning that their peaks and troughs coincide, as shown in Fig. 34-6. Having chosen the y direction for the electric field and the z direction for the magnetic field, we can then write the fields of our plane electromagnetic wave as

$$\mathbf{E}(x, t) = E_p \sin(kx - \omega t)\hat{\mathbf{j}} \qquad (34\text{-}10)$$

and

$$\mathbf{B}(x, t) = B_p \sin(kx - \omega t)\hat{\mathbf{k}}, \qquad (34\text{-}11)$$

where the peak amplitudes E_p and B_p are constants and where $\hat{\mathbf{j}}$ and $\hat{\mathbf{k}}$ are unit vectors in the y and z directions. Figure 34-6a is a "snapshot" of some field vectors of this wave at points on the x axis, shown at a fixed instant of time. That $\mathbf{E}$ and $\mathbf{B}$ are perpendicular is obvious from the figure, as is the fact that they're perpendicular to the propagation direction, in this case the x direction. You can also see the sinusoidal variation, as the field vectors get alternately longer, then shorter, then reverse direction, and so on. And you can see that $\mathbf{E}$ and $\mathbf{B}$ are in phase: they peak at the same points, and are zero at the same points. We emphasize that Fig. 34-6a shows field *vectors* for points on the x axis only; the fields extend forever throughout space, and because this is a plane wave, a picture of field vectors along any line parallel to the x axis would look just the same.

We can also draw field *lines* for our wave, in contrast to the field vectors of Fig. 34-6a. We can't draw complete field lines, because they extend forever in both directions. So in Fig. 34-6b we've shown the field lines only in a rectangular slab; that's enough to give a picture of what the fields look like everywhere. You should convince yourself that Figs. 34-6a and 34-6b show exactly the same thing, namely a plane electromagnetic wave described by Equations 34-10 and 34-11. In one case we use field *vectors,* whose lengths are proportional to the field magnitudes, and in the other we use field *lines,* which extend forever and whose spacing indicates the field magnitudes.

We'll now use Maxwell's equations to show that the electric and magnetic fields pictured in Fig. 34-6 and described by Equations 34-10 and 34-11 really do satisfy Maxwell's equations. We've chosen a sinusoidal waveform for our wave fields because of its mathematical simplicity. But the superposition principle holds for electric and magnetic fields, and we know from Section 16-6 that by superposition we can represent *any* waveform in terms of sinusoidal waveforms. So our proof that electromagnetic waves can exist actually holds for any wave shape (see Problem 74 here and Problem 54 in Chapter 16). That means we can use electromagnetic waves to communicate the complex waveforms of music, TV images, or computer data encoded as pulses of light.

We have four Maxwell equations to satisfy: the two Gauss's laws, and the laws of Faraday and Ampère.

Gauss's Laws

In vacuum, Gauss's laws for the electric and magnetic fields both have zero on the right-hand side (Equations 34-6 and 34-7), reflecting the absence of charge. That means, as we've seen many times before, that the field lines can't begin or end; they either form closed loops or extend to infinity. Our electromagnetic wave is a plane wave, meaning that no wave property varies in directions perpendicular to the wave propagation. Therefore the field lines shown partially in Fig. 34-6*b* must extend, straight, forever in both directions. So they don't begin or end, and thus the two Gauss laws are satisfied.

Faraday's Law

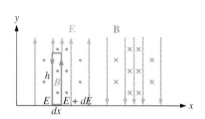

FIGURE 34-7 Cross section of Fig. 34-6 in the *x-y* plane. Also shown is a rectangular loop for evaluating the line integral in Faraday's law.

To see that Faraday's law is satisfied, consider an observer looking directly toward the *x-y* plane in Fig. 34-6. Such an observer would see electric field lines going up and down and magnetic field lines coming straight in and out, as shown in Fig. 34-7. Consider the small rectangular loop of height *h* and infinitesimal width *dx* shown in the figure. Evaluating the line integral of the electric field **E** around this loop, we get no contribution from the short ends because they are at right angles to the field. Going around counterclockwise, we get a contribution $-Eh$ as we go down the left side against the field direction. Then we get a positive contribution going up the right side. Because of the variation in field strength with position, the field strength on the right side of the loop is different from that on the left. Let the change in field be *dE*, so the field on the right side of the loop is $E + dE$, giving a contribution of $(E + dE)h$ to the line integral. Then the line integral of **E** around the loop is

$$\oint \mathbf{E} \cdot d\boldsymbol{\ell} = -Eh + (E + dE)h = h\, dE.$$

Physically, this nonzero line integral implies an induced electric field. Induced by what? By a changing magnetic flux through the loop. The electric field of the wave arises because of the changing magnetic field of the wave. The area of the loop is $h\, dx$, and the magnetic field **B** is at right angles to this area, so the magnetic flux through the loop is just

$$\phi_B = Bh\, dx.$$

The rate of change of flux through the loop is then

$$\frac{d\phi_B}{dt} = h\, dx\, \frac{dB}{dt}.$$

Faraday's law relates the line integral of the electric field to the rate of change of flux:

$$\oint \mathbf{E} \cdot d\boldsymbol{\ell} = -\frac{d\phi_B}{dt},$$

or, using our expressions for the line integral and the rate of change of flux,

$$h\, dE = -h\, dx\, \frac{dB}{dt}.$$

Dividing through by $h\,dx$, we have

$$\frac{dE}{dx} = -\frac{dB}{dt}. \tag{34-12a}$$

In deriving this equation, we considered changes in E with position at a fixed instant of time, as pictured in Fig. 34-7, so our derivative dE/dx means the rate of change of E with position while time is held fixed. Similarly, in evaluating the derivative of magnetic flux, we were concerned only with the time rate of change at the fixed position of our loop. Both our derivatives represent rates of change with respect to one variable while the other variable is held fixed, and are therefore partial derivatives (see Math Toolbox on p. 400 if you're not familiar with partial derivatives). Equation 34-12a should then be written more properly:

$$\frac{\partial E}{\partial x} = -\frac{\partial B}{\partial t}. \tag{34-12b}$$

Equation 34-12b—which is just Faraday's law applied to our electromagnetic wave—tells us that the rate at which the electric field changes with *position* is related to the rate at which the magnetic field changes with *time*.

Ampère's Law

Now imagine an observer looking down on Fig. 34-6 from above. This observer sees the magnetic field lines lying in the x-z plane, and electric field lines emerging perpendicular to the x-z plane as shown in Fig. 34-8. We can apply Ampère's law (Equation 34-9) to the infinitesimal rectangle shown, just as we applied Faraday's law to a similar rectangle in the x-y plane. Going counterclockwise around the rectangle, we get no contribution to the line integral of the magnetic field on the short sides, since they lie perpendicular to the field. Going down the left side, we get a contribution Bh to the line integral. Going up the right side, against the field, we get a negative contribution $-(B + dB)h$, where dB is the change in B from one side of the rectangle to the other. So the line integral in Ampère's law is

$$\oint \mathbf{B} \cdot d\boldsymbol{\ell} = Bh - (B + dB)h = -h\,dB.$$

The electric flux through the rectangle is simply $Eh\,dx$, so the rate of change of electric flux is

$$\frac{d\phi_E}{dt} = h\,dx\,\frac{dE}{dt}.$$

Ampère's law relates the line integral of the magnetic field to this time derivative of the electric flux, giving

$$-h\,dB = \varepsilon_0\mu_0 h\,dx\,\frac{dE}{dt}.$$

Dividing through by $h\,dx$ and noting again that we are really dealing with partial derivatives, we have

$$\frac{\partial B}{\partial x} = -\varepsilon_0\mu_0\frac{\partial E}{\partial t}. \tag{34-13}$$

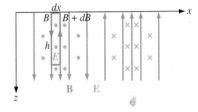

FIGURE 34-8 Cross section of Fig. 34-6 in the x-z plane, showing a rectangular loop for evaluating the line integral in Ampère's law.

Equations 34-12 and 34-13—derived from Faraday's and Ampère's laws—express fully the requirements that Maxwell's universal laws of electromagnetism pose on the field structure of Fig. 34-6. The two equations are remarkable in that each describes an induced field that arises from the changing of the other field. That other field, in turn, arises from the changing of the first field. Thus we have a self-perpetuating electromagnetic structure, whose fields exist and change without the need for charged matter. If Equations 34-10 and 34-11, which describe the fields in Fig. 34-6, can be made consistent with Equations 34-12 and 34-13, then we will have demonstrated that our electromagnetic wave does indeed satisfy Maxwell's equations and is thus a possible configuration of electric and magnetic fields.

Faraday, Ampère, and the Wave Fields

To see that Equation 34-12 is satisfied, we differentiate the electric field of Equation 34-10 with respect to x, and the magnetic field of Equation 34-11 with respect to t:

$$\frac{\partial E}{\partial x} = \frac{\partial}{\partial x}[E_p \sin(kx - \omega t)] = kE_p \cos(kx - \omega t)$$

and

$$\frac{\partial B}{\partial t} = \frac{\partial}{\partial t}[B_p \sin(kx - \omega t)] = -\omega B_p \cos(kx - \omega t).$$

Putting these expressions in for the derivatives in Equation 34-12 gives

$$kE_p \cos(kx - \omega t) = -[-\omega B_p \cos(kx - \omega t)].$$

The cosine term cancels from this equation, showing that the equation holds if

$$kE_p = \omega B_p. \tag{34-14}$$

To see that Equation 34-13 is also satisfied, we differentiate the magnetic field of Equation 34-11 with respect to x and the electric field of Equation 34-10 with respect to t:

$$\frac{\partial B}{\partial x} = kB_p \cos(kx - \omega t)$$

and

$$\frac{\partial E}{\partial t} = -\omega E_p \cos(kx - \omega t).$$

Using these expressions in Equation 34-13 then gives

$$kB_p \cos(kx - \omega t) = -\varepsilon_0 \mu_0[-\omega E_p \cos(kx - \omega t)].$$

Again, the cosine term cancels, showing that this equation is satisfied if

$$kB_p = \varepsilon_0 \mu_0 \omega E_p. \tag{34-15}$$

Our analysis has shown that electromagnetic waves whose form is given by Fig. 34-6 and Equations 34-10 and 34-11 can exist, provided that the amplitudes E_p and B_p, and the frequency ω and wave number k, are related by Equations 34-14 and 34-15. Physically, the existence of these waves is possible because a change in either kind of field—electric or magnetic—induces the other kind of field, giving rise to a self-perpetuating electromagnetic field structure. Maxwell's theory thus leads to the prediction of an entirely new phenomenon—the electromagnetic wave. We will now explore some properties of these waves.

34-5 THE SPEED OF ELECTROMAGNETIC WAVES

In Chapter 16 we found that the speed of a sinusoidal wave is given by the ratio of the angular frequency and wave number:

$$\text{wave speed} = \frac{\omega}{k}.$$

To determine the speed of our electromagnetic wave, we solve Equation 34-14 for E_p:

$$E_p = \frac{\omega B_p}{k},$$

and use this expression in Equation 34-15:

$$kB_p = \varepsilon_0 \mu_0 \omega E_p = \frac{\varepsilon_0 \mu_0 \omega^2 B_p}{k}.$$

Solving for the wave speed ω/k then gives

$$\text{wave speed} = \frac{\omega}{k} = \frac{1}{\sqrt{\varepsilon_0 \mu_0}}. \tag{34-16}$$

This remarkably simple result shows that the speed of an electromagnetic wave in vacuum depends only on the electric and magnetic constants ε_0 and μ_0. All electromagnetic waves in vacuum, regardless of frequency or amplitude, share this speed. Although we derived this result for sinusoidal waves, the superposition principle ensures that it holds for any wave shape.

We can easily calculate the speed given in Equation 34-16:

$$\frac{1}{\sqrt{\varepsilon_0 \mu_0}} = \frac{1}{[(8.85 \times 10^{-12} \text{ F/m})(4\pi \times 10^{-7} \text{ H/m})]^{1/2}} = 3.00 \times 10^8 \text{ m/s}.$$

But this is precisely the speed of light!

As early as 1600, Galileo had tried to measure the speed of light by uncovering lanterns on different mountaintops. He was able to conclude only that "If not instantaneous, it is extraordinarily rapid." The first evidence for a finite speed of light came in the 1670s from observations by the Danish astronomer Ole Römer. He noted that eclipses of Jupiter's moons occurred at different times than predicted as Jupiter's distance from Earth changed. Römer interpreted the changes as being due to the different times for light traveling at a finite speed from Jupiter to Earth. Römer's data implied a speed of 2.3×10^8 m/s, about three quarters of the actual value. In 1728, James Bradley used changes in the apparent positions of stars resulting from Earth's orbital motion to calculate a value of 2.95×10^8 m/s for the speed of light—in error by less than 2%. As we saw in Chapter 1, the exact value $c = 2.99792458 \times 10^8$ m/s was adopted in

FIGURE 34-9 This image of Venus was made using data that include surface altitude determined by very accurate measurements of the travel time for radar signals reflected from Venus' surface. Radar, like all electromagnetic waves, travels at the speed of light.

1983 to define the meter. So we no longer measure the speed of light; instead, that speed provides an accurate way to measure distances (Fig. 34-9).

Do other properties of light besides its speed fit our picture of electromagnetic waves? In 1678—some 200 years before Maxwell—the Dutch physicist Christian Huygens had suggested that light is a wave. In 1801, Thomas Young experimented with a 2-slit system to show that light undergoes interference, giving conclusive evidence for the wave nature of light (see Fig. 16-25). But neither experiment nor theory could say what kind of wave light might be. Then, in the 1860s, came Maxwell. Using a theory developed from laboratory experiments involving electricity and magnetism, with no reference whatever to optics or light, Maxwell showed how the interplay of electric and magnetic fields could result in electromagnetic waves. The speed of those waves—calculated from the quantities ε_0 and μ_0 that were determined in laboratory experiments having nothing to do with light—was precisely the known speed of light. Maxwell was led inescapably to the conclusion that light is an electromagnetic wave.

Maxwell's identification of light as an electromagnetic phenomenon is a classic example of the unification of knowledge toward which science is ever striving. With one simple calculation, Maxwell brought the entire science of optics under the umbrella of electromagnetism. Maxwell's work stands as a crowning intellectual triumph, an achievement whose implications are still expanding our view of the universe.

34-6 PROPERTIES OF ELECTROMAGNETIC WAVES

Our demonstration that electromagnetic waves satisfy Maxwell's equations places definite constraints on the properties of those waves. The wave frequency ω and wave number k are not both arbitrary, but must be related through

$$\frac{\omega}{k} = c,$$
(34-17a)

where $c = 1/\sqrt{\varepsilon_0 \mu_0}$ is the speed of light. In Chapter 16 we related the angular frequency ω and wave number k to the more familiar frequency f and wavelength λ through the equations $\omega = 2\pi f$ and $k = 2\pi/\lambda$. Therefore we can also write Equation 34-17a in the form

$$f\lambda = c.$$
(34-17b)

Furthermore, Equation 34-14 shows that

$$E = \frac{\omega}{k}B = cB.$$
(34-18)

Thus, the field magnitudes in the wave are not independent but are in the ratio of the speed of light. Also, Fig. 34-6 and Equations 34-10 and 34-11 have the electric and magnetic fields perpendicular to each other and to the direction of wave propagation, with the electric and magnetic fields in phase. It is in fact the case that only waves with this form—**E** and **B** in phase and with **E**, **B**, and the propagation direction all perpendicular—can satisfy Maxwell's equations in vacuum (see Problem 11).

EXAMPLE 34-2	*Laser Light*

A laser beam with wavelength 633 nm is propagating in the $+z$ direction. Its electric field is parallel to the x axis and has amplitude 6.0 kV/m. Find the wave frequency, and the direction and amplitude of the magnetic field.

Solution
Equation 34-17b relates the wavelength and frequency to the speed of light. Solving for f gives

$$f = \frac{c}{\lambda} = \frac{3.00 \times 10^8 \text{ m/s}}{633 \times 10^{-9} \text{ m}} = 4.74 \times 10^{14} \text{ Hz} .$$

If we imagine reorienting the wave of Fig. 34-6 so it propagates along the z direction, then rotate it about the z direction so the electric field is parallel to the x axis, we find that the

magnetic field is parallel to the y axis. The magnetic field amplitude follows from Equation 34-18:

$$B_p = \frac{E_p}{c} = \frac{6.0 \times 10^3 \text{ V/m}}{3.00 \times 10^8 \text{ m/s}} = 2.0 \times 10^{-5} \text{ T} .$$

EXERCISE An electromagnetic wave is propagating in the $-y$ direction, with its magnetic field parallel to the x axis. The magnetic field amplitude is 8.0 μT. Write an expression for the wave's electric field vector at the point where the magnetic field points in the $+x$ direction and is at its peak value.

Answer: $\mathbf{E} = -2.4\hat{\mathbf{k}}$ kV/m

Some problems similar to Example 34-2: 24–27

Got It!

Light and radio waves are both electromagnetic waves; of the two, light has a much higher frequency. Does that mean light waves travel faster than radio waves? Regardless of your answer, are any other properties of these waves different?

34-7 THE ELECTROMAGNETIC SPECTRUM

Although an electromagnetic wave's frequency and wavelength must be related by Equation 34-17b, one or the other of these quantities is completely arbitrary. That means we can have electromagnetic waves of any frequency, or, equivalently, any wavelength. Direct measurement shows that visible light occupies a wavelength range from about 400 nm to 700 nm, corresponding to frequencies from 7.5×10^{14} Hz to 4.3×10^{14} Hz. The different wavelengths or frequencies correspond to different colors, with red at the long-wavelength, low-frequency end of the visible region and blue at the short-wavelength, high-frequency end (see the enlargement in Fig. 34-10).

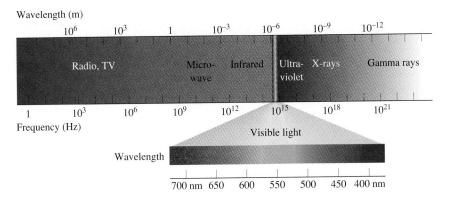

FIGURE 34-10 The electromagnetic spectrum ranges from radio waves to gamma rays, with visible light occupying only a narrow range of wavelengths and frequencies. Note the logarithmic scale, in which intervals between numbered tick marks correspond to factors-of-1000 changes in frequency and wavelength.

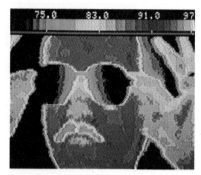

FIGURE 34-11 Subtle variations in body temperature are color coded in this infrared image of a human face. Regions at different temperatures emit different frequencies of infrared; these are coded into the image's visible colors according to the temperature scale at the top.

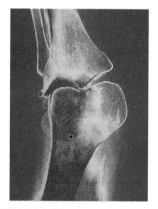

FIGURE 34-12 X rays are high-frequency, short wavelength electromagnetic waves that readily penetrate soft tissues but not bone. Here, an X-ray image reveals rheumatoid arthritis in a human knee joint.

Figure 34-10 shows the entire **electromagnetic spectrum**, including frequencies and wavelengths that differ by many orders of magnitude either way from those of visible light. The invisible electromagnetic waves beyond the narrow visible range were unknown in Maxwell's time. A brilliant confirmation of Maxwell's theory came in 1888, when the German physicist Heinrich Hertz succeeded in generating and detecting electromagnetic waves of much lower frequency than visible light. Hertz intended his work only to verify Maxwell's modification of Ampère's law, but the practical consequences have proven enormous. In 1896, the Italian scientist Guglielmo Marconi demonstrated that he could generate and detect the so-called Hertzian waves. In 1901, he transmitted electromagnetic waves across the Atlantic Ocean, creating a public sensation. From the pioneering work of Hertz and Marconi, spurred by the theoretical efforts of Maxwell, came the entire technology of radio, television, and microwaves that so dominates modern society. We now consider all electromagnetic waves in the frequency range from a few Hz to about 3×10^{11} Hz as radio waves, with ordinary AM radio at about 10^6 Hz, FM radio at 10^8 Hz, and microwaves used for radar, cooking, and satellite communications at 10^9 Hz and above.

Between radio waves and visible light lies the infrared frequency range. Electromagnetic waves in this region are emitted by warm objects, even when they are not hot enough to glow visibly. For this reason, infrared cameras are used to determine subtle body temperature differences in medical diagnosis, to examine buildings for heat loss, and to study the birth of stars in clouds of interstellar gas and dust (Fig. 34-11).

Beyond the visible region are the ultraviolet rays responsible for sunburn, then the highly penetrating X rays (Fig. 34-12), and finally the gamma rays whose primary terrestrial source is radioactive decay. All these phenomena, from radio to gamma rays, are fundamentally the same: They are all electromagnetic waves, differing only in frequency and wavelength. All travel with speed c, and all consist of electric and magnetic fields produced from each other through the induction processes described by Faraday's and Ampère's laws. Naming the different types of electromagnetic waves is just a matter of convenience; there are no gaps in the continuous range of allowed frequencies and wavelengths. Practical differences arise because waves of different wavelengths interact differently with matter; in particular, shorter wavelengths tend to be generated and absorbed most efficiently by smaller systems.

APPLICATION	*The New Astronomy*

Figure 34-10 shows that visible light occupies only a small part of the electromagnetic spectrum. For centuries our only information about the universe beyond Earth—except for an occasional meteorite—came from visible light. Processes like those occurring on the visible surface of our Sun and many other stars produce predominantly visible light. Optical astronomy, utilizing visible light, gave a good picture of the universe to the extent that it consists of objects not too different from the visible part of the Sun. The restriction to optical astronomy was in part imposed by Earth's atmosphere. Transparent to visible light, the atmosphere is largely opaque to other forms of electromagnetic radiation, although "windows" of relative transparency exist in parts of the radio and infrared bands. The

discovery by Bell Telephone Laboratories electrical engineer Karl Jansky in 1931 that radio waves from outer space can be detected on Earth led to the development of radio astronomy. For decades, radio astronomy has given a picture of the universe that complements the optical view, showing phenomena that are simply not detectable by optical means (Fig. 34-13).

The onset of the space age in the late 1950s finally opened the rest of the electromagnetic spectrum to astronomers. Before this time there were surprisingly few suggestions that anything interesting might be found beyond the visible range. But satellites carrying infrared, ultraviolet, X-ray, and gamma-ray detectors have literally revolutionized our view of the universe

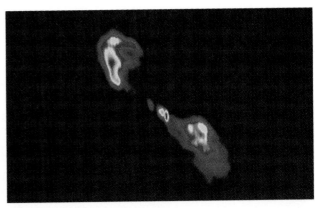

(a)   (b)

FIGURE 34-13 (a) Some of the 27 dish antennas that comprise the Very Large Array (VLA) radio telescope in New Mexico. Each dish is 25 m in diameter, and the array can be configured to occupy an area larger than metropolitan Washington, DC. (b) The galaxy Centaurus A, a powerful radio emitter, imaged with the VLA. The two lobes are jets of material ejected from the galaxy's central core. The VLA was tuned to a wavelength of 20 cm for this observation.

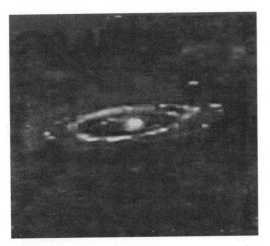

FIGURE 34-14 This false-color infrared image of the Andromeda galaxy was taken with the Infrared Astronomical Satellite. Yellow indicates regions of brightest infrared emission, corresponding to places where new stars are probably forming.

(Fig. 34-14). Exotic objects such as neutron stars and black holes are now objects of astronomical study. The opening of the entire electromagnetic spectrum has brought a new richness to astronomy, showing that our universe contains some of the most unusual objects that the laws of physics permit. Phenom-

ena that were once bizarre conjectures of theoreticians are now observed regularly. For example, astronomers are convinced that massive black holes—with the mass of a million Suns— lurk at the centers of galaxies, including our own. Closer to home, observations of the Sun with ultraviolet and X-ray instruments have brought new understandings of the star that sustains us. And by turning space-borne infrared detectors toward Earth, we have learned much about the structure and resources of our own planet (Fig. 34-15).

FIGURE 34-15 This satellite image documents destruction of the Brazilian rainforest by human activities. False colors enhance the distinction between healthy forest (dark green) and cleared areas (light green, pink).

34-8 POLARIZATION

The fields of an electromagnetic wave in vacuum (and in common materials such as air and glass) are perpendicular to the propagation direction, but within the plane perpendicular to the wave propagation the orientation of one field is still arbitrary. **Polarization** is a wave property that specifies the electric field

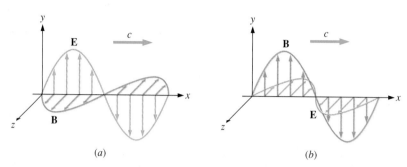

(a)   (b)

FIGURE 34-16 Field vectors for two electromagnetic waves. Both are propagating in the $+x$ direction, but have different polarizations. The polarization direction is that of the electric field, so the wave in (a) is vertically polarized (i.e., its electric field is in the y direction), while the wave in (b) is horizontally polarized (i.e., in the z direction). Unpolarized light would be a mix of such waves with their electric fields oriented at random in many different directions.

16.4
Polarizer

direction; since the two fields are perpendicular, polarization also determines the magnetic field direction (Fig. 34-16).

Electromagnetic waves used in radio, TV, and radar originate from antennas whose configuration gives the waves a definite polarization. The light waves produced by most lasers are also polarized. In contrast, visible light from hot sources such as the Sun or a light bulb is **unpolarized**, consisting of a mixture of electromagnetic waves with random field orientations.

Unpolarized light may be polarized either by reflection off surfaces or when it passes through substances whose molecular or crystal structure has a pre-ferred direction called the **transmission axis**. Many crystals and synthetic ma-terials such as the plastic Polaroid have this property. For example, sunlight reflecting off the hood of a car becomes partially polarized in the horizontal direction. Polaroid sunglasses, with their transmission axis vertical, block this reflected glare with only a modest reduction in overall light intensity.

A polarizing material passes unattenuated only that component of the wave's electric field that lies along its preferred direction. If θ is the angle between the field and the polarizer's preferred direction, then the field component in the preferred direction is $E\cos\theta$. As we will show shortly, the intensity S of an electromagnetic wave is proportional to the square of the field strength; as a result a wave of intensity S_0 incident on a polarizer emerges with intensity given by the so-called **Law of Malus**:

$$S = S_0 \cos^2\theta. \tag{34-19}$$

This equation shows that electromagnetic waves will be blocked completely if $\theta = 90°$, a situation that occurs when unpolarized light passes through one polarizer to give it a definite polarization, then through another oriented at $90°$ to the first (Fig. 34-17).

When unpolarized light passes through a polarizer its intensity is cut in half. You can see this from Equation 34-19 because the unpolarized light includes a mix of waves with random polarization angles θ. Averaging over all possible angles in Equation 34-19 amounts to taking the average of $\cos^2\theta$ over a full cycle. We've seen on several occasions that the average of the square of a sinusoidal function is $\frac{1}{2}$ (recall Fig. 16-16), so a polarizer does indeed cut the intensity of unpolarized light in half.

FIGURE 34-17 Two pairs of Polaroid sunglasses with their transmission axes at right angles. Where they overlap, no light can get through.

| **EXAMPLE 34-3** | *Multiple Polarizers* |

Unpolarized light with intensity S_0 is incident on a "stack" of three polarizers. The first has its polarization axis vertical, the second is at 25° to the vertical, and the third is at 70° to the vertical (Fig. 34-18). What is the intensity of light emerging from this stack?

Solution

We've just seen that the first polarizer cuts the unpolarized intensity in half, giving $\frac{1}{2}S_0$ for the intensity incident on the second polarizer. Equation 34-19 shows that the second and third polarizers each reduce the intensity by a factor $\cos^2 \theta$, where θ is the angle between the incident polarization direction—established by one polarizer—and the next polarizer's axis. For the second polarizer this angle is 25°; for the third it is $70° - 25° = 45°$. Thus light emerges from the stack with intensity

$$S = (\tfrac{1}{2})(\cos^2 25°)(\cos^2 45°)S_0 = 0.205 S_0 .$$

Interestingly, this is greater than the intensity we would get passing light through a vertical polarizer followed by a single polarizer at 70°. And, as the exercise below shows, it is much

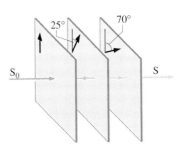

FIGURE 34-18 A stack of polarizers. Arrows on the sheets indicate directions of the polarization axes.

greater than what we would get by interchanging the second and third polarizers. Can you see why?

EXERCISE Rework Example 34-3 with the second and third polarizers interchanged.

Answer: $S = 0.029 S_0$

Some problems similar to Example 34-3: 35, 36, 72

Polarization can tell us much about sources of electromagnetic waves or about materials through which the waves travel. Many astrophysical processes produce polarized waves; measuring the polarization then gives clues to the mechanisms operating in distant objects. Polarization of light as it passes through materials helps geologists to understand the composition and formation of rocks (Fig. 34-19) and helps engineers to locate stresses in structures (Fig. 34-20).

FIGURE 34-19 Photomicrograph of a thin section of rock placed between crossed polarizers. Individual mineral crystals, here a few mm in size, rotate the light's electric field, altering the transmitted light intensity.

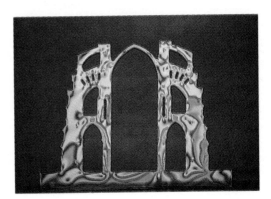

FIGURE 34-20 Plastic model of a Gothic cathedral, photographed between polarizing sheets. The resulting patterns reveal stresses, helping architects and engineers understand the response of the building to wind and weight loading—topics related to our study of static equilibrium in Chapter 14.

APPLICATION	*Liquid Crystal Displays and Electro-Optic Modulation*

They're everywhere, from watches, calculators, and gas pumps to laptop computers—the **liquid-crystal displays** (LCDs) that convert electrical signals into letters, numbers, pictures, and graphs that we can read. Fundamental to their operation is the polarization of light.

In Fig. 34-17 we saw that two polarizers oriented at right angles block all light from getting through the pair. But if we could rotate the light's polarization direction through 90° while it's between the polarizers, then light from the first polarizer would reach the second aligned with the latter's preferred direction, and so would pass through. That's just what happens in an LCD—but it happens selectively, under control of an electrical signal, allowing the transmission of light to be turned on or off.

In Chapter 23 we introduced liquid crystals as systems of long dipole-like molecules that align with an applied electric field. Figure 34-21 shows how this property is used to make a display. The liquid crystal is contained between two transpar-

ent striated plates that cause the molecules to align with their striations. The two plates' striations are mutually perpendicular, so the molecules' alignment gradually changes through the device. The electric field of a light wave interacts with the molecules, with the result that the polarization direction of the light rotates through 90° as it passes through the liquid crystal. The whole system is between crossed polarizers and so, because of the 90° rotation of the polarization, light incident on the system gets through (Fig. 34-21*a*).

Now suppose a voltage is applied between the plates confining the liquid crystal. This results in an electric field that aligns the molecules as shown in Fig. 34-21*b*. In this new orientation the liquid crystal no longer rotates the polarization of the light, so the situation is just like that of Fig. 34-17, and the light is blocked. There's one such system for each of the segments that make up the numbers and letters of a liquid crystal display, and each segment can be turned on or off to make the desired symbol

FIGURE 34-21 Polarization plays a central role in the operation of a liquid-crystal display.

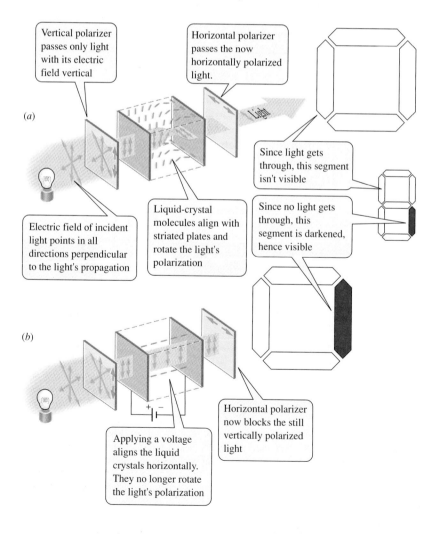

In Fig. 34-21 we show light incident from the back of the display and emerging from the front for viewing. In many LCDs the light at the back is replaced by a mirror that reflects ambient light. Then there's no power needed to provide light, and the LCD operates at minimal electrical power. Low power consumption is one of the key advantages of liquid-crystal displays.

Liquid crystals are rather slow in their response, so they aren't good for rapid switching of light. But some solid crystals have much the same property as the liquid-crystal system of Fig. 34-21, in that they selectively rotate the polarization of light depending on the presence or absence of an electric field (in this case, it takes a field to produce the rotation). This is known as the **electro-optic effect**.

Placing an electro-optic crystal between crossed polarizers makes an **electro-optic modulator** (EOM) that can switch light on timescales as short as 10^{-10} s. Such devices, used as electronic shutters to interrupt laser beams and thus produce very short pulses of light, have been used to make some of the most accurate measurements of the speed of light. Applying a varying voltage to the EOM causes the light transmission to vary continuously. Voice or music, for example, can be transmitted on a laser beam by applying the amplified signal from a microphone to an EOM. EOMs are used in a wide variety of scientific and commercial applications. An especially important use is the conversion of electrical signals to light pulses on the highest-speed fiber optic communications systems.

34-9 PRODUCING ELECTROMAGNETIC WAVES

We have shown that electromagnetic waves can exist, and have explored some of their properties. But how do these waves originate?

All that's necessary is to produce a changing electric or magnetic field. Once a changing field of either type exists, Faraday's and Ampère's laws ensure the production of the other type—and so on, to give a propagating electromagnetic wave. Ultimately, changing fields of either type occur when we alter the motion of electric charge. Therefore:

▮ *Accelerated* **electric charge is the source of electromagnetic waves.**

In a radio transmitter, the accelerated charges are electrons moving back and forth in an antenna, driven by an alternating voltage from an *LC* circuit (Fig. 34-22). In an X-ray tube, high-energy electrons decelerate rapidly as they

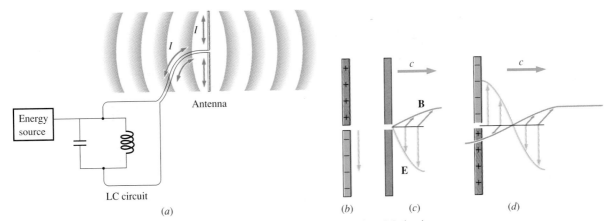

FIGURE 34-22 (a) Simplified diagram of a radio transmitter. Oscillations of an *LC* circuit drive alternating current (green arrows) in the antenna, while a power source replenishes energy carried away in electromagnetic waves. (b)–(d) A changing electric field arises from the changing charge distribution in the antenna. The changing electric field induces a changing magnetic field, and the field structure propagates away from the antenna at the speed of light. Frames (b) and (d) are half a wave period apart in time, at times when charge separation in the antenna is a maximum.

slam into a target; their deceleration is the source of the electromagnetic waves, now in the X-ray region of the spectrum. In the magnetron tube of a microwave oven, electrons circle in a magnetic field; their centripetal acceleration is the source of the microwaves that cook your food. And the altered movement of electrons in atoms—although described accurately only by quantum mechanics—is the source of most visible light. If the motion of the accelerated charges is periodic, then the wave frequency is that of the motion; more generally, systems are most efficient at producing (and receiving) electromagnetic waves whose wavelength is comparable to the size of the system. That's why TV antennas are on the order of 1 m in size, while nuclei—some 10^{-15} m in diameter—produce gamma rays.

Calculation of electromagnetic waves emitted by accelerated charges presents challenging but important problems for physicists and communications engineers. Figure 34-23a shows a "snapshot" of the electric field produced by a single point charge undergoing simple harmonic motion, while Fig. 34-23b shows the field of an oscillating dipole—a configuration approximated by many systems from antennas to atoms and molecules. Both figures show that the waves are strongest in the direction at right angles to the acceleration of the charge distribution and that there is no radiation in the direction of the acceleration. This accounts for, among other phenomena, the directionality of radio and TV antennas, which transmit and receive most effectively perpendicular to the long direction of the antenna.

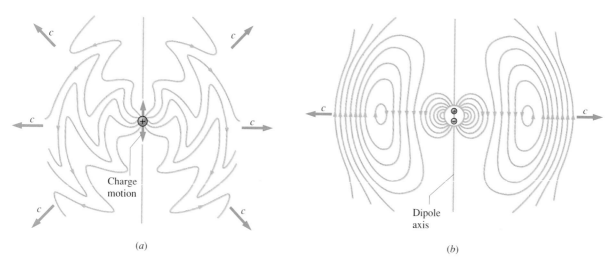

(a)   (b)

FIGURE 34-23 "Snapshots" showing the electric fields of oscillating charge distributions. (a) A single point charge executing simple harmonic motion in the horizontal plane. Note that the field close to the charge approximates the radial field of a stationary point charge, but that farther out the "kinks" in the field—resulting from the accelerated motion—are more prominent and become essentially perpendicular to the radial direction. These transverse kinks move outward at the speed of light, and constitute the wave fields. (b) The electric field of an oscillating dipole. Note that the field forms closed loops, detached from the dipole. These are the outward propagating wave fields. The larger field loops shown were formed when the oscillating dipole had the opposite orientation. Not shown in either figure are the equally important magnetic fields.

The fields shown in Fig. 34-23 seem to bear little resemblance to the plane-wave fields of Fig. 34-7 that we used to demonstrate the possibility of electromagnetic waves. We could produce true plane waves only with an infinite sheet of accelerated charge—an obvious impossibility. But far from the source, the curved field lines evident in Fig. 34-23b, for example, would appear straight, and the wave would begin to approximate a plane wave. So our plane-wave analysis is a valid approximation at great distances—typically many wavelengths—from a localized wave source. Closer to the source more complicated expressions for the wave fields apply, but these, too, satisfy Maxwell's equations.

34-10 ENERGY IN ELECTROMAGNETIC WAVES

We showed in previous chapters that electric and magnetic fields contain energy. Here we have considered electromagnetic waves, in which a combination of electric and magnetic fields propagates through space. As the wave moves, it must transport the energy contained in those fields.

We define **intensity**, S, as the rate at which an electromagnetic wave transports energy across a unit area. This is the same definition we used for wave intensity in Chapter 16, and the units are also the same: power per unit area, or W/m². We can calculate the intensity of a plane electromagnetic wave by considering a rectangular box of thickness dx and cross-sectional area A with its face perpendicular to the wave propagation (Fig. 34-24). Within this box are wave fields **E** and **B** whose energy densities are given by Equations 26-3 and 32-11:

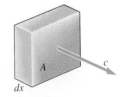

FIGURE 34-24 A box of length dx and cross-sectional area A at right angles to the propagation of an electromagnetic wave.

$$u_E = \tfrac{1}{2}\varepsilon_0 E^2$$

$$u_B = \frac{B^2}{2\mu_0}.$$

If dx is sufficiently small, the fields don't change much over the box, so the total energy in the box is just the sum of the electric and magnetic energy densities multiplied by the box volume $A\,dx$:

$$dU = (u_E + u_B)\,A\,dx = \frac{1}{2}\left(\varepsilon_0 E^2 + \frac{B^2}{\mu_0}\right)A\,dx.$$

This energy moves with speed c, so all the energy contained in the box length dx moves out of the box in a time $dt = dx/c$. The rate at which energy moves through the cross-sectional area A is then

$$\frac{dU}{dt} = \frac{1}{2}\left(\varepsilon_0 E^2 + \frac{B^2}{\mu_0}\right)\frac{A\,dx}{dx/c} = \frac{c}{2}\left(\varepsilon_0 E^2 + \frac{B^2}{\mu_0}\right)A.$$

So the intensity S, or rate of energy flow per unit area, is

$$S = \frac{c}{2}\left(\varepsilon_0 E^2 + \frac{B^2}{\mu_0}\right).$$

We can recast this equation in simpler form by noting that, for an electromagnetic wave, $E = cB$ and $B = E/c$. Using these expressions to replace one of

(a)

(b)

FIGURE 34-25 (a) The intensity of candle light is only a few W/m². (b) This laser produces a modest 3W of power, but because its beam diameter is less than 0.5 mm, its intensity is some 20 MW/m²—2000 times that of bright sunlight.

the E's in the term E^2 with B and similarly one of the B's in the term B^2 with E, we have

$$S = \frac{c}{2}\left(\varepsilon_0 c EB + \frac{EB}{\mu_0 c}\right) = \frac{1}{2\mu_0}(\varepsilon_0 \mu_0 c^2 + 1)\,EB.$$

But $c = 1/\sqrt{\varepsilon_0 \mu_0}$, so $\varepsilon_0 \mu_0 c^2 = 1$, giving

$$S = \frac{EB}{\mu_0}. \tag{34-20a}$$

Although we derived Equation 34-20a for an electromagnetic wave, it is in fact a special case of the more general result that nonparallel electric and magnetic fields are accompanied by a flow of electromagnetic energy. In general, the rate of energy flow per unit area is given by

$$\mathbf{S} = \frac{\mathbf{E} \times \mathbf{B}}{\mu_0}. \tag{34-20b}$$

Here a vector $\mathbf{S}$ is used to signify not only the magnitude of the energy flow, but also its direction. For an electromagnetic wave in vacuum, in which $\mathbf{E}$ and $\mathbf{B}$ must be at right angles, Equation 34-20b reduces to Equation 34-20a, with the direction of energy flow the same as the direction of wave travel. The vector intensity $\mathbf{S}$ is called the **Poynting vector** after the English physicist J. H. Poynting, who suggested it in 1884. Poynting's name is especially fortuitous, for the Poynting vector points in the direction of energy flow. Problem 76 explores an important application of the Poynting vector to fields that do not constitute an electromagnetic wave.

Equations 34-20 give the intensity at the instant when the fields have magnitudes E and B. In an electromagnetic wave the fields oscillate, and so does the intensity. We're usually not interested in this rapid oscillation. For example, an engineer designing a solar collector doesn't care that sunlight intensity oscillates at about 10^{14} Hz. What she really wants is the *average* intensity, $\bar{S}$. Because the instantaneous intensity of Equation 34-20a contains a product of sinusoidally varying terms, which are in phase, the average intensity is just half the peak intensity:

$$\bar{S} = \frac{\overline{EB}}{\mu_0} = \frac{E_p B_p}{2\mu_0} \quad \text{(average intensity)} \tag{34-21a}$$

(This follows because, as we've seen on several occasions, the average of $\sin^2 \omega t$ over one cycle is $\frac{1}{2}$.) Typical values for $\bar{S}$ in visible light range from a few W/m² in the faint light of a candle to many MW/m² in the most intense laser beams (Fig. 34-25).

We wrote Equation 34-21a in terms of both the electric and magnetic fields, but we can use the wave condition $E = cB$ to eliminate either field in terms of the other:

$$\bar{S} = \frac{E_p^{\,2}}{2\mu_0 c} \tag{34-21b}$$

and

$$\bar{S} = \frac{cB_p^{\,2}}{2\mu_0}. \tag{34-21c}$$

Got It!

Lasers 1 and 2 emit light of the same color, and the electric field in the beam from laser 1 is twice as strong as that in laser 2's beam. How do their (a) magnetic fields, (b) intensities, and (c) wavelengths compare?

EXAMPLE 34-4	*Solar Energy*

The average intensity of sunlight on a clear day at noon is about 1 kW/m^2 (Fig. 34-26). What are the electric and magnetic fields in sunlight? How many solar collectors would you need to replace a 4.8-kW electric water heater in noonday sun, if each collector has an area of 2.0 m^2 and converts 40% of the incident sunlight to heat?

Solution

Solving Equation 34-21b for the electric field gives

$$E_p = \sqrt{2\mu_0 c \bar{S}}$$

$$= [(2)(4\pi \times 10^{-7}\ \text{H/m})(3.0 \times 10^8\ \text{m/s})(1 \times 10^3\ \text{W/m}^2)]^{1/2}$$

$$= 0.87\ \text{kV/m}.$$

The peak magnetic field is then given by $B_p = E_p/c$, so

$$B_p = \frac{E_p}{c} = \frac{870\ \text{V/m}}{3.0 \times 10^8\ \text{m/s}} = 3 \times 10^{-6}\ \text{T}.$$

At 1 kW/m^2, we would then need 4.8 m^2 of collector area if the collectors were 100% efficient. At 40% efficiency, we therefore need 4.8 m^2/0.40 = 12 m^2, for a total of 6 collectors.

FIGURE 34-26 In bright sunlight, energy is incident on each square meter of these solar collectors at the rate of about 1000 watts.

EXERCISE A laser produces an average power of 7.0 W in a light beam 1.0 mm in diameter. Find (a) the average intensity and (b) the peak electric field of the laser light.

Answers: (a) 8.9 MW/m^2; (b) 82 kV/m

Some problems similar to Example 34-4: 38–41, 43

Waves from Localized Sources

As an electromagnetic wave propagates through empty space, its total energy does not change. With plane waves the intensity—power per unit area—does not change either. But when a wave originates in a localized source such as an atom, a radio transmitting antenna, a light bulb, or a star, its wavefronts are not planes but expanding spheres (recall Fig. 16-18). The wave's total energy remains the same, but as it expands that energy is spread over the area of an ever larger sphere—whose area increases as the square of the distance from the source. Therefore, as we found in Chapter 16, the power per unit area—the intensity—decreases as the inverse square of the distance:

$$S = \frac{P}{4\pi r^2}. \tag{34-22}$$

Here S and P can be either the peak or average intensity and power, respectively, and r is the distance from a localized source. This intensity decrease occurs not because electromagnetic waves "weaken" and lose energy but because that energy gets spread ever more thinly.

Because the intensity of an electromagnetic wave is proportional to the *square* of the field strengths (Equations 34-21), Equation 34-22 shows that the *fields* of a spherical wave decrease as $1/r$. Contrast that with the $1/r^2$ decrease in the electric field of a stationary point charge, and you can see why the electromagnetic wave fields associated with an accelerated charge dominate in all but the immediate vicinity of the charge (see Fig. 34-23a).

EXAMPLE 34-5	*A Garage-Door Opener*

A radio-activated garage-door opener responds to signals with average intensity as weak as 20 μW/m². If the transmitter unit produces a 240-mW signal, broadcast in all directions, what is the maximum distance at which the transmitter will activate the door opener? What is the minimum value for the peak electric field to which the unit responds?

Solution

Since the waves spread out in all the directions, Equation 34-22 applies. Solving for r gives

$$r = \sqrt{\frac{P}{4\pi S}} = \sqrt{\frac{240 \times 10^{-3} \text{ W}}{(4\pi)(20 \times 10^{-6} \text{ W/m}^2)}} = 31 \text{ m}.$$

Solving Equation 34-21b gives the electric field corresponding to the unit's 20-μW/m² sensitivity:

$$E_p = \sqrt{2\mu_0 c \overline{S}}$$

$$= \sqrt{(2)(4\pi \times 10^{-7} \text{ H/m})(3.00 \times 10^8 \text{ m/s})(20 \times 10^{-6} \text{ W/m}^2)}$$

$$= 0.12 \text{ V/m}.$$

The sensitivity of radio receiving equipment is often expressed in terms of the minimum electric field strength.

EXERCISE A stereo receiver's AM tuner section has a rated sensitivity of 2.1 mV/m. What is the maximum distance at which this unit can receive broadcasts from a radio station's 5.0-kW transmitter, assuming the signal is broadcast in all directions?

Answer: 261 km

Some problems similar to Example 34-5: 49, 51, 52, 61, 62

34-11 WAVE MOMENTUM AND RADIATION PRESSURE

We know from mechanics that moving objects carry both energy and momentum. The same is true for electromagnetic waves. Maxwell showed that the wave energy U and momentum p are related by

$$p = \frac{U}{c}. \tag{34-23}$$

If an electromagnetic wave is incident on an object and the object absorbs the wave energy (as, for example, a black object exposed to sunlight), then the object also absorbs the momentum given by Equation 34-23. If the wave's average intensity is $\overline{S}$, then it carries energy per unit area at the average rate $\overline{S}$ J/s/m². According to Equation 34-23 it therefore carries momentum per unit area at the rate $\overline{S}/c$. Newton's law in its general form $\mathbf{F} = d\mathbf{p}/dt$ tells us that the rate of change of an object's momentum is equal to the net force on the object. Therefore, if an object absorbs electromagnetic wave momentum $\overline{S}/c$ per unit area per unit time, it experiences a force per unit area of this magnitude. Since force per unit area is pressure, we call this quantity the **radiation pressure**:

$$P_{\text{rad}} = \frac{\overline{S}}{c}. \tag{34-24}$$

FIGURE 34-27 The bright dot at the center of this picture is a 20-micron particle levitated by a laser beam reflected upward by the prism shown at the bottom.

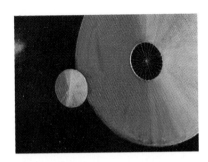

FIGURE 34-28 Two-stage sailing spacecraft proposed for interstellar travel. At the target star, laser light beamed all the way from the solar system would reflect from the large sail to the smaller one, bringing the latter to a stop. The diameter of the large sail is 1000 km.

The radiation pressure is doubled if an object reflects electromagnetic waves, in the same way that bouncing a basketball off a backboard changes the ball's momentum by $2mv$ and, therefore, delivers momentum $2mv$ to the backboard.

The pressure exerted by ordinary light is very small, but Dartmouth College physicists E. F. Nichols and G. F. Hull demonstrated its existence in a sensitive experiment performed in 1903. With high-energy laser light or with objects of low mass and large area, radiation pressure can be appreciable. Lasers exert enough light pressure to levitate small particles (Fig. 34-27), and the pressure of light has been suggested as a means of driving interstellar "sailing ships" (Fig. 34-28). Finally, the idea that electromagnetic waves carry momentum played a crucial role in Einstein's development of his famous equation $E = mc^2$.

EXAMPLE 34-6	*Star Wars*

A proposed ballistic missile defense system calls for a laser that can focus 25 MW of light on an attacking warhead. The weapon works by heating the warhead to the point of destruction, but it also delivers momentum that alters the warhead's trajectory. If the beam dwells on a 200-kg warhead for 15 s, what velocity change does it impart to the warhead? Estimate the distance by which the warhead will be knocked off course over its remaining 30 minutes of flight.

Solution

The energy delivered in a 25-MW beam acting for 15 s is (25 MW)(15 s) = 375 MJ. According to Equation 34-23, the associated momentum is

$$p = \frac{U}{c} = \frac{375 \times 10^6 \text{ J}}{3.00 \times 10^8 \text{ m/s}} = 1.25 \text{ kg·m/s} .$$

The change in the warhead's velocity is given by $m\Delta v = \Delta p$, where Δp is the change in its momentum. Assuming the warhead absorbs all the beam's momentum, we then have

$$\Delta v = \frac{\Delta p}{m} = \frac{1.25 \text{ kg·m/s}}{200 \text{ kg}} = 0.00625 \text{ m/s} .$$

This is insignificant compared with a typical warhead speed of 7 km/s. Even though we don't know the direction of the velocity change, we can estimate crudely the error Δx in the impact point by multiplying this change by the flight time:

$$\Delta x = \Delta v \, t = (0.00625 \text{ m/s})(30 \text{ min})(60 \text{ s/min}) = 11 \text{ m} .$$

This is totally negligible, especially for a nuclear warhead. Even with this enormously powerful laser, radiation pressure has an insignificant effect. It's the energy delivered, not the momentum, that matters here.

EXERCISE A laser delivers 5.0 MW/m^2. If the beam is directed upward, what is the maximum mass for a 100-μm-diameter particle to be suspended in the beam?

Answer: 1.3×10^{-11} kg

Some problems similar to Example 34-6: 56–59

CHAPTER SYNOPSIS

Summary

1. Maxwell's modification of Ampère's law adds a **displacement current** term $\varepsilon_0 d\phi_E/dt$, showing that changing electric flux is a source of magnetic field. This modified law completes the set of **Maxwell's equations**—the four equations that govern the behavior of electromagnetic fields.

2. The interplay of electric and magnetic fields described by Faraday's and Ampère's laws gives rise to **electromagnetic waves**. When they propagate through vacuum, these waves
   a. Travel at the speed of light, $c = 1/\sqrt{\varepsilon_0\mu_0} = 3.00\times10^8$ m/s.
   b. Have their electric and magnetic fields at right angles to each other and to the direction of wave propagation.
   c. Have their fields in phase, with magnitudes related by $E = cB$.
   d. Can have any frequency or wavelength, provided the two are related by the equivalent expressions $f\lambda = c$ or $\omega/k = c$.

3. Radio waves, television, microwaves, infrared, visible light, ultraviolet, X rays, and gamma rays are all forms of electromagnetic radiation. They differ only in frequency and wavelength, and together comprise the **electromagnetic spectrum**.

4. **Polarization** describes the orientation of a wave's electric field in the plane perpendicular to the propagation direction. When a polarized wave passes through a polarizing material, its intensity is reduced by a factor $\cos^2\theta$, where θ is the angle between the wave polarization and the preferred axis of the material.

5. Electromagnetic waves are produced by accelerated electric charges, as in the alternating current of a radio antenna.

6. Electromagnetic waves carry energy. The rate at which energy is transported per unit area is the wave **intensity**. The **Poynting vector**,

$$\mathbf{S} = \frac{\mathbf{E} \times \mathbf{B}}{\mu_0},$$

describes this energy transport for any configuration of electromagnetic fields. The average intensity has half the peak value, or

$$\overline{S} = \frac{E_p B_p}{2\mu_0}.$$

The intensity of a plane wave remains constant, while the intensity from a localized source decreases as the inverse square of the distance from the source.

7. An electromagnetic wave with energy U also carries momentum $p = U/c$. As a result, it exerts a **radiation pressure** $P_{rad} = \overline{S}/c$ on an object that absorbs the wave and twice this pressure on a reflecting object.

Terms You Should Understand

(Pairs are closely related terms whose distinction is important; number in parentheses is chapter section where term first appears.)

displacement current (34-2)
Maxwell's equations (34-3)
electromagnetic wave (34-4)
electromagnetic spectrum (34-7)
polarization (34-8)
intensity, Poynting vector (34-10)
radiation pressure (34-11)

Symbols You Should Recognize

$\varepsilon_0 d\phi_E/dt$ (34-2)
$S, \mathbf{S}, \overline{S}$ (34-10)
c (34-5)
P_{rad} (34-11)

Problems You Should Be Able to Solve

evaluating induced magnetic fields in symmetric situations (34-2)
relating frequency and wavelength of electromagnetic waves (34-6)
relating electric and magnetic field strengths in electromagnetic waves (34-6)
calculating light intensity emerging from one or more polarizers (34-8)
relating wave intensity and fields (34-10)
evaluating wave intensity and fields as a function of distance from localized sources (34-10)
calculating radiation pressure and its effects (34-11)

Limitations to Keep in Mind

The description of electromagnetic waves developed in this chapter applies strictly only in vacuum.

QUESTIONS

1. Why is Maxwell's modification of Ampère's law essential to the existence of electromagnetic waves?
2. The presence of magnetic monopoles would require modification of Gauss's law for magnetism. Which of the other Maxwell equations would also need modification?
3. There is displacement current between the plates of a charging capacitor, yet no charge is moving between the plates. In what sense is the word "current" appropriate here?
4. Is there displacement current in an electromagnetic wave? Is there ordinary conduction current?
5. List some similarities and differences between electromagnetic waves and sound waves.
6. What aspect of the electromagnetic wave considered in Section 34-4 ensures that Gauss's laws for electricity and magnetism are satisfied?
7. Explain why parallel electric and magnetic fields in vacuum could not constitute an electromagnetic wave.
8. The speed of an electromagnetic wave is given by $c = \lambda f$. How does the speed depend on frequency? On wavelength?
9. When astronomers observe a supernova explosion in a distant galaxy, they see a sudden, simultaneous rise in visible light and other forms of electromagnetic radiation. How is this evidence that the speed of light is independent of frequency?
10. Turning a TV antenna so its rods point vertically may change the quality of your TV reception. Why? Think about polarization.
11. Unpolarized light is incident on two sheets of Polaroid with their polarization directions at right angles, and no light gets through. A third sheet is inserted between the other two, and now some light gets through. How can this be?
12. Why is it not possible to define exactly where the visible region of the spectrum ends?
13. Why did the field of X-ray astronomy flourish only after the advent of space flight?
14. The Sun emits most of its electromagnetic wave energy in the visible region of the spectrum, with the peak in the yellow-green. Our eyes are sensitive to the same range, with peak sensitivity in the yellow-green. Is this a coincidence?
15. Suppose your eyes were sensitive to radio waves rather than light. What things would look bright?
16. An LC circuit is made entirely from superconducting materials, yet its oscillations eventually damp out. Why?
17. If you double the field strength in an electromagnetic wave, what happens to the intensity?
18. The intensity of light falls off as the inverse square of the distance from the source. Does this mean that electromagnetic wave energy is lost? Explain.
19. When your picture is taken with a flash camera, why doesn't the momentum of the light flash knock you over?
20. Some long-distance power transmission lines use DC rather than AC, despite the need to convert between DC and AC at either end. Why might this be? What energy loss mechanism occurs with AC but not DC?
21. Electromagnetic waves do not readily penetrate metals. Why might this be?

PROBLEMS

Section 34-2 Ambiguity in Ampère's Law

1. A uniform electric field is increasing at the rate of 1.5 V/m·μs. What is the displacement current through an area of 1.0 cm^2 at right angles to the field?
2. A parallel-plate capacitor has square plates 10 cm on a side and 0.50 cm apart. If the voltage across the plates is increasing at the rate of 220 V/ms, what is the displacement current in the capacitor?
3. A parallel-plate capacitor of plate area A and spacing d is charging at the rate dV/dt. Show that the displacement current in the capacitor is equal to the conduction current flowing in the wires feeding the capacitor.
4. A capacitor with circular plates is fed with long, straight wires along the axis of the plates. Show that the magnetic field *outside* the capacitor, in a plane that passes through the interior of the capacitor and is perpendicular to the axis, is given by $B = \dfrac{\mu_0 \varepsilon_0 R^2}{2rd} \dfrac{dV}{dt}$. Here R is the plate radius, d the spacing, dV/dt the rate of change of the capacitor voltage, and r the distance from the axis.
5. A parallel-plate capacitor has circular plates with radius 50 cm and spacing 1.0 mm. A uniform electric field between the plates is changing at the rate 1.0 MV/m·s. What is the magnetic field between the plates (a) on the symmetry axis, (b) 15 cm from the axis, and (c) 150 cm from the axis?
6. An electric field points into the page and occupies a circular region of radius 1.0 m, as shown in Fig. 34-29. There are no electric charges in the region, but there is a magnetic field forming closed loops pointing clockwise, as shown. The magnetic field strength 50 cm from the center of the

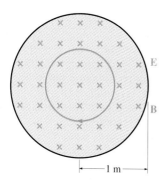

FIGURE 34-29 Problem 6.

FIGURE 34-30 Problem 14.

region is 2.0 μT. (a) What is the rate of change of the electric field? (b) Is the electric field increasing or decreasing?

Section 34-4 Electromagnetic Waves

7. At a particular point the instantaneous electric field of an electromagnetic wave points in the $+y$ direction, while the magnetic field points in the $-z$ direction. In what direction is the wave propagating?
8. The fields of an electromagnetic wave are $\mathbf{E} = E_p \sin(kz + \omega t)\hat{\mathbf{j}}$ and $\mathbf{B} = B_p \sin(kz + \omega t)\hat{\mathbf{i}}$. Give a unit vector in the direction of propagation.
9. The electric field of a radio wave is given by $\mathbf{E} = E \sin(kz - \omega t)(\hat{\mathbf{i}} + \hat{\mathbf{j}})$. (a) What is the peak amplitude of the electric field? (b) Give a unit vector in the direction of the magnetic field at a place and time where $\sin(kz - \omega t)$ is positive.
10. Show by differentiation and substitution that Equations 34-12b and 34-13 can be satisfied by fields of the form $E(x, t) = E_p f(kx \pm \omega t)$ and $B(x, t) = B_p f(kx \pm \omega t)$, where f is any function of the argument $kx \pm \omega t$.
11. Show that it is impossible for an electromagnetic wave in vacuum to have a time-varying component of its electric field in the direction of its magnetic field. *Hint:* Assume $\mathbf{E}$ does have such a component, and show that you cannot satisfy both Gauss and Faraday.

Section 34-5 The Speed of Electromagnetic Waves

12. A light-minute is the distance light travels in one minute. Show that the Sun is about 8 light-minutes from Earth.
13. Your intercontinental telephone call is carried by electromagnetic waves routed via a satellite in geosynchronous orbit at an altitude of 36,000 km. Approximately how long does it take before your voice is heard at the other end?
14. An airplane's radar altimeter works by bouncing radio waves off the ground and measuring the round-trip travel time (Fig. 34-30). If that time is 50 μs, what is the altitude?

15. Roughly how long does it take light to go 1 foot?
16. If you speak via radio from Earth to an astronaut on the moon, how long is it before you can get a reply?
17. "Ghosts" on a TV screen occur when part of the signal goes directly from transmitter to receiver, while part takes a longer route, reflecting off mountains or buildings (Fig. 34-31). The electron beam in a 50-cm-wide TV tube "paints" the picture by scanning the beam from left to right across the screen in about 10^{-4} s. If a "ghost" image appears displaced about 1 cm from the main image, what is the difference in path lengths of the direct and indirect signals?

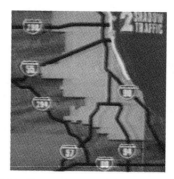

FIGURE 34-31 Ghost images of highways appear on this TV traffic report (Problem 17).

18. A computer can fetch information from its memory in 3.0 ns, a process that involves sending a signal from the central processing unit (CPU) to memory and awaiting the return of the information. If signals in the computer's wiring travel at $0.60c$, what is the maximum distance between the CPU and the memory? Your answer shows why high-speed computers are necessarily compact.
19. Problem 69 shows that the speed of electromagnetic waves in a transparent dielectric is given by $1/\sqrt{\kappa \varepsilon_0 \mu_0}$, where κ is the dielectric constant described in Chapter 26. An experimental measurement gives 1.97×10^8 m/s for the speed of light in a piece of glass. What is the dielectric constant of this glass at optical frequencies?

Section 34-6 Properties of Electromagnetic Waves

20. What are the wavelengths of (a) a 100-MHz FM radio wave, (b) a 3.0-GHz radar wave, (c) a 6.0×10^{14}-Hz light wave, and (d) a 1.0×10^{18}-Hz X ray?

21. A 60-Hz power line emits electromagnetic radiation. What is the wavelength?

22. Antennas for transmitting and receiving electromagnetic radiation usually have typical dimensions on the order of half a wavelength. Look at a TV antenna, and estimate the wavelength and frequency of a TV signal.

23. A CB radio antenna is a vertical rod 2.75 m high. If this length is one-fourth of the CB wavelength, what is the CB frequency?

24. A microwave oven operates at 2.4 GHz. What is the distance between wave crests in the oven?

25. What would be the electric field strength in an electromagnetic wave whose magnetic field equalled that of Earth, about 50 μT?

26. Dielectric breakdown in air occurs at an electric field strength of about 3×10^6 V/m. What would be the peak magnetic field in an electromagnetic wave with this value for its peak electric field?

27. A radio receiver can detect signals with electric fields as low as 320 μV/m. What is the corresponding magnetic field?

Section 34-8 Polarization

28. An electromagnetic wave is propagating in the z direction. What is its polarization direction, if its magnetic field is in the y direction?

29. Polarized light is incident on a sheet of polarizing material, and only 20% of the light gets through. What is the angle between the electric field and the polarization axis of the material?

30. Vertically polarized light passes through a polarizer whose polarization axis is oriented at 70° to the vertical. What fraction of the incident intensity emerges from the polarizer?

31. A polarizer blocks 75% of a polarized light beam. What is the angle between the beam's polarization and the polarizer's axis?

32. An electro-optic modulator is supposed to switch a laser beam between fully off and fully on, as its crystal rotates the beam polarization by 90° when a voltage is applied. But a power-supply failure results in only enough voltage for a 72° beam rotation. What fraction of the laser light is transmitted when it is supposed to be fully on?

33. Unpolarized light of intensity S_0 passes first through a polarizer with its polarization axis vertical, then through one with its axis at 35° to the vertical. What is the light intensity after the second polarizer?

34. Vertically polarized light passes through two polarizers, the first at 60° to the vertical and the second at 90° to the vertical. What fraction of the light gets through?

35. Unpolarized light with intensity S_0 passes through a stack of five polarizing sheets, each with its axis rotated 20° with respect to the previous one. What is the intensity of the light emerging from the stack?

36. Unpolarized light of intensity S_0 is incident on a "sandwich" of three polarizers. The outer two have their transmission axes perpendicular, while the middle one has its axis at 45° to the others. What is the light intensity emerging from this "sandwich?"

37. Polarized light with average intensity S_0 passes through a sheet of polarizing material which is rotating at 10 rev/s. At time $t = 0$ the polarization axis is aligned with the incident polarization. Write an expression for the transmitted intensity as a function of time.

Section 34-10 Energy in Electromagnetic Waves

38. A typical laboratory electric field is 1000 V/m. What is the average intensity of an electromagnetic wave with this value for its peak field?

39. What would be the average intensity of a laser beam so strong that its electric field produced dielectric breakdown of air (which requires $E_p = 3 \times 10^6$ V/m)?

40. Estimate the peak electric field inside a 625-W microwave oven under the simplifying approximation that the microwaves propagate as a plane wave through the oven's 750-cm^2 cross-sectional area.

41. A radio receiver can pick up signals with peak electric fields as low as 450 μV/m. What is the average intensity of such a signal?

42. Show that the electric and magnetic energy densities in an electromagnetic wave are equal.

43. A laser blackboard pointer delivers 0.10 mW average power in a beam 0.90 mm in diameter. Find (a) the average intensity, (b) the peak electric field, and (c) the peak magnetic field.

44. The laser of Example 34-6 produces a spot 80 cm in diameter at its target. What are the rms electric and magnetic fields at the target?

45. The United States' safety standard for continuous exposure to microwave radiation is 10 mW/cm^2. The glass door of a microwave oven measures 40 cm by 17 cm and is covered with a metal screen that blocks microwaves. What fraction of the oven's 625-W microwave power can leak through the door window without exceeding the safe exposure to someone right outside the door? Assume the power leaks uniformly through the window area.

46. A 1.0-kW radio transmitter broadcasts uniformly in all directions. What is the intensity of its signal at a distance of 5.0 km from the transmitter?

47. Use the fact that sunlight intensity at Earth's orbit is 1368 W/m^2 to calculate the Sun's total power output.

48. About two-thirds of the solar energy at Earth's orbit reaches the planet's surface. At what rate is solar energy incident on the entire Earth? See the previous problem,

and compare your result with the roughly 10^{13} W rate at which humanity consumes energy.

49. During its 1989 encounter with Neptune, the Voyager 2 spacecraft was 4.5×10^9 km from Earth (Fig. 34-32). Its images of Neptune were broadcast by a radio transmitter with a mere 21-W average power output. What would be (a) the average intensity and (b) the peak electric field received at Earth if the transmitter broadcast equally in all directions? (The received signal was actually somewhat stronger because Voyager used a directional antenna.)

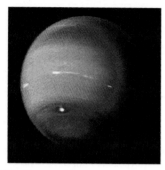

FIGURE 34-32 Neptune, photographed by the Voyager II spacecraft when it was 4.5×10^9 km from Earth. How long did it take the radio signal carrying this image to reach Earth? (Problem 49)

50. A quasar 10 billion light-years from Earth appears the same brightness as a star 50,000 light-years away. How does the power output of the quasar compare with that of the star?

51. At 1.5 km from the transmitter, the peak electric field of a radio wave is 350 mV/m. (a) What is the transmitter's power output, assuming it broadcasts uniformly in all directions? (b) What is the peak electric field 10 km from the transmitter?

52. The peak electric field at a point 25 m from a point source of electromagnetic waves is 4.2 kV/m. What is the peak magnetic field 1.0 m from the source?

53. A typical fluorescent lamp is a little over 1 m long and a few cm in diameter. How do you expect the light intensity to vary with distance (a) near the lamp but not near either end and (b) far from the lamp?

Section 34-11 Wave Momentum and Radiation Pressure

54. A camera flash delivers 2.5 kW of light power for 1.0 ms (Fig. 34-33). Find (a) the total energy and (b) the total momentum carried by the flash.

55. What is the radiation pressure exerted on a light-absorbing surface by a laser beam whose intensity is 180 W/cm²?

56. A laser beam shines vertically upward. What laser power is necessary for this beam to support a flat piece of aluminum foil with mass 30 μg and diameter equal to that of the beam? Assume the foil reflects all the light.

FIGURE 34-33 How much energy and momentum are in light from the camera flash? (Problem 54)

57. The average intensity of noonday sunlight is about 1 kW/m². What is the radiation force on a solar collector measuring 60 cm by 2.5 m if it is oriented at right angles to the incident light and absorbs all the light?

58. Serious proposals have been made to "sail" spacecraft to the outer solar system using the pressure of sunlight. How much sail area must a 1000-kg spacecraft have if its acceleration at Earth's orbit is to be 1 m/s²? Assume the sails are made from reflecting material. You can neglect the Sun's gravity. (Why?)

59. A 65-kg astronaut is floating in empty space. If the astronaut shines a 1.0-W flashlight in a fixed direction, how long will it take the astronaut to accelerate to a speed of 10 m/s?

60. A "photon rocket" emits a beam of light instead of the hot gas of an ordinary rocket. How powerful a light source would be needed for a photon rocket with thrust equal to that of a space shuttle (35 MN)? Compare your answer with humanity's total electric power-generating capability, about 10^{12} W.

Paired Problems

(Both problems in a pair involve the same principles and techniques. If you can get the first problem, you should be able to solve the second one.)

61. Find the peak electric and magnetic fields 1.5 m from a 60-W light bulb that radiates equally in all directions.

62. At 4.6 km from a radio transmitter, the peak electric field in the radio wave measures 380 mV/m. What is the transmitter's power, assuming it broadcasts equally in all directions?

63. Unpolarized light is incident on two polarizers with their axes at 45°. What fraction of the incident light gets through?

64. Find the angle between two polarizers if unpolarized light incident on the pair emerges with 10% of its incident intensity.

65. What is the radiation force on the door of a microwave oven if 625 W of microwave power hits the door at right angles and is reflected?
66. What is the power output of a laser whose beam exerts a 55-mN force on an absorbing object oriented at right angles to the beam? The object is larger than the beam's cross section.
67. A 60-W light bulb is 6.0 cm in diameter. What is the radiation pressure on an opaque object at the bulb's surface?
68. A white dwarf star is approximately the size of Earth but radiates about as much energy as the Sun. Estimate the radiation pressure on an absorbing object at the white dwarf's surface.

Supplementary Problems

69. Maxwell's equations in a dielectric resemble those in vacuum (Equations 34-6 through 34-9), but with ϕ_E in Ampère's law replaced by $\kappa\phi_E$, where κ is the dielectric constant introduced in Chapter 26. Show that the speed of electromagnetic waves in such a dielectric is $c/\sqrt{\kappa}$.
70. Use appropriate data from Appendix E to calculate the radiation pressure on a light-absorbing object at the Sun's surface.
71. A radar system produces pulses consisting of 100 full cycles of a sinusoidal 70-GHz electromagnetic wave. The average power while the transmitter is on is 45 MW, and the waves are confined to a beam 20 cm in diameter. Find (a) the peak electric field, (b) the wavelength, (c) the total energy in a pulse, and (d) the total momentum in a pulse. (e) If the transmitter produces 1000 pulses per second, what is its average power output?
72. In a stack of polarizing sheets, each sheet has its polarization axis rotated 14° with respect to the preceding sheet. If the stack passes 37% of the incident, unpolarized light, how many sheets does it contain?
73. The peak electric field measured at 8.0 cm from a light source is 150 W/m², while at 12 cm it measures 122 W/m². Describe the shape of the source.
74. Show that Equations 34-12b and 34-13 may be combined to yield a wave equation like Equation 16-13. *Hint:* Take the partial derivative of one equation with respect to x and of the other with respect to t, and use the fact that

$$\frac{\partial}{\partial x}\left(\frac{\partial f}{\partial t}\right) = \frac{\partial}{\partial t}\left(\frac{\partial f}{\partial x}\right)$$

for any well-behaved function $f(x, t)$.
75. Studies of the origin of the solar system suggest that sufficiently small particles might be blown out of the solar system by the force of sunlight. To see how small such particles must be, compare the force of sunlight with the force of gravity, and solve for the particle radius at which the two are equal. Assume the particles are spherical and have density 2 g/cm³. Why do you not need to worry about the distance from the Sun?
76. A cylindrical resistor of length ℓ, radius a, and resistance R carries a current I. Calculate the electric and magnetic fields at the surface of the resistor, assuming the electric field is uniform throughout, including at the surface. Calculate the Poynting vector, and show that it points into the resistor. Calculate the flux of the Poynting vector (that is, $\int \mathbf{S} \cdot d\mathbf{A}$) over the surface of the resistor to get the rate of electromagnetic energy flow into the resistor, and show that the result is just I^2R. Your result shows that the energy heating the resistor comes from the fields surrounding it. These fields are sustained by the source of electrical energy that drives the current.

PART 4 *Cumulative Problems*

These problems combine material from chapters throughout the entire part or, in addition, from chapters in earlier parts, or they present special challenges.

1. An air-insulated parallel-plate capacitor has plate area 100 cm² and spacing 0.50 cm. The capacitor is charged and then disconnected from the charging battery. A thin-walled, nonconducting box of the same dimensions as the capacitor is filled with water at 20.00°C. The box is released at the edge of the capacitor and moves without friction into the capacitor (Fig. 1). When it reaches equilibrium the water temperature is 21.50°. What was the original voltage on the capacitor?

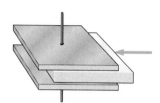

FIGURE 1 Cumulative Problem 1.

2. A wire of length ℓ and resistance R is formed into a closed rectangular loop twice as long as it is wide. It is mounted on a nonconducting horizontal axle parallel to its longer dimension, as shown in Fig. 2. A uniform magnetic field **B** points into the page, as shown. A long string of negligible mass is wrapped many times around a drum of radius a attached to the axle, and a mass m is attached to the string. When the mass is released it falls and eventually reaches a speed that, averaged over one cycle of the loop's rotation, is constant from one rotation to the next. Find an expression for that average terminal speed.

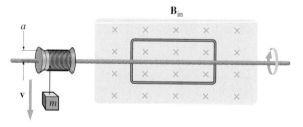

FIGURE 2 Cumulative Problem 2.

3. Five wires of equal length 25 cm and resistance 10 Ω are connected as shown in Fig. 3. Two solenoids, each 10 cm in diameter, extend a long way perpendicular to the page. The magnetic fields of both solenoids point out of the page; the field strength in the left-hand solenoid is increasing at

50 T/s while that in the right-hand solenoid is decreasing at 30 T/s. Find the current in the resistance wire shared by both triangles. Which way does the current flow?

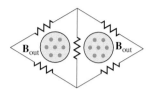

FIGURE 3 Cumulative Problem 3.

4. A long solenoid of length ℓ and radius R has a total of N turns. The solenoid current is increasing linearly with time: $I(t) = bt$, where b is a constant. (a) Find an expression for the rate at which the magnetic energy in the solenoid is increasing. (b) Find an expression for the induced electric field at the inner edge of the solenoid coils. (c) Evaluate the Poynting vector at the inner edge of the coils, and show by integration that electromagnetic energy is flowing into the solenoid at a rate equal to the buildup of magnetic energy.

5. A coaxial cable consists of an inner conductor of radius a and an outer conductor of radius b; the space between the conductors is filled with insulation of dielectric constant κ (Fig. 4). The cable's axis is the z axis. The cable is used to carry electromagnetic energy from a radio transmitter to a broadcasting antenna. The electric field between the conductors points radially from the axis, and is given by $E = E_0(a/r)\cos(kz - \omega t)$. The magnetic field encircles the axis, and is given by $B = B_0(a/r)\cos(kz - \omega t)$. Here E_0, B_0, k, and ω are constants. Show, using appropriate closed surfaces and loops, that these fields satisfy Maxwell's equations. Your result shows that the cable acts as a "waveguide," confining an electromagnetic wave to the space between the conductors.

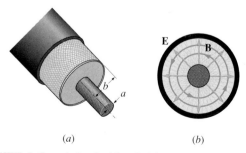

(a)   *(b)*

FIGURE 4 Cumulative Problem 5. (*a*) A coaxial cable. (*b*) Cross section, showing the electric and magnetic fields. The fields also vary with position z along the cable axis, according to the equations given.

Part Five

Optics

In "Prismatic Abstract," multiple light beams converge on a prism to create a dazzlingly colorful effect. Photographic artist Pete Saloutous exploited the principles of optics in creating this work.

Imagine a world without light. We see because light reflects off objects; our eyes form images because light refracts in our corneas and lenses; and the more subtle effect of interference lets us make some of the most precise measurements possible and is behind the operation of everyday technologies like compact discs. Although the behavior of light is ultimately grounded in Maxwell's equations of electromagnetism, we can learn much about light from the simpler perspective of optics. The next three chapters explore the behavior of light, images and optical instruments, and the phenomena of interference.

35 Reflection and Refraction

Reflection and refraction guide light in a wide range of natural and technological applications. Here the image of a bee's head appears in a large-scale version of the optical fibers that are essential to modern communications.

Maxwell's brilliant work shows that the phenomena of **optics**—that is, the behavior of light—are manifestations of the laws of electromagnetism. Except in the atomic realm, where it is necessary to use quantum mechanics, all optical phenomena can be understood in terms of electromagnetic wave fields as described by Maxwell's equations. But often we need not resort to the full electromagnetic or even wave description of light to understand optics.

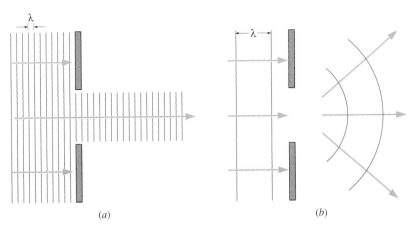

FIGURE 35-1 Light waves incident on an opaque barrier with a hole in it. (*a*) When the hole diameter is much greater than the wavelength λ, light emerges from the hole in essentially a straight line. In this case it is appropriate to treat the light as traveling in straight rays except where it actually hits something. (*b*) When the hole diameter is comparable to or smaller than the wavelength, then interference causes the wavefronts to bend, and the ray approximation is no longer adequate.

When the objects with which light—or, for that matter, any other wave—interacts are much larger than the wavelength, then to a good approximation the light travels in straight lines called rays (Fig. 35-1). Geometrical optics is the study of light under conditions when the ray approximation is valid. In this chapter we show how geometrical optics describes the behavior of light at interfaces between two different materials. In the next chapter we will show how geometrical optics explains optical systems including mirrors, lenses, the human eye, and many optical instruments.

35-1 REFLECTION AND TRANSMISSION

When a light ray propagating in one medium strikes the interface with a second medium, some light may be **reflected** back into the original medium and some **transmitted** into the new medium. Properties of the two materials, and the propagation direction of the incident light, determine the details of the reflection and transmission.

Some materials—notably metals—reflect nearly all the light incident on them. It's no coincidence that these materials are also good electrical conductors. The oscillating electric field of a light wave drives the metal's free electrons into oscillatory motion, and this accelerated motion, in turn, produces electromagnetic waves. The effect of all the oscillating electrons together is simply to reradiate the wave back into the original medium. Ultimately, that's why metals appear shiny.

In other materials, the atomic and molecular configurations are such that the material absorbs most of the incident light energy. Such materials therefore appear dark and opaque. Since an opaque material basically destroys light that's transmitted into it by converting the light to other forms of energy, these materials play little role in our exploration of optics.

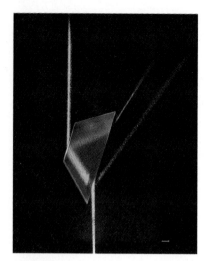

FIGURE 35-2 A laser beam incident on a glass prism shows partial reflection and partial transmission at the interfaces between air and glass. Can you tell which is the incident beam?

Still other materials are essentially transparent, allowing light to propagate with little energy loss. These materials are generally insulators whose electrons, bound to individual atoms, cannot respond freely to the fields of an incident wave. The electrons do respond in a more limited way, however, effectively producing oscillating molecular dipoles. Although a microscopic description of this process is complicated, the net effect in most simple dielectric materials is a reduction in the propagation speed of electromagnetic waves from the speed in a vacuum c, as wave energy is absorbed and reradiated by the molecular dipoles.

In this chapter we explore the processes that occur at the interfaces between transparent and reflective materials and between different transparent materials. Reflection is the significant process in the former case, while in the latter both reflection and transmission generally occur (Fig. 35-2).

35-2 REFLECTION

Reflection returns some or all of the light incident on an interface to its original medium. Whether the reflection is essentially complete, as from a metal, or partial, as from a transparent material, it satisfies the same geometrical condition. Experiment—as well as analysis based on Maxwell's equations—shows that the incident ray, the reflected ray, and the normal to the interface between the two materials all lie in the same plane, and that the angle θ_1' that the reflected ray makes with the normal is equal to the angle θ_1 made by the incident ray (Fig. 35-3a). That is,

$$\theta_1' = \theta_1, \tag{35-1}$$

where the subscript 1 designates angles in the first medium. These angles are designated the **angle of reflection** and **angle of incidence**, respectively.

When a beam of parallel light rays reflects off a smooth surface, each ray in the beam reflects at the same angle, and the entire beam is thus reflected without distortion (Fig. 35-3b). This process is called **specular reflection**. But if the surface is rough, then individual rays, while still obeying Equation 35-1, reflect from differently oriented pieces of the surface. As a result the reflection is **diffuse**, with the original beam spreading in all directions (Fig. 35-3c). White wall paint is a good example of a diffuse reflector, while the aluminum or silver coating of a mirror is an excellent specular reflector. When we speak of reflection we generally mean specular reflection.

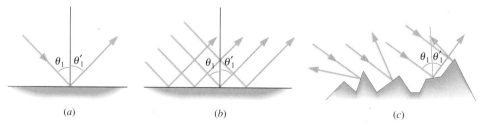

FIGURE 35-3 (a) The angles of reflection and incidence are equal. (b) In specular reflection, a smooth surface reflects a light beam undistorted. (c) A rough surface results in diffuse reflection. The law of reflection still holds for each individual ray.

| **EXAMPLE 35-1** | *The Corner Reflector* |

Two mirrors are joined at right angles, as shown in Fig. 35-4. Show that any light ray incident in the plane of the page will return antiparallel to its incident direction.

Solution

The law of reflection ensures that the two angles marked θ in Fig. 35-4 are equal, as are the two marked ϕ. But the mirrors make a 90° angle, and therefore $\phi = 90° - \theta$. The incident and first reflected ray make an angle 2θ, while the first reflected ray and the outgoing ray make an angle $2\phi = 180° - 2\theta$. Thus these two angles sum to 180°, which shows that the incident and outgoing rays are antiparallel. This result holds regardless of the actual value of the incidence angle θ.

Adding a third mirror at right angles to the other two makes a corner reflector that returns any beam in the direction from which it came—regardless of the orientation of the beam or the reflector (Fig. 35-5*b*). Corner reflectors, often made with prisms rather than mirrors, are widely used in optics. A corner

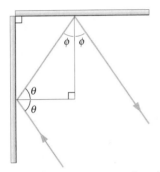

FIGURE 35-4 Two-dimensional corner reflector, made from two mirrors at right angles. Any ray incident in the horizontal plane returns parallel to its original direction.

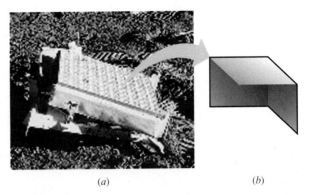

(*a*)   (*b*)

FIGURE 35-5 (*a*) Astronauts left this array of corner reflectors on the moon. Reflecting pulses of laser light off the array allows determination of the moon's position to within 15 cm. (*b*) Each reflector is functionally equivalent to three mutually perpendicular mirrors, although the reflectors are actually made from partial cubes of glass and work by the mechanism of total internal reflection that we'll explore in Section 35-4.

reflector left on the moon allows laser-based measurements of the moon's distance to within about 15 cm (Fig. 35-5*a*).

EXERCISE Two mirrors make an angle of 135°. A light ray is incident on the first mirror at an angle of 60° to the mirror's normal. Find (a) the angle of incidence on the second mirror and (b) the angle between the original incident beam and the final outgoing beam.

Answers: (a) 75°; (b) 90°

Some problems similar to Example 35-1: 2, 4, 5

35-3 REFRACTION

Figures 35-2 and 35-6 show that light passing between two transparent media is partially reflected and partially transmitted at their interface. In addition, the transmitted beam changes direction at the interface—a phenomenon known as **refraction**.

Physically, refraction occurs because the wave speeds in the two media are different. That difference results from delays introduced by the interaction of the electromagnetic wave fields with atomic electrons. But the wave frequency

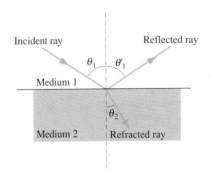

FIGURE 35-6 Reflection and refraction at an interface. This case, where the refracted ray is bent *toward* the normal, occurs when medium 2 has a higher refractive index and therefore a lower wave speed. Angles θ_1, θ_1', and θ_2 are, respectively, the angles of incidence, reflection, and refraction.

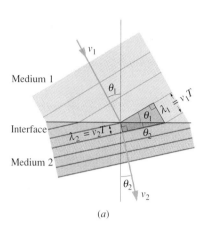

(a)

(b)

FIGURE 35-7 (*a*) Waves refract at an interface because wave speeds—and therefore the wave-lengths—are different in the two media. Two shaded triangles have a common hypotenuse, whose length is $vT/\sin\theta$, where v and θ are taken on either side of the interface. (*b*) Water waves refract as they pass over a triangular patch of shallower water. Note the decreased wavelength and different orientations of the waves within the shallow region. Reflection at the interfaces has re-sulted in waves propagating in several directions. (Wave speed in shallow water depends on depth, so a change in depth corresponds to a change in medium for light waves.)

15.1, 15.2

Reflection and Refraction

f—and thus the wave period $T = 1/f$—must be the same on both sides of the interface; otherwise, on one side of the interface more wave crests would pass in a given time than on the other side, implying the creation or destruction of waves at the interface. In Fig. 35-7a waves in medium 1 travel at speed v_1, and the wavelength—the distance between wave crests—is therefore $v_1 T$. We'll assume that in medium 2 the speed has some lower value v_2, so the wavelength $v_2 T$ is correspondingly shorter. The shaded triangles in Fig. 35-7a are right triangles with a common hypotenuse, and the ratio of the opposite side to the length of this hypotenuse defines the sines of the angles θ_1 and θ_2. Equating expressions for the hypotenuse length (opposite side divided by sine) in terms of these two angles gives

$$\frac{v_1 T}{\sin\theta_1} = \frac{v_2 T}{\sin\theta_2},$$

or

$$\frac{\sin\theta_2}{\sin\theta_1} = \frac{v_2}{v_1}.$$

We characterize the effect of a transparent medium on light through its **index of refraction**, n, defined as the ratio of the speed c of light in vacuum to the speed v of light in the medium:

$$n = \frac{c}{v}. \qquad \text{(index of refraction)} \qquad (35\text{-}2)$$

(Again there's an electromagnetic connection: the index of refraction is just the square root of the dielectric constant that we introduced in Chapter 26. But don't try to calculate refractive indices from the dielectric constants of

Table 26-1; the dielectric constant is frequency dependent, and its value at optical frequencies is significantly different from the DC values of Table 26-1.) Table 35-1 lists some indices of refraction. Note that for gases the index of refraction is essentially 1, the same as that of vacuum.

Using the definition 35-2 in our ratio of the sines of the angles of refraction and incidence, and then cross multiplying, gives **Snell's law**:

$$n_1 \sin \theta_1 = n_2 \sin \theta_2. \quad \text{(Snell's law)} \quad (35\text{-}3)$$

This law was developed geometrically in 1621 by Willebrord van Roijen Snell of the Netherlands and described analytically in the 1630s by René Descartes of France, where it is known to this day as Descartes' law. It allows us to predict what will happen to light at an interface, provided we know the refractive indices of the two media. As a special case, note that when $n_1 = n_2$ there's no change in angle; in general, the more different the refractive indices of the two media, the greater the change in angle.

Snell's law applies whether light goes from a medium of lower to higher refractive index or the reverse, as you can see by reversing the path of the light in Fig. 35-7. In the former case the refracted ray bends *toward* the normal, while in the latter case it bends *away* from the normal. Example 35-2 treats both cases.

TABLE 35-1 *Indices of Refraction**

SUBSTANCE	INDEX OF REFRACTION, n
Gases	
Air	1.000293
Carbon dioxide	1.00045
Liquids	
Water	1.333
Ethyl alcohol	1.361
Glycerine	1.473
Benzene	1.501
Diiodomethane	1.738
Solids	
Ice (H_2O)	1.309
Polystyrene	1.49
Glass	1.5–1.9
Sodium chloride (NaCl)	1.544
Diamond (C)	2.419
Rutile (TiO_2)	2.62

*At 1 atm pressure and temperatures ranging from 0°C to 20°C, measured at a wavelength of 589 nm (the yellow line of sodium).

EXAMPLE 35-2	*In and Out: Parallel Rays*

In Fig. 35-8, a light ray propagating in air strikes a transparent slab of thickness d and refractive index n with incidence angle θ_1. Show that the ray emerges from the slab propagating parallel to its original direction.

Solution

Applying Snell's law to the upper interface gives

$$\sin \theta_2 = \frac{\sin \theta_1}{n},$$

where we've taken $n_1 = 1$ for air and $n_2 = n$ for the slab. At the lower interface, with the light going from the slab to air, we have $n_1 = n$ and $n_2 = 1$, so Snell's law gives

$$\sin \theta_4 = n \sin \theta_3.$$

But the slab faces are parallel so, as the figure suggests, $\theta_3 = \theta_2$. Combining our two versions of Snell's law then gives

$$\sin \theta_4 = n \left(\frac{\sin \theta_1}{n} \right) = \sin \theta_1,$$

showing that the incident and outgoing rays are indeed parallel. They are, however, displaced by the distance x shown in the figure. You can find that displacement in Problem 54.

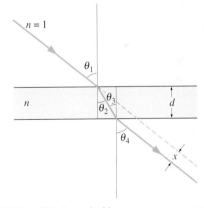

FIGURE 35-8 A light beam incident on a transparent slab emerges with its original direction, but is displaced from its original path.

EXERCISE A piece of glass with $n = 1.52$ is immersed in diiodomethane. A light ray strikes the glass with incidence angle 40°. Find the angle the refracted beam in the glass makes with the normal to the interface.

Answer: 47.3°

Some problems similar to Example 35-2: 11, 13, 54

EXAMPLE 35-3	CD Music

The laser beam that "reads" information from a compact disc is 0.737 mm wide at the point where it strikes the underside of the disc and forms a converging cone with half-angle 27°, as shown in Fig. 35-9. It then travels through a 1.2-mm-thick layer of transparent plastic with refractive index 1.55 before reaching the very thin, reflective information layer near the disc's top surface. What is the beam diameter (d in Fig. 35-9) at the information layer?

Solution

Figure 35-9 shows that $d = D - 2x$, where $D = 0.737$ mm is the beam diameter as it hits the disc. From the figure we also see that $x = t \tan\theta_2$, where $t = 1.2$ mm is the thickness of the plastic. Finally, Snell's law gives $\theta_2 = \sin^{-1}\left(\dfrac{\sin\theta_1}{n}\right)$, where we set the refractive index of air to 1. Putting these relations together gives

$$d = D - 2t \tan\left[\sin^{-1}\left(\frac{\sin\theta_1}{n}\right)\right]$$

$$= 737\ \mu\text{m} - (2)(1200\ \mu\text{m}) \tan\left[\sin^{-1}\left(\frac{\sin 27°}{1.55}\right)\right]$$

$$= 1.8\ \mu\text{m},$$

which is a little larger than the "pits" cut into the CD to store its information. This narrowing of the beam plays a crucial role in keeping CDs noise free. The tiniest dust speck would blot out information at the μm-scale information layer, but at the point where the laser beam actually enters the disc—the closest dust can get to the information layer—it would take mm-size dust to cause problems.

In Chapter 37 we'll see more on how optical phenomena are at the heart of CD technology.

EXERCISE Figure 35-10 shows a polystyrene cylinder whose height is equal to its diameter. What is the maximum incidence angle θ_1 at which a light ray striking the top center of the cylinder will emerge through the bottom without first striking the side? The medium surrounding the cylinder is air.

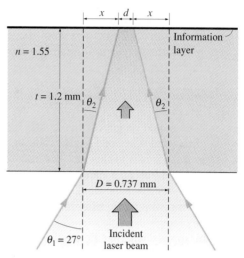

FIGURE 35-9 Section through a compact disc, showing convergence of the laser beam to a narrow spot at the information layer. All CDs share a common refractive index of 1.55 (Example 35-3).

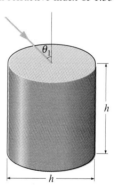

FIGURE 35-10 What is the maximum θ_1 for which the beam will emerge through the bottom of the polystyrene cylinder?

Answer: 42°

Some problems similar to Example 35-3: 14, 15, 17, 18

We derived Snell's law using Fig. 35-7a, which shows the wavelength change that occurs as the wave speed changes between two media. There we argued that the frequencies in the two media must be the same. But wavelength, frequency, and wave speed are related by $\lambda f = v$; therefore, since wave speeds depend inversely on refractive index (Equation 35-2), so do the wavelengths. Thus the wavelengths in the two media are related by

$$\frac{\lambda_2}{\lambda_1} = \frac{n_1}{n_2}. \tag{35-4}$$

EXAMPLE 35-4	*Light and Diamond*

Light with wavelength 589 nm in vacuum enters a diamond. Find the light speed and wavelength in the diamond.

Solution

Equation 35-2 gives

$$v = \frac{c}{n} = \frac{3.00 \times 10^8 \text{ m/s}}{2.419} = 1.24 \times 10^8 \text{ m/s} .$$

The refractive index of vacuum is 1, so Equation 35-4 gives

$$\lambda_{\text{diamond}} = \frac{\lambda_{\text{vacuum}}}{n} = \frac{589 \text{ nm}}{2.419} = 243 \text{ nm} .$$

The wavelength and speed are reduced by the same factor, as they must be to keep the wave frequency unchanged.

EXERCISE Microwaves propagate through glass at about 1.4×10^8 m/s. What is the refractive index of glass at microwave frequencies?

Answer: 2.14

Some problems similar to Example 35-4: 8, 9, 19

Got It!

Figure 35-11 shows the path of a light ray through three different media. Rank the media according to their indices of refraction.

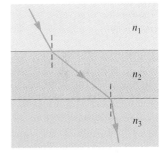

FIGURE 35-11 How do the refractive indices compare?

Multiple Refractions

Engineered optical systems often use several layers of refractive material to minimize reflective losses and certain types of distortion. To describe the path of a light ray in such a system, we need only apply Snell's law at each of the interfaces using the appropriate pair of refractive indices (Fig. 35-12a). When the layers are parallel the angular deflection of a light ray is the same as if it had gone through a single interface from the first medium to the last (see Problem 48). In many natural situations, including the human eye and Earth's atmosphere, the index of refraction is a continuously varying function of position (Fig. 35-12b). We can approximate such a case as a sequence of thin layers, each with a different refractive index. Going toward the limit of infinitely many infinitesimal layers gets us arbitrarily close to the exact solution, in which the

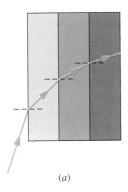

(a)

(b)

FIGURE 35-12 (a) Light propagating through a series of slabs with increasing refractive indices. At each interface the light bends more toward the normal. (b) Light follows a curved path in a medium with a continuously increasing refractive index.

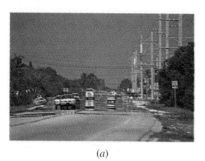

(a)

FIGURE 35-13 (a) Mirages on a hot road. (b) The mirage occurs because hot air near the highway surface has a lower refractive index, resulting in a curved path for the light. The apparent position of the vehicle is not its actual position. Can you see why it appears upside down?

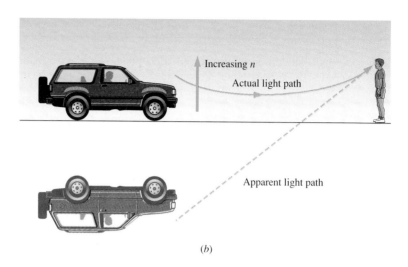

(b)

light follows a curved path. The mirage shown in Fig. 35-13 results from the fact that the refractive index of air is temperature dependent, causing the path of light rays to bend continuously.

35-4 TOTAL INTERNAL REFLECTION

Figure 35-14 shows light propagating inside a glass block and striking the interface with the surrounding air. Since air's refractive index is lower than that of glass, rays are bent *away* from the normal as they leave the glass. As the incidence angle increases, so does the angle of refraction—and Snell's law shows that the latter is always greater than the incidence angle. So at some incidence angle (see ray 3 in Fig. 35-14) the angle of refraction reaches 90°. What then?

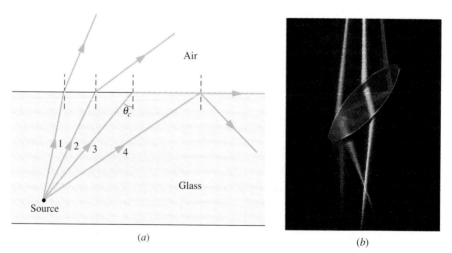

(a)   (b)

FIGURE 35-14 (a) Light propagating inside a glass block is refracted away from the normal at the glass-air interface. Ray 3, incident at the critical angle, just skims along the interface. At higher incidence angles, as with ray 4, the light undergoes total internal reflection at the interface. Not shown are weak reflected rays at angles less than the critical angle. (b) Three light beams strike a lens and are refracted at the air-glass interface. The red beam strikes the subsequent glass-air interface at an incidence angle greater than the critical angle and undergoes total internal reflection.

If the incidence angle is increased further, we find that the light is *totally* reflected at the interface. (There is always *some* reflection back into the glass, but now it's *all* reflected.) This phenomenon is called **total internal reflection**, and the incidence angle at which it first occurs is the **critical angle**, θ_c. We can find θ_c by setting $\theta_2 = 90°$ (i.e., $\sin\theta_2 = 1$) in Snell's law (Equation 35-3). The critical angle is then θ_1, and we have

$$\sin\theta_c = \frac{n_2}{n_1}. \qquad (35\text{-}5)$$

Since the sine of an angle cannot exceed 1, we must have $n_2 \leq n_1$ in order for this equation to have a solution. Thus, total internal reflection occurs only when light propagating in one medium strikes an interface with a medium of lower refractive index, and it occurs whenever the incidence angle exceeds the critical angle. You can simulate total internal reflection with ActivPhysics Activity 15.1, by clicking on the "Larger *n* region" button and varying the incidence angle until the refracted ray disappears.

Total internal reflection makes uncoated glass an excellent reflector when it's oriented appropriately (Fig. 35-15). Corner reflectors (Example 35-1) use total internal reflection in solid cubes of glass, rather than individual mirrors at right angles. For an observer inside a medium of higher refractive index, the existence of the critical angle affects the view of the outside world, as the example below shows. Finally, total internal reflection is the basis of the optical fibers now widely used in communications.

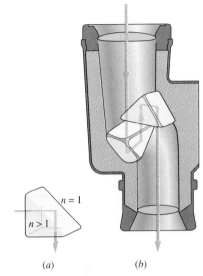

FIGURE 35-15 (*a*) A glass prism redirects light through total internal reflection. (*b*) Binoculars use a pair of prisms to "fold" the light path, allowing a more compact design.

EXAMPLE 35-5	*Whale Watch*

Planeloads of whale watchers fly above the ocean, as shown in Fig. 35-16. A whale looks upward, watching the planes. Within what range of viewing angles can the whale see the planes?

Solution

If the whale emitted light, that light would emerge from the ocean surface only for incidence angles less than the critical angle—that is, those angles within the cone shown in Fig. 35-16. Since the path of light is reversible, the whale can see objects above the surface only when it looks within this cone. For the water-air interface Equation 35-5 gives

$$\theta_c = \sin^{-1}\left(\frac{1}{1.333}\right) = 48.6°,$$

where we found water's refractive index in Table 35-1. The geometry of Fig. 35-16 then shows that this is also the half-angle of the cone, so the whale must look within 48.6° of the vertical to see out.

Can the whale see a plane only if it's *actually* within this angle? No. As the strongly refracted ray from the right-hand plane suggests, the entire outside world appears to the whale compressed into a cone of half-angle θ_c. If the whale looks beyond this cone, it will see instead reflections of objects below the surface.

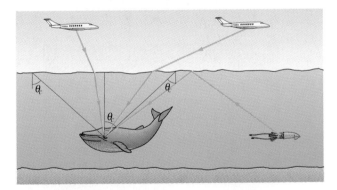

FIGURE 35-16 The whale sees the entire world above the surface in a cone of half-angle θ_c. Looking beyond this cone, it sees reflections of objects below the surface.

EXERCISE A diamond is submerged in water. What is the critical angle at the diamond-water interface?

Answer: 33.4°

Some problems similar to Example 35-5: 22, 23, 26, 28, 33

APPLICATION	*Optical Fibers and Lightwave Communication*

Refraction and total internal reflection are the basis for **optical fibers**, which revolutionized communications in the 1980s. Some three *billion* km of optical fiber were installed in the United States alone during that decade, and today they carry telephone conversations, television signals, computer data, and other information. Undersea fibers link the entire planet in a fiber-optic network.

A typical fiber consists of a glass core only 8 μm in diameter, surrounded by a so-called cladding consisting of glass with a lower refractive index than the core. The propagation of light in the fiber is a process whereby the core-cladding interface guides the light along the fiber. In some fibers this takes place by abrupt internal reflection at the interface (Fig. 35-17), while in others gradual refraction in the cladding guides the light. The glass used in optical fibers is so pure that a 1-km thick slab would appear as transparent as an ordinary window pane. Today's fibers use infrared light at wavelengths of 0.85 μm, 1.31 μm, and 1.55 μm. A recent development are optical fibers that actually regenerate signals as they travel long distances, extracting energy from an additional laser beam; these fibers are now used on some intercontinental and other ultra-long fiber communications systems.

FIGURE 35-18 The thin fiber-optic cable and the much bulkier cable of copper wires carry information at the same rate.

Optical fibers offer several advantages over copper wire or open-air transmission of electromagnetic waves. The main advantage is their very high **bandwidth**—the amount of information they carry per unit time. This large bandwidth results because the information carried on fiber is encoded on infrared radiation with a frequency on the order of 10^{14} Hz—much higher than the microwave frequencies used in conventional communication systems. A single fiber, for example, can carry tens of thousands of telephone conversations (Fig. 35-18).

Fibers are lighter and more rugged than copper cables and are less easy to "tap" illicitly. Because they are insulators, optical fibers are also less susceptible to electrical "noise" and are therefore used to carry information in electrically noisy environments like power plants or high-energy physics laboratories.

Optical fibers play a key role in the global Internet that links nearly all the world's computers. Computers on one floor or within a building may be connected in a small, relatively low-bandwidth network with copper wire. But connections between buildings are nearly always made with optical fibers, linking individual local networks into larger institution-wide networks. Entire institutions—corporations, universities, government laboratories, and the like—are then linked by very high speed fiber-optic "superhighways" that carry the Internet's burgeoning information "traffic."

Optical fiber technology requires more than just fiber: appropriate opto-electronic devices are needed at each end to convert information from light to electrical forms and vice versa. Such devices include miniature lasers made from semiconductors, and high-speed light-sensitive diodes. As the cost of these devices drops, high-speed optical fiber is becoming available to individual homes and offices, allowing nearly instant access to telecommunications, video resources, libraries, and databases.

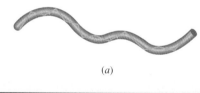

(a)

(b)

FIGURE 35-17 (a) A beam of light undergoes a series of total internal reflections that guide it along an optical fiber. (b) A bundle of actual fibers.

35-5 DISPERSION

Refraction ultimately occurs because of the interaction of electromagnetic wave fields with atomic electrons. Although the details of that interaction require a quantum description, it should not be surprising that the index of refraction depends on frequency. After all, as we found in Chapter 15, the response of a system (here an atom) generally depends on the frequency of the driving force (here the oscillating fields of a wave).

Because the index of refraction depends on frequency, different frequencies—different colors for visible light—will refract through different angles. A light beam containing many colors will therefore spread into its constituent colors, a process called **dispersion** (Fig. 35-19). The classic example of dispersion is Newton's demonstration that white light is really a mixture of all the colors in the visible spectrum. Newton not only broke white light into its constituent colors, as in Fig. 35-19, but he also recombined the colors to produce the original white light.

In most materials in most frequency ranges, the index of refraction increases with increasing frequency and therefore decreases with increasing wavelength (Fig. 35-20). That means colors toward the violet end of the spectrum are refracted through the greatest angles, as is evident in Fig. 35-19.

Dispersion is the basis for the widely used technique of **spectral analysis** or **spectroscopy**, in which substances are identified and characterized by analyzing their **spectra**—meaning the range of wavelengths of electromagnetic radiation they emit, transmit, or absorb. Hot, dense objects, for example, emit a continuous spectrum of radiation, while diffuse gases radiate at only a few specific wavelengths (Fig. 35-21). The existence of those discrete spectra provided some of the strongest evidence for the nature of the atom, and today spectral analysis allows astronomers to identify and measure the abundances of elements in

FIGURE 35-19 Dispersion of white light by a glass prism. The refractive index of the glass is greater at higher frequencies—shorter wavelengths—and therefore results in greater refraction at the blue end of the spectrum. The incident beam comes in from the lower left edge, and a white reflected beam leaves the prism going straight downward. This beam has undergone an additional refraction that has again combined its colors.

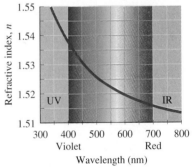

FIGURE 35-20 Index of refraction as a function of wavelength for high-dispersion crown glass.

FIGURE 35-21 (Top) The solar spectrum is an essentially continuous band of wavelengths, produced by the hot, dense gases of the Sun's visible surface. Dark lines are discrete wavelengths absorbed by overlying gases in the solar atmosphere. (Bottom) Spectrum of a diffuse gas—in this case hydrogen—consists of light at discrete wavelengths. The pattern of lines allows identification of the emitting material.

distant astrophysical objects. Geologists use spectral analysis to identify minerals, and chemists use infrared spectra to study molecules. Spectral analysis is a powerful tool in nearly every branch of science. Although early spectroscopes used prisms, most modern instruments use instead diffraction gratings, whose operation we describe in Chapter 37.

Dispersion can be a nuisance in optical systems. Glass lenses, for example, focus different colors at different points, resulting in a distortion known as chromatic aberration. This effect can be minimized by making composite lenses of materials with different refractive indices.

EXAMPLE 35-6	*How Much Dispersion?*

White light strikes the prism in Fig. 35-22 normal to one surface. The prism is made of the glass whose refractive index is plotted in Fig. 35-20. Find the angle between outgoing red (700 nm) and violet (400 nm) light.

Solution
There is no refraction at the air-glass interface since the incident ray is normal to the surface. At the second interface medium 2 is air with $n_2 = 1$, and medium 1 is the glass whose indices at the two wavelengths we can read from Fig. 35-20: $n_{400} = 1.538$, $n_{700} = 1.516$. The geometry of Fig. 35-22 shows that the incidence angle at the second interface is the angle $\alpha = 40°$ at the top of the prism. The angles of refraction are then given by solving Snell's law for the two values of θ_2:

$$\theta_{400} = \sin^{-1}(n_{400}\sin\alpha) = \sin^{-1}[(1.538)(\sin 40°)] = 81.34°,$$

and

$$\theta_{700} = \sin^{-1}(n_{700}\sin\alpha) = \sin^{-1}[(1.516)(\sin 40°)] = 77.02°.$$

The angle between the two outgoing beams is therefore $\theta_{400} - \theta_{700} = 4.32°$, with the violet beam (400 nm) experienc-

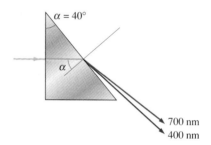

FIGURE 35-22 Example 35-6.

ing the greatest deflection. This 4.32° spread is called the *angular dispersion* of the beam.

EXERCISE If the angle α in Fig. 35-22 is increased, what is the maximum angular dispersion that can be achieved by refracting both the 400 nm and 700 nm beams? At what α does this occur?

Answer: $\Delta\theta = 9.7°$ at $\alpha = \sin^{-1}(1/n_{400}) = 40.556°$

Some problems similar to Example 35-6: 34–38

APPLICATION	*The Rainbow*

Nature provides a beautiful application of dispersion and internal reflection in the rainbow (Fig. 35-23), which occurs when sunlight strikes rain or other water droplets in the air. An observer standing between the Sun and the rain then sees the circular arc of colored bands. Figure 35-24 shows that the center of that arc lies on the line joining the Sun to the observer's eye. That means each observer sees a different rainbow! Furthermore, the rainbow's arc always subtends an angle of approximately 42°. How does the rainbow form, and why does it have this geometry?

Theories of the rainbow date back many centuries. By 1635 Descartes had produced a nearly complete explanation of the rainbow's shape and apparent location, but because he did not

FIGURE 35-23 Reflection, refraction, and dispersion all act to produce a rainbow.

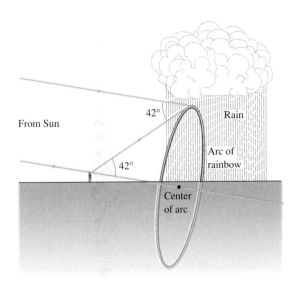

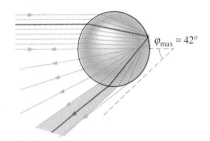

FIGURE 35-26 Parallel rays striking a water drop. The minimum angle through which a ray is deflected is about 138°, corresponding to a maximum of about 42° in the angle ϕ of Fig. 35-25. Furthermore, rays tend to "bunch" at this angle, as suggested by the broad outgoing beam defined by three nearly parallel rays. This "bunching" causes an observer to see a bright arc at 42° from the antisolar direction in Fig. 35-24. The thicker ray undergoes the minimum deviation and has, correspondingly, the maximum ϕ.

FIGURE 35-24 The rainbow is a circular arc located at 42° from the line that includes the Sun, the observer, and the center of the arc. The Sun is so far away that its rays are essentially parallel. Here part of the rainbow is blocked by the ground; however, observers in aircraft can sometimes see the entire circle.

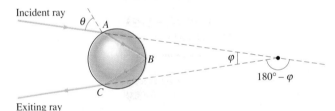

FIGURE 35-25 A light ray passing through a spherical raindrop undergoes refraction at each interface and internal reflection at the back of the drop. (Not shown are the reflected rays at interfaces *A* and *C* and the transmitted ray at interface *B*.) The ray undergoes an overall deflection of $180° - \phi$.

know about dispersion he could not account for the colors. A few years later Newton, in his *Optics,* produced a full explanation.

Figure 35-25 shows a light ray passing through a spherical raindrop. The incidence angle θ in Fig. 35-25 is arbitrary, and

parallel light rays striking the curved surface of the drop will experience a range of values for θ. There will, therefore, be a range of angles ϕ between the incident and outgoing rays. As Fig. 35-26 shows, however, there is a maximum angle ϕ_{max} of about 42° and more light is returned at angles close to ϕ_{max} than at other angles. That's why a bright band—the rainbow—appears in the sky at an angle of about 42° to the direction of the Sun's rays. Problems 58 and 59 show how to find ϕ_{max}.

The "bunching" of light rays near ϕ_{max} explains why a bright band should appear, but why should it be colored? Because the refractive index varies with wavelength, so does ϕ_{max}. Each color will therefore appear brightest at a slightly different angle. For water, the refractive index in the visible region ranges from $n_{red} = 1.330$ to $n_{violet} = 1.342$. Using these values with the results of Problems 58 and 59 yields $\phi_{red} = 42.53°$ and $\phi_{violet} = 40.78°$. Thus the rainbow is seen as a band, itself subtending an angle of about 1.75°, with red at the top.

One occasionally sees a fainter and larger arc above the primary rainbow. This secondary rainbow results from two internal reflections, and as a result the order of its colors is reversed. Problem 60 explores the secondary rainbow.

35-6 REFLECTION AND POLARIZATION

Geometrical optics describes the paths of light rays at interfaces between different media, but doesn't tell how much of the light is reflected and how much transmitted at an interface. Application of Ampère's and Faraday's laws to electromagnetic wave fields at an interface does give that information. We won't undertake the calculation here, but will instead describe briefly the results.

FIGURE 35-27 Reflection in a plate-glass window is especially prominent at oblique incidence angles.

When light is incident on an interface, some fraction of it is reflected. The ratio of the reflected to the incident intensity is called the **reflection coefficient**. In general, the least reflection occurs with normal incidence—i.e., with light incident perpendicular to the interface. For glass with refractive index $n = 1.5$, for example, only about 4 percent of normally incident light is reflected—meaning the reflection coefficient in this case is 0.04. You usually don't notice this faint reflection, except when you're inside a lighted room at night; then there's no light coming through the windows from outside to overwhelm the reflection.

The reflection coefficient generally increases at oblique angles, approaching 1 as the incidence angle approaches 90°. You've undoubtedly experienced this effect when standing in front of a plate-glass window; as you look along the window at an oblique angle, the reflection of objects on your side of the window becomes more prominent (Fig. 35-27).

The Polarizing Angle

Reflection ultimately involves an interaction of the electric field of an incident light wave with electrons near the surface of the reflecting medium. It's not surprising, therefore, that the reflection coefficient depends on the orientation of a light wave's electric field relative to the interface. In Chapter 34 we defined the polarization direction of an electromagnetic wave as the direction of the wave's electric field; thus, the reflection coefficient depends on polarization.

For all but normal incidence, the incident, reflected, and refracted rays are in different directions and together define a plane (see Fig. 35-28, where that plane is the plane of the page). The electric field of the incident light may lie in that plane, or be perpendicular to it, or be at some angle in between. When the field lies in the plane defined by the three rays, there's a special angle at which incident light does not undergo any reflection, and instead is transmitted 100 percent across the interface. This special angle is called the **Brewster angle** or the **polarizing angle**, and designated θ_p. The name "polarizing angle" is apt because if light incident at this angle has a mix of polarizations, only the component with electric field perpendicular to the plane of Fig. 35-28 will be reflected; thus the reflected beam becomes completely polarized.

Why is there no reflection of the preferred polarization at this special angle? In Chapter 34 we saw that electromagnetic waves result from accelerated charge; Fig. 34-23 showed, nevertheless, that no electromagnetic radiation is emitted in the direction of a charged particle's acceleration. Knowing that, we can use Fig. 35-28 to understand the reason for the polarizing angle. For glass with refractive index $n = 1.5$, the polarizing angle is 56.3°. At this incidence angle, Snell's law gives an angle of refraction $\theta_2 = \sin^{-1}(\sin\theta_p/n) = 33.7°$. Now $56.3° + 33.7° = 90°$ and that means, as Fig. 35-28 shows, that any reflected ray would be perpendicular to the refracted ray. But the reflected ray really arises from the acceleration of the electrons in the glass—acceleration

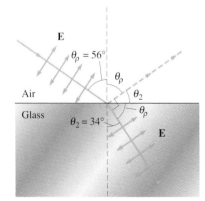

FIGURE 35-28 An electromagnetic wave polarized in the plane of the figure is incident on an interface. When the angles of incidence and refraction sum to 90°, the reflected ray would be in the direction of the electric field in the lower medium. Since there is no radiation in the direction of charged-particle acceleration, there is no reflected ray in this special case. Numbers shown are for an air-glass interface.

which, according to Newton's law of motion, is in the direction of the driving force. But here the driving force comes from the wave's electric field, and with polarization in the plane of Fig. 35-28, that field is itself parallel to the direction the reflected ray would take. But we've seen that there is no radiation in the direction of the acceleration, and hence for this special geometrical condition there is no reflected ray.

Figure 35-28 shows that the condition of no reflection will be met when the angles of incidence and refraction sum to 90°: $\theta_p + \theta_2 = 90°$, where we've set the incidence angle equal to the polarizing angle. This, in turn, implies that $\sin \theta_2 = \cos \theta_p$. But with the incidence angle $\theta_1 = \theta_p$, Snell's law gives $\sin \theta_2 = (n_1/n_2) \sin \theta_p$. Applying our condition $\sin \theta_2 = \cos \theta_p$, we then have $\cos \theta_p = (n_1/n_2) \sin \theta_p$. Multiplying both sides by $n_2/n_1 \cos \theta_p$ then gives

$$\tan \theta_p = \frac{n_2}{n_1}. \qquad (35\text{-}6)$$

For an air-glass interface with $n_1 = 1$ and $n_2 = 1.5$, this equation indeed gives $\theta_p = 56.3°$.

The polarizing angle is important in the construction of lasers, which require nearly loss-free transmission of light reflected from external mirrors back into the medium that generates the laser light. The common red-light helium-neon laser used in physics demonstrations and supermarket scanners, for example, includes a glass tube containing a helium-neon mixture; the ends of the tube are formed at the polarizing angle so that light with the correct polarization enters the tube without reflecting. Because zero reflection occurs only for light polarized in the plane of the incident and refracted rays, the laser itself produces light with this polarization. (We'll see more on how lasers work in Chapter 39 or, for extended-version readers, in Chapter 41).

A phenomenon similar to the polarizing angle occurs for reflection from metals and other surfaces, again because of the interaction of the electric field of the light wave with electrons. Somewhat similarly, scattering of sunlight by air molecules partially polarizes the light. Reduction of glare using Polaroid sunglasses or a camera's polarizing filter works by blocking the component of reflected or scattered light that has the enhanced polarization (Fig. 35-29).

(a)

(b)

FIGURE 35-29 Identical views of a storefront, photographed (a) without and (b) with a polarizing filter. Light reflecting obliquely from the glass is partially polarized. The polarizing filter eliminates this component, allowing the inside of the store to show much more clearly.

CHAPTER SYNOPSIS

Summary

1. **Geometrical optics** treats the behavior of light under the approximation that it travels in straight lines—**rays**—except at interfaces between different materials. This approximation is valid whenever waves interact with systems that are much larger than their wavelength.
2. **Reflection** occurs to some extent at nearly all interfaces. When a light ray reflects, the **angle of incidence** and **angle of reflection**—both measured from the normal to the interface—are equal. **Specular reflection** occurs from smooth surfaces, while rough surfaces produce **diffuse reflection**.
3. **Refraction** is the bending of light at an interface between transparent materials. The directions of the incident and refracted rays are related by **Snell's law**:

$$n_1 \sin \theta_1 = n_2 \sin \theta_2,$$

where θ_1 and θ_2 are the angles of incidence and refraction, respectively. The **indices of refraction** are n_1 and n_2, defined as the ratios of the speed of light in vacuum to the speed in a given medium.
4. **Total internal reflection** occurs when light propagating in a medium with refractive index n_1 is incident on an

interface at an angle greater than the **critical angle** θ_c given by

$$\sin \theta_c = \frac{n_2}{n_1}.$$

Total internal reflection is possible only when $n_2 < n_1$.

5. The index of refraction generally depends on frequency. This results in **dispersion** of the different colors as they refract through different angles. Dispersion is the basis of **spectroscopy**.

6. Some light is usually reflected at an interface, even with a transparent material. Generally, reflection increases as the angle of incidence becomes more oblique. But for the special case of light whose polarization is in the plane defined by incident and refracted rays, there's no reflection when the angle of incidence is equal to the **polarizing angle**, also called the **Brewster angle**. As a result, unpolarized light incident at this angle becomes completely polarized on reflection.

Terms You Should Understand

(Pairs are closely related terms whose distinction is important; number in parentheses is chapter section where term first appears.)

geometrical optics (introduction)
ray (introduction)
angles of incidence, reflection, refraction (35-2, 35-3)
specular reflection, diffuse reflection (35-2)
refraction, index of refraction (35-3)
Snell's law (35-3)

total internal reflection (35-4)
critical angle (35-4)
optical fiber (35-4)
dispersion (35-5)
spectroscopy (35-5)
reflection coefficient (35-6)
polarizing angle (35-6)

Symbols You Should Recognize

θ_1, θ_1', θ_2 (35-2, 35-3)
n (35-3)
θ_c (35-4)
θ_p (35-6)

Problems You Should Be Able to Solve

determining the directions of reflected and refracted rays at interfaces (35-2 and 35-3)
evaluating conditions for total internal reflection (35-4)
analyzing dispersion (35-5)
determining reflected and transmitted intensities at normal incidence (35-6)
evaluating the polarizing angle (35-6)

Limitations to Keep in Mind

Geometrical optics is an approximation valid only when light interacts with systems much larger than its wavelength.
Characterizing the optical properties of a material by a single number, the index of refraction, is a simplification. In many materials optical properties depend on direction, and include absorption as well as transmission.

QUESTIONS

1. Are light rays real? Discuss.
2. It's usually inappropriate to consider low-frequency sound waves as traveling in rays. Why? Why is it more appropriate for high-frequency sound and for light?
3. Describe why a spoon appears bent when it's in a glass of water.
4. Why do a diamond and an identically shaped piece of glass sparkle differently?
5. Specular reflection occurs with "smooth" surfaces. But on the microscopic scale all surfaces are rough. What do you suppose should be the criterion for "smoothness" in dealing with reflection?
6. White light goes from air through a glass slab with parallel surfaces. Will its colors be dispersed when it emerges from the glass?
7. Would light behave as in Fig. 35-15a if the refractive index of the prism were 1.25? Explain.

8. You send white light through two identical glass prisms, oriented as shown in Fig. 35-30. Describe the beam that emerges from the right-hand prism.

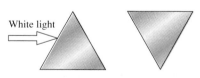

FIGURE 35-30 Question 8.

9. Why can optical fibers carry much more information than copper wires?
10. What would happen if you scratched the outside of the reflecting surface of a prism used for total internal reflection?

11. Lightning produces a sudden burst of static in a nearby radio receiver. The static comprises a broad band of radio frequencies. But in a very distant receiver the "noise" from the flash arrives over an extended time. What does this say about the frequency dependence of the refractive index of Earth's atmosphere for radio waves?

12. What does a fish see as it looks around in directions above the horizontal? Explain.

13. In glass, which end of the visible spectrum has the lowest critical angle for total internal reflection?

14. Looking out the window of a lighted room at night, you see clear reflections of the room's interior. In the daytime those reflections would be much less obvious, yet the reflection coefficient has not changed. Explain.

15. Why can't you walk to the end of the rainbow?

16. What is wrong with the painting in Fig. 35-31? *Hint:* The rainbow subtends a half-angle of 42°.

FIGURE 35-31 What's wrong with this painting (*Niagara,* by Harry Fenn)? (Question 16)

17. Suppose the refractive index of water were not frequency dependent. Would anything like the rainbow occur?

FIGURE 35-32 Question 18.

18. Figure 35-32 shows a ball inside a transparent sphere inside an aquarium tank. The transparent sphere and the tank can each be filled with water. Explain which combination is occurring in each frame.

19. Why are polarizing sunglasses better than glasses that simply cut down on the total amount of light?

20. Does the transmitted intensity always exceed the reflected intensity at an air-glass interface?

21. Under what conditions will the polarizing angle be less than 45°?

PROBLEMS

ActivPhysics can help with these problems:
Activities 15.1, 15.2

Section 35-2 Reflection

1. Through what angle should you rotate a mirror in order that a reflected ray rotate through 30°?

2. The mirrors in Fig. 35-33 make a 60° angle. A light ray enters parallel to the symmetry axis, as shown. (a) How many reflections does it make? (b) Where and in what direction does it exit the mirror system?

3. To what angular accuracy must two ostensibly perpendicular mirrors be aligned in order that an incident ray returns on a path within 1° of its incident direction?

4. If a light ray enters the mirror system of Fig. 35-33 propagating in the plane of the page and parallel to one mirror, through what angle will it be turned?

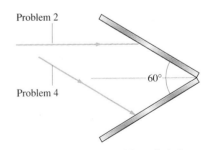

FIGURE 35-33 Problems 2, 4, 5.

5. Suppose the angle in Fig. 35-33 is changed to 75°. A ray enters the mirror system parallel to the axis. (a) How many reflections does it make? (b) Through what angle is it turned when it exits the system?

6. Two plane mirrors make an angle ϕ. For what value of ϕ will a light ray reflecting once off each mirror be turned through the same angle ϕ?

7. Two plane mirrors make an angle ϕ. A light ray enters the system and is reflected once off each mirror. Show that the ray is turned through an angle $360° - 2\phi$.

Section 35-3 Refraction

8. In which substance in Table 35-1 does the speed of light have the value 2.292×10^8 m/s?

9. Information in a compact disc is stored in "pits" whose depth is essentially one-fourth of the wavelength of the laser light used to "read" the information. That wavelength is 780 nm in air, but the wavelength on which the pit depth is based is measured in the $n = 1.55$ plastic that makes up most of the disc. Find the pit depth.

10. Light is incident on an air-glass interface, and the refracted light in the glass makes a 40° angle with the normal to the interface. The glass has refractive index 1.52. Find the incidence angle.

11. A light ray propagates in a transparent material at 15° to the normal to the surface. When it emerges into the surrounding air, it makes a 24° angle with the normal. What is the refractive index of the material?

12. Light propagating in the glass ($n = 1.52$) wall of an aquarium tank strikes the interior edge of the wall with incidence angle 12.4°. What is the angle of refraction in the water?

13. A block of glass with $n = 1.52$ is submerged in one of the liquids listed in Table 35-1. For a ray striking the glass with incidence angle 31.5°, the angle of refraction is 27.9°. What is the liquid?

14. A meter stick lies on the bottom of the rectangular trough in Fig. 35-34, with its zero mark at the left edge of the trough. You look into the long dimension of the trough at a 45° angle, with your line of sight just grazing the top edge of the tank, as shown. What mark on the meter stick do you see if the trough is (a) empty, (b) half full of water, and (c) full of water?

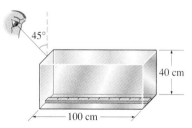

FIGURE 35-34 Problem 14.

15. You look at the center of one face of a solid cube of glass, on a line of sight making a 55° angle with the normal to the cube face. What is the minimum refractive index of the glass for which you will see through the opposite face of the cube?

16. The cylindrical tank in a public aquarium is 10 m deep, 11 m in diameter, and is full to the brim with water. If a flashlight shines on the tank from above, what is the minimum angle its beam can make with the horizontal if it is to illuminate part of the tank bottom?

17. You're standing 2.3 m horizontally from the edge of a 4.5-m-deep lake, with your eyes 1.7 m above the water surface. A diver holding a flashlight at the lake bottom shines the light so you can see it. If the light in the water makes a 42° angle with the vertical, at what horizontal distance is the diver from the edge of the lake?

18. You've dropped your car keys at night off the end of a dock into water 1.6 m deep. A flashlight held directly above the dock edge and 0.50 m above the water illuminates the keys when it's pointed at 40° to the vertical, as shown in Fig. 35-35. What is the horizontal distance x from the edge of the dock to the keys?

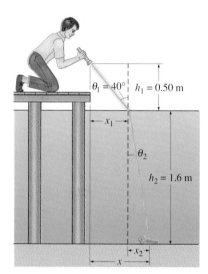

FIGURE 35-35 What is the horizontal distance x from the edge of the dock to the lost keys? (Problem 18)

19. A light ray is propagating in a crystal where its wavelength is 540 nm. It strikes the interior surface of the crystal with an incidence angle of 34° and emerges into the surrounding air at 76° to the surface normal. Find (a) the light's frequency and (b) its wavelength in air.

20. The prism in Fig. 35-36 has $n = 1.52$, $\alpha = 60°$, and is surrounded by air. A light beam is incident at $\theta_1 = 37°$. Find the angle δ through which the beam is deflected.

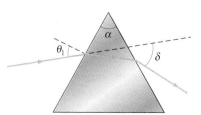

FIGURE 35-36 Problems 20, 51, 55.

Section 35-4 Total Internal Reflection

21. Find the critical angle for total internal reflection in (a) ice, (b) polystyrene, and (c) rutile. Assume the surrounding medium is air.

22. A drop of water is trapped in a block of ice. What is the critical angle for total internal reflection at the water-ice interface?

23. What is the critical angle for light propagating in glass with $n = 1.52$ when the glass is immersed in (a) water, (b) benzene, and (c) diiodomethane?

24. Total internal reflection occurs at an interface between a plastic and air at incidence angles greater than $37°$. What is the refractive index of the plastic?

25. Light propagating in a medium with refractive index n_1 encounters a parallel-sided slab with index n_2. On the other side is a third medium with index $n_3 < n_1$. Show that the condition for avoiding internal reflection at *both* interfaces is that the incidence angle at the n_1-n_2 interface be less than the critical angle for an n_1-n_3 interface. In other words, the index of the intermediate material doesn't matter.

26. An aquarium measures 30 cm front to back, as shown in Fig. 35-37. It is made of glass with thickness much less than the size of the aquarium and is full of water with $n = 1.333$. You put your eye right up to the center of the aquarium's front wall and can still see the entire back wall. What is the maximum value of the aquarium's width w? *Hint:* You can ignore the glass; see the preceding problem.

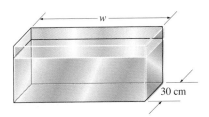

FIGURE 35-37 Problem 26.

27. What is the minimum refractive index for which total internal reflection will occur as shown in Fig. 35-15a? Assume the surrounding medium is air and that the prism is an isosceles right triangle.

28. Where and in what direction would the main beam emerge if the prism in Fig. 35-15a were made of ice?

29. What is the speed of light in a material for which the critical angle at an interface with air is $61°$?

30. The prism of Fig. 35-15a has $n = 1.52$. When it is immersed in a liquid, a beam incident as shown in the figure ceases to undergo total reflection. What is the minimum value for the liquid's refractive index?

31. A compound lens is made from crown glass ($n = 1.52$) bonded to flint glass ($n = 1.89$). What is the critical angle for light incident on the flint-crown interface?

32. Find a simple expression for the speed of light in a material in terms of the critical angle at an interface between the material and vacuum.

33. A scuba diver sets off a camera flash a distance h below the surface of water with refractive index n. Show that light emerges from the water surface through a circle of diameter $2h/\sqrt{n^2 - 1}$.

Section 35-5 Dispersion

34. Blue and red laser beams strike an air-glass interface with incidence angle $50°$. If the glass has refractive indices of 1.680 and 1.621 for the blue and red light, respectively, what will be the angle between the two beams in the glass?

35. Suppose the red and blue beams of the preceding problem are now propagating in the same direction *inside* the glass. For what range of incidence angles on the glass-air interface will one beam be totally reflected and the other not?

36. White light propagating in air is incident at $45°$ on the equilateral prism of Fig. 35-38. Find the angular dispersion γ of the outgoing beam, if the prism has refractive indices $n_{red} = 1.582$, $n_{violet} = 1.633$.

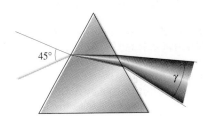

FIGURE 35-38 Problem 36 (angles of dispersed rays are not accurate).

37. Two of the prominent spectral lines—discrete wavelengths of light—emitted by glowing hydrogen are hydrogen-α at 656.3 nm and hydrogen-β at 486.1 nm. Light from glowing hydrogen passes through a prism like that of Fig. 35-22, then falls on a screen 1.0 m from the prism. How far apart will these two spectral lines be? Use Fig. 35-20 for the refractive index.

38. Light from glowing sodium contains the two discrete wavelengths 589.0 nm and 589.6 nm. This light is passed through a prism like that of Fig. 35-22 and then allowed to fall on a screen 2.0 m distant. For wavelengths near 600 nm, the refractive index of the prism is $n = 1.546 - 4.47 \times 10^{-5}\lambda$, with λ the wavelength in nm. What must be the prism's apex angle α in order that the two sodium wavelengths be separated on the screen by 1.5 mm?

Section 35-6 Reflection and Polarization

39. Find the polarizing angle for diamond when light is incident from air.

40. What is the refractive index of a material for which the polarizing angle in air is 62°?

41. What is the polarizing angle for light incident from below on the surface of a pond?

42. For the interface between air (refractive index 1) and a material with refractive index n, show that the critical angle and the polarizing angle are related by $\sin \theta_c = \cot \theta_p$.

Paired Problems

(Both problems in a pair involve the same principles and techniques. If you can get the first problem, you should be able to solve the second one.)

43. Light propagating in air strikes a transparent crystal at incidence angle 35°. If the angle of refraction is 22°, what is the speed of light in the crystal?

44. A laser beam with wavelength 633 nm is propagating in air when it strikes a transparent material at incidence angle 50°. If the angle of refraction is 27°, what is the wavelength in the material?

45. A cylindrical tank 2.4 m deep is full to the brim with water. Sunlight first hits part of the tank bottom when the rising Sun makes a 22° angle with the horizon. Find the tank's diameter.

46. For what diameter tank in the preceding problem will sunlight strike some part of the tank bottom whenever the Sun is above the horizon?

47. Light is incident from air on the flat wall of a polystyrene water tank. If the incidence angle is 40°, what angle does the light make with the tank normal in the water?

48. A parallel-sided slab with refractive index n_2 separates two media with indices n_1 and n_3. Show that a light ray incident on the n_1-n_2 interface then enters the third medium with the same angle of refraction it would have had if the slab had not been present. (Assume total internal reflection does not occur at either interface.)

49. Light strikes a right-angled glass prism ($n = 1.52$) in a direction parallel to the prism's base, as shown in Fig. 35-39. The point of incidence is high enough that the refracted ray hits the opposite sloping side. (a) Through which side of the prism does the beam emerge? (b) Through what angle has it been deflected?

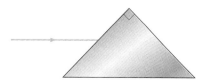

FIGURE 35-39 Problems 49, 50.

50. Repeat the preceding problem if the prism has refractive index 1.15.

51. Repeat Problem 20 for the case $n = 1.75$, $\alpha = 40°$, and $\theta_1 = 25°$.

52. The surfaces of a glass sheet are not quite parallel, but rather make an angle of 10°. The glass has refractive index $n = 1.52$. A light beam strikes one side of the sheet at incidence angle 35°, coming in on the thicker side of the normal. Through what angle is the beam direction changed when it emerges on the opposite side of the glass sheet?

Supplementary Problems

53. A cubical block is made from two equal-size slabs of materials with different refractive indices, as shown in Fig. 35-40. Find the index of the right-hand slab if a light ray is incident on the center of the left-hand slab and then describes the path shown.

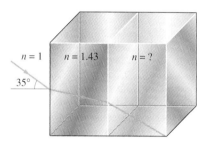

FIGURE 35-40 Problem 53.

54. Find an expression for the displacement x in Fig. 35-8, in terms of θ_1, d, and n.

55. Light is incident with incidence angle θ_1 on a prism with apex angle α and refractive index n, as shown in Fig. 35-36. Show that the angle δ through which the outgoing beam deviates from the incident beam is given by

$$\delta = \theta_1 - \alpha + \sin^{-1}\left\{n \sin\left[\alpha - \sin^{-1}\left(\frac{\sin \theta_1}{n}\right)\right]\right\}.$$

Assume the surrounding medium has $n = 1$.

56. Taking $n = 1.5$ and $\alpha = 60°$, plot the deviation δ of the preceding problem over the range $45° < \theta_1 < 50°$, and use your plot to find the incidence angle for minimum deviation. Trace the incident beam for this value of θ_1. Your result should be the symmetric path shown in Fig. 35-41; in fact, the minimum deviation always occurs with the incidence angle that gives this path, for any n and α.

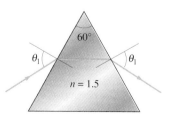

FIGURE 35-41 Minimum deviation through an equilateral prism occurs when the path is symmetric (Problem 56).

57. Show that a three-dimensional corner reflector (three mirrors in three mutually perpendicular planes, or a solid cube in which total internal reflection occurs) turns an incident light ray through 180°, so it returns in the direction from which it came. *Hint:* Let $\mathbf{q} = q_x\hat{\mathbf{i}} + q_y\hat{\mathbf{j}} + q_z\hat{\mathbf{k}}$ be a vector in the direction of propagation. How does this vector get changed on reflection by a mirror in a plane defined by two of the coordinate axes?

58. Show that the angle ϕ that appears in Fig. 35-25 is given by $\phi = 4 \sin^{-1}\left(\dfrac{\sin\theta}{n}\right) - 2\theta$, where θ is the angle of incidence.

59. (a) Differentiate the result of the preceding problem to show that the maximum value of ϕ occurs when the incidence angle θ is given by $\cos^2\theta = \frac{1}{3}(n^2 - 1)$. (b) Use this result and that of the preceding problem to find ϕ_{max} in water with $n = 1.333$.

60. Figure 35-42 shows the approximate path of a light ray that undergoes internal reflection twice in a spherical water drop. Find the maximum angle ϕ for this case, taking $n = 1.333$. This is the angle at which the secondary rainbow appears.

61. *Fermat's principle* states that the path of a light ray between two points is such that the time to traverse that

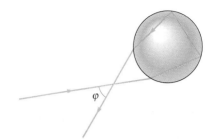

FIGURE 35-42 Problem 60.

path is an extremum (either a minimum or a maximum) when compared with the times for nearby paths. Consider two points A and B on the same side of a reflecting surface, and show that a light ray traveling from A to B via a point on the reflecting surface will take the least time if its path obeys the law of reflection. Thus, the law of reflection (Equation 35-1) follows from Fermat's principle.

62. Use Fermat's principle (see preceding problem) to show that a light ray going from point A in one medium to point B in a second medium will take the least time if its path obeys Snell's law. Thus, Snell's law follows from Fermat's principle.

36 Image Formation and Optical Instruments

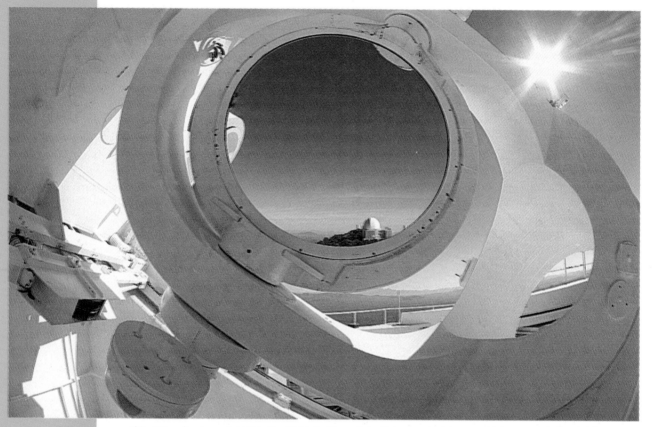

This mirror directs sunlight into the McMath–Pierce Solar Telescope in Arizona, which uses optical technology to form a detailed image of the Sun's surface.

Reflection and refraction alter the direction of light propagation, following laws we developed in the preceding chapter. Microscopes, telescopes, cameras, contact lenses, photocopiers, and your own eyes are among the many natural and technological systems that use reflection or refraction to form **images**—patterns of light that provide visual representations of reality. As you read this page, for example, refraction in your eye forms an image on the retina at the back of the eye. Your optic nerve conveys this image to your brain, which processes it to give you the conscience sense of seeing. In this chapter we study image formation using the approximation of geometrical optics—an approximation that remains valid as long as we consider only length scales much greater than the wavelength of light.

When we view an object with an optical system, we perceive light that seems to come straight from the object but whose path has actually been altered. As a result we see an image that may be different in size, orientation, or apparent position from the actual object. In some cases light actually comes from the image to our eyes; the image is then called a **real image**. In other cases light only apparently comes from the image location; the image is then called a **virtual image**.

36-1 PLANE MIRRORS

When you look at yourself in a flat mirror, you see an image that appears to be behind the mirror by the same distance that you are in front of it. The image is upright and the same size as you are, but appears reversed. Why?

Figure 36-1 shows how the image in a plane mirror comes about. In Fig. 36-1a we concentrate on a small object, in this case an arrowhead. (We'll frequently use arrows to represent objects in image-forming situations because they're both simple and sufficiently asymmetric that we can see whether images are inverted or upright.) We've drawn three light rays that leave the object, reflect off the mirror, and enter the observer's eye. The rays reflect at the mirror with equal angles of incidence and reflection. As Fig. 36-1a shows, light looks to the observer like it's coming from a point behind the mirror. That point is the location of the arrowhead's image. In this case the image is virtual because no light actually comes from behind the mirror.

Since two nonparallel lines define a point, we need only two rays to locate the arrowhead in Fig. 36-1a. We've repeated this image-location process in Fig. 36-1b, using as one of the rays the ray that reflects normally. The same procedure also locates the bottom of the arrow, and we could obviously fill in additional points to locate the entire arrow; the resulting image is shown in Fig. 36-1b.

Note that the triangles OPQ and $O'PQ$ in Fig. 36-1b share a common side and that the angles OPQ and $O'PQ$ are both right angles. And because the angles of incidence and reflection are equal, so are the angles OQP and $O'QP$. Therefore triangles OPQ and $O'PQ$ are congruent, showing that the distance PO' that the arrowhead's image lies behind the mirror is equal to the distance OP from the actual arrowhead to the mirror. A similar analysis applies to the rays from the bottom of the arrow, so we can conclude that the image appears as far behind the mirror as the object is in front. Furthermore, since extensions of the rays from the top and bottom of the arrow normal to the mirror pass through the top and bottom of the image, respectively, the image must be the same height as the object itself.

15.3
Plane Mirrors

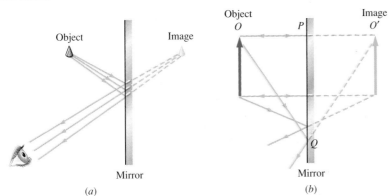

FIGURE 36-1 Image formation in a plane mirror. (a) Light reflected off the mirror seems to come from an image behind the mirror. Since there is really no light coming from behind the mirror, this is a virtual image. (b) Two rays from each point on an object serve to locate that point's image. Triangles OPQ and $O'PQ$ are congruent, showing that object and image are equidistant from the mirror.

EXAMPLE 36-1	*What Size Mirror to Buy?*

You want the smallest mirror that will show your full image. How tall must it be?

Solution

Figure 36-2 shows the situation. Because the angles of incidence and reflection are equal, light from your foot reflects from the mirror at a point that's vertically halfway between your eye and the floor. Similarly, light from the top of your head reflects midway between that point and your eye. The total distance from top to bottom of the mirror then needs to be half your eye-foot distance plus half the distance from your eye to the top of your head—for a total of half your height. Note that this result does not depend on how far from the mirror you stand. It does, however, require that you fix the mirror to the wall at just the right height.

EXERCISE You buy a mirror that's half your height, but you affix it to the wall 2 cm below its optimum location. How much of your image will be cut off?

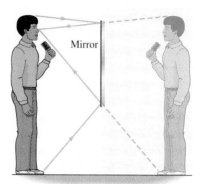

FIGURE 36-2 A mirror half your height shows your entire image.

Answer: Top 4 cm

Some problems similar to Example 36-1: 1, 2

Image Reversal

Stand in front of a plane mirror and you appear reversed left to right; for example, your image's left hand is the image of your *right* hand (Fig. 36-3). It's not that the image of your left hand appears opposite your right hand, any more than the image of your head appears opposite your feet. A more accurate description is that the mirror reverses front to back. Figure 36-4 shows that the effect is to alter only one of the three coordinate axes, and that alters handedness, rotation, and all other phenomena connected with the right-hand rules we've been using.

Although image formation in a single plane mirror is straightforward, multiple reflections with more than one mirror can produce many—in some cases infinitely many—images; see Problem 2.

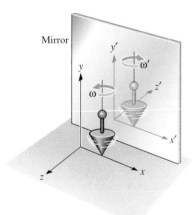

FIGURE 36-4 A plane mirror reverses front to back, reversing the direction of the z axis and making the image coordinate system a left-handed one. The rotation of the spinning top is reversed in the mirror, but its angular velocity vector still points upward because a left-hand rule applies in the "mirror world."

FIGURE 36-3 The image of a right hand is the image's left hand—but it's still the image of the *right* hand.

36-2 CURVED MIRRORS

In contrast to plane mirrors, curved mirrors form images that may be upright or inverted, virtual or real, and whose sizes need not be those of the original objects.

Parabolic Mirrors

A parabola—the curve generated by a quadratic function like $y = x^2$—has the property that a line drawn parallel to the parabola's axis makes the same angle to the normal as does a second line drawn to a special point called the **focus** or **focal point** (Fig. 36-5a). That means a concave mirror of parabolic shape will reflect rays parallel to the parabola's axis so they converge at the focus (Fig. 36-5b). This effect can be used to concentrate light to very high intensities (Fig. 36-6a). Conversely, a point source of light at the focus will emerge from the mirror in a beam of parallel rays (Fig. 36-6b).

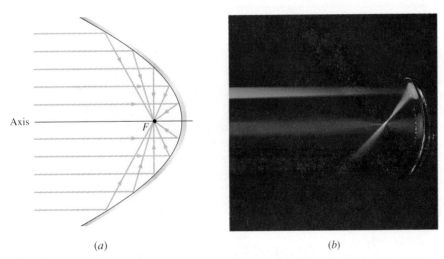

(a)   (b)

FIGURE 36-5 A parabolic mirror reflects rays parallel to its axis to a common focus. (a) Ray diagram. (b) Photo shows rays reflecting from an actual mirror.

(a)   (b)

FIGURE 36-6 (a) This solar furnace uses a huge parabolic reflector to concentrate sunlight. It's used to study properties of materials at high temperatures. (b) A flashlight has a light bulb near the focus of a parabolic mirror and thus produces a beam of nearly parallel light rays.

Spherical Mirrors

Near the apex of the parabolic mirror in Fig. 36-6, you can't tell whether the mirror's shape is parabolic or spherical; parabola and sphere are essentially the same over a limited range. Because a sphere is a more regular shape and thus easier to form, most mirrors used for focusing are, in fact, spherical. The slight distortion caused by the deviation from a perfect parabola—called **spherical aberration**—is minimized by making the actual mirror only a tiny fraction of the entire sphere. In that case the focal length is much larger than the size of the mirror, and light rays from distant objects strike the mirror only if they're close to and nearly parallel to the mirror axis. Such rays are called **paraxial rays**, and it's only for them that the approximation of a parabola by a sphere results in accurate focusing. We assume paraxial rays in what follows. For clarity, however, our diagrams show mirrors much more curved than they should be for distortion-free focusing, and consequently not all the rays we draw will seem paraxial.

APPLICATION	*Hubble Trouble*

The Hubble Space Telescope was launched in 1990 as the flagship of a new generation of space-based astronomical observatories. Although Hubble is smaller than many ground-based telescopes, its vantage point above the atmosphere was to make it optically superior in resolving astronomical objects. Furthermore, Hubble can observe in infrared, visible, and ultraviolet wavelengths.

In the months following Hubble's launch, engineers and scientists checking the telescope were frustrated by their inability to achieve a clear focus. They came reluctantly to the conclusion that Hubble's 2.4-m-diameter primary mirror was flawed. Subsequent investigation showed that an error of 1.3 mm in the placement of instruments used during manufacture of the mirror had resulted in its being ground to the wrong curvature. The mirror itself is off by only 2.3 μm at its edge, but this is an enormous flaw in an optical system designed to be accurate to a small fraction of the wavelength of light. Hubble specifications called for 70% of the light energy from a point source to fall within an angular diameter of 0.1 second of arc; because of its spherical aberration, at best 16% of the light fell in the prescribed zone.

Although the Hubble mirror could not be replaced or repaired, in 1993 astronauts managed to install corrective mirrors that restored Hubble's optical system to better than its original design specifications. The result is a superb astronomical instrument with image quality greatly superior to that of ground-based telescopes (Fig. 36-7).

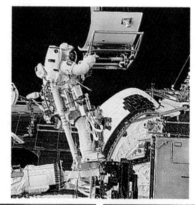

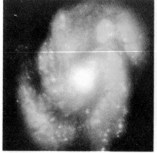 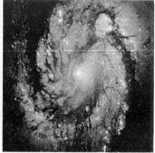

FIGURE 36-7 (Top) An astronaut installing new optical equipment on the Hubble Space Telescope. (Bottom) Hubble images of M-100, a galaxy 50 million light-years from Earth, taken before and after the repair.

We can see how spherical mirrors form images by tracing two rays from each of several points on the object, just as we did for plane mirrors. Some special rays make this process simple; their properties all follow from the law of reflection and the special properties of a spherical mirror in the paraxial approximation:

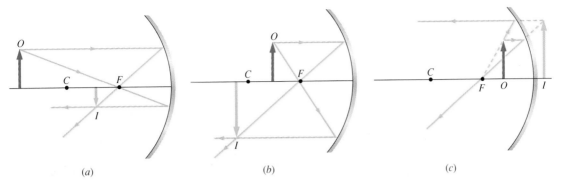

(a)   (b)   (c)

FIGURE 36-8 Image formation in a concave spherical mirror, using the fact that light passing through the focal point F reflects parallel to the mirror axis, and vice versa. O denotes the object and I its image. (a) With the object beyond the mirror's center of curvature C, the mirror forms a real image that is inverted and reduced in size. (b) With the object between the center of curvature and focus, the image is real, inverted, and magnified. (c) When the object is closer than the focus, the image is enlarged, upright, and virtual. Note, in this case, to get the ray including the object and the focus we had to extend the actual light path back toward the focus.

1. Any ray parallel to the mirror axis reflects through the focal point.
2. In the converse of (1), any ray that passes through the focal point reflects parallel to the axis.
3. Any ray that strikes the center of the mirror reflects symmetrically about the mirror axis.
4. Any ray through the center of curvature strikes the mirror normal to the mirror surface, and thus returns on itself.

Any two of these rays suffice to locate an image.

Figure 36-8 shows ray tracings, using our special rays (1) and (2) that go through the focal point, to find the image location in three cases. In all three cases symmetry ensures that the bottom of the image arrow will be on the axis, so we haven't bothered to trace it. In Fig. 36-8a we see that an object beyond the mirror's center of curvature (C) forms a smaller, inverted image. Light actually emerges from this image, so it's a *real* image. If you looked from the left in Fig. 36-8a you would actually see the image in space in front of the mirror (Fig. 36-9).

As the object moves closer to the mirror the real image grows; with the object between the center of curvature and the focus, the image is larger than the object, and farther from the mirror (Fig. 36-8b). As the object moves toward the focus the image grows larger and moves rapidly away from the mirror. With the object right at the focus the rays emerge in a parallel beam and there is no image. Finally, rays from an object closer to the mirror than the focus diverge after reflection. To an observer they appear to come from a point behind the mirror. Thus there is a virtual image, in this case upright and enlarged (Fig. 36-8c).

ActivPhysics Activity 15.4 provides a simulation of Fig. 36-8 in which you can move the object to any point.

FIGURE 36-9 A bear meets its real image, formed by the concave mirror at rear. The bear and its image are both in *front* of the mirror.

15.4
Spherical Mirrors

Got It!

Where would you place an object so its real image is the same size as the object?

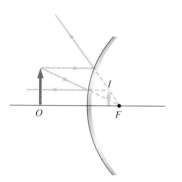

FIGURE 36-10 Image formation using a convex mirror. The image is always virtual, upright, and reduced in size.

Convex Mirrors

A convex mirror reflects on the outside of its spherical curvature, causing light to diverge rather than focus. Therefore, there is no possibility of forming a real image with a convex mirror. But Fig. 36-10 shows that the mirror can still form a virtual image. Although the focus has less obvious physical significance in this case, its location still controls the geometry of reflected rays. As Fig. 36-10 shows, we can still draw a ray parallel to the axis and another ray that would go through the focus if the mirror weren't in its way. By tracing these rays through the mirror we can see the directions in which they reflect. The reflected rays appear to diverge from a common point behind the mirror, showing that there is a virtual image, upright and reduced in size, behind the mirror. By considering different object positions, you can convince yourself that for a convex mirror the image always has these characteristics. Convex mirrors are widely used where an image of a broad region needs to be captured in a small space (Fig. 36-11).

The Mirror Equation

Drawing ray diagrams helps give an intuitive feel for image formation. More precise image locations and sizes follow from the **mirror equation**, which we now derive. This time we'll find the image using our special rays parallel to the axis and striking the mirror's center, as shown in Fig. 36-12a. The ray that strikes the center of the mirror reflects symmetrically about the axis; therefore, the two shaded triangles are similar. Then the **magnification**—the ratio image height h' to the object height h—is the same as the ratio of the image and object distances from the mirror. We'll consider the image height negative if the image is inverted; then from Fig. 36-12 we have

FIGURE 36-11 Reflecting spheres are convex mirrors, forming reduced, virtual, upright images.

$$M = \frac{h'}{h} = -\frac{\ell'}{\ell}. \tag{36-1}$$

Here object and image are both in front of the mirror, so we take object and image distances ℓ and ℓ' as positive quantities; the negative sign in Equation 36-1 then shows that in this case the image is inverted. Also, for the object

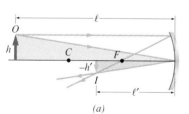

(a)

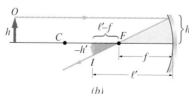

(b)

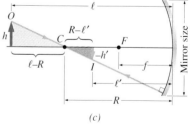

(c)

FIGURE 36-12 Finding the image I using the ray from the object O parallel to the axis, along with the ray that reflects from the center of the mirror. (a) Since the latter ray reflects symmetrically about the axis, the shaded triangles are similar, and allow us to relate the object and image heights h and h' to their distances ℓ and ℓ' from the mirror. (b) Another pair of similar triangles lets us relate the focal length f to the heights and distances. Length of the image arrow is marked $-h'$ because h' is considered negative for an inverted image. (c) The ray through the center of curvature strikes the mirror at 90°, so it reflects back on itself. Once again the shaded triangles are similar; now they let us relate the curvature radius to the heights and distances and thus, through the mirror equation, to the focal length. The curvature radius R proves to be twice the focal length f. The mirror size indicated should actually be considerably smaller than the curvature radius for the descriptions and equations of this section to be accurate.

location of Fig. 36-12, it's clear that $|M| < 1$, meaning the image is reduced rather than enlarged.

Figure 36-12b is the same as Fig. 36-12a except that now we show only the ray that reflects through the focus. We've also labeled the **focal length** f—i.e., the distance from the mirror to the focal point—and have shaded a different pair of similar triangles. From these triangles you can see that

$$\frac{-h'}{h} = \frac{\ell' - f}{f}.$$

Here we put the minus sign on h' because we've defined h' as a negative quantity for the inverted image, while comparing similar triangles requires a ratio of positive quantities. But Equation 36-1 shows that the ratio h'/h is the magnification $M = -\ell'/\ell$. So we have

$$-\frac{\ell'}{\ell} = \frac{\ell' - f}{f}$$

or, dividing both sides by ℓ' and doing a little algebra,

$$\frac{1}{\ell} + \frac{1}{\ell'} = \frac{1}{f}. \quad \text{(mirror equation)} \qquad (36\text{-}2)$$

Equations 36-1 and 36-2 together give us all the information we would get from ray tracing.

Although we derived the mirror equation using a real image, the equation applies to virtual images with the convention that a *negative* image distance ℓ' means the image is *behind* the mirror—as are virtual images (recall Fig. 36-8c). And we can handle *convex* mirrors as well by taking the focal length to be a *negative* quantity. Table 36-1 summarizes these sign conventions.

We can extract one more useful piece of information by considering the ray that passes through the center of curvature, C. This point is the center of the sphere of which the mirror is a part; therefore, its distance from the mirror is the mirror's curvature radius, R. That's why a ray through C hits normal to the mirror; it's following a radius, which intersects the sphere at right angles. So a ray through C reflects back on itself. We show this ray in Fig. 36-12c, along with yet another pair of similar triangles. From them, you can see that

$$\frac{R - \ell'}{\ell - R} = \frac{-h'}{h} = \frac{\ell'}{\ell},$$

where again we write $-h'$ because the inverted image has negative height according to our sign conventions, and we need a ratio of positive distances. The

TABLE 36-1 *Sign Conventions for Mirrors*

FOCAL LENGTH f[1],	OBJECT DISTANCE, ℓ	IMAGE DISTANCE[2], ℓ'	TYPE OF IMAGE
+	+, $\ell > f$	+	Real, inverted, enlarged for $\ell < 2f$, reduced for $\ell > 2f$
+	+, $\ell < f$	−	Virtual, upright, enlarged
−	+	−	Virtual, upright, reduced

[1] + for concave mirror, − for convex.
[2] − means behind mirror.

last step in this equality follows from Equation 36-1. Solving the mirror equation for ℓ' and using the result in the equation above (see Problem 16) then yields

$$f = \frac{R}{2}. \tag{36-3}$$

Thus the focal length of a spherical mirror is half its curvature radius.

15.7

Spherical Mirror Problems

We emphasize that the results derived in this section are approximations based on the assumption that the spherical mirror is a good approximation to a parabola. Equivalent ways of describing this approximation are (1) that the curvature radius is large compared with the mirror's size as indicated in Fig. 36-12c and (2) that all rays reflecting from the mirror are close to and nearly parallel to the mirror axis (the paraxial approximation). Again, our drawings can't accurately reflect these conditions while at the same time showing clearly the ray paths.

EXAMPLE 36-2	*Sizing Up Hubble: A Concave Mirror*

During assembly of the Hubble Space Telescope, a technician stood 3.85 m in front of the telescope's concave mirror and viewed his image (Fig. 36-13). Given the telescope's focal length of 5.52 m, find (a) the location and (b) the magnification of the technician's image. (c) Repeat for the case when the technician stands 15.0 m from the mirror.

Solution

Since the mirror is *concave,* the focal length f is *positive.*
(a) We can solve the mirror equation (Equation 36-2) to get

$$\frac{1}{\ell'} = \frac{1}{f} - \frac{1}{\ell} = \frac{\ell - f}{f\ell},$$

or

$$\ell' = \frac{f\ell}{\ell - f} = \frac{(5.52 \text{ m})(3.85 \text{ m})}{3.85 \text{ m} - 5.52 \text{ m}} = -12.7 \text{ m}.$$

Why the *negative* answer? Because the technician is closer to the mirror than the focal point, so this is a *virtual* image located *behind* the mirror.
(b) Equation 36-1 gives the magnification:

$$M = -\frac{\ell'}{\ell} = -\frac{(-12.7 \text{ m})}{3.85 \text{ m}} = 3.30.$$

This *positive* answer indicates an *upright* image, enlarged about three times as shown in Fig. 36-13.
(c) If the technician stands 15.0 m from the mirror, similar calculations give

$$\ell' = \frac{f\ell}{\ell - f} = \frac{(5.52 \text{ m})(15.0 \text{ m})}{15.0 \text{ m} - 5.52 \text{ m}} = 8.73 \text{ m}$$

and

$$M = -\frac{\ell'}{\ell} = -\frac{8.73 \text{ m}}{15.0 \text{ m}} = -0.582.$$

FIGURE 36-13 A technician standing in front of the Hubble Space Telescope mirror. Where and how big is the technician's image?

Now ℓ' is *positive,* so the image is *real* and in *front* of the mirror; the *negative* magnification shows that it's *inverted,* and it's reduced in size.

EXERCISE You're scrutinizing your nose using a handheld concave mirror with curvature radius 2.2 m. How far from your face should you hold the mirror to see your nose doubled in size?

Answer: 55 cm

Some problems similar to Example 36-2: 3–9, 11–14

EXAMPLE 36-3 | *Jurassic Park: A Convex Mirror*

In the film *Jurassic Park,* horrified passengers in a car watch in the convex side-view mirror as a tyrannosaurus rex pursues them. Printed on the mirror is the warning "OBJECTS IN MIRROR ARE CLOSER THAN THEY SEEM." If the mirror's curvature radius is 12 m, and if the T-rex is actually 9.0 m from the mirror, by what factor does its image appear reduced in size?

Solution

This is a *convex* mirror, so its focal length is *negative.* Since the focal length is half the curvature radius, we have $f = -6.0$ m. Here we're asked for the magnification, given by Equation 36-1. For that we need the image distance ℓ'. We found an expression for ℓ' in the preceding example, and that expression holds here because the mirror equation from which it was derived works for both concave and convex mirrors. So Equation 36-1 becomes

$$M = -\frac{\ell'}{\ell} = -\frac{f\ell/(\ell - f)}{\ell} = -\frac{f}{\ell - f}$$

$$= -\frac{-6.0 \text{ m}}{9.0 \text{ m} - (-6.0 \text{ m})} = 0.40 .$$

The T-rex in the mirror appears only 40 percent of its actual size, and thus it "seems" further away. Note that the mirror's warning isn't really a comparison of the image and object *distances,* but of the apparent versus actual *size* of objects. Image distances in a convex mirror are always *smaller* than object distances, so the images are always *reduced* and we therefore perceive objects viewed in a convex mirror as being farther way.

EXERCISE An object 30 cm from a convex mirror appears reduced to one-fourth of its actual size when viewed in a convex mirror. What is the mirror's curvature radius?

Answer: 20 cm

Some problems similar to Example 36-3: 10, 15, 62

APPLICATION | *Nonimaging Optics and the Quest for Solar Energy*

Sometimes we want to concentrate light energy without necessarily forming an image. In solar energy systems producing heat, for example, concentrated sunlight leads to higher temperature and thus to higher efficiency; with photovoltaic systems inexpensive reflectors can be used to concentrate solar energy onto more expensive photovoltaic cells, reducing the cell area needed.

Nonimaging optics is a new field, and the design of concentrators is an ongoing challenge for optical engineers. Figure 36-14 shows a popular concentrator design, called a compound parabolic concentrator. Unlike a parabolic mirror designed for image formation, this concentrator is made from parabolic segments that do not form a single complete parabola. As Fig. 36-14a shows, all light entering the concentrator

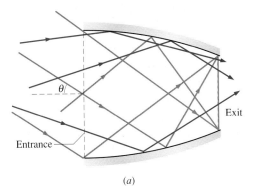

(a)

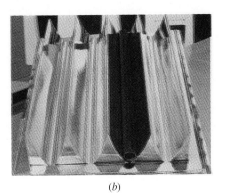

(b)

FIGURE 36-14 (*a*) A compound parabolic concentrator. Rays (blue) entering at the angle θ to the concentrator axis are reflected to the edge of the exit aperture. Rays incident at smaller angles (red) pass through the exit aperture after at most one reflection; thus all light entering over the angular range 2θ is concentrated at the exit. (*b*) A section of parabolic concentrators used to concentrate solar energy on a black tube carrying a heat-transfer fluid. A piece of pipe lies at the exit of one concentrator; since light paths are reversible, the fact that the entire concentrator appears black confirms that the path of an incident light ray ends up on the black tube.

from a broad range of angles ends up at the narrow exit end. The light doesn't converge to form an image, but its intensity has nevertheless been increased because its energy is spread over a smaller area. Thus, the concentrator acts as a "funnel" for light. Figure 36-14*b* shows a section of a compound parabolic reflector used to concentrate light onto a tube carrying heat-transfer fluid in a solar thermal power plant. Because the concentrator accepts light from a broad angular range, it works without the need for expensive tracking equipment that would keep it facing the Sun.

Nonimaging concentrators have other applications as well. The first compound parabolic concentrator, built in 1965, was designed to collect light from a high-energy physics experiment. Nonimaging optics in the infrared were used on the Cosmic Background Explorer satellite that has provided crucial evidence in support of the Big Bang theory of the origin of the universe. And under development are solar-powered lasers that use nonimaging concentrators as the "pump" that supplies energy to run the laser.

36-3 LENSES

A **lens** is a transparent piece of material that uses refraction of light to form images. As with mirrors, lenses can be either concave or convex. But light goes through a lens, while it reflects off a mirror, so the roles of the two types are reversed. A convex lens focuses parallel rays to a **focal point**, and is therefore called a **converging lens** (Fig. 36-15). As we'll soon see, a convex lens can form real and virtual images, depending on the object location. A concave lens, in contrast, is a **diverging lens**; it refracts parallel rays so they appear to be diverging from a common focus. Like a *convex* mirror, a *concave* lens can form only virtual images (Fig. 36-16).

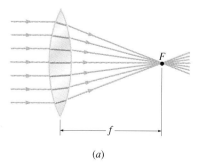

(a)

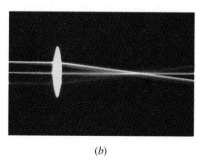

(b)

FIGURE 36-15 A convex lens brings parallel light rays to a focus *F*. The focal length *f* is the distance from the lens to the focal point. You can see in (*a*) that light is refracted at each surface of the lens, but as the lens is thin we can treat the two refractions as a single change of direction at the center plane of the lens. Because the lens surfaces are parallel at the center of the lens, any ray through the center passes undeflected.

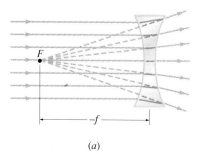

(a)

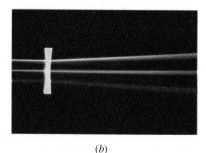

(b)

FIGURE 36-16 Parallel light rays passing through a concave lens diverge so it looks as though they are coming from a common focus. But light doesn't actually come from the focus, so this type of lens can produce only virtual images.

In Section 36-4 we'll examine the detailed behavior of light as it refracts at the interfaces between a lens and the surrounding medium. First, we explore the simpler situation of a **thin lens**—one whose thickness is small compared with the curvature radii of its two surfaces. Although light refracts once as it enters a lens and once as it exits, in the thin-lens approximation the two lens surfaces are so close that it suffices to consider that the light bends just once, as it crosses the center plane of the lens. Unlike a mirror, light can go either way through a lens; that means the lens has two focal points, one on either side. For a thin lens, the focal length proves to be the same in either direction, so it doesn't matter which way we orient the lens. We'll justify the thin-lens approximation mathematically in Section 36-4.

Lens Images by Ray Tracing

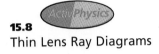

15.8

Thin Lens Ray Diagrams

As with mirrors, two rays serve to fix the image formed by a lens. For lenses, two special rays make ray tracing easy:

1. Any ray parallel to the lens axis refracts through the focal point.
2. Any ray through the center of the lens passes undeflected.

Figure 36-17 shows ray tracings for different object placements in relation to a converging lens. In Fig. 36-17*a* we see that an object farther out than two focal lengths produces a smaller, inverted real image on the other side of the lens.

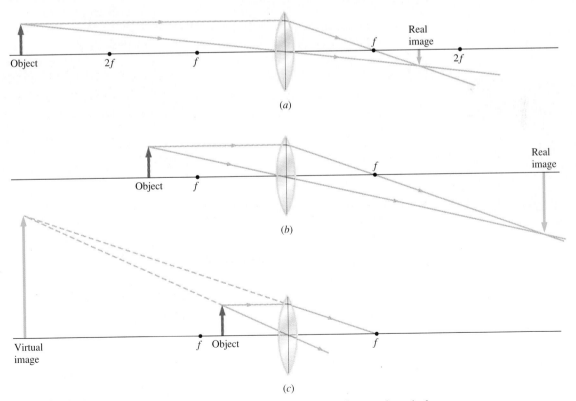

FIGURE 36-17 Image formation with a converging lens. Marks on axis are distances from the lens center, in units of the focal length *f*. In (*a*) and (*b*), an object distance greater than the focal length results in an inverted real image. The image is enlarged if the object distance is between one and two focal lengths, as shown in (*b*). In (*c*) a virtual image forms when the object is within the focal length. You can simulate these situations with ActivPhysics Activity 15.8.

FIGURE 36-18 Simplified diagram of a movie projector. The film lies just beyond the focal length, and thus the lens produces an enlarged real image on the distant screen. The audience normally views the image from the projector side of the screen. Note that the film is upside down.

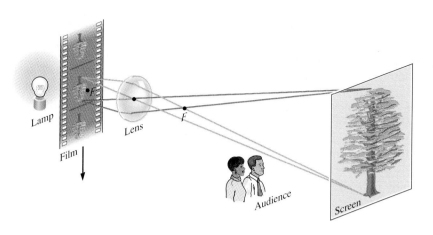

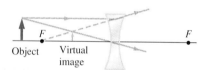

FIGURE 36-19 A diverging lens always forms a reduced, upright, virtual image, visible only through the lens.

Since light really emanates from this image, you could see it without actually looking through the lens. As the object moves toward the lens, the image moves away and grows in size. When the object is between one and two focal lengths from the lens, the image has moved beyond 2f, and is enlarged. The image on a movie screen is formed in this way (Fig. 36-18). Moving the object closer than the focal point produces an enlarged virtual image that can be seen only by an observer looking *through* the lens (Fig. 36-17c).

Figure 36-19 shows ray tracings for a diverging lens. Like a convex mirror, this lens produces only virtual images that are upright and reduced in size. Like the virtual image of Fig. 36-17c these virtual images are visible only through the lens. You should convince yourself that the basic geometry of Fig. 36-19 does not change even if the object moves within the focal length.

Got It!

Before going on to the mathematics of lenses, try answering the following simple questions about the image shown in Fig. 36-20. (Remember that answers to GOT IT! boxes are in the back of the book.)
a. What would happen if the bottom half of the lens were covered?
b. What would happen if the lens were removed?
c. What would happen if the screen's distance from the lens were doubled?
d. Would there be an image in the absence of the screen?

FIGURE 36-20 A simple optical system, consisting of an object (the candle), a converging lens, and a white screen on which the image appears. This system is a realization of Fig. 36-17b.

A Lens Equation

We can locate lens images quantitatively by deriving an equation like we did for mirrors. Note in Fig. 36-21 that the two unshaded right triangles formed by

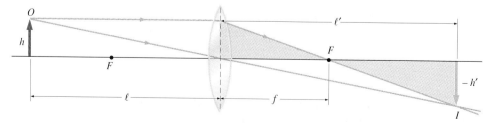

FIGURE 36-21 Ray diagram for deriving the lens equation. The unshaded pair of right triangles formed by the object and image arrows with their distances ℓ and ℓ' are similar, as are the pair of shaded triangles.

TABLE 36-2 *Sign Conventions for Lenses*

FOCAL LENGTH f^1,	OBJECT DISTANCE, ℓ	IMAGE DISTANCE^2, ℓ'	TYPE OF IMAGE
+	+, $\ell > f$	+	Real, inverted, enlarged for $\ell < 2f$, reduced for $\ell > 2f$
+	+, $\ell < f$	−	Virtual, upright, enlarged
−	+	−	Virtual, upright, reduced

^{1} + for convex lens, − for concave.
^{2} − means on same side of lens as object.

the object and image arrows with their distances ℓ and ℓ' are similar. Therefore, the magnification is

$$M = \frac{h'}{h} = -\frac{\ell'}{\ell},\qquad(36\text{-}4)$$

where again we take a negative height to signify an inverted image. Thus, the magnitude of the magnification is the ratio of object to image distance, as it was with mirrors. The two shaded triangles in Fig. 36-21 are also similar, and therefore

$$\frac{-h'}{\ell' - f} = \frac{h}{f}.$$

Combining this result with Equation 36-4 and doing some algebra then gives

$$\frac{1}{\ell} + \frac{1}{\ell'} = \frac{1}{f},\qquad \text{lens equation}\qquad(36\text{-}5)$$

which is identical to the mirror equation 36-2. Note that putting the object at infinity ($\ell = \infty$) gives $\ell' = f$ and that putting the object at the focus ($\ell = f$) gives $\ell' = \infty$. Thus, Equation 36-5 reflects our ray-tracing diagrams that show parallel rays (such as those from an object at a great distance) converging at the focal point, and vice versa.

Although we derived Equation 36-5 for the case of a real image, the equation holds for virtual images if we consider the image distance negative; in that case the image is on the same side of the lens as is the object. And it holds for diverging lenses if we consider the focal length negative. Table 36-2 summarizes these sign conventions for lenses, while Fig. 36-22 describes graphically the sizes and types of images formed at different object distances.

Got It!

You look through a lens at this page and see the words magnified. Is the image you observe real or virtual? Is the lens concave or convex?

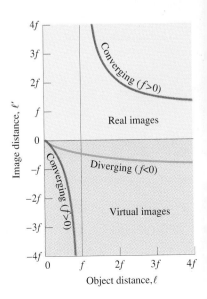

FIGURE 36-22 Image versus object distances for lenses. Real images correspond to positive image distances, virtual images to negative image distances. Red curves are for converging lenses, for which object distances below the focal length result in virtual images ($\ell' < 0$). The image moves toward infinity as the object approaches the focal point from either direction, and concurrently the image grows arbitrarily large. For diverging lenses (blue curve), images are always virtual and reduced in size.

EXAMPLE 36-4	*Slide Show*

You're projecting slides onto a wall 2.6 m from a slide projector whose single lens has focal length 12.0 cm. (a) How far should the slides be from the lens? (b) How big will be the image of a 35-mm slide?

Solution

We want the image focused on the screen, so the image distance ℓ' is 2.6 m. Solving Equation 36-5 for the object distance ℓ then gives

$$\ell = \left(\frac{1}{f} - \frac{1}{\ell'}\right)^{-1} = \left(\frac{1}{12 \text{ cm}} - \frac{1}{260 \text{ cm}}\right)^{-1} = 12.58 \text{ cm} .$$

This is just beyond the focal length, as Figs. 36-17 and 36-22 suggest it should be to get an enlarged, distant, real image.

Equation 36-4 then gives the height h' of the image formed of a 35-mm slide:

$$h' = -h\frac{\ell'}{\ell} = -(3.5 \text{ cm})\left(\frac{260 \text{ cm}}{12.58 \text{ cm}}\right) = -72 \text{ cm} .$$

The minus sign indicates inversion, showing that the slide must go in the projector upside down to get an upright image.

EXERCISE If the slide in Example 36-4 moves 1 mm farther from the lens, what will happen to the position of the image?

Answer: moves 36 cm toward projector

Some problems similar to Example 36-4: 18–30

EXAMPLE 36-5	*Fine Print*

You're using a magnifying glass (a converging lens) with 30 cm focal length to read a telephone book (Fig. 36-23). How far from the page should you hold the lens in order to see the print enlarged 3 times?

Solution

Here the image is virtual, so ℓ' is negative and $3\times$ magnification then corresponds to $\ell' = -3\ell$. So Equation 36-5 becomes

$$\frac{1}{\ell} - \frac{1}{3\ell} = \frac{2}{3\ell} = \frac{1}{f} = \frac{1}{30 \text{ cm}},$$

whence $\ell = (2)(30 \text{ cm})/3 = 20 \text{ cm}$. Figure 36-23 confirms that the image appears further from the lens than the actual page.

EXERCISE A magnifying glass enlarges print by 50% when it's held 9.0 cm from a page. What is its focal length?

FIGURE 36-23 A magnifying glass is a converging lens used in its virtual-image mode.

Answer: 27 cm

Some problems similar to Example 36-5: 18–30

36-4 REFRACTION IN LENSES: THE DETAILS

We now examine in detail the refraction effects that cause lenses to form images. Every lens has two refracting surfaces, at least one of which is curved. We therefore look first at image formation due to refraction at a *single* curved interface. To understand the behavior of a lens we will then consider two such interfaces, using the image formed by the first as the object for the second.

Refraction at a Curved Surface

Figure 36-24 shows part of a spherically curved piece of transparent material with curvature radius R and refractive index n_2, surrounded by a medium with

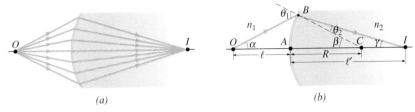

FIGURE 36-24 Refraction at an interface with a curved surface. (*a*) Rays from an object at *O* are refracted at the interface and converge to form an image at *I*. (*b*) Geometry for relating the object and image distances ℓ and ℓ'. All the labeled angles are considered small, even though the drawing doesn't show them as such.

index n_1 (typically air). A point-like object O lies on an axis through the center of curvature of the refracting surface. As we will now show, light rays diverging from this object at small angles to the optic axis are refracted to a common image point (Fig. 36-24*a*). The restriction to small angles is the same paraxial approximation we applied for spherical mirrors; again, our drawings don't always show the angles as being small.

In Fig. 36-24*b* we show a single ray in detail. Under the paraxial approximation the labeled angles in this figure are all small, and we can use the approximation $\sin x \simeq \tan x \simeq x$, where $x \ll 1$ with x an angle measured in radians. Then Snell's law—$n_1 \sin \theta_1 = n_2 \sin \theta_2$—becomes simply

$$n_1 \theta_1 = n_2 \theta_2 .$$

From triangles BCI and OBC, we see that $\theta_2 = \beta - \gamma$ and $\theta_1 = \alpha + \beta$. Using these results in our small-angle version of Snell's law gives

$$n_1(\alpha + \beta) = n_2(\beta - \gamma) .$$

Furthermore, in the small-angle approximation the arc BA is so close to a straight line that we can write $\alpha \simeq \tan \alpha \simeq BA/\ell$, with $\ell = OA$ the object's distance from the refracting surface. Similarly, $\beta \simeq BA/R$, and $\gamma \simeq BA/\ell'$. Thus, our expression of Snell's law becomes

$$n_1\left(\frac{BA}{\ell} + \frac{BA}{R}\right) = n_2\left(\frac{BA}{R} - \frac{BA}{\ell'}\right)$$

or, on canceling the arc length BA and rearranging,

$$\frac{n_1}{\ell} + \frac{n_2}{\ell'} = \frac{n_2 - n_1}{R} . \tag{36-6}$$

Notice that the angle α does not appear in this equation. Therefore, this relation between the object and image distances holds for *all* rays as long as they satisfy the small-angle approximation. That means all such rays come to a common focus at I, as in Fig. 36-24*a*, so an image must appear at this point.

Although we derived Equation 36-6 for a case of real image formation, as usual it holds for virtual images as well if we consider the image distance negative. It also works for surfaces that are concave toward the object—the opposite of Fig. 36-24—if we take R as a negative number. And it even works for flat surfaces, with $R = \infty$, as the exercise following Example 36-6 shows.

EXAMPLE 36-6	A Cylindrical Aquarium

An aquarium is made from a thin-walled tube of transparent plastic 70 cm in diameter (Fig. 36-25a). For a cat looking directly into the aquarium, what is the apparent distance to a fish 15 cm from the aquarium wall?

Solution

We can neglect the aquarium wall; since it's thin and has essentially parallel faces, light suffers no net deflection in passing through the wall. The surface is concave toward the object, so $R = -35$ cm. With $\ell = 15$ cm, $n_1 = 1.333$ for water, and $n_2 = 1$ for air, we can solve Equation 36-6 for the image distance ℓ':

$$\ell' = \frac{n_2}{\left(\dfrac{n_2 - n_1}{R} - \dfrac{n_1}{\ell}\right)} = \frac{1}{\left(\dfrac{1 - 1.333}{-35 \text{ cm}} - \dfrac{1.333}{15 \text{ cm}}\right)}$$

$$= -12.6 \text{ cm}.$$

The negative answer indicates that we have a virtual image, as shown in Fig. 36-25b.

A special case of Equation 36-6 is a flat surface, for which $R = \infty$. The right-hand side is then zero, but the equation still relates object and image distances. Looking down into a swimming pool from above, for example, you see virtual images of objects in the pool. The objects appear closer than they actually are, as Fig. 36-26 and the following exercise illustrate.

EXERCISE The bottom of a swimming pool looks to be 1.5 m below the surface. What is the pool's actual depth?

Answer: 2.0 m

Some problems similar to Example 36-6: 30, 31, 32, 34–36

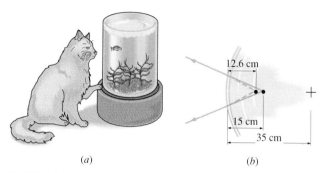

FIGURE 36-25 (a) A cylindrical aquarium. (b) Top view, showing formation of a virtual image of a fish that is actually 15 cm from the aquarium wall.

FIGURE 36-26 Refraction at a flat surface produces an image I that appears closer than the object O. Objects at the bottom of a swimming pool, for example, appear closer than they really are.

Lenses, Thick and Thin

Figure 36-27 shows a lens of arbitrary thickness t made from material with refractive index n. For simplicity we will consider the lens surrounded by air or

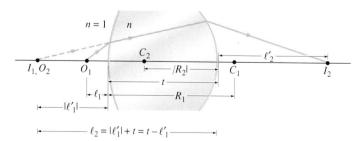

FIGURE 36-27 A thick lens. The left-hand surface forms the virtual image I_1, which is also labelled O_2 because it forms the object for the right-hand surface. Together, the two surfaces then produce the final real image I_2. Absolute value signs are used on distances whose algebraic signs in Equation 36-6 are negative—i.e., the distance ℓ'_1 to the virtual image and the curvature radius R_2 of the right-hand surface, which is concave toward the incident light.

vacuum, with refractive index equal to 1. An object O_1 lies a distance ℓ_1 to the left of the left-hand surface. This surface focuses light from O_1 to form image I_1. Light from this image impinges on the right-hand surface, forming a second image I_2. We want to relate the original object O_1 and final image I_2.

We developed Equation 36-6, our description of refraction at a single curved surface, using Fig. 36-24. In that figure we considered formation of a real image, but we quickly noted that Equation 36-6 applies to virtual and real images alike. In considering a two-surface lens it proves more convenient to place the object where its image in the first surface is a virtual one, as in Fig. 36-27. Again, our final result will apply whatever the object placement.

At the left-hand surface in Fig. 36-27, the quantities in Equation 36-6 are $\ell = \ell_1$, $\ell' = \ell'_1$, $n_1 = 1$, $n_2 = n$, and $R = R_1$, so Equation 36-6 becomes

$$\frac{1}{\ell_1} + \frac{n}{\ell'_1} = \frac{n-1}{R_1}. \qquad \text{(left-hand surface)}$$

The "object" O_2 for the right-hand surface is the image I_1 since light incident on that surface looks like it's coming from I_1. The distance ℓ in Equation 36-6 for this "object" is $\ell = \ell_2 = t - \ell'_1$, with t the lens thickness. Why minus? Because I_1 is a *virtual* image, so, according to our sign conventions, ℓ'_1 is a *negative* quantity. The physical distance between the image and the lens is then the positive quantity $-\ell'_1$, and that quantity adds to the lens thickness to give the distance from this intermediate image to the right-hand surface. Also at the right-hand surface, $\ell' = \ell'_2$, $n_1 = n$, $n_2 = 1$, and $R = R_2$. Thus, at the right-hand surface Equation 36-6 reads

$$\frac{n}{t - \ell'_1} + \frac{1}{\ell'_2} = \frac{1-n}{R_2}. \qquad \text{(right-hand surface)}$$

Now we'll let the lens become arbitrarily thin, taking the limit $t \to 0$. Then the first term in our right-surface equation becomes $-n/\ell'_1$. But the term n/ℓ'_1 also occurs in the left-surface equation. So we can add the two equations to eliminate the intermediate-image distance ℓ'_1. Since we'll be left with only one object distance, ℓ_1, and one image distance, ℓ'_2, we can drop the subscripts 1 and 2 on these quantities. The result is

$$\frac{1}{\ell} + \frac{1}{\ell'} = (n-1)\left(\frac{1}{R_1} - \frac{1}{R_2}\right). \qquad (36\text{-}7)$$

The left-hand side of this equation is identical to the left-hand side of Equation 36-5. So we can equate the right-hand sides of the two equations to get an expression for the focal length of our lens:

$$\frac{1}{f} = (n-1)\left(\frac{1}{R_1} - \frac{1}{R_2}\right). \qquad \text{(lensmaker's formula)} \qquad (36\text{-}8)$$

We emphasize that the radii R_1 and R_2 in Equation 36-8 may be positive or negative, depending on the lens curvature. In Fig. 36-27, for example, R_1 is positive because the left-hand surface is convex toward the incident light but R_2 is negative because the right-hand surface is concave toward the light. One of the radii can also be infinite if the corresponding surface is flat.

Lenses are made in a variety of shapes, as shown in Fig. 36-28. Those that are thicker at the center are converging lenses, for which Equation 36-8 gives a positive focal length. Those that are thinner at the center are diverging lenses, with negative focal length. These characterizations of lens behavior reverse if

Plano-convex   Double convex   Convex meniscus

Plano-concave   Double concave   Concave meniscus

FIGURE 36-28 Common lens types.

the medium surrounding the lens has a higher refractive index than the lens itself (see Problem 73, which generalizes Equation 36-8 for an arbitrary refractive index in the surrounding medium).

EXAMPLE 36-7	A Plano-Convex Lens

The plano-convex lens in Fig. 36-28 is made from material with refractive index n. Given that the curved surface has curvature radius R, find an expression for the focal length of the lens. Show that the focal length is the same whether light is incident on the lens from right or left.

Solution

With light incident from the left in Fig. 36-28, $R_1 = R$. A flat surface has infinite curvature, so $R_2 = \infty$. Then Equation 36-18 gives

$$f = \left[(n-1)\left(\frac{1}{R} - \frac{1}{\infty} \right) \right]^{-1} = \frac{R}{n-1},$$

since $1/\infty = 0$. If light is incident from the right, then $R_1 = \infty$ and, since the curved surface is now concave toward the light,

$R_2 = -R$. Then

$$f = \left[(n-1)\left(\frac{1}{\infty} - \frac{1}{-R} \right) \right]^{-1} = \frac{R}{n-1},$$

showing that the two focal points are indeed equidistant from the lens.

EXERCISE A double-convex lens (see Fig. 36-28) is made of glass with $n = 1.75$. If the curvature radii of the two sides are equal, what should that radius be in order to give the lens a 25-cm focal length?

Answer: 37.5 cm

Some problems similar to Example 36-7: 38–47

Lens Aberrations

Lenses exhibit several types of optical defects. We've already described **spherical aberration** in connection with mirrors; this defect occurs because a spherical mirror only approximates the ideally focusing shape of a parabola. Lenses with spherical surfaces also exhibit spherical aberration (Fig. 36-29a). In our analysis of image formation by a curved refracting surface we had to make the small-angle approximation; otherwise, we would not have reached the conclusion that all rays from an object come to a common focus. Spherical aberration can be minimized by ensuring that incident rays are as close and as parallel as possible to the lens axis. That's easy for distant objects but harder with objects close to the lens. Using only the central portion of the lens eliminates those rays at larger angles (Fig. 36-29b), leading to a sharper focus. That's why a camera focuses over a wider range when it is "stopped down," the outer part of its lens

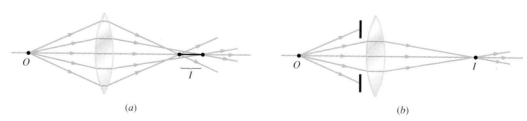

(a)   (b)

FIGURE 36-29 (a) Spherical aberration occurs because rays striking the lens farther from the axis and at greater angles focus closer to the lens than do near-axial rays. The result is a "smearing" of the image. (b) This defect can be minimized by using only the central portion of the lens, at the expense of a dimmer image.

FIGURE 36-30 Chromatic aberration occurs because the refractive index varies with wavelength, causing different colors to focus at different points.

covered by an adjustable diaphragm. The trade-off, of course, is that there is less light available.

Another optical defect is **chromatic aberration** (Fig. 36-30), which occurs because the refractive index varies with wavelength. High-quality optical systems minimize this defect by using composite lenses made from different materials whose differing refractive indices allow several colors to focus at the same point. Chromatic aberration is unique to lenses since mirrors reflect light of all colors in exactly the same way. Figure 36-31 shows both spherical and chromatic aberration in a simple magnifying lens.

FIGURE 36-31 This magnifying lens shows both spherical aberration (distortion of the lines) and chromatic aberration (colors).

APPLICATION	*Fresnel Lenses*

Large-diameter lenses are impractically thick. Lighthouses, in particular, cannot use single lenses to concentrate their intense beams because too much light would be absorbed in the glass. To solve this problem the French scientist Augustin Fresnel, in 1822, devised a way of making large lenses thin. A Fresnel lens consists of concentric rings shaped to approximate segments of an ordinary lens surface, with steplike jumps to keep the overall structure thin (Fig. 36-32a). Fresnel lenses are still used in

lighthouses (Fig. 36-32b), while Fresnel lenses made from plastic sheets appear in home, office, and car windows to provide magnification or wide-angle views (Fig. 36-32c). They are also used in some overhead projectors.

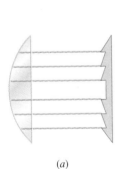

(a)

(b)

(c)

FIGURE 36-32 (a) A Fresnel lens approximates a normal curved lens by a series of short segments. (b) A giant Fresnel lens from a nineteenth-century lighthouse. (c) Fresnel lens made from sheet plastic mounted on the rear window of a van provides a wide-angle view of what's behind the van.

36-5 OPTICAL INSTRUMENTS

Numerous optical instruments make use of mirrors and/or lenses. We've already considered some simple applications using a single lens or mirror, including film projectors, magnifying glasses, and side-view mirrors. More complicated systems use several optical elements (lenses or mirrors), but the principles we have developed still apply. In particular, we trace light through a sequence of optical elements by using the image formed by one element as the object for the next.

The Eye

15.3

The Eye

Our eyes are our primary optical instruments. Each eye is a complex optical system with several refracting surfaces and mechanisms to vary both the focal length and the amount of light admitted. Figure 36-33*a* shows that the eye is essentially a fluid-filled ball about 2.3 cm in diameter. Light enters through the hard, transparent cornea and passes through a fluid called the aqueous humor before entering the lens. On exiting the lens, light traverses the vitreous humor that fills the main body of the eyeball and finally strikes the retina. The retina is covered with light-sensitive cells of two types (Fig. 36-33*b*). Cells called cones are sensitive to different colors but require moderate amounts of light, while rod cells function at low intensity but lack color discrimination. Both types of cells produce electrochemical signals that carry information to the brain.

A properly functioning eye produces a well-focused real image on the retina. Contrary to general belief, most of the refraction is provided not by the lens but by the cornea. The lens, however, is the adjustable element. Muscles pulling on the lens alter its focal length, allowing fine adjustment of the eye's focus—a process known as accommodation. Other muscles automatically adjust the iris, enlarging or contracting the pupil opening to compensate for different light levels.

When the muscles are relaxed, the lens is relatively flat, with focal length about 1.7 cm. But for nearsighted (myopic) people, the image still forms in front

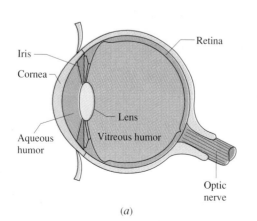

(*a*)

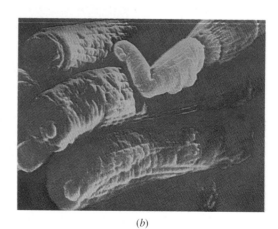

(*b*)

FIGURE 36-33 (*a*) The human eye. (*b*) Scanning-electron-microscope image showing rods and a cone (blue structure) in a human retina.

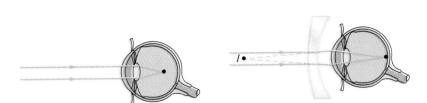

FIGURE 36-34 (a) A myopic eye focuses light from distant objects in front of the retina. (b) A diverging lens corrects the problem, creating a virtual image closer to the eye. The eye's image of this virtual image then falls on the retina.

of the retina, causing distant objects to appear blurred (Fig. 36-34a). Diverging corrective lenses produce closer intermediate images that the myopic eye can then focus (Fig. 36-34). In farsighted (hyperopic) eyes, the image of nearby objects would focus behind the retina, and converging corrective lenses are used (Fig. 36-35). Actually, everyone is farsighted, in the sense that there is a minimum distance, called the **near point**, below which the eye cannot focus sharply. In the typical human the near point is at about 25 cm, and this value is taken as a standard. By the time one is 50, however, the typical near point is at about 40 cm, and it may be several meters.

ActivPhysics Activity 15.13 simulates both near- and farsighted eyes.

Prescriptions for corrective lenses usually specify the corrective power, P, in **diopters**, where the diopter measure of a lens is the inverse of its focal length in meters. Thus, a 1-diopter lens has $f = 1$ m, while a 2-diopter lens has $f = 0.5$ m and is more powerful in that it refracts light more sharply.

Since even the closest objects we view are many centimeters from the eye, it doesn't matter whether a corrective lens is a few cm away from the eye, as with glasses, or right on the cornea, as with a contact lens. Today's soft contact lenses are more than 50 percent water and provide a natural-seeming addition to the cornea that corrects simple vision defects. Contact lenses can be quite thin because, as Equation 36-8 shows, it's the curvature radii rather than the lens thickness that establishes the focal length. On the other hand, glasses remain somewhat more versatile, with variable-focus lenses available that can compensate for defects in both near and far vision. A more radical approach is laser surgery to reshape the cornea; when successful, it can eliminate the need for corrective lenses.

The human eye is a complex biological system, in many ways a direct extension of the brain. Although we understand its optical behavior, we understand much less clearly how visual perception actually occurs. Recently biologists and computer scientists have teamed to produce an electronic "silicon retina" whose behavior mimics many subtle aspects of the natural eye and may therefore shed light on the process of perception.

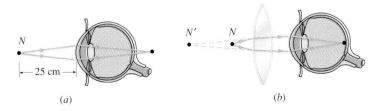

FIGURE 36-35 (a) A farsighted eye cannot focus light from the standard 25-cm near point at N. (b) A converging corrective lens makes light from an object at the near point appear to come from the point N' which is at the minimum distance where this eye can focus.

EXAMPLE 36-8	*Lost Your Glasses!*

You're on vacation and have lost your reading glasses; without them, your eyes can't focus closer than 70 cm. Fortunately you can buy nonprescription reading glasses in a pharmacy, where they come in increments of 0.25 diopter. Which glasses should you buy?

Solution

Correcting your vision problem means bringing the range for clear focus to the standard 25-cm near point. According to Fig. 36-35b, that means you want a lens that will produce a virtual image at 70 cm of an object at 25 cm. The required power follows directly from Equation 36-5:

$$P = \frac{1}{f} = \frac{1}{\ell} + \frac{1}{\ell'} = \frac{1}{0.25 \text{ m}} + \frac{1}{-0.70 \text{ m}} = 2.57 \text{ diopters},$$

where the image distance is negative because the image is virtual. You'll do fine with 2.5-diopter glasses.

EXERCISE A nearsighted person cannot see clearly beyond 80 cm. Prescribe a lens power that will image the most distant objects at 80 cm, giving clear vision at all distances.

Answer: −1.25 diopters, the minus sign signifying a diverging lens

Some problems similar to Example 36-8: 48–50, 69

Got It!

You and your roommate have gotten your boxes of disposable contact lenses mixed up. One box is marked "−1.75 diopter," the other "+2.25 diopter." You're farsighted and your roommate is nearsighted. Which contact lenses are yours?

Cameras

A camera is much like the eye, except that in place of the eye's retina it focuses its image on film or a light-sensitive electronic device (Fig. 36-36). Most still cameras use the long-established technology of film based on light-sensitive chemicals, but light-sensitive silicon chips known as charge-coupled devices (CCDs) have already made film obsolete in astronomical imaging and, with the proliferation of digital cameras, are rapidly challenging conventional photography.

All but the simplest cameras have movable lenses that adjust, either manually or automatically, for optimum focus with different distances to the subject. Most

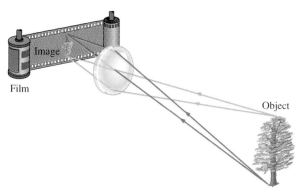

FIGURE 36-36 Optical system of a simple camera.

(a)	(b)

FIGURE 36-37 Photos taken from the same point with (a) short and (b) long focal length settings of an adjustable zoom lens.

cameras also have an adjustable diaphragm that covers part of the lens to regulate the amount of incoming light; "stopping down" the lens by closing the diaphragm admits less light but permits a broader range of distances to be in reasonably clear focus. Many cameras have zoom lenses whose focal lengths can be altered to provide different views of the same subject (Fig. 36-37).

Magnifiers and Microscopes

We wouldn't need optical instruments to examine small objects if we could bring our eyes arbitrarily close to the objects. But we've seen that the average human eye can't focus much closer than about 25 cm. We therefore use lenses to put enlarged images of small objects at distances where our eyes can focus.

What matters is not so much the actual size of the image, but how much of our field of view it occupies. Consequently we define the **angular magnification** m as the ratio of the angle subtended by an object seen through a lens to the angle subtended as seen by the naked eye when the object is at the standard 25-cm near point. Figure 36-38a shows that the former angle, α, is given

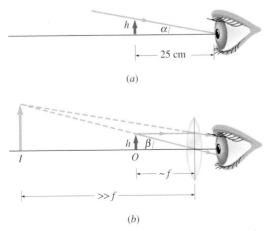

(a)

(b)

FIGURE 36-38 (a) An object of height h subtends a small angle $\alpha \simeq h/25$ cm at the standard 25-cm near point. (b) Putting the object near the focus of a converging lens gives an image that subtends an angle $\beta \simeq h/f$. The angular magnification is the ratio $m = \beta/\alpha$.

by $\alpha = h/25$ cm, where h is the object height and α is in radians. The maximum magnification would occur with the image itself at the near point (see Problem 53), but it's more comfortable to view a very distant image. We therefore place the object at just inside the focal length, forming an enlarged virtual image at a great distance. Figure 36-38b shows this geometry, from which we see that the angle β subtended by the image is essentially h/f. Then the magnification is

15.11

Two-Lens Systems

$$m = \frac{\beta}{\alpha} = \frac{h/f}{h/25 \text{ cm}} = \frac{25 \text{ cm}}{f} \qquad \text{(simple magnifier)}. \qquad \text{(36-9)}$$

This angular magnification is achieved only with the eye very close to the lens, which is not the way we normally hold an ordinary magnifying glass. But it is the way we place our eyes on instruments such as microscopes and telescopes that use simple magnifying lenses for their eyepieces.

15.14

Microscope

Single lenses can produce angular magnifications of about 4 before aberrations compromise the image quality. Higher power magnification therefore requires more than one lens. A **compound microscope** is a two-lens system in which a lens of short focal length called the **objective** forms a magnified real image. This image is then viewed with a second lens, the **eyepiece**, positioned as a simple magnifier (Fig. 36-39). The object being viewed is positioned just beyond the focal length of the objective lens, and its image falls just inside the focal length of the eyepiece. If both focal lengths are small compared with the distance between the lenses, then the object distance for the objective lens is approximately the objective focal length f_o, and the resulting image distance is approximately the lens spacing L. The real image formed by the objective lens is larger than the object by the ratio of the image to object distance, or $-L/f_o$. The eyepiece enlarges the image further, by a factor of its angular magnification $25 \text{ cm}/f_e$. Then the overall magnification of the microscope is

$$M = M_o m_e = -\frac{L}{f_o}\left(\frac{25 \text{ cm}}{f_e}\right), \qquad \text{(compound microscope)} \quad \text{(36-10)}$$

where, as usual, the minus sign signifies an inverted image.

Optical microscopes work well as long as the approximation of geometrical optics holds—that is, when the object being viewed is much larger than the wavelength of light. Viewing smaller objects requires waves of shorter wavelength than visible light. In the widely used electron microscope, those "waves" are electrons, whose wavelike nature we will examine in Chapter 39.

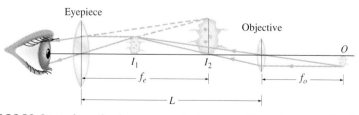

FIGURE 36-39 Image formation in a compound microscope. Figure is not to scale; distance L should be much greater than either focal length, and the image I_1 should be very near the eyepiece's focus, resulting in greater magnification.

You can "build" and experiment with 2-lens optical systems, such as the microscope, using ActivPhysics Activity 15.11.

Telescopes

A telescope collects light from distant objects, either forming an image or supplying light to instruments for analysis. Telescopes are classified as **refracting** or **reflecting**, depending on whether the main light-gathering element is a lens or mirror. Small hand-held telescopes and binoculars are refracting instruments, as are telephoto camera lenses and some older astronomical telescopes. Modern astronomical telescopes are invariably reflectors.

The simplest refracting telescope consists of a single lens that images distant objects at essentially its focal point. Film or a CCD placed at that point captures the image, or an eyepiece is used to view the image. The world's largest refracting telescope, at Yerkes Observatory in Wisconsin, has a 1-m-diameter lens with 12-m focal length. Photographers can think of it as a 12,000-mm telephoto lens. Figure 36-40 shows the imaging process in an astronomical refracting telescope. The focal points of the objective and eyepiece lenses are nearly coincident, so the real image of a distant object that forms at the objective's focus is then seen through the eyepiece as a greatly enlarged virtual image. The angular magnification is the ratio of the angle β subtended by the final image to the angle α subtended by the actual object; Fig. 36-40 shows that this ratio is

15.12
The Telescope

$$m = \frac{\beta}{\alpha} = \frac{f_o}{f_e}. \qquad \text{(refracting telescope)} \qquad (36\text{-}11)$$

Since a real image is inverted and a virtual image is upright, a two-lens refracting telescope gives an inverted image. This is fine for astronomical work, but telescopes designed for terrestrial use have an extra lens, a diverging eyepiece (see Problem 72) or a set of reflecting prisms (as in binoculars; see Fig. 35-15) to produce an upright image.

Reflecting telescopes offer many advantages over refractors. Mirrors have reflective coatings on their front surfaces, eliminating chromatic aberration because light need not pass through glass. Having only one optically active

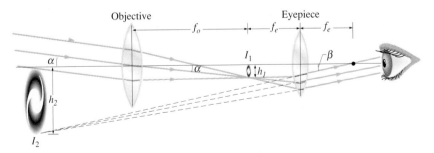

FIGURE 36-40 Image formation in a refracting telescope. A distant object, in this case a galaxy, is imaged first at the focus of the objective lens (image I_1). An eyepiece with its focus at nearly the same point then gives an enlarged virtual image (I_2). The angles α and β are given by $\alpha = h_1/f_o$ and $\beta = h_1/f_e$ in the small-angle approximation, leading to Equation 36-11 for the angular magnification.

FIGURE 36-41 One of the two identical Keck telescopes that occupy adjacent observatory domes atop Hawaii's Mauna Kea. Each telescope has a hexagonal mirror 10 m across, consisting of 36 individually adjustable segments; here the entire mirror is visible through the slit in the dome. The two Keck telescopes are being joined optically with four smaller telescopes to form an instrument with the resolving power of an 85-m telescope. (More on how this works in the next chapter.)

surface allows much larger reflectors to be built since the mirrors can be supported across their entire back surfaces—unlike lenses, which can be supported only at the edges. Where the largest refracting telescope ever built has a 1-m-diameter lens, the newest reflectors boast diameters in the 10-m range (Fig. 36-41). These designs incorporate segmented and/or flexible mirrors whose shape can be adjusted under computer control for optimum focusing; with so-called adaptive optics, such systems may adjust rapidly enough to compensate for the atmospheric turbulence that has traditionally limited the resolution of ground-based telescopes.

The simplest reflecting telescope is a curved mirror with a CCD or film at its focus. Superb image quality results, in principle limited only by wave effects we will discuss in the next chapter. More often the telescope is used as a "light bucket," collecting light from stars or other distant sources too small to image even with today's large optical telescopes. Then a secondary mirror sends light to a focus at a point that's convenient for telescope-mounted instrumentation. Optical fibers may also be used to bring light collected by the primary mirror to fixed instruments. Alternatively, an eyepiece can be mounted to examine the image visually. Figure 36-42 shows several common designs for reflecting telescopes.

Magnification is not a particularly important quantity in astronomical telescopes, which are used more for spectral and other analysis than for direct imaging. More important is the light-gathering power of the instrument, which is determined simply by the area of its objective lens or primary mirror. The 10-m Keck telescope, for instance, has 100 times the light-gathering power of the 1-m Yerkes refractor and more than 17 times the power of the 2.4-m Hubble Space Telescope.

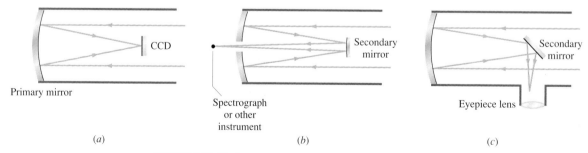

(a) (b) (c)

FIGURE 36-42 Common arrangements for reflecting telescopes. (a) Placing a CCD or film at the prime focus gives the best image quality. (b) In the Cassegrain design light reflects from a secondary mirror and passes through a hole in the primary. The secondary may be either plane or convex. This design is widely used in large telescopes, with the added option of placing detectors directly at the prime focus as in (a). (c) The Newtonian design, used primarily in small telescopes, has an angled secondary mirror to direct light to the eyepiece.

CHAPTER SYNOPSIS

Summary

1. Reflection and refraction can result in **images**, which are **real** or **virtual** depending on whether light actually comes from the image location.

2. Plane mirrors form only virtual images, equal in size to the object being imaged. Concave curved mirrors have a **focal point** at which parallel rays converge after reflection. Concave mirrors form either real or virtual images, depending on the object location. For convex mirrors, parallel rays reflect as though diverging from the focal point; such mirrors can form only virtual images. The **mirror equation** quantifies the relation between object and image distances ℓ and ℓ':

$$\frac{1}{\ell} + \frac{1}{\ell'} = \frac{1}{f},$$

where the **focal length** f is the distance from the mirror's apex to its focus. The **magnification** is the ratio $M = -\ell'/\ell$, where a negative ℓ' corresponds to a virtual image and therefore to a positive M and so to an upright image.

3. **Lenses**, made from transparent materials, refract light to a focus. In the **thin-lens** approximation, the curvature radii of the lens surfaces are much greater than the thickness of the lens. Such a lens has two foci, located equal distances f on either side of the lens. The object and image distances and magnification then obey equations identical to those for mirrors. The focal length of a thin lens is given by the **lensmaker's equation**:

$$\frac{1}{f} = (n - 1)\left(\frac{1}{R_1} - \frac{1}{R_2}\right),$$

where R_1 and R_2 are the curvature radii of the lens surfaces, taken as positive when the surface is convex toward the incident light. A positive focal length f corresponds to a **converging lens** and a negative f to a **diverging lens**. Lens **aberrations** are focusing defects resulting from imperfect lens shapes and the variation of refractive index with wavelength.

4. Optical instruments use lenses and/or mirrors to form useful images. The power of instrument lenses is often given in **diopters**—the inverse of the focal length in meters.

Terms You Should Understand

(Pairs are closely related terms whose distinction is important; number in parentheses is chapter section where term first appears.)

real image, virtual image (introduction)
focal point, focal length (36-2)
magnification (36-2)
thin lens (36-3)
converging lens, diverging lens (36-3)
spherical aberration, chromatic aberration (36-2, 36-3)
near point (36-5)
diopter (36-5)
angular magnification (36-5)
compound microscope (36-5)
reflecting telescope, refracting telescope (36-5)

Symbols You Should Recognize

ℓ, ℓ' (36-2, 36-3)
f (36-2, 36-3)
M, m (36-2–36-4)

Problems You Should be Able to Solve

finding mirror images and their sizes using ray tracing and algebraic techniques (36-2)
finding lens images and their sizes using ray tracing and algebraic techniques (36-3)
analyzing image formation at a single refracting surface (36-4)
designing lenses and analyzing their focal properties (36-4)
designing and analyzing simple optical instruments (36-5)

Limitations to Keep in Mind

Our description of imaging is based on the approximation of geometrical optics, valid only when objects and optical components are much larger than the wavelength of light.
Formulas for image formation in spherical mirrors and lenses are approximations, valid under the conditions that the curved surfaces used form only a small portion of a full sphere, and that all light rays are nearly parallel to the mirror or lens axis.

QUESTIONS

1. How can you see a virtual image, when it really "isn't there"?

2. You're trying to photograph yourself in a mirror, using an autofocus camera that sets its focus by bouncing ultrasound waves off the subject at which the camera is pointed. Why might the photo come out blurred?

3. You lay a magnifying glass (which is just a converging lens) on a printed page. Looking toward the glass, you move it away from the page. Explain the changes in what you see, especially as you move the lens beyond its focal length.

4. Under what circumstances will the image in a concave mirror be the same size as the object?

5. Describe the shapes of the mirrors making the images in Fig. 36-43.

FIGURE 36-43 Question 5.

6. If you're handed a converging lens, what can you do to estimate quickly its focal length?
7. What is the meaning of a negative object distance? Of a negative focal length?
8. A diverging lens always makes a reduced image. Could you use such a lens to start a fire by focusing sunlight? Explain.
9. Is there any limit to the temperature you can achieve by focusing sunlight? Think about the second law of thermodynamics.

10. Can a concave mirror make a reduced real image? A reduced virtual image? An enlarged real image? An enlarged virtual image? Give conditions for each image that is possible.
11. If you placed a screen at the location of a virtual image, would you see the image on the screen? Why or why not?
12. Where must the object be placed to form a reduced real image with a concave mirror or converging lens?
13. Where should you place a flashlight bulb in relation to the focus of its reflector?
14. Is the image on a movie screen real or virtual? How do you know?
15. Does a fish in a spherical bowl appear larger or smaller than it actually is?
16. A block of ice contains a hollow, air-filled space in the shape of a double-convex lens. Describe the optical behavior of this space.
17. The refractive index of the human cornea is about 1.38. If you can see clearly in air, why can't you see clearly underwater? Why do goggles help?
18. The compound microscope and the refracting telescope are both two-lens optical systems. How do their designs reflect their different uses?
19. Cheap binoculars sometimes show blurred images with different colors evident across the blurred region. Why?
20. Do you want a long or short focal length for the objective lens of a telescope? Of a microscope?
21. Give several reasons reflecting telescopes are superior to refractors.
22. Given that star images cannot be resolved even with telescopes, why are large telescopes superior to ordinary cameras for studying stars?

PROBLEMS

ActivPhysics can help with these problems: All activities in Section 15

Sections 36-1 and 36-2 Plane and Curved Mirrors

1. A shoe store uses small floor-level mirrors to let customers view prospective purchases. At what angle should such a mirror be inclined so that a person standing 50 cm from the mirror with eyes 140 cm off the floor can see her feet?
2. Two plane mirrors occupy the first four meters of the positive x and y axes, as shown in Fig. 36-44. Find the locations of all images of an object at $x = 2$ m, $y = 1$ m.
3. (a) What is the focal length of a concave mirror if an object placed 50 cm in front of the mirror has a real image 75 cm from the mirror? (b) Where and what type will the image be if the object is moved to a point 20 cm from the mirror?

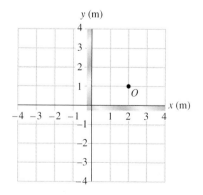

FIGURE 36-44 Problem 2.

4. A candle is 36 cm from a concave mirror with focal length 15 cm and on the mirror axis. (a) Where is its image? (b) How do the image and object sizes compare? (c) Is the image real or virtual?

5. An object is five focal lengths from a concave mirror. (a) How do the object and image heights compare? (b) Is the image upright or inverted?

6. The McMath-Pierce solar telescope at Kitt Peak National Observatory (Fig. 36-45) uses a single concave mirror to produce a real solar image 80 cm in diameter. (a) What is the focal length of the mirror? (b) How far is the image from the mirror? *Hint:* Consult Appendix E.

FIGURE 36-45 The McMath-Pierce solar telescope (Problem 6).

7. A virtual image is located 40 cm behind a concave mirror with focal length 18 cm. (a) Where is the object? (b) By how much is the image magnified?

8. (a) Where on the axis of a concave mirror would you place an object in order to produce a full-size image? (b) Will the image be real or virtual?

9. A 12-mm-high object is 10 cm from a concave mirror with focal length 17 cm. (a) Where, (b) how high, and (c) what type is its image?

10. Repeat the preceding problem for a convex mirror, assuming all numbers stay the same.

11. An object's image in a 27-cm-focal-length concave mirror is upright and magnified by a factor of 3. Where is the object?

12. What is the curvature radius of a concave mirror that produces a 9.5-cm-high virtual image of a 5.7-cm-high object, when the object is located 22 cm from the mirror?

13. When viewed from Earth, the moon subtends an angle of 0.5° in the sky. How large an image of the moon will be formed by the 3.6-m-diameter mirror of the Canada-France-Hawaii telescope, which has a focal length of 8.5 m?

14. At what two distances could you place an object from a 45-cm-focal-length concave mirror in order to get an image 1.5 times the object's size?

15. You look into a reflecting sphere 80 cm in diameter and you see an image of your face at one-third its normal size (Fig. 36-46). How far are you from the sphere's surface?

FIGURE 36-46 Problem 15.

16. Carry out the algebraic steps described just before Equation 36-3 to complete the proof that the focal length of a spherical mirror is half its curvature radius.

Section 36-3 Lenses

17. A light bulb is 56 cm from a convex lens, and its image appears on a screen located 31 cm on the other side of the lens. (a) What is the focal length of the lens? (b) By how much is the image enlarged or reduced?

18. By what factor is the image magnified when an object is placed 1.5 focal lengths from a converging lens? Is the image upright or inverted?

19. A lens with 50-cm focal length produces a real image the same size as the object. How far from the lens are image and object?

20. By holding a magnifying glass 25 cm from my desk lamp, I find I can focus an image of the lamp's bulb on a wall 1.6 m from the lamp. What is the focal length of my magnifying glass?

21. A simple camera uses a single converging lens to focus an image on its film. If the focal length of the lens is 45 mm, what should be the lens-to-film distance for the camera to focus on an object 80 cm from the lens?

22. A real image is 4 times as far from a lens as is the object. What is the object distance, measured in focal lengths?

23. How far from a page should you hold a lens with 32-cm focal length in order to see the print magnified 1.6 times?

24. A converging lens has a focal length of 4.0 cm. A 1.0-cm-high arrow is located 7.0 cm from the lens with its lowest point 5.0 mm above the lens axis. Make a full-scale drawing of the situation, and use ray tracing to locate the image. Confirm using the lens equation.

25. The largest refracting telescope in the world, at Yerkes Observatory, has a 1-m-diameter lens with focal length 12 m (Fig. 36-47). If an airplane flew 1 km above the telescope, where would its image occur in relation to the images of the very distant stars?

FIGURE 36-47 The Yerkes Observatory boasts the world's largest refracting telescope (Problem 25).

26. A small magnifying glass can focus sunlight sufficiently to ignite paper. Calculate the actual size of the solar image produced by a magnifying glass consisting of an optically perfect lens with 25-cm focal length. *Hint:* You'll need to consult Appendix E.

27. A lens has focal length $f = 35$ cm. Find the type and height of the image produced when a 2.2-cm-high object is placed at distances (a) $f + 10$ cm and (b) $f - 10$ cm.

28. How far apart are object and image produced by a converging lens with 35-cm focal length when the object is (a) 40 cm and (b) 30 cm from the lens?

29. A candle and a screen are 70 cm apart. Find two points between candle and screen where you could put a convex lens with 17 cm focal length to give a sharp image of the candle on the screen.

30. An object is placed two focal lengths from a diverging lens. (a) What type of image forms, (b) what is the magnification, and (c) where is the image?

Section 36-4 Refraction in Lenses: The Details

31. You're standing in a wading pool and your feet appear to be 30 cm below the surface. How deep is the pool?

32. A tiny insect is trapped 1.0 mm from the center of a spherical dew drop 4.0 mm in diameter. As you look straight into the drop at the insect, what is its apparent distance from the edge of the drop?

33. Use Equation 36-6 to show that an object at the center of a glass sphere will appear to be its actual distance—one radius—from the edge. Draw a ray diagram showing why this result makes sense.

34. You're underwater, looking through a spherical air bubble (Fig. 36-48). What is its actual diameter if it appears, along your line of sight, to be 1.5 cm in diameter?

FIGURE 36-48 Problem 34.

35. Rework Example 36-6 for a fish 15 cm from the *far* wall of the tank.

36. Consider the inverse of Example 36-6: You're inside a 70-cm-diameter hollow tube containing air, and the tip of your nose is 15 cm from the wall of the tube. The tube is immersed in water, and a fish looks in. To the fish, what is the apparent distance from your nose to the tube wall?

37. Two specks of dirt are trapped in a crystal ball, one at the center and the other halfway to the surface. If you peer into the ball on a line joining the two specks, the outer one appears to be only one-third of the way to the other. What is the refractive index of the ball?

38. My magnifying glass is a double convex lens with equal curvature radii of 32 cm. If the lens glass has $n = 1.52$, what is its focal length?

39. A contact lens is in the shape of a convex meniscus (see Fig. 36-28); the inner surface is curved to fit the eye, with a curvature radius of 7.80 mm. The lens is made from plastic with refractive index $n = 1.56$. If it's to have a focal length of 44.4 cm, what should be the curvature radius of its outer surface?

40. For what refractive index would the focal length of a plano-convex lens be equal to the curvature radius of its one curved surface?

41. An object is 28 cm from a double convex lens with $n = 1.5$ and curvature radii 35 cm and 55 cm. Where and what type is the image?

42. A double convex lens has equal curvature radii of 35 cm. An object placed 30 cm from the lens forms a real image at 128 cm. What is the refractive index of the lens?

43. A plano-convex lens has curvature radius 20 cm and is made from glass with $n = 1.5$. Use the generalized lens-maker's formula given in Problem 73 to find the focal length when the lens is (a) in air, (b) submerged in water ($n = 1.333$), and (c) embedded in glass with $n = 1.7$. Comment on the sign of your answer to (c).

44. A slide projector has a double convex lens with equal curvature radii, and is made from glass with $n = 1.58$. (a) What should be the curvature radius to give a focal length of 104 mm? (b) With this focal length, how far from the focal point should the slide be placed to focus its image on a screen 3.1 m distant from the lens?

45. Two plano-convex lenses are geometrically identical, but one is made from crown glass ($n = 1.52$), the other from flint glass. An object at 45 cm from the lens focuses to a real image at 85 cm with the crown-glass lens and at 53 cm with the flint-glass lens. Find (a) the curvature radius (common to both lenses) and (b) the refractive index of the flint glass.

46. A double convex lens with equal 38-cm curvature radii is made from glass with refractive indices $n_{red} = 1.51$, $n_{blue} = 1.54$ at the edges of the visible spectrum. If a point source of white light is placed on the lens axis at 95 cm from the lens, over what range will its visible image be smeared?

47. An object placed 15 cm from a plano-convex lens made of crown glass focuses to a virtual image twice the size of the object. If the lens is replaced with an identically shaped one made from diamond, what type of image will appear and what will be its magnification? See Table 35-1.

Section 36-5 Optical Instruments

48. You find that you have to hold a book 55 cm from your eyes for the print to be in sharp focus (Fig. 36-49). What power lens is needed to correct your farsightedness?

55 cm

FIGURE 36-49 Problem 48.

49. Grandma's new reading glasses have 3.8-diopter lenses to provide full correction of her farsightedness. Her old glasses were 2.5 diopters. (a) Where is the near point for her unaided eyes? (b) Where will be the near point if she wears her old glasses?

50. A particular eye has a focal length of 2.0 cm instead of the 2.2 cm that would be required for a sharply focused image on the retina. (a) Is this eye nearsighted or farsighted? (b) What power of corrective lens is needed?

51. A camera's zoom lens covers the focal length range from 38 mm to 110 mm. You point the camera at a distant object and photograph it first at 38 mm and then with the camera zoomed out to 110 mm. Compare the sizes of its images on the two photos.

52. A camera can normally focus as close as 60 cm, but it has provisions for mounting additional lenses at the outer end of the main lens to provide closeup capability. What type and power of auxiliary lens will allow the camera to focus as close as 20 cm? The distance between the two lenses is negligible.

53. The maximum magnification of a simple magnifier occurs with the image at the 25-cm near point. Show that the angular magnification is then given by $m = 1 + \dfrac{25 \text{ cm}}{f}$, where f is the focal length.

54. A compound microscope has objective and eyepiece focal lengths of 6.1 mm and 1.7 cm, respectively. If the lenses are 8.3 cm apart, what is the magnification of the instrument?

55. A 300-power compound microscope has a 4.5-mm-focal-length objective lens. If the distance from objective to eyepiece is 10 cm, what should be the focal length of the eyepiece?

56. To the unaided eye, the planet Jupiter has an angular diameter of 50 arc seconds. What will be its angular size when viewed through a 1-m-focal-length refracting telescope with an eyepiece whose focal length is 40 mm?

57. A Cassegrain telescope like that shown in Fig. 36-42b has 1.0-m focal length, and the convex secondary mirror is located 0.85 m from the primary. What should be the focal length of the secondary in order to put the final image 0.12 m behind the front surface of the primary mirror?

58. The Hubble Space Telescope is essentially a Cassegrain reflector like that shown in Fig. 36-42b. The focal lengths of the concave primary and convex secondary mirrors are 5520.00 mm and −679.00 mm, respectively. The secondary is located at 4906.071 mm from the apex of the primary. Draw a ray diagram showing the path of initially parallel incident rays through the telescope, and use appropriate equations to determine where in Fig. 36-42b such rays are finally focused.

Paired Problems

(Both problems in a pair involve the same principles and techniques. If you can get the first problem, you should be able to solve the second one.)

59. (a) How far from a 1.2-m-focal length concave mirror should you place an object in order to get an inverted image 1.5 times the size of the object? (b) Where will the image be?

60. (a) How far from a 48-cm-focal length concave mirror should you place an object in order to get an upright image 1.5 times the size of the object? (b) Where will the image be?

61. Find the focal length of a concave mirror if an object 15 cm from the mirror has a virtual image 2.5 times the object's actual size.

62. An object is held 6.0 cm from the surface of a reflecting ball, and its image appears three-quarters full size. What is the ball's diameter?

63. How far from a 1.6-m focal length concave mirror should you place an object to get an upright image magnified by a factor of 2.5?

64. How far from a 25-cm-focal-length lens should you place an object to get an upright image magnified by a factor of 1.8?

65. An object and its lens-produced real image are 2.4 m apart. If the lens has 55-cm focal length, what are the possible values for the object distance and magnification?

66. An object and its converging-lens-produced virtual image are 2.4 m apart. If the lens has 55-cm focal length, what are the possible values for the object distance and magnification?

67. An object is 68 cm from a plano-convex lens whose curved side has curvature radius 26 cm. The refractive index of the lens is 1.62. Where and of what type is the image?

68. Both surfaces of a double concave lens have curvature radii of 18 cm, and the refractive index is 1.5. If a virtual image appears 14 cm from the lens, where is the object?

Supplementary Problems

69. My contact lens prescription calls for +2.25-diopter lenses with an inner curvature radius of 8.6 mm to fit my cornea. (a) If the lenses are made from plastic with $n = 1.56$, what should be the outer curvature radius? (b) Wearing these lenses, I hold a newspaper 30 cm from my eyes. Where is its image as viewed through the lenses?

70. Show that the powers of closely spaced lenses add; that is, placing a 1-diopter lens in front of a 2-diopter lens gives the equivalent of a single 3-diopter lens.

71. Show that identical objects placed equal distances on either side of the focal point of a concave mirror or converging lens produce images of equal size. Are the images of the same type?

72. Galileo's first telescope used the arrangement shown in Fig. 36-50, with a double convex eyepiece placed slightly before the focus of the objective lens. Use ray tracing to show that this system gives an upright image, which makes the design useful for terrestrial observing.

73. Generalize the derivation of the lensmaker's formula (Equation 36-8) to show a lens of refractive index n_{lens} in an external medium with index n_{ext} has focal length given

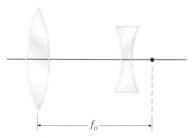

FIGURE 36-50 Problem 72.

by

$$\frac{1}{f} = \left(\frac{n_{lens}}{n_{ext}} - 1\right)\left(\frac{1}{R_1} - \frac{1}{R_2}\right).$$

74. An object is located 40 cm from a lens made from glass with $n = 1.5$. In air, the resulting image is real and is located 32 cm from the lens. When the entire system is immersed in a liquid, the image becomes virtual and is reduced to half the object's size. Use the result given in the preceding problem to find the refractive index of the liquid.

75. A Newtonian telescope like that of Fig. 36-42c has a primary mirror with 20-cm diameter and 1.2-m focal length. (a) Where should the flat diagonal mirror be placed to put the focus at the edge of the telescope tube? (b) What shape should the flat mirror have to minimize blockage of light to the primary?

76. A parabola is described by the equation $y = x^2/4f$, where f is the distance from vertex to focus. (a) Find the equation for the circle (which would be a sphere in three dimensions) that closely approximates the parabola $y = x^2$. *Hint:* How are the focal length and curvature radius of a spherical mirror related? (b) Solve the circle's equation for y, and use the binomial theorem to show that the equation reduces to that of the parabola for $x \ll 1$.

77. Just before Equation 36-7 are two equations describing refraction at the two surfaces of a lens with thickness t. Combine these equations to show that the object distance ℓ and image distance ℓ' for such a lens are related by

$$\frac{1}{\ell} + \frac{1}{\ell'} - \frac{[(n-1)\ell - R_1]^2 t}{\ell R_1[t(\ell + R_1) + n\ell(R_1 - t)]}$$
$$= (n-1)\left(\frac{1}{R_1} - \frac{1}{R_2}\right).$$

78. Use the result of the preceding problem to find an expression for the focal length of a transparent sphere with radius R and refractive index n, as measured from the exit surface.

Interference and Diffraction 37

Interference of light plays an important role in extracting information from compact discs. Here adjacent tracks of the microscopic "pits" that code the CD's information produce interference that results in a rainbow of colors. This chapter explores many applications of wave interference and diffraction, including the operation of CDs and the newer DVDs.

The preceding chapters considered reflection and refraction, and their application in image formation, from the approximation of geometrical optics—an approximation valid when we can ignore the wave nature of light. We now turn to **physical optics**, which treats optical phenomena for which the wave nature of light plays an essential role. Two related phenomena, interference and diffraction, are central to much of physical optics.

37-1 COHERENCE AND INTERFERENCE

We introduced wave **interference** in Chapter 16, showing how wave displacements add in a manner that may be constructive or destructive depending on the relative phases of the waves. Interference of electromagnetic waves—including light—occurs in the same way; since the electric and magnetic fields separately obey the superposition principle, the net electric and magnetic fields at any point are the vector sums of the fields of individual waves. The superposition of those fields may result in an increase (constructive interference) or decrease (destructive interference) in the field strength.

Coherence

Although interference occurs any time two waves interact, we get steady interference patterns only when the interacting waves are **coherent**, meaning that they maintain a constant phase relation. Ordinary sources such as light bulbs or the Sun produce light that is coherent only over very short distances. That's because light from these sources consists of short wavetrains emitted with random phases (Fig. 37-1a). Lasers, in contrast, produce relatively long wavetrains that maintain coherence over many wavelengths (Fig. 37-1b). The typical length of a wavetrain is the **coherence length** for a given light source.

Regardless of the source, it takes two or more waves to interfere. It's virtually impossible for two different light sources to maintain coherence, so such interference usually results only when light from a single source splits, travels different paths, and then recombines. Even light from an ordinary light bulb will produce interference patterns provided the light in the two recombining light beams originated at nearly the same place and time. With the more coherent light of a laser, interference occurs over a wider range of path differences.

Coherence requires that the interfering light beams have exactly the same frequency and therefore wavelength or color. With a white-light source such as sunlight, interference occurs separately for each different color. Again, lasers make things easier: their light is very nearly **monochromatic**, consisting of a narrow band of wavelengths. Very slight deviations from exactly equal

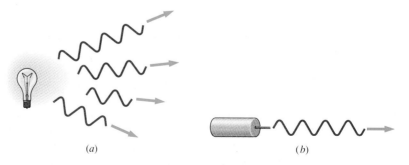

(a) (b)

FIGURE 37-1 (*a*) Light bulbs emit many short wavetrains whose phases are related in random ways. Coherent interference can occur only with light originating from a spatially limited region, so that a single wavetrain interferes with itself. The coherence length is defined as the average length of a wavetrain, here about 3 wavelengths. (*b*) Lasers produce light with much greater coherence length, making it easier to produce coherent interference with laser light.

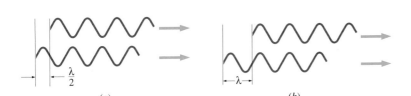

FIGURE 37-2 Two waves that started out in phase but have traveled different paths before coming together. (*a*) Here the lower wave travels half a wavelength farther, so the two come together 180° out of phase, and their superposition results in destructive interference. (*b*) When the lower wave travels a full wavelength farther, the two come together in phase and the interference is constructive.

frequency and wavelength may still permit observable interference, and yield the optical equivalent of the beats we introduced in Section 16-5.

Destructive and Constructive Interference

Consider light waves that originate together at a single source, travel two different paths, and then come together again. Suppose one wave's path is exactly half a wavelength longer. Then when the waves recombine they will be out of phase by half a wavelength (Fig. 37-2*a*), and thus their superposition will have lower amplitude (zero, if the two interfering waves have exactly the same amplitude). If, on the other hand, the path lengths don't differ, or differ by a full wavelength, then the two waves recombine in phase (Fig. 37-2*b*) and their superposition has greater amplitude. These two cases correspond, respectively, to **destructive interference** and **constructive interference**. It doesn't really matter whether path lengths for the waves in Fig. 37-2*a* differ by half a wavelength, or $1\frac{1}{2}$ wavelengths, or $2\frac{1}{2}$ wavelengths—as long as the difference is an odd multiple of a half wavelength, the waves recombine out of phase and destructive interference results. Thus:

> **Destructive interference results when light paths differ by an odd integer multiple of a half wavelength.**

Similarly, it doesn't matter whether the path lengths in Fig. 37-2*b* are the same, or differ by 1, 2, 3, or any other integer number of wavelengths. Thus

> **Constructive interference results when light paths differ by an integer multiple of the wavelength.**

We'll use these two statements to build an understanding of interference in both simple and complicated situations.

There's one caveat to our statements: the path difference can't be greater than the coherence length that we defined in connection with Fig. 37-1. Otherwise the interfering waves will be from different wavetrains, and won't be coherent. Once again, laser light has the advantage here, because of its greater coherence length.

Of course, light paths don't have to differ by half or full multiples of the wavelength. In intermediate cases interfering waves superpose to make a composite wave whose amplitude may be enhanced or diminished, depending on the relative phase as determined by the path-length difference.

APPLICATION	*CD Music, Continued*

Example 35-3, "CD Music," showed how refraction in a compact disc (CD) helps focus the laser beam that "reads" information from the disc. Interference, too, plays a crucial role in "reading" a CD.

Information on a CD—whether an audio signal or computer data—is stored digitally in a sequence of "pits"—depressions stamped into a reflective metallic "information layer" (Fig. 37-3). The pits vary in length, but their depth is the same—very nearly one-quarter wavelength of the laser light used to "read" the CD. From the transparent underside of the disc, where the laser beam enters, each pit appears as an elevated bump. Since the bumps stick down one-quarter

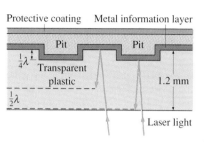

FIGURE 37-4 Structure of a CD, showing that pits appear as bumps to the laser beam shining from below the disc. Path lengths for the laser beam differ by a half wavelength depending on whether the light reflects off a bump, resulting in destructive interference when the beam strikes a bump and the surrounding disc surface.

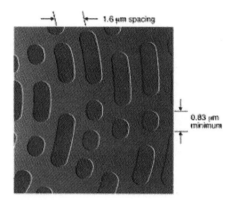

FIGURE 37-3 Information on a standard CD is stored in "pits" stamped into a metallic "information layer." The pits form a continuous spiral track that winds around the disc. Adjacent turns of the spiral are 1.6 μm apart, and the minimum pit length is 0.83 μm. Depth of the pits is approximately a quarter wavelength of the laser light used to "read" the CD.

wavelength, light reflecting off a bump follows a round-trip path that's shorter by half a wavelength compared with the path of light reflecting off the undisturbed information layer (Fig. 37-4). The laser beam that "reads" the disc is somewhat wider than the pit, so the reflected beam includes light both from the undisturbed disc as well as from the bump. The two interfere destructively, just as we showed in Fig. 37-2, making a much less intense reflected beam when a bump is present. As the disc spins, the result is a pattern of fluctuating light intensity conveying the information associated with the pattern of pits on the CD. A photodetector converts that pattern to electrical signals for processing by the electronic circuitry of the CD player or computer.

The new DVD discs introduced in the late 1990s work in exactly the same way, except—as we'll see later in this chapter—they can store much more information.

37-2 DOUBLE-SLIT INTERFERENCE

In Chapter 16 we looked briefly at interference patterns produced by a pair of coherent sources. With light, such a pair can be made by passing light from a single source through two narrow slits. In 1801 Thomas Young used this approach in a historic experiment that confirmed the wave nature of light. Young first admitted sunlight to his laboratory through a hole small enough to ensure coherence of the incoming light. The light then passed through a pair of narrow, closely spaced slits, after which it illuminated a screen. Each slit acts as a source of cylindrical wavefronts that interfere in the region between slits and screen (Fig. 37-5a). Constructive and destructive interference result in alternating regions of light and dark on the screen, as shown in Fig. 37-5b for laser light passed through double slits. The light and dark regions in Fig. 37-5b are called **interference fringes**.

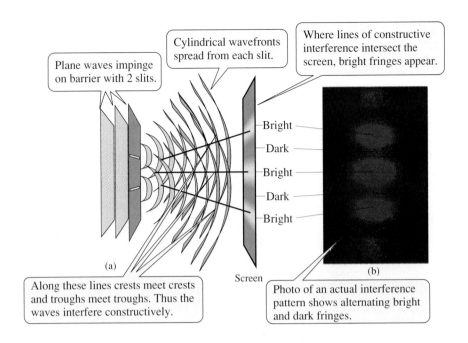

Plane waves impinge on barrier with 2 slits.

Cylindrical wavefronts spread from each slit.

Where lines of constructive interference intersect the screen, bright fringes appear.

Bright
Dark
Bright
Dark
Bright

(a)

Screen

Along these lines crests meet crests and troughs meet troughs. Thus the waves interfere constructively.

(b)

Photo of an actual interference pattern shows alternating bright and dark fringes.

FIGURE 37-5 Double-slit interference results when light from a single source passes through a pair of closely spaced slits. Photo in (b) was made by replacing the screen with film in an actual double-slit apparatus using laser light.

We can understand the occurrence and location of fringes in double-slit interference by applying our criteria for constructive and destructive interference. The bright fringes represent constructive interference, and therefore they occur where the difference in the path length for light traveling from the two different slits is a multiple of the wavelength. When the distance L from slits to screen is much larger than the slit spacing d, Fig. 37-6 then shows that the path difference from the two slits to a point on the screen is $d\sin\theta$, where θ is the angular position of a point on the screen, measured from an axis perpendicular to slits and screen. So our criterion for constructive interference—that this difference be an integer number of wavelengths—becomes

$$d\sin\theta = m\lambda. \qquad \text{(bright fringes)} \qquad (37\text{-}1a)$$

The integer m is the **order** of the fringe, with the central bright fringe being the zeroth order fringe and with higher order fringes on either side.

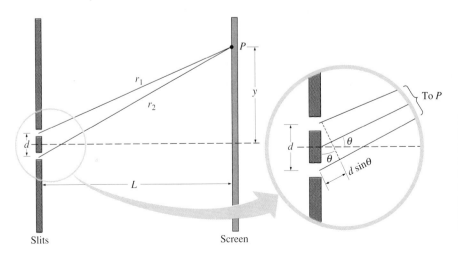

FIGURE 37-6 Geometry for finding locations of the interference fringes. A bright fringe occurs when the path-length difference $r_2 - r_1$ is an integer multiple of the wavelength. In the blowup you can see that for $L \gg d$ the paths to P are nearly parallel, and the difference in their lengths is $d\sin\theta$. Can you find similar triangles to prove that the angles labeled θ are indeed the same?

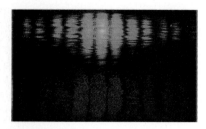

FIGURE 37-7 Interference patterns made with the same double-slit system, using two different wavelengths of light. The different fringe spacings reflect the wavelength dependence in Equations 37-2.

16.5
Two-Source Interference

Waves interfere destructively when they arrive at the screen 180° out of phase, which occurs when their path lengths differ by an odd integer multiple of a half wavelength:

$$d \sin \theta = (m + \tfrac{1}{2})\lambda, \qquad \text{(dark fringes)} \qquad (37\text{-}1b)$$

where m is any integer.

In a typical double-slit experiment, L may be on the order of 1 m, d a fraction of 1 mm, and λ the sub-μm wavelength of visible light. Then we have the additional condition that $\lambda \ll d$. This makes the fringes very closely spaced on the screen, so the angle θ in Fig. 37-6 is small even for large orders m. Then $\sin \theta \simeq \tan \theta = y/L$, and Equations 37-1 and the geometry of Fig. 37-6 show that a fringe's position y on the screen, measured from the central maximum, is given by

$$y_{\text{bright}} = m\frac{\lambda L}{d} \qquad \text{and} \qquad y_{\text{dark}} = (m + \tfrac{1}{2})\frac{\lambda L}{d}. \qquad (37\text{-}2a, b)$$

These equations show that the fringe spacing depends on wavelength, as confirmed experimentally in Fig. 37-7. Measurement of fringe spacing enabled Young to determine the wavelength of light. You can simulate two-slit interference—including the effect of varying wavelength—with ActivPhysics Activity 16.5.

Got It!

If you increase the slit separation in a 2-slit system, do the interference fringes become closer together or farther apart?

EXAMPLE 37-1	*Laser Wavelength*

A pair of narrow slits are 0.075 mm apart and are located 1.5 m from a screen. Laser light shining through the slits produces an interference pattern whose third-order bright fringe is 3.8 cm from the screen center. Find the wavelength of the light.

Solution

Here we have $m = 3$, $L = 1.5$ m, and $d = 0.075$ mm, so we can solve Equation 37-3a for the wavelength λ:

$$\lambda = \frac{y_{\text{bright}}d}{mL} = \frac{(0.038 \text{ m})(0.075 \times 10^{-3} \text{ m})}{(3)(1.5 \text{ m})} = 633 \text{ nm}.$$

This is in fact the wavelength of the red light from low-power helium-neon lasers commonly used in physics demonstrations.

EXERCISE What slit spacing will produce bright fringes 1.8 cm apart on a screen 85 cm from the slits, if the slits are illuminated with 589-nm light?

Answer: 27.8 μm

Some problems similar to Example 37-1: 2–5, 10

Intensity in the Interference Pattern

Geometric arguments allowed us to find the positions of the maxima and minima of a two-slit interference pattern. We can find the actual intensity variation by algebraically superposing the interfering waves. You might think this could be done by adding the wave intensities. But no! It's the electric and magnetic fields that obey the superposition principle, not the wave intensities. Intensity is proportional to the *square* of either field; if we added intensities we could never get the cancellation that occurs in destructive interference.

Consider again a point P on the screen of a double-slit apparatus (Fig. 37-8). Since light from the two slits reaches P over paths of different lengths, we expect that the waves will have different intensities when they reach P. In the approximation $d \ll L$, however, the path-length difference $d \sin \theta$ is so small that we can neglect this effect. So we consider that the two waves arriving at P have electric fields of equal amplitude, given by expressions like Equation 34-10. Since we're considering a fixed point P, it's convenient to take the origin at P to eliminate the kx term in Equation 34-10. Then we can express the electric fields of the two waves at P in the form

$$E_1 = E_p \sin \omega t \quad \text{and} \quad E_2 = E_p \sin(\omega t + \phi),$$

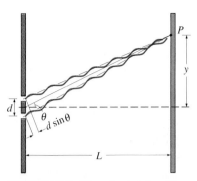

FIGURE 37-8 Waves leaving the slits with the same phase arrive at P displaced by the path-length difference $d \sin \theta$. This corresponds to phase difference $\phi = d \sin \theta (2\pi/\lambda)$.

where E_p is the common amplitude, ω the common frequency, and ϕ the phase difference that occurs because of the different path lengths. We don't bother with vector notation because both waves, since they originate in the same source, are polarized in the same direction and thus their electric fields will simply add algebraically. Then net electric field at P is

$$E = E_1 + E_2 = E_p[\sin \omega t + \sin(\omega t + \phi)].$$

In Appendix A we find the trigonometric identity $\sin \alpha + \sin \beta = 2 \sin[(\alpha + \beta)/2] \cos[(\alpha - \beta)/2]$, which, with $\alpha = \omega t$ and $\beta = \omega t + \phi$, transforms our expression for E into

$$E = 2E_p \sin\left(\omega t + \frac{\phi}{2}\right) \cos\left(\frac{\phi}{2}\right).$$

We also used $\cos(-x) = \cos x$ to eliminate a minus sign in the argument of the cosine. Thus, the electric field at P oscillates with the wave frequency ω, and its overall amplitude is scaled by the factor $\cos(\phi/2)$.

What is the phase difference ϕ? We've already seen that the path-length difference is $d \sin \theta$, with d the slit spacing and θ the angle subtended at the slits between P and the slit centerline. If this difference is one-half wavelength λ, then we have a phase difference of $180°$ or π radians. More generally, the phase difference in radians is whatever fraction of the full cycle (2π radians) the path difference $d \sin \theta$ is of the wavelength:

$$\phi = 2\pi \frac{d \sin \theta}{\lambda}.$$

Using this result in our expression for the electric field at P gives

$$E = 2E_p \sin\left(\omega t + \frac{\phi}{2}\right) \cos\left(\frac{\pi d \sin \theta}{\lambda}\right).$$

This equation describes a field whose peak amplitude is not E_p but $2E_p \cos(\pi d \sin \theta/\lambda)$. The average intensity then follows from Equation 34-20b:

$$\bar{S} = \frac{[2E_p \cos(\pi d \sin \theta/\lambda)]^2}{2\mu_0 c} = 4\bar{S}_0 \cos^2\left(\frac{\pi d \sin \theta}{\lambda}\right), \quad (37\text{-}3)$$

where $\bar{S}_0 = E_p^2/2\mu_0 c$ is the average intensity of either wave alone. Equation 37-3 shows that the intensity varies between zero and $4\bar{S}_0$ as the angular position changes. We can also write Equation 37-3 in terms of position y on the screen. Under the approximation $d \gg \lambda$ even high-order fringes will occur at

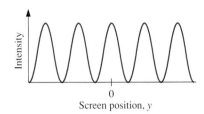

FIGURE 37-9 Intensity as a function of position y on the screen of a double-slit system. This intensity variation is reflected in Fig. 37-7, although saturation effects of the bright laser light on the film prevents the photo from showing accurately the sinusoidal dependence.

small angles θ, so we can write $\sin\theta \simeq \tan\theta \simeq y/L$, giving

$$\overline{S} = 4\overline{S}_0 \cos^2\!\left(\frac{\pi d}{\lambda L}y\right). \qquad (37\text{-}4)$$

Now, $\cos^2\alpha$ has its maximum value, 1, when its argument is an integer multiple of π. Thus, the maxima of Equation 37-4 occur when $dy/\lambda L$ is an integer m, or when $y = m\lambda L/d$. This is just the condition of Equation 37-2a, showing that our intensity calculation is fully consistent with the simpler geometrical analysis. But the intensity calculation tells us more: it gives not only the positions of bright and dark fringes, but also the intensity variation in between, as shown in Fig. 37-9.

37-3 MULTIPLE-SLIT INTERFERENCE AND DIFFRACTION GRATINGS

Systems with multiple slits play a crucial role in optical instrumentation and in the analysis of materials. As we will soon see, gratings manufactured with several thousand slits per centimeter make possible high-resolution spectroscopic analysis. At a much smaller scale the regularly spaced rows of atoms in a crystal act much like a multiple-slit system for X rays, and the resulting X-ray patterns reveal the crystal structure.

Figure 37-10 shows waves from three evenly spaced slits interfering at a screen. Maximum intensity requires that all three waves either be in phase, or differ in phase by an integer number of wavelengths. Our criterion for the maximum in a two-slit pattern, $d\sin\theta = m\lambda$, ensures that waves from two adjacent slits will add constructively. Since the slits are evenly spaced with distance d between each pair, waves coming through a third slit will be in phase with the other two if this criterion is met. So the criterion for a maximum in an N-slit system is still Equation 37-1a:

$$d\sin\theta = m\lambda. \qquad \text{(maxima in multi-slit interference)}$$

With more than two waves, however, the criterion for destructive interference is more complicated. Somehow all the waves need to sum to zero. Figure 37-11 shows that this happens for three waves when each is out of phase with the others by one-third of a cycle. Thus, the path-length difference $d\sin\theta$ must be either $(m + \frac{1}{3})\lambda$ or $(m + \frac{2}{3})\lambda$, where m is an integer. The case $(m + \frac{3}{3})\lambda$ is excluded because then the path lengths differ by a full wavelength, giving constructive interference and thus a maximum in the interference pattern. More generally we can write

$$d\sin\theta = \frac{m}{N}\lambda, \qquad (37\text{-}5)$$

for destructive interference in an N-slit system, where m is an integer *but not an integer multiple of N*. The reason for the exclusion is that when m is an integer multiple of N then m/N is an integer; then the path-length difference is an integer number of wavelengths, resulting in constructive rather than destructive interference. Mathematically, when m/N is an integer, Equation 37-5 becomes equivalent to Equation 37-1a that gives the condition for constructive interference.

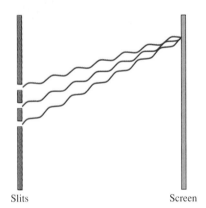

FIGURE 37-10 Waves from three evenly spaced slits interfere constructively when they arrive at the screen in phase.

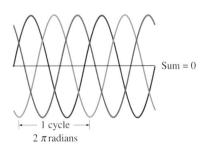

FIGURE 37-11 Waves from three slits must be out of phase by one-third of a cycle in order to interfere destructively. With this phase relationship the three waves sum to zero at every point.

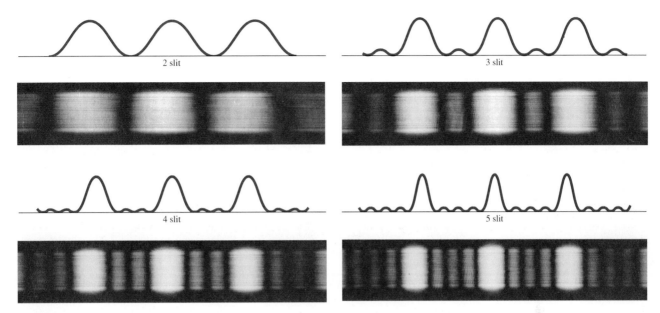

FIGURE 37-12 Interference patterns for multiple slit systems with the same slit spacing. The bright fringes stay in the same place, but become narrower and brighter as the number of slits increases. Intensity plots do not have the same vertical scale; peak intensity in fact scales as the *square* of the number of slits.

Figure 37-12 shows interference patterns and intensity plots from some multiple-slit systems. Note that the bright, or *primary,* maxima are separated by several minima and fainter, or *secondary,* maxima. Why this complex pattern? Our analysis of the three-slit system shows two minima between every pair of primary maxima; for example, we considered the minima at $d \sin \theta$ equal to $(m + \frac{1}{3})\lambda$ or $(m + \frac{2}{3})\lambda$, which lie between the maxima at $d \sin \theta$ equal to $m\lambda$ and $(m + 1)\lambda$. More generally, Equation 37-5 shows that there are $N - 1$ minima between each pair of primary maxima given by Equation 37-2a. The secondary maxima that lie between these minima result from interference that is neither fully destructive nor fully constructive. The figure shows that the primary maxima become much brighter and narrower as the number of slits increases, while the secondary maxima become relatively less bright. With a large number N of slits, then, we should expect a pattern of bright but narrow primary maxima, with broad, essentially dark regions in between.

Diffraction Gratings

A set of many very closely spaced slits is called a **diffraction grating** and proves very useful in the spectroscopic analysis of light. Diffraction gratings commonly measure several cm across and have several thousand slits—usually called lines—per cm. Gratings are made by photoreducing images of parallel lines or by ruling with a diamond stylus on aluminum-plated glass (Fig. 37-13). Gratings like the slit systems we have been discussing are **transmission gratings** since light passes through the slits. **Reflection gratings** produce similar interference effects by reflecting incident light.

We've seen that the maxima of the multi-slit interference pattern are given by the same criterion, $d \sin \theta = m\lambda$, that applies to a two-slit system. For $m = 0$

FIGURE 37-13 A diffraction grating disperses white light into its constituent colors. The enlarged spectrum at rear results from reflecting the diffracted beam off a concave mirror.

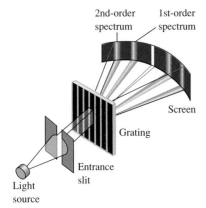

2nd-order spectrum
1st-order spectrum
Screen
Grating
Entrance slit
Light source

FIGURE 37-14 Essential elements of a grating spectrometer. The entrance slit regulates the amount of light entering the instrument. The grating disperses the light into its component wavelengths, which reach the screen to produce spectra of the different orders. An electronic detector would normally be used in place of the screen.

this equation implies that all wavelengths peak together at the central maximum, but for larger values of m the angular position of the maximum depends on wavelength. Thus, a diffraction grating can be used in place of a prism to disperse light into its component wavelengths, and the integer m is therefore called the **order** of the dispersion. Figure 37-14 shows a grating spectrometer working on this principle. Because the maxima in N-slit interference are very sharp for large N (recall Fig. 37-12), a grating with many slits diffracts individual wavelengths to very precise locations. Incidentally, the rainbow of colors produced by the compact disc in this chapter's opening photo results because adjacent "tracks" of CD pits (see Fig. 37-3) act as a diffraction grating.

EXAMPLE 37-2	*A Grating Spectrometer*

Light from glowing hydrogen contains discrete wavelengths ("spectral lines") called hydrogen-α and hydrogen-β, at 656.3 nm and 486.1 nm, respectively. Find the angular separation between these two wavelengths in a spectrometer using a grating with 6000 slits per cm. Consider both the first-order ($m = 1$) and second order ($m = 2$) dispersion.

Solution

With 6000 slits/cm, the slit spacing is $d = (1/6000)$ cm $= 1.667$ μm. Applying the criterion $d\sin\theta = m\lambda$ for the first-order spectrum, we then have

$$\theta_{1\alpha} = \sin^{-1}\left(\frac{\lambda}{d}\right) = \sin^{-1}\left(\frac{0.6563\ \mu\text{m}}{1.667\ \mu\text{m}}\right) = 23.2°$$

and

$$\theta_{1\beta} = \sin^{-1}\left(\frac{\lambda}{d}\right) = \sin^{-1}\left(\frac{0.4861\ \mu\text{m}}{1.667\ \mu\text{m}}\right) = 17.0°\ .$$

Thus, the angular separation is 6.2°. Repeating the same calculation with $m = 2$ gives $\theta_{2\alpha} = 51.9°$ and $\theta_{2\beta} = 35.7°$, for an angular spread of 16.2°. This wider spacing is characteristic of higher-order dispersion.

EXERCISE The bright yellow light emitted by glowing sodium vapor actually consists of two spectral lines at 589.0 nm and 589.6 nm. Find the angular separation of these lines in a second-order spectrum taken with a 4800-slit/cm grating.

Answer: 0.04°

Some problems similar to Example 37-2: 17–19

16.3

Multiple Slits Diffraction

In Example 37-2 the two lines are near the ends of the visible spectrum, and the values calculated for the angular positions show that there is no overlap between the first- and second-order visible spectra. But higher-order spectra do overlap, a fact that astronomers use in high-resolution spectroscopy when they wish to observe two different spectral lines simultaneously. Problem 21 explores this situation, while Fig. 37-15 shows the relative positions of the different orders.

Resolving Power

The detailed shapes and wavelengths of spectral lines contain a wealth of information about the systems in which light originates. Studying these details requires a high dispersion in order to separate nearby spectral lines or to analyze the intensity versus wavelength profile of a single line. Suppose we pass light

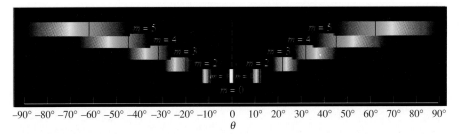

$$-90° \quad -80° \quad -70° \quad -60° \quad -50° \quad -40° \quad -30° \quad -20° \quad -10° \quad 0 \quad 10° \quad 20° \quad 30° \quad 40° \quad 50° \quad 60° \quad 70° \quad 80° \quad 90°$$
$$\theta$$

FIGURE 37-15 Positions of the different orders in a grating spectrum. The vertical separation between orders has been introduced for clarity; in actuality they would overlap. The central line of each spectrum is at 550 nm. Note the increased dispersion of the higher orders.

containing two spectral lines of nearly equal wavelengths λ and λ' through a grating. Figure 37-16 shows that we will just be able to distinguish two spectral lines if the peak of one line corresponds to the first minimum of the other; any closer and the lines will blur together. Suppose wavelength λ has its mth-order maximum at angular position θ. The criterion for this maximum is, as usual, $d \sin \theta_{max} = m\lambda$. We can equally well write this as $d \sin \theta_{max} = \dfrac{mN}{N}\lambda$, with N the number of slits in the grating. Equation 37-5 then shows that we get an adjacent minimum if we add 1 to the numerator mN. Thus, there is an adjacent minimum whose position satisfies

$$d \sin \theta_{min} = \frac{mN + 1}{N}\lambda .$$

Our criterion that the two wavelengths λ and λ' be just distinguishable is that the maximum for λ' fall at the location of this minimum for λ. But the maximum for λ' satisfies $d \sin \theta'_{max} = m\lambda' = \dfrac{mN}{N}\lambda'$, so for $\theta'_{max} = \theta_{min}$ we must have

$$(mN + 1)\lambda = mN\lambda' .$$

It's convenient to express this result in terms of the wavelength difference $\Delta\lambda = \lambda' - \lambda$. Solving our equation relating λ and λ' for λ' and using the result to write $\Delta\lambda$ in terms of λ alone then gives

$$\frac{\lambda}{\Delta\lambda} = mN . \qquad \text{(resolving power)} \qquad (37\text{-}6)$$

The quantity $\lambda/\Delta\lambda$ is the **resolving power** of the grating, a measure of its ability to distinguish closely spaced wavelengths. The higher the resolving power, the smaller the wavelength difference $\Delta\lambda$ that can be distinguished in the spectrum. Equation 37-6 shows that the resolving power increases with the number of lines, N, on the grating, and also with the order, m, of the spectrum we observe. Both these points make sense. We saw in Fig. 37-12 that the intensity of the maxima increases and their width decreases with increasing N, making different wavelengths easier to distinguish, while Fig. 37-15 shows that higher-order spectra are more dispersed and thus, again, make it easier to distinguish different wavelengths.

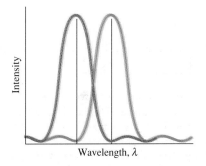

FIGURE 37-16 A plot of intensity versus wavelength for spectral lines of slightly different wavelengths, as observed with a spectrometer. The lines are just distinguishable if the maximum of one falls on the first minimum of the other; any closer and they blur together.

| EXAMPLE 37-3 | "Seeing" a Double Star |

A certain double star system consists of a massive star essentially at rest, with a smaller companion in circular orbit. The stars are far too close to each other, and the system far too distant from Earth, for the pair to appear as anything but a single point in even the largest telescopes. Yet astronomers can "see" the companion star through the Doppler shift in the wavelengths of its spectral lines that occurs because of the star's motion. In the system under observation the hydrogen-α line from the companion star, at 656.272 nm when the source is at rest, is shifted to 656.215 nm (this corresponds to an orbital speed of about 26 km/s) when the companion is moving toward Earth. If the telescope's spectrometer grating has 2000 lines/cm and measures 2.5 cm across, what order spectrum will resolve the hydrogen-α lines from the stationary star and its orbiting companion?

Solution

Here $N = (2000 \text{ lines/cm})(2.5 \text{ cm}) = 5000$ lines. Solving Equation 37-6 for m then gives

$$m = \frac{\lambda}{N\,\Delta\lambda} = \frac{656.272 \text{ nm}}{(5,000)(656.272 \text{ nm} - 656.215 \text{ nm})} = 2.3 \,.$$

Since the order number must be an integer, the observation must be made in third order.

EXERCISE Putting atoms in a magnetic field causes what are normally single spectral lines to split, as the atoms produce light of two slightly different wavelengths. In a particular case, a spectral line of mercury at 435.8 nm splits into two lines separated in wavelength by 0.027 nm. To the nearest thousand, how many lines must a grating have to resolve these wavelengths in first order?

Answer: 16,000

Some problems similar to Example 37-3: 26–29

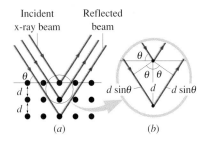

FIGURE 37-17 (a) X rays reflecting off the planes of atoms in a crystal. (b) X rays striking a lower plane travel an extra distance $2d \sin\theta$. The outgoing beam is enhanced by constructive interference when this distance is an integer multiple of the X-ray wavelength.

X-Ray Diffraction

The wavelengths of X rays, around 0.1 nm, are far too short to be dispersed with diffraction gratings produced mechanically or photographically. The regular spacing of atoms in a crystal, however, provides a "grating" of the appropriate scale. In the classical electromagnetic description, the reflection of electromagnetic waves occurs as electrons in each atom are set into oscillation by the electric field of the incident X-ray beam. The oscillating electrons then reradiate the energy they have absorbed, and the combined beam from all the atoms obeys the law of reflection. When the atomic spacing is regular, and comparable to the wavelength, however, interference enhances the reflected radiation at certain angles. Figure 37-17 shows an X-ray beam interacting with the layers of atoms in a crystal. In Fig. 37-17b we see that waves reflecting at one layer travel a total distance $2d \sin\theta$ farther than those reflecting at the layer above, where θ is the angle between the incident beams and the atomic planes. The outgoing beams will interfere constructively when this difference is an integer multiple of the wavelength:

$$2d \sin\theta = m\lambda \,. \quad \text{(Bragg condition)} \quad (37\text{-}7)$$

First derived by W. L. Bragg, this **Bragg condition** allows one to use a crystal with known spacing as a diffraction grating at X-ray wavelengths. More important is the converse: much of what we know about crystal structure comes from probing crystals with X rays and using the resulting patterns to deduce the positions of their atoms (Fig. 37-18).

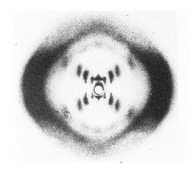

FIGURE 37-18 This X-ray diffraction image of DNA, made by the British scientist Rosalind Franklin in 1952, was crucial in establishing the structure of the DNA molecule.

APPLICATION	*Acousto-Optic Modulation*

Anything containing regularly spaced structures—like the lines in a diffraction grating or the atoms in a crystal—can act as a diffraction grating for waves of suitable wavelength. A very useful technological development, the **acousto-optic modulator** (AOM), uses diffraction from the periodic variations in the structure of a quartz crystal caused by the presence of a sound wave in the crystal.

Figure 37-19 shows a diagram of an AOM. Attached to the crystal is a transducer—a loudspeaker-like device that converts an alternating voltage into sound waves that propagate through the quartz. The regular spacing of the acoustic wavefronts constitutes a diffraction grating whose spacing may be varied by changing the driving frequency. Light incident on the quartz is diffracted at preferred angles given by Equation 37-7, just as are X rays by regularly spaced atomic planes. Changing the sound frequency allows the diffracted beam to be scanned in direction; turning the sound on and off switches the diffracted beam on and off. These effects are widely used in lightwave communication and other optical technologies; most laser printers, for example, use AOMs to control the laser beam that "paints" a picture of the printed page on a light-sensitive surface.

AOMs are also used to encode audio and video signals onto light, allowing transmission of these signals by light beams. Setting up the AOM's "diffraction grating" requires propagating sound waves into the crystal. Since this takes time, the AOM is not as fast a lightwave modulator as is the electro-optic modulator discussed in Chapter 34. The AOM is, however, much less expensive and less demanding of the associated electronic circuitry.

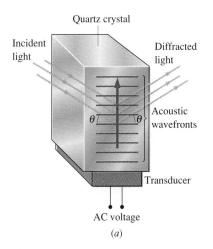

(a)

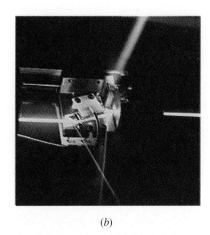

(b)

FIGURE 37-19 (*a*) Schematic diagram of an acousto-optic modulator. The transducer drives sound waves into the crystal, and the acoustic wavefronts act like a moving diffraction grating to incident light. (*b*) An acousto-optic modulator. A laser beam enters the transparent crystal while electrical signals supplied by the cable in the foreground generate sound waves that act as a diffraction grating to modify the beam's propagation direction and frequency. Such modulators are used in laser printers and many other applications.

37-4 THIN FILMS AND INTERFEROMETERS

We treated the double-slit system first because it's one of the most straightforward examples of interference. Then we turned to the more complicated case of multiple-slit interference. But there are many ways to produce interfering light waves besides passing light through slits. All have in common the separation of light into two or more beams that travel on different paths, then recombine. Here we examine a few such examples.

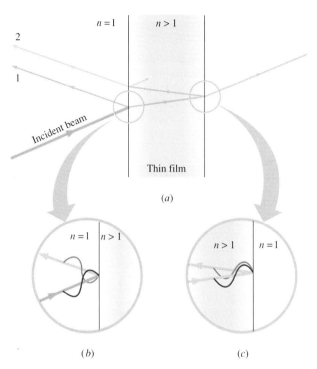

FIGURE 37-20 (*a*) Reflection and refraction at a thin layer of transparent material. (*b*) The reflected and incident beams are 180° out of phase when they reflect at an interface that goes from a lower to a higher refractive index. (*c*) There is no phase difference on reflection when the incident medium has a higher refractive index.

Interference in Thin Films

We saw in Section 35-6 that light is partially reflected and partially transmitted at an interface between two transparent media. Figure 37-20 shows what happens when light propagating in air strikes a thin film of transparent material. Partial reflection at both surfaces results in two beams propagating back into the air. Since these beams derive from the same source they're coherent, and therefore they interfere. (Additional reflections actually result in multiple beams, but they're successively fainter and we neglect them.)

In Section 17-5 we saw how waves on a string reflect when the end of the string is fixed, free, or tied to another string. Light incident from air on a medium with higher refractive index is like a wave on a string that's fixed or tied to a heavier string; the reflected wave undergoes a 180° phase change, as we showed in Figs. 17-5a and 17-6. Going the other way, from the medium with the higher refractive index to air, there's no phase change on reflection; here the situation is more like Fig. 17-5b or a string tied to a lighter string. So the incident light from air onto the film reflects with a 180° phase change, while light incident from inside the film on its rear surface reflects with no phase change. Figures 37-20b and c show these phase relations.

If the film in Fig. 37-20 were negligibly thin compared with the wavelength of the light, then the reflected beams 1 and 2 would be 180° out of phase because there's a 180° phase change at the first surface but none at the second. But if the film has thickness d, then there will be an additional phase difference due to the additional distance that beam 2 travels. We'll consider the case when light is incident on the film at nearly normal incidence, so that extra distance is essentially $2d$. In Section 37-1 we established that a path difference equal to an integer number of wavelengths results in constructive interference (recall Fig. 37-2), while an odd integer number of half wavelengths gives destructive interference. Here, though, we have an extra 180° phase change due to the reflections at the different surfaces of the film. Therefore a phase change of 180° due to the path length difference will combine with the reflection-caused 180° phase change to put the waves back in phase—giving constructive interference. Thus our usual criteria for constructive and destructive interference are reversed; for example, the condition for constructive interference is that the path difference be an integer multiple of a half wavelength, or

$$2d = (m + \tfrac{1}{2})\lambda_n ,$$

where λ_n is the wavelength in the film, whose refractive index is n.

In Chapter 35 we saw that the wavelength in a material with refractive index n is reduced by a factor $1/n$ from its value λ in air or vacuum; thus $\lambda_n = \lambda/n$, and our criterion for constructive interference can be written

$$2nd = (m + \tfrac{1}{2})\lambda . \quad \text{(constructive interference, thin film)} \quad (37\text{-}8a)$$

Conversely, destructive interference occurs when

$$2nd = m\lambda . \quad \text{(destructive interference, thin film)} \quad (37\text{-}8b)$$

The destructive interference is not complete, however, since the two beams do not have the same intensity.

Suppose a film is illuminated with light of a single color—that is, a single wavelength λ. If the thickness of a film varies with position, then constructive interference described by Equation 37-8a will occur at different places. Thus there will be bright bands separated by darker areas in which destructive interference occurs. If, on the other hand, the film is illuminated with white light, then the interference conditions will be satisfied at different places for the different wavelengths of the colors that comprise white light. The bands of color you see in a soap bubble or oil slick result from such thin-film interference (Fig. 37-21). If part of the film is too thin to meet the constructive interference condition of Equation 37-8a for *any* visible wavelength, then that part of the film will appear dark. You can see this effect at the top of the soap film in Fig. 37-21.

FIGURE 37-21 Interference patterns formed in a soap film illuminated with white light. The film's thickness increases toward the bottom, resulting in constructive interference for a given wavelength occurring at several different vertical positions. The film is too thin at the top for constructive interference at any visible wavelength, so it appears dark.

EXAMPLE 37-4	A Soap Film

A rectangular wire loop 20 cm high is dipped into a soap solution and then held vertically, producing a soap film whose thickness varies linearly from essentially zero at the top to 1.0 μm at the bottom (Fig. 37-22). (a) If the film is illuminated with 650-nm light, how many bright bands (as shown in Fig. 37-21) will appear? (b) What region of the film would be dark if it were illuminated with white light? The refractive index of the film is that of water, $n = 1.33$.

Solution

The film thickness at the position of a bright band is given by Equation 37-8a. To find the number of bright bands, we can solve this equation for the value of m at which the thickness d would equal the maximum film thickness:

$$m = \frac{2nd}{\lambda} - \frac{1}{2} = \frac{(2)(1.33)(1.0\ \mu m)}{0.65\ \mu m} - \frac{1}{2} = 3.6\ .$$

Since m must be an integer, the largest m corresponding to a thickness within the 1.0-μm maximum is 3. Since m ranges from zero to 3, there are a total of 4 bright bands.

At a given wavelength the minimum thickness for constructive interference occurs at $m = 0$. Taking the minimum wavelength for visible light at 400 nm = 0.40 μm, Equation 37-8a with $m = 0$ then gives

$$d = \frac{\lambda}{4n} = \frac{0.40\ \mu m}{(4)(1.33)} = 0.0752\ \mu m\ .$$

Since the film goes linearly from zero thickness to a maximum of 1.0 μm over its 20-cm height, this thickness occurs 0.0752

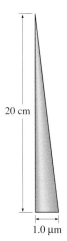

FIGURE 37-22 Cross section through a vertical soap film. The angle between the surfaces is greatly exaggerated.

20 cm

1.0 μm

of the way from the top edge, or at (0.0752)(20 cm) = 1.5 cm. Above this level the film is too thin for constructive interference in visible light, so the top 1.5 cm of film appears darker.

EXERCISE At what distances from the top of the film will bright bands appear if the film in Example 37-4 is illuminated with 450-nm light?

Answer: 1.69 cm, 5.08 cm, 8.46 cm, 11.8 cm, 15.2 cm, 18.6 cm

Some problems similar to Example 37-4: 31–33, 35

We derived Equations 37-8 on the assumption that our thin film was surrounded by air. Frequently, though, a thin film is sandwiched between two different media—as when an oil film floats on water. If the intermediate medium has a higher refractive index than the medium at its rear (i.e., at the right in Fig. 37-20), then our results still apply. But if the rear medium has a greater refractive index than the thin film, then there will be an additional 180° phase change at the rear interface, and therefore, our interference conditions will reverse (see the application below, as well as Problems 67 and 68).

APPLICATION	Antireflection Coatings

Partial reflection limits the amount of light that can be transmitted from one transparent material into another, reducing the light-gathering power of cameras, binoculars, and other lens-based instruments and of nonimaging devices such as windows and solar collectors.

Coating lenses, photovoltaic cells, and other critical light-gathering components with thin layers of appropriate materials can reduce reflection through the use of destructive interfer-

ence. Normally such **antireflection coatings** have refractive indices between those of air and glass; consequently, there is a 180° phase change at *each* interface, and thus, Equation 37-8a rather than 37-8b gives the condition for *destructive* interference. Thus, the minimum thickness for an antireflection coating, given by Equation 37-8a with $m = 0$, is $d = \lambda/4n$. Since this result depends on wavelength, antireflection coatings are not equally effective for all colors. With composite lenses and multiple layers, however, reduced reflection is possible over the visible spectrum.

A perfect antireflection coating might seem impossible, even in principle, since the reflected rays 1 and 2 in Fig. 37-20 do not have the same intensity. But the situation is actually more complicated. There are additional rays resulting from multiple reflections inside the transparent material, and these also interfere. A full solution of the problem involving the application of

Maxwell's equations at both interfaces shows that the reflection becomes exactly zero when the antireflection layer has not only the right thickness but also refractive index $n_2 = \sqrt{n_1 n_3}$, where n_1 and n_3 are the indices of the two media separated by the antireflection coating. A widely used antireflection coating, magnesium fluoride (MgF$_2$), has $n = 1.38$, a value that approximates the zero-reflection condition for high-index flint glasses in air.

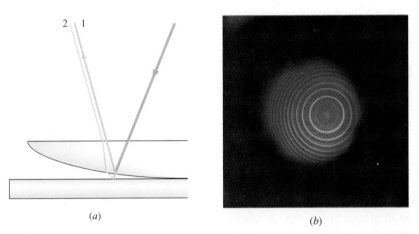

(a)

(b)

FIGURE 37-23 (a) Portion of a lens sitting on a flat glass plate. Newton's rings arise from the difference in path lengths between rays like 1 and 2. (b) Ring pattern produced in a test of a telescope's optical system.

Interference in thin layers is the basis of some very sensitive optical measuring techniques. The shape of a lens, for example, can be checked for accuracy to within a fraction of the wavelength of light using **Newton's rings**—interference patterns formed by interference of light reflected between the lens and a perfectly flat glass plate (Fig. 37-23; see also Problems 73–74).

The Michelson Interferometer

A number of optical instruments use interference for precise measurement of small distances. Among the simplest and most important of these is the **Michelson interferometer**, invented by the American physicist Albert Michelson and used in the 1880s by Michelson and his colleague Edward W. Morley in a famous experiment that paved the way for the theory of relativity. We discuss the Michelson-Morley experiment in the next chapter; here we describe the interferometer, which is still used for precision measurements.

Figure 37-24 shows the basic design of the Michelson interferometer. The key idea is that light from a monochromatic source is split into two beams by a half-silvered mirror called a **beam splitter**. The beam splitter is set at a 45° angle, so the reflected and transmitted beams travel perpendicular paths. Each then reflects off a flat mirror and returns to the beam splitter. The beam splitter again transmits and reflects half the light incident on it, with the result that some light from the originally separated beams is recombined. The recombined beams interfere, and the interference pattern is observed with a viewing lens at the bottom of Fig. 37-24.

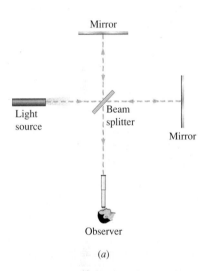

(a)

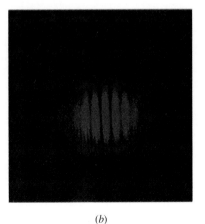

(b)

FIGURE 37-24 (a) Schematic diagram of a Michelson interferometer. The beam splitter splits incident light into reflected and transmitted beams of equal intensity. (b) The observer looking through the viewer sees interference fringes arising from differing optical path lengths.

Suppose the path lengths in the two perpendicular arms of the interferometer were exactly the same or differed by a multiple of the wavelength. When the beams recombined they would then undergo fully constructive interference. If the path-length difference were a multiple of a half wavelength, on the other hand, the beams would interfere destructively. In reality, however, the mirrors are never exactly perpendicular, and therefore light reflecting from different parts of the mirrors experiences slightly different path lengths and thus recombines with different phase lags. To the observer, the result is a series of alternating light and dark fringes corresponding to constructive and destructive interference.

Now suppose one mirror is moved slightly. The path-length differences change and therefore, the interference pattern shifts. Moving the mirror a mere quarter wavelength adds an extra half wavelength to the round-trip path. That results in an additional 180° phase shift, moving dark fringes to where light ones were, and vice versa. An observer looking through the viewer as the mirror moves sees the fringes shift to their new positions. Shifts of a fraction of the distance between fringes are readily detected, allowing measurement of mirror displacements to within a small fraction of the wavelength.

A similar fringe shift occurs if a transparent material is placed in one path, retarding the beam because of its refractive index. This approach allows accurate measurements of the refractive indices of gases, which are so close to one that conventional methods would not be useful (see Problem 46).

Measurements with the Michelson interferometer depend not on the interference pattern itself but on *changes* in that pattern. Therefore, it doesn't really matter whether the path lengths are exactly equal. Whatever those lengths, there will be an interference pattern, and changes in that pattern will reflect changes in the relative optical paths.

EXAMPLE 37-5	*Sandstorm!*

A sandstorm has pitted the aluminum mirrors of a desert solar energy installation, and engineers want to know the depths of these pits so they can estimate the mirrors' useful lifetimes. They construct a Michelson interferometer with a sample from one of the pitted mirrors in place of one of the flat mirrors. With a 633-nm laser as the light source, the interference pattern shown in Fig. 37-25 results. What is the approximate depth of the pit?

Solution

The "bumps" in the interference pattern correspond to light that has traveled the extra distance into the bottom of the pit and back. A shift of one full cycle in the interference pattern would correspond to a full wavelength change in the path. As Fig. 37-25 shows, the pit causes a fringe shift corresponding to about 0.2 wavelengths. Since light makes a round trip through the pit, its actual depth is therefore 0.1λ, or 63 nm. Try measuring that with a meter stick!

EXERCISE A Michelson interferometer uses sodium light with wavelength 589.6 nm. As one mirror is moved, a photocell

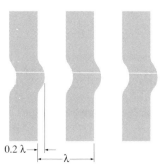

FIGURE 37-25 Fringe pattern resulting from a pitted mirror. The size of the bump is a measure of the pit depth.

connected to a counter "watches" a fixed point through the viewer. If the counter records 4878 fringes passing that point, how far did the mirror move?

Answer: 1.438 mm

Some problems similar to Example 37-5: 44–46

37-5 HUYGENS' PRINCIPLE AND DIFFRACTION

The interference we've been studying in this chapter isn't the only optical phenomenon where the wave nature of light is important. There's also **diffraction**—the bending of light or other waves as they pass by objects. Interference and diffraction are closely related, and the double- and multiple-slit interference we've studied actually involves diffraction as well; hence the term "diffraction grating."

Diffraction, like other optical phenomena, is ultimately governed by Maxwell's equations of electromagnetism. But we can understand diffraction of light and other waves more readily using **Huygens' principle**, articulated in 1678 by the Dutch scientist Christian Huygens, who was first to suggest that light might be a wave. Huygens' principle states that

> All points on a wavefront act as point sources of spherically propagating "wavelets" that travel at the speed of light appropriate to the medium. At a short time Δt later, the new wavefront is the unique surface tangent to all the forward-propagating wavelets.

Figure 37-26 shows how Huygens' principle accounts for the propagation of plane and spherical (or cylindrical) waves. It is also possible to derive the laws of reflection and refraction from Huygens' principle.

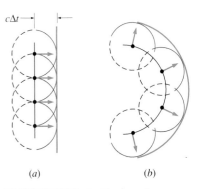

FIGURE 37-26 Application of Huygens' principle to (*a*) plane and (*b*) spherical waves. In each case the wavefront acts like a set of point sources that emit circular waves. A short time Δt later the wavelets have expanded to radius $c\Delta t$, and the new wavefront is the surface tangent to the wavelets. To follow the propagation further one could draw new wavelets originating on the new wavefront.

Diffraction

Figure 37-27 shows plane waves incident on an opaque barrier containing a hole. Since the waves are blocked by the barrier, Huygens' wavelets produced near each barrier edge cause the wavefronts to bend at the barrier (see blowups in Fig. 37-27). When the width of the hole is much greater than the wavelength, as in Fig. 37-27*a*, this diffraction is of little consequence, and the waves effectively propagate straight through the hole in a beam defined by the hole size. But when

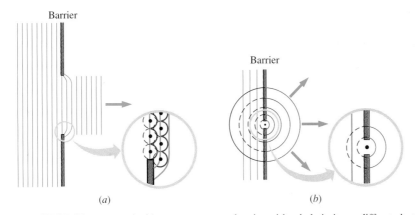

FIGURE 37-27 Plane waves incident on an opaque barrier with a hole in it are diffracted at the edges of the hole, as shown by Huygens' wavelet constructions. (*a*) When the hole size is much larger than the wavelength this diffraction is negligible, and the waves essentially propagate in a straight beam defined by the hole. (*b*) When the hole size and wavelength are comparable, the emerging wavefronts spread in a broad beam, approaching circular wavefronts as the hole size becomes negligibly small.

the hole size and wavelength are comparable, then wavefronts emerging from the hole spread in a broad pattern (Fig. 37-27*b*). Here diffraction is the dominant effect on the propagation. Thus diffraction, although it always occurs when waves pass an object, is significant only on length scales comparable to or smaller than the wavelength. That's why we could ignore diffraction and assume that light always travels through a single medium in straight lines, when we considered optical systems with dimensions much larger than the wavelength of light.

Diffraction ultimately limits our ability to image small objects and to focus light with arbitrary precision. Next, we'll see why this is so by examining quantitatively the behavior of light as it passes through a single slit. The result will help us understand optical challenges ranging from telescopic imaging of distant astrophysical objects, to "star wars" antimissile systems, to the development of the new digital video discs (DVDs) that hold a full-length movie on a disc identical in size to a standard audio CD.

37-6 SINGLE-SLIT DIFFRACTION

In treating double-slit and multiple-slit interference in Section 37-2, we assumed that plane waves passing through a slit emerged with circular wavefronts. According to Fig. 37-27, that assumption is vaild only if the width of the slits is very small compared with the wavelength, so the slit can be treated as a single, localized source of new waves. When the slit width is not small, Huygens' principle implies that we have to consider each point in the slit as a separate source—and then we can expect interference from waves originating at different points in the same slit. Thus a single wide slit is really like a multiple-slit system with infinitely many slits!

Figure 37-28 shows light incident on a slit of width *a*. Each point in the slit acts as a source of spherical wavelets propagating in all directions to the right of the slit. In Fig. 37-28 we focus on a particular direction described by the angle θ and will look at interference of light from the five points shown. Figure 37-28*b* concentrates on the points from which rays 1, 2, and 3 originate and shows that the path lengths for rays 1 and 3 differ by $\frac{1}{2}a\sin\theta$. These two beams will interfere destructively if this distance is half the wavelength; that is, if $\frac{1}{2}a\sin\theta = \frac{1}{2}\lambda$ or $a\sin\theta = \lambda$. But if rays 1 and 3 interfere destructively, so do rays 3 and 5, which have the same geometry, and so do rays 2 and 4, for the same reason. In fact, a ray leaving *any* point in the lower half of the slit will interfere destructively with the point located a distance $a/2$ above it. Therefore, an observer viewing the slit system at the angle θ satisfying $a\sin\theta = \lambda$ will see no light.

Similarly, the sources for rays 1 and 2 are $a/4$ apart and will therefore interfere destructively if $\frac{1}{4}a\sin\theta = \frac{1}{2}\lambda$, or $a\sin\theta = 2\lambda$. But then so will rays 2 and 3, and rays 3 and 4; in fact, any ray from a point in the lower three quarters of the slit will interfere destructively with a ray from the point $a/4$ above it, and therefore, an observer looking at an angle satisfying $a\sin\theta = 2\lambda$ will see no light.

We could equally well have divided the slit into six sections with seven evenly spaced points; we would then have found destructive interference if $\frac{1}{6}a\sin\theta = \frac{1}{2}\lambda$, or $a\sin\theta = 3\lambda$. We could obviously continue this process for any number of points in the slit, and therefore, we conclude that destructive

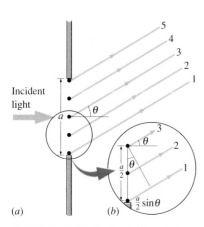

FIGURE 37-28 Each point in a slit acts as a source of Huygens' wavelets, which interfere in the region to the right of the slit. (*a*) Here we consider 5 points within the slit, and the relative phases of their light as viewed at an angle θ. (*b*) The path-length difference for two beams is their separation times $\sin\theta$.

interference occurs for all angles satisfying

$$a \sin \theta = m\lambda, \quad \text{(destructive interference, single-slit diffraction)} \quad (37\text{-}9)$$

with m any nonzero integer and a the slit width. Note that the case $m = 0$ is excluded; it produces not destructive interference but a central maximum in which all waves are in phase.

16.1
Diffraction

Tip

Interference and Diffraction Equation 37-9 for the *minima* of a single-slit diffraction pattern looks just like Equation 37-1a for the *maxima* of a multi-slit interference pattern, except that the slit width a replaces the slit spacing d. What's going on? Why does the same equation give the minima in one case and the maxima in another? Because we're dealing with two distinct but related phenomena. In the multi-slit case leading to Equation 37-1a, we considered each slit to be so narrow that it could be considered a single source, thus neglecting the interference of waves originating within the same slit. In the single-slit case leading to Equation 37-9, the diffraction pattern occurs precisely because of the interference of waves from different points within the same slit.

EXAMPLE 37-6	*Diffraction: A Narrow Slit*

For what slit width, in terms of wavelength, will the first minimum lie at an angular position of 45°?

Solution
With $m = 1$, Equation 37-9 gives

$$a = \frac{\lambda}{\sin \theta} = \frac{\lambda}{\sin 45°} = \sqrt{2}\lambda.$$

Here, with the slit width nearly equal to the wavelength, diffraction dominates the wave propagation. The incident light is therefore spread over a wide angular range. The exercise below shows that the beam spreading decreases as the slit width grows.

EXERCISE Light is incident on a slit whose width is 20 times its wavelength. Find the angular spread of the beam, taken as the angle between the first minima on either side of the central maximum.

Answer: 5.7°

Some problems similar to Example 37-6: 49–51

Intensity in Single-Slit Diffraction

We can find the intensity of the single-slit diffraction pattern by adding the electric fields of the individual beams, as we did for two-slit interference. Since there are infinitely many points along the slit, each constituting a point source of light, we might set up and evaluate a complicated integral. Instead we use the graphical method of phasors, introduced in Chapter 33 to deal with alternating currents and voltages of different phases. We have a similar situation here, as we want to combine waves with different phases that arise from different points on the slit. The phasor method is entirely equivalent to integrating over the electric field contributions from the individual sources in the slit.

We use phasors to represent the electric fields of the individual waves originating from points in the slit when they arrive at the screen. The length of a phasor gives the field amplitude E, and its direction gives its phase. Consider N such points, spaced evenly across a slit of width a, like the five points in Fig. 37-28.

These divide the slit into $N - 1$ sections, each of width $a/(N - 1)$. At some angle θ, the phase difference, in radians, of light coming from two adjacent points will be the ratio of their path-length difference to the wavelength, times the 2π radians that comprise a complete cycle. As usual, the path-length difference is the point spacing times $\sin \theta$ (see Fig. 37-28b). Here the point spacing is $a/(N - 1)$, so we have

$$\Delta\phi = \left(\frac{a}{N - 1} \sin \theta\right)\left(\frac{2\pi}{\lambda}\right) \tag{37-10}$$

for the phase difference between waves from adjacent points. All the waves have essentially the same amplitude, so we now need to add N equal-length phasors each of which differs in phase by $\Delta\phi$ from its nearest neighbors.

Consider first the case $\theta = 0$. Then Equation 37-10 gives $\Delta\phi = 0$ so, as Fig. 37-29a shows, the phasors are all in the same direction and sum to give a large total amplitude. This is the central maximum of the diffraction pattern. If, on the other hand, $\Delta\phi$ is such that the N phasors sum to a closed path, then the total amplitude—the net displacement from the beginning to the end of the phasor diagram—is zero (Fig. 37-29b). Here we have a point of zero intensity in the interference pattern. More generally, the phasors sum to give an amplitude E_θ that is neither zero nor as great as a simple sum of the individual amplitudes, as shown in Fig. 37-29c.

Now each point in the slit differs in phase by $\Delta\phi$ from its immediate neighbors. Thus, the second point differs by $\Delta\phi$ from the first point, the third point by $2\Delta\phi$ from the first point, and so forth until the Nth point differs in phase by $(N - 1)\Delta\phi$ from the first point. But this last quantity $(N - 1)\Delta\phi$ is just the total phase difference ϕ from one end of the slit to the other. Using Equation 37-10, we can write this phase difference as

$$\phi = (N - 1)\left(\frac{a}{N - 1} \sin \theta\right)\left(\frac{2\pi}{\lambda}\right) = \frac{2\pi}{\lambda} a \sin \theta. \tag{37-11}$$

To consider all points in the slit, we take the limit as $N \to \infty$; then the end-to-end chain of phasors in Fig. 37-29c becomes a circular arc of radius R, as shown in

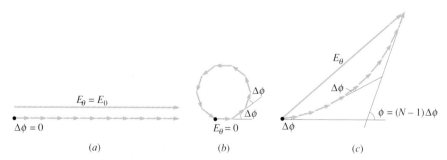

FIGURE 37-29 Phasor addition to find the amplitude in single-slit diffraction. (*a*) When $\theta = 0$ in Fig. 37-28 all waves have the same phase, and their amplitudes add to produce the central maximum. (*b*) When the phasor sum is a closed loop, the net phasor displacement is zero and so is the wave amplitude. (*c*) In general, the phasors add to produce an amplitude that is neither zero nor as great as in the central maximum. The angle between the first and last phasor is $N\Delta\phi$. Here $N = 10$ in all three frames, and in general we designate the resultant amplitude by E_θ. When the phasors all have the same phase, E_0 is the resultant amplitude.

Fig. 37-30. If we stretched this arc into a line, its length would be the electric field amplitude E_0 of Fig. 37-29a; therefore, E_0 is also the length of the arc. From the geometry of Fig. 37-30 we see that

$$\sin(\phi/2) = \frac{E_\theta/2}{R}.$$

We can also write the angle $\phi/2$ using the definition of an angle in radians as the ratio of arc length to radius. Here $\phi/2$ subtends an arc of length $E_0/2$, so we have

$$\phi/2 = \frac{E_0/2}{R}.$$

Dividing these two equations gives the ratio of the amplitudes:

$$\frac{E_\theta}{E_0} = \frac{\sin(\phi/2)}{\phi/2}.$$

But the wave intensity $\bar{S}$ is proportional to the square of the amplitude, so

$$\bar{S}_\theta = \bar{S}_0 \left[\frac{\sin(\phi/2)}{\phi/2} \right]^2, \qquad (37\text{-}12)$$

where ϕ is given by Equation 37-11.

Figure 37-31 shows plots of Equation 37-12 for several values of the slit width a in relation to the wavelength λ. Note that for wide slits—slit width a large compared with the wavelength λ—the central peak is very narrow and the secondary peaks are much smaller. Here diffraction is negligible, and the beam essentially propagates through the slit in the ray approximation of geometrical optics. But as the slit narrows the diffracted beam spreads, until, with $a = \lambda$, it covers an angular width of some 120°.

The intensity given by Equation 37-12 will be zero when the numerator on the right-hand side is zero—that is, when the argument of the sine function is an integer multiple of π. That occurs when $\frac{\phi}{2} = \frac{\pi a}{\lambda} \sin\theta = m\pi$, or when $a \sin\theta = m\lambda$. Thus, we recover our earlier result of Equation 37-9 for the angular positions where destructive interference gives zero intensity.

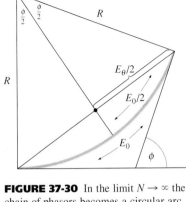

FIGURE 37-30 In the limit $N \to \infty$ the chain of phasors becomes a circular arc of length E_0.

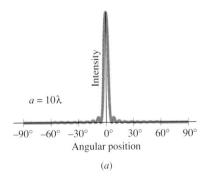

(a)

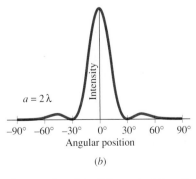

(b)

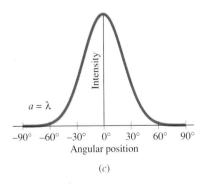

(c)

FIGURE 37-31 Intensity in single-slit diffraction, as a function of the angle θ from the centerline, for three values of slit width a, expressed in units of wavelength λ. When the slit is much wider than the wavelength, most of the light is concentrated in a narrow central peak. But as the slit width approaches the wavelength, the diffracted beam becomes very wide.

EXAMPLE 37-7	*Other Peaks*

Secondary maxima lie approximately midway between the minima of the diffraction pattern. Use this fact to find the intensity at the first of these secondary maxima, in terms of the central-peak intensity $\bar{S}_0$.

Solution

The first and second minima are at positions given by $a \sin\theta_1 = \lambda$ and $a \sin\theta_2 = 2\lambda$, respectively. With the first of the secondary maxima midway between them, its angular position is given by $a \sin\theta = \frac{3}{2}\lambda$. (Here we assume θ is small, so $\sin\theta \simeq \theta$, and midway in angular position θ is therefore also midway in $\sin\theta$.) Then $\frac{a}{\lambda}\sin\theta = \frac{3}{2}$, so Equation 37-11 gives $\frac{\phi}{2} = \frac{\pi a}{\lambda}\sin\theta = \frac{3\pi}{2}$. Using this result in Equation 37-12, we

have

$$\bar{S} = \bar{S}_0 \left[\frac{\sin(\phi/2)}{\phi/2} \right]^2 = \bar{S}_0 \left[\frac{\sin(3\pi/2)}{3\pi/2} \right]^2 = \frac{4\bar{S}_0}{9\pi^2} = 0.045\bar{S}_0 .$$

Thus, the intensity at the first secondary maximum is only about 4.5% of the central-peak intensity. Note that this result is independent of the slit width, provided the secondary peak exists (which it may not; see Fig. 37-31c).

EXERCISE Show that the intensity in single-slit diffraction has half its maximum value when $\sin\theta = 1.3916\dfrac{\lambda}{\pi a}$.

Some problems similar to Example 37-7: 49–53

In analyzing single-slit diffraction we considered only parallel rays in the diffraction region. To make the diffraction pattern actually appear on a screen, we have to focus those rays with a lens between slit and screen (Fig. 37-32). Diffraction associated with parallel rays is called **Fraunhofer diffraction**. In general, Fraunhofer diffraction occurs when the distance from the diffracting system is large compared with the wavelength. Fraunhofer diffraction is an approximation to the more general case of **Fresnel diffraction**, whose analysis is more complicated because it also accounts for nonparallel rays that exist near a diffracting system.

Multiple Slits and Other Diffracting Systems

In treating multiple-slit systems in Section 37-2, we assumed the slits were so narrow compared with the wavelength that the central diffraction peak spread into the entire space beyond the slit system. When the slit width is not negligible, then the waves from each slit produce a single-slit diffraction pattern. The result is a pattern that combines single-slit diffraction with multiple-slit interference (Fig. 37-33).

FIGURE 37-32 Single-slit diffraction pattern produced by focusing light from a single slit onto a screen. Note the bright central peak and secondary maxima separated by regions of destructive interference.

FIGURE 37-33 When the slit width is not negligible, the double-slit pattern shows the regular variations of double-slit interference within a single-slit diffraction pattern.

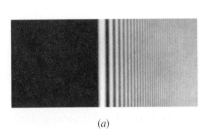

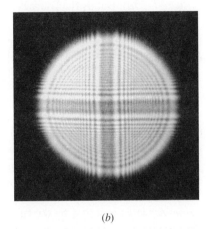

(a) (b)

FIGURE 37-34 (a) Light waves diffract as they pass by the straight edge of an opaque barrier. Photo shows the resulting interference pattern on a screen some distance beyond the barrier, whose shadow is the black region at left. (b) Diffraction of monochromatic light by a pair of crosshairs in a circular aperture. Diffraction effects from both the crosshairs (straight fringes) and the aperture itself (circular fringes) are evident.

Diffraction occurs any time light passes a sharp, opaque edge like the edges of the slits we've been considering. Close examination of the shadow produced by a sharp edge shows parallel fringes resulting from interference of the diffracting wavefronts (Fig. 37-34a). More complex diffraction patterns result from objects of different shape (Fig. 37-34b). The presence of such diffraction patterns limits our ability to form sharp optical images, as we show in the next section.

37-7 THE DIFFRACTION LIMIT

Diffraction imposes a fundamental limit on the ability of optical systems to distinguish closely spaced objects. Consider two point sources of light illuminating a slit. The sources are so far from the slit that waves reaching the slit are essentially plane waves, but the different source positions mean the waves reach the slit at different angles. We assume the sources are incoherent, so they don't

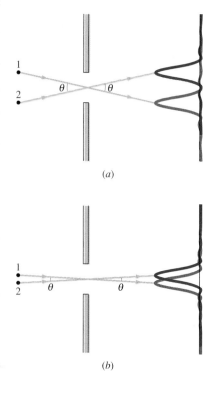

(a)

(b)

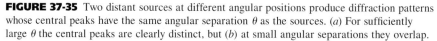

FIGURE 37-35 Two distant sources at different angular positions produce diffraction patterns whose central peaks have the same angular separation θ as the sources. (a) For sufficiently large θ the central peaks are clearly distinct, but (b) at small angular separations they overlap.

produce a regular interference pattern. Then light diffracting at the slit produces two single-slit diffraction patterns, one for each source. Because the sources are at different angular positions, the central maxima of these patterns don't coincide, as shown in Fig. 37-35.

If the angular separation between the sources is great enough, then the central maxima of the two diffraction patterns will be entirely distinct. In that case the eye or any other optical system can clearly distinguish the two sources (Fig. 37-35a). But as the sources get closer the central maxima begin to overlap (Fig. 37-35b). The two sources remain distinguishable as long as the total intensity pattern shows two peaks. Since the sources are incoherent the total intensity is just the sum of the individual intensities. Figure 37-36 shows how that sum loses its two-peak structure as the diffraction patterns merge. In general, two peaks are barely distinguishable if the central maximum of one coincides with the first minimum of the other. This condition is called the **Rayleigh criterion**, and when it is met we say that the two sources are just barely **resolved**.

What does all this have to do with optical instruments and images? Simply this: All optical systems are analogous to the single slit we've been considering. Every system has an aperture of finite size through which light enters the system. That aperture may be an actual slit or hole, like the diaphragm that "stops down" a camera lens, or it may be the full size of a lens or mirror. So all optical systems ultimately suffer loss of resolution if two sources—or two parts of the same extended object—have too small an angular separation. Thus, diffraction fundamentally limits our ability to probe the structure of objects that are either very small or very distant.

Figure 37-35 shows that the angular separation between the diffraction peaks is equal to the angular separation between the sources themselves. Then the Rayleigh criterion is just met if the angular separation between the two sources is equal to the angular separation between a central peak and the first minimum. We found earlier that the first minimum in single-slit diffraction occurs at angular position given by

$$\sin\theta = \frac{\lambda}{a},$$

with a the slit width and with θ measured from the central peak. In most optical systems the wavelength is much less than the size of any apertures, so we can use the small-angle approximation $\sin\theta \simeq \theta$ with θ in radians. Then the Rayleigh criterion—the condition that two sources be just resolvable—for single-slit diffraction becomes

$$\theta_{min} = \frac{\lambda}{a}. \qquad \text{(Rayleigh criterion, slit)} \qquad (37\text{-}13a)$$

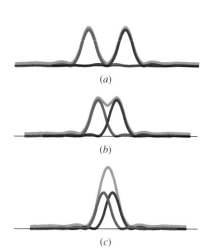

(a)

(b)

(c)

FIGURE 37-36 Since the two sources are incoherent, the total intensity is just the sum of the intensities of the two diffraction patterns. Here we see the intensities in two patterns and their sum (light blue). (a) Fully resolved; (b) barely resolved (Rayleigh criterion); (c) unresolved.

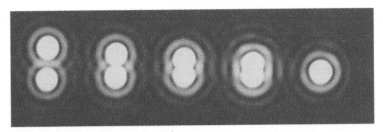

FIGURE 37-38 Diffraction patterns produced by a pair of point sources imaged through a circular hole. The angular separation of the sources decreases going from left to right, and when the sources are too close they cannot be resolved.

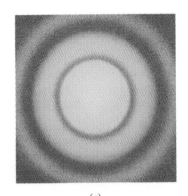

(a)

Most optical systems have circular apertures rather than slits. The diffraction pattern from such an aperture is a series of concentric rings (Fig. 37-37). A more involved mathematical analysis shows that the angular position of the first ring relative to the central peak, and therefore, the minimum resolvable source separation for a circular aperture, is

$$\theta_{min} = \frac{1.22\lambda}{D}, \quad \text{(Rayleigh criterion, circular aperture)} \quad (37\text{-}13b)$$

with D the aperture diameter. In most optical systems the angle θ is very small, and Equations 37-13a and b hold for this case. For larger angles, θ_{min} in both equations should be replaced with $\sin\theta_{min}$. Figure 37-38 shows the loss of resolution as two nearby sources are imaged through a circular aperture. You can simulate this effect using ActivPhysics Activity 16.6.

Equations 37-13 show that increasing the aperture size allows smaller angular differences to be resolved. In optical instrument design, that means larger mirrors, lenses, and other components. An alternative is to decrease the wavelength used, which may or may not be an option depending on the source. In high-quality optical systems diffraction is often the limiting factor preventing perfectly sharp image formation; such systems are said to be **diffraction limited**. For example, the diffraction limit sets a minimum size for objects resolvable with optical microscopes; that's why electron microscopes—with shorter effective wavelength—are used to image the smallest biological structures. Large ground-based telescopes are an exception to the diffraction limit; their image quality is limited by atmospheric turbulence, although this can be reduced with adaptive optics that we mentioned in Chapter 36. From its vantage point above the atmosphere, the Hubble Space Telescope is the first large diffraction-limited astronomical telescope.

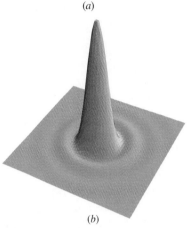

(b)

FIGURE 37-37 (a) Diffraction pattern produced by a circular aperture. (b) Three-dimensional plot of intensity versus position.

16.6
Resolving Power

Got It!

You're a biologist trying to resolve details of structures within a cell, but they look fuzzy even at the highest power of your microscope. Why won't it help to substitute a new eyepiece with shorter focal length, as suggested by Equation 36-10?

EXAMPLE 37-8 | *Asteroid Alert!*

An asteroid appears on a collision course with Earth, at a distance of 20×10^6 km. What is the minimum size asteroid that the 2.4-m-diameter diffraction-limited Hubble Space Telescope could resolve at this distance, using 550-nm reflected sunlight?

Solution

Resolving the asteroid means being able to distinguish its opposite edges in the telescope image and therefore to assess its size. Suppose the asteroid's long dimension (it might not be spherical) is ℓ. Then at a distance $L \gg \ell$ it subtends an angle given very nearly by $\theta = \ell/L$. Using this result in Equation 37-13b with the mirror diameter and wavelength given, we have

$$\frac{\ell}{L} = \frac{1.22\lambda}{D},$$

or

$$\ell = \frac{1.22\lambda L}{D} = \frac{(1.22)(550 \times 10^{-9} \text{ m})(20 \times 10^9 \text{ m})}{2.4 \text{ m}} = 5.6 \text{ km}.$$

This is a potentially dangerous object, comparable in size to the asteroid that scientists believe caused the extinction of the dinosaurs, and somewhat larger than the comet fragments that slammed into Jupiter in 1994, causing Earth-sized disturbances on the giant planet.

EXERCISE Two ants stand 1 cm apart. Assuming diffraction limited vision, at what distance could a human eye, with an iris aperture of 4 mm, tell that two are indeed separate creatures? Assume a wavelength of 550 nm, near the middle of the visible spectrum. (Other limitations of the human eye prevent its realizing this diffraction limit.)

Answer: 60 m

Some problems similar to Example 37-8: 55–59

APPLICATION | *Movies on Disc: From CD to DVD*

Standard audio CDs have a maximum playing time of 74 minutes—a value that's set by the optical diffraction limit. In the Application "CD Music, Continued" earlier in this chapter, we showed how a CD encodes information in "pits" 1.6 μm apart and as short as 0.83 μm in length. Standard CDs are read with 780-nm infrared laser light and the pit size and separation are chosen to ensure that diffraction effects at this wavelength don't cause the CD player's optical system to confuse adjacent pits. Ultimately, therefore, the 74-minute playing time is limited by the laser wavelength.

When CDs were first developed, inexpensive semiconductor lasers were available only in the infrared. But today's semiconductor lasers produce light well into the visible—with significantly shorter wavelengths than the infrared light used in CD players and CD-ROM drives. The new DVDs introduced in the late 1990s (read either "digital video disc" or "digital versatile disc") exploit these shorter-wavelength lasers.

Using laser wavelengths of 635 and 650 nm, DVDs can function with significantly lower pit sizes and spacings because of the lower diffraction limit at these shorter wavelengths (Fig. 37-39). Coupled with a two-layer structure (as opposed to the standard CD's single information layer) and more sophisticated data-compression schemes, the smaller pits and pit spacing give DVDs more than 12 times the information-storage capacity of standard CDs. That translates into more than two hours of high quality video and audio, as opposed to the CD's 74 minutes of audio alone. In computer use, it means a DVD can hold some 8.5 gigabytes of information as opposed to a CD's 680 megabytes (by comparison, a 3.5″ floppy disc holds only 1.44 MB). And DVDs can be made in two-sided versions, providing another doubling in capacity. Despite their high capacity, DVDs are physically the same size as CDs, and DVD players are compatible with standard CDs as well.

FIGURE 37-39 A comparison of a standard CD and a DVD. The smaller pit size and closer pit spacing of the DVD result in a much higher information storage capacity, and are made possible by the lower diffraction limit associated with the DVD player's shorter wavelength laser light. Both images are microphotographs of the same size region, about 8 μm on a side. The pits lie on a single spiral track that covers most of the disc.

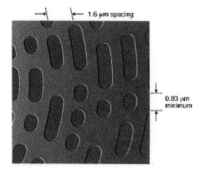

(a)

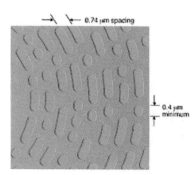

(b)

APPLICATION	*Interferometry*

At a given wavelength, Equations 37-13 show that resolving small angular separations requires a large aperture. To see detail in distant astronomical objects, in particular, requires impractically large apertures. A technique called **interferometry** provides a way around this problem. Used most commonly at radio wavelengths, interferometry employs two or more individual apertures (i.e., radio telescopes), usually separated by a considerable distance. Signals from each are combined with their phases intact, so that they interfere. A two-telescope interferometer works like a two-slit system in reverse: the system is most sensitive to radiation from angular positions that produce constructive interference (Fig. 37-40). The resolution of an interferometer is approximately that of a single slit-like aperture whose width is the spacing between the telescopes.

Today's interferometers include installations with many radio telescopes at a single site (Fig. 37-41), as well as coordinated instruments spread across the globe. The first interferometric arrays of optical telescopes began operation in the 1990s, and astronomers look forward to radio interferometers using the Earth-moon distance as their "aperture."

FIGURE 37-40 A radio interferometer consists of two or more radio telescopes at different locations. The interferometer can detect very slight changes in phase of the incoming wavefronts and can therefore resolve very small differences in angular position of objects in the sky.

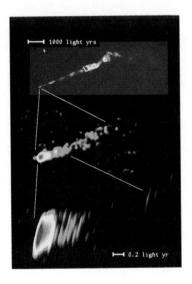

FIGURE 37-41 Radio images of the active galaxy M87 show a jet of material emerging from the galactic core. (*top*) Image made with the Very Large Array (VLA) in New Mexico. The VLA consists of 27 radio telescopes whose separation gives an effective aperture of 27 km. (*bottom two images*) Much higher resolution is obtained with the Very Long Baseline Array (VLBA), whose radio telescopes extend from Hawaii to Puerto Rico. The resulting effective aperture of 8,000 km has a much lower diffraction limit, hence the higher resolution.

CHAPTER SYNOPSIS

Summary

1. **Interference** and **diffraction** are wave phenomena that constitute the subject of physical optics. Interference effects require two or more beams of **coherent** light, which maintain a fixed phase relation. Such coherent beams can be produced by allowing light from a single source to travel two different paths. If the path lengths differ by an integer multiple of the wavelength, **constructive interference** results when the beams recombine. If the path lengths differ by an integer multiple of a half wavelength, the result is **destructive interference**.

2. When coherent light of wavelength λ passes through a pair of narrow slits with spacing d, the resulting interference pattern shows bright fringes at maxima given by

$$d \sin \theta = m\lambda,$$

where m is an integer. The average intensity in the interference pattern is given by

$$\bar{S} = 4\bar{S}_0 \cos^2\left(\frac{\pi d \sin \theta}{\lambda}\right),$$

where $\bar{S}_0$ is the average intensity incident on the slits.

3. A multiple-slit system has primary interference maxima in the same position as a double-slit system, with multiple minima and secondary maxima in between. For large numbers of slits the primary maxima are narrow and bright and the region between them relatively dark. A system with many slits constitutes a **diffraction grating**, which disperses light into its component wavelengths. A grating produces spectra of many **orders**, corresponding to the integer m in the equation that locates the interference maxima. The **resolving power** of an N-slit grating is given by

$$\frac{\lambda}{\Delta\lambda} = mN,$$

where $\Delta\lambda$ is the minimum separation between wavelengths that can be distinguished in the mth-order spectrum. Other periodic systems, like the layers of atoms in a crystal, can serve as diffraction gratings for appropriate wavelengths.

4. Interference occurs in thin transparent films when light reflected from the front and back surfaces of the film recombines. For a film whose refractive index is larger than that of its surroundings, the interference is constructive when the film thickness d, refractive index n, and the light wavelength λ are related by $2nd = (m + \frac{1}{2})\lambda$, where m is an integer.

5. The **Michelson interferometer** utilizes the interference of light traveling on two perpendicular paths to make precise distance measurements.

6. **Huygens' principle** treats each point on a wavefront as a source of expanding spherical wavelets. Superposition of the wavelets describes the propagation of the wavefront and shows that waves undergo **diffraction** when passing by an opaque edge.

7. When the width of a single slit is not negligible compared with the wavelength, interference of light passing through different parts of the slit produces a **diffraction pattern** with a central maximum surrounded by lesser maxima separated by points of zero intensity.

8. The **diffraction limit** in optical systems arises because diffraction effects merge the images of two objects when their angular separation is sufficiently small. The **Rayleigh criterion** gives the minimum angular separation that can be resolved by a given aperture. For a circular aperture of diameter D, the Rayleigh criterion is

$$\theta_{\min} = \frac{1.22\lambda}{D},$$

where $\theta_{\min}$ is in radians. Large apertures are therefore necessary to resolve objects with small angular separation.

Terms You Should Understand

(Pairs are closely related terms whose distinction is important; number in parentheses is chapter section where term first appears.)

physical optics, geometrical optics (introduction and preceding chapters)
interference (37-1)
coherence (37-1)
monochromatic light (37-1)
interference fringe (37-2)
order (37-2, 37-3)
diffraction grating (37-3)
resolving power (37-3)
Bragg condition (37-3)
Michelson interferometer (37-4)
diffraction (37-5)
Huygens' principle (37-5)
diffraction limit (37-7)
Rayleigh criterion (37-7)

Symbols You Should Recognize

m (37-1, 37-2, 37-3) $\theta_{\min}$ (37-7)

Problems You Should Be Able to Solve

analyzing double-slit interference patterns (37-2)
finding locations of maxima and minima in multiple-slit interference (37-3)
analyzing dispersion of light with diffraction gratings (37-3)
determining conditions for constructive and destructive interference in thin films (37-4)
analyzing experiments using Michelson interferometers (37-4)
finding minima and beam widths in single-slit diffraction (37-6)
finding the diffraction limit in optical systems (37-7)

Limitations to Keep in Mind

This chapter's analysis of double-slit interference assumes slit widths much smaller than the wavelength; otherwise the pattern combines diffraction and interference.

Our analysis of diffraction applies only in the Fraunhofer limit, in which the incident light is essentially parallel and the pattern is formed at large distances from the diffracting aperture.

QUESTIONS

1. A prism bends blue light more than red. Is the same true of a diffraction grating?
2. Why does an oil slick show colored bands?
3. Would a Michelson interferometer work even if its two arms were not exactly the same length?
4. Why does a soap bubble turn colorless just before it dries up and breaks?
5. Why don't you see interference effects between the front and back of your eyeglasses?
6. Hold two fingers very close together while looking through them at a source of light. Explain what you see.
7. Figure 37-42 shows the shadow cast by a ball bearing on the end of a needle, under monochromatic laser light. Explain the existence of the fringes shown and of the white spot at the center of the ball bearing's shadow.

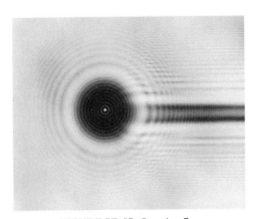

FIGURE 37-42 Question 7.

8. You can hear around corners but you can't see around corners. Why the difference?
9. In deriving the intensity in double-slit interference, we could not simply add the intensities from the two slits. Why not?
10. In sketching the intensity pattern for two incoherent sources imaged through a single slit, we could simply add the intensities from the two sources. Why?
11. The primary maxima in multiple-slit interference are in the same angular positions as those in double-slit interference. Why, then, do diffraction gratings have thousands of slits instead of just two?
12. In what way is a widely separated pair of small radio telescopes superior to a single large one? In what way is it inferior?
13. Describe the change in the diffraction pattern of a single slit as the slit is narrowed.
14. What pattern would result from passing red and blue light simultaneously through a double-slit system?
15. When the moon passes in front of a star, the intensity of the starlight fluctuates instead of dropping abruptly. Explain.
16. In analyzing crystal structure using X-ray diffraction, it is necessary to take data with the crystal in several different orientations. Why?
17. A double-slit system has one slit much narrower than the wavelength of the incident light, the other much wider. Describe the resulting intensity pattern.
18. Sketch roughly the diffraction pattern you would expect for light passing through a square hole a few wavelengths wide.

PROBLEMS

ActivPhysics can help with these problems:
Activities in Section 16, Physical Optics

Section 37-2 Double-Slit Interference

1. A double-slit system is used to measure the wavelength of light. The system has slit spacing $d = 15 \ \mu m$ and slit-to-screen distance $L = 2.2$ m. If the $m = 1$ maximum in the interference pattern occurs 7.1 cm from screen center, what is the wavelength?
2. A double-slit experiment with $d = 0.025$ mm and $L = 75$ cm uses 550-nm light. What is the spacing between adjacent bright fringes?
3. A double-slit experiment has slit spacing 0.12 mm. (a) What should be the slit-to-screen distance L if the bright fringes are to be 5.0 mm apart when the slits are illuminated with 633-nm laser light? (b) What will be the fringe spacing with 480-nm light?
4. With two slits separated by 0.37 mm, the interference pattern has bright fringes with angular spacing 0.065°. What is the wavelength of the light illuminating the slits?
5. The green line of gaseous mercury at 546 nm falls on a double-slit apparatus. If the fifth dark fringe is at 0.113° from the centerline, what is the slit separation?
6. What is the angular position θ of the second-order bright fringe in a double-slit system with 1.5-μm slit spacing if the light has wavelength (a) 400 nm or (b) 700 nm?
7. Light shines on a pair of slits whose spacing is three times the wavelength. Find the locations of the first- and second-order bright fringes on a screen 50 cm from the slits. *Hint:* Do Equations 37-2 apply?

8. A double-slit experiment has slit spacing 0.035 mm, slit-to-screen distance 1.5 m, and wavelength 500 nm. What is the phase difference between two waves arriving at a point 0.56 cm from the center line?

9. For a double-slit experiment with slit spacing 0.25 mm and wavelength 600 nm, at what angular position is the path difference equal to one-fourth of the wavelength?

10. A screen 1.0 m wide is located 2.0 m from a pair of slits illuminated by 633-nm laser light, with its center on the centerline of the slits. Find the highest-order bright fringe that will appear on the screen if the slit spacing is (a) 0.10 mm; (b) 10 μm.

11. Laser light at 633 nm falls on a double-slit apparatus with slit separation 6.5 μm. Find the separation between (a) the first and second and (b) the third and fourth bright fringes, as seen on a screen 1.7 m from the slits.

12. A tube of glowing gas emits light at 550 nm and 400 nm. In a double-slit apparatus, what is the lowest-order 550-nm bright fringe that will fall on a 400-nm dark fringe, and what are the corresponding orders?

Section 37-3 Multiple-Slit Interference and Diffraction Gratings

13. In a 5-slit system, how many minima lie between the zeroth-order and first-order maxima?

14. In a 3-slit system the first minimum occurs at an angular position of 5°. Where is the first maximum?

15. A 5-slit system with 7.5-μm slit spacing is illuminated with 633-nm light. Find the angular positions of (a) the first 2 maxima and (b) the 3rd and 6th minima.

16. On the screen of a multiple-slit system, the interference pattern shows bright maxima separated by 0.86° and 7 minima between each bright maximum. (a) How many slits are there? (b) What is the slit separation if the incident light has wavelength 656.3 nm?

17. Green light at 520 nm is diffracted by a grating with 3000 lines per cm. Through what angle is the light diffracted in (a) first and (b) fifth order?

18. Find the angular separation between the red hydrogen-α spectral line at 656 nm and the yellow sodium line at 589 nm if the two are observed in 3rd order with a 3500 line/cm grating spectrometer.

19. Light is incident normally on a grating with 10,000 lines per cm. What is the maximum order in which (a) 450-nm and (b) 650-nm light will be visible?

20. Visible light has wavelengths between 400 nm and 700 nm. What is the lowest pair of consecutive orders for which there will be some overlap between the visible spectra as dispersed by a grating?

21. A solar astronomer is studying the Sun's 589-nm sodium spectral line with a 2500 line/cm grating spectrometer whose fourth order dispersion puts the wavelength range from 575 nm to 625 nm on a detector. The astronomer is interested in observing simultaneously the so-called calcium-K line, at 393 nm. What order dispersion will put this line also on the detector?

22. (a) What portions of the 4th and 5th order visible spectra overlap in a 3000 lines/cm grating spectrometer? (b) How would your answer change for a 1000 lines/cm grating? (c) For a 10,000 lines/cm grating?

23. Estimate the number of lines per cm in the grating used to produce Fig. 37-15.

24. A grating spectrometer's detector covers an angular range of 10° and can be swung at any angle within ±75° of the normal to the grating. If the grating has 1200 lines/cm, in what orders can the hydrogen-α spectral line at 656 nm and the calcium-K line at 393 nm both fall on the detector? (b) What will be the angular position of the K line under these conditions?

25. When viewed in 6th order, the 486.1-nm hydrogen-β spectral line is flanked by another line that appears at the position of 484.3 nm in the 6th order spectrum. Actually the line is from a different order of the spectrum. What are the possible visible wavelengths of this line?

26. (a) Find the resolving power of a grating needed to separate the sodium-D spectral lines, which are at 589.0 nm and 589.6 nm. (b) How many lines must the grating have to achieve this resolution in first order? (This is very low resolution by present-day spectroscopic standards.)

27. Echelle spectroscopy uses relatively coarse gratings in high order. Compare the resolving power of an 80 line/mm echelle grating used in 12th order with a 600 line/mm grating used in 1st order, assuming the two have the same width.

28. The International Ultraviolet Explorer satellite carries a spectrometer with a 2.0-cm-wide grating ruled at 102 lines/mm. What is the minimum wavelength difference it can resolve in 12th order when observing in the ultraviolet at 155 nm?

29. You wish to resolve the calcium-H line at 396.85 nm from the hydrogen-ε line at 397.05 nm in a 1st-order spectrum. To the nearest hundred, how many lines should your grating have?

30. X-ray diffraction in potassium chloride (KCl) results in a first-order maximum when the X rays graze the crystal plane at 8.5°. If the X-ray wavelength is 97 pm, what is the spacing between crystal planes?

Section 37-4 Thin Films and Interferometers

31. Find the minimum thickness of a soap film ($n = 1.33$) in which 550-nm light will undergo constructive interference.

32. Light of unknown wavelength shines on a precisely machined wedge of glass with refractive index 1.52. The

closest point to the apex of the wedge where reflection is enhanced occurs where the wedge is 98 nm thick. Find the wavelength.

33. Monochromatic light shines on a glass wedge with refractive index 1.65, and enhanced reflection occurs where the wedge is 450 nm thick. Find all possible values for the wavelength in the visible range.

34. White light shines on a 100-nm-thick sliver of fluorite ($n = 1.43$). What wavelength is most strongly reflected?

35. As a soap bubble ($n = 1.33$) evaporates and thins, the reflected colors gradually disappear. (a) What is its thickness just as the last vestige of color vanishes? (b) What is the last color seen?

36. An oil film ($n = 1.25$) floats on water, and a soap film ($n = 1.33$) is suspended in air. Find the minimum thickness for each that will result in constructive interference with 500-nm green light.

37. Light reflected from a thin film of acetone ($n = 1.36$) on a glass plate ($n = 1.5$) shows maximum reflection at 500 nm and minimum at 400 nm. Find the minimum possible film thickness.

38. What minimum thickness of a coating with refractive index 1.35 should you use on a glass lens to minimize reflection at 500 nm, the approximate center of the visible spectrum?

39. An oil film with refractive index 1.25 floats on water. The film thickness varies from 0.80 μm to 2.1 μm. If 630-nm light is incident normally on the film, at how many locations will it undergo enhanced reflection?

40. Microwave ovens operate at a frequency of 2.4 GHz. What is the minimum thickness for a plastic tray with refractive index 1.45 that will cause enhanced reflection of microwaves incident normal to the plate?

41. Two perfectly flat glass plates are separated at one end by a piece of paper 0.065 mm thick. A source of 550-nm light illuminates the plates from above, as shown in Fig. 37-43. How many bright bands appear to an observer looking down on the plates?

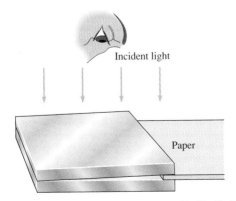

FIGURE 37-43 An air wedge (Problems 41, 42, 43, 72).

42. An air wedge like that shown in Fig. 37-43 shows N bright bands when illuminated from above. Find an expression for the number of bands that will appear if the air is replaced by a liquid of refractive index n different from that of the glass.

43. You apply a slight pressure with your finger to the upper of a pair of glass plates forming an air wedge as in Fig. 37-43. The wedge is illuminated from above with 500-nm light, and you place your finger where, initially, there is a dark band. If you push gently so the band becomes light, then dark, then light again, by how much have you deflected the plate?

44. A Michelson interferometer uses light from glowing hydrogen at 486.1 nm. As you move one mirror, 530 bright fringes pass a fixed point in the viewer. How far did the mirror move?

45. What is the wavelength of light used in a Michelson interferometer if 550 bright fringes go by a fixed point when the mirror moves 0.150 mm?

46. One arm of a Michelson interferometer is 42.5 cm long and is enclosed in a box that can be evacuated. The box initially contains air, which is gradually pumped out to create a vacuum. In the process, 388 bright fringes pass a fixed point in the viewer. If the interferometer uses light with wavelength 641.6 nm, what is the refractive index of the air?

47. The evacuated box of the previous problem is filled with chlorine gas, whose refractive index is 1.000772. How many bright fringes pass a fixed point as the tube fills?

48. Your personal stereo is in a dead spot caused by direct reception from an FM radio station at 89.5 MHz interfering with the signal reflecting off a wall behind you. How much farther from the wall should you move in order that the interference be fully constructive?

Sections 37-6 and 37-7 Single-Slit Diffraction and the Diffraction Limit

49. For what ratio of slit width to wavelength will the first minima of a single-slit diffraction pattern occur at $\pm 90°$?

50. Light with wavelength 633 nm is incident on a 2.5 μm wide slit. Find the angular width of the central peak in the diffraction pattern, taken as the angular separation between the first minima.

51. A beam of parallel rays from a 29-MHz citizen's band radio transmitter passes between two electrically conducting (hence opaque to radio waves) buildings located 45 m apart. What is the angular width of the beam when it emerges from between the buildings?

52. Use trial-and-error with a calculator, or a more sophisticated root-finding method, to verify the number 1.3916 in the exercise following Example 37-7.

53. Find the intensity as a fraction of the central peak intensity for the second secondary maximum in single-slit

diffraction, assuming the peak lies midway between the second and third minima.

54. A proposed "star wars" antimissile laser is to focus 2.8-μm wavelength infrared light to a 50-cm-diameter spot on a missile 2500 km distant. Find the minimum diameter for a concave mirror that can achieve this spot size, given the diffraction limit. Your answer suggests one of the many technical difficulties faced by antimissile defense systems.

55. The movie *Patriot Games* has a scene in which CIA agents use spy satellites to identify individuals in a terrorist camp (Fig. 37-44). Suppose that a minimum resolution for distinguishing human features is about 5 cm. If the spy satellite's optical system is diffraction limited, what diameter mirror or lens is needed to achieve this resolution from an altitude of 100 km? Assume a wavelength of 550 nm.

FIGURE 37-44 CIA agents using satellite imaging to identify terrorists in the film *Patriot Games*. How big a mirror or lens must the satellite's optical system have? (Problem 55)

56. Suppose one of the 10-m-diameter Keck telescopes in Hawaii could be trained on San Francisco, 3400 km away. Would it be possible to read (a) newspaper headlines or (b) a billboard sign at this distance? Justify your answers by giving the minimum separation resolvable with Keck at 3400 km, assuming 550-nm light. (c) Repeat for the case of the Keck optical interferometer, formed from the two 10-m Keck telescopes and several smaller ones, with an effective aperture of 50 m.

57. A camera has an $f/1.4$ lens, meaning that the ratio of focal length to lens diameter is 1.4. Find the smallest spot diameter (defined as the diameter of the first diffraction minimum) to which this lens can focus parallel light with 580-nm wavelength.

58. The distance from the center of a circular diffraction pattern to the first minimum on a screen 0.85 m distant from the diffracting aperture is 15,000 wavelengths. What is the aperture diameter?

59. While driving at night, your eyes' irises have dilated to 3.1-mm diameter. If your vision were diffraction limited, what would be the greatest distance at which you could see as distinct the two headlights of an oncoming car, which are spaced 1.5 m apart? Take $\lambda = 550$ nm.

60. Two stars are 4.0 light-years apart, in a galaxy 20×10^6 light-years from Earth. What minimum separation of two radio telescopes, acting together as an interferometer, is needed to resolve them? The telescopes operate at 2.1 GHz and are pointing straight upward; the stars are directly overhead.

61. Under the best conditions, atmospheric turbulence limits the resolution of ground-based telescopes to about 1 arc second (1/3600 of a degree) as shown in Fig. 37-45. For what aperture sizes is this limitation more severe than that of diffraction at 550 nm? Your answer shows why large ground-based telescopes do not produce better images than small ones, although they do gather more light.

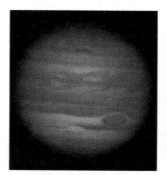

FIGURE 37-45 Jupiter, photographed with a ground-based telescope (left) and from space (right). Atmospheric turbulence limits the ground-based image quality while diffraction limits the space-based image (Problem 61).

62. Two objects are separated by approximately one wavelength of the light with which an observer is attempting to resolve them. Show that the Rayleigh criterion then requires that the distance to the objects be less than the diameter of the observing aperture, and thus the Fraunhofer diffraction approximation is violated. It is in fact impossible to resolve two objects as close as one wavelength.

Paired Problems

(Both problems in a pair involve the same principles and techniques. If you can get the first problem, you should be able to solve the second one.)

63. Find the total number of lines in a 2.5-cm-wide diffraction grating whose third-order spectrum has the 656-nm hydrogen-α spectral line at an angular position of 37°.

64. Light is diffracted by a 5000 line/cm grating, and a detector sensitive only to visible light finds a maximum intensity at 28° from the central maximum. (a) What is the wavelength of the light? (b) In what order is it seen at the 28° position?

65. A 400 line/mm diffraction grating is 3.5 cm wide. Two spectral lines whose wavelengths average to 560 nm are just barely resolved in the 4th-order spectrum of this grating. What is the difference between their wavelengths?

66. What order is necessary to resolve wavelengths of 647.98 nm and 648.07 nm using a 4500-line grating?

67. A thin film of toluene ($n = 1.49$) floats on water. What is the minimum film thickness if the most strongly reflected light has wavelength 460 nm?

68. Oil with refractive index 1.38 forms a 210-nm-thick film on a piece of glass. What color of visible light is most strongly reflected?

69. What diameter optical telescope would be needed to resolve a Sun-sized star 10 light-years from Earth? Take $\lambda = 550$ nm. Your answer shows why stars appear as point sources in optical astronomy.

70. Could the 305-m radio telescope at Arecibo in Puerto Rico resolve the star in the preceding problem, if it were observing at a wavelength of 1.0 cm?

Supplementary Problems

71. White light shines on a 250-nm-thick layer of diamond ($n = 2.42$). What wavelength *of visible light* is most strongly reflected?

72. An air wedge like that of Fig. 37-43 displays 10,003 bright bands when illuminated from above. If the region between the plates is then evacuated, the number of bands drops to 10,000. Calculate the refractive index of the air.

73. In Fig. 37-23 the mth Newton's ring appears a distance r from the center of the lens. Show that the curvature radius of the lens is given approximately by $R = r^2/(m + \frac{1}{2})\lambda$, where the approximation holds when the thickness of the air space is much less than the curvature radius.

74. Given the result of the preceding problem, how many bright Newton's rings would be seen with a 2.5-cm-diameter glass lens with curvature radius 7.5 cm, when illuminated with 500-nm light?

75. How many rings would be seen if the system of the preceding problem were immersed in water ($n = 1.33$)?

76. A thin-walled glass tube of length L containing a gas of unknown refractive index is placed in one arm of a Michelson interferometer using light of wavelength λ. The tube is then evacuated, and during the process m bright fringes pass a fixed point as seen in the viewer. Find an expression for the refractive index of the gas.

77. The signal from a 103.9-MHz FM radio station reflects off a building 400 m away, effectively producing two sources of the same signal. You're driving at 60 km/h along a road parallel to a line between the station's antenna and the building and located a perpendicular distance of 6.5 km

from them. How often does the signal appear to fade when you're driving roughly opposite the transmitter and building?

78. A satellite dish antenna 45 cm in diameter receives TV broadcasts at a frequency of about 12 GHz. (a) What is the angular size of its beam, defined as the full width of the central diffraction peak? (b) How many communications satellites could fit in geosynchronous orbit above Earth's equator if antennas like this one were not to pick up signals from more than one satellite? Your answer shows why geosynchronous orbit is such valuable "real estate."

79. The component of a star's velocity in the radial direction relative to Earth is to be measured using the doppler shift in the hydrogen-β spectral line, which appears at 486.1 nm when the source is stationary relative to the observer. What is the minimum speed that can be detected by observing in 1st order with a 10,000 line/cm grating 5.0 cm across? *Hint:* See Equation 17-9.

80. Light is incident on a diffraction grating at an angle α to the normal. Show that the condition for maximum light intensity becomes $d(\sin\theta \pm \sin\alpha) = m\lambda$.

81. In a double-slit experiment, a thin glass plate with refractive index 1.56 is placed over one of the slits. The fifth bright fringe now appears where the second dark fringe previously appeared. How thick is the plate if the incident light has wavelength 480 nm?

82. An arrangement known as Lloyd's mirror (Fig. 37-46) allows interference between a direct and a reflected beam from the same source. Find an expression for the separation of bright fringes on the screen, given the distances d and D in Fig. 37-46, and the wavelength λ of the light. *Hint:* Think of two sources, one the virtual image of the other.

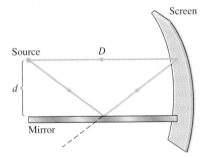

FIGURE 37-46 Lloyd's mirror (Problem 82).

PART 5 *Cumulative Problems*

These problems combine material from chapters throughout the entire part or, in addition, from chapters in earlier parts, or they present special challenges.

1. A *grism* is a grating ruled onto a prism, as shown in Fig. 1. The grism is designed to transmit undeviated one wavelength of the spectrum in a given order, as refraction in the prism compensates for the deviation at the grating. Find an equation relating the separation d of the grooves that constitute the grating, the wedge angle α of the prism, the refractive index n, the undeviated wavelength λ_0, and order m_0.

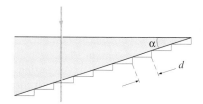

FIGURE 1 A grism (Cumulative Problem 1).

2. A double-slit system consists of two slits each of width a, with separation d between the slit centers ($d > a$). Light of intensity S_0 and wavelength λ is incident on the system, perpendicular to the plane containing the slits. Find an expression for the outgoing intensity as a function of angular position θ, taking into account both the slit width and the separation. Plot your result for the case $d = 4a$, and compare with Fig. 37-33.
3. A closed cylindrical tube whose glass walls have negligible thickness measures 5.0 cm long by 5.0 mm in diameter. It is filled with water, initially at 15°C, and placed with its long dimension in one arm of a Michelson interferometer. The water is not perfectly transparent, and it absorbs 3.2% of the light energy incident on it. The laser power incident on the water is 50 mW, and the wavelength is 633 nm. The refractive index of water in the vicinity of 15°C is given approximately by $n = 1.335 - 8.4\times10^{-5}T$, where T is the temperature in °C. As the water absorbs light energy, how long does it take the interference pattern to shift by one whole fringe?
4. A radio antenna broadcasts a 6.5-MHz signal in all directions. The antenna is on top of a tower 300 m above sea level, and the tower is located 2.0 km from the shore. An airplane is flying toward the tower, at twice the altitude of the tower top, as shown in Fig. 2. Radio waves from the tower reflect off the ocean surface with a 180° phase change, but there is no significant reflection off the land. As the plane heads toward the tower, at what horizontal distance or distances from the tower will its radio equipment detect a minimum in the radio signal amplitude due to destructive interference of the direct and reflected radio waves?
5. In one type of optical fiber, called a *graded-index fiber*, the refractive index varies in a way that results in light rays

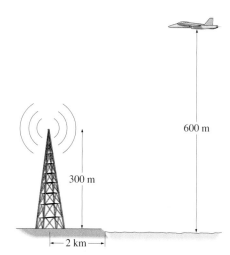

FIGURE 2 Cumulative Problem 4 (figure is not to scale).

being guided along the fiber on curved trajectories, rather than undergoing abrupt reflections. Figure 3 shows a simple model that demonstrates this effect; it also describes the basic optical effect in mirages. A slab of transparent material has refractive index $n(y)$ that varies with position y perpendicular to the slab face. A light ray enters the slab at $x = 0$, $y = 0$, making an angle θ_0 with the normal just inside the slab. The refractive index at this point is $n(y = 0) = n_0$. (a) By writing $\sin\theta$ in Snell's law in terms of the components dx and dy of the ray path, show that that path (written in the form of x as a function of y) is given by

$$x = \int_0^y \frac{n_0 \sin\theta_0}{\sqrt{[n(y)]^2 - n_0^2\sin^2\theta_0}}\,dy\,.$$

(b) Suppose $n(y) = n_0(1 - ay)$, where $n_0 = 1.5$ and $a = 1.0$ mm^{-1}. If $\theta_0 = 60°$, find an explicit expression for x as a function of y, and plot your result to give the actual ray path. Explain the shape of your curve in terms of what happens when the ray reaches a point where $n(y) = n_0 \sin\theta_0$. What happens beyond this point?

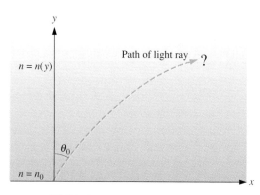

FIGURE 3 Cumulative Problem 5.

APPENDIX A
Mathematics

A-1 ALGEBRA AND TRIGONOMETRY

Quadratic Formula

If $ax^2 + bx + c = 0$ then $x = \dfrac{-b \pm \sqrt{b^2 - 4ac}}{2a}$

Circumference, Area, Volume

Where $\pi \simeq 3.14159 \ldots$

circumference of circle	$2\pi r$
area of circle	πr^2
surface area of sphere	$4\pi r^2$
volume of sphere	$\frac{4}{3}\pi r^3$
area of triangle	$\frac{1}{2}bh$
volume of cylinder	$\pi r^2 \ell$

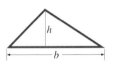

Trigonometry

definition of angle (in radians): $\theta = \dfrac{s}{r}$

2π radians in complete circle
1 radian $\simeq 57.3°$

Trigonometric Functions

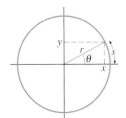

$$\sin \theta = \frac{y}{r}$$

$$\cos \theta = \frac{x}{r}$$

$$\tan \theta = \frac{\sin \theta}{\cos \theta} = \frac{y}{x}$$

Values at Selected Angles

$\theta \rightarrow$	0	$\dfrac{\pi}{6}$ (30°)	$\dfrac{\pi}{4}$ (45°)	$\dfrac{\pi}{3}$ (60°)	$\dfrac{\pi}{2}$ (90°)
$\sin\theta$	0	$\dfrac{1}{2}$	$\dfrac{\sqrt{2}}{2}$	$\dfrac{\sqrt{3}}{2}$	1
$\cos\theta$	1	$\dfrac{\sqrt{3}}{2}$	$\dfrac{\sqrt{2}}{2}$	$\dfrac{1}{2}$	0
$\tan\theta$	0	$\dfrac{\sqrt{3}}{3}$	1	$\sqrt{3}$	∞

Graphs of Trigonometric Functions

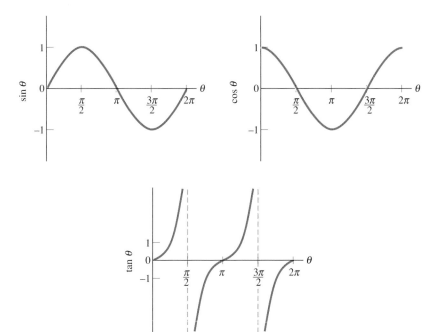

Trigonometric Identities

$\sin(-\theta) = -\sin\theta$

$\cos(-\theta) = \cos\theta$

$\sin\left(\theta \pm \dfrac{\pi}{2}\right) = \pm\cos\theta$

$\cos\left(\theta \pm \dfrac{\pi}{2}\right) = \mp\sin\theta$

$\sin^2\theta + \cos^2\theta = 1$

$\sin 2\theta = 2\sin\theta\cos\theta$

$$\cos 2\theta = \cos^2 \theta - \sin^2 \theta = 1 - 2\sin^2 \theta = 2\cos^2 \theta - 1$$

$$\sin(\alpha \pm \beta) = \sin\alpha\cos\beta \pm \cos\alpha\sin\beta$$

$$\cos(\alpha \pm \beta) = \cos\alpha\cos\beta \mp \sin\alpha\sin\beta$$

$$\sin\alpha \pm \sin\beta = 2\sin[\tfrac{1}{2}(\alpha \pm \beta)]\cos[\tfrac{1}{2}(\alpha \mp \beta)]$$

$$\cos\alpha + \cos\beta = 2\cos[\tfrac{1}{2}(\alpha + \beta)]\cos[\tfrac{1}{2}(\alpha - \beta)]$$

$$\cos\alpha - \cos\beta = -2\sin[\tfrac{1}{2}(\alpha + \beta)]\sin[\tfrac{1}{2}(\alpha - \beta)]$$

Laws of Cosines and Sines

Where A, B, C are the sides of an arbitrary triangle and α, β, γ the angles opposite those sides:

Law of cosines

$$C^2 = A^2 + B^2 - 2AB\cos\gamma$$

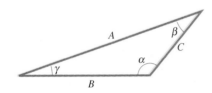

Law of sines

$$\frac{\sin\alpha}{A} = \frac{\sin\beta}{B} = \frac{\sin\gamma}{C}$$

Exponentials and Logarithms

Graphs

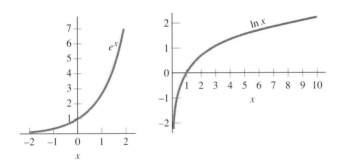

Exponential and Natural Logarithms Are Inverse Functions

$$e^{\ln x} = x, \quad \ln e^x = x \quad e = 2.71828\ldots.$$

Exponential and Logarithmic Identities

$$a^x = e^{x \ln a} \qquad \ln(xy) = \ln x + \ln y$$

$$a^x a^y = a^{x+y} \qquad \ln\left(\frac{x}{y}\right) = \ln x - \ln y$$

$$(a^x)^y = a^{xy} \qquad \ln\left(\frac{1}{x}\right) = -\ln x$$

$$\log x \equiv \log_{10} x = \ln(10)\ln x \approx 2.3\ln x$$

Expansions and Approximations

Series Expansions of Functions

Note: $n! = n(n - 1)(n - 2)(n - 3) \cdots (3)(2)(1)$

$$e^x = 1 + x + \frac{x^2}{2!} + \frac{x^3}{3!} + \cdots \quad \text{(exponential)}$$

$$\sin x = x - \frac{x^3}{3!} + \frac{x^5}{5!} - \cdots \quad \text{(sine)}$$

$$\cos x = 1 - \frac{x^2}{2!} + \frac{x^4}{4!} - \cdots \quad \text{(cosine)}$$

$$\left. \right\} \ (x \text{ in radians})$$

$$\ln(1 + x) = x - \frac{x^2}{2} + \frac{x^3}{3} - \cdots \quad \text{(natural logarithm)}$$

$$(1 + x)^p = 1 + px + \frac{p(p - 1)}{2!}x^2 + \frac{p(p - 1)(p - 2)}{3!}x^3 + \cdots$$

(binomial, valid for $|x| < 1$)

Approximations

For $|x| \ll 1$, the first few terms in the series provide a good approximation; that is,

$$e^x \approx 1 + x$$

$$\sin x \approx x$$

$$\cos x \approx 1 - \tfrac{1}{2}x^2 \qquad \left. \right\} \text{ for } |x| \ll 1$$

$$\ln(1 + x) \approx x$$

$$(1 + x)^p \approx 1 + px$$

Expressions that do not have the forms shown may often be put in the appropriate form. For example:

$$\frac{1}{\sqrt{a^2 + y^2}} = \frac{1}{a\sqrt{1 + \dfrac{y^2}{a^2}}} = \frac{1}{a}\left(1 + \frac{y^2}{a^2}\right)^{-1/2}$$

For $y^2 \ll a^2$, this may be approximated using the binomial expansion $(1 + x)^p \simeq 1 + px$, with $p = -\frac{1}{2}$ and $x = y^2/a^2$:

$$\frac{1}{a}\left(1 + \frac{y^2}{a^2}\right)^{-1/2} \simeq \frac{1}{a}\left(1 - \frac{1}{2}\frac{y^2}{a^2}\right).$$

Vector Algebra

Vector Products

$\mathbf{A} \cdot \mathbf{B} = AB\cos\theta$

$|\mathbf{A} \times \mathbf{B}| = AB\sin\theta$, with direction of $\mathbf{A} \times \mathbf{B}$ given by right-hand rule:

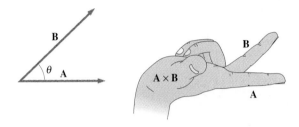

Unit Vector Notation

An arbitrary vector $\mathbf{A}$ may be written in terms of its components A_x, A_y, A_z and the unit vectors $\hat{\mathbf{i}}$, $\hat{\mathbf{j}}$, $\hat{\mathbf{k}}$ that have length 1 and lie along the x, y, z axes:

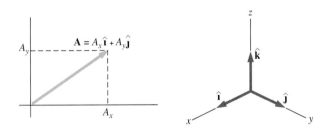

In unit vector notation, vector products become

$\mathbf{A} \cdot \mathbf{B} = A_x B_x + A_y B_y + A_z B_z$

$\mathbf{A} \times \mathbf{B} = (A_y B_z - A_z B_y)\hat{\mathbf{i}} + (A_z B_x - A_x B_z)\hat{\mathbf{j}} + (A_x B_y - A_y B_x)\hat{\mathbf{k}}$

Vector Identities

$\mathbf{A} \cdot \mathbf{B} = \mathbf{B} \cdot \mathbf{A}$

$\mathbf{A} \times \mathbf{B} = -\mathbf{B} \times \mathbf{A}$

$\mathbf{A} \cdot (\mathbf{B} \times \mathbf{C}) = \mathbf{B} \cdot (\mathbf{C} \times \mathbf{A}) = \mathbf{C} \cdot (\mathbf{A} \times \mathbf{B})$

$\mathbf{A} \times (\mathbf{B} \times \mathbf{C}) = (\mathbf{A} \cdot \mathbf{C})\mathbf{B} - (\mathbf{A} \cdot \mathbf{B})\mathbf{C}$

A-2 CALCULUS

Derivatives

Definition of the Derivative

If y is a function of x $[y = f(x)]$, then the **derivative of y with respect to x** is the ratio of the change Δy in y to the corresponding change Δx in x, in the limit of arbitrarily small Δx:

$$\frac{dy}{dx} = \lim_{\Delta x \to 0} \frac{\Delta y}{\Delta x}.$$

Algebraically, the derivative is the rate of change of y with respect to x; geometrically, it is the slope of the y versus x graph—that is, of the tangent line to the graph at a given point:

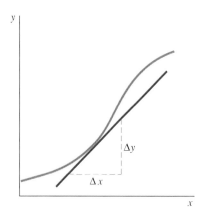

Derivatives of Common Functions

Although the derivative of a function can be evaluated directly using the limiting process that defines the derivative, standard formulas are available for common functions:

$$\frac{da}{dx} = 0 \quad (a \text{ is a constant})$$

$$\frac{dx^n}{dx} = nx^{n-1} \quad (n \text{ need not be an integer})$$

$$\frac{d}{dx}\sin x = \cos x$$

$$\frac{d}{dx}\cos x = -\sin x$$

$$\frac{d}{dx}\tan x = \frac{1}{\cos^2 x}$$

$$\frac{de^x}{dx} = e^x$$

$$\frac{d}{dx}\ln x = \frac{1}{x}$$

Derivatives of Sums, Products, and Functions of Functions

1. Derivative of a constant times a function

$$\frac{d}{dx}[af(x)] = a\frac{df}{dx} \quad (a \text{ is a constant})$$

2. Derivative of a sum

$$\frac{d}{dx}[f(x) + g(x)] = \frac{df}{dx} + \frac{dg}{dx}$$

3. Derivative of a product

$$\frac{d}{dx}[f(x)g(x)] = g\frac{df}{dx} + f\frac{dg}{dx}$$

Examples

$$\frac{d}{dx}(x^2 \cos x) = \cos x \frac{dx^2}{dx} + x^2 \frac{d}{dx}\cos x = 2x \cos x - x^2 \sin x$$

$$\frac{d}{dx}(x \ln x) = \ln x \frac{dx}{dx} + x \frac{d}{dx}\ln x = (\ln x)(1) + x\left(\frac{1}{x}\right) = \ln x + 1$$

4. Derivative of a quotient

$$\frac{d}{dx}\left[\frac{f(x)}{g(x)}\right] = \frac{1}{g^2}\left(g\frac{df}{dx} - f\frac{dg}{dx}\right)$$

Example

$$\frac{d}{dx}\left(\frac{\sin x}{x^2}\right) = \frac{1}{x^4}\left(x^2\frac{d}{dx}\sin x - \sin x\frac{dx^2}{dx}\right) = \frac{\cos x}{x^2} - \frac{2\sin x}{x^3}$$

5. Chain rule for derivatives

If f is a function of u and u is a function of x, then

$$\frac{df}{dx} = \frac{df}{du}\frac{du}{dx}.$$

Examples

a. Evaluate $\dfrac{d}{dx}\sin(x^2)$. Here $u = x^2$ and $f(u) = \sin u$, so

$$\frac{d}{dx}\sin(x^2) = \frac{d}{du}\sin u \frac{du}{dx} = (\cos u)\frac{dx^2}{dx} = 2x\cos(x^2).$$

b. $\dfrac{d}{dt}\sin \omega t = \dfrac{d}{d\omega t}\sin \omega t \dfrac{d}{dt}\omega t = \omega \cos \omega t.$ (ω a constant)

c. Evaluate $\dfrac{d}{dx}\sin^2 5x$. Here $u = \sin 5x$ and $f(u) = u^2$, so

$$\frac{d}{dx}\sin^2 5x = \frac{d}{du}u^2\frac{du}{dx} = 2u\frac{du}{dx} = 2\sin 5x\frac{d}{dx}\sin 5x$$

$$= (2)(\sin 5x)(5)(\cos 5x) = 10\sin 5x\cos 5x = 5\sin 2x.$$

Second Derivative

The second derivative of y with respect to x is defined as the derivative of the derivative:

$$\frac{d^2y}{dx^2} = \frac{d}{dx}\left(\frac{dy}{dx}\right).$$

Example

If $y = ax^3$, then $dy/dx = 3ax^2$, so

$$\frac{d^2y}{dx^2} = \frac{d}{dx}3ax^2 = 6ax.$$

Partial Derivatives

When a function depends on more than one variable, then the partial derivatives of that function are the derivatives with respect to each variable, taken with all other variables held constant. If f is a function of x and y, then the partial derivatives are written

$$\frac{\partial f}{\partial x} \quad \text{and} \quad \frac{\partial f}{\partial y}.$$

Example

If $f(x, y) = x^3\sin y$, then

$$\frac{\partial f}{\partial x} = 3x^2\sin y \quad \text{and} \quad \frac{\partial f}{\partial y} = x^3\cos y.$$

Integrals

Indefinite Integrals

Integration is the inverse of differentiation. The **indefinite integral**, $\int f(x)\,dx$, is defined as a function whose derivative is $f(x)$:

$$\frac{d}{dx}\left[\int f(x)\,dx\right] = f(x).$$

If $A(x)$ is an indefinite integral of $f(x)$, then because the derivative of a constant is zero, the function $A(x) + C$ is also an indefinite integral of $f(x)$, where C is any constant. Inverting the derivatives of common functions listed in the preceding section gives the integrals on the next page (a more extensive table appears at the end of this appendix).

$$\int a\,dx = ax + C$$

$$\int \cos x\,dx = \sin x + C$$

$$\int x^n\,dx = \frac{x^{n+1}}{n+1} + C, \quad n \neq -1$$

$$\int e^x\,dx = e^x + C$$

$$\int \sin x\,dx = -\cos x + C$$

$$\int x^{-1}\,dx = \ln x + C$$

Definite Integrals

In physics we are most often interested in the **definite integral**, defined as the sum of a large number of very small quantities, in the limit as the number of quantities grows arbitrarily large and the size of each arbitrarily small:

$$\int_{x_1}^{x_2} f(x)\,dx \equiv \lim_{\substack{\Delta x \to 0 \\ N \to \infty}} \sum_{i=1}^{N} f(x_i)\,\Delta x,$$

where the terms in the sum are evaluated at values x_i between the limits of integration x_1 and x_2; in the limit $\Delta x \to 0$, the sum is over all values of x in the interval.

The definite integral is used whenever we need to sum over a quantity that is changing—for example, to calculate the work done by a variable force (Chapter 7), the entropy change in a system whose temperature varies (Chapter 22), or the flux of an electric field that varies with position (Chapter 24).

The key to evaluating the definite integral is provided by the **fundamental theorem of calculus**. The theorem states that, if $A(x)$ is an *indefinite* integral of $f(x)$, then the *definite integral* is given by

$$\int_{x_1}^{x_2} f(x)\,dx = A(x_2) - A(x_1) \equiv A(x)\Big|_{x_1}^{x_2}.$$

Geometrically, the definite integral is the area under the graph of $f(x)$ between the limits x_1 and x_2:

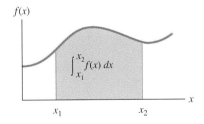

Evaluating Integrals

The first step in evaluating an integral is to express all varying quantities within the integral in terms of a single variable. For example, in evaluating $\int E\,dr$ to calculate an electric potential (Chapter 25), it is necessary first to express E as a function of r. This procedure is illustrated in many examples throughout this text; Example 23-7 provides a typical case.

Once an integral is written in terms of a single variable, it is necessary to manipulate the integrand—the function being integrated—into a form whose integral you know or can look up in tables of integrals. Two common techniques are especially useful:

1. **Change of variables**
   An unfamiliar integral can often be put into familiar form by defining a new variable. For example, it is not obvious how to integrate the expression

   $$\int \frac{x \, dx}{\sqrt{a^2 + x^2}}.$$

   where a is a constant. But let $z = a^2 + x^2$. Then

   $$\frac{dz}{dx} = \frac{da^2}{dx} + \frac{dx^2}{dx} = 0 + 2x = 2x,$$

   so $dz = 2x \, dx$. Then the quantity $x \, dx$ in our unfamiliar integral is just $\frac{1}{2} dz$, while the quantity $\sqrt{a^2 + x^2}$ is just $z^{1/2}$. So the integral becomes

   $$\int \tfrac{1}{2} z^{-1/2} \, dz = \frac{\frac{1}{2} z^{1/2}}{(1/2)} = \sqrt{z},$$

   where we have used the standard form for the integral of a power of the independent variable. Substituting back $z = a^2 + x^2$ gives

   $$\int \frac{x \, dx}{\sqrt{a^2 + x^2}} = \sqrt{a^2 + x^2}.$$

2. **Integration by parts**
   The quantity $\int u \, dv$ is the area under the curve of u as a function of v between specified limits. In the figure below, that area can also be expressed as the area of the rectangle shown minus the area under the curve of v as a function of u. Mathematically, this relation among areas may be expressed as a relation among integrals:

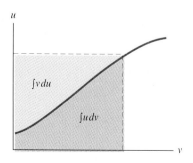

$$\int u \, dv = uv - \int v \, du. \qquad \text{(integration by parts)}$$

This expression may often be used to transform complicated integrals into simpler ones.

Example

Evaluate $\int x \cos x \, dx$. Here let $u = x$, so $du = dx$. Then $dv = \cos x \, dx$, so $v = \int dv = \int \cos x \, dx = \sin x$. Integrating by parts then gives

$$\int x \cos x \, dx = (x)(\sin x) - \int \sin x \, dx = x \sin x + \cos x,$$

where the $+$ sign arises because $\int \sin x \, dx = -\cos x$.

Table of Integrals

[More extensive tables are available in many mathematical and scientific handbooks; see, for example, *Handbook of Chemistry and Physics* (Chemical Rubber Co.) or Dwight, *Tables of Integrals and Other Mathematical Data* (Macmillan).] Increasingly, sophisticated computer software is used instead of tables for the symbolic evaluation of integrals; among the most widely used are *Maple*, *Mathematica*, and *Derive*.

In the expressions below, a and b are constants. An arbitrary constant of integration may be added to the right-hand side.

$$\int e^{ax} \, dx = \frac{e^{ax}}{a}$$

$$\int \sin ax \, dx = -\frac{\cos ax}{a}$$

$$\int \cos ax \, dx = \frac{\sin ax}{a}$$

$$\int \tan ax \, dx = -\frac{1}{a} \ln(\cos ax)$$

$$\int \sin^2 ax \, dx = \frac{x}{2} - \frac{\sin 2ax}{4a}$$

$$\int \cos^2 ax \, dx = \frac{x}{2} + \frac{\sin 2ax}{4a}$$

$$\int x \sin ax \, dx = \frac{1}{a^2} \sin ax - \frac{1}{a} x \cos ax$$

$$\int x \cos ax \, dx = \frac{1}{a^2} \cos ax + \frac{1}{a} x \sin ax$$

$$\int \frac{dx}{\sqrt{a^2 - x^2}} = \sin^{-1}\left(\frac{x}{a}\right)$$

$$\int \frac{dx}{\sqrt{x^2 \pm a^2}} = \ln(x + \sqrt{x^2 \pm a^2})$$

$$\int \frac{dx}{x^2 + a^2} = \frac{1}{a} \tan^{-1}\left(\frac{x}{a}\right)$$

$$\int \frac{x \, dx}{\sqrt{a^2 - x^2}} = -\sqrt{a^2 - x^2}$$

$$\int \frac{x \, dx}{\sqrt{x^2 \pm a^2}} = \sqrt{x^2 \pm a^2}$$

$$\int \frac{dx}{(x^2 \pm a^2)^{3/2}} = \frac{\pm x}{a^2 \sqrt{x^2 \pm a^2}}$$

$$\int x e^{ax} \, dx = \frac{e^{ax}}{a^2}(ax - 1)$$

$$\int x^2 e^{ax} \, dx = \frac{x^2 e^{ax}}{a} - \frac{2}{a}\left[\frac{e^{ax}}{a^2}(ax - 1)\right]$$

$$\int \frac{dx}{a + bx} = \frac{1}{b} \ln(a + bx)$$

$$\int \frac{dx}{(a + bx)^2} = -\frac{1}{b(a + bx)}$$

$$\int \ln ax \, dx = x \ln ax - x$$

The International System of Units (SI)

This material is from the United States edition of the English translation of the sixth edition of "Le Système International d'Unités (SI)," the definitive publication in the French language issued in 1991 by the International Bureau of Weights and Measures (BIPM). The year the definition was adopted is given in parentheses.

unit of length (meter): The meter is the length of the path traveled by light in vacuum during a time interval of 1/299 792 458 of a second. (1983)

unit of mass (kilogram): The kilogram is the unit of mass; it is equal to the mass of the international prototype of the kilogram. (1889)

unit of time (second): The second is the duration of 9 192 631 770 periods of the radiation corresponding to the transition between the two hyperfine levels of the ground state of the cesium-133 atom. (1967)

unit of electric current (ampere): The ampere is that constant current which, if maintained in two straight parallel conductors of infinite length, of negligible circular cross section, and placed 1 meter apart in vacuum, would produce between these conductors a force equal to 2×10^{-7} newton per meter of length. (1948)

unit of thermodynamic temperature (kelvin): The kelvin, unit of thermodynamic temperature, is the fraction 1/273.16 of the thermodynamic temperature of the triple point of water. (1957) Also, the unit kelvin and its symbol K should be used to express an interval or a difference of temperature.

unit of amount of substance (mole): (1) The mole is the amount of substance of a system that contains as many elementary entities as there are atoms in 0.012 kilogram of carbon 12. (1971) (2) When the mole is used, the elementary entities must be specified and may be atoms, molecules, ions, electrons, other particles, or specified groups of such particles.

unit of luminous intensity (candela): The candela is the luminous intensity, in a given direction, of a source that emits monochromatic radiation of frequency 540×10^{12} hertz and that has a radiant intensity in that direction of (1/683) watt per steradian. (1979)

▲ *SI Base and Supplementary Units*

QUANTITY	SI UNIT NAME	SI UNIT SYMBOL
Base Unit		
Length	meter	m
Mass	kilogram	kg
Time	second	s
Electric current	ampere	A
Thermodynamic temperature	kelvin	K
Amount of substance	mole	mol
Luminous intensity	candela	cd
Supplementary Units		
Plane angle	radian	rad
Solid angle	steradian	sr

▲ *SI Prefixes*

FACTOR	PREFIX	SYMBOL
10^{24}	yotta	Y
10^{21}	zetta	Z
10^{18}	exa	E
10^{15}	peta	P
10^{12}	tera	T
10^{9}	giga	G
10^{6}	mega	M
10^{3}	kilo	k
10^{2}	hecto	h
10^{1}	deka	da
10^{0}	—	—
10^{-1}	deci	d
10^{-2}	centi	c
10^{-3}	milli	m
10^{-6}	micro	μ
10^{-9}	nano	n
10^{-12}	pico	p
10^{-15}	femto	f
10^{-18}	atto	a
10^{-21}	zepto	z
10^{-24}	yocto	y

▲ *Some SI Derived Units with Special Names*

QUANTITY	SI UNIT NAME	SI UNIT SYMBOL	EXPRESSION IN TERMS OF OTHER UNITS	EXPRESSION IN TERMS OF SI BASE UNITS
Frequency	hertz	Hz		s^{-1}
Force	newton	N		$m \cdot kg \cdot s^{-2}$
Pressure, stress	pascal	Pa	N/m^2	$m^{-1} \cdot kg \cdot s^{-2}$
Energy, work, heat	joule	J	$N \cdot m$	$m^2 \cdot kg \cdot s^{-2}$
Power	watt	W	J/s	$m^2 \cdot kg \cdot s^{-3}$
Electric charge	coulomb	C		$s \cdot A$
Electric potential, potential difference, electromotive force	volt	V	J/C	$m^2 \cdot kg \cdot s^{-3} \cdot A^{-1}$
Capacitance	farad	F	C/V	$m^{-2} \cdot kg^{-1} \cdot s^4 \cdot A^2$
Electric resistance	ohm	Ω	V/A	$m^2 \cdot kg \cdot s^{-3} \cdot A^{-2}$
Magnetic flux	weber	Wb	$V \cdot s$	$m^2 \cdot kg \cdot s^{-2} \cdot A^{-1}$
Magnetic field	tesla	T	Wb/m^2	$kg \cdot s^{-2} \cdot A^{-1}$
Inductance	henry	H	Wb/A	$m^2 \cdot kg \cdot s^{-2} \cdot A^{-2}$
Radioactivity	becquerel	Bq	1 decay/s	s^{-1}
Absorbed radiation dose	gray	Gy	J/kg, 100 rad	$m^2 \cdot s^{-2}$
Radiation dose equivalent	sievert	Sv	J/kg, 100 rem	$m^2 \cdot s^{-2}$

APPENDIX C
Conversion Factors

The listings below give the SI equivalents of non-SI units. To convert from the units shown to SI, multiply by the factor given; to convert the other way, divide. For conversions within the SI system see table of SI prefixes in Appendix B, Chapter 1, or inside front cover. Conversions that are not exact by definition are given to, at most, 4 significant figures.

Length

1 inch (in.) = 0.0254 m
1 foot (ft) = 0.3048 m
1 yard (yd) = 0.9144 m
1 mile (mi) = 1609 m
1 nautical mile = 1852 m

1 angstrom (Å) = 10^{-10} m
1 light-year (ly) = 9.46×10^{15} m
1 astronomical unit (AU) = 1.5×10^{11} m
1 parsec = 3.09×10^{16} m
1 fermi = 10^{-15} m = 1 fm

Mass

1 slug = 14.59 kg
1 metric ton (tonne; T) = 1000 kg

1 unified mass unit (u) = 1.660×10^{-27} kg

Force units in the English system are sometimes used (incorrectly) for mass. The units given below are actually equal to the number of kilograms multiplied by g, the acceleration of gravity.

1 pound (lb) = weight of 0.454 kg
1 ton = 2000 lb = weight of 908 kg

1 ounce (oz) = weight of 0.02835 kg

Time

1 minute (min) = 60 s
1 hour (h) = 60 min = 3600 s

1 day (d) = 24 h = 86 400 s
1 year (y) = 365.2422 d* = 3.156×10^7 s

*The length of the year changes very slowly with changes in Earth's orbital period.

Area

1 hectare (ha) = 10^4 m^2 1 acre = 4047 m^2
1 square inch (in.^{2}) = 6.452×10^{-4} m^2 1 barn = 10^{-28} m^2
1 square foot (ft^2) = 9.290×10^{-2} m^2 1 shed = 10^{-30} m^2

Volume

1 liter (L) = 1000 cm^3 = 10^{-3} m^3 1 gallon (U.S.; gal) = 3.785×10^{-3} m^3
1 cubic foot (ft^3) = 2.832×10^{-2} m^3 1 gallon (British) = 4.546×10^{-3} m^3
1 cubic inch (in.^{3}) = 1.639×10^{-5} m^3
1 fluid ounce = 1/128 gal = 2.957×10^{-5} m^3
1 barrel = 42 gal = 0.1590 m^3

Angle, Phase

1 degree (°) = $\pi/180$ rad = 1.745×10^{-2} rad
1 revolution (rev) = 360° = 2π rad
1 cycle = 360° = 2π rad

Speed, Velocity

1 km/h = (1/3.6) m/s = 0.2778 m/s   1 ft/s = 0.3048 m/s
1 mi/h (mph) = 0.4470 m/s   1 ly/y = 3.00×10^8 m/s

Angular Speed, Angular Velocity, Frequency, and Angular Frequency

1 rev/s = 2π rad/s = 6.283 rad/s (s^{-1})   1 rev/min (rpm) = 0.1047 rad/s (s^{-1})
1 Hz = 1 cycle/s = 2πs^{-1}

Force

1 dyne = 10^{-5} N   1 pound (lb) = 4.448 N

Pressure

1 dyne/cm^2 = 0.10 Pa   1 lb/in.^{2} (psi) = 6.895×10^3 Pa
1 atmosphere (atm) = 1.013×10^5 Pa   1 in. H$_2$O (60°F) = 248.8 Pa
1 torr = 1 mm Hg at 0°C = 133.3 Pa   1 in. Hg (60°F) = 3.377×10^3 Pa
1 bar = 10^5 Pa = 0.987 atm

Energy, Work, Heat

1 erg = 10^{-7} J   1 Btu* = 1.054×10^3 J
1 calorie* (cal) = 4.184 J   1 kWh = 3.6×10^6 J
1 electron-volt (eV) = 1.602×10^{-19} J   1 megaton (explosive yield; Mt)
1 foot-pound (ft·lb) = 1.356 J   = 4.18×10^{15} J

---

* Values based on the thermochemical calorie; other definitions vary slightly.

Power

$$1 \text{ erg/s} = 10^{-7} \text{ W}$$
$$1 \text{ horsepower (hp)} = 746 \text{ W}$$

$$1 \text{ Btu/h (Btuh)} = 0.293 \text{ W}$$
$$1 \text{ ft·lb/s} = 1.356 \text{ W}$$

Magnetic Field

$$1 \text{ gauss (G)} = 10^{-4} \text{ T}$$

$$1 \text{ gamma } (\gamma) = 10^{-9} \text{ T}$$

Radiation

$$1 \text{ curie (ci)} = 3.7 \times 10^{10} \text{ Bq}$$

$$1 \text{ rad} = 10^{-2} \text{ Gy}$$
$$1 \text{ rem} = 10^{-2} \text{ Sv}$$

▲   *Energy Content of Fuels*

ENERGY SOURCE	ENERGY CONTENT
Coal	2.9×10^7 J/kg $= 7300$ kWh/ton $= 25 \times 10^6$ Btu/ton
Oil	43×10^6 J/kg $= 39$ kWh/gal $= 1.3 \times 10^5$ Btu/gal
Gasoline	44×10^6 J/kg $= 36$ kWh/gal $= 1.2 \times 10^5$ Btu/gal
Natural gas	55×10^6 J/kg $= 30$ kWh/100 ft^3 $= 1000$ Btu/ft^3
Uranium (fission)	
Normal abundance	5.8×10^{11} J/kg $= 1.6 \times 10^5$ kWh/kg
Pure U-235	8.2×10^{13} J/kg $= 2.3 \times 10^7$ kWh/kg
Hydrogen (fusion)	
Normal abundance	7×10^{11} J/kg $= 3.0 \times 10^4$ kWh/kg
Pure deuterium	3.3×10^{14} J/kg $= 9.2 \times 10^7$ kWh/kg
Water	1.2×10^{10} J/kg $= 1.3 \times 10^4$ kWh/gal $= 340$ gal gasoline/gal
H_2O	
100% conversion, matter to energy	9.0×10^{16} J/kg $= 931$ MeV/u $= 2.5 \times 10^{10}$ kWh/kg

The Elements

The atomic weights of stable elements reflect the abundances of different isotopes; values given here apply to elements as they exist naturally on Earth. For stable elements, parentheses express uncertainties in the last decimal place given. For elements with no stable isotopes (indicated in boldface), sets of most important isotopes are given. (Exceptions are the unstable elements thorium, protactinium, and uranium, for which atomic weights reflect natural abundances of long-lived isotopes.) See also periodic table inside back cover.

ATOMIC NUMBER	NAMES	SYMBOL	ATOMIC WEIGHT
1	Hydrogen	H	1.00794 (7)
2	Helium	He	4.002602 (2)
3	Lithium	Li	6.941 (2)
4	Beryllium	Be	9.012182 (3)
5	Boron	B	10.811 (5)
6	Carbon	C	12.011 (1)
7	Nitrogen	N	14.00674 (7)
8	Oxygen	O	15.9994 (3)
9	Fluorine	F	18.9984032 (9)
10	Neon	Ne	20.1797 (6)
11	Sodium (Natrium)	Na	22.989768 (6)
12	Magnesium	Mg	24.3050 (6)
13	Aluminum	Al	26.981539 (5)
14	Silicon	Si	28.0855 (3)
15	Phosphorus	P	30.973762 (4)
16	Sulfur	S	32.066 (6)
17	Chlorine	Cl	35.4527 (9)
18	Argon	Ar	39.948 (1)
19	Potassium (Kalium)	K	39.0983 (1)
20	Calcium	Ca	40.078 (4)
21	Scandium	Sc	44.955910 (9)
22	Titanium	Ti	47.88 (3)
23	Vanadium	V	50.9415 (1)
24	Chromium	Cr	51.9961 (6)
25	Manganese	Mn	54.93805 (1)
26	Iron	Fe	55.847 (3)
27	Cobalt	Co	58.93320 (1)

ATOMIC NUMBER	NAMES	SYMBOL	ATOMIC WEIGHT
28	Nickel	Ni	58.69 (1)
29	Copper	Cu	63.546 (3)
30	Zinc	Zn	65.39 (2)
31	Gallium	Ga	69.723 (1)
32	Germanium	Ge	72.61 (2)
33	Arsenic	As	74.92159 (2)
34	Selenium	Se	78.96 (3)
35	Bromine	Br	79.904 (1)
36	Krypton	Kr	83.80 (1)
37	Rubidium	Rb	85.4678 (3)
38	Strontium	Sr	87.62 (1)
39	Yttrium	Y	88.90585 (2)
40	Zirconium	Zr	91.224 (2)
41	Niobium	Nb	92.90638 (2)
42	Molybdenum	Mo	95.94 (1)
43	**Technetium**	**Tc**	**97, 98, 99**
44	Ruthenium	Ru	101.07 (2)
45	Rhodium	Rh	102.90550 (3)
46	Palladium	Pd	106.42 (1)
47	Silver	Ag	107.8682 (2)
48	Cadmium	Cd	112.411 (8)
49	Indium	In	114.82 (1)
50	Tin	Sn	118.710 (7)
51	Antimony (Stibium)	Sb	121.75 (3)
52	Tellurium	Te	127.60 (3)
53	Iodine	I	126.90447 (3)
54	Xenon	Xe	131.29 (2)
55	Cesium	Cs	132.90543 (5)
56	Barium	Ba	137.327 (7)
57	Lanthanum	La	138.9055 (2)
58	Cerium	Ce	140.115 (4)
59	Praseodymium	Pr	140.90765 (3)
60	Neodymium	Nd	144.24 (3)
61	**Promethium**	**Pm**	**145, 147**
62	Samarium	Sm	150.36 (3)
63	Europium	Eu	151.965 (9)
64	Gadolinium	Gd	157.25 (3)
65	Terbium	Tb	158.92534 (3)
66	Dysprosium	Dy	162.50 (3)
67	Holmium	Ho	164.93032 (3)
68	Erbium	Er	167.26 (3)
69	Thulium	Tm	168.93421 (3)
70	Ytterbium	Yb	173.04 (3)
71	Lutetium	Lu	174.967 (1)
72	Hafnium	Hf	178.49 (2)
73	Tantalum	Ta	180.9479 (1)
74	Tungsten (Wolfram)	W	183.85 (3)
75	Rhenium	Re	186.207 (1)
76	Osmium	Os	190.2 (1)
77	Iridium	Ir	192.22 (3)
78	Platinum	Pt	195.08 (3)
79	Gold	Au	196.96654 (3)
80	Mercury	Hg	200.59 (3)
81	Thallium	Tl	204.3833 (2)
82	Lead	Pb	207.2 (1)
83	Bismuth	Bi	208.98037 (3)

ATOMIC NUMBER	NAMES	SYMBOL	ATOMIC WEIGHT
84	Polonium	Po	209, 210
85	Astatine	At	210, 211
86	Radon	Rn	211, 220, 222
87	Francium	Fr	223
88	Radium	Ra	223, 224, 226, 228
89	Actinium	Ac	227
90	Thorium	Th	232.0381 (1)
91	Protactinium	Pa	231.03588 (2)
92	Uranium	U	238.0289 (1)
93	Neptunium	Np	237, 239
94	Plutonium	Pu	238, 239, 240, 241, 242, 244
95	Americium	Am	241, 243
96	Curium	Cm	243, 244, 245, 246, 247, 248
97	Berkelium	Bk	247, 249
98	Californium	Cf	249, 250, 251, 252
99	Einsteinium	Es	252
100	Fermium	Fm	257
101	Mendelevium	Md	255, 256, 258, 260
102	Nobelium	No	253, 254, 255, 259
103	Lawrencium	Lr	256, 258, 259, 261
104	Rutherfordium	Rf	257, 259, 260, 261
105	Dubnium	Db	260, 261, 262
106	Seaborgium	Sg	259, 260, 261, 263
107	Bohrium	Bh	261, 262
108	Hassium	Hs	264, 265
109	Meitnerium	Mt	266
110	—	—	269
111	—	—	272
112	—	—	277

Astrophysical Data

SUN, PLANETS, PRINCIPAL SATELLITES

BODY	MASS (10²⁴ kg)	MEAN RADIUS (10⁶ m EXCEPT AS NOTED)	SURFACE GRAVITY (m/s²)	ESCAPE SPEED (km/s)	SIDEREAL ROTATION PERIOD* (days)	MEAN DISTANCE FROM CENTRAL BODY† (10⁶ km)	ORBITAL PERIOD	ORBITAL SPEED (km/s)
Sun	1.99×10^6	696	274	618	36 at poles 27 at equator	2.6×10^{11}	200 My	250
Mercury	0.330	2.44	3.70	4.25	58.6	57.6	88.0 d	48
Venus	4.87	6.05	8.87	10.4	−243	108	225 d	35
Earth	5.97	6.37	9.81	11.2	0.997	150	365.3 d	30
Moon	0.0735	1.74	1.62	2.38	27.3	0.385	27.3 d	1.0
Mars	0.642	3.38	3.74	5.03	1.03	228	1.88 y	24.1
Phobos	9.6×10^{-9}	9-13 km	0.001	0.008	0.32	9.4×10^{-3}	0.32 d	2.1
Deimos	2×10^{-9}	5-8 km	0.001	0.005	1.3	23×10^{-3}	1.3 d	1.3
Jupiter	1.90×10^3	69.1	26.5	60.6	0.414	778	11.9 y	13.0
Io	0.0889	1.82	1.8	2.6	1.77	0.422	1.77 d	17
Europa	0.478	1.57	1.3	2.0	3.55	0.671	3.55 d	14
Ganymede	0.148	2.63	1.4	2.7	7.15	1.07	7.15 d	11
Callisto	0.107	2.40	1.2	2.4	16.7	1.88	16.7 d	8.2
and 13 smaller satellites								
Saturn	569	56.8	11.8	36.6	0.438	1.43×10^3	29.5 y	9.65
Tethys	0.0007	0.53	0.2	0.4	1.89	0.294	1.89 d	11.3
Dione	0.00015	0.56	0.3	0.6	2.74	0.377	2.74 d	10.0
Rhea	0.0025	0.77	0.3	0.5	4.52	0.527	4.52 d	8.5
Titan	0.135	2.58	1.4	2.6	15.9	1.22	15.9 d	5.6
Iapetus	0.0019	0.73	0.2	0.6	79.3	3.56	79.3 d	3.3
and 12 smaller satellites								
Uranus	86.6	25.0	9.23	21.5	−0.65	2.87×10^3	84.1 y	6.79
Ariel	0.0013	0.58	0.3	0.4	2.52	0.19	2.52 d	5.5
Umbriel	0.0013	0.59	0.3	0.4	4.14	0.27	4.14 d	4.7
Titania	0.0018	0.81	0.2	0.5	8.70	0.44	8.70 d	3.7
Oberon	0.0017	0.78	0.2	0.5	13.5	0.58	13.5 d	3.1
and 11 smaller satellites								
Neptune	103	24.0	11.9	23.9	0.768	4.50×10^3	165 y	5.43
Triton	0.134	1.9	2.5	3.1	5.88	0.354	5.88 d	4.4
and 7 smaller satellites								
Pluto	0.015	1.2	0.4	1.2	−6.39	5.91×10^3	249 y	4.7
Charon	0.001	0.6			−6.39	0.02	6.39 d	0.2

*Negative rotation period indicates retrograde motion, in opposite sense from orbital motion. Periods are sidereal, meaning the time for the body to return to the same orientation relative to the distant stars rather than the Sun.

†Central body is galactic center for Sun, Sun for planets, and planet for satellites.

Got It! Answers

Chapter 2

p. 24 Average speed and average velocity are the same for direct and Kansas City stop flights; average speed is greater for Minneapolis stop flight

p. 27 (b) has constant speed; (a) reverses direction; (d) speeds up

Chapter 3

p. 52 (c)

Chapter 4

p. 70 None are true

Chapter 5

p. 95 The straight line

p. 99 $T > F_g$ for upward a; $T < F_g$ for downward a; $T = F_g$ for constant speed in either direction

p. 102 No; for example, a car slowing down is moving in the direction opposite the force that's slowing it

p. 107 The statement is nonsense. If there were no gravity in space, spacecraft, astronauts, and the moon would all move in straight lines and we would never see them again!

p. 109 Upward acceleration does not imply upward velocity; cable tension exceeds weight in (a) and (d)

p. 111 No, the force on the larger block is 1.5 N

Chapter 6

p. 134 Both 1 N

p. 139 Because the gravitational force is just enough to keep them accelerating in a circular path

p. 144 Because the objects were on sloping surfaces, and therefore the normal force was not equal to the weight

p. 153 The larger one; it has a greater ratio of mass to surface area

Chapter 7

p. 172 No, it's only 5 J, as the spring hasn't exerted 2 N the whole way

p. 177 Both do the same work; the faster hiker produces more power

Chapter 8

p. 200 Because an *increase* in potential energy (positive dU/dx) means one is doing work moving *against* a force

Chapter 10

p. 244 Second one from the top

p. 247 $30\hat{\jmath}$ kg·m/s

p. 249 Both skaters' momenta increase; the basketball's momentum reverses sign; system momentum is unchanged

Chapter 11

p. 264 The first two

p. 271 The object initially at rest

Chapter 12

p. 290 12-6b

p. 297 Because its mass is farther from the rotation axis

p. 304 The solid ball

Chapter 13

p. 323 The boy brings no additional angular momentum to the system, while the girl does

p. 327 Upward

Chapter 14

p. 339 The diagonal pair

Chapter 15

p. 369 Frequency and period are the same; amplitude and phase constants are different

p. 375 (a) no change; (b) doubles; (c) doubles

Chapter 17

p. 422 No, it drops by 20 dB

Chapter 18

p. 450 No, the water level stays the same

p. 451 Because you'll put the center of gravity over the center of buoyancy, making the canoe unstable as in Fig. 18-17b

p. 458 Lower

Chapter 19

p. 480 The rock

p. 486 Radiation; (a) conduction; (b) convection

Chapter 20

p. 504 100°C

Chapter 21

p. 526 In an isothermal process T is constant so pressure and volume are inversely proportional. But temperature changes in an adiabatic process, so P and V are not inversely proportional. Thus there's no contradiction between the two equations

Chapter 23
p. 576 (a) $-\hat{\mathbf{i}}$; (b) $\sqrt{2}/2(-\hat{\mathbf{i}} + \hat{\mathbf{j}})$
p. 583 (a) 200 N/C; (b) 100 N/C
p. 585 Because P isn't the same distance from **all** parts of the rod

Chapter 24
p. 606 (a) $\phi = 0$ for A, B; $\phi = Es^2$ for C; (b) $\phi = 0$ for A, $\phi = s^2 E \cos 45° = \sqrt{2}s^2 E/2$ for B, C
p. 608 ϕ doesn't change; $\mathbf{E}$ generally does
p. 611 (a) remains zero; (b) doubles
p. 617 (a) $E = \dfrac{Q}{-(2)(1\ m)^2(\varepsilon_0)}$ (b) $E = \dfrac{kQ}{(1000\ m)^2}$
p. 619 No

Chapter 25
p. 633 (a) doubles; (b) doubles; (c) becomes zero; (d) changes sign
p. 633 $W_\alpha = 2W_p$
p. 635 Proton: toward negative ΔV; electron: toward positive ΔV
p. 636 b, a, c
p. 637 More
p. 644 (a)
p. 645 Yes to both

Chapter 26
p. 666 They're the same
p. 670 Twice the working voltage
p. 673 (a) parallel; (b) series; (c) the series combination 1/2 C

Chapter 27
p. 686 (a) current to left; (b) upward current; (c) current to left; (d) no current; (e) no current
p. 700 (a) (2); (b) (1)

Chapter 28
p. 713 (a) 3 V; (b) 0 V; (c) 6 V
p. 716 (a) 2R; (b) 1/2 R
p. 718 A will be brightest; with C disconnected both A and B will have equal brightness
p. 732 (a) 6 mA; (b) 2 mA

Chapter 29
p. 746 Greatest force in (a); least (0) in (c); direction in (a) and (b) is into page
p. 749 Counterclockwise
p. 755 Upward

Chapter 30
p. 777 (a) into the page at P, out of the page at Q; (b) stronger at P
p. 778 Tighten, independent of the current direction
p. 780 Into the page
p. 782 (b) only

Chapter 31
p. 811 Same direction as in Fig. 31-11; you still do work
p. 812 Counterclockwise
p. 814 Harder
p. 817 (a) clockwise; (b) counterclockwise

Chapter 32
p. 838 Increasing
p. 843 Only when it's opened

Chapter 33
p. 857 The capacitor
p. 864 Smaller, by a factor of 10^{-4}
p. 866 Above

Chapter 34
p. 895 Both have the same speed; light has a much smaller wavelength
p. 905 (a) $B_1 = 2B_2$; (b) $S_1 = 4S_2$; (c) $\lambda_1 = \lambda_2$

Chapter 35
p. 923 $n_3 > n_1 > n_2$

Chapter 36
p. 943 At the mirror's center of curvature
p. 950 (a) The intensity diminishes, but the full image remains (b) there would be no image (c) there would be no image, or it would be very out of focus (d) yes, but not obviously visible except when looking straight toward lens
p. 951 Virtual, convex
p. 960 +2.25 diopter

Chapter 37
p. 976 Closer together

Chapter 38
p. 1020 When the twins move at the same speed they are the same age; the twin making the longer trip is younger
p. 1029 Less, although insignificantly so at these low relative speeds
p. 1033 Very nearly c

Answers to Odd-Numbered Problems

Chapter 1
3. 100,000 times bigger
   5.0.108 782 775 7 ns
7. 10^8
9. 0.79 rad
11. 28 g
13. 10^6
15. 7%
17. Less by about 3 mi/h
19. 30 AU
21. 143 m^2/kg
23. Approximately 0.0175 rad
25. L/T^2
27. (c) Actually, the speed is given by
   $v = \sqrt{\lambda g/2\pi}$
29. 2.5×10^6 m
31. 7.4×10^6 m/s²
33. (a) 2.5×10^{-11} m²; (b) 5.0 μm
35. 280 K
37. 41 m
39. 7
43. $\sim 1.3 \times 10^6$
45. About 0.1%
47. (a) $\sim 1.4 \times 10^{18}$ m³; (b) $\sim 1.3 \times 10^{12}$
49. ~ 10 times as much in stars
51. $\sim 10^4$
53. $d_{Sun}/d_{moon} = 380$;
   $R_{Sun} \sim 7 \times 10^5$ km
   (a) 4 μm; (b) 7500
55. (a) $\sim 10^{28}$; (b) $\sim 10^{14}$
59. $\sqrt{F_0/\mu}$; this is in fact the equation
   for the wave speed

Chapter 2
1. 10.16 m/s
3. 5.30 m/s
5. (a) 24 km north; (b) 9.6 km/h;
   (c) 16 km/h; (d) 0; (e) 0
7. 28.5 km/h
9. 48 mi/h

11. 1 m/s = 2.24 mi/h
13. 51 ft/s = 35 mi/h
15. (a) 84 km/h; (b) 55 h
17. 2.6 h later; 1800 km from New
   York
21. (a) 2.0 m/s; (b) 0; (c) -5.0 m/s; (d)
   1.2 m/s; (e) 0.17 m/s
23. (a) $b - 2ct$; (b) 8.4 s after launch
25. (a) $t = 0$ s, 0.13 s, 2.5 s;
   (b) $v = 3bt^2 - 2ct + d$;
   (c) $v_0 = 1.0$ m/s;
   (d) $t = 0.065$ s, 1.7 s
27. 125 m/s²
29. 15 m/s²
31. 31 s
33. (a) 126 m/s; (b) 0.46 m/s²
35. $a = 6bt - 2c$
37. 100 m by both methods
41. (a) 46 m/s²; (b) 61 s
43. (a) 2.0 m/s²; (b) 150 m
45. 5×10^{-12} m
47. 12 km/s
49. (a) 0.014 s; (b) 0.51 m
51. 886 m
53. Yes, $a = 370$ m/s²
55. No collision; 10 m apart
57. 4.6×10^{-3} m/s²
59. Collide at 12 km/h
61. 11.3 m/s
63. (a) 27 m; (b) 4.7 s
65. Mars
67. 273 m
69. 2.0 m/s
71. 2.4 s
73. (a) 25 km/h; (b) 13 km/h
75. (a) 4.6 s; (b) 8.7 m/s
77. 0.196 s
79. 5.0 s; 17 km/h
81. (a) 7.0 m/s; (b) in 2.3 s
83. 83.113 m

85. (b) 3.8 s; (c) 19 m; (d) 100 m
87. (a) $v = \omega x_0 \cos \omega t$,
   $a = -\omega^2 x_0 \sin \omega t$;
   (b) $v_{max} = \omega x_0$, $a_{max} = \omega^2 x_0$
89. (a) 20 cm
91. 1.19 m

Chapter 3
1. 266 m, 34° N of W
3. 702 km, 21.3° E of N
5. $C = 5.0$ m; 127° clockwise from $\mathbf{A}$
7. (a) $0.68A$ vertically upward;
   (b) $1.88A$, to the right
9. (a) L, $-x$ direction; (b) $\sqrt{3}L$,
   $+ y$ direction; (c) 0; (d) $2L$,
   $- x$ direction
11. $\mathbf{V} = 105\hat{\mathbf{i}} + 58\hat{\mathbf{j}}$ km
13. $\mathbf{A} = 8.19\hat{\mathbf{i}} + 5.74\hat{\mathbf{j}}$;
   $\mathbf{B} = -3.44\hat{\mathbf{i}} - 4.91\hat{\mathbf{j}}$;
   $\mathbf{C} = -3.38\hat{\mathbf{i}} + 7.25\hat{\mathbf{j}}$
15. $\mathbf{A} + \mathbf{B} = 4.8\hat{\mathbf{i}} + 0.82\hat{\mathbf{j}}$;
   $\mathbf{A} - \mathbf{B} = 12\hat{\mathbf{i}} + 11\hat{\mathbf{j}}$;
   $\mathbf{A} + \mathbf{C} = 4.8\hat{\mathbf{i}} + 13\hat{\mathbf{j}}$;
   $\mathbf{A} + \mathbf{B} + \mathbf{C} = 1.4\hat{\mathbf{i}} + 8.1\hat{\mathbf{j}}$
17. $\mathbf{C} = -15\hat{\mathbf{i}} + 9\hat{\mathbf{j}} - 18\hat{\mathbf{k}}$
19. (a) $1.37\hat{\mathbf{i}} + 8.07\hat{\mathbf{j}}$;
   (b) $8.25\hat{\mathbf{i}} + 17.9\hat{\mathbf{j}}$; (c) $10.5\hat{\mathbf{i}} - 17.6\hat{\mathbf{j}}$
21. $0.19\hat{\mathbf{i}} + 0.88\hat{\mathbf{j}}$ km;
   (b) 1.0 km at 79° N of E
23. (a) $A_x = 5.9$, $A_y = 8.1$; $A'_x = 5.4$,
   $A'_y = 8.4$ units
25. $\hat{\mathbf{i}} + \hat{\mathbf{j}} + \hat{\mathbf{k}}$; magnitude $= \sqrt{3}$
27. (a) in x-y system $\Delta\mathbf{r} = 5.0\hat{\mathbf{i}} +$
   $3.5\hat{\mathbf{j}}$ km; in x'-y' system
   $\Delta\mathbf{r} = 6.1\hat{\mathbf{i}} + 0.50\hat{\mathbf{j}}$ km;
   (b) $\Delta r = 6.1$ km
29. (a) 5.4 mi at 32° E of N;
   (b) 15 mi/h at 32° E of N
31. (a) 264 km/h, 29° west of north;
   (b) $-128\hat{\mathbf{i}} + 231\hat{\mathbf{j}}$ km/h

33. $19\hat{\imath} + 4.5\hat{\jmath} + 0.26\hat{k}$ km/h
35. (a) $24\hat{\imath} + 10\hat{\jmath}$ m;
    (b) $12\hat{\imath} + 5.0\hat{\jmath}$ m/s;
    (c) $12\hat{\imath} - 5.0\hat{\jmath}$ m/s
37. 5.12 m/s^2, 41° S of W (221° from x axis)
39. (a) $\bar{\mathbf{v}} = -0.8\hat{\jmath}$ cm/h;
    (b) $\bar{\mathbf{a}} = -0.42\hat{\imath}$ cm/h^2
41. (a) $10\hat{\imath} - 21\hat{\jmath}$ m/s; (b) 13.0 m/s;
    (c) 89.0°
43. 6.7$\hat{\imath}$ m/s; (b) 1.66 s; (c) 8.24 m/s
45. (a) 18 km/h, 14 km/h, 10 km/h,
    14 km/h; (b) 21 km/h, 17 km/h,
    13 km/h, 17 km/h
47. $30\hat{\imath} + 64\hat{\jmath}$ km/s
49. (a) 1.6 m, 2.8 m/s, both vertically
    downward; (b) 2.03 m, 3.57 m/s,
    both at 38.1° to the vertical;
    (c) 9.8 m/s^2, vertically downward in
    both frames of reference
51. 16.2 m
53. (a) 1.8 km/h/s = 0.50 m/s^2;
    (b) 142°
55. (a) 0.32 cm/s; (b) 0.034 cm/s^2;
    (c) 90°
57. 25° upstream
59. (a) 1.30×10^6 m; (b) 7.78 km/s;
    (c) 9.19 m/s^2, almost g
61. $-b\hat{\imath} + a\hat{\jmath}$, $b\hat{\imath} - a\hat{\jmath}$
63. $\frac{\sqrt{2}}{2}\hat{\imath} + \frac{\sqrt{2}}{2}\hat{\jmath}$
67. 53.8°, 13.9 km/h

Chapter 4

1. 0°
3. $1.3\hat{\imath} + 2.3\hat{\jmath}$ m/s
5. 6.0 m/s at 53° below x axis
7. (a) 23°; (b) 5.4×10^3 km
9. 1.83 m
11. (a) $t = 18$ s; (b) 300 m; (c) 22 m/s,
    at 120° to x axis
13. (a) 2.6×10^{17} cm/s^2, upward;
    (b) parabolic
15. (a) 1.34 s; (b) 14.7 m
17. 5.7 m/s
19. 34 nm
21. 8.3 m/s at 61°
23. Yes
25. -14.6 m/s
27. (a) 6.64 km/s; (b) 16.0 min;
    (c) 8.28 km/s
29. 1.1 s
31. 1090 m

35. (a) 8.8 m; (b) 0.53 m
37. 11.2 m/s
41. 31.2° or 65.7°
43. 2.8×10^{-3} m/s^2
45. 54 min
47. 2.27 km
59. 5.07×10^3 s
51. $a_r = 0.947$ m/s^2;
    $a_t = 6.28\times10^{-2}$ m/s^2
53. $t = \sqrt{r/a_t}$
55. 89 m/s
57. 32 m
59. 19 m
61. 300 m, 119 m
63. $\mathbf{v}_0 = 6.36\hat{\imath} + 10.3\hat{\jmath}$ m/s,
    or 12.1 m/s at 58.3°
65. 83°
71. 7.2 m/s at 77° to horizontal
75. 38°
77. $2v_0 \sin\theta_0/g$
79. 892 m/s^2
81. 364 m

83. (a) $\tan^{-1}\left(\tan\theta_0 - \dfrac{gt}{v_0\cos\theta_0}\right)$;

    (b) $\tan^{-1}\left(\tan\theta_0 - \dfrac{gx}{v_0^2\cos^2\theta_0}\right)$

Chapter 5

1. 3.8 MN
3. 1.5×10^3 kN
5. 10^{-4} N
7. (a) $m_B = 3.0m_A$; (b) 2.0 m/s^2
9. Quadruples
11. (a) 11 m; (b) 24 m; (c) 43 m;
    (d) 53 m
13. $F_{driver} = 5.7$ kN; $F_{passenger} =$
    125 kN, 22 times greater
15. 5.77 N at 72.2° to the x axis
17. Venus
19. (a) 3.3 N; (b) 12 oz
21. 9.1×10^3 kg
23. 7.7×10^{12} m/s^2
25. 4.26 m/s^2
27. 385 N
29. 2.9 m/s^2, downward
31. (a) 3.1×10^7 N; (b) 9.4×10^2 N
33. 0.53 s
35. 55 kN
37. 2.0 N
39. 1.3×10^{-21} cm

41. (a) 5.26 kN; (b) 1.08 kN;
    (c) 494 N; (d) 589 N
43. 130 N
45. 33 cm
47. 1.9 m/s^2
49. 830 g
51. (a) 132 cm; (b) 127 cm;
    (c) 120 cm; (d) 40 m/s^2
53. 30.7 kN
55. 4.1 cm
57. Apparent weight is 55% of actual
    weight
59. 240 N
61. 4.3 cm
63. 7.2 m
65. (a) 0.40mg; (b) 2.40mg; (c) 1.40mg
67. (a) 16 kN; (b) 1.5 kN
69. (a) $a = \dfrac{m_f - m_s}{m_s}g$;

    (b) $y = \dfrac{m_f a_s h}{(m_f - m_s)(g + a_s)}$
71. $\ell + nm(a + g)/k$, where n is the
    spring number measured from the
    bottom
75. 900 N

Chapter 6

1. $2.7\hat{\imath} + 5.5\hat{\jmath}$ N, or 6.1 N at 64° to
   the x axis
3. (a) 2.0 kN; (b) 1.4 kN
7. 43 cm
9. 530 N; 3.6 times the weight
11. 98 N in horizontal string; $98\sqrt{2}$ N
    in vertical string
13. 230 N in short rope; 84 N in long
    rope
15. (a) 6.3 m/s^2; (b) 0.44 s
17. Right-hand mass 2.5 times left-hand
    mass
19. (a) 7.1 kg; (b) 3.9 kg
21. Left to right, 56.9 N, 34.4 N,
    89.2 N
23. 8.18×10^{-8} N
27. (a) 13 m/s; (b) 4.4°
29. 132 m
31. (a) 310 N; (b) 0; (c) nothing
33. (a) 35°; (b) 22°
35. 24 m/s = 86 km/h
37. 17 m/s
39. 579 N
41. 5.43 kN
43. 0.21

45. 25.3 s
47. 11.4 m/s^2
49. 133 m
51. 2.7 cm
53. (a) 1.6 m/s^2; (b) 3.3 N
55. 4.2 m/s^2
57. 95 km/h
61. 0.72
63. 2.6 N
65. 4.7 m/s
67. 0.70 m/s^2, upward
69. 7.75 m/s
71. 1.40 s
73. (a) 0.12; (b) toward the inside of the turn
75. 2.0 rpm
79. (a) lower at equator, where a net downward force is needed to keep you accelerating with Earth's rotation; (b) 0.34%
85. 28 cm

Chapter 7
1. 900 J
3. 0.15 NJ
5. 9.6 MJ
7. (a) 400 J; (b) 31 kg
9. 4.4 MN
13. (a) 86.9 units^2; (b) 20.3 units^2
15. (a) 0; (b) 90°
19. 169 J
21. 622 J
23. (a) 60 kJ; (b) 20 kJ
25. (a) 360 J; (b) 350 J; (c) 357.5 J; (d) 359.375 J
27. $k_B = 8k_A$
29. 190 J
31. (a) 33 J; (b) 60 J; (c) 78 J
33. $F_0\left(x + \dfrac{x^2}{2\ell_0} + \dfrac{\ell_0^2}{\ell_0 + x} - \ell_0\right)$
35. (a) 0; (b) $2FR$; (c) πFR
37. 135 J
41. 2.56×10^{-15} J = 16.0 keV
43. 116 km/h
45. 1 : 2
47. 113 m/s
49. 2.82 kN = 635 lbs
51. (a) 83.6 MJ; (b) 256 km/h; (c) 2.14 s; (d) 33.3 m/s^2
53. (a) 60 kW; (b) 1 kW; (c) 40 W
55. 9.4 MJ
57. (a) 36 MW; (b) 1.1 MW

61. 2.7 h
63. 430 million gal/day
65. 2.1 MJ
67. 7.7°
69. 1.9 m
71. $\frac{1}{2}F_0 x_0$
73. 70.5°
75. (a) 28 kJ; (b) 18 kJ
77. (a) 450 W; (b) 8.0 kJ
79. (a) $W = \frac{1}{2}bt^2$; (b) $a = \sqrt{b/m}$
81. (a) 71 kW·y; (b) 93 kW·y
83. About 450 J
85. (a) 33 J; (b) 167 J

Chapter 8
1. (a) $-2\mu mg\,\ell$; (b) $-\sqrt{2}\mu mg\,\ell$
3. (a) 0; (b) $F_0 a$
5. (a) 1.3 MJ; (b) 59 kJ
9. (a) 1.07 J; (b) 1.12 J
11. 5.2 J
13. 55 cm
15. 2.9 J
17. $U = -\frac{1}{3}ax^3 - bx$
19. $U = F_0\left(x + \dfrac{x^2}{2\ell} + \dfrac{\ell^2}{\ell + x} - \ell\right)$
21. 50 m/s (180 km/h)
23. 92 m
27. (a) 16 m/s; (b) 29%
29. 26 MN/m
31. 3.6 m/s = 13 km/h
35. 2.6 m/s
39. ± 2.0 m
43. (a) $U = -\dfrac{a}{2}x^2 + \dfrac{b}{4}x^4$; (b) $x = 0.66$ m, $x = 2.1$ m
45. (a) -6.7 N; (b) 0; (c) 4.5 N
49. (a) 30 cm; (b) 10.4 N/m
51. 35%
53. 19%
55. 0.36
57. 2.6 m/s
59. 0.036
61. 62 cm from left end of frictional zone
63. 1000 MW, twice that of the coal plant
65. $x = 2(h_1 - h_2)$
69. (a) $v = \sqrt{\sqrt{2}g\ell}$; (b) $T = \dfrac{3}{\sqrt{2}}mg$
71. ± 25 cm

73. 14 m
75. (a) 2.53×10^5 m/s; (b) 2.91×10^5 m/s; (c) 2.93×10^5 m/s
77. 54.6 mJ
79. 75 cm
81. (a) 1.74 cm; (b) 0.78 cm; (c) 7.4×10^7 m/s
83. (a) $v = \left[\dfrac{x^2}{m}\left(a - \frac{1}{2}bx^2\right)\right]^{1/2}$; (c) $v_{max} = a/\sqrt{2mb}$
85. $v = [2ax^{|b+1|}/m|b + 1|]^{1/2}$
87. 14.5 m

Chapter 9
1. $R_E/\sqrt{2}$
3. 58%
5. 8.6 kg
7. 46 nN
9. $(\sqrt{2} - 1)R_{planet} \simeq 0.41R_{planet}$
11. 1.2×10^{-7}
13. 3.1 km/s
15. 1.8 days
17. 1.0 hour
19. 2.6×10^{41} kg, about 10^{11} solar masses
21. 6.3×10^{10} m
23. 2.64×10^{10} m
25. 2.47 times Earth's orbital radius
27. No
29. 3.2×10^9 J
31. 530 km
33. 58 MJ
35. $R_E/99 = 64$ km; underestimate
37. 3%
39. $\sqrt{2}$
41. 7.7 Mm
43. (a) 11.2 km/s; (b) 9.74 km/s; (c) no
47. $v = \sqrt{2GM\left(\dfrac{3}{R} + \dfrac{1}{r}\right)}$
49. 8.1×10^{11} m, just beyond Jupiter
53. 109 min
55. 15 km/s, 23 km/s
57. 7.95 km/s
59. 8.85×10^5 m
61. (a) 9.0×10^{10} m; (b) 5.3×10^{11} J; (c) 38 km/s
63. 4.60×10^{10} m
65. (b) 8.8 mm; (c) 2.9 km
67. 1400 km lower

Chapter 10

1. 0.75 m from the center
3. 14 m to the right, 4.5 m upward in Fig. 10-23
5. $\ell/2\sqrt{3}$ along the perpendicular bisector of any side
7. $X = 44$ cm, $Y = 55$ cm, with origin at lower left
9. 0.115a above the vertex of the missing triangle
11. 6.5 pm from the oxygen
13. $\mathbf{R} = (t^2 + \frac{10}{3}t + \frac{7}{3})\hat{\mathbf{i}} + (\frac{2}{3}t + \frac{8}{3})\hat{\mathbf{j}}$; $\mathbf{V} = (2t + \frac{10}{3})\hat{\mathbf{i}} + \frac{2}{3}\hat{\mathbf{j}}$; $\mathbf{A} = 2\hat{\mathbf{i}}$
15. $\sim 10^{-10}$ m, the diameter of a hydrogen atom
17. $m_{\text{mouse}} = \frac{1}{4}m_{\text{bowl}}$
19. Moves in the opposite direction at 67 cm/s
21. 21 g, $-x$ direction
23. 498 m/s
25. 8.4 km/h
27. (a) 0.14 N/m^2; (b) 0.014 mm
29. (a) 0.99 m; (b) 3.9 m/s
31. 3.9 km/h
33. $26\hat{\mathbf{i}} + 16\hat{\mathbf{j}}$ m/s
35. 1100 kg
37. (a) 3.3×10^6 N (b) 3.4×10^5 kg
39. 0.22
41. $K_{\text{cm}} = 1.1 \times 10^{-14}$ J before and after; $K_{\text{int}} = 0$ before, $K_{\text{int}} = 1.3 \times 10^{-14}$ J after
43. before: $K_{\text{cm}} = 1.6$ MJ, $K_{\text{int}} = 21$ kJ; after: $K_{\text{cm}} = 1.6$ MJ, $K_{\text{int}} = 0$
45. (a) 1.7 cm above the bottom; (b) 2.7 cm above the bottom
47. 20 m
49. $-47\hat{\mathbf{i}} - 68\hat{\mathbf{j}}$ m/s
51. (a) 3.5 m; (b) 1.3 m/s; (c) 0
53. (a) 0.096 m/s^2; (b) 6.2 m/s
55. 9.3 m/s
57. (a) $m = \dfrac{\pi\rho h^2}{2a}$; (b) $Z = \frac{2}{3}h$
59. 3.0 mN
61. (a) 37.7°; (b) 0.657 m/s
63. 5.8 s after explosion
65. (a) thrust $= m\dfrac{dv}{dt} =$
$[(1 + f)V_{\text{ex}} - V]\dfrac{dM_{\text{in}}}{dt}$;
(b) 1504 lb

67. $v_1 = \left(\dfrac{m_2 k x^2}{m_1^2 + m_1 m_2}\right)^{1/2}$;

$v_2 = \left(\dfrac{m_1 k x^2}{m_2^2 + m_1 m_2}\right)^{1/2}$

Chapter 11

1. 52 N·s
3. 4.3×10^3 N, 7.1mg
5. (a) $-2.6\hat{\mathbf{i}} + 0.74\hat{\mathbf{j}}$ N·s; (b) $-51\hat{\mathbf{i}} + 14\hat{\mathbf{j}}$ N
7. 0.46 s
9. (a) 7.3 MN·s; (b) 5.6 MN
11. (a) 6.8×10^{-3} N·s; (b) 2.3 N
13. $\Delta P/P = 2\%$
15. 12 ms
17. (a) 5.4 mi/h; (b) 13%
19. 19 kg
23. 10^{21} kg
25. $4.0\hat{\mathbf{i}} + 21.5\hat{\mathbf{j}}$ Mm/s
29. 1.3 μJ
31. 120°
33. 46 m/s
35. $v_{1f} = -11$ Mm/s; $v_{2f} = 6.9$ Mm/s
37. $3 + 2\sqrt{2} \approx 5.8$; it doesn't matter which is more massive
39. $v_A = -\frac{1}{3}v$; $v_B = \frac{2}{9}v$; $v_C = \frac{8}{9}v$
45. 22°
47. ($v_{1i} = 0.833$ m/s, $v_{2i} = 1.22$ m/s, $\theta_{2i} = 28.3°$); ($v_{1i} = 1.20$ m/s, $v_{2i} = 1.12$ m/s, $\theta_{2i} = 31.2°$)
49. 13 m/s at 27° to horizontal
51. $v_A = -\frac{1}{5}v_0\hat{\mathbf{i}}$; $v_B = \frac{3}{5}v_0\hat{\mathbf{i}} + \frac{1}{5}\sqrt{3}v_0\hat{\mathbf{j}}$; $v_C = \frac{3}{5}v_0\hat{\mathbf{i}} - \frac{1}{5}\sqrt{3}v_0\hat{\mathbf{j}}$
53. 350 N
55. 52 km/h at 33° north of east
57. $m_{\text{truck}} = 7.6 m_{\text{car}}$
59. (a) $m_1 = 3m_2$; (b) $v_{2f} = 2v$
61. $v_{1f} = 1.66$ m/s; $v_{2f} = 0.703$ m/s; $\theta_{2f} = 67°$ clockwise from initial velocity of the first ball
63. (a) 12.0 m; (b) 15.4 m/s
65. 0.88
69. $v_{1\text{kg}} = 4.0$ m/s; $v_{4\text{kg}} = 1.0$ m/s at 50° clockwise from the x axis
71. $v_{1200} = 2.2$ km/h, $v_{1800} = 18$ km/h
73. (a) $v_1 = 0.28v_0$, $v_2 = 0.48v_0$; (b) 3, 0.26v_0, 0.31v_0

Chapter 12

1. (a) 7.27×10^{-5} rad/s; (b) 1.75×10^{-3} rad/s; (c) 1.45×10^{-4} rad/s; (d) 31.4 rad/s

3. (a) 75.4 rad/s; (b) 0.24 mrad/s; (c) 6283 rad/s; (d) 2.0×10^{-7} rad/s
5. (a) 66 rpm; (b) 3.7 s
7. (a) 21.7 rad/s, 207 rpm; (b) 34.7 rad/s, 331 rpm
9. (a) 0.068 rpm/s; (b) 7.1×10^{-3} rad/s^2
11. (a) 12 min; (b) 2.2×10^4
13. 1.3 rad/s^2
15. (a) 2.0 s; (b) 1.0 rev
17. 1.2 m
19. 0.079 N·m
21. 0.15 N·m
23. (a) 0.70 N·m, counterclockwise; (b) $\mathbf{F}_1$ and $\mathbf{F}_5$
25. 614 kg·m^2
27. (a) $\frac{2}{3}m\ell^2$; (b) $\frac{2}{3}m\ell^2$; (c) $\frac{4}{3}m\ell^2$
29. 45 kg·m^2
33. (a) 1×10^{38} kg·m^2; (b) 2.6×10^{19} N·m
35. (a) 1.29×10^{38} kg·m^2; (b) 6.45×10^{33} N·m
39. (a) 430 min; (b) 1900 rev
41. 1900 N·m
43. 170 rpm
45. $m_{\text{pulley}} = 0.49$ kg; $m_1 = 0.41$ kg; $m_2 = 0.58$ kg
47. (a) 450 J; (b) 140 W
49. 0.089%
51. 12.2 rad/s
53. 7.0 m/s

55. $v = \sqrt{\dfrac{2gh}{\alpha + 1}}$

57. 17%
59. hollow
61. (a) 0.156; (b) 0.070 rad/s

63. $\dfrac{253}{512}MR^2 = 0.494MR^2$

65. (a) 310 N; (b) 165 kg
67. (a) 3.5 m/s; (b) 24%
69. $\frac{27}{10}R$
71. $\omega = \sqrt{2A/I}$
73. $I = \frac{1}{2}Mb^2$
75. $2\sqrt{2g/3R}$
77. $\frac{1}{2}Mg\ell\cos\phi$

Chapter 13

1. 63 rad/s, west
3. 0.52 rad/s^2, $-37°$
5. 16.6 rad/s

7. (a) $-z$; (b) z; (c) in the x-y plane, 45° clockwise from the x axis
9. (a) $-12\hat{k}$ N·m; (b) $36\hat{k}$ N·m; (c) $12\hat{i} - 36\hat{j}$ N·m
11. $-9.0\hat{k}$ N·m
13. Parallel to the x axis or 120° clockwise from x axis
17. $F_x = 1.33F_y - 3.13$ N
19. 414 kg·m²/s
21. 7.6 rad/s
23. 0.017 kg·m²/s
25. 37 kg·m²/s
27. 2.7×10^5 kg·m²/s, out of page in Fig. 13-30
29. 0.21 kg·m²
31. (a) 0.17 rev/s; (b) 386 J
33. (a) 142 rpm; (b) 21%
35. 2.5 days
37. (a) 23.7 rpm; (b) 3.49 mJ
39. (a) $\dfrac{2M\omega_0}{2M + 3m}$; (b) $\dfrac{M\omega_0}{M + 6m}$; (c) same as (b)
41. (a) 0.537 rad/s; (b) 6.44 m/s; (c) 207 N
43. 6.0 cm
45. $I = \dfrac{mgd}{2\omega\Omega}$
47. $\tan^{-1}(\frac{1}{2}) = 26.6°$
49. 0.37 rev/s
51. 22 g
53. $\dfrac{I}{I + mR^2}$
55. (a) 1.61; (b) 2.22
59. Sun's rotation 2.8%; Jupiter's orbital motion 60%
61. $v = \left[\dfrac{8(m + M)g\ell}{m^2}(\frac{1}{4}m + \frac{1}{3}M)\right]^{1/2}$
63. (a) $\dfrac{m\sqrt{2gh}}{(\frac{1}{2}M + m)R}$;
(b) $\dfrac{\sqrt{2gm[hm - (\frac{1}{2}M + m)R]}}{(\frac{1}{2}M + m)R}$;
(c) $h = \dfrac{(\frac{1}{2}M + m)R}{m}$
65. (a) $\frac{2}{7}\omega_0$; (b) $2\omega_0R/7\mu_k g$

Chapter 14
1. (a) $\frac{1}{3}\ell F_3 - \frac{2}{3}\ell F_2 + \ell F_1 = 0$;
(b) $\frac{1}{2}\ell F_1 - \frac{1}{6}\ell F_2 - \frac{1}{6}\ell F_3 + \frac{1}{2}\ell F_4 - \frac{1}{2}\ell F_5 = 0$

3. (b) $\tau_{\text{origin}} = -7\hat{k}$ N·m
5. (a) A vector of length $\sqrt{2}\,F$, oriented 45° clockwise from the negative y axis, applied at the point $x = 0$ m, $y = +1$ m or anywhere on the line $y = (1 + x)$ m.
(b) Not possible; the first two vectors sum to zero but produce a nonzero torque, so any other vector applied to balance torques will upset force balance.
7. Both sets have $-F_1 + F_2 \sin\phi + F_3 = 0$, $-F_2 \cos\phi + F_4 = 0$; torque equations are
(a) $\ell_2 F_4 \cos\phi - \ell_2 F_3 \sin\phi - \ell_1 F_2 = 0$; (b) $(\ell_2 - \ell_1)F_2 - \ell_2 F_1 \sin\phi = 0$.
9. (a) $\tau_A = \frac{1}{2}\ell mg$; (b) $\tau_B = 0$; (c) $\tau_C = \frac{1}{2}\ell mg$
11. $\frac{1}{6}L$
13. (a) 61 cm from left end; (b) 1.4 m from left end
15. 120 N
17. 11.7 kN
19. (a) 40 N·m; (b) 1300 N
21. Vertical forces both 73.5 N, downward, horizontal forces both 33.6 N, away from door jamb at top, toward jamb at bottom
23. 5.0 kN; tension
25. 0.87
27. 500 N
29. 7.3°
31. 50 kN
33. 6.05 kN
35. $\frac{1}{8}$
37. Maximum height of CM is at sphere center; lower for clown (b)
39. Two equilibria for $|a| > 2\sqrt{3}$; one metastable, other unstable
41. 1.2 m
43. 170 N
45. 74 kg
47. $\frac{1}{2}(\sqrt{3} - 1)mgs$
49. $\mu = \dfrac{\sin 2\theta}{3 + \cos 2\theta}$
51. $mg/2k$
53. 28°
55. Left scale 16.3 N; right scale 22.9 N
57. Tip
59. Slide

61. (a) $0.44mg$, at 12° to Earth's polar axis; (b) $0.036mgR_E$, out of the plane of Fig. 14-57

Part 1 Cumulative Problems
1. 16.5 m from the post
3. $a = \dfrac{2g[(m_1 + m_2)\sin\theta - \mu m_1 \cos\theta]}{2m_1 + 3m_2}$
5. (a) $v = \frac{2}{7}\omega R$; (b) $\Delta x = \dfrac{2\omega^2 R^2}{49\mu g}$

Chapter 15
1. $T = 0.780$ s; $f = 1.28$ Hz
3. 11.5 fs
5. $A = 20$ cm, $\omega = \pi/2$ s^{-1}, $\phi = 0$; $A = 30$ cm, $\omega = 2.0$ s^{-1}, $\phi = -\pi/2$; $A = 40$ cm, $\omega = \pi/2$ s^{-1}, $\phi = \pi/4$
7. 63.3 kg
9. 1.7 kN/m
11. 0.69 s
13. (a) $\pi\sqrt{m/k}$; (b) $v_0\sqrt{m/k}$
17. (a) 1.0 cm; (b) 6.2 m; (c) 3.6 km
19. 0.11 N·m/rad
21. (a) $2\pi\sqrt{\ell/g}$; (b) $2\pi\sqrt{2\ell/3g}$; (c) $2\pi\sqrt{2\ell/3g}$; (d) infinite
23. 0.34 s
25. $R = \sqrt{2\kappa/k}$
27. Within 1 μm
33. 5.0 g
35. $\omega^2 = \dfrac{k_1 k_2}{m(k_1 + k_2)}$
37. a and b are the amplitudes in the x and y directions, respectively
39. 400 J, or 1.4×10^{-3} of the total KE
41. $t = (0.14 + n)$ s, $t = (0.53 + n)$ s, n an integer; $x = \pm 37$ cm
45. $\omega = \sqrt{2k/3M}$
47. 34
49. 77% at 0.90ω; 66% at 1.1ω
53. (a) 19 s^{-1}; (b) 0.33 s; (c) 92 m/s²
55. (a) 6.5 cm; (b) 0.51 s
57. 1.64 s
59. 300 g
61. (a) $E_2 = \frac{1}{4}E_1$; (b) $a_{2\,\text{max}} = \frac{1}{4}a_{1\,\text{max}}$
63. 2.1 m/s²
65. 0.44
67. $2\pi\sqrt{7/10ga}$
69. $f = 0.54$ Hz; $A = 22$ cm; $\phi = -0.11$ rad
71. $T = 2\pi\sqrt{R/g}$
73. $T = 2\pi\sqrt{mL/2F_0}$

Chapter 16

1. 3.4 s
3. 3.38 m
5. 1.81×10^8 m/s $= 0.604c$
7. (a) 400 nm; (b) 0.3 mm
9. 11 m
11. (a) 0.58 m^{-1}; (b) 1.53 s^{-1}
13. (a) 13.7 s^{-1}; (b) 0.393 cm^{-1};
    (c) $y = 2.5\cos(0.393x + 13.7t)$
15. (a) 25 cm; (b) 0.37 Hz; (c) 12 m;
    (d) 4.4 m/s
17. $y = \dfrac{2}{(x - 3t)^4 + 1}$
19. (a) 3.0 m; (b) 1.5 s; (c) 2.0 m/s;
    (d) $+x$
21. 250 m/s
23. (a) 7.6 N; (b) 1.7 m/s
25. 364 m/s
27. 94 N
29. 7.64 g/cm^3
31. 585 m/s
33. 9.9 W
35. 35 cm
37. $4\pi^2 A^2 F/\lambda$
39. 12 mW/m^2
41. (a) 9.1 kW/m^2; (b) 0.88 W/m^2
43. (a) 6.4 kW/m^2; (b) 4.9 W/m^2
45. 5.1 m
47. (a) 2 cm; (b) pulse 1 at $x = 0$,
    direction $+x$, pulse 2 at $x = 5$,
    direction $-x$; (c) $t = 2.5$ s
49. Every 6 s
51. 5.34 m
53. $\sqrt{gh}$
55. (a) 1.5 cm; (b) 63 cm; (c) 11 ms;
    (d) 56 m/s;
    (e) 18 W
57. $v = \sqrt{k\ell(\ell - \ell_0)/m}$
59. 10 m
61. Every 30 s
63. $u < 0.063v$
67. 5.2 km
69. 67 m

Chapter 17

3. $\lambda = 34$ cm; $T = 1.0$ ms;
    $\omega = 6.3 \times 10^3 \text{ s}^{-1}$;
    $k = 0.18 \text{ cm}^{-1}$
5. 0.29 s
7. 0.14 kg/m^3
9. monatomic
11. 739 m/s
13. 190 m/s

15. 4.4 nm
17. (a) 3.8 mW/m^2; (b) 96 dB;
    (c) 1.8 N/m^2; (d) 1.6 μm
19. 1 kHz to 6.5 kHz
21. (a) 3.2 $\mu\text{W/m}^2$, 0.051 N/m^2;
    (b) 3.2×10^{-13} W/m^2;
    1.6×10^{-5} N/m^2
23. (a) 20 dB; (b) approximately
    250 Hz
27. 6.3 m
29. 1
31. 3.2 km/s
33. 0.75 mm
35. 39 μs
37. no; $F = 31$ kN
39. (a) 280 Hz; (b) 70 Hz; (c) 210 Hz
45. (a) 16.6 cm; (b) 424–457 Hz
47. 0.33 Hz
49. 91 Hz
51. 253 m/s
53. 400 Hz
55. 43 m/s $= 154$ km/h
57. (a) 2800 Hz; (b) 933 Hz
59. 25 m/s
63. $u/v = 1/\sin 45° = 1.4$
65. (a) 5.5×10^{-4} W/m^2; (b) 87 dB
67. (a) 112 m/s; (b) 4, 5
69. 960 m/s
71. 0.445 s
73. (a) $\lambda = 5.0$ m, $f = 0.56$ Hz;
    (b) $\lambda = 2.5$ m; $f = 0.79$ Hz
75. 1.36
77. $\Delta f = 2uf/(v - u)$
79. 16 kHz

Chapter 18

1. 1.2 kg
3. 10^{-14}
5. (a) 81 N; (b) 65 N
7. 1 in. $\text{H}_2\text{O} = 249$ Pa
9. 2×10^7 N, or 2000 tons
11. 21 N
13. 0.25 m^2
15. No; $F = 2.3 \times 10^4$ N, or 2.5 tons
17. 1700 kg/m^3
19. ~90 m
21. 890 Pa gauge
23. 8.1×10^{10} N
25. 3.6 mm
27. 93 cm higher in the eye
29. 8.11×10^3 kg
31. 44 kg
33. 0.75 %
35. 59 g

37. 27 m
39. (a) 49 kg; (b) 2500 kg
43. (a) 1.8×10^4 m^3/s; (b) 1.5 m/s
45. 1.75 m/s
47. (a) $h_2 = h_1$; (b) $h_2 = h_1 - \dfrac{3v^2}{2g}$
49. 14.3 m
51. 7.2 cm^3/s
53. (a) no; (b) yes
55. 13
57. 70%
59. $A\sqrt{2gh}$
61. (a) 14 m/s; (b) 2.2 m
65. (a) 25 L/s; (b) 55 m/s; (c) 1.8 kPa
67. $t = \dfrac{A_0}{A_1}\sqrt{\dfrac{2h}{g}}$
69. $P = P_a + \rho g h_0 + \frac{1}{2}\rho\omega^2 r^2$;
    (b) $h = h_0 + \dfrac{\omega^2 r^2}{2g}$
71. (a) $\rho(h) = \dfrac{P_0}{h_0 g}e^{-h/h_0}$; (b) 5.7 km

Part 2   Cumulative Problems

1. (a) $\ell = \dfrac{4M}{\pi d^2 \rho}$; (b) $T = 4\sqrt{\dfrac{\pi M}{d^2 \rho g}}$
5. 17.2 cm

Chapter 19

1. 720
3. 20°C
5. -40
7. $-196°$C, $-321°$F
9. (a) 138 kPa; (b) 33.4 kPa;
    (c) 233 kPa
11. 1.37 L
13. 586 mm
15. 240 kcal
17. 0.36 kg
19. 24 days
21. (a) 23 kJ; (b) 337 kJ; (c) 65 kJ
23. 7.5 kW
25. 2.4 kg
27. (a) 560 g; (b) 0.27 K/s
29. 1.8 kg
31. 0.70 K
33. 1.6 K/s
35. 197 g
37. 56.2°C
39. 55 kW
41. 0.293 W
43. 25 $\text{ft}^2\cdot°\text{F}\cdot\text{h/Btu}$
45. 200 W

47. (a) 12.3 ft²·°F·h/Btu;
    (b) 715 Btu/h
49. Will save 10 gallons/month
51. 23°C
53. 80%
55. −25°C
57. Drop by 5.9 K
59. 24°C
61. 480 W
63. 1151 K
65. −2.5°C
67. (a) $87; (b) $10
69. 4.65%
71. $\Delta T_{copper} = 0.16$ K; $\Delta T_{iron} = 2.1$ K
73. 2.9 J
77. 10 hours

Chapter 20
1. 2.6 m³
3. 1.8 MPa
5. (a) 27 L; (b) 330 K
7. 2.7×10^7
9. 11 L
11. 515 kPa
13. (a) 1.27 atm; (b) 0.0268 mol;
    (c) 0.786 atm
15. H_2
17. 268 K, compared with ideal gas
    292 K
19. 1.76 MPa
21. (a) 9.1×10^{20}; (b) 2.0×10^{20}
23. 22 kJ
25. 3.9 kg
27. 5.96 MJ
29. 1.3×10^{10} kg
31. 564 W
33. 44 minutes
35. 48 min
37. (a) 117 s
39. 3.55 MJ
41. 64°C
43. 177 g
45. 135 g solid in 865 g liquid, at 234 K
47. 5.0 kg
49. 4.9°C
51. 1.00021 cm
53. 3.9 km
55. 43.6 mm³
57. 307 K
59. $d = \frac{1}{2}L_0 \sqrt{2\alpha \, \Delta T + (\alpha \, \Delta T)^2}$
61. 120 mol/m³
63. 19 kW
65. 79 g
67. 1.2 kg ice, 0.80 kg water, all at 0°C

69. 50 min
71. (a) 61 h; (b) 52 h
77. 34 km

Chapter 21
1. 29 kJ
3. Increases by 250 J
5. (a) 310 MW; (b) 54%
7. 0.02°C
9. $2P_1 V_1$
11. 1.2 kJ
13. 4.3 kJ
15. 190 K
17. 1.99 kJ
19. (a) 399 J; (b) 264 kPa
21. (a) 571 kPa; (b) 438 J
23. 440°C
25. $V = 0.18 V_0$
27. (b) Gas does 13 J of work;
    (c) 22 J heat lost from gas
29. (a) 300 K, 1.5 kJ; (b) 336 K, 0 J;
    (c) 326 K, 429 J
31. (a) 39.9 kPa; (b) 83.3 kPa;
    (c) 80.2 kJ
33. 928 J
35. (a) 211 J; (b) 12.9 L
37. 75°C
39. 128 J
41. (a) −9.0°C; (b) stable
43. 57.7%
45. 79%
47. 20 mol
49. Drops 23.1 K
51. 343 K
53. 28 kPa
55. (a) 598 J; (b) 2500 J flows in
57. 25 m
59. $\frac{4}{3}P_1 V_1$
63. (a) 2.5 kJ; (b) 447 K
69. (a) $M = \dfrac{P_0 A}{g}\left[\dfrac{h_1}{h_2} - 1\right]$;

    (b) $M = \dfrac{P_0 A}{g}\left[\left(\dfrac{h_1}{h_2}\right)^{\gamma} - 1\right]$

Chapter 22
1. (a) 12!/6!, or 6.7×10^5 states;
    (b) about 1 in 1000
3. 5×10^{24} J, assuming oceans cover
    75% of Earth to an average depth
    of 3 km; this is about 20,000 times
    annual use
5. (a) 27%; (b) 7.0%; (c) 77%
7. 0.95 K
9. 52% winter, 48% summer
11. (a) 1.75 GW; (b) 43%; (c) 505 K
13. 2×10^7 kg/s, slightly more than the
    Mississippi's flow
15. (a) 39%; (b) 550 J; (c) 190°C
17. 53.3 kJ
19. (a) 4.3; (b) maximum COP = 11
23. (a) $COP_{summer} = 13$, $COP_{winter} = 3.5$;
    (b) 0.076 J; (c) 0.22 J
25. (a) 561.7 J; (b) 464.1 J;
    (c) 97.66 J; (d) 17.4%;
    (e) $T_c = 403$ K, $T_h = 487$ K
29. 718 K
31. 1.22 kJ/K
33. 8.9°C
35. 1.36×10^8 J/K
39. (a) 53 J/K; (b) 74 J/K; (c) 0
41. (a) −109 J/K; (b) 122 J/K;
    (c) 13 J/K
43. $\Delta S_{AB} = 68.5$ J/K, $\Delta S_{BC} = 45.7$ J/K,
    $\Delta S_{CA} = -114.2$ J/K
45. 470 kPa
47. (a) 69%; (b) 967 K
49. Decrease in $T_{minimum}$
51. $58
53. (a) $W = Q = 345$ J; (b) $e = 24\%$
55. 598 J/K
57. About 30 km for 200 kg of water
    and a 60 kg bather
59. 166 MW
61. (a) $1 - 5^{1-\gamma}$; (b) $3T_{min}(5^{\gamma - 1})$;
    (c) $e_{Carnot} = 1 - \frac{1}{3}(5^{1-\gamma})$
63. (a) 7.94; (b) 5.26; (c) $P_n = 2.96 P_s$
65. (a) $T_h = T_{h0}e^{-P_0 t/mc(T_{h0} - T_c)}$;
    (b) $P = 0$ at
    $t = \dfrac{mc(T_{h0} - T_c)}{P_0} \ln\left(\dfrac{T_{h0}}{T_c}\right)$
67.

	P	V	T	$U - U_A$	$S - S_A$
A					
B			$3.4\,T_0$	$6.0\,P_0 V_0$	$3.1\,P_0 V_0/T_0$
C	$1.5\,P_0$	$2.2\,V_0$	$3.4\,T_0$	$6.0\,P_0 V_0$	$3.8\,P_0 V_0/T_0$
D			$3.0\,T_0$	$5.0\,P_0 V_0$	$3.8\,P_0 V_0/T_0$

Part 3 Cumulative Problems

1. $e = 1 - r^{1-\gamma}\left[\dfrac{r_c^\gamma - 1}{\gamma(r_c - 1)}\right]$

3. $W = an^2\left(\dfrac{1}{V_2} - \dfrac{1}{V_1}\right) +$

$nRT\ln\left(\dfrac{V_2 - bn}{V_1 - bn}\right)$

5. (a) $t_1 = \dfrac{L_f M T_h}{P_h T_0}$;

(b) $P = P_h\left[1 - \dfrac{T_0}{T_h}e^{P_h(t-t_1)/McT_h}\right]$,

(c) $t_2 = t_1 + \dfrac{McT_h}{P_h}\ln\dfrac{T_h}{T_0}$, with L_f
the heat of fusion of ice and c the
specific heat of water.

Chapter 23

1. Several coulombs
3. (a) *uud*; (b) *udd*
5. About 10^9 N; about 10^6 times typical human weight
7. 8.2×10^{-8} N
9. $21.8\ \mu C$
11. $-0.18\hat{\imath} + 0.64\hat{\jmath}$ nN
13. (a) $\hat{\jmath}$; (b) $-\hat{\imath}$; (c) $(\hat{\imath} + 3\hat{\jmath})/$ $\sqrt{10} \approx 0.032\hat{\imath} + 0.95\hat{\jmath}$
15. $14\hat{\imath} - 7.4\hat{\jmath}$ N
17. $15\ \mu C$
19. $1.6\hat{\imath} - 0.33\hat{\jmath}$ N
21. $\dfrac{kq^2}{a^2}(\sqrt{2} + \tfrac{1}{2})$
23. $q_2 = 143\ \mu C$; $q_3 = 116\ \mu C$
25. 3.8×10^9 N/C
27. (a) 2.2 MN/C; (b) 77 N
29. 5.15×10^{11} N/C
31. (a) $26\hat{\jmath}$ MN/C; (b) $-5.15\hat{\jmath}$ MN/C; (c) $-58\hat{\jmath}$ MN/C
33. $-4e$
35. (a) $\mathbf{E} = \dfrac{2kqy}{(a^2 + y^2)^{3/2}}\hat{\jmath}$; (b) $y = \pm a/\sqrt{2}$
37. (a) $8.0\hat{\jmath}$ GN/C; (b) $190\hat{\jmath}$ MN/C; (c) $216\hat{\jmath}$ kN/C
39. 39 pm
41. (a) $\mathbf{E} = 2\sqrt{3}\ kqa/x^3\hat{\imath}$; (b) $p = \sqrt{3}\ qa$
43. 2.1 MN/C
45. $-\dfrac{2k\lambda_0}{\pi\ell}\hat{\imath}$

47. -137 nC
51. 1.1 kN/C
53. (a) $2.5\ \mu C/m$; (b) 3.0×10^5 N/C; (c) 1.8 N/C
55. 3.3×10^{-12} kg
57. (a) 1.35 cm; (b) reverses direction, accelerates and exits field region at 3.8×10^5 m/s
59. $v > \ell\sqrt{qE/md}$
61. 2.8 Mm/s
63. $-14\ \mu C/m$
65. (a) 3.0 mN·m; (b) 11 mJ
67. (b) Attractive
69. $x = -8.09$ nm
71. $\dfrac{k\lambda_0}{\ell}\hat{\imath}$
73. $2\sqrt{2}kQ/\pi a^2$
75. 1.4 cm
77. $33.3\ \mu C$
79. $-4q$, a distance $3a$ to the right of $-q$
81. 50.7 kN/C, downward
83. 7.0 cm; $0.54\ \mu C$
85. (a) $(2kep/r^3)\hat{\imath}$; (b) $(-2kep/r^3)\hat{\imath}$, with the $+x$ direction to the right

Chapter 24

1. $+3\ \mu C$
5. (a) 1.7 kN·m²/C; (b) 1.2 kN·m²/C; (c) 0
7. 490 N·m²/C
9. $\pi R^2 E$
11. (a) $-q/\varepsilon_0$; (b) $-2q/\varepsilon_0$; (c) 0; (d) 0
13. 4.9×10^4 N·m²/C
15. (a) 0.69 MN·m²/C (b) -0.69 MN·m²/C (c) 0
17. 10 kN/C
19. 1.8×10^{12} N/C
21. (a) 2.2×10^5 N/C, outward; (b) 2.5×10^4 N/C, outward; (c) 4.0×10^3 N/C, inward
23. (a) $8kQ/R^2$, inward; (b) $kQ/4R^2$, inward; (c) (a) would not change, (b) would become 0
25. (a) 3.6 MN/C; (b) 3.8 MN/C; (c) (a) would not change, (b) would nearly double
27. as $1/r$
29. $6.3\ \mu C/m^3$
33. 3.6 mC/m³
35. 58 nC/m²
37. $E_1 = \sigma/2\varepsilon_0$, left; $E_2 = \sigma/2\varepsilon_0$, right; $E_3 = 3\sigma/2\varepsilon_0$, right; $E_4 = \sigma/2\varepsilon_0$, right

39. 18 N/C
41. (a) $x < 1.83$ cm; (b) $x > 54.5$ cm
43. 1.6×10^5 N/C
45. (a) $\rho = 0$; (b) $\sigma = 4.0$ mC/m²; (c) other charges would destroy the symmetry, making σ nonuniform
47. (a) $0.50\ \mu C/m^2$; (b) 56 kN/C
49. (b) $-Q$
51. 1.8 MN/C
53. (a) 0; (b) 180 kN/C; (c) 0; (d) 20 kN/C
57. (a) $4kq/R^2$; (b) $3kq/4R^2$
59. (a) 0; (b) 1.3 MN/C; (c) 0
61. (a) 1.9×10^{11} N/C; (b) 3.6×10^{10} N/C
63. $\dfrac{\rho r}{3\varepsilon_0} - \dfrac{\rho a^3}{3\varepsilon_0 r^2}$
65. $\tfrac{1}{3}E_0 a^2$
67. $0.39\ \mu s$
69. $E_{\text{in}} = \rho_0 x^2/2\varepsilon_0 d$; $E_{\text{out}} = \rho_0 d/8\varepsilon_0$
73. (a) 0; (b) $(ac/\varepsilon_0 r^2)(e^{-1} - e^{-r/a})$; (c) $(ac/\varepsilon_0 r^2)(e^{-1} - e^{-b/a})$
77. $+10.6\ \mu C/m^2$ on both outer faces, $\pm36.9\ \mu C/m^2$ on inner faces

Chapter 25

1. $600\ \mu J$
3. 3.0 kV
5. 910 V
7. 5.6 kV/m
9. Proton and He⁺ both gain 100 eV $= 1.6\times10^{-17}$ J; α gains 200 eV $= 3.2\times10^{-17}$ J
11. 4.5 V
13. 0.23 MC
17. $6.1\ \mu C$
19. 27.2 V
21. $Q = 5.4$ nC, $r = 17$ cm
23. (a) 442 kV; (b) 9.2 Mm/s
25. kQ/R.
27. $V(x) = -\tfrac{1}{2}ax^2$
29. 52 nC/m
31. $x = -a/2$, $x = a/4$
33. (a) 2.6 kV; (b) 1.8 kV; (c) 0
35. $kQ\left(\dfrac{2}{c} + \dfrac{1}{b} - \dfrac{1}{a}\right)$
37. $2kQ/R$
39. $2\pi k\sigma(\sqrt{x^2 + b^2} - \sqrt{x^2 + a^2})$
41. (a) $V(x, y) = -E_0(x + y) = -150(x + y)$ V/m; (b) 150V
45. (a) $\mathbf{E} = -ay\hat{\imath} - ax\hat{\jmath}$
47. (a) 4 V; (b) $E_x = 1$ V/m, $E_y = -12$ V/m, $E_z = 3$ V/m

49. $\mathbf{E} = \dfrac{kQx}{(x^2 + a^2)^{3/2}}\hat{\mathbf{i}}$

51. $E = V_0/R$, radially outward

53. 3 kV

55. (a) 34 kV, -9.0 kV; (b) 12.6 kV on each; (c) 24 nC

57. (a) 43 kV; (b) 1.7 MV/m; (c) 540 V; (d) 0

59. 1.55 keV $= 2.47 \times 10^{-16}$ J

61. (a) $\dfrac{2kqx}{x^2 - a^2}$; (b) $\dfrac{2kq}{x}$

63. (a) 27 kV; (b) no change

65. -7.5 V

67. (a) $x = -3$ m, 0 m, 1 m; (b) $\mathbf{E} = (3x^2 + 4x - 3)\hat{\mathbf{i}}$; (c) $x = -1.87$ m, 0.535 m

69. (a) 7.2 kV; (b) 14.4 kV

71. 14 cm, 1.7 nC

73. 23 nC/m

75. (a) $V(x) =$ $\dfrac{k\lambda_0 x}{\ell^2}\left[x \ln\left(\dfrac{2x + \ell}{2x - \ell}\right) - \ell\right]$; (b) $\frac{1}{12}\lambda_0\ell$; (c) $\dfrac{k\lambda_0\ell}{12x}$

77. $y^2 + (x - \frac{5}{3}a)^2 = (\frac{4}{3}a)^2$; i.e., a circle

79. $\dfrac{kq}{2a}\ln\left(\dfrac{\sqrt{2} + 1}{\sqrt{2} - 1}\right) \simeq \dfrac{0.881\,kq}{a}$

Chapter 26

1. $3kq^2/\ell$

3. 4.88 kJ

5. $v = 2q\sqrt{\dfrac{k}{m\ell}}$

7. $6kq^2/a$

9. (a) 2.0 MV/m; (b) 9.9 kV; (c) 5.5 mJ

11. (a) 0.74 μC; (b) 40 kV

13. $\frac{1}{2}kQ^2\left(\dfrac{1}{a} - \dfrac{1}{b}\right)$

15. (b) $dW = 2kq\,dq/a$; (c) $W = kQ^2/a$

17. 1 km³

19. 9×10^{30} J/m³

21. 24 μJ

25. $(kQ^2/R)(2^{2/3} - 1) = 0.60$ mJ

27. $U/\ell = \pi a^4 \rho^2/16\varepsilon_0$

29. ± 14 C

31. 6.5 mF

33. 0.74 nF

35. 55 pF

39. 70 nF

41. 1 μF stores 15 times as much energy

43. (a) 30 μF; (b) 0.1 μF; (c) 0.01 μF

45. (a) 5.0 kW; (b) 250 μF; (c) 0.50 W

47. (a) Increases by factor of 2.5; (b) drops to 40% of its original value

51. Equal

53. (a) 6.0 μF; (b) 0.55 μF; (c) 0.83 μF, 1.3 μF, 1.5 μF, 2.2 μF, 2.8 μF, 3.7 μF

55. (a) 2 series pairs in parallel or two parallel pairs in series; (b) 4 in series

57. 0.86 μF

61. $\pm 1\%$

63. (a) 64 V; (b) drops from 16 mJ to 14 mJ

65. (a) 3.5 mm; (b) 87 kV

67. 126 pF

69. (a) 50 nC, 170 nC; (b) 23 μJ, 77 μJ

71. 1.4 mm

73. (a) 0.90 J; (b) 1.8 J; energy comes from work done by agent separating the plates

75. (a) 1.2 μF; (b) 24 μC

77. 13 min

79. $\dfrac{kq^2}{a}(2\sqrt{3} - \frac{15}{2}) \simeq -4.04\dfrac{kq^2}{a}$

81. (a) $C = \frac{1}{2}(\kappa + 1)C_0$; (b) $U = \dfrac{C_0 V_0^2}{\kappa + 1}$; (c) $F = \dfrac{2C_0 V_0^2(\kappa - 1)}{L(\kappa + 1)^2}$, into capacitor

83. (a) 75 mF; (b) 1.4×10^{12} J

85. (a) $Q^2/2\varepsilon_0 a$; (b) $Q^2/\varepsilon_0 a$; (a) is right since (b) includes the fields of *both* plates, and a plate doesn't experience a force from its own field

87. $31d^2kp^2/1280\ell^5$

89. 7.2 pF/m

Chapter 27

1. 9.4×10^{18}

3. 2.9×10^5 C

5. 1.9×10^{11}

7. 7.65 MA/m²

9. 1.23 cm/s

11. 0.31 mA

13. (a) 37 A/m²; (b) 86%

15. 9.71 μC

17. 0.17 V/m

19. 2.2×10^{-6} $\Omega \cdot$m

21. (a) 5.95×10^7 $(\Omega \cdot$m$)^{-1}$; (b) 4.5 $(\Omega \cdot$m$)^{-1}$

23. 6.4×10^{-15} s

25. 253°C

27. 25 Ω

29. 2.34 mA

31. 25 mA

33. 1.5 kA

35. (a) 17 mΩ; (b) 86 A; (c) 18 MA/m²; (d) 1.7 V/m

37. $d_{Al} = 1.26\,d_{Cu}$

39. (a) 2.07 cm; (b) 2.60 cm; (c) aluminum

41. 34 mΩ

43. 1.38 kW

45. 160 μA

47. 240 Ω

49. 48 W

51. 960 W$\cdot$h $= 3.5$ MJ

53. Resistor with more power has $\sqrt{2}$ times greater diameter

55. (a) 150 A; (b) 3.4 km

57. 0.54 mA

59. 0.94 Ω

61. (a) 8.7 kA; (b) 15%

63. 2.9 A

65. 2.5 A

67. 120 A

69. 17 J/K

Chapter 28

5. 1.4 hours

7. 6.0 V

9. 229 kΩ

11. 1.5 A

13. 0.02 Ω

15. 45 Ω

17. 30 A

19. R_1 for each

21. 24

23. (a) 162 Ω; (b) 125 mW

25. (a) $\dfrac{R_1\mathcal{E}}{R + 2R_1}$; (c) $\frac{1}{2}\mathcal{E}$

27. 2.45 W

29. $(\mathcal{E}_2 R_1 - \mathcal{E}_1 R_2)/(R_1 + R_2)$

31. $\frac{7}{5}R$

33. $I_1 = 2.79$ A, $I_2 = 2.36$ A, $I_3 = 0.429$ A

35. $\mathcal{E}_2 > 5.49$ V

37. 8.5 nA, downward

39. 1.6% low

41. 1.2 kW41.24.99 kΩ

43. (a) 20 V; (b) 3.0 mA

49. (a) 9.0 V; (b) 1.5 ms; (c) 0.32 μF

51. (a) 0.35 s; (b) 0.17 s

53. 3.4 μF

55. (a) $I_1 = 25$ mA, $I_2 = 0$, $V_C = 0$; (b) $I_1 = I_2 = 10$ mA, $V_C = 60$ V; (c) $I_1 = 0$, $I_2 = 10$ mA, $V_C = 60$ V; (d) $I_1 = I_2 = 0$, $V_C = 0$

57. (a) $3\mathcal{E}/4R$; (b) $2\mathcal{E}/3R$

59. 3.4 kΩ

61. (a) 4.51 V; (b) 35.2 Ω

63. 1.07 A, left to right

65. (a) 13.0 V; (b) 2.23 mA

67. 15.9 ms

69. 83 μs

71. (a) 0; (b) 1.0 A; (c) 0.75 A; (d) 0; (e) 1.0 A; (f) 3.0 A; (g) 3.0 A; (h) 1.0 A

73. (b) 22 hours

Chapter 29

1. (a) 1.6 mT; (b) 2.3 mT

3. (a) 2.0×10^{-14} N; (b) 1.0×10^{-14} N; (c) 0

5. (a) $-1.1\hat{\mathbf{i}} + 1.5\hat{\mathbf{j}} + 1.7\hat{\mathbf{k}}$ mN

7. $\mathbf{B} = 0.13\hat{\mathbf{k}}$ T; $\mathbf{v}_2 = -14\hat{\mathbf{i}}$ km/s

9. $-24.9\hat{\mathbf{i}} - 40.1\hat{\mathbf{j}} - 87.3\hat{\mathbf{k}}$ fN

11. 40.1° or 140°

13. (a) $1.2\hat{\mathbf{i}} + 0.45\hat{\mathbf{j}}$ fN; (b) $-1.2\hat{\mathbf{i}} + 35\hat{\mathbf{j}} - 15\hat{\mathbf{k}}$ fN

15. 3.9 mm

17. 1.5 mT

19. $r_{\text{proton}} = 43\, r_{\text{electron}}$

21. (a) 86 mT; (b) 1.01 keV

23. 1.3 μs

25. (a) 15 MHz; (b) 19 MeV; (c) 6467

29. 0.43%

31. 1.1 mm, 2.6 mm

33. 0.38 N

35. (a) 49 mT; (b) 0.73 N/m

37. 43 kN

39. 0.12 T

41. 21 mN, diagonally toward the upper right

45. 76 mT

47. (a) 1.1 mA·m²; (b) 1.0 mN·m

49. 0.15 A·m²

51. (a) 0.35 A·m²; (b) 4.2×10^{-2} N·m

53. 1.97×10^{-25} J = 1.23 μe V

55. $42\hat{\mathbf{i}} + 88\hat{\mathbf{j}} - 25\hat{\mathbf{k}}$ fN

57. 30 km

59. 0.27 N, to right

61. 0.010 T

63. 6.8 mm

65. (a) 12.8 N/m; (b) 24.9 cm

67. $I = Mg/2Bd$

69. 77 mT

73. $\mu = 9.25\times10^{-24}$ A·m²

Chapter 30

1. 12 cm

3. 1.23 mT

5. 3.8 GA

7. 0.875 cm²

9. 732

11. Between the wires, 2.0 cm from center of 5.0-A wire

13. 23° west of magnetic north

15. $\mu_0 I/4a$, into page

17. $\dfrac{\mu_0 I}{4ab}(b - a)$, out of the page

19. 5 μN

21. 3.8 mm

23. 13.2 μN/m, at 71.6° below right-pointing horizontal

25. 23.5 mN

27. 7.0 A

29. 24 A

31. 123 mA

33. (a) 0; (b) 0.36 mT; (c) 1.9 mT; (d) 0.50 mT

35. (a) $\mu_0 J_0 r^2/3R$; (b) $\mu_0 J_0 R^2/3r$

37. (a) 5.3 mm; (b) maximum; (c) 130 A

41. (a) 0; (b) $\dfrac{\mu_0 I(r^2 - a^2)}{2\pi r(b^2 - a^2)}$; (c) $\dfrac{\mu_0 I}{2\pi r}$

43. 17 T

45. (a) 38 mT; (b) 5.9 μT

47. 3.3 m

49. $1/2\pi nR$

51. $\chi_M = -1.6\times10^{-3}$; diamagnetic

53. 7.2×10^3

55. $I_{\text{outer}} = 2I_{\text{inner}}$, in opposite direction

57. Out of page

59. 1 km

61. (a) 8.0 μT; (b) 4.0 μT; (c) 0

63. (a) 0.40 mT; (b) 1.0 nT

65. $B = \mu_0 I/\ell$ inside, $B = 0$ outside

67. 55A

Chapter 31

3. 1.4×10^{-4} T·m²

5. 160 T/s

7. (a) 0.30 A; (b) 0.20 A

9. $B^2\ell^3 v/R$

11. 39 V

13. 0.32 V

15. 9.0 μA, counterclockwise in Fig. 31-5

17. (a) $I = -25$ mA for $0 < t < 2$ s; $I = 0$ for 2 s $< t < 3$ s; $I = +25$ mA for 3 s $< t < 5$ s; (b) $P = 3.1$ mW for $0 < t < 2$ s and 3 s $< t < 5$ s; otherwise 0

19. (a) Left to right; (b) 140 μA; (c) 28 μA

21. (a) $I_R = -I_{\text{peak}} \cos \omega t$, where (b) $I_{\text{peak}} = 110$ mA; (c) 0

23. 0.16 s

25. 7.1 mV

27. (a) Downward; (b) $(B\ell v)^2/R$

29. $v_{\text{final}} = \mathcal{E}/B\ell$; R affects time to reach final speed

31. (a), (b) Both 6.7 mA, counterclockwise; (c) 0.44 mW in both cases

33. (a) 25 mA; (b) 1.25 mN; (c) 2.5 mW; (d) 2.5 mW

35. (a) 77 mV; (b) 94 mV

37. 1.57 μN

39. $dB/dt = 10$ T/s

41. $E = \frac{1}{2}bh$, to the left above the field region and to the right below

43. $\frac{16}{3}B_0 x_0^2$

45. 42 mA, clockwise

47. $mgR/B^2\ell^2$

49. $\frac{1}{2}BR^2\omega$

51. 58 T/ms

53. $I = at^2$, with $a = 0.81$ A/s²

57. (a) 2.4 km; (b) 2.89 kW; (c) \$6.94; (d) their generators get harder to turn, so they use more fuel

59. (a) $J = rb/2\rho$; (b) $P = \pi b^2 a^4 h/8\rho$

Chapter 32

1. 120 V

3. 12 V

5. (a) $-2\pi fMI_p \cos 2\pi ft$; (b) 133 mH

7. $\mu_0 n^2 \pi R^2 \ell$

9. $\dfrac{\mu_0 \ell}{2\pi} \ln\left(\dfrac{a + w}{a}\right)$

11. 3.2 mH

13. 40 kV

15. 1350

17. (a) 2.1 A; (b) −1.5 A (minus indicates direction reversal)

19. 26 A/ms

21. 11 A

25. 130 Ω

27. 15 s

29. (a) 0.11 H; (b) 20 mA

31. (a) 76 mA; (b) 4.4 V (c) 7.6 V; (d) 2.2 A/s; (e) 0.58 W

33. 400 Ω

35. 50 Ω

37. (a) 2.0 A; (b) 6.0 A; (c) 60 V

39. 100 mA

41. (a) 52 J; (b) 1.8 s

43. (a) 2.5 kW; (b) no

45. 15 W

47. (a) 5.7 MJ; (b) 31 mΩ; (c) 39 s

49. 9.9×10^8 J/m^3

51. 10^{11} times that of gasoline; 2600 times that of U-235

53. Smaller by factor $1/4n^2R^2$

55. 10^{18} J

57. $|\mathcal{E}| = 2Mbt$

59. 48 H

61. (a) 18.4 V; (b) 0; (c) 70 V

63. $(\mu_0 I^2 \ln 100)/4\pi$

65. (a) $L = \dfrac{\mu_0 N^2 \ell}{2\pi} \ln\left(\dfrac{R + \ell}{R}\right)$

67. (a) $P = I_0^2 R e^{-2Rt/L}$

69. $E/B = 1/\sqrt{\mu_0 \varepsilon_0} = 3.0 \times 10^8$ m/s $= c$

Chapter 33

1. $V = 325 \sin(314t)$, with V in volts and t in seconds.

3. 9.9 V

5. (a) 350 mA; (b) 1.50 kHz

9. $V_{\rm rms} = V_p/\sqrt{3}$

11. $I_1 = I_p \cos\phi$, $I_2 = I_p \sin\phi$

13. 45 mA

15. (a) 804 Ω; (b) 48.2 Ω; (c) 2.41 Ω

17. 1.47 μF

19. 15.9 kHz

21. (a) 10 mA; (b) 14 V; (c) 7.7 mA

23. 2.7 mC

25. 0.32 A

27. 8.23 kHz or 5.17×10^4 s^{-1}

29. 4.9 pF to 42 pF

31. 3.65 F

33. (a) 1.63 A; (b) 4.58 μs

35. (a) 63 V; (b) 89 V; (c) 764 mA; (d) 99 μJ

37. (a) $1/\sqrt{2}$; (b) 1/2; (c) $-1/\sqrt{2}$; (d) 1/2

39. Close switch B for 702 ms, then simultaneously close A and open B. After 351 ms, open A; (b) 400 V

41. 0.22 μF

43. 16.2 V

45. (a) 0.43 μH; (b) $R > 16$ Ω

47. (a) $V_{Rp} = 23.86$ V, $V_{Cp} = 28.19$ V, $V_{Lp} = -28.05$ V; (b) $V_{R\rm rms} = 16.9$ V, $V_{C\rm rms} = 256$ V, $V_{L\rm rms} = 255$ V

49. (a) above; (b) current lags by approximately 49°

51. (a) I leads V by 63.6°; (b) I lags V by 81.7°

53. 500 W

55. (a) 80 Ω; (b) 97 Hz

57. (a) 5.5%; (b) 9.1%; (c) large

59. 5.0 mA

61. (a) 8.91 V; (b) 1.38 kΩ

63. $4f_1$

65. 13.2 V

67. 0.64 Ω

69. 8.25 V

71. 36.2 nF, 11.5 nF

73. $C = \dfrac{L[\ln(U_0/U_1)]^2}{4\pi^2 N^2 R^2}$

77. $R = 400$ Ω, $L = 67$ mH, $C = 0.094$ μF

79. 1.3 kN/m

Chapter 34

1. 1.3 nA

5. (a) 0; (b) 8.33×10^{-13} T; (c) 9.26×10^{-13} T

7. $-x$

9. (a) $\sqrt{2}E$; (b) $(\hat{\jmath} - \hat{\imath})/\sqrt{2}$

13. 0.24 s

15. 1 ns

17. 600 m

19. 2.32

21. 5000 km

23. 27.3 MHz

25. 15 kV/m

27. 1.1 pT

29. 63°

31. 30°

33. $0.34S_0$

35. $0.304S_0$

37. $S = S_0 \cos^2 \omega t$, with $\omega = 20\pi$ s^{-1}

39. 12 GW/m^2

41. 2.7×10^{-10} W/m^2

43. (a) 157 W/m^2; (b) 344 V/m; (c) 1.15 μT

45. 1.1%

47. 3.9×10^{26} W

49. (a) 8.3×10^{-26} W/m^2; (b) 7.9×10^{-12} V/m

51. (a) 4.6 kW; (b) 52.5 mV/m

53. (a) as $1/r$; (b) as $1/r^2$

55. 6.0 mPa

57. 5.0 μN

59. 6.18×10^3 years

61. $E_p = 40$ V/m, $B_p = 0.13$ μT

63. 1/4

65. 4.2 μN

67. 17.7 μPa

71. (a) 1.0 MV/m; (b) 4.3 mm; (c) 64 mJ; (d) 2.1×10^{-10} kg·m/s; (e) 64 W

73. Long, with cylindrical symmetry

75. 0.3 μm

Part 4 Cumulative Problems

1. 6.0 MV

3. 15.7 mA, top to bottom

5. (b) $c/\sqrt{\kappa}$

Chapter 35

1. 15°

3. ±0.5°

5. (a) 2; (b) 210°

9. 126 nm

11. 1.57

13. Ethyl alcohol

15. 1.83

17. 5.1 m

19. (a) 3.20×10^{14} Hz; (b) 937 nm

21. (a) 49.8°; (b) 42.2°; (c) 22.4°

23. (a) 61.3°; (b) 80.9°; (c) there is none

27. $\sqrt{2}$

29. 2.62×10^8 m/s

31. 53.5°

35. 36.5° to 38.1°

37. About 3.4 cm

39. 67.5°

41. 36.9°

43. 1.96×10^8 m/s

45. 2.32 m

47. 28.8°

49. (a) base; (b) 63.2°

51. 35.2°

53. $n = 1.17$

59. (b) 42.1°

Chapter 36

1. Mirror surface 55° to horizontal
3. (a) 30 cm; (b) virtual, 60 cm behind mirror
5. (a) Image height is 1/4 object height; (b) inverted
7. (a) 12.4 cm in front of mirror; (b) 3.22 times
9. (a) 24.3 cm behind the mirror; (b) 29 mm; (c) virtual
11. 18 cm in front of mirror
13. 7.42 cm
15. 40 cm
17. (a) 20 cm; (b) reduced to 55% actual size
19. 12 cm
21. 47.7 mm
23. 2.3 mm
27. (a) Real, inverted, 7.7 cm high; (b) virtual, upright, 7.7 cm high
29. 29 cm or 41 cm from the candle
31. 40 cm
35. $\ell' = -67.9$ cm
37. 2
39. 7.56 mm
41. Virtual image, 81 cm from lens on same side as object
43. (a) 40 cm; (b) 160 cm; (c) −170 cm (the lens becomes a diverging lens)
45. (a) 15.3 cm; (b) 1.63
47. Real image, magnified 2.74 times
49. (a) 5.0 m; (b) 37 cm
51. (a) Enlarged 2.9 times at 110 mm
55. 1.85 cm
57. −17.7 cm
59. (a) 2.0 m; (b) 3.0 m in front of the mirror
61. 25 cm
63. 96 cm
65. $(\ell = 85.4$ cm, $m = -1.81)$; $(\ell = 155$ cm, $m = -0.552)$
67. Real image, 109 cm on other side of lens
69. (a) 8.31 mm; (b) 92 cm from my eye
71. No, one is virtual, the other real
75. (a) 1.1 m from primary; (b) elliptical

Chapter 37

1. 484 nm
3. (a) 95 cm; (b) 3.8 mm
5. 1.25 mm
7. 17.7 cm, 44.7 cm
9. 0.034°

11. (a) 17.1 cm; (b) 20.0 cm
13. 4
15. (a) 4.8°, 9.7°; (b) 2.9°, 6.8°
17. (a) 8.97°; (b) 51.3°
19. (a) 2nd; (b) 1st
21. 6th order
23. 3200
25. 415 nm, 581 nm
27. Echelle grating has 60% greater resolving power
29. 2000
31. 103 nm
33. 424 nm, 594 nm
35. (a) 75.2 nm; (b) violet
37. 368 nm
39. 5
41. 236
43. 375 nm (i.e., $\frac{3}{4}\lambda$)
45. 545 nm
47. 1022
49. $a/\lambda = 1$
51. 26.6°
53. 0.0162
55. 1.3 m
57. 2.0 μm
59. 6.9 km
61. For diameters greater than 14 cm
63. 7645
65. 0.01 nm
67. 77.2 nm
69. 46 m
71. 484 nm
75. 5542
77. Every 2.8 s
79. 6.0 km/s
81. 3.0 μm

Part 5 Cumulative Problems

1. $m_0 = (n - 1)d(\sin\alpha)/\lambda_0$
3. 3.2 min
5. (b) $x = \dfrac{\sqrt{3}}{2a}\ln\left[2(1 - ay - \sqrt{\tfrac{1}{4} - 2ay + a^2y^2})\right]$

Chapter 38

1. (a) 4.50 h; (b) 4.56 h; (c) 4.62 h
3. (a) $v/c = \tan\theta$, with θ the amplitude of the sine curve. Here $\theta = 20''$ (20/3600 degree), giving $v = 29$ km/s; (b) the orbit is nearly circular
5. 41 cm
7. (a) 8.26 h; (b) 6.28 h
9. (a) 0.857c; (b) 9.69 min
11. 0.14c

13. $c/\sqrt{2}$
15. Twin A: 83 years; twin B: 40 years
17. 0.96c
19. 0.996c
21. (a) B first, by 5.74 min; (b) A first, by 13.1 min; (c) essentially simultaneous
23. A, by 6.4 My
27. (a) 21.7 m; (b) 12.4 m
29. 0.918c
31. 3.4
33. (a) 2.1 MeV; (b) 1.6 MeV
35. 0.36c
37. 5.3×10^{-8} kg·m/s, about the same as the insect
39. 5.9×10^{-30} kg
41. (a) 0.020c; (b) 0.55c; (c) 0.94c; (d) essentially c
47. (a) -0.75×10^{10} ly^2; (b) 99×10^{10} ly^2; events can be causally related only if $(\Delta s)^2 > 0$
49. 0.274c
51. (a) 16 ns; (b) 4.8 m
53. (a) 4.2 ly; (b) −2.4 years (i.e., B occurs earlier)
55. 0.395c
57. 0.9999953c
59. 598 m
61. 0.95c

Chapter 39

1. (a) 4.1 neV; (b) 2.1 eV; (c) 12.4 keV
3. (a) 1.6×10^{-24} J; (b) 3.9×10^{26} photons/s
5. (a) 1.7×10^{28} s^{-1}; (b) 3.2×10^{15} s^{-1}; (c) 1.3×10^{18} s^{-1}
7. β $(n_1 = 5)$
9. $n = 229$
11. 73 cm/s
13. 1.6 km/s
15. Electron: no; proton: yes
17. 12 pm
19. 0.0034°
21. 2.5 h
23. 20 minutes
25. 0.64 kg
27. 0
29. $u\,\bar{u}\,\bar{d}$
31. $+e$
33. (a) 10.2 eV; (b) $n_1 = 2$, $n_2 = 1$
35. The proton
37. 1.16×10^6 m/s
39. 18 pm
41. (a) 1 eV; (b) 5 MeV
43. 10–20 billion years

Index

Page numbers in *italics* refer to illustrations; page numbers followed by t refer to tables.

GEOPHYSICAL AND ASTROPHYSICAL DATA

EARTH

Mass	5.97×10^{24} kg
Mean radius	6.37×10^6 m
Orbital period	3.16×10^7 s (365.3 days)
Mean distance from Sun	1.50×10^{11} m
Mean density	5.5×10^3 kg/m^3
Surface gravity	9.81 m/s^2
Surface pressure	1.013×10^5 Pa
Magnetic moment	8.0×10^{22} A·m^2

SUN

Mass	1.99×10^{30} kg
Mean radius	6.96×10^8 m
Orbital period (about galactic center)	6×10^{15} s (200 My)
Mean distance from galactic center	2.6×10^{20} m
Power output (luminosity)	3.85×10^{26} W
Mean density	1.4×10^3 kg/m^3
Surface gravity	274 m/s^2
Surface temperature	5.8×10^3 K

MOON

Mass	7.35×10^{22} kg
Mean radius	1.74×10^6 m
Orbital period	2.36×10^6 s (27.3 days)
Mean distance from Earth	3.85×10^8 m
Mean density	3.3×10^3 kg/m^3
Surface gravity	1.62 m/s^2

COMPARATIVE ENERGIES

Supernova explosion	10^{46} J	World per capita energy use, per second	2×10^3 J
Sun's output, per second	4×10^{26} J	Food energy used by human body,	
Solar energy incident on Earth, per second	2×10^{17} J	per second	10^2 J
Explosive yield of MX missile		Energy to lift this book 1 foot	8 J
(10 350-kiloton nuclear warheads)	1×10^{16} J	Particle energy in Superconducting	3.2×10^{-6} J
Human energy use, per second	10^{13} J	Super Collider	(20 TeV)
1 ounce uranium-235	2.3×10^{12} J	Energy release in U-235 fission (200 MeV)	3.2×10^{-11} J
1 gallon seawater		Energy release in deuterium-tritium fusion	2.8×10^{-12} J
(with deuterium content as fusion fuel)	4.7×10^{10} J		(17.6 MeV)
1 ton of coal	2.6×10^{10} J	Energy release in forming hydrogen atom	2.2×10^{-18} J
Electrical output of large power plant,			(13.6 eV)
per second	10^9 J	Thermal energy kT at room temperature	4×10^{-21} J
1 gallon of gasoline	1.3×10^8 J		(0.025 eV)
1500-kg car going 60 mph	6.3×10^5 J	Thermal energy kT associated with cosmic	4×10^{-23} J
U.S. per capita energy use, per second	10^4 J	background radiation	(0.23 meV)